Shakespeare's England

From the painting by Marcus Gheeraerts in the collection of the Earl of Ilchester at Melbury

VISIT OF QUEEEN ELIZABETH TO BLACKFRIARS, JUNE 16, 1600

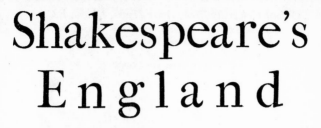

Shakespeare's England

An Account of the
Life & Manners
of his Age
Volume
I

Clarendon Press Oxford

Oxford University Press, Amen House, London E.C.4

GLASGOW NEW YORK TORONTO MELBOURNE WELLINGTON
BOMBAY CALCUTTA MADRAS KARACHI LAHORE DACCA
CAPE TOWN SALISBURY NAIROBI IBADAN ACCRA
KUALA LUMPUR HONG KONG

FIRST PUBLISHED 1916
REPRINTED 1916, 1926, 1932, 1950, 1962

PRINTED IN GREAT BRITAIN

PREFACE

THE purpose of this book is to describe the habits of the English people during Shakespeare's lifetime. The attempt would be worth making even if Shakespeare had never lived. It has been made in the belief that an understanding of the world he lived in is a step to the understanding of Shakespeare. Language is, no doubt, a great preservative, and Shakespeare speaks directly every day to many people who never trouble themselves with the changes that have come over England since he was buried at Stratford. Nevertheless, they would understand him better if they knew more of his surroundings and of the audience that he addressed. Half the errors and fantasies of popular Shakespeare criticism find their opportunity in indifference to these matters, or in ignorance of them.

This kind of study of Shakespeare, which deals with bare, and often trivial, matter of fact, does not appeal to the metaphysician, or to any of those who covet the glow that comes from brisk exercise in large empty spaces. But no apology need be offered to the artist, for the artist knows that life is a hand-to-mouth affair, and that happiness, which is the spirit of life, is concerned not with the interstellar distances, but with that small portion of space which is more or less under our control. To order it rightly and pleasantly is art. The body must be fed and clothed, and a shelter must be built for it from the weather ; when these things are done, the mind must still be occupied and humoured with play, which mimics the labours that it seeks to escape from.

The truth was well handled by Sir Toby Belch and Sir Andrew Aguecheek, in their profound discussion of human life. 'Does not our life consist of the four elements?' said Sir Toby. 'Faith, so they say,' said Sir Andrew, 'but I think it rather consists of eating and drinking.' Sir Andrew is a foolish gentleman, but those who want to know what Shakespeare thinks must not neglect what his fools say. After all, how does one age differ from another? The elements remain the same; earth, air, fire, and water; birth, marriage, and death; these are not much altered from century to century. It is the little things that change, and in their change serve as an index to the character of a man or of an age. Everything in one sense remains the same; everything in another sense is different. Some slight changes in material conditions alter manners, customs, values, and the meanings of spoken language.

Shakespeare's book is not the only book that is sometimes read with imperfect intelligence. In the authorized translation of the Bible, produced in King James's reign, and in the Book of Daniel, the people are told to fall down and worship the golden image when they hear the sound of 'the cornet, flute, harp, sackbut, psaltery, dulcimer, and all kinds of music'. It might be thought that those are the instruments which were played in King Nebuchadnezzar's time. They are the music of Elizabethan England.

Elizabethan England is reflected everywhere in Shakespeare's works; he held the mirror up to nature, but the nature that passed across it was English nature of the time of Elizabeth. He said many things that are true for all time; but if we understand the world that he moved in and the language that he spoke, we are saved from mistaking the accidents of his time for the essentials of his thought.

The English school of Shakespeare criticism has always been strong in antiquarian lore. Theobald, Malone, Drake, Furnivall, and a score of others have served Shakespeare's fame well, and have drawn a better meaning out of his plays than the philosophers have read into them. The best that can be hoped for this book, the work of many hands, is that it may be judged to be not unworthy of its ancestry, and of the service to which it is dedicated.

So long ago as 1905 Sir WALTER RALEIGH sketched the first plan of this book, and in 1909 Sir SIDNEY LEE undertook its production. He arranged for the writing of most of the treatises now published, set on foot the first selection of the illustrations by which they are accompanied, and made additions from his own collections and from fresh researches. In 1911 he was obliged to postpone work upon the book, and in 1914 to relinquish the hope of completing it. Successive editors who took up the task were withdrawn by war work in the course of 1914–15, and owing to these inevitable delays, not by design, the book appears in the tercentenary year of Shakespeare's death, and in the midst of the Great War.

The Clarendon Press esteems itself fortunate to have been able to employ for the completion of the work the practised hand of Mr. ONIONS, co-editor of the Oxford Dictionary and author of the Shakespeare Glossary, which at long last has given us a complete and authoritative survey by an English scholar of such Shakespearian words and meanings as are no longer current in English speech. The minute examination of the vocabulary of Shakespeare and his contemporaries, made for the purposes of the glossary, has been very profitable to the present work : it has tended to secure completeness and has called attention to or thrown light upon sundry passages and allusions which might have escaped notice. Mr. Onions desires to acknowledge on his own behalf the benefits he has received from the constant counsel and encouragement of Sir Walter Raleigh, and in the later stages of the editorial work, from collaboration most kindly undertaken by Mr. Nichol Smith. Mr. P. E. Matheson, also, has helped with the final reading of the proofs, and throughout much assistance and advice has been given by Mr. C. F. Bell, Mr. Percy Simpson, and Mr. Emery Walker, and, on special points, by Mr. F. P. Barnard, Mr. Raymond Beazley, Sir William Osler, and Dr. C. W. Singer. The verification of references and the reading of proofs have been largely in the hands of Mr. Yockney and Mr. Dadley of the Oxford Dictionary; the index of proper names was prepared by Mr. Ostler of the Clarendon Press and Mrs. A. F. New. The new editor and the publishers, at the completion of an undertaking upon which no pains have been spared, express their thanks to the authors who have waited patiently for publication, or have made possible the very considerable additions of letterpress and illustrations which have been collected during the editorship of Mr. Onions.

Acknowledgements for permission to reproduce title-pages, prints, and pictures are in the first place due to the Director of the British Museum and the Librarian of the Bodleian Library at Oxford ; the illustrations which form part of this book are in a large proportion derived from treasures of which they are the guardians. Other institutions or corporate bodies to which acknowledgements are due are : the Ashmolean Museum, for the portraits of John Dee and John Bull, and Pieter Breughel's print of 'An Alchemist'; the National Portrait Gallery, for the portraits of Prince Henry by P. van Somer, Sir Walter Ralegh, and Sir Edward Coke by Cornelius Jansen van Ceulen, and the perspective portrait of Edward VI; the Public Record Office, for Shakespeare's signature to a deposition; Somerset House, for the three signatures of Shakespeare to his will; the Library of the Guildhall, London, for Shakespeare's signature to the Blackfriars deed; the University of Cambridge, for the title-page of Camden's Greek Grammar; the University of Edinburgh, for a plate from Derricke's *Image of Ireland*; the Fitz-william Museum, Cambridge, for the picture of the Palace of Sheen; the Society of Antiquaries, London, for per-mission to reproduce an engraving from a picture in their possession of 'Preaching at St. Paul's Cross', and for the use of their negative of the Earl of Derby's Elizabethan picture of a card-party; to the Governors of Dulwich College, for the portraits of Alleyn, Field, and Burbage; to the Worshipful Company of Barbers, for permission to reproduce an engraving of the picture in their possession of Henry VIII conferring a charter; to the Trustees and Guardians of Shakespeare's Birthplace, for the Quiney letter and tradesmen's tokens.

Many private persons have kindly given permission for the photographing of subjects for reproduction in this book: His Grace the Duke of Devonshire, eight designs by Inigo Jones for the staging of Ben Jonson's *Masque of Queens*, at Chatsworth; His Grace the Duke of Portland, the portrait of the third Earl of Southampton, at Welbeck Abbey; His Grace the Duke of Richmond and Gordon, the picture of Court of Wards and Liveries, at Goodwood; the Right Honourable the Earl of Derby, the picture of an Elizabethan card-party, at Knowsley; the Right Honourable the Earl of Ilchester, the picture by Marcus Gheerarts of Queen Elizabeth's visit to Blackfriars, at Melbury; the Most Honourable the Marquess of Salisbury, the picture by Hoefnagel of a marriage fête at Horsleydown, at Hatfield; the Viscount Dillon, the portrait of Queen Elizabeth, at Ditchley; the Reverend Wentworth Watson, the garden mount at Rockingham Castle; Mr. Percy Macquoid, three pieces of furniture in his collection; Mr. W. H. Godfrey, the reconstructive sketch by him of The Fortune theatre.

Mr. John Hogg has kindly given permission for the reproduction of two illustrations from Sir W. H. St. John Hope's *Heraldry for Craftsmen and Designers*; Messrs. Batsford for four architectural pictures from Mr. J Alfred Gotch's *Early Renaissance Architecture in England*; the editor of *The Architectural Review* for the use of the block of Mr. W. H. Godfrey's reconstruction of the Fortune Theatre, and Mr. Freeman O'Donoghue for his photograph of Viscount Dillon's portrait of Queen Elizabeth. The negative of the Shakespeare bust at Stratford-on-Avon was specially made for Captain Purchas.

CONTENTS

VOLUME I

VOLUME II

LIST OF ILLUSTRATIONS

VOLUME I

ABBREVIATIONS EMPLOYED IN QUOTATIONS
FROM SHAKESPEARE'S WORKS

All's W.	= All's Well that Ends Well	M. Wives	= The Merry Wives of Windsor
Ant. & Cleop.	= Antony and Cleopatra	Mid. N. D.	= A Midsummer Night's Dream
A. Y. L.	= As You Like It	Much Ado	= Much Ado about Nothing
Com. of E.	= Comedy of Errors		
Cor.	= Coriolanus	Oth.	= Othello
Cymb.	= Cymbeline	Pass. Pilg.	= The Passionate Pilgrim.
Haml.	= Hamlet		
1 Hen. IV	= The First Part of King Henry IV	Pericles	= Pericles
		Rich. II	= King Richard II
2 Hen. IV	= The Second Part of King Henry IV	Rich. III	= King Richard III
		Rom. & Jul.	= Romeo and Juliet
Hen. V	= King Henry V	Sonnets	= Sonnets
1 Hen. VI	= The First Part of King Henry VI	Tam. Sh.	= The Taming of the Shrew
2 Hen. VI	= The Second Part of King Henry VI	Temp.	= The Tempest
		Timon	= Timon of Athens
3 Hen. VI	= The Third Part of King Henry VI	Tit. Andr.	= Titus Andronicus
		Troilus	= Troilus and Cressida
John	= King John	Tw. N.	= Twelfth Night
Jul. Caes.	= Julius Caesar	Two Gent.	= The Two Gentlemen of Verona
Lear	= King Lear		
Lover's Comp.	= A Lover's Complaint	Ven. & Ad.	= Venus and Adonis
Love's L. L.	= Love's Labour's Lost	Wint. Tale	= The Winter's Tale
Lucr.	= The Rape of Lucrece	chor.	= chorus
Macb.	= Macbeth	epil.	= epilogue
Meas. for M.	= Measure for Measure	ind.	= induction
Merch. of V.	= The Merchant of Venice	prol.	= prologue
		st. dir.	= stage direction

The text used is that of the Oxford Shakespeare, except where for special reasons it has been necessary to set it aside.

O D E

ON THE TERCENTENARY COMMEMORATION

OF

SHAKESPEARE

BY

ROBERT BRIDGES Poet Laureate

1916

KIND dove-wing'd Peace, for whose green olive-crown
The noblest kings would give their diadems,
Mother, who hast ruled our home so long,
  How suddenly art thou fled !
Leaving our cities astir with war ;
And yet on the fair fields deserted
Lingerest, wherever the gaudy seasons
  Deck with excessive splendour
  The sorrow-stricken year,
Where cornlands bask and high elms rustle gently,
And still the unweeting birds sing on by brae and bourn.

The trumpet blareth & calleth the true to be stern :
Be then thy soft reposeful music dumb ;
  Yet shall thy lovers awhile give ear
    —An' tho' full-arm'd they come—
  To the praise of England's gentlest son ;
Whom, when she bore, the Muses lov'd
Above the best of eldest honour
    —Yea, save one without peer—
    And by great Homer set,
Not to impugn his undisputed throne,
The myriad-hearted by the mighty-hearted one.

For God of His gifts pour'd on him a full measure,
And gave him to know Nature & the ways of men :
   And he dowr'd with inexhaustible treasure
     A world-conquering speech,
   Which surg'd as a river high-descended
   That, gathering tributaries of many lands,
   Rolls through the plain a bounteous flood,
     Picturing towers & temples
     And ruin of bygone times,
And floateth the ships deep-laden with merchandise
Out to the windy seas to traffic in foreign climes.

Thee, SHAKESPEARE, to-day we honour ; and evermore,
Since England bore thee, the master of human song,
   Thy folk are we, children of thee,
     Who, knitting in one her realm
   And strengthening with pride her sea-borne clans,
   Scorn'st in the grave the bruize of death.
   All thy later-laurel'd choir
     Laud thee in thy world-shrine :
     London's laughter is thine ;
One with thee is our temper in melancholy or might,
And in thy book Great-Britain's rule readeth her right.

Her chains are chains of Freedom, & her bright arms
Honour, Justice and Truth and Love to man.
   Though first from a pirate ancestry
     She took her home on the wave,
   Her gentler spirit arose disdainful,
   And, smiting the fetters of slavery,
   Made the high seaways safe & free,
     In wisdom bidding aloud
     To world-wide brotherhood,

Till her flag was hail'd as the ensign of Liberty,
And the boom of her guns went round the earth in salvos
   of peace.

And thou, when Nature bow'd her mastering hand
To borrow an ecstasy of man's art from thee,
  Thou, her poet, secure as she
    Of the shows of eternity,
  Didst never fear thy work should fall
  To fashion's craze nor pedant's folly
  Nor devastator, whose arrogant arms
    Murder and maim mankind ;
    Who, when in scorn of grace
He hath batter'd & burn'd some loveliest dearest shrine,
Laugheth in ire & boasteth aloud his brazen god.

    *   *   *   *   *   *

I SAW the Angel of Earth from strife aloof
Mounting the heavenly stair with Time on high,
  Growing ever younger in the brightening air
    Of the everlasting dawn :
  It was not terror in his eyes nor wonder,
  That glance of the intimate exaltation
  Which lieth as Power under all Being,
    And broodeth in Thought above—
    As a bird wingeth over the ocean,
Whether indolently the heavy water sleepeth
Or is dash'd in a million waves, chafing or lightly laughing.

I hear his voice in the music of lamentation,
In echoing chant and cadenced litany,
  In country song and pastoral piping
    And silvery dances of mirth :

And oft, as the eyes of a lion in the brake,
    His presence hath startled me . . .
In austere shapes of beauty lurking,
        Beautiful for Beauty's sake ;
        As a lonely blade of life
Ariseth to flower, whensoever the unseen Will
Stirreth with kindling aim the dark fecundity of Being.

Man knoweth but as in a dream of his own desire
    The thing that is good for man, and he dreameth well :
        But the lot of the gentle heart is hard
            That is cast in an epoch of life,
        When evil is knotted and demons fight,
        Who know not, they, that the lowest lot
        Is treachery hate and trust in sin
            And perseverance in ill,
            Doom'd to oblivious Hell,
To pass with the shames unspoken of men away,
Wash'd out with their tombs by the grey unpitying tears
    of Heaven.

But ye, dear Youth, who lightly in the day of fury
    Put on England's glory as a common coat,
        And in your stature of masking grace
            Stood forth warriors complete,
        No praise o'ershadoweth yours to-day,
        Walking out of the home of love
        To match the deeds of all the dead.—
            Alas ! alas ! fair Peace,
            These were thy blossoming roses.
Look on thy shame, fair Peace, thy tearful shame !
Turn to thine isle, fair Peace ; return thou & guard it well !

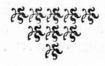

I

THE AGE OF ELIZABETH

BY

SIR WALTER RALEIGH

THE Age of Elizabeth is the most glorious, and in some ways the most significant, period of English history. To be an Englishman is to be the fellow countryman of Cromwell and Milton, of Chatham and Johnson. Yet not a few Englishmen would renounce even these high titles before they would renounce their fellowship with Drake and Sidney, Bacon and Ralegh, Spenser and Shakespeare. If these names could pass into oblivion, half the national pride would go with them. They are ours more completely than the great men of a later time. They express the national temper; they were not lonely prophets and reformers. Drake was an English seaman. Bacon was a lawyer, who sought and found employment in affairs of State. Shakespeare was a jovial actor and manager, who spent some part of his leisure in the midst of congenial company at the Mermaid tavern in Bread Street. If they seem more than human, that is an illusion of memory; their figures are illuminated by the flood of light which suddenly revealed to Englishmen that England was a great nation, and was to bear a hand in shaping the destinies of the world.

It was in a kind of lull between two storms that England was found ready to challenge the might of Spain. The two notable civil wars of English history belong to the fifteenth and the seventeenth centuries. When Elizabeth came to the throne, the Wars of the Roses were long over, and the Tudor monarchy was firmly established. The Puritan Revolution was still in the distance. That storm was heralded by mutterings continually growing in volume during the hundred years that passed from the birth of

Elizabeth to the quarrel of King Charles with the Scottish Parliament. But during the Queen's own reign these omens did not much disturb the national mind; they are treated with levity by Shakespeare. The Reformation of the Church in England was imposed upon the people by the power of the State, and was essentially a working compromise. It went further, perhaps, than the bulk of the people desired, and it did not satisfy the reforming party. Throughout the reign of Elizabeth the Church of England

The Entrance of Q. Elizabeth.

From Carleton, *A Thankfull Remembrance,* 1627.

was engaged with its enemies on two fronts, Rome and Geneva. But this was mainly an affair of ecclesiastical politicians; the people of England were not passionately involved in it, and were free to give their minds to those great secular changes which are called the Renaissance. The World, not the Church, called the tune to which the Age of Elizabeth danced and sang. Two new surprising vistas, revealed at the same time, widened the world so enormously, that the imagination of the age was intoxicated by a new sense of power and freedom, and, forgetting the miseries and squalors of the human estate, gave itself over to poetry. The civilization of the ancient world was discovered by the enthusiasm of scholars, and was made real and brought near to the people by the labour of translators. At the same time the illimitable possibilities of the new world beyond the seas were discovered and published by the voyagers. The truths thus revealed were too wonderful to be expressed in prose, and prose almost went out of fashion. In the preface to his *Discourse of English Poetrie* (1586) William Webbe speaks no more than the truth. 'Among the innumerable sortes of Englyshe Bookes', he says, 'and infinite fardles of printed pamphlets, wherewith thys Countrey is pestered, all shoppes stuffed, and euery study furnished : the greatest part I thinke in any one kinde, are such as are either meere Poeticall, or whiche tende in some respecte (as either in matter or forme) to Poetry.' In the disputations of the learned and in the traffic of daily life, prose, of course, held its own, but for whole realms of exhilarating facts it was felt to be an inadequate form of speech. In Marlowe and Shakespeare it is dedicated chiefly to the base and comic aspects of life. Drayton wrote his gazetteer of England and Wales in verse; and all his contributions to English history are, like Samuel Daniel's history of the Civil Wars, poetical in substance and form. There is the lift and impulse of poetry even in the work of the prose chroniclers, who laboured to give their country a place in the world's esteem along with countries of older fame. It would be difficult to find another period of English history to furnish fit company for Shakespeare, and when the age is called the Age of Shakespeare, the compliment is double-edged, for the age was worthy of the man.

Honour must first be paid where Shakespeare was never slow to pay it, to the great Queen who ruled the England of his youth and early manhood. In *A Midsummer Night's Dream*, which is certainly one of his earliest plays, he offered a magnificent tribute to 'a fair vestal throned by the west', whom Cupid assailed in vain :

> But I might see young Cupid's fiery shaft
> Quench'd in the chaste beams of the wat'ry moon,
> And the imperial votaress passed on,
> In maiden meditation, fancy-free. (*Mid. N. D.* ii. i. 161–4)

In the latest of all the plays that he had a hand in, *King Henry VIII*, the memory of Elizabeth's greatness is cast

into the form of a prophecy, spoken at her christening by
Archbishop Cranmer :

> This royal infant,—heaven still move about her !—
> Though in her cradle, yet now promises
> Upon this land a thousand thousand blessings,
> Which time shall bring to ripeness : she shall be—
> But few now living can behold that goodness—
> A pattern to all princes living with her,
> And all that shall succeed : Saba was never
> More covetous of wisdom and fair virtue
> Than this pure soul shall be : all princely graces
> That mould up such a mighty piece as this,
> With all the virtues that shall attend the good,
> Shall still be doubled on her ; truth shall nurse her ;
> Holy and heavenly thoughts still counsel her ;
> She shall be lov'd and fear'd ; her own shall bless her ;
> Her foes shake like a field of beaten corn,
> And hang their heads with sorrow ; good grows with her.
> In her days every man shall eat in safety
> Under his own vine what he plants, and sing
> The merry songs of peace to all his neighbours.
> God shall be truly known ; and those about her
> From her shall read the perfect ways of honour,
> And by those claim their greatness, not by blood.
>
> (*Hen. VIII*, v. v. 18–39)

In later ages the character of Elizabeth has not found
many admirers. A hundred stories are told of her to illustrate her vanity, her love of flattery, her wilfulness, her
stinginess to her allies, her meanness to her dependants, her
cold-blooded calculation of chances. But she ruled England
and saved England, at a crisis when more amiable qualities
in the ruler might easily have ruined the country. There
is an old saying that it is better to have a queen than a king,
for under a queen the country is ruled by men, and under
a king by women. It is true that England was ruled by
men under Elizabeth ; Cecil and Walsingham were her right
and left hands ; but she was the daughter of her father,
and a Tudor, and she kept control. 'The principall note
of her Reign', says Sir Robert Naunton, 'will be, that she
ruled much by faction and parties, which her self both
made, upheld, and weakened, as her own great judgement
advised.' To prove his point, Naunton tells a story of a
sharp answer of the Queen to Leicester, at the time when
that nobleman was high in the royal favour. One Bowyer,

a gentleman of the Black Rod, had orders to be very precise in admitting courtiers to the Privy Chamber, and repulsed a very gay captain, a follower of Leicester's, at the door. Thereupon 'Leicester, coming into the contestation, said publikely (which was none of his wont) that he was a Knave, and should not continue long in his office ; and so turning about to go in to the Queen, Bowyer (who was a bold Gentleman and well beloved) stept before him, and fell at her Majesties feet, related the story, and humbly craves her Graces pleasure ; and whether my Lord of Leicester was King, or her Majesty Queen ? Whereunto she replyed with her wonted oath :

Gods death, my Lord, I have wisht you well, but my favour is not so lockt up for you, that others shall not partake thereof ; for I have many servants, unto whom I have, and will at my pleasure bequeath my favour, and likewise resume the same ; and if you think to rule here, I will take a course to see you forth-coming : I will have here but one Mistress, and no Master, and look that no ill happen to him, lest it be severely required at your hands.

Which so quelled my Lord of Leicester, that his fained humility was long after one of his best virtues.' She was almost as short with Burghley himself, when he urged on her that only the Protestants were her friends, and dissuaded her from treating with France about Scottish affairs. Elizabeth was not willing to run the risk of uniting the great Catholic powers against her, and she told him so in very clear language :

Mr. Secretary, I mean to have done with this business ; I shall listen to the proposals of the French King. I am not going to be tied any longer to you and your brethren in Christ.[1]

She knew, as all good rulers must know, when to ask and take advice, and she had one of the best of a ruler's talents, for she was a shrewd judge of character. In passionate love for her country and people she has never been surpassed. Soon after she came to the throne, the Lower House of Parliament, troubled by the question of the succession, sent a deputation to her to urge her to marry. Her reply is recorded by Camden :

Concerning Marriage, which ye so earnestly move me to, I have beene long since persuaded that I was sent into this world by God to think and do these things chiefly which may tend to his Glory. Hereupon have I chosen that kind of life which is most free from

[1] Beesly, p. 89. The French report runs : Quoiqu'il y ait, Maistre Secretaire, dict elle, je veulx sortir hors de ceste affaire, et entendre à ce que le Roy me mande, et ne m'en arrester plus à vous aultres frères en Christ.

the troublesome Cares of this world, that I might attend the Service of God alone. From which if either the tendered Marriages of most potent Princes, or the danger of Death intended against me, could have removed me, I had long agone enjoyed the honour of an Husband. And these things have I thought upon when I was a private person. But now that the public Care of governing the Kingdom is laid upon me, to draw upon me also the Cares of Marriage may seem a point of inconsiderate Folly. Yea, to satisfy you, I have already joined myself in Marriage to an Husband, namely, the Kingdom of England. And behold, said she, which I marvel ye have forgotten, the pledge of this my Wedlock and Marriage with my Kingdom. And therewith she drew the ring from her Finger, and shewed it, wherewith at her Coronation she had in a set form of words solemnly given herself in Marriage to her Kingdom. Here having made a pause, And do not, saith she, upbraid me with miserable lack of Children; for every one of you, and as many as are Englishmen, are Children and Kinsmen to me; of whom if God deprive me not, (which God forbid) I cannot without injury be accounted Barren. But I commend you that ye have not appointed me an Husband, for that were most unworthy the Majesty of an absolute Princess, and unbeseeming your Wisdom, which are Subjects born. Nevertheless if it please God that I enter into another course of life, I promise you I will do nothing which may be prejudicial to the Commonwealth, but will take such a Husband, as near as may be, as will have as great a care of the Commonwealth as myself. But if I continue in this kind of life I have begun, I doubt not but God will so direct mine own and your Counsels, that ye shall not need to doubt of a Successor which may be more beneficial to the Commonwealth than he which may be born of me, considering that the Issue of the best Princes many times degenerateth. And to me it shall be a full satisfaction, both for the memorial of my Name, and for my Glory also, if, when I shall let my last breath, it be engraven upon my Marble Tomb: Here lieth Elizabeth, which Reigned a Virgin, and died a Virgin.

When we read the words spoken by the Queen, we begin to understand something of her devotion to her subjects, and something also of the devotion that she commanded from them. She gained their confidence, and from that time forward her voice was the voice of England. Towards the close of her reign the King of Denmark offered to mediate between England and Spain. The Queen declined his offer, adding a few words of explanation:

I would have the King of Denmark and all Princes Christian and Heathen to know, that England hath no need to crave peace; nor myself endured one hour's fear since I attained the crown thereof, being guarded with so valiant and faithful subjects.

ROBERT DUDLEY by F HOGENBERG (?)

When the ruler could command utterances like these it is no wonder that Englishmen were ready to forget their religious differences in their love of queen and country. John Stubbs, the Puritan, when he was sentenced to have his right hand cut off for writing a book against the proposed French marriage of 1579, 'after his Right hand was cut off, put off his Hat with his Left, and said with a loud voice, "God save the Queen". The Multitude about was deeply silent.' Mary Queen of Scots will continue to attract more sympathy as a woman, and to supply more matter for the use of tragic poetry. But Elizabeth was every inch a queen. She belongs to that small class of statesmen who are content to serve their country and are sufficiently rewarded when they succeed in making themselves necessary. She led a long life of unbroken loneliness in the single-minded pursuit of her duty to her people. They were not deceived in their opinion of her, which, after the first few years, never wavered. The foibles of the Queen, and the gossip and rumours concerning her which passed from lip to lip, were not mistaken in her own day for the history of her reign. They amused those who repeated them, but they were seen against the background of her steadfast political service. Her courage and her loyalty are reflected in the deeds of the gentlemen privateers who made the name of England feared upon the seas, and in the enormous adulation of the poets who strained language and sense in the endeavour to praise her. In George Peele's play, *The Arraignment of Paris*, presented before the Queen's Majesty by the Children of her Chapel, and printed in 1584, not only do the three goddesses, Juno, Pallas, and Venus, willingly yield the prize to the nymph Eliza, but the very Fates, who preside over the destinies of man's life, give into her hands the implements of their office. This goes beyond the limits of poetic licence, but it seemed a permissible extravagance to the subjects of Elizabeth, who worshipped in her the guardian of their safety and their honour.

The political beliefs and habits of thought which seem to express themselves in Shakespeare's plays were the average beliefs of the time. In some of the plays, where the story invites a treatment of the problems of government, Shakespeare pays no heed to the invitation. *Julius Cæsar*, for instance, deals with a great constitutional crisis of the world's history ; yet the play, as Shakespeare handles it, is not a political play. Plutarch, who was his authority, is interested mainly in drama and character, and Shakespeare was well content to follow Plutarch. The English historical plays, in the same way, treat the clash of personalities, and exhibit human character tested by great events, but hardly touch on political theory. There is nothing to wonder at in this ; authors and craftsmen who have taken human nature for their province commonly stand aloof from the politics of their age. But the fact is that the political issues which exercised the imagination of the ordinary intelligent man in Shakespeare's day were few and simple. Indeed it might truly be said that there was only one live question, or at least that there was one question so real and insistent and practical that it overshadowed all the rest. That question was how political unity and power might be achieved and consolidated against the forces of anarchy, against domestic treason and foreign aggression. It is the question treated by Machiavel in the wonderful little book which dominated all the political thought of the sixteenth century. But even if the problem of the Prince had never been mooted in literature, it would have been brought home to the minds of men by experience. There was hardly a kingdom in western Europe which had not been long troubled by disputed successions and by continual attempts at rebellion. In the Wars of the Roses, and the rebellions against Henry VII, England had had her lesson, and, as if to enforce it, there followed the divisions and doubts which the changes in religion and the divorce of Henry VIII brought in their train. Under Elizabeth the nation longed for unity and peace ; the maintenance and security of the powers of government was what concerned the people ; and it was not till a later time that the question of the balance and subdivision of political power became the chief problem for thinkers. Even in the seventeenth century the most notable treatises aim, like Hobbes's *Leviathan* and Filmer's *Patriarcha*, at vindicating sovereignty, and supplying it with a solid basis in theory or history. That the sovereign powers of the State might be exercised by a corporation or council was a possibility which had to be considered by Machiavel, but it was too remote from English thought and habit to claim attention in England. The attempts made

on the life of Elizabeth by Babington's conspiracy, or by
Lopez, the royal physician who is mentioned in *Dr. Faustus*,
were regarded as attempts on the life of England ; and the
fervent loyalty of the people to the Queen was not a little
inspired by regard for their own independence and welfare.

In this matter Shakespeare is simply a man of his time.
He believed in rank and order and subordination.   His
speeches in favour of these things have nothing ironical
about them, and are never answered by equally good
speeches on the other side.   Indeed they may all be paralleled
from the works of his contemporaries.   Lyly puts the loyal

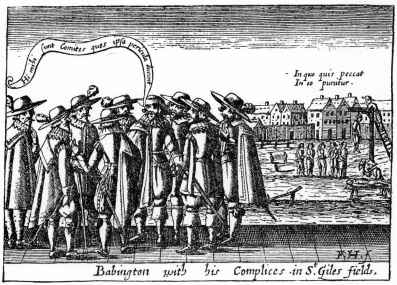

From Carleton, *A Thankfull Remembrance*, 1627.

creeds of a courtier quite succinctly in the argument of the
old bee-keeper, Fidus :

I have learned by experience, that to reason of Kings or Princes,
hath ever bene much mislyked of the wise, though much desired
of fooles, especially wher old men, which should be at their beads,
be too busie with the court, and young men, which shold follow their
bookes, be to inquisitive in the affaires of princes.   We shold not
looke at that we cannot reach, nor long for that we shold not have :
things above us, are not for us, and therfore are princes placed under
the Gods, that they should not see what they do, and we under
princes, that we might not enquire what they doe.

The greatest of Shakespeare's dramatic speeches on

politics is spoken to this same effect, and is put into the
mouth of Ulysses, the wisest of the Greeks :

> The heavens themselves, the planets, and this centre
> Observe degree, priority, and place,
> Insisture, course, proportion, season, form,
> Office, and custom, in all line of order :
> And therefore is the glorious planet Sol
> In noble eminence enthron'd and spher'd
> Amidst the other ; whose med'cinable eye
> Corrects the ill aspects of planets evil,
> And posts, like the commandment of a king,
> Sans check, to good and bad : but when the planets
> In evil mixture to disorder wander,
> What plagues, and what portents, what mutiny,
> What raging of the sea, shaking of earth,
> Commotion in the winds, frights, changes, horrors,
> Divest and crack, rend and deracinate
> The unity and married calm of states
> Quite from their fixure ! O ! when degree is shak'd,
> Which is the ladder to all high designs,
> The enterprise is sick. How could communities,
> Degrees in schools, and brotherhoods in cities,
> Peaceful commerce from dividable shores,
> The primogenitive and due of birth,
> Prerogative of age, crowns, sceptres, laurels,
> But by degree, stand in authentic place ?
> Take but degree away, untune that string,
> And, hark ! what discord follows ; each thing meets
> In mere oppugnancy : the bounded waters
> Should lift their bosoms higher than the shores,
> And make a sop of all this solid globe :
> Strength should be lord of imbecility,
> And the rude son should strike his father dead :
> Force should be right ; or rather, right and wrong—
> Between whose endless jar justice resides—
> Should lose their names, and so should justice too.
> Then every thing includes itself in power,
> Power into will, will into appetite ;
> And appetite, a universal wolf,
> So doubly seconded with will and power,
> Must make perforce a universal prey,
> And last eat up himself.   (*Troilus*, I. iii. 85–124)

Popular orators, from Antony to Jack Cade, who pander
to the restless desires of the mob, get from the dramatist no
such measure of sympathy as went to the making of this
speech. Shakespeare, it is sometimes said, never takes
a side. It is true that for the most part he takes his stand

with average humanity, and is hardly ever eccentric. But he had a meaning, even while drama was his trade; in this matter of politics he was on the side of the Government, and of all but a very few of the people who were proud to call themselves the subjects of the Queen.

Immense changes were wrought in the daily life of the people during the half-century covered by Shakespeare's lifetime. These changes, no doubt, had a much longer history than the life of any one man; already in the fifteenth century they were visible in the rapid growth of towns and the break-up of the old country life, and they were not formally completed until feudal tenures were abolished in the reign of Charles II. But the crisis of the passing of Feudalism belongs to the sixteenth century. During the reign of Elizabeth there was a great advance in national prosperity; the nation became a first-class power; manufacture, commerce, and wealth increased immensely; the education of the people in the grammar schools was improved and strengthened; intercourse with foreign nations, France, Italy, Germany, and Spain became more frequent, and introduced new customs and new fashions. Old men who lived on into the reign of James I found themselves in a world utterly unlike the world of their boyhood. The change from *Gorboduc* to *King Lear* is hardly greater than the change that came over the daily life of the people in the years that elapsed between these two productions.

Men are seldom able to judge truly of the changes that take place before their eyes. A few, a very few, of the writers of Shakespeare's time record some of the changes as matter for congratulation. But the greater part lament them, and see in increased wealth and vigour only increased luxury and wantonness. The Puritan Philip Stubbes, in his *Anatomie of Abuses* (1583), written in the time of Shakespeare's youth, says that for pride of ' mouth, heart, and apparel ' there is not a people ' more abrupt, wicked, and perverse upon earth ' than the English. And besides the extreme Puritans, who would have liked to introduce the discipline of Geneva, or of Munster, there were many liberal-minded men who yet had sinkings at heart when they saw the innovations around them, and the pace at which old ideals were giving way to new. William

Harrison, who wrote the *Description of England* in Holinshed's *Chronicle* (1577–87), finds the use of oak in the building of private houses a sign of the decay of morality:

In times past men were contented to dwell in houses builded of sallow, willow, plumtree, hardbeame, and elme, so that the use of oke was in maner dedicated wholie unto churches, religious houses, princes palaces, noblemens lodgings, and navigation ; but now all these are rejected, and nothing but oke anie whit regarded. And yet see the change, for when our houses were builded of willow, then had we oken men ; but now that our houses are come to be made of oke, our men are not onlie become willow, but a great manie through Persian delicacie crept in among us altogither of straw, which is a sore alteration. In those, the courage of the owner was a sufficient defense to keepe the house in safetie ; but now the assurance of the timber, double doores, lockes and bolts, must defend the man from robbing. Now have we manie chimnies, and yet our tenderlings complaine of rheumes, catarhs, and poses. Then had we none but reredosses, and our heads did never ake. For as the smoke in those daies was supposed to be a sufficient hardning for the timber of the house, so it was reputed a far better medicine to keepe the goodman and his familie from the quacke or pose, wherewith as then verie few were oft acquainted.

This passage on the degeneracy of English courage was written only a year or two before Drake started on his voyage round the world, and not many years before the defeat of the Spanish Armada.

Perhaps nothing caused more disquiet to those who remembered the glories of old England than the introduction of newer and deadlier weapons. The popular outcry against the villanies of gunpowder had almost ceased in Shakespeare's day, though it is echoed in the speech of the fop who talked with Hotspur at the battle of Homildon Hill (*1 Hen. IV*, I. iii. 29–64). Roger Ascham, a scholar and patriot of the old school, in the reigns of Edward and Mary, had written a treatise in defence and praise of the famous long-bow, which won so many victories over the French. But the long-bow was doomed. Harrison says that the Frenchmen and ' Rutters ' (or German horsemen), clad in corslets, deride the English archers, and tauntingly expose themselves in open skirmish, crying ' Shoot, English ! ' But he adds that ' our countrie men wex skilfull in sundrie other points, as in shooting in small peeces, the caliver, the handling of the pike, in the severall uses whereof they are become verie expert '. In Elizabeth's reign young gallants practised much with the 'dag', or pistol, and gave up the old-fashioned sword and buckler in favour of the newer, more stylish, and deadlier rapier. The age of the sober-suited civilian was not yet; young men of good position went armed in the streets, and quarrels were frequent. 'Englishmen,' says Fynes Moryson, who gathered his impressions of English life at the close of the sixteenth century, 'especially being young and unexperienced, are apt to take things in snuffe. Of olde, when they were fenced with Bucklers, as with a Rampire, nothing was more common with them, then to fight about taking the right or left hand, or the wall, or upon any unpleasing countenance.' Such a young Englishman is described by Shakespeare when he makes Mercutio rail at Benvolio :

Thou art like one of these fellows that when he enters the confines of a tavern claps me his sword upon the table, and says, ' God send me no need of thee ! ' and by the operation of the second cup draws it on the drawer when indeed there is no need . . . Thou ! why, thou wilt quarrel with a man that hath a hair more or a hair less in his beard than thou hast. Thou wilt quarrel with a man for cracking nuts, having no other reason but because thou hast hazel eyes . . . Thou hast quarrelled with a man for coughing in the street, because he hath wakened thy dog that hath lain asleep in the sun . . . and yet thou wilt tutor me from quarrelling ! (*Rom. & Jul.* iii. i. 5–33)

In 1571 or thereabouts, says Stow, pikes of bucklers were first made ten or twelve inches long, ' wherewith they meant either to break the swords of their enemies, if it hit upon the pike, or else suddenly to run within them and stab, and thrust their buckler with the pike into the face, arm, or body of their adversary; but this continued not long: every haberdasher then sold bucklers.' In 1580, says Camden, a proclamation reduced swords to three feet, daggers to twelve inches besides the handle, and pikes of bucklers to two inches long. The rapier must have come into general use about the date of *Romeo and Juliet*, for Benvolio carries the old-fashioned arms, and Tybalt, in the same play, is the newer type of Italianate gallant, armed with a rapier :

He fights as you sing prick-song ; keeps time, distance, and proportion ; rests me his minim rest, one, two, and the third in your bosom ; the very butcher of a silk button, a duellist, a duellist ; a gentleman of the very first house, of the first and second cause. Ah ! the immortal passado ! the punto reverso ! the hay !

(*Rom. & Jul.* ii. iv. 22–8)

Henry Porter, the dramatist, in *The Two Angrie Women of Abington*, written in the closing years of the century, makes the jovial Dick Coomes lament the dearth of good swords and the passing of sword and buckler fight. 'I am sorry for it,' he says. 'I shall never see good manhood againe ; if it be once gone, this poking fight of rapier and dagger will come up then. Then a man, a tall man, a good sword and buckler man, will be spitted like a cat or a cunney.' Fynes Moryson, on the other hand, approves the change, and defends it by Scriptural precedent ; David, he says, made use of an unaccustomed weapon, and his innovation stood him in good stead when he fought with Goliath.

This revolution in weapons is only one instance of changes that affected all the habits of daily life. Harrison describes the great increase in solid building, and in the comforts of life. The older type of country house, he says, was built of timber beams and posts, and the walls of clay, with the stables and offices all under one roof. There was more comfort than show in the old style, so that the Spaniard of Queen Mary's time remarked, ' These English have their houses made of sticks and dirt, but they fare commonly as well as the King'. With the increase of wealth, houses in the country were enlarged and made more solid, and the dairy, stable, and brewhouse were put under separate roofs, adjoining the main building. Also glass was brought in, not only for windows, instead of the older wooden lattice-work or panels made of horn, but in a more delicate kind, for drinking-vessels, in preference even to gold and silver goblets. The nobility had fine Venice glasses, made at Murano, and the poorer classes followed suit with coarse glass made of fern and burnt stone. When Dame Quickly presses Sir John Falstaff for the debt he owes her, she says, ' I must be fain to pawn both my plate and the tapestry of my dining chambers ', and he replies by appealing to her sense of the fashionable usage—' Glasses, glasses, is the only drinking ' (*2 Hen. IV*, II. i. 159). Moreover, the farmers began to have furniture in greater plenty—arras hangings, silver and pewter plate, brass and linen—which, by capitalizing their savings, kept them from the rack-renting landlord. ' There are old men yet dwelling in the village where I remaine,' says Harrison (it was Radwinter in Essex), 'who have noted a general amendment of lodging ; for, said they, our fathers, yea, and we ourselves also have lain full oft upon straw pallets, on rough mats covered only with a sheet . . . and a good round log under their heads instead of a bolster or pillow. If it were so that our fathers, or the goodman of the house, had within seven years after his marriage purchased a mattress or flock-bed, and thereto a stack of chaff to rest his head upon, he thought himself to be as well lodged as the lord of the town, that peradventure lay seldom in a bed of down or whole feathers ; so well were they content, and with such base kind of furniture ; which also is not very much amended as yet in some parts of Bedfordshire.'

If the houses were sometimes scantily furnished, among all but the poorer classes there was great plenty and variety of meats—beef, mutton, veal, lamb, kid, pork, cony, capon, red deer, fish, and wild fowl, as well as venison pasty and brawn, which were dishes proper to England. In the nobleman's hall many of these were placed on the table at one time in silver dishes ; the reversion went to the servants, and from them to the poor at the gates. Dinner among the upper classes was commonly at eleven o'clock, and they sometimes sat at table till two or three. Busier people, both merchants and husbandmen, dined an hour later. Hospitality was general, except in London, where ' a cup of wine or beere with a napkin to wipe their lips, and an "You are heartelie welcome" is thought to be great interteinement'. There is a pleasant picture in Shakespeare's *Winter's Tale* of country hospitality:

> Fie, daughter ! when my old wife liv'd, upon
> This day she was both pantler, butler, cook ;
> Both dame and servant ; welcom'd all, serv'd all,
> Would sing her song and dance her turn ; now here,
> At upper end o' the table, now i' the middle ;
> On his shoulder, and his ; her face o' fire
> With labour ; and the thing she took to quench it
> She would to each one sip. (IV. iii. 55–62)

According to Harrison, there were about fifty-six sorts of light wine, and thirty kinds of stronger wine, Italian, Grecian, Spanish, Canary, and others. Beer, made of malt and hops, was a new-fangled drink in the age of

Elizabeth, and deserves more particular mention.   According to the old rhyming proverb, which has many variants,

> Turkeys, carps, hops, pickerel, and beer
> Came into England all in one year.

The year was somewhere between the tenth and the fifteenth year of King Henry VIII.   Andrew Borde, the physician of King Henry VIII's time, calls beer 'a naturall drynke for a Dutche man.   And nowe of late dayes it is moche used in Englande to the detryment of many Englysshe men.'   The habit of inordinate beer-drinking was distasteful to the aesthetic sense of the Latin peoples and to the moral sense of the English.   'I giue God thankes', says Della Casa, the author of the famous book of courtesy called *Il Galateo*,[1] 'that amongest many the Plagues that haue creapt ouer the Alpes, to infect vs : hitherto this worst of all the rest, is not come ouer : that we should take a pleasure and praise, to be drunke.'   Competitive social beer-drinking seems to have come into England by way of the Low Countries.   'In our time', says Fynes Moryson, 'some Gentlemen and Commanders from the warres of Netherland brought in the custome of the Germans large garaussing.'   Drunkenness is proper to no single nation, but the very word 'carouse', which means to empty the cup at a single draught, is a present to England from the Germans.   The practice became fashionable in the later years of the Queen, and in 1607 King James passed a statute against drunkenness, with suitable fines.

The most significant of Shakespeare's speeches against drunkenness is spoken by Hamlet, while he is waiting to see the Ghost, and hears the sound of trumpets and of ordnance shot off :

> *Ham.* The king doth wake to-night and takes his rouse,
> Keeps wassail, and the swaggering up-spring reels ;
> And, as he drains his draughts of Rhenish down,
> The kettle-drum and trumpet thus bray out
> The triumph of his pledge.
> *Hor.*   Is it a custom ?
> *Ham.* Ay, marry, is 't :
> But to my mind,—though I am native here
> And to the manner born,—it is a custom

---

[1] Translated into English by R. Peterson, 1576.

More honour'd in the breach than the observance.
This heavy-headed revel east and west
Makes us traduc'd and tax'd of other nations ;
They clepe us drunkards, and with swinish phrase
Soil our addition.   (*Haml.* i. iv. 8–20)

The visit of the English ambassador in 1603 to the Court of Denmark was the occasion of uproarious merrymaking at Copenhagen. Stow concludes his account thus :

To be briefe, it were superfluous to tell you all the superfluities that were used, and it would make a man sick to hear of their drunken healths : use hath brought it into a fashion, and fashion made it a habit, which ill beseemes our nation to imitate.

In the same year Ben Jonson wrote his *Ode* 'Αλληγορική in Hugh Holland's *Pancharis* ; among the nations he mentions

the Danes that drench
Their cares in wine.

The second quarto of *Hamlet* in which the lines against drunkenness first occur was published in 1604. They were omitted from the 1623 edition of the plays, perhaps because they came too near to censuring the vices of Queen Anne of Denmark's court. They have little dramatic value, and illustrate Shakespeare's habit of making room in his plays for any topic that is uppermost in his mind.

Foreign critics often charged the English with gross feeding and a senseless variety of meats. Fynes Moryson confesses that dainties invite to eat without hunger, and that the custom of sitting long at table makes men unawares eat more. But the Italians, he retorts, will eat a charger full of herbs and roots, with three pennyworth of bread. Now ' all fulness is ill, and that of bread worst '. So Falstaff thought, when he spent but one halfpenny on bread.

Elizabethan table manners were not delicate. Tom Coryat, among the observations he made during his travels (1608–9), records especially his first sight of forks used in eating :

This forme of feeding I understand is generally used in all places of Italy, their forkes being for the most part made of yron or steele, and some of silver, but those are used only by Gentlemen. The reason of this their curiosity is, because the Italian cannot by any meanes endure to have his dish touched with fingers, seeing all mens fingers are not alike cleane. Hereupon I my selfe thought good to imitate the Italian fashion by this forked cutting of meate, not only while I was in Italy, but also in Germany, and oftentimes in England since I came home.

The silver fork and the case of toothpicks, carried on the person, was the mark, later in King James's reign, of the travelled exquisite.[1] But in Shakespeare's England the meat was cut with a knife and taken in the hand. There is a vivid story in the *Merrie Conceited Jests of George Peele* (1607), a collection which perhaps better than any other gives a picture of the wealth and poverty, the squalor and magnificence of Elizabethan London. Peele, the story runs, was invited to a festive supper at the White Horse in Friday Street, and on his way thither met with a friend who had neither meat nor money, and felt ill at the stomach to hear of George's good luck. He was out at elbows, so George could not take him to the party, but they made an agreement together ; the friend, who is called ' H. M.', watched his time below, and when the meat was carried up, followed it into the room.

' You whoreson rascal,' quoth George, ' what make you here ? ' ' Sir,' quoth he, ' I am come from the party you wot of.' ' You rogue,' quoth George, ' have I not forewarned you of this ? ' ' I pray you, Sir,' quoth he, ' hear my errand.' ' Do you prate, you slave ? ' quoth George, and with that he took a rabbit out of the dish, and threw it at him. Quoth he, ' You use me very hardly.' ' You dunghill,' quoth George, ' do you outface me ? ' and with that took the other rabbit, and threw it at his head ; after that a loaf ; then, drawing his dagger, making an offer to throw it, the gentleman stayed him. Meanwhile H. M. got the loaf and the two rabbits, and away he went : which when George saw he was gone, after a little fretting, he sat quietly. So by that honest shift he helped his friend to his supper, and was never suspected for it of the company.[2]

The guests sat on stools, even at ceremonial banquets :

> now they rise again,
> With twenty mortal murders on their crowns,
> And push us from our stools.   (*Macb.* III. iv. 80-2)

Barnabe Rich in *The Honestie of this Age* (1614) tells how a certain Lord Mayor being ready to set himself down to dinner with his company, there thronged into the room of a sudden a company of uninvited strangers. The Lord

---

[1] Massinger, *The Great Duke of Florence*, iii.
[2] *The Works of George Peele*, ed. Bullen, 1888, vol. ii, p. 387.

Mayor was very hospitable, but this was more than he liked. ' Whereupon one of the officers coming to the Lord Mayor, said unto him, " If it please your Lordship, here be too few stools." "Thou liest, knave," answered the Mayor, "there are too many guests." ' There was certainly less formality in Elizabethan table manners than is found at a later time. When De Flores, the hired bravo in Middleton's great play, *The Changeling*, produces the ring-finger of the man whom Beatrice has ordered him to kill, she protests in horror.

> *De F.* Why, is that more than killing the whole man ? . . .
> A greedy hand thrust in a dish at court
> In a mistake hath had as much as this.

There were fierce contrasts in Elizabethan life, as in Elizabethan drama. Life was less private than it is to-day, and the extremes of wealth and poverty were more in evidence. But the great middle class, in town and country, was prosperous and prodigal. There are three devouring cankers in England, says Philip Stubbes, which, if they be not checked, will eat up the Commonwealth—dainty fare, gorgeous buildings, and sumptuous apparel.

> For I have heard my Father say, that in his dayes, one dish, or two of good wholsome meate was thought sufficient, for a man of great worship to dyne withall. . . . A good peece of beef was thought than, good meat, and able for the best, but now, it is thought too grosse: for their tender stomachs are not able to digest such crude and harsh meats.

When Katharine in *The Taming of the Shrew* was willing to take the beef without the mustard, and spoke of beef as

> A dish that I do love to feed upon,   (IV. iii. 24)

she had been reduced to a more tolerant frame of mind.

The clothing of Shakespeare's time was so diverse and brilliant, and the fashions changed so often, that a full account of it is hardly feasible. Burckhardt, the historian of the Italian Renaissance, tells how in Florence, by the year 1390, there were no reigning modes ; every one dressed as he pleased, and created his own costume. Something of this experimental independence persisted in the age of Elizabeth. Modern uniformity of costume saves time and trouble, and gives ease and scope to those who work for impersonal aims. But where costume is a means of self-expression, as it was in that great age of the adventurer, diversity and change is the rule. The English had the name, at that time, of being the most feather-headed, imitative race on earth.

> Th' English Apes and very Zanies be
> Of every thing that they doe heare and see,

says Drayton [1]; and again,

> My Muse is rightly of the English straine,
> That cannot long one Fashion intertaine.[2]

The grave prose writers tell the same story. To count the fashions in England, says one, would be to number the stars of heaven and the sands of the sea. The sober Camden, writing of the year 1574, says:

In these dayes had very great excesse of Apparell spred it selfe all over England, and the habite of our own Countrey, through a peculiar Vice incident to our apish Nation, grew into such contempt, that men by their new-fashioned Garments, and apparell too gawdy, discovered a certaine deformitie and insolencie of minde, whilest they jetted up and downe in theyr Silkes, glittering with gold and silver eyther imbroydered or laced.

Stow says that in his time gentlemen, citizens, and yeomen wore better habit and household ornaments than any Earl or Countess in former ages. Men of mean rank wore garters, and rosettes on their shoes, of more than five pounds price; and some wore scarfs (also a new fashion) from ten pounds apiece unto thirty pounds or more. The milliners' shops were stored with rich and curious embroidered waistcoats of the value of ten, twenty, and forty pounds, and there were more silk shops in Cheapside during the latter years of Elizabeth than there had formerly been in all England. The process of weaving and knitting silk by machinery was perfected by William Lee, Master of Arts; and tufted taffetas, wrought velvets, and branched satins were made in Shoreditch. 'The sum of a hundred pounde', says one writer, 'is not to be accompted much in these dayes to be bestowed of apparell for one gentleman.'[3] The conversation between Petruchio and the tailor in *The Taming of the Shrew*, gives

---

[1] *Epistle to H. Reynolds*, 1627.   [2] *Idea*, To Reader, ed. 1619.
[3] *The Institution of a Gentleman*, 1555.

some idea of the elaborate fashions of the time and of Shakespeare's opinion concerning them :

> *Pet.* What's this ? a sleeve ? 'tis like a demi-cannon :
> What ! up and down, carv'd like an apple-tart ?
> Here's snip and nip and cut and slish and slash,
> Like to a censer in a barber's shop. . . .
> *Tai.* You bid me make it orderly and well,
> According to the fashion and the time.
> *Pet.* Marry, and did: but, if you be remember'd
> I did not bid you mar it to the time.   (*Tam. Sh.* IV. iii. 88–95)

Stubbes, out of the wealth of his indignation, gives a very full account of the various garments worn,—the steeple-crowned hats ; the battlemented hats, of silk, velvet, taffeta and sarsenet, with hat-bands of black, white, russet, red, green, or yellow, never the same for two days ; the great bunches of feathers of diverse colours ('many get good living by dying and selling of them,' says Master Stubbes, thinking of his Puritan friends in Blackfriars) ; the monstrous padded doublets of satin and taffeta with gold and silver lace ; the hose after the French and Venetian fashions ; the silk stockings, costing more than an entire costume used to cost aforetime ; the shoes of various-coloured leather, slashed and embroidered with gold or silver, raised from the ground on cork, ornamented with buckles or rosettes, and collecting the mud from the ill-tended streets ; the shirts of cambric or lawn, wrought with silk needle-work—'in so much as I have heard of Shirtes that have cost, some ten shillynges, some twentie, some fortie, some five pound, some twentie Nobles, and (whiche is horrible to heare) some ten pounde a peece.' The cost of Falstaff's shirts, it will be remembered, was a matter of controversy :

> *Quickly.* I bought you a dozen of shirts to your back.
> *Falstaff.* Dowlas, filthy dowlas : I have given them away to bakers' wives, and they have made bolters of them.
> *Quickly.* Now, as I am true woman, holland of eight shillings an ell.   (*1 Hen. IV*, III. iii. 77–83)

Falstaff, at this time, had in his pocket nothing but tavern reckonings and one poor pennyworth of sugar-candy. To find the price of a costume gentlemen sold their lands (Harrison knew one who sold sixty woods to buy a pair of galligascons) ; gallants starved themselves and dined with

Duke Humphrey or at a threepenny ordinary ; country squires pinched themselves that their sons might appear as gentlemen. Hall, the satirist, describes such a squire :

> Himselfe goes patch'd like some bare cottyer
> Least he might ought the future stocke appeyre.

As for the son, he changes his suit three times a day, in order to air his wardrobe :

> Bearing his paune-layd lands upon his backe,
> As snayles their shels, or pedlers doe their packe.

It is no wonder, in view of the almost fabulous extravagance and variety of the fashions, that many men in England felt as much indignation as Hotspur himself at the affectations of their younger fellow-countrymen. The Puritans, remembering the garden of Eden, held that clothes are a mark of man's fall, and a badge of his disgrace ; they therefore thought it a horrible sign of pride that he should deck and paint the body they despised, and glory in his shame. The elder statesmen, and Elizabeth herself, regarded with anxiety the deportation of gold from England to pay for these foreign novelties. All the staider members of the commonwealth disapproved of the upheaval of social barriers and the confusion of social distinctions which the fuller life of the time brought with it. It was hard, they complained, to know who was noble, who was worshipful, who was a gentleman, and who was not, when all men, even those of base birth and below the yeomanry in standing, went daily in silks, velvets, damasks, taffetas, and such-like. The name of ' Master ' began to be claimed by every butcher, shoemaker, tailor, cobbler, husbandman ; ' yea, every tinker, pedlar and swineherd must be called by the vain name.' Moreover, the rapid change of fashions was very expensive for sober-minded men, who, not wishing to appear singular, were compelled to go with the crowd. Fynes Moryson tells, by way of fable, how Jupiter once sent a shower of rain which made fools of all that it wetted. Only one philosopher, who was studying in his room, escaped. So when he came out for his daily walk he found himself the only sane man in a foolish city. But he was so taunted and mocked and pelted for his singularity, that he ran home and prayed Jupiter to send another shower, that he might be a fool with the rest. The fashions rid post, and changed every

Th'admired Empresse throwgh the worlde applauded,
For supreme vertues rarest Imitatien,
Whose Scepters rule sunes lowde-voyc'd trumpet laudeth,
Untill the eares of euery forraigne Nation,
Cannopey'd vnder powrefull Angells winges
To her Immortall praise sweete Science singes.

Willms   Rogers sculp.

QUEEN ELIZABETH by WILLIAM ROGERS

year or two. Hose from being wide became narrow and then wide again. The French and Venetian hose were narrow, as may be seen by the speech of the porter at Macbeth's gate : ' Faith, here's an English tailor come hither for stealing out of a French hose : come in, tailor; here you may roast your goose ' (*Macb.* II. iii. 15–17). The Burgundian hose were wide, and both they and the doublet came to be padded and stuffed until the wearer resembled Punch in figure.

In their imitation of foreign peoples the English were eclectic, and early got a name for incongruous mixtures. ' How oddly he is suited ! ' says Portia of the young English baron, Falconbridge, ' I think he bought his doublet in Italy, his round hose in France, his bonnet in Germany, and his behaviour everywhere ' (*Merch. of V.* I. ii. 78–81). This accusation is a commonplace of the satirists ; here is Drayton's portrait of the Englishman who has lost his native character :

> Some travell hence t'enrich their minds with skill,
> Leave heere their good, and bring home others ill ;
> Which seeme to like all Countries but their owne,
> Affecting most where they the least are knowne.
> Their leg, their thigh, their back, their neck, their head,
> There form'd, there fetch'd, there found, there borrowed.
> In their attire, their jesture, and their gate,
> Fond in each one, in all Italionate.
> Italian, French, Dutch, Spanish altogether,
> Yet not all these, nor one entirely neyther.
> So well in all deformity in fashon,
> Borrowing a limne of ev'ry severall Nation ;
> And nothing more than England hold in scorne,
> So live as strangers whereas they were borne.[1]

This character is a stock figure of the drama and of satire ; Shakespeare sketched it, in passing, more than once, and criticized it in the words of Rosalind :

Farewell, Monsieur Traveller : look you lisp, and wear strange suits, disable all the benefits of your own country, be out of love with your nativity, and almost chide God for making you that countenance you are ; or I will scarce think you have swam in a gondola.   (*A. Y. L.* IV. i. 34–40)

But these severe judgements are not the final verdict on the extravagances of the Renaissance ; these light things

---

[1] Drayton, *Heroical Epistles*, Geraldine to Surrey (1599), 119–32.

speak more convincingly than any bookish borrowings to
the strength of the tide which brought scholarship and art
into England. Where the imagination is touched, it will
not be satisfied with a discipleship which leaves life where
it was, and tries unreal experiments in literature. The
English travellers who overran the Continent were eager to
copy all they saw. Women's fashions are perhaps a surer
testimony than books to the influence of one civilization
upon another. Masks, fans, busks, muffs, periwigs, and
bodkins, among other novelties, were all introduced from
Italy by way of France during the earlier part of Elizabeth's
reign, at a time when many Englishmen were serving in
France as volunteer soldiers. Bodkins were the little knives
or daggers that ladies carried about them ; Juliet had one
to kill herself with if the poison should fail. Periwigs, or
false hair, are treated often, and with some acrimony, by
Shakespeare.

> Look on beauty,
> And you shall see 'tis purchas'd by the weight ; . . .
> So are those crisped snaky golden locks
> Which make such wanton gambols with the wind,
> Upon supposed fairness, often known
> To be the dowry of a second head,
> The skull that bred them, in the sepulchre.
>
> (*Merch. of V*. III. ii. 88–96)

Of all classes of the community, says Harrison, the merchants and citizens of London kept most gravity in their
attire, and altered it the least ; but ' the yoonger sort of their
wives ', he adds, ' both in attire and costlie housekeeping
can not tell when and how to make an end, as being women
in deed in whome all kind of curiositie is to be found and
seene, and in farre greater measure than in women of higher
calling '. They were fond of foreign rarities, according to
the old proverb, ' Far fet and dear bought is good for ladies ',
and they took up with all the new fashions. Early in Elizabeth's reign they discarded the little white knit caps of
woollen yarn which they formerly wore, and began to haunt
the shops of the ' puppet-making tailors '. The tailors
delighted in quick changes, and when the wheel of fashion
revolved too slowly, were willing to jog it. They and the
merchants, we are told, when the fashions of France and
Italy were all run through, sent out new patterns and stuffs
to be made abroad, and so ' taught strangers to serve our

lightness with such inventions as themselves never knew before '.

Shakespeare's characters are almost all plain gentle or simple ; he does not anatomize the burgess, or draw any really familiar picture of the burgess's ambitious and fashionable young wife. It is easy to discern from his plays that he was at home in the country, and was a visitor and lodger in the town. The inn-yard, the tavern, the theatre, the street, and all that drifting populace which plies its trade or takes its ease in these places, he knew by heart. Of the classes who had social aspirations, and of those who kept themselves to themselves, he knew very little. But in *Eastward Hoe* (1605), Jonson, or Chapman, or Marston, has drawn a life-like portrait of the young city wife. Her name is Gertrude, and she is to be married to a kind of a knight, called Sir Petronel Flash. She models her be- haviour accordingly :

I must be a Lady and I will be a Lady. I like some humors of the Citty Dames well, to eate Cherries onely at an Angell a pound, good ; to dye rich Scarlet black, prety ; to line a Grogarom gowne cleane thorough with velvet, tollerable ; their pure linen, their smocks of 3 pounde a smock are to be borne withall. But your minsing niceries, taffata pipkins, durance petticotes, and silver bodkins— Gods my life, as I shal be a Lady I cannot indure it.

(*Eastward Hoe*, I. i.)

The race of fashion may be well illustrated by a brief history of the Rise, Progress, Decline, and Fall of the Ruff. The original of the ruff was the band, or falling-band, a wide embroidered collar of linen or cambric, worn round the neck. King Henry VIII is said to have been the first person in England to wear a band round his neck—very plain, without lace, and an inch or two in depth. Before very long the ruff proper, a large circular pleated collar, standing out from the neck, came in from France. This earlier type of ruff may be seen in some of the portraits of Mary Queen of Scots. Ruffs came to be called picardels or picadils, and were made by one Higgins, a tailor, who lived on the outskirts of the town in a road which was first called Piccadilly in the reign of Elizabeth. Then began the race for distinction among makers and wearers of ruffs. Ruffs were made of finer and finer material, were more deeply pleated and embroidered, and grew larger and larger in size.

At first it was difficult to wear them very large of fine, limp material, for to hold them out from the neck they had to be underpropped by wire frameworks, which were called ' supportasses '. But in 1564 a certain Mistress Dinghen, the daughter of a Dutch gentleman, arrived in England, and taught the use of starch. The citizens' wives flocked to her ; her fees were—to teach starching, £5 ; to teach the seething of starch, 20s. So skilful was she at starching even the flimsiest materials that it was jestingly said that she would soon make ruffs out of spiders' webs. Thereupon the use of lawn and cambric for ruffs increased, until by the end of Elizabeth's reign there was more lawn and cambric in an ordinary linen-draper's shop than there had been before with all the merchants of London. Foreign nations were soon left behind ; ruffs were still called ' the French fashion ', but the French, says Stow, call us monsters for wearing them. Their size increased till they were a foot deep, and a man's head looked like a head on a platter. Moreover, the introduction of steel poking-sticks,[1] about 1570, in place of the old setting-sticks of bone or wood, facilitated the making of elaborate ruffs. So that whereas an ordinary gentleman's ruff in 1560 cost twelve pence only, in 1620 it cost no less than four pounds.[2] Queen Elizabeth tried in vain to limit the size of ruffs, equally in vain the Puritans inveighed against them. One of the best of the moral stories in *The Anatomie of Abuses* is the story of the awful judgement that fell on a young woman of Antwerp. She had great trouble with her ruffs for a wedding-party, and at last in her impatience wished that the devil might take her if ever she wore one of those neckerchers again. With that a pleasant and courteous young man came in to assist her, and, sad to relate, twisted her neck. At her funeral the coffin proved too heavy to lift, and when it was opened, there was found within it a lean and deformed black cat, setting of ruffs and frizzling of hair. These things happened on the 27th of May, 1582.

There is a wild eloquence in Stubbes's invectives against the gallants of his day. They have great and monstrous ruffs, he says, made of cambric, holland, or lawn, and a quarter of a yard or more deep. If the wind blow and

---

[1] See *Winter's Tale*, IV. iii. 228.
[2] Walter Cary, *The Present State of England*, 1627.

hit upon the crazy bark of their bruised ruffs then they go flip-flap in the wind, like rags flying about, and lie upon their shoulders like the dish-clout of a slut. But the devil, who first invented ruffs, has invented also two mainstays or pillars for the kingdom of ruffs, the one being the wire supportass, the other starch. Starch is the devil's liquor, the starching houses are consecrate to ' Belzebub and Cerberus, arch-devils of great ruffs ', the ruffs themselves are the ' cartwheels of the devil's chariot of pride, leading the direct way to the dungeon of hell '. This is all very violent, but the information it conveys is borne out by others. Dekker, who was no harsh Puritan, speaks of

your trebble-quadruple Daedalian ruffes . . . your stiffenecked re-batoes, (that have more arches for pride to row under, then can stand under five London Bridges).

Ruffs were not only monstrous in size, but were worn one above another, step by step, the minor ruffs below, the ' master devil ruff ', as Stubbes calls it, on the top, and raised at the back of the head. These tiers of ruffs are called ' cabbage ruffs ' by Samuel Rowlands.

Moreover starch was made of sundry colours. One Mistress Anne Turner, the widow of a doctor of physic, remarkable for her great beauty, was the inventor of yellow starch. This Mistress Turner was afterwards one of the minor agents in the murder of Sir Thomas Overbury, and Lord Chief Justice Coke, in condemning her to death, ordered that ' as she was the person who had brought yellow starched ruffs into vogue, she should be hanged in that dress, that the same might end in shame and detesta-tion '. Even the hangman was decorated with yellow ruffs for the occasion.[1]

So yellow starch went partly out of fashion, and large ruffs followed it before the end of King James's reign. Plain bands or collars succeeded; then the laced neck-cloths of Charles II's time. The Eton collar is the nearest representative of the old falling-band, and the band-box, which was a box for keeping bands or ruffs, is the funeral monument which serves to recall the past.

Many of the novelties of Elizabeth's reign were of the kind that works a change in the customs of daily life. Coryat, on his travels, noted certain things made of

---

[1] *Works of Sir Thomas Overbury*, ed. Rimbault, 1856, p. xxxvii *note*.

leather in the form of a canopy, and hooped inside,—
' called in the Italian tongue *umbrellas.*' These were
destined not to be seen in England for nearly two centuries
more. It was early in the reign of Elizabeth that coaches
first came into general use. William Boonen, a Dutchman
and the Queen's coachman, first built coaches in England
in the year 1564, and within twenty years after there was
a great trade in them. ' After a while,' says Stow, ' divers
great ladies, with as great jealousy of the Queen's displeasure, made them coaches, and rid them up and down
the countries to the great admiration of all beholders.'
Before that time long wagons plied from London to Canterbury, Ipswich, Norwich, and other places, carrying passengers and commodities. But the private coach, or
caroche, was common by the end of the century. Fynes
Moryson, writing in 1617 says :

Sixtie or seventy yeeres agoe, Coaches were very rare in England,
but at this day pride is so farre increased, as there be few Gentlemen of any account (I meane elder Brothers) who have not their
Coaches, so as the streetes of London are almost stopped up with
them.

Drayton, addressing his lady in a magnificent sonnet,
alludes to this new fashion, and to women's habit of
painting their faces :

How many paltry, foolish, painted things
That now in Coaches trouble ev'ry Street
Shall be forgotten, whom no Poet sings,
Ere they be well wrap'd in their winding Sheet !
Where I to thee Eternitie shall give,
When nothing else remayneth of these dayes,
And Queenes hereafter shall be glad to live
Upon the Almes of thy superfluous prayse ;
Virgins and Matrons reading these my Rimes,
Shall be so much delighted with thy story,
That they shall grieve, they liv'd not in these Times,
To have seene thee, their Sexes onely glory :
    So shalt thou flye above the vulgar Throng,
    Still to survive in my immortall Song.[1]

Tobacco, ' an herb so generally received in the courts of
Princes, the chambers of nobles, the bowers of sweet ladies,
the cabins of soldiers ',[2] was another of these novelties.
The cat is never mentioned in Holy Writ, and tobacco is

---

[1] *Idea* (1619), vi.   [2] Jonson. *Every Man in his Humour.*

never mentioned by Shakespeare; but it must not be forgotten. For the neglect of the sovereign weed by his friend and fellow Ben Jonson made plentiful amends. Stow asserts categorically (and there is no reason to doubt his word) that tobacco was first brought into England in 1565 by Sir John Hawkins. Camden tells how some fifteen years later the practice of 'tobacco-drinking' became common, and how Fletcher, Bishop of London and father of the dramatist, died of excessive tobacco-taking after the death of his wife. Sir Walter Ralegh's name is wrongly connected with the introduction of tobacco into the country, though no doubt he did much by his example to make it fashionable at Court. The story commonly told of Ralegh, that his serving-man, seeing smoke issue from his mouth, threw a tankard of beer over him to quench the fire, is told by Barnabe Riche, in *The Irish Hubbub* (1619), of a Welshman newly come to London, and occurs also in the collection of Tarlton's *Jests*. Barnabe Riche estimates that early in King James's reign there were at least seven thousand shops in London which sold tobacco, and by reckoning the takings of a single shop at half a crown a day, arrives at the conclusion that the annual takings of the trade amount to £319,375,—'all spent in smoke.'[1] These are exact figures inexactly obtained, after the manner of statisticians. But Rich's evidence is good. He tells how tobacco was sold not only in special shops (like Abel Drugger's), but also in taverns, inns, alehouses, and by apothecaries, grocers, and chandlers. A lively pamphlet war on the merits and demerits of tobacco was carried on for years, and the King himself condescended to issue a *Counterblast to Tobacco* (1604), calling on his subjects not to imitate the base Indians, 'slaves to the Spaniards, refuse to the world, and as yet aliens from the holy Covenant of God'. He found an able second in Joshua Sylvester, the translator of Du Bartas, who produced a long poem, sufficiently described by its title—*Tobacco Battered, and the Pipes Shattered (about their Ears that idlely Idolize so base and barbarous a Weed; or at least-wise over-love so loathsome Vanitie): by a Volley of Holy Shot Thundered from Mount Helicon.* King James followed up his pamphlet with an imposition of six shillings and eightpence a pound laid

---

[1] *The Honestie of this Age* (1614).

upon the drug ; but if he scotched the practice of ' tobacconing ', he did not kill it.

France and Italy, which were ahead of England in the arts of civilized life, lent England many of their improvements. The custom of sending noblemen's and gentlemen's sons for a period of travel abroad began in the time of Henry VII, and became general in the sixteenth century. In Harrison's day it was the rule for university men (especially those who studied medicine) to travel abroad to complete their education. The history of English scholarship and literature is a sufficient record of the benefits attending this practice. But it was an age-long complaint of the sober patriots at home that many of these students brought back only foreign vices. Harrison speaks of the ' atheism, vicious conversation, and ambitious and proud behaviour ' that were imported from Italy. One travelled gentleman of his acquaintance held discourse like this : ' Faith and truth is to be kept where no loss or hindrance of a future purpose is sustained by holding of the same ; and forgiveness only to be showed when full revenge is made.' These two lessons, the playing fast and loose with a pledged word, and the free use of the dagger and the poison-bowl, were easily to be learned in Italy. Fortunately England did not learn them. The Italian vendetta, of which so many terrible pictures are to be found in the dramatists, came into English literature rather than into English life, and the worst immediate effect of English intercourse with Italy was the importation of affected manners of speech and gesture. It is worth noting that the bravo, or hired ruffian, who will commit any sin for money, and who plays so conspicuous a part in many fine tragedies, did not interest Shakespeare. The murderers in *Macbeth* are perhaps as near to the type as any of his characters ; he needs them for the plot, and sketches them hastily in a few lines. When he came to draw Iago he raised him to a pitch of wickedness far above the mercenary crimes of broken and reckless soldiers. On the other hand, he takes delight in the vanities of the man who has made the tour of Europe :

> Now your traveller,
> He and his toothpick at my worship's mess,
> And when my knightly stomach is suffic'd,
> Why then I suck my teeth, and catechize

My picked man of countries : ' My dear sir,'—
Thus, leaning on mine elbow, I begin,—
' I shall beseech you,'—that is question now ;
And then comes answer like an absey-book :
' O, sir,' says answer, ' at your best command ;
At your employment ; at your service, sir.'
' No, sir,' says question, ' I, sweet sir, at yours : '
And so, ere answer knows what question would,
Saving in dialogue of compliment,
And talking of the Alps and Apennines,
The Pyrenean and the river Po,
It draws towards supper in conclusion so.
But this is worshipful society
And fits the mounting spirit like myself. (*John*, I. i. 189–206)

James Howell, in his *Instructions for Forreine Travel*, gives the best account we have of the travel of that age. For what is called scenery he cares nothing ; his purpose is to study humanity and to collect notes on manners and customs. He would ' rather travel fifty miles to hear a wise man than five to see a fine city ' ; yet he prefers the city to the country, and both to the mountains, which bear nothing useful to man or beast. He advises all those who travel abroad to stay for some time in each place, and to acquaint themselves with the manners of the inhabitants. Even Tom Coryat, ' the leg-stretcher of Odcombe', who is commonly regarded as a buffoon and a zany, is preoccupied with the same interests, and records the dimensions of churches, the inscriptions on tombs, the curious customs preserved at universities or boroughs, with all the zeal of an antiquary.

Another foot-traveller, as poor as Coryat, and no less witty, wrote a premature epitaph on Coryat, in which he taunts him with a pettifogging concern for antiquities :

> Who now will take the height of every gallows ?
> And who'll describe the sign of every alehouse ?

But Taylor himself, in his journeys to Scotland, Wales, Cornwall, or Holland, pays attention to the same things that attracted Coryat. There is nothing he is fonder of describing than that common wayside object, a gallows ; and where the human interest fails the road has no attraction for him. It is true that once at Netherstowey, where he stopped at the Rose and Crown Inn on his way to Cornwall, he records that ' being weary of the house I went and sat for three hours in the road ', but he was repelled by the house, and he does not mention the beauties of the Quantock Hills. There had been trouble about some powdered beef and carrots, very hospitably offered, but not forthcoming, for the only servant was tending hogs in the fields. After waiting three hours for the beef and carrots, Taylor spent two more waiting for an egg and parsley, which had been mentioned as a possible substitute ; then, finding there were no eggs to be had, he got a piece of bread and butter, and went to bed in a rage, but, for various reasons, not to sleep.

The Rose and Crown Inn at Netherstowey was not a fair example of English country inns. Travellers of the better sort, who arrived on horseback, would be more carefully waited on than the poor poet, who, for all that his verses were highly esteemed by King James, was threadbare and on foot. The well-to-do traveller was subject to other annoyances. There were many rogues, or ' knaves in buckram ', ready to waylay him and lighten him of his money. These men, says Harrison, often carried staves ' thirteen or fourteen foot long, beside the pike of twelve inches '. The traveller was forced, in self-protection, to carry a ' case of dags ', and even so, he often was robbed. Ministers of the gospel, we are told, would not carry weapons except a dagger or hanger.

There is no doubt about it, the complaints come on all hands ; the England of Queen Elizabeth's time was overrun by idle vagabonds. They were a symptom and consequence of the great change which was passing over the country. Some of them were serving-men out of employ, dismissed from the retinues of noblemen or gentlemen, and compelled to shift for themselves. Some were old soldiers, who had come home from the wars ; they were accustomed to living on booty, and found no standing army to discipline and control them. Others were labourers, thrown out of work by the immense enclosures and the conversion of tillage into pasturage. The multitude of these, having no choice but crime or starvation, occasioned the first English Poor Law in 1601. The whole country was in the throes of the transformation from its old sober estate to its new commercial opportunities. Many of the men who carved out the greatness of the Elizabethan Age had adventure thrust upon them by the break-up of the old order.

Men are more conscious of the past that they see vanishing than of the future that awaits them, and the air rang with complaints of the change from the settled feudal order to a new untried civilization. The great families and the great houses were breaking and failing. The change was slow ; and many of the new men gained applause by imitating the old usages. Sir Christopher Hatton was praised for his housekeeping at Holdenby in Northampton-shire. The house was a new erection, with separate chimneys—that is to say, with fireplaces in the private rooms. Yet the old generosity was imitated.

And such worthie porte and daiely hospitalitie kepte, that although the owner hymself useth not to come there once in twoo yeares, yet I dare undertake, there is daiely provision to be founde convenient, to entertaine any noble manne with his whole traine that should hap to call in of a sodain. And how many Gentlemen and straungers, that comes but to see the house, are there daiely welcomed, feasted, and well lodged. From whence should he come, be he riche, bee he poore, that should not there bee entertained, if it please hym to call in ? To bee short, Holdenby giveth daiely relief to suche as bee in wante, for the space of sixe or seven miles' compasse.[1]

The owner useth not to come there once in two years— there is the secret of the change. He was following his fortune elsewhere, and if he kept a good house, it was merely a rich man's fancy, as a stockbroker may amuse himself with a model farm. The poor did not much trouble their heads about economic causes, but everywhere they witnessed the decay of the old order, under which the great house had been the mainstay of a district, the centre of employment and charity ; and they lamented the corruption of the times. The song and ballad writers (they were many) who took this for their theme do sometimes show an insight into the meaning of the change. Here is a song from *The Servingman's Comfort*, a pamphlet of 1598 ; the writer seems to understand that wealth has broken out from its old channels, and that there is no sufficient motive to keep noble families on their estates :

> When Countreys causes did require,
> Each Nobleman to keepe his house,
> Then Blew coates had what they desyre,
> Good cheare, with many a full carouse :
> > But now not as it wont to be,
> > For dead is Liberalitie.

[1] *Riche his Farewell to Militarie profession,* 1581.

The Haull boordes-end is taken up,
No Dogges do differ for the bones,
Blacke-jack is left, now Glasse or Cup,
It makes mee sigh with many groones,
    To thinke what was, now thus to be
    By death of Liberalitie.

The golden worlde is past and gone,
The Iron age hath runne his race,
The lumpe of Lead is left alone
To presse the poore in every place :
    Nought els is left but miserie,
    Since death of Liberalitie.

Some twenty years earlier than this lament the whole
question, and it was the most important question of the time,
was discussed dialogue-fashion in a pamphlet on *Cyvile and
Uncyvile Lyfe* (1579).   The town gentleman criticizes the
enormous number of useless retainers who are gathered about
a country house.   The country gentleman is shocked by the
proposal that he shall keep only enough for necessary uses :

Doo you so say Sir ? . . . If wee Gentlemen should so doo, how
should wee furnish our Halles ? how should wee bee ready for
quarrellers ? or how should our Wives bee wayted on when they
ride abroade, as commonly their custome is, cheefely in Sommer,
the faire season and hunting time ?

The town gentleman admits that retainers were necessary
in the time of the Barons' Wars, but what use are they
now ?   The country gentleman undertakes their defence :

Our serving men . . . can well and decently weare their garments,
and cheefely their lyvery coates, their swords and bucklers ; they
can also carve very cumly at your table, as to unlase a Conny, to
raise a Capon, trompe a Crane, and so likewise handle all other
dishes, and meates that are set on the board before you : Some of
them also can wrestle, leape well, run, and daunce.   There are also
of those that can shoote in longe Bowes, crosse Bowes, or handgunne :
Yea there wanteth not some that are both so wise, and of so good
audacitie, as they can, and doo (for lacke of better company) entertaine their Maister with table talke, bee it his pleasure to speake
either of Hawkes, or houndes, fishinge, or fowling, sowing or graf-
finge, ditchinge or hedginge, the dearth or cheapenes of grayne, or
any such matters, wherof Gentlemen commonly speake in the
Country.

Their counsel for the defence does not mention that they
also acted interludes at times, but he tells how they take
part in outdoor sports and indoor games :

Some to Ticktacke, some Lurche, some to Irish game, or Dublets:
Other sit close to the Cardes, at Post and Paire, at Ruffe, or
Colchester Trumpe, at Mack or Maw: yea, there are some ever so fresh
gamesters, as wil bare you company at Novem Quinque, at Faring,
Trey trip, or one and thirty, for I warrant you, we have right good
fellowes in the countrey, sumtimes also (for shift of sports, you know,
is delectable) we fall to slide thrifte, to Penny prick, and in winter
nights we use certaine Christmas games very propper, and of much
agilitie ; wee want not also pleasant madheaded knaves, that bee
properly learned, and will reade in diverse pleasant bookes, and good
Authors : As Sir Guy of Warwicke, foure Sonnes of Amon, the
Ship of Fooles, the Budget of Demaundes, the Hundreth merry
Tales,[1] the Booke of Ryddles,[2] and many other excellent writers, both
witty and pleasaunt.

In the end the townsman carries the debate at all points,
and converts the countryman, whom he bids ' most hartely
welcome to our town habitation, as a place fittest for
a Gentleman '. In fact, gentlemen more and more resorted
thither until the life and administration of the country
threatened to fall to pieces, and a law of Charles I was
passed, in 1633, compelling country gentlemen to spend
some part of the year on their estates. But the law did
not avail to check the rush to the towns. All through
Shakespeare's lifetime the tide was flowing in that direction, and all classes went with the tide. The gentlemen
sought new polite interests—music, poetry, dress, diver-
sion ; the serving-men, like Edgar in *King Lear*, were
proud in heart and mind, curled their hair, wore gloves in
their caps, and imitated their old masters. London, with
its court and palaces, its river and shipping, its theatres
and taverns, and its never-failing life of the streets, was as
full of possibilities and surprises as the Bagdad of Haroun
Alraschid. It was a city packed with humanity, rich in
adventure, crime, and disorder. The theatre itself was
a perfect expression of the new age ; it belonged to the
suburbs, and to the new roving population ; the grave
merchants and the civic authorities opposed it steadfastly
at every stage of its growth. Even the theatre was no
more than an artificial reflection of that fuller and more
disordered life of masquerades and plots which surged in
the streets. The pamphlets which were written by the poet,
Robert Greene, in the last two years of his life, give a wonder-

---

[1] Cf. *Much Ado*, II. i. 137.   [2] Cf. *M. Wives*, I. i. 209.

ful vivid picture of the London that he lived in. The ostensible purpose of these cony-catching pamphlets is moral, to warn ignorant youth against the thousand and one devices of rogues and sharpers. But their value to us is rather in their realistic description of the life of the town that Shakespeare knew. There was one cunning knave who used to await outside citizens' houses till they were busy in their shops.

Then would he step up the stairs (for there was and is another door to the house besides that which entereth into the shop), and what was next hand come ever away with. One time above the rest, in an evening about Candlemas, when day light shuts in about six of the clock, he watched to do some feat in the house, and seeing the mistress go forth with her maid, the goodman and his folks very busy in the shop, up the stairs he goes as he was wont to do, and lifting up the latch of the hall portal door, saw nobody near to trouble him ; when stepping into the next chamber, where the Citizen and his wife usually lay, at the bed's feet there stood a handsome trunk, wherein was very good linen, a fair gilt salt, two silver French bowls for wine, two silver drinking-pots, a stone jug covered with silver, and a dozen of silver spoons. This trunk he brings to the stairs' head, and making fast the door again, draws it down the steps so softly as he could, for it was so big and heavy as he could not easily carry it ; having it out at the door, unseen of any neighbour or anybody else, he stood struggling with it to lift it up on the stall, which by reason of the weight troubled him very much. The goodman coming forth of his shop, to bid a customer or two farewell, made the fellow afraid he should now be taken for altogether, but calling his wits together to escape if he could, he stood gazing up at the sign belonging to the house, as though he were desirous to know what sign it was, which the Citizen perceiving, came to him and asked him what he sought for. ' I look for the sign of the Blue Bell, Sir,' quoth the fellow, ' where a gentleman having taken a chamber for this Term-time hath sent me hither with this his trunk of apparel.' Quoth the Citizen, ' I know no such sign in this street, but in the next ' (naming it) ' there is such a one indeed, and there dwelleth one that letteth forth chambers to gentlemen.' ' Truly, Sir,' quoth the fellow, ' that's the house I should go to ; I pray you, Sir, lend me your hand but to help the trunk on my back, for I thinking to ease me a while upon your stall, set it short, and now I can hardly get it up again.' The Citizen, not knowing his own trunk, but indeed never thinking on any such notable deceit, helps him up with the trunk, and so sends him away roundly with his own goods. When the trunk was missed, I leave to your conceits what household grief there was on all sides.

This short story, better than any bare description, gives a view of a citizen's house and shop, the sign hanging above it,

the stall or bulk in front of it, and, upstairs, the solid trunk
at the bed's foot for the treasuring of linen and silver.   In
like fashion Greene gives us glimpses of dealings in shops,
of chance encounters and conversations in the street or
in St. Paul's, and of acquaintance made in taverns.   His
pamphlets are the nearest thing we have to a handbook
of Elizabethan London.   Here is another of his stories,
which tells of two musical young men, and how they were
left to pay the bill :

Two young men of familiar acquaintance, who delighted much
in music, because themselves therein were somewhat expert, as on
the virginals, bandora, lute, and such like, were one evening at
a common inn of this town, as I have heard, where the one of them
showed his skill on the virginals to the no little contentment of the
hearers.   Now as divers guests of the house came into the room to
listen, so among the rest entered an artificial coney-catcher, who,
as occasion served, in the time of ceasing between the several toys
and fancies he played, very much commended his cunning, quick
hand, and such qualities praiseworthy in such a professor.   The time
being come when these young men craved leave to depart, this
politic varlet stepping to them, desired that they would accept a
quart of wine at his hand, which he would—most gladly he would
—bestow upon them ; besides, if it liked him that played on the
virginals to instruct, he would help him to so good a place as happily
might advantage him for ever.   These kind words, delivered with
such honest outward show, caused the young men, whose thoughts
were free from any other opinion than to be as truly and plainly
dealt withal as themselves meant, accepted his offer, because he
that played on the virginals was desirous to have some good place
of service ; and hereupon to the tavern they go, and being set, the
wily companion calleth for two pints of wine, a pint of white, and
a pint of claret, casting his cloak upon the table, and falling to his
former communication of preferring the young man.   The wine is
brought, and two cups withal, as is the usual manner, when, drinking to them of one pint, they pledge him, not unthankful for his
gentleness.   After some time spent in talk, and as he perceived fit
for his purpose, he takes the other cup and tastes the other pint of
wine, wherewith he finding fault, that it drank somewhat hard, said
that rose-water and sugar would do no harm ; whereupon he leaves
his seat, saying he was well acquainted with one of the servants of
the house, of whom he could have two pennyworth of rose-water for
a penny, and so of sugar likewise, wherefore he would step to the
bar unto him.   So, taking the cup in his hand, he did, the young
men never thinking on any such treachery as ensued, in that he
seemed an honest man, and beside left his cloak lying on the table
by them.   No more returns the younker with rose-water and sugar,
but stepping out of doors, unseen of any, goes away roundly with the

cup. The young men not a little wondering at his long tarrying, by the coming of the servants to see what they wanted, who took no regard of his sudden departure, find themselves there left, not only to pay for the wine, but for the cup also, being rashly supposed by the master and his servants to be copartners with the treacherous villain ; but their honest behaviour well-known, as also their simplicity, too much abused, well witnessed their innocency. Notwithstanding, they were fain to pay for the cup, as afterward they did, having nothing towards their charge but a thread-bare cloak not worth two shillings.

Our most intimate knowledge of Elizabethan England is given us by writers who found in the life and changes of the time matter for complaint and protest. Town or country makes no difference ; all were agreed that the world was hastening to decay. One very significant complaint is made by Harrison ; he laments that the taking of interest on moneys has become common, and that the usual rate of interest has risen to twelve per cent. To him, as to all old-fashioned philosophers, who made no allowance for the necessities of trade, interest was merely usury, the taking advantage of a man's poverty and ill fortune. The rise in the rate of interest is recorded in that satirical mock-epitaph on Combe, the usurer of Stratford, which is attributed to Shakespeare both by Aubrey and by Rowe. Aubrey's version of it runs thus :

> Ten in the hundred the devil allows,
> But Combe will have twelve, he swears and he vows ;
> If anyone asks who lies in this tomb,
> ' O ho,' quoth the devil, ' 'tis my John a Combe.'

The sharp practices recorded by Greene had for their victims chiefly rustics or country gentlemen who had come up to town on a visit, or for business connected with the law ; another class of sharpers lay in wait for the fashionable gallants who ruffled it in silks and lace and prided themselves on their knowledge of London life. Greene's fellow dramatist, Thomas Lodge, was the son of a Lord Mayor of London, and, probably from personal experience, knew much about usurers. In his *Alarum against Usurers* he describes their methods. They buy up refuse commodities—lustrings, hobby-horses, brown or grey paper, sugar, spices, hops, or what not—at remnant prices. Then they set ' some old soaking undermining solicitor ' to haunt Paul's and the ordinaries, to take up with

young heirs.　A loan is negotiated, at ruinous interest, but
only part of the advance is in money, the rest is in some
of these same commodities, which are offered as an extraordinary bargain, and in the sequel prove almost unsaleable.
The business is as old as sin, and flourishes to-day ; but
the Elizabethan debtor who failed to repay the loan was
often thrown into prison, a noisome and deadly place.　In
Measure for Measure the clown in the prison enumerates
the prisoners and the causes that brought them there :

Here's young Master Rash, he's in for a commodity of brown
paper and old ginger, nine-score and seventeen pounds, of which
he made five marks, ready money. . . . Then is there here one Master
Caper, at the suit of Master Three-pile the mercer, for some four suits
of peach-colour'd satin, which now peaches him a beggar.

(Meas. for M. IV. iii. 4–12)

In the country Harrison inveighs chiefly against land-
grabbing, by the enclosing of commons, rack-renting
(rents had increased tenfold in his own time), and fore-
stalling or engrossing on the part of wealthy farmers and
landowners.　Of this last he gives a very minute account,
telling how the poor grower is obliged to sell his crop in
time of plenty and buy it back piecemeal in time of dearth.
There was a favourite Elizabethan story, which illustrates
this practice ; it is alluded to by the porter in *Macbeth* :

Knock, knock, knock !　Who's there, i' the name of Beelzebub?
Here's a farmer that hanged himself on the expectation of plenty :
come in time.　(II. iii. 3–6)

Malone used this passage as an argument for assigning the
play to 1606, in which year the harvest was especially
plentiful.　But the story was a common one.　Reference is
made to it by Ben Jonson in *Every Man out of his Humour*
(III. ii), by Hall in his *Satires* (IV. 6), by Nashe, and by
John Taylor the water-poet.　It is told long before Shakespeare's time by Castiglione in his book of the Courtier
(1516), and after Shakespeare's time by Peacham in *Truth
of our Times revealed* (1638).　Taylor's version tells how
there was

a miserly farmer, that had much corn in his barns, and did expect
a scant or barren harvest, that through want and scarcity he might
sell his corn at what dear rates he pleased, but (contrary to his
wicked hopes) the harvest proved abundantly plentiful, wherefore
he being in an extraordinary merry or mad vein, put himself to the

charge of the buying a twopenny halter, and went into his barn as
secretly as he could, and putting the halter about his neck with
a riding-knot, he fastened the other end to a beam, and most neatly
hanged himself. But (as ill luck would have it) his man presently
came into the barn, and espied his master so bravely mounted.
The unlucky knave drew his knife and cut the halter, crying out
for help as loud as he could, rubbing and chafing his master with
all care and diligence to recover him to life again. At the last he
awakened out of his trance and fetched a deep groan, began to
stare and look about him, and taking the end of the cut halter in
his hand, his first words to his man was ' Sirrah, who did cut this ? '
' O, Master,' said the fellow, ' it was I that did it, and I thank God
that I came in good time to do it, and I pray you to take God in
your mind, and never more to hazard your soul and body in such
a wicked manner.' To which good counsel of the poor fellow the
caitiff replied, ' Sirrah, if you would be meddling, like a saucy busy
rogue, you might have untied it, that it might have served another
time ; such an unthrifty rascal as thou will never be worth such
a halter ; it cost me twopence, and I will abate the price of it in
thy quarter's wages.' And when the quarter day came he did abate
the said twopence, for the which the fellow would dwell no longer
with him, but went and got him another service.

These were some of the abuses that were lamented on
all hands when Shakespeare was at the height of his power
and fame. Men looked back with regret to the England
of their fathers and grandfathers. ' It was never merry
world in England', says John Holland, ' since gentlemen
came up' (2 *Hen. VI*, iv. ii. 10–11). Merry England was
not the England of Elizabeth ; it was the England which
the men of that age cherished and celebrated in memory.
The new world that they lived in bewildered them ; the
country had got loose from its moorings, and was drifting
none knew whither. The contrast between the old order
and the new is expressed in the famous ballad of the Old
Courtier, which is both a lively dramatic poem and an
historical document of first-rate importance :

THE OLD COURTIER OF THE QUEEN'S[1]

With an old song made by an old aged pate
Of an old gentleman that had an old wealthy estate,
Who kept an old house, at an old bountiful rate,
And an old porter to relieve poor people at his gate:
     Like an old Courtier of the Queen's,
     And the Queen's old Courtier.

[1] From MS. Ashm. 38, fo. 113, with the spelling modernized.

With an old lady whose anger one word assuages,
Which every quarter pays her servants their wages,
Who never knew what belonged to footmen or pages,
But kept fifty stout fellows with blue coats and badges;
    Like an old Courtier, &c.

With an old study filled full of old learned books,
And an old reverend parson you may judge by his old looks,
And an old buttery hatch worn off the old hooks,
And an old kitchen that maintained half a dozen old cooks;
    Like an old Courtier, &c.

With an old hall hung round with pikes, guns, and bows,
And old blades and bucklers that hath bidden many old blows,
And an old frisadoe coat, to cover his worship's trunk hose,
And a cup of old sack to burnish out his honourable nose;
    Like an old Courtier, &c.

With an old fashion when Christmas is come,
To call out his old neighbours, with an old bagpipe and drum,
And meat enough to furnish out every old room,
And old beer that will make a cat speak and a wise man dumb;
    Like an old Courtier, &c.

With an old falconer and huntsman and a kennel of hounds,
Who never hawked but in his grandfather's old grounds,
Who like a wise man kept yearly within his old bounds
And when he died gave each child a thousand old pounds;
    Like an old Courtier of the Queen's,
    And the Queen's old Courtier.

But to his son and heir his house and land he assigned,
With an old will and charge to hold the same bountiful mind,
To be good to his neighbours and to his tenants kind,
But in the ensuing ditty you shall hear how he was inclined;
    Like a new Courtier of the King's,
    And the King's new Courtier.

With a new flourishing gallant, new come to his land,
Who kept a brace of new painted creatures to be at his hand,
And could take up a thousand readily upon his own new bond,
And be drunk in a new tavern till he be not able to go or stand;
    Like a new Courtier, &c.

With a new lady whose face is beautiful and fair,
Who never knew what belongs to housekeeping or care,
But purchased seven new fans to play with the air,
And seventy new dressings of other women's hair;
    Like a new Courtier, &c.

With a new study stuffed full of pamphlets and plays,
And a new pedagogue chaplain that swears faster than he prays,
And a new buttery hatch that opens once in five or six days,
And a new French cook to devise kickshaws and toys;
  Like a new Courtier, &c.

With a new hall where the old hall stood,
And a new chimney that burns neither coals nor wood,
And a new shovel-a-bord table whereon meat never stood,
Hung round with pictures that do the poor no good;
  Like a new Courtier, &c.

With a new fashion when Christmas is coming on,
With a new journey to London they must all be gone,
Leaving none to keep in the country but his new man John,
Who relieves the poor people with a new thump of a stone;
  Like a new Courtier, &c.

With a new gentleman usher whose carriage is complete,
With a new coachman and two footmen to carry up his meat,
With a new waiting gentlewoman whose dressing is very neat,
Who, when her lady and master hath dined, leaves her fellows little
 to eat;
  Like a new Courtier, &c.

With new titles purchased with his father's old gold,
For which many of his grandfather's old manors newly are sold,
And hath a new reason why housekeeping is grown so cold,
That is the new course that most of our new gallants do hold;
  Like a new Courtier of the King's,
  And the King's new Courtier.

The New Courtier, it will be noticed, belongs to the time of King James; it was against his frivolous innovations that Sir Thomas Bodley provided, when in founding the great library at Oxford he decreed that plays and such-like riff-raffs should be excluded from its shelves.[1] The Old Courtier is treated as a man of Queen Elizabeth's time, though indeed he was old even then, and belongs of right to a somewhat earlier period. But the change that was coming over England was hastened and made more visible by the passing of the Tudor dynasty. While the Queen yet lived, something of the sense of power and unity which uplifted the nation after the repulse of the Armada was still

---

[1] ' I can see no good Reason, to alter my Opinion, for excluding such Books, as Almanacks, Plays, and an infinite Number, that are daily Printed, of very unworthy matters and handling, such, as methinks, both the Keeper and Underkeeper should Disdain to seek out, to deliver to any Man. Haply some Plays may be worthy the Keeping: But hardly one in Forty ' (Hearne's *Reliquiae Bodleianae*, 1703, p. 277).

BEATI PACIFICI

Crownes haue their compasse, length of dayes their date,
Triumphes their tombes, felicitie See fate:
Of more then earth, can earth make none partaker,
But knowledge makes the KING most like his maker.

Simon Passeus sculp: Lond.   Ioh: Bill excudit.

JAMES I by SIMON DE PASSE

in the air. Yet in the life of a nation, as in the life of a man, these exultations are momentary things, flashes of insight,

> Too like the lightning, which doth cease to be
> Ere one can say ' It lightens '.

No sooner was the foreign danger out of men's minds, than civil differences, taking courage, began to prepare their age-long drama. The state prosecutions in matters of religion, which for thirty years had been directed mainly against the Catholics, now changed their object, and began to harry the Puritans. The King of Spain, the villain of the earlier acts, was baffled, and passed off the stage ; at once, with no intermission, Martin Marprelate, an anonymous and scurrilous assailant of the Church of England, took his place in the drama of public affairs. The people of England, when they are not under the pressure of immediate danger to the national life, always quarrel among themselves ; it is their school of war, the exercise that keeps them fit to deal with foreign aggression. So it was in the later years of Queen Elizabeth ; the parties which were to fight it out during the whole of the seventeenth century began to formulate their causes of division, to organize their resources, and to measure out the battle-field. The absolutism of the Tudors assumed a darker complexion when it was professed from the throne by a Stuart. The ears of the people of England are distinguishing, as Burke remarked. They heard their king speak broad. A certain heaviness of mind, natural in men who feel that they are committed to a huge task with no clearly foreseen issue, is observable in all the greater and graver literature of King James's reign. It is perhaps not fantastic to connect Shakespeare's tragedies with this atmospheric change. The glad confident morning temper of the later sixteenth century passed away, and the only gaiety that remained was the gaiety which is first cousin to recklessness. The love songs of the Cavaliers, wonderful as they are in their vivacity and charm, are the songs of a mood or a whim ; they shine with the brightness of jewels against a dark background ; they have the fervour of a protest against the tyranny of political necessity. The love songs of Shakespeare, Marlowe, and the Elizabethans are the songs of a May morning, which belongs to the whole world without difference of class or creed. That

sort of unity of temper has not been found in England since
Shakespeare died.

So it is that Elizabethan literature has all the virtue of
a prophecy, which has been fulfilled in part, from time to
time, but has never been overtaken by achievement. We
have had some measure of political unity at times—in
the Seven Years' War, against the tyranny of Napoleon,
or against the bloodthirsty vanity of that meaner and
poorer tyranny which threatens us to-day. We have spread
ourselves over the surface of the habitable globe, and have
established our methods of government in new countries.
But the poets are still ahead of us, pointing the way. It
was they, and no others, who first conceived the greatness
of England's destinies, and delivered the doctrine that was
to inspire her. They were adventurers, to a man, and
they enjoyed a freedom unknown to their successors. The
language was as free to them as the seas of the world, and,
like the seas, it was uncharted, with no lighthouses, and
few pilots. They subdued it to their purposes, and made
it the servant of their magnanimous ideas. Above them all,
Shakespeare speaks for the English race. His works are
not the eccentricities of a solitary genius ; they are the
creed of England. It is not a dogmatic or a narrow creed ;
it is full of thought and question, so that no one who reads
him with intelligence can escape from the torment of
thought. But in that great world of tides and currents
and whirlpools which is Shakespeare's thought, unbroken
by the shock of the waves and undimmed by the rainbow cloud of the spray, the landmarks stand out like
headlands, and are never shaken. He questions everything, except the obligations laid on weak humanity; he
laughs at everything, except the affections of the heart.
He has an enormous tolerance, as well befits the greatest
poet of a race which has taught the practice of toleration
to Europe. But for all his tolerance, and all his sympathy,
there are things which he cannot tolerate, so that when he
defends them his drama becomes lurid with irony, and
when he pleads against them his voice vibrates with
passion. He hates pedantry—all that complicated mechan-
ism of theory and regulation which systematic men attempt
to impose upon human flesh and blood. He hates cruelty,
the ugly daughter of pedantry ; and if the voice of Shake-

speare as prompter is ever to be heard in all his plays, it is to be heard in the wonderful pleading for mercy by Portia in *The Merchant of Venice* and by Isabella in *Measure for Measure*. His descriptions of the hunted deer in *As You Like It*, and of the hunted hare in *Venus and Adonis* go beyond the stolid sympathies of average selfish humanity ; they are the work of a tragic genius, who cares chiefly, even when he deals with the beasts of the chase, for the sufferings of the mind.

In these things, as in how many others, Shakespeare is English to the core. He is quicker and more sensitive than the vast majority of his fellow-countrymen, or he could not be their poet and their teacher. But what he teaches was learnt in their company, whether in the City of London or in the woods and meadows of the midland counties, and is congenial to their instincts and habits. The English love of compromise is strong in him. If it be examined it will be found to have its origin, not in intellectual timidity, but in a deep reverence for the complexity of human nature and for the sacredness of the elemental instincts. No one ever did more with the intellect than Shakespeare, but he dares not trust it. If its compelling logic drives over the hearts of men, he refuses to follow, and declares for the rights of the heart.

He has many disciples and admirers in foreign lands, some of whom partly understand him. The best translations of his work into foreign tongues, made by poets of repute, are strongest in rendering his drama, weakest in rendering his subtle passages of daring poetry. There is enough and to spare in his drama to enthral the attention of the children of all nations ; it is by his gifts as a teller of stories and a coiner of moral proverbs that he holds his world-wide fame. His appeal to his countrymen is deeper than this, and closer. He speaks to them in a language rich in associations with their daily life and their daily habits of thought. His characters— the soldiers, the ladies, the fools, the rogues—are English characters, studied from the life. His poetry, which overflows and sometimes confuses his drama, is the highest reach of the only art in which England has attained to supreme excellence. This poetry is what Englishmen most value in him, so that the best English critics of Shake-

speare—Johnson, Hazlitt, and Lamb, among others—
have consistently refused to accept the stage presentation
of his plays as a sufficient expression of his genius. They
follow the engraver's advice, and by preference 'look,
not on his picture, but his book'. The magic lines and
sentences of Shakespeare lose most of their virtue when
they are translated ; as his own Norfolk says :

> The language I have learn'd these forty years,
> My native English, I must now forego ;
> And now my tongue's use is to me no more
> Than an unstringed viol or a harp,
> Or like a cunning instrument cas'd up,
> Or, being open, put into his hands
> That knows no touch to tune the harmony.

(Rich. II, I. iii. 159–163)

Shakespeare's admirers abroad do credit to him and to
themselves, but they cannot teach the love of him to his
friends at home. Their public homage is an empty thing
to those who celebrate him more intimately, who love him
best not for his power but for his humanity, and who,
while he still drew breath among them, invented for him
a name which can never be bettered, the name of the
gentle Shakespeare.

BIBLIOGRAPHY.—The earliest history of the reign of Queen Elizabeth is
WILLIAM CAMDEN's *Annales Rerum Anglicarum, et Hibernicarum, regnante
Elizabetha ad annum salutis, M.D.LXXXIX*, 1615, the first translation of which
was made from the French of P. de Bellegent by Abraham Darcie, and
appeared in 1625 as *Annales The True and Royall History of the famous Empresse
Elizabeth Queene of England France and Ireland &c.* The second part of
Camden's history (1589 onwards) was published posthumously in 1627 as
Tomus Alter Annalium Rerum Anglicarum [etc.]., and was translated into
English by T. Browne, *Tomus Alter, & Idem : Or The Historie of the life and
reigne of that Famous Princesse, Elizabeth*, 1629. A new and better version
of the whole work was put out by R. N. (apparently Robert Norton), and
entitled *The Historie of the most Renowned and Victorious Princesse Elizabeth,
Late Queene of England. Contayning all the Important and Remarkeable Passages
of State both at Home and Abroad, during her Long and Prosperous Raigne.
Composed by Way of Annals. Never heretofore so Faithfully and fully Published
in English*, 1630 ; another edition of this appeared in 1635 ; a third edition
is described on the title-page as *Written by William Camden, Clarenceux King
at Arms. The Third Edition, Revised and compared with the Originall,
whereby many gross Faults are amended, severall Periods before omitted are
added in their due places, and the English Phrase much altered, more consonant
to the Mind of the Authour*, 1675. Next in importance is JOHN STOW's *Annales*,
1573, &c. (which was continued by EDWARD HOWES, 1615, &c.), and his
Survay of London, 1598, 1603, &c. ; reprinted from 1603, ed. C. L. Kingsford,
2 vols., 1908.

The political, ecclesiastical, and social conditions of the time are specifically
treated in Sir THOMAS SMYTH's *De Republica Anglorum*, 1584, &c.; by WILLIAM

HARRISON in *A Description of England* contributed to Holinshed's *Chronicle*, 1577, 1587 ; and by PHILIP STUBBES in *The Anatomie of Abuses*, 1583 ; the two latter have been reprinted by the New Shakspere Society. The characters of Queen Elizabeth and her ministers are portrayed in Sir ROBERT NAUNTON's *Fragmenta Regalia*, 1641 (two editions), reprinted by Arber. A review of the reigns of Queen Elizabeth and her successor by GEORGE CARLETON is entitled *A Thankfull Remembrance of Gods Mercy in the Deliverance of the Church and State in the reigns of Elizabeth and James I*, 1624, 1627, 1630. Another retrospect is WILLIAM CARY's *The Present State of England expressed in this Paradox, Our Fathers were very rich with little, And Wee poore with much*, 1627.

Much is to be gleaned concerning the conditions and customs of the Shakespearian period from the works of the poets and dramatists, of the pamphleteers, especially Dekker, Nashe, Greene, Peele, Harvey, Gosson, Riche, and of the satirists and humorists such as JOSEPH HALL(*Virgidemiarum Sixe Bookes*, 1597-8), SAMUEL ROWLANDS (*Works*, Hunterian Club, 1880, &c.), and JOHN TAYLOR, the Water-poet (*Works*, 1630, fol. ; reprinted by the Spenser Society, 1868, &c., with those not included in the 1630 ed., 1870, &c.).

There are many lives of Queen Elizabeth and histories of her reign : the following are among the best : LUCY AIKIN's *Memoirs of the Court of Queen Elizabeth*, 2 vols., 1818 (often reprinted) ; THOMAS WRIGHT's *Queen Elizabeth and her Times*, 1838 ; AGNES STRICKLAND's life in *Lives of the Queens of England*, 1840-8 (several times reprinted) ; BP. CREIGHTON's *The Age of Elizabeth* (Epochs of Modern History), 1876, and *Queen Elizabeth*, 1896 ; E. S. BEESLY's *Queen Elizabeth* (Twelve English Statesmen), 1892.

II

RELIGION

BY

THE REV. RONALD BAYNE

THE ELIZABETHAN SETTLEMENT: THE DISCIPLINARIAN
CONTROVERSY: PAPIST AND PURITAN

THE modern world is to be distinguished from the
mediaeval mainly by its attitude to religion. European
civilization after the destruction of the Roman Empire
was so largely the work of the Church, and statecraft,
except on its purely military side, was so much the business
of the higher clergy, that social and political life became
departments of religion. But, as the modern nations
developed and the arts increased, kings and nobles acquired
a measure of culture and learning and the layman began to
compete with the ecclesiastic and to challenge his supremacy,
first in the domain of law and politics, and finally in social
life and even in religion itself. The Renaissance and the
Reformation are terms which, taken together, describe the
whole process by which political, intellectual, civil, and
religious energies became independent, so that they were
no longer of necessity connected with the organization of
the Church. This process culminated in England in the
Puritan Revolution of the seventeenth century, and therefore a fundamental difference between pre-Restoration and
post-Restoration times is the greater urgency and importance
in the former of religious questions. Elizabethan England
was still more mediaeval than modern. But if religion
dominated men's minds in the Elizabethan era to an
extent not easily comprehended by the modern world, it
was nevertheless an era of rest in comparison with the
reigns of Edward VI and Mary before it and the Puritan
epoch after it. Queen Elizabeth and her statesmen established a temporary equilibrium in Church and State—

a government which was essentially a compromise between the old and the new spirit. They called a halt in the process of revolutionary change and insisted that the nation should produce some fruits of peace and order before proceeding further in social experiments. The fruits produced were the modern English Church and the English drama. Neither of these would have come into being if Puritanism had run its course unchecked. The most striking feature of the marvellous activity of the Elizabethan age is its free humanity, the energy and variety of its manhood. This activity was possible because the yoke of Rome was shaken off and the yoke of Geneva not yet bound on. Between the two dominations came the Elizabethan age—the age of the layman uncontrolled either by priest or presbyter.

It is difficult succinctly to summarize the religious history of Elizabeth's reign, because many problems still await investigation and few writers have written on the subject without bias. In the *Devise for alteratione of Religione*[1] at the *first Year of Queen Elizabeth* it is foreseen that a moderate alteration in which ' some old ceremonies be left still ', will be condemned by extreme reformers as ' a cloaked papistry or a mingle-mangle '. But this danger was deliberately incurred by Cecil, with the result that about eighty parish priests only, and rather more than a hundred of the higher clergy, refused to accept the new régime and were deprived.[2] The attempt to conciliate the old-fashioned and conservative elements in the nation was successful for the first ten years of Elizabeth's reign. The flight of Mary Queen of Scots into England in 1568 was the chief cause of the rising of the Northern Earls in 1569, but that rising was a failure, and the conformity of the Roman party in England to the Elizabethan settlement was checked only by the bull *Regnans in excelsis* of Pius V in 1570, which excommunicated Elizabeth, and forced her Roman Catholic subjects into schism against her settlement. ' Then ', says Fuller, ' began the word recusant to be first born and bred in men's mouths ; which,

---

[1] ' Religion ' here means religion as an institution, organized and sanctioned by the nation.

[2] Camden gives the total number at 189. Gee's investigations, based on episcopal registers, establish the substantial accuracy of the numbers : consult his book *The Elizabethan Clergy*, but see also H. N. Birt's *The Elizabethan Religious Settlement*.

though formerly in being to signify such as refused to obey the edicts of lawful authority, was now confined in common discourse to express those of the Church of Rome.' The massacre of Huguenots on St. Bartholomew's Day in 1572 accentuated the alarm and resentment caused in England by the Pope's interference. The foreign seminaries began presently to send their missionaries into the country. The first priest to suffer death was Cuthbert Mayne, executed in November 1577. The Jesuits, Parsons and Campion,

Raro antecedentem Scelestum:

Campian

F. Parſons et Campian F H ſecit

Rebellion the effect of Monaſteries.

From Carleton, *A Thankfull Remembrance*, 1627.

reached England in 1580. Severe legislation against Roman Catholics culminated in the bill of 1584, which made Jesuits and seminary priests liable to the penalties of high treason and the harbouring of them a felony. Edward Arden of Park Hall, near Warwick, was one of the victims of these penal laws; he was executed in 1583. He was probably related [1] to Mary Arden of Wilmcote, the mother of Shakespeare, through whom some knowledge of the refinement of ladies of gentle birth may perhaps have reached the dramatist. Between 1570, when John Felton was

[1] Edward Arden's father was probably second cousin to Mary Arden. Arden was convicted of instigating Somerville to shoot the Queen: his religion may be held to have caused his conviction.

executed for posting upon the door of London House the Pope's bull against the Queen, and 1603, it is calculated that 180 Romanists suffered death under the penal laws.

To modern feeling, these laws which controlled the treatment of the seminary priests were mercilessly cruel, but if the general character of Elizabethan punishments be taken into account, they cannot be judged extraordinary, and they called forth no protest on the part of the people. We can discover no clear reference to them in Shakespeare's plays, although the dramatist may have had in mind the courage with which the victims of the anti-Catholic penal legislation faced death when he wrote somewhat enigmatically in *Sonnet* cxxiv :

> the fools of time,
> Which die for goodness, who have liv'd for crime.[1]

One of his earlier historical plays, *King John*, expresses very vigorously and freely the general feelings of Englishmen with regard to the bull of Pius V against their Queen. *King John* is founded upon an earlier play which was acted after *Tamburlaine* had taken the town by storm, probably in 1588. In this older play the politics of the sixteenth century are carried back into the twelfth; the Pope is ' The Arche prowd titled Priest of Italy '; the Prologue terms him ' the Man of Rome '; and because monks are ' lazy lubbers ' John proposes to ' Ransacke the Abbeys, Cloysters, Priories ', and ' Convert their coyne unto my souldiers use '; none is to go ' to Rome for justice and for law ', on pain of being held a traitor to the state and an enemy to England. Shakespeare modifies in many ways the rude bluntness of the earlier play, and he omits an abbey-robbing scene, but it cannot be said that in the crucial passage he weakens at all the impeachment of Rome. It is worth while to compare the two versions. To Pandulph's challenge John makes this answer in the old play :

And what hast thou or the Pope thy maister to doo to demaund of me, how I employ mine own ? Know, Sir Priest, as I honour the Church and holy Churchmen, so I scorne to be subject to the greatest Prelate in the world. Tell thy Maister so from me, and say, John of England said it, that never an Italian Priest of them all, shal either have tythe, tole, or polling penie out of England : but as I am

[1] Palgrave explains : ' apparently, the plotters and political martyrs of the age.'

King, so will I raigne next under God, supreame head both over
spiritual and temrall : and hee that contradicts me in this, Ile
make him hoppe headlesse.

This is the popular conception of bluff King Hal speaking
with all his accustomed vigour in the person of John.
Shakespeare's version runs thus :

> What earthy name to interrogatories
> Can task the free breath of a sacred king ?
> Thou canst not, cardinal, devise a name
> So slight, unworthy and ridiculous,
> To charge me to an answer, as the pope.
> Tell him this tale ; and from the mouth of England
> Add thus much more : that no Italian priest
> Shall tithe or toll in our dominions ;
> But as we under heaven are supreme head,
> So under him that great supremacy,
> Where we do reign, we will alone uphold,
> Without the assistance of a mortal hand :
> So tell the pope ; all reverence set apart
> To him, and his usurp'd authority.   (*John*, III. i. 147–60)

The speech of King John in both plays causes King
Philip to exclaim that the English king blasphemes.
According to the old play John retorts :

> Philip, though thou and all the Princes of Christendome suffer
> themselves to be abusde by a Prelates slauery, my minde is not of
> such base temper. If the Pope will be King in England, let him winne
> it with the sword, I know no other title he can alleage to mine
> inheritance.

Shakespeare's expansion of this introduces new matter
of his own :

> Though you and all the kings of Christendom
> Are led so grossly by this meddling priest,
> Dreading the curse that money may buy out ;
> And, by the merit of vile gold, dross, dust,
> Purchase corrupted pardon of a man,
> Who in that sale sells pardon from himself ;
> Though you and all the rest so grossly led
> This juggling witchcraft with revenue cherish ;
> Yet I alone, alone do me oppose
> Against the pope, and count his friends my foes.
> (III. i. 162–71)

Pandulph's excommunication, also, is in Shakespeare's
version more definite and pointed in its reference to Queen
Elizabeth's case. The old play discharges John's subjects

from all duty and obedience, and promises pardon and
forgiveness of sin to any that shall carry arms against him
or murder him. Shakespeare expands the last point:

> And meritorious shall that hand be call'd,
> Canonized and worshipp'd as a saint,
> That takes away by any secret course
> Thy hateful life. (III. i. 176–9)

These passages seem to make it clear that about 1595
Shakespeare was willing to gratify popular feeling in
London against the papal claims which had been intensified
by the bull of 1570 and the plottings of the Jesuit
priests. But it does not appear that he recast the old play
because it contained this anti-Papal matter, nor does it
absorb much of his attention. The dramatist's main interest
is in the very unecclesiastical character of the Bastard and
the passionate sorrow of Constance ; while his art finds its
sweetest and purest expression in the beautiful colloquy
between Hubert and Arthur.

But Shakespeare shows no tendency to represent Roman
Catholic priests and clergy as specially wicked—he has no
animus against them. It has even been maintained that
his appreciative sketches of friars and his acquaintance
with the details of Roman Catholic religious customs and
rites prove the truth of the report that ' he died a Papist '.
The character of Friar Laurence in *Romeo and Juliet* is
specially appealed to in this connexion. It is alleged that
the portrait of the friar is much fuller and also more complimentary than that of any parson or minister sketched by
Shakespeare. His ministers, as we shall see, are generally
laughing-stocks and of no importance in the plays. But
the case of Friar Laurence will not bear the construction
put upon it. Shakespeare in *Romeo and Juliet* made use
of Arthur Brooke's lengthy poem (*The Tragicall Historye
of Romeus and Juliet*[1]) on the subject, and probably had
before him an earlier play which has been lost. Brooke
thinks it necessary to insert a very Protestant address to
the reader in which he says that he describes the 'unfortunate lovers ' . . . as ' conferring their principall counsels
with drunken gossyppes and superstitious friers, the naturally fitte instrumentes of unchastitie ', and ' using auricular

---

[1] It contains 3,020 lines. Consult P. A. Daniel's introduction to his edition
for Shakespeare's use of it.

confession'. But Brooke's poem does not at all correspond
to his preface. His sketch of the Friar embodies all the
kindly features of Bandello's novel; he is 'that good
barefooted fryre'; 'no mark of defame Did seeme to blot
or touch at all the honor of his name'. Shakespeare gets
all his main motives from Brooke's verse, and Brooke's
example is sufficient proof that Shakespeare's procedure
had no religious significance. Shakespeare's other friar,
Francis, in *Much Ado about Nothing,* uses no technical
or professional language, and the two characters entitle us
only to say that Shakespeare was not unwilling, when the
exigences of his art put pressure upon him, to draw friars
whose kindness of heart, sound judgement, and delicacy of
feeling would do honour to any religion. But in these
creations Shakespeare approaches his characters on their
human side; they are not champions or even types of their
own religion; and their goodness of heart is evidence of the
temper of London theatre-goers rather than of Shakespeare.
The dramatist does not refrain from representing a priest
as intolerant when Ophelia is refused full Christian burial.
The irritation of Laertes when he asserts

> I tell thee, churlish priest,
> A ministering angel shall my sister be,
> When thou liest howling,   (*Haml.* v. i. 262–4)

expresses the point of view of a layman who resents theological dogma when it seems to him harsh and inhuman.
The fatherly priest, sympathizing with and consoling
distress and suffering is honoured; but the dogmatic
ecclesiastic is frowned upon.

It may at this point be noted, before we pass on to consider the reformed religion, that Shakespeare's use of
technical terms connected with the old religion seems on
the whole less than we should expect from one whose
vocabulary was so large and whose use of the semi-technical
words and phrases of all classes and professions was so
profuse. When in the speech of the Ghost in *Hamlet* we
get technical expressions like those in the line

> Unhousel'd, disappointed, unanel'd,[1]   (I. v. 77)

we find them all in this place only; the word 'purgatory'
occurs only twice in all the plays (*Rom. & Jul.* III. iii. 18;

---

[1] The line is not found in the first quarto.

JOHN WHITGIFT

Oth. iv. iii. 77) ; and if we compare the Ghost's description
of his prison-house with Claudio's references to ' fiery
floods ', ' thick-ribbed ice', and ' viewless winds', when
' the delighted spirit ' goes ' we know not where ', we shall
feel that Shakespeare's thoughts of the next life were not
confined within the limits of Roman Catholic orthodoxy.

The more eager spirits in the party of reform were
expected by the author of the *Devise for alteratione of
Religione* to resent the *via media* established by Elizabeth
and her advisers. The burning at the stake of Cranmer,
Latimer, and Ridley, with a number of their followers,
was the chief cause of that widespread horror and fear of
Rome which for centuries was to be a characteristic of
the English people. Gardiner and Bonner, when their
party was in opposition, had not been burnt. It was
therefore an innovation, due to foreign influence, the
influence of Rome and Spain, that when the reform party
was in opposition under Mary, they were treated as both
parties were in the habit of treating atheists and other
extreme heretics, and were burnt at the stake. That
a punishment reserved usually for supposed blasphemous
outcasts should be inflicted as publicly and openly as
possible upon nearly three hundred persons, including among
them some of the most famous and venerated men in the
land, produced an impression which sank deep into the minds
of Englishmen, and made the position that the Pope or the
Roman See was the Antichrist of Revelation not a mere
eccentricity of theologians and Puritan preachers but the
sober conviction of multitudes entirely ignorant of divinity.
When we add to the fires of Smithfield the massacre of St.
Bartholomew and the menace of the Armada we cannot be
surprised at the fierceness of the extreme reformers and the
Protestantism of the mob in London and other towns. But
even before the death of Edward VI there was a party
among the reformers who were prepared to criticize even
his second Prayer Book as not thoroughgoing enough in
its rejection of prayers and ceremonial that had been
tainted by use in the mediaeval ritual of worship. Under
Mary such men sought refuge on the Continent, where
they were offered hospitality and brotherly sympathy,
not by the Lutheran cities but by the more advanced
towns of Switzerland and the Rhine which followed Calvin

as their prophet. In Geneva and other cities where the Genevan spirit was dominant, the English exiles learnt lessons which could not be applied to England and English conditions without arousing protracted and bitter conflict. In matters religious, political, and social Calvin had established a method of life in Geneva which seemed to the exiles a far more clear and logical realization of evangelical aspirations than anything they had been acquainted with in England. The tract known as *The Brief Discourse of the Troubles begun at Frankfort in Germany*, A.D. 1554, relates how the English exiles quarrelled among themselves as to the form of prayer they should use, and drew from Calvin a criticism of the second Prayer Book of Edward VI which was practically a condemnation of it. Although many of the exiles refused in a foreign country to join in this attack upon the English Prayer Book, yet they could not resist the influence upon their thoughts and feelings of a church polity and worship much more extreme than their own. The Elizabethan compromise therefore could not be congenial to them. It seemed the work of men who by a cowardly conformity in Queen Mary's day had escaped both persecution and exile, and it commanded no enthusiasm. At first dislike of the new Prayer Book fastened upon one point, the surplice. Hooper, in Edward's reign, had scrupled to wear the cope and surplice, and Nonconformity under Elizabeth began by refusing to wear the surplice, which was required by Archbishop Parker's *Advertisements* in 1566. To officiate without it remained throughout the reign the chief method of asserting Nonconformist opinions. Shakespeare has one allusion to the matter ; the Clown says to the Countess in *All's Well* when he is ordered off :

> Though honesty be no Puritan, yet it will do no hurt ; it will wear the surplice of humility over the black gown of a big heart.
>
> (I. iii. 97–101)

The words seem to recognize some pride in the refusal to don the surplice and yet to imply a respect for the zeal which distinguished the wearers of the black gown.

It was a consequence of the proceedings of the authorities in 1566 that in the next year we hear of private meetings at which those who were dissatisfied with the established form of worship met together to use the Service which the exiles had used in Geneva and to enjoy the ministrations of deprived preachers. It was to the members of such private congregations that the word Puritan was first applied, about the year 1567, probably in derision. But for the time being the activity of the Nonconformists died down.

It is not necessary to describe in detail the steps by which insistence on the surplice grew into the disciplinarian controversy, which demanded the establishment of a Presbyterian discipline like that of Geneva. The controversy may be said to begin with the two Admonitions presented to the Parliament of 1572 and to end with the publication of Richard Hooker's five books *Of Ecclesiastical Polity*.[1] On the Puritan side the two leading writers were Thomas Cartwright and Walter Travers ; the Marprelate Tracts were a by-product of the dispute.

This immense disciplinarian controversy did not in Elizabeth's reign produce any political results, but its social and religious influence was very great. The Puritan's demand for pure religion and clean living was combined with two evil tendencies. Puritanism in political life made for liberty, but in private life it was constantly tyrannical and eager to force the ordinary man to be moral against his will. In the second place, the bugbear of popery was constantly setting up an irrational prejudice against all old customs and old sports and merriments as ' the dregs of Antichrist '. The narrower Puritan contracted into the smallest limits all forms of recreation. Life was for him made up of business and religious services. The large neutral ground between work on the one hand and religious services on the other, in which flourish so many of the arts—painting, music, dancing, poetry, the drama—and all forms of sport, was by the extreme Puritan reduced to the narrowest limits. All these activities were dangerous, either as temptations, or as tainted by their use in the mediaeval Church. The Puritan attack upon the stage began very early. The literature and legislation directed against players and playhouses are dealt with in Chapter XXIV, vol. ii. 240–5.

Shakespeare has several definite allusions to Puritans

[1] Books I to IV, 1593. Book V, 1597.

and sectaries. In *Twelfth Night*, Maria is asked by Sir Toby
to tell him something of Malvolio; she answers :

> Marry, sir, sometimes he is a kind of Puritan.
> *Sir Andrew.* O ! if I thought that, I'd beat him like a dog.
> *Sir Toby.* What, for being a Puritan ? thy exquisite reason, dear
> knight ?
> *Sir And.* I have no exquisite reason for 't, but I have reason good
> enough.
> *Mar.* The devil a Puritan that he is, or anything constantly but
> a time-pleaser. (II. iii. 153–62)

The reference to the surplice in *All's Well* has been quoted
already. Shortly before that allusion the Clown declares
that ' young Charbon the Puritan and old Poysam the
Papist, howsome'er their hearts are severed in religion'
(I. iii. 36), as married men, run the same risks. Malone
suggests that the nicknames are derived from the fiery
zeal of the Puritan and the Papist's fish diet on fast days.
Again, in *Pericles*, in a scene which has some Shakespearian
touches in it, it is said of Marina that

> She would make a Puritan of the devil if he should cheapen a kiss
> of her. (IV. vi. 9)

Finally, the Clown in *The Winter's Tale*, speaking of the
shearers, says that there is

> but one Puritan amongst them, and he sings psalms to hornpipes.
> (IV. ii. 47–8)

In *Twelfth Night* there is a mention of a separatist sect, when
Sir Andrew remarks :

> Policy I hate : I had as lief be a Brownist as a politician.
> (III. ii. 35–6)

These references are all slight and casual. That Shakespeare was not a Puritan, any more than he was a Papist,
we gather from the general tenor of his plays and the central
facts of his life rather than from any direct attacks upon
Puritanism in his writings. The sketch of the credulous
self-love of Malvolio was no doubt suggested in the main
by Puritan preciseness, but Shakespeare's treatment of
the character is kindly and could give offence to no
reasonable person. At the same time, in Sir Toby's
exclamation

> Dost thou think, because thou art virtuous, there shall be no more
> cakes and ale ? (*Tw. N.* II. iii. 124–5)

we have a proof that Shakespeare fully understood the
problem of which Puritanism always desired to cut the knot.
Still more impartial and extraordinary even among Shakespeare's dramas for its infinite suggestiveness is the play of
Measure for Measure. In Angelo the Puritan is dealt with
seriously, almost tragically, just as in Malvolio he is dealt
with comically, with admirable tact. It is not the Puritan
as a political person who is the subject of the drama, but
the universal Puritan who is a part of every man's mental
and moral equipment.

But in Shakespeare's plays we find not only Puritans and
Papists; we have also parish priests—Sir Topas, the curate,
who comes to visit Malvolio; Sir Nathaniel, the curate in
Love's Labour's Lost; Sir Hugh Evans, a Welsh parson,
in *The Merry Wives*; Sir Oliver Martext, a vicar in *As You
Like It.* ' Sir ' was a translation of ' Dominus ', a title given
to such clergy as had taken the first degree of bachelor of
arts. It came to be applied especially to the old-fashioned
or ignorant priest who could only read the services and was
not able to preach. The reforming party were unwilling
that such readers should be recognized as clergy, and the
more extreme among them insisted on the necessity of
the ' ministry of the word ' or preaching, to constitute
a valid ministry. Politically, it was satisfactory that the
change of religion at Elizabeth's accession was carried out
with little friction and that very few of the parish clergy
either resigned or were deprived, but the circumstance
promoted a low level of spiritual zeal and sincerity. The
changes at Edward's accession, at Mary's accession, and
at Elizabeth's accession, tended generally to eliminate the
best parish priests, and to lower the standard both of piety
and learning among those that were left. The abuse of
patronage led to the same result. Latimer in 1550 spoke
out manfully :

But what do you patrons ? Sell your benefices, or give them to
your servants for their service, for keeping of hounds or hawks, for
making of your gardens. These patrons regard no souls, neither
their own nor other men's. What care they for souls, so they have
money, though they perish, though they go to the devil ?

The poor pay of the parish priest was a main cause of his
illiteracy and inefficiency. The scholar in *The Pilgrimage
to Parnassus* meets, at the foot of the hill of learning,

' a companie of ragged vicars and forlorne schoolemaisters'.
Harrison says much the same in his interesting account
of the state of the English Church, written for Holinshed's
Chronicle in 1577. But, on the other hand, the extreme
Puritan aggravated the difficulties of the situation by
inveighing fiercely against the ' blind Sir Johns ', by
denouncing ' bare reading ', and by contending that

prayers and sacraments, forasmuch as they take effect by the
preaching of the word, where that is not, those do not only not feed,
but are ordinarily to further condemnation.

The scarcity of preachers is dwelt upon and lamented by
a long list of authorities—by Latimer, by Jewel, by Sandys,
by Harrison. The Puritan, therefore, would have done well
to lay to heart the words of the Helvetian Confession :

We condemn all unmeet ministers not endued with gifts necessary
for a shepherd that should feed his flock. Howbeit we acknowledge
that the harmless simplicity of some shepherds in the old church
did sometimes more profit the Church, than the great, exquisite, and
fine or delicate, but a little too proud, learning of some others ;
wherefore we reject not nowadays the good simplicity of certain, so
that they be not altogether unskilful of God and His Word.

Shakespeare's Sir Johns reflect very accurately the type
of parish priest common in his day. Sir Nathaniel and Holofernes are only too anxious to appear learned and their
respectability is above suspicion. Costard's ' censure ' of
Sir Nathaniel is surely Shakespeare's, and it is an interesting
comment on the passage we have just quoted from the
Helvetian Confession. Sir Nathaniel, in the part of Alexander the Great, is put out of countenance by the jokes of
the courtiers. Costard apologizes for him :

There, an't shall please you : a foolish mild man ; an honest man,
look you, and soon dash'd. He is a marvellous neighbour, faith, and
a very good bowler ; but, for Alisander, alas ! you see how 'tis ;—
a little o'erparted. (*Love's L. L.* v. ii. 581–5)

Sir Hugh Evans is more peppery than Sir Nathaniel, as
befits his Welsh extraction, but again, when we have
allowed for some comic exaggeration, we perceive that
Shakespeare intends us to respect Sir Hugh. It is part of
his office to compose quarrels :

If Sir John Falstaff have committed disparagements unto you,
I am of the Church, and will be glad to do my benevolence, to make
atonements and compromises between you. (*M. Wives,* i. i. 31–4)

He is the village schoolmaster and his catechizing of Master William Page a transcript from the life of the day; he points the moral against Ford and Falstaff:

> Sir John Falstaff! Serve Got, and leave your desires, and fairies will not pinse you. *(M. Wives,* v. v. 139–40)

He is not idealized, but he is a part of the honest wholesome English burgess society of the play. In Sir Oliver Martext, a more disreputable type of hedge-priest is for a moment brought on the stage by Shakespeare, and though he is treated with characteristic gentleness—

> 'Tis no matter; ne'er a fantastical knave of them all shall flout me out of my calling *(A. Y. L.* iii. iii. 113–14)

—yet the difference is made clear between such as he and ' a good priest that can tell you what marriage is '. If Shakespeare's picture of the parson is compared with that given in other dramas—in *The Weakest goeth to the Wall,* for instance, and in the extant first part of *Sir John Oldcastle*— we shall perceive how much coarseness and caricature Shakespeare avoided. This coarseness was largely an inheritance from the interlude, where the priest, the friar, or the pardoner is generally treated with gross disrespect. A comparison of Shakespeare's parsons with his priests will suggest that the latter were ideal portraits, whereas the former were drawn from personal observation and memory.

The passage in which he finely suggests the character of a true father in God may well conclude this examination of his attitude towards the clergy:

> Who hath not heard it spoken
> How deep you were within the books of God?
> To us the speaker in his parliament;
> To us the imagin'd voice of God himself;
> The very opener and intelligencer
> Between the grace, the sanctities of heaven,
> And our dull workings. *(2 Hen. IV,* iv. ii. 16–22)

RELIGION IN CHURCH, PARISH, AND HOME. PREACHING.

The Prayer Book of Queen Elizabeth was ordered by the Act of Uniformity of her first Parliament to come into use on St. John's Day, the 24th of June, 1559. To get a broad picture of church and parish activities as organized by the Elizabethan Settlement, it will be convenient to summarize the articles of inquiry issued by Archbishop Grindal for the province of York in 1571. Grindal was Elizabeth's first Bishop of London. On his appointment to York he was followed in the see of London by Edwin Sandys, who issued, also in 1571, articles for the London diocese, which very closely followed those of Grindal for York. These two sets of articles have the advantage of exhibiting to us the aims of the central London authorities at a time when the new order of worship and parish life had acquired stability and definite form.

The services for parish churches on Sundays were fixed by authority 'at due and convenient hours'. This meant generally 7 to 8 a.m. for Morning Prayer, to be followed immediately by the Litany and Communion; and 2 to 3 p.m. for Evening Prayer. In cathedrals, colleges, and schools services began much earlier—at 5 a.m. in summer and 6 in winter.[1] It is clear from the payments for candles in church-wardens' accounts that as a rule lights were not used in parish churches except at Christmas, when there were early services. Prayer began after daylight and ended before dark.

The articles of Grindal and Sandys issued in 1571 show that in cathedral churches and colleges the Holy Communion was administered upon the first or second Sunday of each month 'at the least', in order to secure that communicants might receive three times in the year at the least. Canterbury used the first Sunday; St. Paul's, London, the second. The celebrant with gospeller and epistoller wore a cope at the cathedral service. In the parish churches 'a comely surplice with sleeves' is to be worn at all services, and there is to be 'a comely and decent table standing on a frame, for the Holy Communion, with a fair linen cloth to lay upon the same, and some covering of silk, buckram, or other such-like for the clean keeping thereof'. There is to be in use also a communion cup of silver, with a cover of silver for paten; and certain books are required

---

[1] The 1559 Visitation articles prescribe for cathedrals a service at these hours, before Morning Prayer. Thomas Lever, preaching in 1550 at Paul's Cross, describes how Cambridge students begin their day at 5 a.m. in chapel (*Sermons*, ed. Arber, p. 122).

From an engraving after a picture in the possession
of the Society of Antiquaries London

PREACHING AT ST PAUL'S CROSS

—'the Book of Common Prayer with the new Kalendar, a Psalter, the English Bible in the largest volume, the two tomes of the Homilies, and the Paraphrases of Erasmus translated into English'. In Grindal's articles the inquiry whether there is a 'convenient pulpit well placed' comes before the article about the communion table. There is great insistence on clear and audible reading of everything read, and inquiry concerning such parts of the prayers as be sung whether 'there be a modest and distinct song' that may be 'as plainly understanded as if they were read without singing'. The over-use of 'organs' is deprecated. The Commination Service is required to be used four times at least in the year. As to preaching, has the parson or vicar or curate preached 'his quarterly or monthly sermons as by the Queen's injunctions he is bound'? If there is no sermon, has 'some part of the Homilies' been read 'distinctly and plainly'? Are the Homilies neglected for exposition of Scripture by any minister not admitted by the Ordinary? Great stress is laid upon the duty of catechizing. 'Before or at the Evening Prayer,' on every Sunday and Holy day, openly in the church, 'for half an hour at the least', the minister was to 'call for, hear, and instruct all the children, apprentices and servants of both the sexes that be of convenient age', in the Catechism. He was to make a list of them 'and by course call certain of them by name every Sunday and Holy day'. The names are asked for of such 'fathers, mothers, masters, and dames' of the parish as do not send their young people, 'being above six years and under twenty'. And again: How many children cannot 'say by heart the said Catechism; what be their names and age, and with whom do they dwell'? It is asked also whether godparents have received the Holy Communion before christenings; whether evil-livers, before admission to the Holy Communion, have done 'due penance to the satisfaction of the congregation'; and generally whether communicants over twenty can say the Ten Commandments, the Creed, and the Lord's Prayer, in English; and those under twenty and over fourteen, their Catechism. The Holy Communion must be received thrice in the year at least, and 'the churchwardens and sworn men' must assist the minister in collecting ignorant people for the necessary instruction. There are stringent questions about church attendance. Do householders attend regularly with their families on the Holy days 'and chiefly upon the Sundays to Morning and Evening Prayer '? Are there any who are irreverent, come late, walk or talk in the church; or use any gaming abroad; or sit in the streets or churchyard or in any tavern or alehouse upon the Sunday in the time of common prayer, sermons or reading of the homilies, either before noon or after noon? The churchwardens are to fine such offenders twelve pence. Innkeepers, alewives, and victuallers must not aid such offenders. Shops must not be open in time of common prayer on Sundays and Holy days. Fairs and common markets must not fall upon the Sunday, nor must there be 'any shewing of wares' before Morning Prayer be done. The minister must openly on Sunday after the second lesson remind churchwardens and sworn men of their duties. Is there a proper confession of fault before the congregation by unmarried mothers before they are churched? It is the duty of the ' substantial men ' of the parish to walk the bounds with the clergy ' on the days of Rogations commonly called the gang days '. On these days are said the psalms and suffrages such as the Queen's Injunctions enjoin; and do they walk ' without wearing any surplices, carrying of banners or hand-bells, or staying at crosses or other suchlike popish ceremonies '? Is the bell tolled ' when any Christian body is in passing ', and is the minister called to comfort the sick person? There must be no ringing ' tending to the maintenance of the popish purgatory or praying for the dead'; there may be 'one short peal' before the burial and another after. The conformity and the manner of life of the 'parson, vicar, or curate' are minutely inquired into; it is asked whether he is resident, holds more than one benefice, and obtained his cure without simony. The churchwardens are also held responsible for the proper upkeep of church and chancel and churchyard and ' the mansion house of your parson ', as well as for the safeguard of all church goods and the administration of legacies to the church or to orphans or to poor maids for marriage or to schools or to highways or to ' any other godly use '. They are, moreover, to control the collectors for the poor, and see that they ' make a just account quarterly ' of their moneys, which include a proportion of the fines paid for non-attendance at church. They are asked whether the hospitals, spitals, and almshouses are 'well and godly used'. All schoolmasters are under their surveillance. They are to give the names of all who teach 'either openly or privately in any noble or gentleman's house'. Are such teachers well-behaved and loyal and properly licensed? Do they use King Henry VIII's Grammar and teach the Catechism in Latin, lately set forth? The questions, after a long article about marriage, end with a general inquiry regarding evil-livers, which begins with 'contentious persons', includes 'any that bruiteth abroad rumours of the alteration of religion received within this realm', as well as blasphemers and adulterers, and ends with witches, common drunkards, and ribalds.

This summary indicates how much disciplinary, educational, and secular work was organized and controlled by ecclesiastical authority. The 'churchwardens and sworn men', upon whom so much depended, were parishioners usually of the tradesman class. It is interesting to recall that Heminge and Condell, members of Shakespeare's company of players and editors of the First Folio, were both London churchwardens. But the religious and social activities summarized by Grindal in 1571 did not sufficiently realize the ideals of the Puritan party. We shall more fully understand the religious life of England at that date if we place beside the articles of the bishops a manifesto of the disciplinarian party. Strype prints such a document, dated 1571, and approved for the town of Northampton by the Bishop, Edmund Scambler, the mayor, and the civic authorities. A few points must be noted. Prayers are to be said not in the choir but in the body of the church, without 'organs'; worshippers file past the table receiving the Holy Communion without kneeling; prayers on Sundays in churches where there is no sermon must be over by 9 o'clock to enable worshippers to attend the sermon in the chief church. In the chief church there are week-day services on Tuesday and Thursday from 9 to 10. Youth are catechized in Calvin's Catechism at the end of Evening Prayer for an hour. There is careful taking of names from house to house before communions, which are quarterly: each parish church had two, one 'for servants and officers to begin at five of the clock with a sermon of an hour and to end at eight', and the other for masters, dames, &c., from nine to twelve, also with a sermon. Every Thursday after the prescribed service there is a disciplinary assembly of the mayor and his brethren, assisted by the preacher, ministers, 'and other gentlemen', for correction of discord made in the town. For the improvement of ministers there are special ' exercises ' for two hours every Saturday morning. These regulations represent the wishes of the more moderate among the reformers. Their ideal is clearly taken from Geneva, but they are anxious to obey the law and to use the Prayer Book. Out of the ' exercises ' last mentioned developed in a few years the ' prophesyings ', which the Queen suppressed in 1577 as dangerous to the State, in spite of the brave protest of Grindal, by that time Archbishop of Canterbury.

But in addition to the services of the Prayer Book there were many occasional services, some of penitence, some of thanksgiving, in which extra prayers put forth by authority were used along with portions of the Prayer Book. Such services were ordered when the Turks attacked Malta in 1565, and in the following year when Hungary was in danger. The Northern Rebellion in 1569, the massacre of St. Bartholomew in 1572, the earthquake in 1580, the conspiracies of Parry in 1585 and Babington in 1586 against the Queen, Drake's success at Cadiz in 1587, and the defeat of the Armada are among the occasions when special services were enjoined. More elaborate were the prayers in connexion with the outbreaks of plague. The first plague was in 1563, brought from France by the English army at Havre de Grace. The Queen addressed a letter to Archbishop Parker requesting him to arrange that ' universal prayer and fasting be more effectually used in this our realm ', and giving him authority to issue a prescribed order. Grindal, Bishop of London, with the help of Nowell, the Dean of St. Paul's, drew up the Form. The Gunpowder Plot was the occasion of the drawing up of a public thanksgiving which formed an integral part of the Prayer Book from 1606 till 1859.

Grindal blamed Protestants for their neglect of fasting, holding ' that in no one thing the adversary hath more advantage against us than in the matter of fast '. Wednesday was appointed as fasting day for all persons between sixteen and sixty (' sick folks and labourers in harvest or other great labours only excepted ') : on that

day ' but one only competent and moderate meal ' was to
be eaten, in which meal 'very sober and spare diet ' was
to be used. ' It shall be indifferent to eat flesh or fish, so
that the quantity be small and no variety or delicacy be
sought.' Parliament (5 Eliz. c. 5), on the other hand, required
that Wednesday 'shall be hereafter observed and kept . . .
as a Fish day . . . as the Saturdays in every week be or ought
to be ', but insisted at some length that its object was merely
secular—the support of fishermen and the navy. The most
interesting features of the ' Fourme to be used in Common
Prayer twyse aweke and also an order of publique fast, &c.'
are the order of a silence for a quarter of an hour for private
prayer and meditation, the use of a psalm composed of a
cento of verses from various parts of the Bible, and the
special homily ' Concerning the Justice of God' composed
by Dean Nowell. There was also issued a ' form of meditation very meet to be daily used of householders in their
houses in this dangerous and contagious time '. It consists
of thirty collects or paragraphs, with the directions : ' The
master kneeling with his family in some convenient place
of his house, perfumed before with Frankincense or some
other wholesome thing, as Juniper, Rosemary, Rose water,
and Vinegar, shall with fervent heart say or cause to be said
this that followeth. The servants and family to every
petition shall say Amen.'

A remarkable feature of Elizabethan and Jacobean
religion was the great vogue of the sermon. A long and
significant list could be drawn up of the sermons at Paul's
Cross, comprising either those ecclesiastically interesting—
such as Jewel's famous ' challenge' sermon in March 1560,
and Pilkington's discourse when the cathedral was burnt in
1561,—or those nationally interesting—such as the sermons
after the defeat of the Armada. But the most striking illustration of this vogue of the sermon is to be found in the
diary of John Manningham of the Middle Temple. The diary
runs from January 1602 to April 1603, and is chiefly remembered for its vivid picture of Queen Elizabeth's death and its
reference to the performance of *Twelfth Night*. The diarist
dislikes Puritans, and is not a person of special piety, but his
note-book contains summaries, some of them of considerable
length, of more than forty sermons. A large number of the
sermons at Paul's Cross are noticed, preached by such eminent

divines as Lancelot Andrewes, James Montague, John King, Henry Parry, and George Abbot. Unfortunately, Manningham does not describe personally the better-known preachers; but occasionally he goes to hear a popular preacher, and gives some account of his appearance and manner. In 'a little church or chappell up stayres' at Blackfriars he heard Mr. Egerton, who had 'a great congregacion, specially of women', and at a church in Foster Lane 'one Clappam, a blacke fellowe, with a sower looke, but a good spirit, bold, and sometymes bluntly witty'. The strangers, in the Temple

PREACHING AT ST. PAUL'S CROSS.

From *St. Paules-Church her bill for the Parliament*, 1621.

Church or at St. Paul's, he describes freely, as, for instance, on December 19 'at Paules', 'one with a long browne beard, a hanging looke, a gloting eye, and a tossing learing jeasture'. The notes of sermons in the diary, if read together, give a remarkably full and vivid picture of preaching in London at the end of Elizabeth's reign.

The most popular among the Elizabethan preachers was probably 'silver-tongued Smith' of St. Clement Danes, who died 1591. A recent writer has said: 'Probably Henry Smith, alone among Elizabethan preachers, shares with Hooker the distinction of finding modern readers.'[1]

[1] *Cambridge History of English Literature*, vol. iv, p. 237.

A picture of the religious life of an Elizabethan gentle-woman of pronounced Puritan views is given in the diary of Margaret Lady Hoby,[1] the wife of Sir Thomas Posthumus Hoby. When she comes to town she goes to hear the Mr. Egerton mentioned by Manningham. At home in the country she has a chaplain, whose 'lectures' she attends. He reads sermons to her and she composes certain spiritual exercises under his direction. Her day begins always with Bible-reading and she retires more than once every day for private prayer ; there is much psalm-singing in the house-hold. The piety of the lady is sincere and beautiful, but a little narrow. The only books mentioned, besides the Bible and sermons, are Foxe's Martyrs and the Herbal.

Shakespeare's references to the religious observances of his own day are not abundant, and when they are introduced it is for the most part to point a phrase or to colour a dia-logue. The practice of attending daily worship is glanced at when Mistress Quickly, recounting to Falstaff the virtues of Mistress Page, is made to say that she is 'one, I tell you, that will not miss you morning nor evening prayer' (*M. Wives*, II. ii. 102–3). In *Pericles* there is 'fish for fasting-days' (II. i. 86), and in *Lucrece* 891 'private feasting' is placed in antithesis to ' public fast '; but there is nothing in the whole of Shakespeare to match the scene in *Every Man in his Humour* (III. iv.), where Cob, the water-carrier, rails at length against fasting-days, how ' they are of a Flemish breed ' because ' they raven up more butter than all the days of the week beside ', and ' they stink of fish and leek-porridge miserably ', and how ' they keep a man devoutly hungry all day' and send him 'supperless to bed'. There is in Shakespeare one matter-of-fact instance of priest and clerk as the ecclesiastical witnesses of a marriage (*Tam. Sh.* IV. iv. 94), but in all the other three passages where the clerk is mentioned it is his responsory function that is the motive, as in :

> I think good thoughts, while others write good words,
> And, like unletter'd clerk, still cry 'Amen '
> To every hymn that able spirit affords
> In polish'd form of well-refined pen. (*Sonnet* lxxxv)

Shakespeare's use of 'catechism', 'homily', and 'sermon' is in every case metaphorical or allusive, and he employs

[1] *Trans. Royal Hist. Soc.*, 3rd Ser., 1906, vol. ii, pp. 160 ff.

' preachment ' and the verb ' sermon ' only to express the
tedious and distasteful aspect of the pulpit. The forms and
formulae of the marriage service are reproduced or referred
to in several passages, the most striking of which is the echo
of ' for better, for worse ' in :

Oph. Still better, and worse.
Ham. So you must take your husbands. (*Haml.* III. ii. 265-6)

The saying of grace is more frequently spoken of than
any other religious custom. The authorized form concluded
with the petition ' God save our Queen and Realm, and send
us peace in Christ. Amen ', and this is played upon in :

First Gent. There's not a soldier of us all, that, in the thanksgiving
before meat, doth relish the petition well that prays for peace.
Second Gent. I never heard any soldier dislike it.
Lucio. I believe thee, for I think that thou never wast where
grace was said.
Second Gent. No ? a dozen times at least.
First Gent. What, in metre ?
Lucio. In any proportion, or in any language.
First Gent. I think, or in any religion. (*Meas. for M.* I. ii. 14-25)

Of Timon's elaborate graces one is in verse, the other in
prose (*Timon*, I. ii. 64-73, III. vi. 79-96).

RELIGIOUS LITERATURE

No account of religion in the Shakespearian age is adequate without some notice of the books which influenced
thought and feeling in the reigns of Elizabeth and James.
Of these the first in importance next to the Bible was Foxe's
Book of Martyrs. During Mary's reign, Foxe, at Basle,
found employment as a reader for the press with the printer
Oporinus, and began his project of producing a history of the
sufferers at the stake in England, both in English and Latin.
He was made the recipient of reports and documents concerning the sufferings and deaths of Bradford, Philpot,
Cranmer, and other martyrs, and was assisted in his undertaking by Grindal and Aylmer, fellow exiles in Germany.
The death of Mary resulted in the transference of the whole
scheme to London, and the hurrying forward of the English
version, which John Day produced in March 1562-3, as *Actes
and Monuments of these latter and perilous Dayes*. The book
was illustrated by excellent woodcuts, and it is impossible to
exaggerate its influence upon English feeling and opinion.

The Catholics angrily nicknamed it 'Foxe's Golden Legend', but the nickname defines very accurately the place taken by the book in the minds of the common people of England. It superseded the mediaeval acts of saints and martyrs from which the Reformation cut them off. The second edition of 1570 was in two volumes, folio, of 934 and 1,378 pages respectively, and there were several later editions. Convocation ordered copies to be placed in cathedral churches, and it was very widely supplied to parish churches. Sir Sidney Lee remarks that Foxe's style ' has the vigour that comes of deep conviction, and there is a pathetic picturesqueness in the forcible simplicity with which he presents his readers with the details of his heroes' sufferings : his popularity is thus amply accounted for '.

A second influence upon the nation, hardly less important than Foxe's book, was the translation of Calvin's sermons and commentaries from French and Latin. The publication at Geneva in 1559 of Calvin's final revision of the *Institutions de la religion chrétienne* led to the translation into English which was made by Thomas Norton, part-author of *Gorboduc*. This came out in 1561, and was reprinted five times before the end of the century. Calvin's death in 1564, no doubt, swelled the stream of translations of his works which poured from the press. The work of Luther was much less read in England, with the exception of his commentary on Galatians, which was translated and went through three editions.

Jewel's books were printed in great numbers. His ' challenge ' sermon caused his elaborate controversy with Harding ; and his *Apologia Ecclesiae Anglicanae*, printed first in 1562, was answered by the same adversary, and resulted in a second series of volumes. The first short *Apologia* was translated into English by Lady Bacon, the mother of Francis Bacon, and both in Latin and English was regarded as the official statement of the position of the Church of England under Elizabeth. In 1609 Jewel's sermons and controversies were published in folio and reprinted in 1611. Like Foxe's *Book of Martyrs*, Jewel's works were frequently placed in the churches. Of the works of the earlier English reformers, Bradford's treatises and Latimer's sermons were the most popular in Elizabeth's reign;

some of the short devotional treatises of Thomas Becon, whose works were carefully printed in three volumes in 1560–4, also enjoyed great popularity. Becon began writing in 1541, his earliest tracts being printed under the name of Theodore Basille. His titles, *The News out of Heaven, A Christmas Banquet, A Potation for Lent, The Pathway unto Prayer, A Pleasant New Nosegay,* were derided by the learned, but found favour with the multitude. *The Sick Man's Salve* was so popular that the Stationers' Company kept it constantly in print till the seventeenth century. *The Pomander of Prayer,* almost as popular as *The Sick Man's Salve,* was ascribed to Becon ; but it is doubtful whether he wrote it. In his revision of his works in 1560–4 he made an endeavour to bring his older tracts up to date, but it is remarkable how much matter is left that reflects the religion of a past age. These treatises must have been useful in avoiding too harsh a break in the habits of piety among the simple-minded. Becon died in 1567. Another very popular devotional writer who wrote sometimes in prose, sometimes in verse, and sometimes in a mixture of the two, was John Norden,—almost certainly not the topographer, although the two began to publish about 1585. In that year appeared *A Sinful Man's Solace,* which was in prose and verse ; and *A Pensive Man's Practice,* described as ' a Treatise for such as are in any way afflicted '. This last went through innumerable editions. An edition, ' newly corrected after forty impressions ', is dated 1627. Another of Norden's tracts, *A Poor Man's Rest,* reached the twelfth by 1631.

All the work that has been described is in the prevailing Genevan school of doctrine and sentiment, and at the end of the century the great popularity of the Cambridge preacher, William Perkins, fully maintained the Calvinist tradition. Perkins united scholastic method with simplicity and fervour, and his heavy tomes were continually reprinted. It was at last the preaching of Andrewes, continuing the teaching of Hooker and Bancroft at the end of the sixteenth century, that produced a reaction against the dominant Calvinism and established at the same time a devotional style and method, which expressing itself first in the prayers of Andrewes and Cosin, became truly popular in the personality and writings of George Herbert.

The popularity of the metrical versions of the Psalms acted as a stimulus upon the output of devotional poetry. John Day held the monopoly for printing what became known as the Old Version and issued many editions from 1562 onwards which were bound up with Bibles and Prayer Books. His title-page may be quoted because it gives the only authorization of the version and at the same time states exactly its use in public worship by all who had Puritan leanings :

> The whole booke of Psalmes newly set forth and . . . allowed to be song in all Churches of all the people together, before & after morning and evening prayer : as also before & after the Sermon and moreover in private houses for their godly solace and comfort, laying aparte all ungodly songes and balades.

Thomas Sternhold, Groom of the Robes to Henry VIII, was the writer of 40 of these psalms and John Hopkins of 60 ; Thomas Norton, William Whittingham, and William Kethe supplied 47 out of the remaining 50. Only William Kethe's 'All people that on earth do dwell' remains in use to-day. The popularity of these psalms produced a whole school of translators of psalms who aimed at versions more poetical or more accurate. Archbishop Parker executed a complete version but did not publish it. Sir Philip Sidney began a version which was finished by his sister, the Countess of Pembroke. Among translators of selected psalms may be mentioned Queen Elizabeth, Spenser, Abraham Fraunce, the Davisons, Donne, Phineas Fletcher, Lord Bacon, Herbert, Crashaw. The versions of George Wither and of George Sandys in the early seventeenth century are from the literary point of view the best. Much paraphrasing of Scripture followed upon the paraphrasing of psalms. Among Roman Catholic poets Robert Southwell reaches a spiritual exaltation rare in religious poetry.

Shakespeare on one occasion quotes the Old Version. Sir Hugh Evans to keep his courage up sings a verse from Marlowe's ' Come live with me ' ; but, his heart failing him, he mixes with Marlowe a line from Whittingham's version of Psalm 137 :

> When as I sat in Pabylon.   (*M. Wives*, III. i. 24)[1]

---

[1] Cf. vol. II, p. 525-6.

TRANSLATIONS OF THE BIBLE :   SHAKESPEARE'S KNOWLEDGE AND USE OF THE BIBLE

Shakespeare was likely to hear familiar texts of the Bible quoted in three differing translations.[1]   In his youth the Great Bible was by no means obsolete.   It was first issued in 1539, and six editions followed in the next two years. It has been calculated that 20,000 copies of the large folio were distributed throughout the country.   This was the version which first openly and heartily satisfied the demand for the Bible in the vulgar tongue, and the eager public reading of it must have exercised a considerable influence upon contemporary speech.   Moreover, this translation of the Great Bible was used in the Book of Common Prayer, and in Elizabeth's Prayer Book the psalms, epistles, and gospels were all from that version.   But during the earlier years of Elizabeth's reign the Geneva Bible of 1560 came into general use and completely superseded the Great Bible in popular esteem.   It was especially the Bible of the Puritan party, and it deserved its popularity by the pains it took to assist its readers.   It was printed in all sorts of handy editions ;   it used roman type ;   it broke up the text into verses ;   it had pictures and maps ;   it provided pithy, scholarly, and scurrilous notes which were none the less appreciated because they were tinged by the Calvinistic theology of the translators. Some two hundred editions of this Bible were issued in the half-century after Elizabeth's accession, and it was so much the most convenient version that even Hooker, the official defender of the Prayer Book against Puritan attacks, does not hesitate to make large use of it in his *Ecclesiastical Polity*.   It is therefore most probable that if Shakespeare wished for any purpose to refer to a Bible he would find the Geneva version most ready to his hand, and the influence of the Geneva Bible on the speech of the people must have been considerable and continuous during Elizabeth's reign. But, thirdly, the authorized version of Elizabeth's reign, so far as there was one, was the Bishops' Bible, issued under Parker's auspices in 1568 and again in 1572.   This was the

---

[1] There is nothing in his works to show that he had any acquaintance with the authorized Roman Catholic versions, viz. the Rheims New Testament of 1582, and the Douay Bible of 1609-10.

THE
NEWE TESTAMENT
OF OVR LORD
IESVS CHRIST,

* ***

Conferred diligently with the Greke, and beſt appro-
ued tranſlacions in diuers languages.

EXOD. XIIII, VER. XIII.

FEARE YE NOT, STAND STIL, AND BE-
holde the ſaluacion of the Lord, which he wil ſhewe to you this day.

THE LORD SHAL FIGHT FOR YOV:
therfore holde you your peace, Exod. 14, vers. 14.

AT GENEVA.

PRINTED BY ROVLAND HALL.

M. D. LX.

Bible read in the churches except when the Prayer Book
was being used. The laws insisting upon attendance at
church were persistently enforced by the authorities, first
against Papists and afterwards against Puritans [1] ; and it
is not likely that a member of the Lord Chamberlain's
company of players which occupied so conspicuous a
position in the public eye and enjoyed such distinguished
patronage would compromise himself and his company by
refusing to conform to the law of the land. Halliwell-
Phillipps, in a short essay long since out of print, raised the
question which version Shakespeare was familiar with. He
pointed out that Shylock's reference to ' parti-coloured
lambs ' in his argument for usury drawn from Jacob's
sheep - breeding, implied a use of the Geneva Bible.
But this instance illustrates the difficulty of arriving at
any certain conclusions on the point. It is almost certain
that there was a pre-Shakespearian play, no longer extant,
which combined the stories of the caskets and the pound
of flesh, and Shakespeare may have found the word ' parti-
coloured ' in this original. In other cases there is no clear
proof that the Geneva Bible was the source. Shakespeare
alludes to the leopard's spots. This is claimed as a clear
use of the Geneva version ; but the leopard with his spots
is found in Lyly's *Euphues*, where there are many other
biblical references and quotations. Falstaff makes many
biblical allusions and occasionally quotes Scripture pro-
fanely. But all that Falstaff's scriptural allusions can be
held to prove is that in the last decade of the sixteenth
century the Bible was becoming very well known to the
English people and had already woven its vocabulary
very thoroughly into ordinary speech. It had done this
by means of all the three versions mentioned above, and we
find in Shakespeare echoes from all three versions. But
the definite echoes of the Bishops' Bible as distinct from the
Geneva, or of the Geneva as distinct from the Great Bible,
are few in comparison with the large vocabulary which is
shared by all three and also by Shakespeare. This points
to the conclusion that Shakespeare had not a favourite Bible
which he read every day. The most elaborate treatment
of Shakespeare's use of Scripture is Mr. Thomas Carter's

---

[1] We find in contemporary documents accusations of non-attendance at
the Holy Communion ' quia papista ' and ' quia puritanus '.

Shakespeare and Holy Scripture: with the Version he used.
The book contains a huge list of alleged parallels between
the language of the plays and the Geneva versions, but
there is no examination of the Bishops' Bible or of the
Great Bible. A truer estimate of Shakespeare's relation
to the Bible is to be obtained from such a survey as
Mr. H. R. D. Anders gives in his *Shakespeare's Books*. It
is probable that some of Shakespeare's biblical knowledge
came by way of the Prayer Book. His attitude to the
Bible was in no sense professional or theological. We
cannot prove from his vocabulary that he shared the
passion for Bible-reading which was so important a result of
the Reformation movement. His religion was the religion
of a man who stood outside all parties of the day without
despising any of them. His religion, in short, is an aspect
or part of his general attitude to life and humanity.
It has the universality, the tolerance, the deep humanity
of his dramatic art.

But while the bulk of his work is pervaded by an atmosphere of natural religion which cuts him off from the
orthodoxies of his day, yet in several places he quite naturally
employs the language of orthodox Christian piety. It is
likely that he employed heartily and sincerely such language
as King Henry's, when he speaks of

> those holy fields
> Over whose acres walk'd those blessed feet
> Which fourteen hundred years ago were nail'd
> For our advantage on the bitter cross;
>
> (*1 Hen. IV*, I. i. 24–7)

or the Bishop of Carlisle's, when he says that Norfolk,
dying at Venice,

> gave
> His body to that pleasant country's earth,
> And his pure soul unto his captain Christ,
> Under whose colours he had fought so long;
>
> (*Rich. II*, IV. i. 97–100)

or Valentine's, when he forgives Proteus so readily, because,

> By penitence the Eternal's wrath's appeased;
>
> (*Two Gent.* v. iv. 81)

or Edward's, when he refers to a murderer as one who has

> defaced
> The precious image of our dear Redeemer;
>
> (*Rich. III*, II. i. 123–4)

or Clarence's, when he charges his murderers,

> as you hope to have redemption
> By Christ's dear blood shed for our grievous sins.
>> (*Rich. III*, I. iv. 198-9)

And in plays of which the tone and setting are either worldly or definitely pagan we find the poet's *anima naturaliter Christiana* strangely and obviously present. Polixenes forgets that he is a Pagan as he denies the accusation brought against him; if it be so, ' O then,' he says, may

> My name
> Be yok'd with his that did betray the Best.
>> (*Wint. Tale*, I. ii. 418-19)

Leontes too speaks as a modern, when, in pregnant phrase, he speaks of the comfort of Camillo's counsel,

> Wherein, priestlike, thou
> Hast cleans'd my bosom.   (*Wint. Tale*, I. ii. 237-8)

It is strange in *Cymbeline* to come across the reference to

> reverence—
> That angel of the world   (*Cymb.* IV. ii. 247-8)

and to find Posthumus pardoning Iachimo in these words :

> The power I have on you is to spare you ;
> The malice towards you, to forgive you. (*Cymb.* V. v. 419-20)

Even Ariel speaks like a saint when he denounces the ' three men of sin ', and assures Alonzo that nothing can guard him from perdition

> but heart-sorrow
> And a clear life ensuing.   (*Temp.* III. iii. 81-2)

BIBLIOGRAPHY.—W. H. Frere has edited for the Alcuin Club *Visitation Articles and Injunctions of the Period of the Reformation*, vols. xiv, xv, xvi. The index may be consulted under Communion, Cope, Service (Divine), Surplice. STRYPE's *Annals of the Reformation in England*, and his lives of Parker, Whitgift, and Aylmer, are a mine of valuable and copious material for the study of religious movements and conditions in Elizabeth's reign. This has been ably summarized with many additional references to contemporary books and pamphlets by HENRY SOAMES in his *Elizabethan Religious History*, 1839. More recently, the beginning of the reign down to 1570 has been elaborately treated in R. W. DIXON's *History of the Church of England*, vols. v and vi, 1902, and in H. GEE's *The Elizabethan Clergy and the Settlement of Religion*, 1898, and his *The Elizabethan Prayer Book and Ornaments*, 1902. The whole period is treated on a smaller scale in W. H. FRERE's *The English Church in the reigns of Elizabeth and James I*, 1904. Special studies of the Puritan movement are contained in BISHOP PAGET's *Introduction to Hooker, Book V*, 1899, and in RONALD BAYNE's essay, ' Disciplinarian Puritanism,' in his edition of Book V of the *Ecclesiastical Polity*, 1902. B. BROOK's *Life of Cartwright*, 1845, is still indispensable for Cartwright's career, but should be supplemented by J. B. MULLINGER's account in chap. iii of *The University of Cambridge*, where there is also a valuable sketch of Travers. Mullinger's life of Cartwright in the *D. N. B.* must also be consulted. Many of the articles in the *D. N. B.*—especially those by Creighton, Mullinger, Dixon, and Lee—contain the most recent and critical summaries of the careers of the chief actors in the Elizabethan religious controversies and of the preachers, translators, and poets mentioned above. The works of Grindal, Sandys, Becon, and Jewel are published by the Parker Society, which includes in its series collections of the ' Liturgies and Occasional Services of the Reign of Queen Elizabeth ' and of the ' Private Prayers ' : see Index volume. The metrical psalms are treated in JULIAN's *Dictionary of Hymnology* under Old Version of Psalter (English). EDWARD FARR's *Select Poetry, chiefly Devotional, of the Reign of Queen Elizabeth* (Parker Society), 2 vols., is a representative selection.

The condition of the English clergy in Shakespeare's lifetime is described and discussed by WILLIAM HARRISON in chap. i of Book II of his *Description of England*, contributed to Holinshed's *Chronicle* ; 1st edition, 1577, 2nd edition, 1587. The notes in the reprint of Harrison by the New Shakspere Society collect useful references—to the scarcity of preachers on pp. 21–2, to the lack of learning and refinement on pp. 26–7. In chap. v of the first part of NATHAN DRAKE's *Shakespeare and his Times* some evidence is given of the state of things in 1609.

The view that Shakespeare was a Roman Catholic is maintained by H. S. BOWDEN in *The Religion of Shakespeare*, 1889, a book founded upon writings left unfinished by Richard Simpson. The opposite opinion that he was a Puritan is asserted by THOMAS CARTER in *Shakespeare, Puritan and Recusant*, 1897, and further supported in the same writer's *Shakespeare and Holy Scripture ; with the version he used*, 1905. A lucid and judicious criticism of these theories will be found in H. C. BEECHING's essay, ' The Religion of Shakespeare,' printed in vol. x of the Stratford Town edition of Shakespeare's Works, 1907. Mention must also be made of BISHOP WORDS-WORTH's *On Shakespeare's Knowledge and Use of the Bible* ; 1st edition, 1864, 4th edition, 1892. Chap. vi of H. R. D. ANDERS's *Shakespeare's Books*, 1904, considers ' The Bible and the Prayer Book '.

III

THE COURT

BY

E. K. CHAMBERS

ENGLAND was 'merrie England' still in the early days
when Henry the Eighth kinged it with Katherine of
Arragon, breaking into her chamber at dawn ' for a gladness
to the queen's grace' as Robin Hood with his merry men
in coats of Kentish green, and filling the great hall of
Placentia, his ' manor of Pleasaunce' at Greenwich, with
revels, the elaborate pageantries of which are recorded alike
in the dusty account-books of the Rolls Office and in the
picturesque pages of Edward Hall's chronicle. A shadow
fell across the mirth when ' the king's secret ', the scruple
sorely trying the royal conscience hitherto so light, was
imparted to Wolsey upon a fateful day in 1527. But the
tradition of courtly splendour survived even through the
troubled reigns of Edward the Sixth and Mary; and was
readily picked up by Elizabeth when, still a girl, and, as
impartial observers averred, of remarkable beauty in spite
of her high nose, she came at last to her own after the years
of repression and personal danger. She shared to the full
the sensuous Tudor love of fine dresses and costly trinkets,
of music and dancing, of riding and of hunting. Before she
had been on the throne a month, the Duke de Feria wrote
to Philip of Spain that he had handed over to her two
of Mary's rings which the king had presented to him,
' because as I saw she was so fond of her jewels I thought
best to give her up even the poorest of them'. During
these first years, all the English correspondence is impressed
with the gaiety of the court, with the banquets, the masques,
the water-parties on the Thames. ' Regina tota amoribus
dedita est,' writes Francis Chaloner to his brother in 1563,
' venationibusque, aucupiis, choreis et rebus ludicris in-
sumens dies noctesque.' Yet one may be sure that this

apparent frivolity of demeanour was not inconsistent with
a very solid application to the practical business of governing ; and likewise that the constant willingness to take part
in the popular amusements of London, the May-games
and morris-dances, the lordships of misrule and the midsummer watches, which Machyn's diary records, had its
origin not merely in a natural taste for spectacle, but in
a deliberate intention to win the hearts of the citizens,
and to be before all things the people's queen.   As Sir
Christopher Hatton was wont to say of his mistress, she
fished for men's souls.   Chaloner's Latin was perhaps
dictated by his allusion to the royal *amores*.   Elizabeth's
court was no less crowded with suitors than Portia's
Belmont.   From all ends of the earth they came trooping,
or sent their likely ambassadors of love before them.
Philip of Spain himself, the Kings of Denmark and Sweden,
the Archdukes Charles and Ferdinand of Austria, the Duke
of Nemours, the Earl of Arran, were among them ; and
the coming and going of their trains, with gifts and compliments, and fantastic devices of bleeding hearts embroidered on their coats, made a brilliant contribution to the
bustling splendour of the palace.   Englishmen, too, were
named as possible consorts : the Earl of Arundel, Sir
William Pickering, Lord Robert Dudley.   The Queen's own
preference for Dudley was unmistakable, and soon led
to comments far from flattering to her reputation.   It is
perhaps improbable that she ever thought seriously of
marrying him, or, for the matter of that, any one else ;
but it is clear that in some sense she was in love with his
good looks, high spirits, and proficiency in all the arts of
a courtier.   And although she was capable of prudish
affectations when it suited her purpose, the Tudor blood
did not dispose her to much reticence of speech or conduct
in private.   A Spanish ambassador reports in 1565 a
characteristic scene which took place while he was riding
with Leicester one morning in Windsor Park :

> We came round by the footpath leading to the riverside through
> the wood to where the Queen lodges, and when we came to her
> apartments Leicester's fool made so much noise calling her, that
> she came undressed to the window.

If Leicester ever had hopes, they vanished.   On the whole,
he appears to have kept his head better than might have

been expected; and save for occasional indiscretions, of which the most serious was his secret marriage with Lettice, Countess of Essex, in 1578, he managed to retain his leading position on the ceremonial and intimate side of court life until his death in 1588. In politics he was no match for Sir William Cecil, and he was careful also not to bring himself into conflict with such men as William Lord Howard of Effingham, or Henry Carey, Lord Hunsdon, who were of Elizabeth's kindred and therefore, as he would say, 'of the tribe of Dan and *noli me tangere*'. Like Cecil himself, he was bitterly hated as an upstart by the older English nobility. In 1566 the court was divided into a purple and a yellow faction, wearing respectively the colours of Leicester and those of the Duke of Norfolk; and the direct intervention of Elizabeth could never do more than patch up the enduring feud between the 'gipsy' favourite and Thomas Radcliffe, Earl of Sussex. Leicester was not the only upstanding young Englishman who found that a good leg and an impudent face were the best passports to fortune under a maiden queen. Both the endearments and the scandal had to be shared with Christopher Hatton, whose performances in a masque opened for him a career which only ended with the Lord Chancellorship. During the 'seventies Edward Vere, Earl of Oxford, won credit for a while, and lost it again through the ill discipline of his life; and in the 'eighties Sir Walter Ralegh and Charles Blount, afterwards Earl of Devonshire and lover of Stella, were contending for the privilege of paying a suit which had by that time become a strained and artificial convention. Both of them, however, had to give way to Robert Earl of Essex, who more than any man after Leicester's death came near to being to Elizabeth's faded heart what Leicester had been to her youth; and whose senseless outbreak in the very last years of her reign cost him his life and the Queen some of the few genuine tears that she ever shed. Thus the court was a place where high prizes were to be won. To the lads of England it offered in anticipation a romantic adventure, and in retrospect too often a memory of sordid intrigue. So confesses Sir John Harington, a godson of the Queen, who fluttered in the wake of Essex, and just escaped being entangled in his fall:

I have spente my time, my fortune, and almoste my honestie, to buy false hope, false friends, and shallow praise;—and be it remembrd, that he who castethe up this reckoning of a cowrtlie minion, will sett his summe like a foole at the ende, for not beinge a knave at the beginninge.

It is precisely this discontent of the finer spirits with the conditions of the courtier's life that gives its burden to the pastoral comedy of *As You Like It.*

By policy or temperament, Elizabeth was averse from the married state. 'The hatred that this queen has of marriage is most strange,' wrote the Spanish ambassador to Philip in 1567. 'They represented a comedy before her last night, which ended in a marriage, and the queen, as she told me herself, expressed her dislike of the woman's part.' Her nearest approach to a match was with Francis, Duke of Alençon, a brother of Henry the Third of France, in 1581. After nearly ten years of dilatory courtship, a treaty was all but signed. Alençon came twice to England, once in secret, and again openly. Elizabeth gave him a golden master-key to every door in her palace, and he sent her a letter with an emerald worth four hundred crowns stuck in the sealing-wax. It is improbable that either party to the negotiation took it seriously. Alençon was squat and pock-marked, with a forked and swollen nose. On his side he complained to the queen-mother that Elizabeth was old, ugly, and consumptive. She had indeed suffered from many ailments during the first twenty years of her reign, and doubtless her girlish good looks were gone, and the curling red-gold hair which Sir James Melville admired under an Italian caul and bonnet in 1564 had given way to the innumerable frizzled wigs of her later portraits. However, the comedy was played out to the end, and when Alençon was summoned to take up the governorship of the Netherlands early in 1582, he was accompanied to Canterbury by a weeping queen, ' la quale, volendo mostrare dolore di questa sua partita, si vesti di nero'. Both must have known very well that he would never come back. Thereafter Elizabeth permanently adopted the pose of a settled and obdurate virginity.

> The imperial votaress passed on
> In maiden meditation, fancy-free ;   (*Mid. N. D.* II. i. 163)

and the protestations of her adorers mingled oddly with neatly turned compliments wherein she figured as Diana, Cynthia, or Belphoebe, unapproachable and chaste. We have it on the word of an early historian that the prolonged festivities of 1581 proved something of a turning-point in court annals.

The coming of the Duke of Alençon into England opened a way to a more free way of living and relaxed very much the old severe form of discipline. . . . Masques . . . were taken up and used. . . . There were then acted comedies and tragedies with much cost and splendour ; from whence proceeded in after times an unrestrainable desire of frequenting these divertisements ; so that there was afterwards a greater concourse at the theatre, than at the sermon.[1]

There is no doubt that at the beginning of the reign Elizabeth's instinct for pleasure was kept in check by the severe need for retrenchment which a ruined exchequer entailed. She is said to have reduced her household to a third of that maintained by Mary. The financial pressure was probably relaxed by 1581, thanks to business-like administration and a good deal of buccaneering enterprise. The expenses of Alençon's visit were in fact largely paid for out of the Spanish loot brought back by Drake in *The Golden Hind*. Gradually the household attained to a more liberal footing. An inquiry in 1601 elicited that the ordinary expenses of maintenance then amounted to £52,000 a year as against £40,000 in 1561. But this Elizabeth resented, and sternly required a reformation, more particularly in view of the dangers attaching to the custom of purveyance, whereby goods and carriages for the royal use were ' taken up ' at fixed rates below the market price. In the next reign this privilege came to be regarded as a grievance, and was certainly abused by the purveyors, who took up more than was needed and sold it at a profit to themselves. In Elizabeth economy, from a necessity, became a habit. And it governed the revels as well as the kitchen. This was a queen who loved better to be entertained than to entertain. The costly masques paid for by her father and her successor find few parallels in her account-books. The extravagances of her reign were committed not by her, but for her.

The organization of the royal household was a traditional one. It fell into three departments, taking responsibility respectively for out-of-doors, downstairs, and upstairs duties, and presided over by three great officers, the Master of the Horse, the Lord Steward, and the Lord Chamberlain.

---

[1] E. Bohun, *Character of Queen Elizabeth*, p. 345, from R. Johnston, *Hist. rerum Brit.* (1655), p. 353 ; cf. R. Carey, *Memoirs* (ed. 1905), p. 2.

These officers, with some of their principal subordinates, were members of the Privy Council, which sat almost daily at court, and served as a board of domestic control, supervising many details of household administration, in addition to exercising the functions of an executive council of state. The ordinary mode of appointing an important household officer was by the delivery of a white staff, which became the symbol of his office, and which at the funeral of the sovereign he solemnly broke over his head before the bier. Certain offices dating from remote antiquity, those of the Lord High Steward, the Lord Great Chamberlain, the Chief Butler of England, had by the time of Elizabeth become mere hereditary dignities, or were at the most confined to the performance of ceremonial functions at a coronation, a state trial, or a parliament. The Mastership of the Horse, unlike the other chief household offices, was conferred by patent. It was held by the Earl of Leicester from 1559 to 1587, by the Earl of Essex from 1587 to 1597, and by Edward Earl of Worcester, first as deputy to Essex, and after 1601 in his own right, from 1597 to 1616. The Master was responsible for the supervision of the Stable, in which he had the assistance of the Chief Avenor. Elizabeth's first Lord Steward was Henry Earl of Arundel. He resigned in 1564 and was succeeded in 1567 by William Earl of Pembroke. After Pembroke's death in 1570, the post seems to have been long kept vacant, and the department supervised, in addition to his own, by the Lord Chamberlain. It was, however, afterwards revived, and held at various times by the Earl of Leicester, by Henry Earl of Derby, and by the Earl of Nottingham. The actual work was no doubt performed by the two subordinate 'white staves', the Treasurer and the Comptroller of the Household. The white staves, together with the Cofferer, who was in general charge of purveyance, and some of the Clerks of the Counting-house, formed the Board of Green Cloth; and under them were the Kitchen, with its array of Clerks, Cooks, and lesser menials, and a number of smaller offices of provision, the Bake-house, the Pantry, the Cellar, the Buttery, the Pitcher-house, the Spicery, the Chandlery, the Wafery, the Confectionery, the Ewery, the Laundry, the Larder, the Boiling-house, the Accatry, where the purchases (Fr. *achat*) were made, the Poultry, the Scalding-house, the Pastry, the

Scullery, and the Wood-yard. Each of these had its appropriate establishment, in nicely defined grades, of Serjeants, Clerks, Yeomen, Grooms, Pages, and Children. To this department also belonged the Almonry under the Chief Almoner, the Porters, and the Marshals, Sewers, and Surveyors of the Hall, a group once of the first importance, but now obsolescent since the sovereign had ceased to dine and sup in the Hall. In a sense the most important branch of the household, as being the most in the public view and the nearest to the Queen's person, was the Chamber. The Lord Chamberlain was responsible for all court entertainments, and his white staff frequently proved of practical service in regulating the eager throng which pressed to see the masques and plays. He became a natural channel of communication with the sovereign, had to bear the brunt of her anger if she was displeased with the service done her, and was a dignified and conspicuous figure in the palace. Polonius was probably a Lord Chamberlain. In the performance of his multifarious duties the Lord Chamberlain had sometimes, although not always, the assistance of a Vice-Chamberlain. The Lords Chamberlain under Elizabeth and James were William Lord Howard of Effingham from 1558 to 1572, Leicester's rival the Earl of Sussex from 1572 to 1583, Charles Lord Howard of Effingham from 1583 to 1585, Henry Lord Hunsdon from 1585 to 1596, William Brooke, Lord Cobham, from 1596 to 1597, George Lord Hunsdon from 1597 to 1603, the Earl of Suffolk from 1603 to 1614, the Earl of Somerset from 1614 to 1615, and William Herbert, Earl of Pembroke, one of the claimants to be the ' M[r] W. H.' of Shakespeare's *Sonnets*, from 1615 to 1626.[1] The Vice-Chamberlains were Sir Edward Rogers from 1558 to 1559, Sir Francis Knollys from 1559 to 1570, Sir Christopher Hatton from 1577 to 1587, Sir Thomas Heneage from 1589 to 1595, and Sir John Stanhope, afterwards Lord Stanhope of Harrington, from 1601 to 1616. The post of Vice-Chamberlain was sometimes combined with that of the Treasurer of the Chamber, a functionary through whom many household payments, including rewards to players at court, were made. The more personal expenses of the sovereign passed through the hands of a different paymaster, the Keeper of the Privy Purse. Under the

---

[1] Cf. *The Elizabethan Lords Chamberlain*, in *Malone Society Collections*, i. 31.

superintendence of the Lord Chamberlain were a number of more or less specialized establishments, such as the Jewel House, the Wardrobe, the Beds, the Serjeants at Arms, the Guard, of which Ralegh was captain from 1587 to 1603, the Gentlemen Pensioners, who attended the Queen, as the cowslips attended Titania, when she came abroad (*Mid. N. D.* II. i. 10), the Chapel, a body of singing men and children, the latter of whom were often trained to perform plays, the Tents, the Revels, the Works, the Queen's Barge, and many others. The Lord Chamberlain was responsible too for the hunting establishments and for such officers as the Physicians, the Serjeant Painter, the Astronomer, the Players of Interludes, and a host of Musicians, some of whom were of Italian extraction. At the beginning of the reign there was a royal Fool, one Robert Grene, but this personage does not seem to have been quite so much in evidence as in some earlier and later courts. Finally, there was the Chamber itself, divided into the Outer Chamber and the Privy Chamber, and comprising—at any rate in theory, since some of the posts were merely honorific—the personal attendants on the sovereign : Gentlemen, Gentlemen Ushers and Grooms of the Privy Chamber, Gentlemen Ushers and Grooms of the Outer Chamber, Carvers, Cupbearers, and Sewers, Clerks of the Closet, where the Queen heard prayers, Esquires of the Body, of whom was John Lyly, Harbingers, who went before the progress, Yeomen Ushers, Pages, and Messengers. In a queen's household some of these posts were naturally duplicated by ladies. Elizabeth had ladies of the Bedchamber, Ladies of the Privy Chamber, Chamberers, and of course the famous Maids of Honour, young girls of good birth, whose business it was to wait upon her, to walk with her, to play, sing, and read to her, and above all to entertain her with dancing, an exercise of which she was remarkably fond, and continued herself to practise, even when on the verge of the grave. Sir James Melville reports her delighted vanity when she had forced him to admit that the Queen of Scots danced not ' so high or disposedly ' as she did. Many of the names of the Maids of Honour are upon record, and their history might well be written. That prince of court gossips, Rowland White, fills his letters to Sir Robert Sidney with details of their bravery and their flirtations. In 1598 he especially notes

QUEEN ELIZABETH

Mrs. Ratcliffe, and her 'whyte sattin gown, all embrodered, richly cutt upon good cloth of silver, that cost £180'. A year or two later Margaret Ratcliffe came to a pathetic end, which won her the honour of an exquisite epitaph by Ben Jonson. She was the daughter of Sir Alexander Ratcliffe of Ordsall, and died of grief for the fall of her brother in the Irish wars. The following account of her in a letter by Philip Gawdy has been recently discovered :

Ther is newes besydes of the tragycall death of Mrs. Ratcliffe, the mayde of honor who euer synce the deathe of Sr Alexander her brother hathe pined in suche straunge manner, as voluntarily she hathe gone about to starue her selfe and by the two dayes together hathe receyued no sustinaunce, whiche meeting withe extreame greife hathe made an ende of her mayden modest dayes at Richmonde vppon Saterdaye last, her Matie being present, who commaunded her body to be opened and founde it all well and sounde, sauing certeyne stringes striped all ouer her harte. All the maydes euer synce haue gone in blacke. I saw it my selfe at court.

When they were not in mourning, the ordinary wear of the maids of honour was white. Sidney's correspondent describes them as ' all in white, excellently brave ' at the reception of the Dutch ambassador in 1600, and Dudley Carleton mentions the presence of Elizabeth ' with all her *candidae auditrices* ' at a play in the Blackfriars during the Christmas of 1601. It was no light matter to serve Elizabeth, who had a sharp eye and a sharp tongue for the frailties and even the vanities of her *entourage*. Nor did the royal temper confine itself to oral reprimands. In the spring of 1597 White writes :

The Queen hath of late used the faire Mrs Bridges with words and blowes of anger, and she, with Mrs Russel, were put out of the Coffer Chamber. They lay 3 nights at my Lady Staffords, but are now returned againe to their wonted waiting. By what I wryt in my last lettre unto you, by post, you may conjecture whence these stormes rise. The cause of this displeasure, sayd to be their taking of phisick, and one day going privatly through the Privy Galleries to see the playing at Ballon.

About the same time the Lady Mary Howard was in trouble. She showed a lamentable unpunctuality when it was her turn to carry the Queen's mantle in the garden or the cup of grace in the privy chamber, or to attend upon her mistress at prayers. She answered back when she was rebuked. Moreover, she was unfortunate enough to possess a velvet suit and a rich border powdered with pearls, finer than anything in the Queen's own wardrobe. The real difficulty of course was that the poor girls could not be got to take the cult of Cynthia seriously, and that the idle young men about the court, who were supposed to be paying their addresses to no one except Elizabeth, were only too ready to abet them in the heresy. The revival of *Love's Labour's Lost* in 1597 thus presents itself as a satire not altogether without topical point. Essex was the disturber of hearts in the case of Mary Howard and Elizabeth Brydges, and for the matter of that in the case of Elizabeth Russell and Elizabeth Southwell also. The intrigue with Mrs. Brydges became serious in 1598, and the many dependants on Essex's favour were seriously disquieted lest the Queen or Lady Essex should hear of it. ' I will hope ', writes Rowland White, ' that there is no such thing, but the malice of a wicked world wherein we live.' But even when the philandering ended in a marriage, Elizabeth was hardly less displeased. Essex himself was more easily forgiven than the Earl of Southampton, who went with an embassy to France in 1598, and 'lefte behynd hym a very desolate gentlewoman, that hath almost wept out her fairest eyes '. This was Elizabeth Vernon, whom Southampton shortly afterwards returned in haste to marry, and thereby earned his committal to the Fleet and the royal displeasure for the rest of the reign. Southampton is, of course, another candidate for the honour of being ' Mr W. H.'

Long before this, in 1591, Robert Dudley, Leicester's doubtfully legitimate son, had been ' commanded from court for kissing Mrs Cavendish ', whom he married: nor was wedlock possible to Ralegh and Elizabeth Throgmorton in 1592, or to Robert Tyrwhitt and Bridget Manners in 1594, without the resentment of the offended goddess of chastity. More fortunate was Elizabeth Russell's sister Anne, who not only obtained the royal sanction to marry Lord Herbert, son of the Earl of Worcester, in 1600, but had even the honour of the queen's presence at her wedding.[1] There was a characteristic little episode. Eight ladies

---

[1] G. Scharf, in *Archaeological Journal*, vol. xxxiii, p. 131, argues that the well-known picture at Sherborne, representing Elizabeth borne in procession in a litter, commemorates this event, and not, as has also been held, a visit to Hunsdon House in Hertfordshire. The contemporary duplicate of this picture, now at Melbury, is reproduced as a frontispiece to this volume

danced a mask, representing the Muses in search of one of their fellows.

Mrs Fitton went to the Queen, and woed her to dawnce; her Majestie asked what she was; *Affection*, she said. '*Affection!*' said the Queen, '*Affection* is false.' Yet her Majestie rose and dawnced.

Mary Fitton afterwards disgraced herself with the Earl of Pembroke, and had the impudence while in waiting to 'put off her head tire and tucke upp her clothes and take a large white cloake, and marche as though she had bene a man to meete the said Earle out of the Courte'. There are still persons who believe that Mary Fitton was the lady of Shakespeare's *Sonnets*. She is much more likely to have been the Maria of *Twelfth Night*. Shakespeare's official duties did not require regular attendance in the household, and *Twelfth Night*, which dates from about 1601–2, is one of the few plays which seems to contain anything more than a very distant echo of court affairs. It is at least tempting to compare the scene (II. iii) in which Malvolio breaks in upon the midnight revels of Maria and the riotous knights with the following episode recorded by Sir Nicholas L'Estrange, in which figures Sir William Knollys, the Treasurer of the Household, who is known to have been an elderly lover of Mary Fitton :

The Lord Knolls, in Queen Elizabeths time, had his lodging at Court, where some of the Ladyes and Maydes of Honour us'd to friske and hey about in the next roome, to his extreame disquiete a nights, though he had often warned them of it ; at last he getts one to bolt their own backe doore, when they were all in one night at their revells, stripps off to his shirt, and so with a payre of spectacles on his nose, and Aretine in his hand, comes marching in at a posterne doore of his owne chamber, reading very gravely, full upon the faces of them. Now let the reader judge what a sadd spectacle and pittiful sight these poor creatures endur'd, for he fac'd them and often traverst the roome in this posture above an houre.

The court had its local habitation wherever the sovereign happened for the time to be lodged. The chief town palace was that indifferently known as Westminster or Whitehall. This had originally belonged to the see of York, and had been taken over and enlarged by Henry the Eighth, upon the fall of Wolsey. It covered some scores of acres with a medley of buildings arranged on no very coherent plan. Through the midst of it ran the highway from London to

Westminster, passing under two gate-houses, of which the northern one had been designed by Holbein. To the west lay a tilt-yard, a cockpit, and many lodgings, backed by St. James's Park; to the east the privy garden, chapel, and apartments of state. On this side the palace extended to the river, from which it was approached by the Whitehall stairs. Opposite, near the Surrey side, was moored the royal barge, and this, drawn by a boatful of rowers, enabled the queen to make free use of the Thames waterway. Whitehall was generally occupied during the winter, and in particular when Parliament was sitting. But it was only one of a large number of residences at the disposal of the court. In its immediate neighbourhood were St. James's and Somerset House, as well as Durham Place, which was generally reserved for the accommodation of ambassadors and other foreign visitors of distinction. The Tower, in London itself, was only used by the sovereign as a lodging for the night before a coronation. It housed traitors, and a collection of caged beasts, including an old lion called Edward the Sixth, a tiger, a lynx, a wolf, a fretful porcupine, and an eagle. Occasionally also the queen lay at the Charterhouse, a disused monastery. The other principal palaces were Greenwich, a few miles down the river; Richmond and Hampton Court, a few miles up; Windsor, the most ancient of all, with its own chapel in which the knightly order of the Garter was installed; and Oatlands and Nonsuch, in Surrey. To Nonsuch Elizabeth was especially attached; to the splendours of Hampton Court, on the other hand, she took a dislike after an attack of small-pox from which she suffered there in 1562. In addition were numerous smaller houses, situated upon royal manors, which the queen occasionally visited, but which for the most part were left in solitude under Keepers, who enjoyed the privileges of herbage and pannage in their parks. Such were Eltham and Otford in Kent, Havering atte Bower in Essex, Hatfield in Hertfordshire, Enfield in Middlesex, Reading Abbey in Berkshire, and Woodstock in Oxfordshire.

The arrangement of the principal rooms of a Tudor palace can perhaps be best studied in the plan of Hampton Court. Upon the dais at the back of the great Hall is the entrance to a Guard or Watching Chamber. Out of this opens the Presence Chamber, and out of this again the Privy Chamber, which gives access to the private apartments of the sovereign. From the opposite end of the Guard Chamber runs a gallery, which passes round two sides of a court and leads to the royal Closet, overlooking and forming part of the Chapel. Into this gallery also opens the Council Chamber. The presence chamber and the privy chamber were the essential elements of the scheme, and these had to be contrived, however humbly the court was lodged. The crowd of courtiers filled the presence chamber, and waited until it was the pleasure of the sovereign to appear in public. Such appearances were accompanied with considerable ceremony. Paul Hentzner, a German who visited London in 1598, describes Elizabeth's procession to chapel on a Sunday at Greenwich :

We were admitted by an order from the lord chamberlain into the presence-chamber, hung with rich tapestry, and the floor after the English fashion strewed with hay,[1] through which the queen commonly passes on her way to chapel : at the door stood a gentleman dressed in velvet, with a gold chain, whose office was to introduce to the queen any person of distinction, that came to wait on her : it was Sunday, when there is usually the greatest attendance of nobility. In the same hall were the archbishop of Canterbury, the bishop of London, a great number of counsellors of state, officers of the crown, and gentlemen, who waited the queen's coming out ; which she did from her own apartment, when it was time to go to prayers, attended in the following manner. First went gentlemen, barons, earls, knights of the garter, all richly dressed and bareheaded ; next came the chancellor, bearing the seals in a red-silk purse, between two ; one of which carried the royal sceptre, the other the sword of state, in a red scabbard, studded with golden fleurs de lis, the point upwards: next came the queen, in the sixty-fifth year of her age, as we were told, very majestic ; her face oblong, fair, but wrinkled ; her eyes small, yet black and pleasant ; her nose a little hooked ; her lips narrow, and her teeth black (a defect the English seem subject to, from their too great use of sugar) ; she had in her ears two pearls, with very rich drops ; she wore false hair, and that red ; upon her head she had a small crown, reported to be made of some of the gold of the celebrated Lunebourg table : her bosom was uncovered, as all the English ladies have it, till they marry ; and she had on a necklace of exceeding fine jewels ; her hands were small, her fingers long, and her stature neither tall nor low ; her air was stately, her manner of speaking mild and obliging. That day she was dressed in white silk, bordered with pearls of the size of beans, and over it a mantle of black silk, shot with silver

---

[1] 'Suppose . . . the grass whereon thou treadest the presence strewed' (*Rich. II*, I. iii. 288).

threads ; her train was very long, the end of it borne by a mar-
chioness ; instead of a chain, she had an oblong collar of gold and
jewels. As she went along in all this state and magnificence, she
spoke very graciously, first to one, then to another, whether foreign
ministers, or those who attended for different reasons, in English,
French, or Italian ; for, besides being well skilled in Greek, Latin, and
the languages I have mentioned, she is mistress of Spanish, Scotch,
and Dutch : whoever speaks to her, it is kneeling ; now and then
she raises some with her hand. While we were there, W. Slawata,
a Bohemian baron, had letters to present to her ; and she, after
pulling off her glove, gave him her right hand to kiss, sparkling
with rings and jewels, a mark of particular favour : where ever she
turned her face, as she was going along, every body fell down on
their knees. The ladies of the court followed next to her, very
handsome and well shaped, and for the most part dressed in white ;
she was guarded on each side by the gentlemen pensioners, fifty in
number, with gilt battle-axes. In the antichapel next the hall where
we were, petitions were presented to her, and she received them most
graciously, which occasioned the acclamation of, Long live Queen
Elizabeth ! She answered it with, I thank you, my good People.

Hentzner then narrates how, while the Queen was at
chapel, the royal dinner was brought in by the yeomen
of the guard ' clothed ', as they are still, ' in scarlet, with
a golden rose upon their backs ', to the music of drums and
trumpets. The service was done with great solemnity, and
a countess, after rubbing the plates with bread and salt,
gave the guard tasting morsels of each dish. The dishes
were then removed by the Queen's ladies into the privy
chamber. Elizabeth had disused the ancient custom of
the English kings, which was afterwards revived by her
successor, of occasionally dining in state in the great hall of the
palace, served by the principal nobles of the realm on the
knee. The presence chamber appears to have been open to
any one who was entitled to appear at court. Access to the
privy chamber, on the other hand, was jealously guarded.
Here the Queen sat with her ladies, and a yeoman usher kept
the door against all except the privileged officers of the
Chamber, and such others as the Queen might honour by
a special summons. Ambassadors seem to have been
sometimes admitted to audience in the privy chamber.
A pendant to Hentzner's description is the account
by the Venetian ambassador, Giovanni Carlo Scaramelli,
of his reception at Richmond in 1603, a few years after
Hentzner's visit, and just before Elizabeth's last and fatal

illness. This, too, was on a Sunday. Scaramelli, escorted by a pensioner, was received by a gentleman at the foot of the stairs, and at the top by the Lord Chamberlain, who led him through the presence chamber into another, where he found Elizabeth. She was loaded with jewels, and sat on a small square dais with two steps. The privy councillors stood around her, and the room was full of ladies and gentlemen and of musicians who had just been playing dance-music. The Queen discoursed with Scaramelli in Italian, and ended the interview by fishing for a compliment on her proficiency in the language. Probably the Queen did not habitually sit even in the privy chamber, and in her absence the gentlemen of the privy chamber played at cards and tables to solace their time of waiting. The maids of honour, when not dancing measures for the Queen's delectation in the privy chamber, or carrying her mantle in the privy garden, seem to have been lodged in an apartment known as the Coffer Chamber.

Until the arrival of Scaramelli in 1603 there had been no Venetian ambassador in England since the reign of Mary. This is regrettable, as the Venetian eye for spectacle and ceremony and the Venetian habit of writing minute reports to the Signory would have added largely to our knowledge of the intimate details of Elizabeth's court. Spain also withdrew her ambassadors after the diplomatic breach with England in 1584. But throughout the reign there was generally a resident or 'lieger' French ambassador, and from France and elsewhere there were frequent 'extraordinary' ambassadors, in whose honour the court put on its most sumptuous and lavish aspect. The programme provided for the commissioners sent to negotiate the marriage treaty between Elizabeth and the Duke of Alençon in 1581 may be taken as an illustration. The commission was preceded in February by Alençon's secretary, Pierre Clausse, Seigneur de Marchaumont. He was graciously received by Elizabeth, and accompanied her to a banquet 'finer than ever had been seen in England since the time of King Henry', on board Drake's ship, *The Golden Hind*, at Deptford. Here a very Elizabethan incident took place. The Queen was wearing a purple and gold garter, which slipped down and was trailing as she entered the ship. Marchaumont stooped and picked it up, but Elizabeth begged him to let her have it, as she had nothing else with which to keep her stocking up, and promised to give it him when she got home. She then put it on before him, and when she reached Westminster fulfilled her promise. Marchaumont sent the garter to Alençon in triumph, with a full account of the episode. Throughout April preparations for the coming festivities were in full swing. It was noted that the Queen would pay no attention to treaty points, and was only concerned to know whether there were any new devices in the jousts, or where a ball was to be given, or what beautiful women were coming to court. She issued an order in council that all stuffs of cloth of gold, velvet, and silk were to be sold at a reduction of twenty-five per cent., in order that lords and ladies might be better able to bedizen themselves. On April 20, the commissioners, of whom the most important were François de Bourbon, Dauphin of Auvergne, and Artur de Cossé, Marshal of France, reached London. They had their first audience a few days later, and then began a round of festivities. On one day they were banqueted by the queen, on another by Leicester, on a third by Burleigh, and on a fourth by Sussex. Each banquet entailed a costly provision of masques and plays. A bear-baiting was arranged for their amusement, and a visit to Hampton Court, where there were jousts led by the Earl of Arundel and Lord Windsor. Finally, in the middle of May, was held one of those great spectacular tournaments which were characteristic of chivalry in its Tudor stage of degeneration. A Fortress of Perfect Beauty was built in the tilt-yard at Westminster, and here Elizabeth was besieged by Arundel and Windsor, with Philip Sidney and Fulke Greville, who proclaimed themselves the Four Foster-children of Desire, and challenged all comers to combat. They had to meet twenty-two defendants, including Sir John Perrott and Anthony Cooke as Adam and Eve, and Sir Henry Lee as an unknown knight. Just such an elaborate foolery of devices furnishes material for Act ii, Scene ii, of *Pericles, Prince of Tyre*. Nothing seems to have proved more attractive to foreign ambassadors than an English bear-baiting. This pastime, under the name of the Queen's Game of Paris Garden, was carried on as part of the royal establishment, under a Master and two Keepers, of the Bears and of the Mastiffs respectively. The public shows were in a ring or bear-garden on the Surrey side of the Thames, but the bears were often brought to Whitehall, so that the Queen and her guests might watch the sport from a gallery of the palace.

The movements of the court followed with some regularity a seasonal cycle. About the beginning of November, the Queen came back from the country to London. The event was a ceremony of state, to which it was customary to invite the ambassadors. Elizabeth rode in a litter, with lords and ladies about her. A great noble bore the sword of state, and the Master of the Horse led her palfrey by the bridle. Shouting citizens thronged the fields, and the Lord Mayor, with some hundreds of burgesses in gold chains, came to bid her welcome. The date of her return was determined partly by the setting in of winter, partly by the desire to be at Westminster for Accession Day, November 17, which was annually observed, after its twelfth return in 1570, as a solemn festival. Bonfires, the ancient folk observance of the beginning of winter, were lit, and it is a curious fact that the day continued to be observed as a public holiday at the Exchequer, and in the schools of Westminster and Merchant Taylors, during the first half of the nineteenth century. In Elizabeth's own court the celebration took the form of a ' triumph ' or ' joust of peace '. This survival of chivalry was conducted under rules laid down by John, Lord Tiptoft and Earl of Worcester, as Lord High Constable of England, in 1466, and adopted by Elizabeth in 1562. Its principal element was the running at tilt, a combat with spears on horseback ; but there were also the tourney, fought with swords on horseback, and the barriers, fought with pikes and swords on foot. Even during the sixteenth century these sports were still to some extent an exercise of arms and horsemanship, but they tended more and more to become mimetic, a matter of ' disguises ' and ' devices ', and an occasion for courtly compliment. A famous tilting of this type is described in George Peele's *Polyhymnia* (1590), and in William Segar's *Honor, Military and Civil* (1602). This was in 1590, when Sir Henry Lee, who had for many years been challenger on Accession Day, resigned his privilege, on the ground of advancing years, to the Earl of Cumberland. Segar describes the device as follows :

Her Majesty, beholding these armed knights comming toward her, did suddenly hear a musicke so sweete and secret, as every one thereat greatly marveiled. And hearkening to that excellent melodie, the earth as it were opening, there appeared a Pavilion, made of white taffata, containing eight score elles, being in proportion like unto the sacred Temple of the Virgins Vestall. This Temple seemed to consist upon pillars of pourferry, arched like unto a church, within it were many lampes burning. Also, on the one side there stood an altar covered with cloth of gold, and thereupon two waxe candles burning in rich candlesticks ; upon the altar also were layd certaine princely presents, which after by three virgins were presented unto her Maiestie. Before the doore of this Temple stood a crowned pillar, embraced by an Eglantine tree, whereon there hanged a table ; and therein written (with letters of gold) this prayer. . . . The gifts which the Vestall maydens presented unto her Maiesty, were these : a vaile of white exceeding rich and curiously wrought ; a cloke and safegard set with buttons of gold, and on them were graven emprezes of excellent devise : in the loope of every button was a noblemans badge, fixed to a pillar richly embrodered. . . . These presents and prayer being with great reverence delivered into her Maiesties owne handes, and he himselfe disarmed offered up his armour at the foot of her Maiesties crowned pillar ; and kneeling upon his knees, presented the Earle of Cumberland, humbly beseeching she would be pleased to accept him for her Knight, to continue the yeerely exercises aforesaid. Her Majesty gratiously accepting of that offer, this aged knight armed the Earle, and mounted him upon his horse. That being done, he put upon his owne person a side coat of blacke velvet pointed under the arme, and covered his head (in liew of a helmet) with a buttoned cap of the countrey fashion.

George Clifford, Earl of Cumberland, seems to have continued to perform the functions of challenger to the end of the reign ; but a prominent figure in the later jousts was the Earl of Essex, for whose devices in 1595 Francis Bacon wrote speeches which are his nearest approach to dramatic literature. In 1588 Elizabeth added to the festival of Accession Day a second celebration on St. Elizabeth's day, November 19, in honour of the Armada ; and this was still kept in 1590.

Christmas, unless plague rendered the neighbourhood of a populous city undesirable, was generally spent by the court at Whitehall. On New Year's Day, it was customary, as it had been customary since the Roman emperors took their *strenae,* to give presents to the sovereign, who rewarded the donors with orders upon the Master of the Jewel House for plate of a value proportionate to their degree. Several rolls setting out these New Year gifts are in existence. The cupidity of Elizabeth was not offended by the offer of twenty ' dimy soveraignes ' in a silken purse ; but many courtiers went to the trouble of thinking out costly and appropriate jewels, while the ladies brought finery and ' sweet bags ', and the humbler household servants prepared with anxious pains symbolical masterpieces of their offices. Thus the apothecary would bring ' one pott of grene gynger, and a pott of orenge flowers ', or the Serjeant of the Pastry ' a greate pye of quynses and wardyns guilte '. Another joust often enlivened the Christmas holidays, which was also the especial period for indoor festivities such as plays and masques. These were generally given in the evening, after supper, on one of the three saint's-days immediately following Christmas, or on New Year's Day or Twelfth Night. They were the charge of a special department of the Household under the control of the Lord Chamberlain, known as the Office of the Revels, and consisting of a Master, with a Clerk, a Clerk Comptroller, and a yeoman as his subordinate staff. The post of Master was held by Sir Thomas Cawarden from 1544 to 1559, by Sir Thomas Benger from 1559 to 1572, by Edmund Tilney from 1578 to 1610, and by Sir George Buck from 1610 to 1622. John Lyly, the dramatist, was an unsuccessful candidate for the succession to Tilney, and at a later date Ben Jonson had a reversion of the office, which he did not live to enjoy. Both plays and masques were sometimes brought to court, at their own expense, by amateurs, such as the gentlemen of the Inns of Court. As examples may be taken the performance of Norton and Sackville's *Gorboduc* or *Ferrex and Porrex* by the Inner Temple on January 18, 1562, and Davison and Campion's masque of *Proteus and the Rock Adamantine* presented by Gray's Inn on March 3, 1595. Ordinarily, however, the Revels office was responsible for providing the entertainment. During the weeks preceding Christmas the officers called in the companies of men and boys then playing publicly in London, made them rehearse their new pieces, and appointed them days on which to produce those selected at the court. Properties and costumes were supplied, when necessary, from the wardrobe of the Revels, and the players received a reward, generally amounting to £10, for which the Privy Council signed a warrant payable by the Treasurer of the Chamber. It is an entry of such a warrant in the Treasurer's account-book which preserves to us the first official record of Shakespeare's name, in 1595. The masques were danced by the lords and ladies of the court themselves, and the purchase of costly materials, with the making, altering, and repairing of the dresses for the dancers and their attendant torchbearers, occupied a large share of the time and attention of the Revels officers. Many interesting details of such work can be pieced together from the surviving records of the office. But full descriptions of Elizabethan masques have rarely been handed down; and, as has been said, it is probable that the royal tendency to economy was unfavourable to that elaboration of spectacle which characterized earlier and later reigns. The influence of the masque upon the drama is, however, to be traced throughout the Shakespearian plays. Thus there is a masque of Muscovites in *Love's Labour's Lost*, while *A Midsummer Night's Dream*, almost certainly written for a court wedding at which Elizabeth was present, resolves itself at the close into a bergomasque and a dance of fairies by way of epithalamium, thus supplying precisely that combination of the grotesque and the dainty which the masque particularly loved. The same play gives a very close illustration of the manner of dramatic performances at court. Philostrate, the 'usual manager of mirth' to Theseus, stands for the Master of the Revels, and the company whose 'play is preferred' are introduced into 'the great chamber' of the palace,

> To wear away this long age of three hours
> Between our after-supper and bed-time.
> (*Mid. N. D.* v. i. 33–4)

Another example of a play at court is to be found in *Hamlet*, Act III, Scene ii. The presence chamber, or at need the great hall, sufficed for the purposes of a play, and here a temporary stage was easily arranged against the screen. A masque, bringing its crowd of spectators by permission from the city as well as the court, required an ampler space, if the evolutions of the dancers and their pageant were to have fair scope. Temporary structures of woodwork, known as 'banqueting houses', were prepared to meet the need, and 1581 saw the erection at Whitehall of a more permanent banqueting-house, although still of flimsy materials, for the entertainment of the French. It is minutely described in Holinshed's *Chronicles*.

A banketting house was begun at Westminster, on the south west side of hir maiesties palace of White hall, made in maner and forme of a long square, three hundred thirtie and two foot in measure about; thirtie principals made of great masts, being fortie foot in length a peece, standing upright; betweene everie one of these masts ten foot asunder and more. The walles of this house were closed with canvas, and painted all the outsides of the same most artificiallie with a worke called rustike, much like to stone. This house had two hundred ninetie and two lights of glasse. The sides within the same house was made with ten heights of degrees for people to stand upon: and in the top of this house was wrought most cunninglie upon canvas, works of ivie and hollie, with pendents made of wicker rods, and garnished with baie, rue, and all maner of strange flowers garnished with spangles of gold, as also beautified with hanging toseans made of hollie and ivie, with all maner of strange fruits, as pomegranats, orenges, pompions, cucumbers, grapes, carrets, with such other like, spangled with gold, and most richlie hanged. Betwixt these works of baies and ivie, were great spaces of canvas, which was most cunninglie painted, the clouds with starres, the sunne and sunne beames, with diverse other cotes of sundrie sortes belonging to the queenes maiestie, most richlie garnished with gold. There were of all maner of persons working on this house, to the number of three hundred seventie and five: two men had mischances, the one brake his leg, and so did the other. This house was made in three weekes and three daies, and was ended the eighteenth daie of Aprill; and cost one thousand seven hundred fortie and foure pounds, nineteene shillings and od monie; as I was crediblie informed by the worshipfull maister Thomas Grave surveior unto hir maiesties workes, who served and gave order for the same, as appeareth by record.

The Elizabethan banqueting-house lasted 'with much propping' until 1607, and was then replaced by James with one of brick and stone. This was burnt, with the records of the Council, Privy Seal and Signet Offices, which were stored beneath it, in 1619. The banqueting-house of Inigo Jones, which is still the glory of Whitehall, was begun almost immediately afterwards.

In strictness the Christmas season ended on Twelfth Night, but the revels were resumed at intervals until Lent, and particularly at Candlemas (February 2) and Shrovetide. For one or both of these feasts the court often moved to Hampton Court, Greenwich, or Richmond, generally returning to Whitehall for a part of the spring and early summer.

The transits were accomplished either by road or by river. They took two days, and the Queen spent a night on the way at the house of some favoured courtier, such as Lord Admiral Howard at Chelsea or the Archbishop of Canterbury or Lord Borough at Lambeth. As she passed, the church-bells broke into jubilation, and the entries of payments to ringers in the churchwardens' accounts of St. Martin's and St. Margaret's, Westminster, and other parishes, make it possible to date many of her journeys. At Easter, it was customary for the sovereign to go through the ceremony of washing the feet of the poor on Maundy Thursday; and on St. George's day, April 23, took place the great feast of the Order of the Garter. This was held, with a procession about the great hall, wherever the court might happen to be; but the head-quarters of the order was in St. George's chapel at Windsor, and when new knights were created they rode to Windsor for their installation with great ceremony and at vast expense. The connexion of Windsor Castle with the Garter is celebrated in *The Merry Wives of Windsor*, v. v. 65–76. Possibly the play was written for a Garter feast.

> The several chairs of order look you scour
> With juice of balm and every precious flower.
> Each fair instalment, coat, and several crest
> With loyal blazon ever more be blest!
> And nightly, meadow-fairies, look you sing,
> Like to the Garter's compass, in a ring.
> The expressure that it bears, green let it be,
> More fertile-fresh than all the field to see;
> And *Honi soit qui mal y pense* write
> In emerald tufts, flowers purple, blue, and white;
> Like sapphire, pearl, and rich embroidery,
> Buckled below fair knighthood's bending knee.

The heats of summer found Elizabeth again at a country palace; and in July or August she generally started on one of those progresses through her dominions, the records of which preserve in memory the most characteristic splendours of the reign. In these sumptuous and costly holidays she expected the attendance of her court, and elaborate pro-grammes or 'gests' were published in advance. Several counties were often traversed, and at most of the places visited the Queen lay for at least two or three nights, occasionally occupying one of her own outlying manor-houses, but more often the residence of some subject upon whom she imposed the honour and the tax of her entertainment. Simple gentlemen, as well as great nobles, were called upon to show their loyalty in this fashion; and although the household brought much of its equipment and was prepared to pay its own food and drink bill, it is not clear that even this concession was always accepted by men of means, and in any case the mere incidental expenses in banquets and revels, and rich gifts proved a heavy burden on many a slender revenue. Lord Burghley received Elizabeth at Theobalds and elsewhere upon twelve several occasions, at a cost of £2,000 or £3,000 each time, for visits which sometimes extended a month or six weeks. ' But,' says the chronicler,

His love to his Sovereigne, and joye to enterteyn her and her traine was so greate, as he thought no troble, care, nor cost too much, and all too little, so it weare bountifully performed to her Majestie's recreation, and the contentment of her traine.

There may have been some grumbling at the cost, one may suspect, when the gaudy train had swept by, and the host was left to meet the lengthening face of his steward. But there is abundant evidence of the popularity which Elizabeth won by these progresses, and of an enthusiasm in receiving her which did not limit itself to the ordinary duties of hospitality, but broke out into elaborate and ingenious devices, often quasi-dramatic in character, of welcome and farewell. The cities through which the progress passed shared in this fantastic pageantry, and the poets and scholars who were employed to plan the entertainments often took the trouble to commit descriptions of them to print, for the glorification of their own ingenuity, and incidentally for the information of posterity. The extent and direction of the progresses varied in different years. Some of the most lengthy or famous were those of 1564 to Cambridge, Huntingdonshire, and Leicestershire; of 1566 to Northamptonshire, Lincolnshire, Warwickshire, and Oxford; of 1572 to Warwickshire and Northamptonshire; of 1573 to Sussex and Kent; of 1574 to Gloucestershire, Somersetshire, Wiltshire, and Hampshire; of 1575 to Northamptonshire, Warwickshire, Staffordshire, Worcestershire, and Oxfordshire; and of 1578 to Suffolk, Norfolk, and Cambridgeshire. Elizabeth does not ever seem to have travelled further north or west than these records indicate. To 1575 belongs the well-known visit to the Earl of Leicester at Kenilworth, of which two minute accounts exist, one by George Gascoigne, who had a share in devising the entertainments, the other by the quaint gossip Robert Laneham, who attended the court as Keeper of the Council Chamber Door. It is a beloved and baseless fancy of Shakespeare's more sentimental biographers that he gazed upon the spectacle as a boy. A brief summary of the festivities may serve to illustrate what took place on a smaller scale whenever the Queen passed. Elizabeth reached Kenilworth on Saturday, July 9, and was met at successive points with speeches by a Sibyl, by the porter dressed as Hercules, by the Lady of the Lake, and by a Poet 'in a long ceruleous garment'. She entered the castle over an elaborately adorned bridge and beneath a shower of fireworks. On the 10th, being Sunday, she attended service in the parish church. In the afternoon there was dancing, and at night another display of fireworks. On the 11th the Queen hunted, and was greeted on her return by a complimentary dialogue between a Savage Man and Echo. The 12th was a day of rest, with music and dancing, and the 13th was also given up to hunting. In the morning of the 14th bears were baited, and in the evening there were fireworks, and an Italian showed feats of agility. The 15th and 16th were days of rest. The 17th, after service, was devoted to rustic festivities, a bride-ale, with a morris-dance and tilting at the quintain, and the Hock-Tide show of the citizens of Coventry. In the evening followed a play and a banquet, which lasted so long that a masque, which had been prepared, was not shown. On the 18th the Queen hunted, and then saw a water-pageant of the Delivery of the Lady of the Lake, with Triton riding upon a mermaid and Arion upon a dolphin. An investiture of knights also took place, and the Queen 'touched' for the king's evil. This the English sovereigns were accustomed to do as claimants to the crown of France. The practice was continued by James, and is described in Act IV, Scene iii, of *Macbeth*. On the 19th the Coventry show was repeated. On the 20th the Queen had purposed to ride to the Earl of Warwick's at Wedgenall and a device of *Zabeta* was prepared ; but the weather proved unpropitious. She stayed yet another week at

Kenilworth, but no further details are preserved, except of a final show, *The Farewell of Silvanus*, which greeted her departure. During the troublous times of the 'eighties there seem to have been comparatively few progresses of any exceptional character. But after the relief from the peril of the Armada, the spirit of gaiety revived. In the summer of 1591 Elizabeth visited Sussex, Hampshire, and Surrey, and in the summer of 1592 Buckinghamshire, Berkshire, Oxfordshire, and Gloucestershire ; and accounts are preserved of her reception by Lord Montagu at Cowdray, by the Earl of Hertford at Elvetham, by Lady Russell and Sir Edward Hoby at Bisham, by Lord Chandos at Sudeley, by Lord Norris at Rycote, and by the University of Oxford. The Elvetham entertainment is particularly interesting, not only for the appearance of Aureola the Fairy Queen and wife of Auberon, but also because the chief device took the form of a water-pageant with a sea-nymph, who sang in a pinnace drawn by sea-gods and tritons. On the following day there were fireworks on the lake ; and it is on the whole probable that this occasion, rather than the far-off revels of 1575 at Kenilworth, gave Shakespeare the hint for his description of how Oberon

> sat upon a promontory,
> And heard a mermaid on a dolphin's back
> Uttering such dulcet and harmonious breath,
> That the rude sea grew civil at her song,
> And certain stars shot madly from their spheres,
> To hear the sea-maid's music. (*Mid. N. D.* ii. i. 149)

The details are not, in all probability, precise. There was no actual mermaid on a dolphin's back, either at Kenilworth or at Elvetham. It is perhaps permissible to conjecture that Elvetham played a part in the love-affair which issued, three or four years later, in the wedding for which *A Midsummer Night's Dream* was written.

Elizabeth continued her progresses indomitably to the end. In 1599 she even extended her original programme, 'by reason of an intercepted letter, wherein the giving over of long voyages was noted to be sign of age'. In 1600 a progress was resolved upon, contrary to the hopes of courtiers, who were themselves getting elderly and liked their ease. Rowland White writes from Nonsuch :

The Lords are sorry for it, but her Majestie bids the old stay

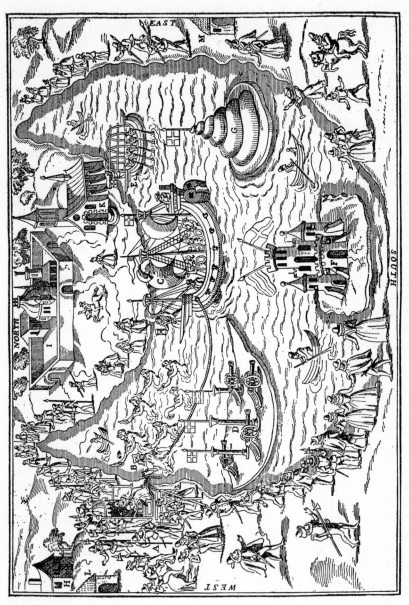

THE ELVETHAM ENTERTAINMENT, 1591, from Nichols's *Progresses*.

behind, and the young and able to go with her. She had just cause to be offended, that at her remove to this place she was soe poorly attended ; for I never saw so small a train.

Elizabeth's last years, indeed, showed renewed signs of that feverish love of amusement which had been more becoming to her youth. In the winter of 1597–8 a correspondent wrote to Spain of a feast at which ' the head of the Church of England and Ireland was to be seen in her old age dancing three or four gaillards '. She was dancing still ' gayement et de belle disposition ', when the French ambassador saw her at Anne Russell's wedding in 1600.[1] In 1601 she went a-Maying at Sir William Cornwallis's house at Highgate, and in the autumn was entertained at several places, notably by Sir William Knollys at Caversham ' with singing dancing and playing-wenches '. In 1602 she Mayed again, with Sir Richard Buckly at Lewisham. In August she was entertained by Sir Thomas Egerton at Harefield, but not, as a forgery of Collier's would have us believe, with *Othello*. She visited Sir Robert Cecil at Cecil Place in December. At Christmas Sir John Harington reported that she ' doth now bear shew of human infirmitie ' ; but during the festive season the court ' flourisht more than ordinarie ' with many plays, and on February 2 the Venetian ambassador found the Queen in excellent health and to all appearance far from the end of her life. A week later the collapse had come, and by March 24 Elizabeth had started upon her last progress, leaving behind her ' a rich wardrobe of more than two thousand gowns, with all things else answerable ', which in a very few months Anne of Denmark was cutting up to furnish a masque.[2] The last scene of all is touched with the irony which waits inevitably on courts. Scaramelli describes it to the Signory :

The body of the late Queen by her own orders has neither been opened, nor, indeed, seen by any living soul save by three of her ladies.

[1] P. P. Laffleur de Kermaingant, *Mission de Jean de Thumery*, i. 415.
[2] Scaramelli, in *Venetian Papers*, x. 64, estimates the number at 6,000. An inventory of the Wardrobes of Robes in 1600 (Nichols, *Elizabeth*, iii. 300) enumerates over 1,000 garments of various kinds.

The Elvetham Entertainment.—The key to the letters in the engraving here reproduced is as follows : A. Her Majesties presence-seate, and traine. B. Nereus, and his followers. C. The pinnace of Neaera, and her musicke. D. The ship-ile. E. A boate with musicke, attending on the pinnace of Neaera. F. The Fort-mount. G. The Snaile-mount. H. The Roome of Estate. I. Her Majesties Court. K. Her Majesties wardrop. L. The place whence Silvanus and his companie issued.

It has been taken to Westminster near London, and lies there in the palace, all hung with mournings. There the Council waits on her continually with the same ceremony, the same expenditure, down to her very household and table service, as though she were not wrapped in many a fold of cerecloth, and hid in such a heap of lead, of coffin, of pall, but was walking as she used to do at this season, about the alleys of her gardens. And so, in accordance with ancient custom, will it continue till the King gives orders for her funeral.

The forms of the court remained under James much what they had been under Elizabeth. When he reached Theobalds, the king adopted the English way of living in place of that to which he had been accustomed in Scotland. The external changes made were of minor importance. The old custom of dining in state in the great hall, with a groaning sideboard of gold and silver vessels, was revived. Certain new festivals were instituted. Naturally James chose his own Accession day, rather than Elizabeth's, for a solemn tilting. He also celebrated August 5, the day of his delivery from the Gowrie conspiracy, and after 1605 November 5, the day of the Gunpowder Plot; and it is interesting to observe that to this day the winter bonfires, lit during Elizabeth's reign on November 17, attached themselves. But although the outer aspect was the same, acute critics were not slow to note a profound modification in the general tone of court life. Everything was done with a profusion which soon brought about financial difficulties, and with a want of dignity which offended those who had known, and for all her whimsies had respected, Elizabeth. Even at his coronation James made himself ridiculous, and worse than ridiculous, by the number of knights he created and the fees he took for the bestowal of the honour. The authors of *Eastward Hoe* got themselves into trouble for their allusion to the ' thirty pound knights '; but that their satire was no more than a fair reflection of popular sentiment is well illustrated by one of Philip Gawdy's letters to his relatives at home :

Ther wer a number of worthy and very choyse knightes made uppon that great day, but with them (lyke cokle amongst good corne) a skumm of suche as it wolde make a man sycke to thinke of them. I have heard your countryes of Norfolke and Suffolke taxed, that ther wer sheapreves, yomans sonns knighted. I cann assuer you ther ar other countryes ar not behynde them in that, and dyvers pedlers sonns of London have receyved the same order ;

amongst the rest Thimblethorpe the attorney, that was called Nimblechappes full of the pox was knighted for seven pounde tenn shillings.

Scaramelli, too, does not refrain from satire in mentioning the transaction :

> Since his accession to the throne the King has created seven hundred knights, and intends to make one thousand, in imitation of King Arthur, who created that number, but among those who had followed him to battle.

Some years later the growing embarrassments of the exchequer drove James and his government to conceive the idea of establishing the new order of Baronet. This scheme is first mentioned in 1611 ; it was carried out with some difficulty, owing to the unwillingness of those selected for the dignity to pay the price. It is not perhaps altogether surprising, in view of the relations between the English and Scottish courts during Elizabeth's reign, that James should have shown himself disinclined to pay any exaggerated deference to either the memory or traditions of his predecessor. He ordered the funeral ceremonies to be abridged, and wore no mourning, ' although', as Scaramelli ironically puts it, ' he knows the Queen wore strict mourning when she took the life of his mother'. On the other hand, the court was not slow to resent his hasty disregard of certain decencies. Writing of the plays during the winter of 1607, John Chamberlain says :

> The king was very anxious to have one on Christmas night, though, as I take it, he and the prince received that day, but the lords told him it was not the fashion. Which answer pleased him not a whit, but said, 'What do you tell me of the fashion? I will make it a fashion.'

After all allowance has been made for the conservatism of flunkeys and the critical mood of the *laudatores temporis acti*, there is ample evidence that the loose-fibred self-indulgence of James and the frivolity of Anne of Denmark permitted a marked degeneration in the standard of court life even as compared with that which had prevailed in ' the spacious times of great Elizabeth '. Some singular things happened in 1606 when Anne's brother, Christian the Fourth of Denmark, paid a visit to England. Sir John Harington, no austere or squeamish person, shall be the narrator :

The sports began each day in such manner and such sorte, as well nigh persuaded me of Mahomets paradise. We had women, and indeed wine too, of such plenty, as woud have astonishd each sober beholder. Our feasts were magnificent, and the two royal guests did most lovingly embrace each other at table. I think the Dane hath strangely wrought on our good English nobles; for those, whom I could never get to taste good liquor, now follow the fashion, and wallow in beastly delights. The ladies abandon their sobriety, and are seen to roll about in intoxication. . . . One day, a great feast was held, and, after dinner, the representation of Solomon his Temple and the coming of the Queen of Sheba was made, or (as I may better say) was meant to have been made, before their Majesties, by device of the Earl of Salisbury and others. But alass! as all earthly thinges do fail to poor mortals in enjoyment, so did prove our presentment hereof. The Lady who did play the Queens part, did carry most precious gifts to both their Majesties; but, forgetting the steppes arising to the canopy, overset her caskets into his Danish Majesties lap, and fell at his feet, tho I rather think it was in his face. Much was the hurry and confusion; cloths and napkins were at hand, to make all clean. His Majesty then got up and woud dance with the Queen of Sheba; but he fell down and humbled himself before her, and was carried to an inner chamber and laid on a bed of state; which was not a little defiled with the presents of the Queen which had been bestowed on his garments; such as wine, cream, jelly, beverage, cakes, spices, and other good matters. The entertainment and show went forward, and most of the presenters went backward, or fell down; wine did so occupy their upper chambers. Now did appear, in rich dress, Hope, Faith, and Charity: Hope did assay to speak, but wine renderd her endeavours so feeble that she withdrew, and hoped the King would excuse her brevity: Faith was then all alone, for I am certain she was not joyned with good works, and left the court in a staggering condition: Charity came to the King's feet, and seemed to cover the multitude of sins her sisters had committed; in some sorte she made obeysance and brought giftes, but said she would return home again, as there was no gift which heaven had not already given his Majesty. She then returned to Hope and Faith, who were both sick and spewing in the lower hall. Next came Victory, in bright armour, and presented a rich sword to the King, who did not accept it, but put it by with his hand; and, by a strange medley of versification, did endeavour to make suit to the King. But Victory did not tryumph long; for, after much lamentable utterance, she was led away like a silly captive, and laid to sleep in the outer steps of the anti-chamber. Now did Peace make entry, and strive to get foremoste to the King; but I grieve to tell how great wrath she did discover unto those of her attendants; and, much contrary to her semblance, most rudely made war with her olive branch, and laid on the pates of those who did oppose her coming. I have much

marvelled at these strange pegeantries, and they do bring to my
remembrance what passed of this sort in our Queens days ; of which
I was sometime an humble presenter and assistant : but I neer did
see such lack of good order, discretion, and sobriety, as I have
now done. I have passed much time in seeing the royal sports of
hunting and hawking, where the manners were such as made me
devise the beasts were pursuing the sober creation, and not man in
quest of exercise or food. I will now, in good sooth, declare to you,
who will not blab, that the gunpowder fright is got out of all our
heads, and we are going on, hereabouts, as if the devil was contriving
every man shoud blow up himself, by wild riot, excess, and devasta-
tion of time and temperance. The great ladies do go well-masked,
and indeed it be the only show of their modesty, to conceal their
countenance ; but alack, they meet with such countenance to uphold
their strange doings, that I marvel not at ought that happens. . . .
I do often say (but not aloud) that the Danes have again conquered
the Britains, for I see no man, or woman either, that can now command himself or herself (*Nugae Antiquae*, i. 349).

Something here is perhaps, as indeed Harington suggests,
to be attributed to a courteous adoption of Danish manners
during the visit. That the Danes were ' traduced and
taxed of other nations' for their intemperance had been
observed some years before by the author of *Hamlet*.[1] But
it is to be feared that this particular exercise of hospitality
was only too congenial to James's private tastes.[2] It is not
necessary here to dwell any further upon the seamy side
of court life under the first Stuarts. Its blackest episodes,
those connected with the name of Frances Howard, lay
beyond the period of Shakespeare's active London life.
The visit of the King of Denmark ended somewhat abruptly,
and in no very good will between himself and James, whose
relations with Anne were constantly strained. James was
far from popular with his new subjects. His immoderate
love of hunting was a grievance alike to the council, whose
business he neglected, and to the farmers, whose crops he
trampled down. The abuses of purveyance were allowed
to flourish unchecked. The quick comedians, although at
considerable risk to their own liberty, appealed to the

---

[1] *Haml.* I. ii. 124; iv. 8. At the meeting of the kings, according to the
French ambassador De la Boderie (*Ambassades*, i. 297), ' la plus remarquable
cérémonie fut des santés qu'ils se portèrent, chacune accompagnée d'une
volée de canons '.

[2] *Secret History of the Court of James the First*, ii. 3. Too much importance
must not be attached to the scandalous memoirs collected in these volumes ;
but the French ambassador wrote of James in 1621, ' The end of all is ever
the bottle' (Raumer, *Sixteenth and Seventeenth Centuries*, ii. 263).

public sentiment in plays against the king, and Anne appears to have been guilty of the impropriety of visiting the theatre, to see her husband's foibles hit off on the stage.[1]

A bright spot in this murky court was the young prince, Henry Frederick, at whose baptismal pageant in 1594 that 'fearful wild fowl' a lion was forbidden to appear lest his presence should fright the ladies. At the time of his father's accession he was ten years old, 'little of body and quick of spirit, ceremonious beyond his years'; and as he grew older, his sobriety of demeanour, his ready understanding, and the high patriotic ideals with which he was credited won him a measure of popular affection, which was only intensified by the fact that he was no favourite with either of his parents. Prince Henry played golf, but cared little for hunting, for which his father rated him and called him 'no sportsman'. His great delight was 'to witch the world with noble horsemanship', and he excelled in the art of equitation and in all martial exercises, such as the tilt and riding at the ring. A fine engraving by William Hole of *Henricus Princeps*[2] with pike and helmet accompanies Michael Drayton's *Poly-Olbion* of 1613. One of the palmary ceremonies of the reign was the creation of Henry as Prince of Wales in 1610, after which he set up his own household, and lived in considerable state. Two years later he was suddenly smitten by typhoid fever, and died amidst universal grief and with some suspicion of foul play. 'Nor can I do aught else', writes the Venetian ambassador Antonio Foscarini, 'than follow his bier with useless tears, with temporal mourning in my dress, and sempiternal dolour in my breast.' The untoward event broke in upon the preparations for another great court ceremony, the wedding of the Princess Elizabeth, afterwards the romantic and unfortunate 'Queen of Hearts', to Frederick V, the Elector Palatine. Amongst the festivities of the occasion was a performance of *The Tempest*, although it is hardly possible to accept the theory that the play was then first written, or to find portraits of the bridal pair in the lineaments of Ferdinand and Miranda. The Elector, indeed, proved an uncouth boor, and Anne of Denmark, who disliked the alliance, took revenge in nicknaming her

---

[1] Raumer, ii. 207.
[2] Probably made from the portrait by an unknown artist in the Picture Gallery at Dulwich, reproduced in Chap. XXII; see vol. ii, p. 205, note.

PRINCE HENRY by P VAN SOMER

daughter as ' Goody Palsgrave '. A common taste, perhaps the only common taste, of the royal family was for drama and spectacle. The King and Queen, Henry and Elizabeth, and their younger brother Charles Duke of York, each gave patronage to at least one company of players, and the winter performances at court reached double or treble the number that had been customary under Queen Elizabeth. The evolution of the masque, retarded by the economical temper of the previous reign, reached its culminating point through a combination of the literary genius and recondite learning of Ben Jonson and the architectural and mechanical skill of Inigo Jones. Originally a mere incursion into the festive hall of a group of dancing neighbours coming, in survival of forgotten sacrificial customs, to bid the lord of the house good fortune, it now became a lyric drama in little, with a skilful juxtaposition of the poetic and the grotesque, in the masque proper and the antimasque; and into its service were pressed all the arts and all the science of its day. In its turn it reacted upon the drama proper, and the introduction of a masque forms a feature of Shakespeare's *Timon of Athens, Cymbeline,* and *The Tempest,* of *Henry VIII,* and *The Two Noble Kinsmen,* and of innumerable plays of other writers.

BIBLIOGRAPHY.—A systematic history of the Royal Household has never been written. The account in this chapter is based mainly on the Household Books printed in Nichols's *Progresses* and in *A Collection of Ordinances and Regulations for the Government of the Royal Household,* published by the Society of Antiquaries in 1700. Most of the details of the royal progresses are taken from J. NICHOLS's *The Progresses and Public Processions of Queen Elizabeth,* in which work the contemporary narratives are reprinted with much illustrative material. Particulars of court life have been drawn chiefly from the following : the Calendars of State Papers, Spanish, Venetian, and Domestic series ; COLLINS's Sydney Papers ; Calendar of Hatfield Papers ; HARINGTON's *Nugae Antiquae* ; NAUNTON's *Fragmenta Regalia* (1797 ed.); *Philip Gawdy's Letters* (Roxburghe Club) ; CAMDEN's *Annals* ; MELVILLE's *Memoirs* ; MACHYN's *Diary* (Camden Society) ; WALSINGHAM's Journal ; MANNINGHAM's *Diary* (Camden Society) ; CHAMBERLAIN's *Letters,* temp. Elizabeth (Camden Society) ; ELLIS's *Original Letters* ; P. HENTZNER's *Travels in England,* in RYE's *England as seen by Foreigners,* 1865 ; LODGE's *Illustrations of British History* ; BIRCH's *Court and Times of James I.* See also E. SHEPPARD's *The Old Royal Palace of Whitehall,* E. LAW's *History of Hampton Court Palace,* and E. K. CHAMBERS's *The Mediaeval Stage.* For the history of the Office of the Revels consult Prof. A. FEUILLERAT's *Documents relating to the Office of Revels* and his *Le Bureau des Menus-Plaisirs (Office of the Revels) et la mise en scène à la cour d'Elizabeth,* 1910 ; also E. K. CHAMBERS's *The Tudor Revels,* 1906. The fullest account of the Jacobean mask is in P. REYHER's *Les Masques Anglais,* 1909. Froude's *History of England* should also be consulted. The subject-matter of the chapter has been rehandled, with full bibliographies, in E. K. CHAMBERS's *The Elizabethan Stage,* 1923.

IV

THE ARMY : MILITARY SERVICE AND EQUIPMENT

§ 1. THE SOLDIER

BY

THE HON. J. W. FORTESCUE

In Shakespeare's England a standing army was unknown. There was no general military organization. The military defence of the realm rested upon two Statutes of Philip and Mary, passed in 1557, the one for Arms and Armour, the other for Taking of Musters. The first required 'every nobleman, gentleman, or other temporal person' to keep, according to his means, a fixed number of weapons, horses, and suits or articles of defensive armour ; the highest income named by the Act being one thousand pounds, and the lowest five pounds. The most interesting point in this Act is the fact that, though the existence of fire-arms is recognized by the obligation of the wealthiest classes to furnish 'haquebuts', the longbow is none the less exalted as the first of missile weapons, and practice at the archery-butts is still strictly enjoined upon the people at large. This was an absurdity, for fire-arms in the hands of skilful Spaniards and Italians had already been brought to considerable perfection, and the famous longbow was practically obsolete.

The Act for Taking Musters is, in virtue of its preamble, a more remarkable document. Two chief reasons were assigned for its enactment. The first was that many men 'had absented themselves from the said musters' ; the second, which Shakespeare helps us to understand, was recited to be that 'many of the most able and likely men have been through friendship or rewards released and discharged of the said service, and some other, not being able or meet, taken, appointed, or chosen thereunto ; and yet the same disability and unaptness notwithstanding, the same

Du̇ctores ordinū pedestriū.
Sergeante of the bande.

THIS WORTHY KNIGHT
Sr Phillip Sidney, in the cause of his god and
true religion, and for the honor of his Prince &
country, spared not to spende his blud as you
haue harde. For his wrtt, learninge, & knowledge
in diuers languages he was muche admired, for
his courtesie & affability towards all men no
less beloued, and for all other his singuler
parts of bounty, courag & liberaliti (bothe to
strangers & his owne country men) as greatly
honored of all that harde his fame (w was spred
about the worlde) as of those that knew him hear
at home. And as he thus liued bring of all beloued,
so moste honorably he dyed & lamentably miured
by the appointment of the right honorable, s
Frances Walsingham knight, principall Secretary,
& one of her Maiesties most honorable preue Coun
cell (his father in lawe) who spared not any coste to
haue this funerall well pformed He was caried from
the Minorites (w is wth out Aldgate) along the
cheefe streets of the Cytye vnto the Cathedrvall
church of S Paules, y w streets all a long were so
thronged with people, that y mourners had skarsly
rome to pass, the houses likewise weare as full as they
might be of w greate multitude ther weare fewe
or none that shed not some tears as the corps
passed by them. Of the mourners eury Gent had
a man, eury knight 2, some Nobleme 12, some more
some less, as also sundry English Capt of the low
Countrie w diuers other Gent that came voluntary
& arr not in this woorke expressed, So that the
whole nobre wree about 700 persons The great
west doore of S Paules (where y mourners nitred)
was kept by some of her Ma Gaard y Quire & hearse
by 2 Harolds of Armes, viz Nico Dethicke als Wind
for & Edm Knight, als Chester, who placed y nobles
& others according to their degrees So when the
sermon was ended y offernges & other seremonies
finished & his body interred y soldiers in y church
yard did by a double volye giue vnto his famous
life & death, a Marciall vale 1588
Tho Lant Jnuen

unable and unmeet persons, upon sums of money or other kind of rewards or exactions by them paid to some such as had the order of the said muster, have been also released and discharged of the said service, to the great impoverishment of the subjects, and chiefly to the great danger and peril of the realm'. To check these abuses it was enacted that any man evading the muster should suffer ten days' imprisonment, unless he preferred to purchase exemption at the price, utterly prohibitive to a poor man, of forty shillings. Muster-masters accepting money to discharge recruits were subjected to a fine of ten times the sum by them taken.

It is not too much to say that in many respects both of these Acts remained dead letters. When the Militia was summoned for service in the north of England in 1569 hardly a horseman was produced, and there were but sixty fire-arms among twenty-five hundred infantry. Thrice at least during Elizabeth's reign the entire force of the shires was called out, in 1558, in 1570, and 1588; and in 1570 the French ambassador reported that one hundred and twenty thousand men were ready to take the field in different parts of the country, while the muster-rolls showed a total of six hundred thousand men. These muster-rolls are still extant, but on the face of them are not to be trusted, for they simply state the numbers of men and arms in each hundred with no further detail whatever. Nevertheless they have an interest of their own, particularly those of Warwickshire, for probably Shakespeare as a little boy of six saw one at least of them made up, and caught his first sight of pompous justices and clumsy recruits.[1]

It is not likely that the forces of the shire were well, if at all, known to Shakespeare, but he certainly learned something of troops of a better stamp. In 1573, the year after the dispatch of the first Englishman to aid the Dutch insurgents against Alva, three thousand men of the London train-bands, from very shame at England's military back-

---

[1] One roll, perused by the present writer, tells unwittingly a curious story. The concluding words are hastily written; there are spots upon the parchment, and in lieu of the seal, which signified the attestation of the muster-master, leaves of a beech-tree have been crushed into the wax. Evidently a shower of rain had fallen during the muster; and the justices had run away to shelter, leaving their clerk to conclude the business as best he could. The leaves, though of course brown and dry, are in perfect preservation—leaves which were green when Shakespeare was a boy.

wardness, were formed and exercised regularly at Mile End. This had been since the days of Henry the Eighth a famous drill-ground, where Justice Shallow, as we know from his own statement, had played his part when a student at Clement's Inn (*2 Hen. IV*, III. ii. 301). Probably some at least of the instructors were foreigners, competent Englishmen being difficult to find; and so Parolles is made to say of his captain Dumain, that ' he had the honour to be the officer at a place there called Mile-end, to instruct for the doubling of files' (*All's W.* IV. iii. 303). Now the doubling of files, with its counterpart the doubling of ranks,[1] constituted the elements of drill, both for cavalry and infantry in those days, and to active citizens, who longed to fire their pieces, must have been extremely tedious. Quite possibly all the little boys shouted ' Double your files' at every train-bandsman whom they saw in the streets, so that a laugh at this allusion on the stage must have been certain. But Shakespeare knew more of drill than this. A file in these days consists of two men. In the sixteenth century it numbered at least ten ; and a knowledge of this fact is necessary to understand the passage in *Cymbeline* (v. iii. 30–1) :

> For three performers are the file when all
> The rest do nothing.

Again, the place of honour to military men has always been the right of the line, and accordingly a captain always drew up his best and choicest men in the right-hand files of his company. ' Do you two know', asks Menenius of Brutus and Sicinius, 'how you are censured here in the city, I mean of us o' the right-hand file ?' (*Cor.* II. i. 24–6).

There are other signs of close observation of the drill at Mile End. The handling of the fire-arms, or, as it is now called,

---

[1] Infantry were in those days drawn up in ten ranks, not shoulder to shoulder, but with intervals between man and man. To convert the ten ranks into five, the word was given ' To the right (or left) double your ranks', whereupon the men of the even ranks moved up into the intervals of the odd ranks. To reconvert the five ranks into ten, the word was ' To the left (or right) double your files ', upon which the men who had moved up from the even ranks moved back to their original places. It must be added that the file was, in those days, the unit (to use a modern phrase) in which the strength of an army was expressed. Men took their places in the *files*, not in the *ranks* of an army.

> Within our files there are,
> Of those that serv'd Mark Antony but late,
> Enough to fetch him in.   (*Ant. & Cleop.* IV. i. 12–14)
> Now, if you have a station in the file,
> Not i' the worst rank of manhood, say it.   (*Macb.* III. i. 102–3)

From T Lant's engraving of the Funeral of Sir Philip Sidney

the manual-exercise, was taught by an infinity of elaborate motions, which no doubt were parodied by Justice Shallow when the caliver was put into Wart's hand at Coventry.

He is not his craft's master, he doth not do it right.   I remember at Mile-end Green . . . there was a little quiver fellow, and a' would manage you his piece thus : and a' would about and about, and come you in, and come you in ; 'rah, tah, tah,' would a' say ; 'bounce,' would a' say ; and away again would a' go, and again would a' come : I shall never see such a fellow.   (*2 Hen. IV*, III. ii. 300–9)

The description points to the action of an alert skirmisher, which is perfectly in accordance with all that we know of the military practice of the time.   Infantry was composed in those days of pikemen and musketeers, who were drawn up in solid square blocks, ten in rank and ten in file, the pikemen in the centre, and the musketeers, or as they were generally called the *shot*,[1] upon each flank.   Very often the musketeers were dispersed in loose order before the pikes ; but, if they fired in close order, the rule was that the first rank fired and ran round to the rear to reload, the second rank fired and did likewise, and so the remaining ranks in succession, until, by the time that the tenth rank had fired the first had reloaded and was ready to fire again.   'Away again would a' go, and away again would a' come' is therefore a correct description enough.   Moreover, the tallest and strongest men were always preferred for the pike, and the little nimble men for the musket.   'O, give me always a little, lean, old, chopp'd, bald shot' (*ibid.* 297), says Falstaff, echoing in part the cant of the time.

Of the pike-exercise, which was even more elaborate than that of the musket, Shakespeare mentions one motion only, the trail.   'To trail a pike'—that is to say, to hold the steel head in the hand and let the butt trail on the ground—was a common phrase to signify service in the infantry, for in those days gentlemen volunteers worked their way up from the ranks, and more than one peer trailed a pike in the regiments of Maurice of Nassau.   'Trail'st thou the puissant pike ?' (*Hen. V*, IV. i. 40) asks Pistol of disguised King Harry on the eve of Agincourt, on hearing that his companion was

[1] Shakespeare has a striking instance of the technical expression 'loose shot' in the speech of the porter's man in *Henry VIII* (v. iv. 60): 'I defied 'em still ; when suddenly a file of boys behind 'em, loose shot, delivered such a shower of pebbles that I was fain to draw mine honour in.'   Sir John Smythe says that musketeers should not be used as 'loose shot' (i.e. marksmen unattached to a company) in skirmishes.

a 'gentleman of a company'.   A special occasion for trailing
a pike was a military funeral, a duty which the train-bands
enjoyed immensely.   The classical instance of a military
funeral at St. Paul's is that of Sir Philip Sidney[1] in 1586.
Shakespeare must have witnessed more than one; and
hence at the close of *Coriolanus* we find Aufidius saying
over the corpse of the hero :

> Take him up :
> Help, three o' the chiefest soldiers ; I'll be one.
> Beat thou the drum, that it speak mournfully ;
> Trail your steel pikes.   (v. v. 149–52)

From Carleton, *A Thankfull Remembrance*, 1627.

It is also evident that Shakespeare had been struck with
the imposing appearance of a forest of pikes carried at
the 'shoulder' :

> . . . thou told'st me thou wouldst hunt the boar . .
> On his bow-back he hath a battle set
> Of bristly pikes, that ever threat his foes.
>
> (*Ven. & Ad.* 614, 619–20)

Another detail which must have been impressed upon
him by the drill-ground at Mile End was the quadrate
formation, already mentioned, of the companies. He

---

[1] In Lant's plates, here reproduced, the pikes are seen reversed.

From Lant's Funeral of Sir Philip Sidney

occasionally uses the technical word squadrons, though it may be doubted whether he understood its true meaning; but there is no mistaking the significance of the following passage, where Antony says of Octavius—

> He at Philippi kept
> His sword e'en like a dancer, while I struck
> The lean and wrinkled Cassius ; and 'twas I
> That the mad Brutus ended : he alone
> Dealt on lieutenantry, and no practice had
> In the brave squares of war. (*Ant. & Cleop.* III. ix. 35–40)

And here must be noticed, with reference to the word lieutenantry, which in this place means subordinate command, that Shakespeare's vocabulary of military titles was singularly meagre. At Mile End he saw Companies commanded by Captains, Lieutenants, and Ensigns or Ancients, with Corporals for non-commissioned officers ; and he seems practically to have been content with these terms. Occasionally he uses the word Regiment, but never the words Colonel or Sergeant-major, which were the titles that belonged to the chief and second-in-command of a regiment, and were in full use before 1588. It is curious that he should have missed the pomp of the word ' coronel ' (an equally authentic form with ' colonel '), which seized the ear of Milton. The word ' sergeant ' he employs occasionally in the modern sense, but more often to signify an officer of police, a use which survives in the title sergeant-at-arms. But here he was right, for it had been officially displaced, as the title of an instructor in drill, by the word ' corporal ', a corruption of the French *caporal,* which in its turn was derived from the Italian *capo di squadra* or head of a square. The two famous corporals of the plays, Bardolph and Nym, were of course a disgrace to the name ; and it is satisfactory to know that both of them were hanged by King Henry the Fifth.

The inference to be drawn from this poverty of military titles is that Shakespeare had no knowledge of larger bodies of troops than companies. He speaks frequently of Generals, but a general's second-in-command is to him a lieutenant, as in the quotation above given, and the third an ancient or ensign. Othello was the commander of a large and important garrison, and is frequently spoken of as the general. Cassio, his second, should have been sergeant-major-general, but is merely a lieutenant, while Iago was, to his great discontent, 'his Moorship's ancient'. As such Iago should have carried the colour, but we never hear him refer to such a thing, though the colour was a very sacred matter in those days. These peculiarities point to no very profound acquaintance with the art of war; and yet there are touches which show that Shakespeare combined with his ignorance some curious details of knowledge. Thus, in a pitched battle, it was a rule that a commander should manœuvre to throw the sun or the wind, or if possible both, in the eyes of his enemy. In *Love's Labour's Lost* (IV. iii. 367–9) Berowne urges the King of Navarre and his lords in the following terms to break their vow and court the ladies of France :

> Advance your standards, and upon them, lords !
> Pell-mell, down with them ! but be first advis'd,
> In conflict that you get the sun of them.

The last words were a common military phrase, which summarized the highest ideas then current concerning tactics. So too Aaron, in *Titus Andronicus* (IV. ii. 133–6), when about to take distrustful counsel with Demetrius, says :

> Then sit we down, and let us all consult,
> My son and I will have the wind of you :
> Keep there.[1]

Again, there is a phrase in *The First Part of Henry VI* (IV. ii. 42–3) which shows that Shakespeare knew something of the use of cavalry for purposes of reconnaissance in war :

> He fables not ; I hear the enemy :
> Out, some light horsemen, and peruse their wings.

Again, in *Julius Cæsar* some note is taken of the dispositions at Philippi, and of the part that may be played by a general-in-chief. It may be doubted whether Shakespeare had ever seen a general dispatch an aide-de-camp with a written order to a subordinate commander, for large bodies of troops were seldom assembled for exercise in time of peace, and, in the deep heavy formations of the time, two or three thousand men occupied but little space. Yet what aide-de-camp could fail to gallop his hardest on receiving such an order as that of Brutus to Messala ?

---

[1] But this last figure may perhaps be taken from the chase ; cf. *Hamlet*, III. ii. 368–9 : 'Why do you go about to recover the wind of me, as if you would drive me into a toil ? '

From Lant's Funeral of Sir Philip Sidney

Ride, ride, Messala, ride, and give these bills
Unto the legions on the other side.
Let them set on at once, for I perceive
But cold demeanour in Octavius' wing,
And sudden push gives them the overthrow.
Ride, ride, Messala : let them all come down.
(Jul. Cæs. v. ii. 1-6)

On the other hand, the numerous battles in the plays as a rule resolve themselves—doubtless owing to the exigencies of the drama—into a series of heroic duels after the Homeric fashion. Nor was this wholly inaccurate, for Elizabeth's generals were expected to lead the fight, and did not disappoint the expectation. But upon the whole it seems most probable that Shakespeare accepted the conventional notion of battle, and had little real knowledge of the refinements of the military art. It would, perhaps, be hypercritical to point out that he makes King John bring cannon before the walls of Angers a century before such engines were invented. The one really fine military stratagem mentioned in the plays has a special interest since, according to report, it was repeated by the Japanese in their late war with Russia. But to the dramatist it served only to fulfil the prophecy that Birnam wood should come to Dunsinane, and for him possessed no further importance. Yet the words of Macduff are worth quoting to show that his purpose, at any rate, was purely military :

Let every soldier hew him down a bough
And bear 't before him ; thereby shall we shadow
The numbers of our host, and make discovery
Err in report of us.　　　(Macb. v. iv. 5-8)

The question then arises as to the sources of Shakespeare's knowledge of things military. Did he gather it from books ? So far as Plutarch could furnish it, no doubt he did, but it seems certain that he had little if any acquaintance with the military treatises which were published in astonishing profusion in England during the latter half of the sixteenth century. Then it was that the renascence of the art of war fairly made itself felt in these islands ; and, though the literature on the subject consisted principally of translations from the Italian, the Spanish, and the Dutch, there were original works in English which were at least of equal value, though the writers had been obliged to draw their experience from service in foreign armies. German landsknechts and

Italian arquebusiers had been imported into England
towards the close of the reign of Henry the Eighth, and there
is evidence which suggests that a certain number of them
married and settled down in the country.   Yet there is little
or no trace of their technical terms to be found in the plays.
The words Infantry and Cavalry, which should have found
their way into Shakespeare's vocabulary through Italian
and French books, do not occur at all.   Of distinctively
German military expressions there is but one—the word
Foreward (*Rich. III*, v. iii. 294), signifying the first line
of embattled troops—but this was as much English as
German, and had displaced the French word Vanguard
in English military language during the reign of Henry
the Eighth.   On the other hand, for the second line
of an army Shakespeare uses the old word Battle or
Battalia, borrowed from the Latin nations, instead of the
current English form, Mid-ward; and for the third line
he accepts the usual bastard word Rear-ward, instead of
Rear-guard.   Singularly enough, the very word Almain,
the usual name for a landsknecht or ' lance-knight ',
occurs only once in the whole body of the dramas.   The
pike and halberd, distinctly Teutonic weapons, find sufficiently frequent mention, but the arquebus, the commonest
name for a fire-arm in the military books, is not to be discovered in any of its numerous corrupted forms.   Setting
artillery aside, Shakespeare speaks of only three fire-arms,
the pistol, the caliver, and, in a single passage, the musket.
The caliver, or arquebus of calibre, was of Spanish origin, as
also was the musket ; and upon the whole there is a preponderance of Spanish military terms in Shakespeare's
military vocabulary.   Such are battalia (*batalla*), though
this might equally be Italian, cavalero (*caballero*), and in
particular *bisoño* (a recruit), in the corrupted form bezonian,
which is found once in a serious passage—' Great men
oft die by vile bezonians' (*2 Hen. VI*, IV. i. 134), and
once in Pistol's bombast—' Under which king, Bezonian ?
speak, or die' (*2 Hen. IV*, v. iii. 116).   Since the Spanish
school was that to which English officers principally resorted
for instruction, and of which English writers had most to say,
this would seem to be natural.   No reader who had digested
books, whether original or translated, concerning the Spanish
army could have failed to use other Spanish expressions,

Das Sechſt Buch. CXL

Ampt vnd Befelch eines jeglichen Kriegß= manns oder Landsknechts.

Jnes jeglichen Kriegßmanns oder Landsknechts Befelch vnd Ampt iſt/ So bald einer von einem Herren angenommen vnd Gelt empfecht/ſo iſt er ſchuldig demſelbigen/darumb er beſtellt/nachzukoṁen/denn dieweil er Gelt

empfangen/ſo hat er ſein Haut/auch Leib vnd Leben/verkaufft/ deṅ vmb das Gelt muß er dem Herren/ſo jn angenoṁen vnd beſtellt hat/gehorſam vnd geſellia ſeyn/ wo er jn denn ſeiner notturfft vnd gelegenheit nach hin brauchen wil / es ſey für die Freund oder Feind/ zu Waſſer oder Land/in Stedten/ Beſatzungen/Schlöſſern/ Flecken / Märckten / Dörffern / in Heer oder Feldtlägern/auff Zügen/ Wachten/

GERMAN LANDSKNECHTE

such as *alferez* instead of ensign or ancient. Pistol's foreign jargon, such as it is, is nearer akin to Italian than to any other language, so that Shakespeare cannot have conceived of Spain as the classical land, which in his time it was, of the military art.

The conclusion to be drawn from the foregoing considerations is that Shakespeare had not read the military literature of the day, but drew his knowledge wholly from the soldiers whom he met in the streets of London. These must have been sufficiently numerous ; for, apart from the gentlemen volunteers, who were serving or had served under the colours of Spain, there were English troops constantly engaged in campaigns against the Irish in Ireland, on behalf of the French Protestants in France, and for the Dutch insurgents in the Low Countries. Most of the officers probably came home during the period of winter-quarters for relaxation or to raise recruits, and there must have been a constant flow of these into and out of London. Some were no doubt pedants, who had read their Arrian, and who furnished the model for the character of Fluellen. Others again were mere rogues and impostors who affected military dress and conversation, either talking big like Pistol, or with an assumed brevity and an attempted laconism like Nym. These last were probably very numerous, for the military profession, setting aside some very great and noble names, was not in good repute in Elizabeth's time. The fact was that the Queen could not be induced to pay her soldiers ; consequently the troops were always seething with mutiny and thinned by desertion, and no gentleman of any self-respect would take command of them. Commissions therefore fell into the hands of scoundrels, who swindled their men and sent them out to plunder the country for their benefit. ' Of late years', wrote Sir Henry Knyvett in a treatise on *The Defence of the Realme*, addressed to the Queen in 1596, ' all private soldiers have been so lightly regarded, yea, so uncharitably and cruelly used, as, were it not for their extraordinary obedience and loyal love which they would bear to Your Most Sacred Majesty, they would more willingly be hanged at their doors than abide shameful martyrdom with many extremities abroad. . . .' ' The corruption of our wars', he adds in a later page, ' springeth only from the rash and evil choice which hath been most commonly made of needy, riotous, licentious, ignorant, and base colonels, captains, lieutenants, sergeants, and such like officers, who have made merchandise of their places, and without regard of their duty or respect of conscience have made porte sale of their soldiers' blood and lives to maintain their unthriftiness and disorders.'

To levy men for such a service was not easy, and accordingly we find that the troops were recruited either by opening the gaols and sweeping the refuse of the nation into the ranks, or simply by resort to the pressgang. It cannot be supposed that the Queen had the slightest legal right to compel men to service abroad, but the legal reservation carried little weight. Ugly scenes, however, occasionally marked Easter Sunday, when, every one being bound by law to take the sacrament, the pressgangs would close the church doors and impress every man of the congregation. It is significant that Shakespeare had no notion of recruiting except by impressment, though he had seen enough of young Englishmen setting out for the wars to know the quality of gentlemen volunteers :

> Rash, inconsiderate, fiery voluntaries,
> With ladies' faces and fierce dragons' spleens,
> Have sold their fortunes at their native homes,
> Bearing their birthrights proudly on their backs,
> To make a hazard of new fortunes here. (*John*, II. i. 67-71)

Thus at the battle of Towton a Lancastrian soldier says :

> From London by the king was I press'd forth ;
> My father, being the Earl of Warwick's man,
> Came on the part of York, press'd by his master.
> (*3 Hen. VI*, II. v. 64-6)

Falstaff's men were all pressed ; and Falstaff treated them exactly in the manner reprobated by the statute of Philip and Mary. Similar proceedings to those of the fat knight had probably been witnessed by Shakespeare himself.

I have misused the king's press damnably. I have got, in exchange of a hundred and fifty soldiers, three hundred and odd pounds. I press me none but good householders, yeomen's sons ; inquire me out contracted bachelors, such as had been asked twice on the banns ; such a commodity of warm slaves, as had as lief hear the devil as a drum, . . . and they have bought out their services ; and now my whole charge consists of ancients, corporals, lieutenants, gentlemen of companies, slaves as ragged as Lazarus in the painted cloth, . . . and such as indeed were never soldiers, but discarded unjust serving-men, younger sons to younger brothers, revolted tapsters and ostlers trade-fallen,[1] the cankers of a calm world and a long peace ; ten times more dishonourable ragged than an old faced ancient : and such have I, to fill up the rooms of them that have bought out their services. . . . No eye hath seen such scarecrows. I'll not march through Coventry with them, that's flat ; nay, and the villains march wide betwixt the legs, as if they had gyves on ; for, indeed I had the most of them out of prison.

(*1 Hen. IV*, iv. ii. 13 ff.)

The last touch, about the gyves, shows that Shakespeare knew the appearance of soldiers recruited from the gaols, who were far too common in the British armies of his day. ' The very scum of the world,' was Francis Vere's comment upon one reinforcement sent to him by Elizabeth, almost in the identical words used, though unjustly, by the Duke of Wellington concerning his army in the Peninsula, two and a half centuries later. ' The worst of everything is thought good enough for this place,' wrote Lord Warwick from Havre, twenty years earlier than Vere, on receiving a similar draft of recruits. Henry, Prince of Wales, it will be remembered, had procured Falstaff a charge of foot. ' I did never see such pitiful rascals,' was his criticism ; and he was answered, ' Tut, tut ; good enough to toss ; food for powder, food for powder ' (*1 Hen. IV*, iv. ii. 71–3). And Falstaff was as good as his word. ' I have led my ragamuffins ', he soliloquizes, ' where they are peppered : there's not three of my hundred and fifty left alive, and they are for the town's end, to beg during life ' (*ibid.* v. iii. 36–40). The object of getting all the men killed was of course that the captain might draw the pay due to them, and put it in his own pocket ; but Shakespeare is a little weak here, for even if Falstaff had led his men into a hot fire, they would assuredly never have followed him. The fate of crippled old soldiers—to beg at the town end for life—is, however, accurately described. Elizabeth, far from feeling compassion for them, was impatient of the very sight of them, and declared that she would not be pestered with the ' miserable creatures '.

[1] It is interesting to compare Oliver Cromwell's speech to Hampden in 1642 : ' Your troops are most of them old decayed serving-men and tapsters : their troops are gentlemen's sons and persons of quality. Do you think the spirits of such base and mean fellows will ever be able to encounter gentlemen who have courage, honour, and resolution in them? You must get men of a spirit that is likely to go as far as gentlemen will go, or you will be beaten still.' Had Oliver this passage of Shakespeare in his mind ?

Then comes the famous scene (*2 Hen. IV*, III. ii), probably
little exaggerated, when six recruits are brought before
Falstaff at Justice Shallow's house. Once again these are
pressed men, legitimately so, the service being within the
kingdom. Moreover, the levy is one taken from parish to
parish, or from hundred to hundred, the quota (to use the
phrase of a later time) of Shallow's jurisdiction being four
men. Shallow, so far as his feeble intellect reaches, has done
his duty. 'I would have you served with the best' (l. 277),
he tells Falstaff; but the parish constables have evidently
been corrupted, for only two of the six men are fit to serve.
All of course are unwilling to become soldiers; and one of
them, Wart, is at first actually rejected by Falstaff as physically unfit; but the two likeliest of the men bribe Bardolph
heavily—for three pounds was a large sum in those days—
to evade service. Falstaff then recants his opinion concerning Wart with his own inimitable wit and dexterity. A pun
upon the name of Simon Shadow hints at another crying
abuse of the time. 'We have a number of shadows to fill up
the muster book' (l. 148), says Falstaff; for the word 'shadow'
was used, together with the expressions 'faggot' and 'dead-
head', to signify fictitious men whose names were borne upon
the muster-rolls in order that their captain might draw their
pay for his own profit. Meanwhile, Feeble's words, when
he finds escape impossible, confirm Knyvett's testimony
as to the loyalty and obedience of the queen's troops, ill
though she treated them.

By my troth, I care not; a man can die but once; we owe God
a death. I'll ne'er bear a base mind: an't be my destiny, so;
an't be not, so. No man 's too good to serve 's prince; and let it go
which way it will, he that dies this year is quit for the next.'

(*2 Hen. IV*, III. ii. 253-8)

On the other hand, Bullcalf's words—'I had as lief be
hanged as go' (l. 241)—anticipate the phrase actually used by
Knyvett to signify the general revolt from military service.
Shakespeare was here evidently drawing upon his own ex-
perience of reluctant recruits, impressed in London for
service abroad, and attributing their feelings to these troops of
Henry the Fourth who were impressed merely to march from
Gloucestershire to York. A minute detail tends to strengthen
this supposition. When the men have been finally enlisted,
Falstaff says, 'Bardolph, give the soldiers coats' (l. 314). Now

in London, where there would certainly be depots of clothing, such an order would be natural and reasonable enough; but to suppose that an army in Elizabeth's day would carry stores of clothing with it, when the roads would scarcely admit of the transport even of provisions, is incredible. As a matter of fact, it was the custom from the reign of Henry the Seventh to give a recruit of the levies of the shire what was called ' coat and conduct money ', that is to say, a fixed sum to enable him to obtain a white smock with a red cross upon it, and to pay the expenses of his journey to the rendezvous.[1]

Though Shakespeare thus turns military service into ridicule, most notably in the persons of Falstaff and his crew and the ' damnable both-sides rogue ', Parolles, yet there are signs that he had conversed with really good officers, who deplored the abuses reigning in the army. This can be seen in Brutus's denunciation of contributions levied upon the poor in any theatre of war :

> By heaven, I had rather coin my heart,
> And drop my blood for drachmas, than to wring
> From the hard hands of peasants their vile trash
> By any indirection. (*Jul. Cæs.* IV. iii. 72–5)

Take again the reproof to Cassius for another of the abuses condemned by Sir Henry Knyvett :

> Let me tell you, Cassius, you yourself
> Are much condemn'd to have an itching palm ;
> To sell and mart your offices for gold.
> (*Jul. Cæs.* IV. iii. 9–11)

Brutus, in fact, stands throughout for the honest, high-minded soldier, the type that was personified among Englishmen by such men as John Norris and Francis Vere. And it is pretty certain that Shakespeare must have met soldiers who had fought in the battle of Dutch independence, for he had learned the meaning of the interminable sieges which were so prominent a feature of the campaigns in the Low Countries :

> There might you see the labouring pioner,
> Begrim'd with sweat, and smeared all with dust ;
> And from the towers of Troy there would appear
> The very eyes of men through loop-holes thrust,
> Gazing upon the Greeks. (*Lucr.* 1380–4)

---

[1] As a matter of fact, the word Cassock (French *casaque*) had displaced the simpler word ' coat ' as the name of the soldier's uniform. ' The muster-file . . . amounts not to fifteen thousand poll ; half of the which dare not shake the snow from off their cassocks, lest they shake themselves to pieces ' (*All 's W.* IV. iii. 189–93).

Again, in *Macbeth* there is a line which recalls all the campaigns in the Netherlands, even to the Walcheren Expedition of 1809:

> Hang out our banners on the outward walls ;
> The cry is still, ' They come ' ; our castle's strength
> Will laugh a siege to scorn ; here let them lie
> *Till famine and the ague eat them up.* (*Macb.* v. v. 1–4)

We cannot suppose that Shakespeare set down all that he observed of military matters in England. It was open to him to write satires upon doting justices and rascally captains, but he could never have dared to tell even a fraction of the real truth, for the simple reason that England's military condition was in the highest degree dangerous, and that the Queen was responsible for it. It was safe to lay the blame upon a few underlings, under the types of Shallow and Falstaff ; and it was safe, in the magnificent passages of *Henry V*, to glorify the powers of the English archer. But to hint at the shameful neglect of (for example) Leicester's troops in the Low Countries, or the appalling confusion at the camp of Tilbury in 1588—to breathe a whisper to the effect that brave and able soldiers like John Norris trembled over the prospect of the landing of a single regiment of Spanish regular soldiers—this would have been perilous to impossibility. Nor need we lament over the fact, since military scenes inspired Shakespeare to give us some of the noblest of his eloquence, and the most incomparable passages of his humour.

BIBLIOGRAPHY.—The following list includes some of the principal military treatises of the time, with which it is at least possible that Shakespeare had some acquaintance : PETER WHITEHORNE'S *The Arte of Warre*, 1560, 1573, 1588 (a translation of the *Dell' Arte della Guerra* of Machiavelli) ; his *Onosandro Platonico, of the Generall Captaine, and of his office*, 1563 ; *The foure bookes of Flavius Vegetius*, 1572 ; BARNABE RICHE'S *A right excelent . . . Dialogue between Mercury and an English Souldier*, 1574, *A pathway to military practise*, 1587, and *A souldiers wishe to Britons welfare*, 1604 ; LEONARD DIGGES'S *The Arte of Warre*, by WILLIAM GARRARD, finished and corrected by Captain *Stratioticos*, 1579 ; ROGER WILLIAMS'S *A Brief Discourse of Warre*, 1590 ; Hitchcock, 1591 ; Sir THOMAS KNYVETT'S *The Defence of the Realme*, 1596 (first printed 1906) ; Sir EDWARD HOBY'S *Theorique and Practise of Warre*, a translation from the Spanish of Mendoza, 1597 ; a translation of François de la Noue's *Discours politiques et militaires*, 1597 ; ROBERT BARRET'S *The Theorike and Practike of moderne Warres*, 1598. For the conditions of military service, the Calendar of State Papers (Domestic) should be consulted for the reigns of Henry VIII, Edward VI, Mary, and Elizabeth. For the history, see the present writer's *History of the British Army*, vol. i, 1899.

§ 2. ARMOUR AND WEAPONS

BY

VISCOUNT DILLON

IN considering the armour and weapons of Shakespeare's time we should first endeavour to discover what opportunities the poet had for seeing any of them, remembering always that, except for pageants and the tilt-yard, armour was fast disappearing. We may well suppose that in his youth in the country he had seen some of the yearly musters of the Warwickshire county forces, and had also no doubt seen the bodies of men drafted from the country for the wars in Ireland and the Low Countries. But when in 1586 he came to London he could have seen the jousters in the tilt-yard on Queen's day, November 17, when Sir Henry Lee, and after him George Earl of Cumberland, presided at those the latest almost of the old sports of the tilt-yard. In 1588 he must have seen the great preparations for the resistance to the invasion of England, and may well have been one of those who at Tilbury under the Earl of Leicester received the Queen. The stirring passage in the chorus to Act II of *King Henry V* seems to breathe the spirit of the general feeling of those days. That scene he may have beheld as a spectator, or perhaps as an actor in the great national movement. If he were one of those there encamped, he would have experienced the hardships and discomforts so fully spoken of by that great military reformer, Sir John Smythe, who for his pains in advocating reforms was sent to prison. The bad quality and fit of the armour supplied to the forces of the Crown was an old story. In 1584 the Lord Deputy and Council of Ireland had sent back to the Ordnance Office three hundred suits, and they told the Privy Council that they could buy better armour in London for twenty-five shillings than that supplied at forty-two shillings a suit. In 1590 Sir John Smythe, speaking of the musters of 1587 and 1588 of the Essex Regiment, while admitting that he had found some good *old* armour amongst them, complained that many of the ordinary corselets had great imperfections in the shallowness of the burgonets (head-pieces), the straightness of the collars (gorgets), and the lack of compass in the pauldrons (shoulder defences). These and

other faults of construction and material made the armour
(much of which was imported) 'unfit for the soldiers, with
ease to fetch their breaths, and to march in', and 'much
armour unfit and uneasy to fight in'. In 1590 Sir George
Carew wrote to Burghley from Cork that the thousand
Hamburg and Flanders corselets could not be issued to the
garrison 'as they are badly shaped and rotten'. The reason
for armour being 'made in Germany' and elsewhere was that
the art of working up English metal was quite in its infancy,
as we may learn from a trial of Foreign and English metal in
1590, described in *Archaeologia*, volume li. Apart from the
inferior make of the armour, the drawbacks of wearing any
armour were beginning to make themselves felt, and conduced
in a few years to the abandonment of the metal protection.

In *2 Henry IV* (IV. v. 29–30) the poet says that majesty is
> Like a rich armour worn in heat of day,
> That scalds with safety.

The gradual disuse of armour is referred to in *Measure for
Measure* (I. ii. 177), when unenforced penalties are likened to
'unscour'd armour hung by the wall'. There were many
who in the poet's early days would, like Benedick before he
was in love, 'have walked ten mile afoot to see a good
armour' (*Much Ado*, II. iii. 17), but later we find that the
English especially are content to wear only a cuirass and
a head-piece, like Edward Stanley at the assault of Zutphen.

The flexible and yet good defences for the body, the
Brigandines, Privy coats, Coats of fence, and Jacks, though
in use in the poet's day, the first two for the rich, and the
last two for the ordinary civilian and soldier, are never
mentioned directly. The Brigandine, composed of small
steel plates overlapping and riveted to a canvas foundation
by rivets, the gilt heads of which showed up bravely on the
velvet or the rich material of the facing, though in use on the
Continent, can only be surmised in Cassio's remark :
> That thrust had been mine enemy indeed
> But that my coat is better than thou know'st ;
> I will make proof of thine.   (*Oth.* v. i. 24–6)

The Jack—composed of small overlying metal plates held in
position between the foundation of canvas and the facing of
some textile fabric by strings passing through and forming
a series of intercrossing lines on the surface—was worn by
naval as well as military men. In appearance, as in the

portrait of Sir Hugh Willoughby at Greenwich, it gives no idea of its defensive power. Shakespeare must have seen many of these coats. He does certainly in *1 Henry VI* (I. i. 85) make Bedford say 'Give me my steeled coat', which might refer to a defence other than plate ; so also Smith the weaver says of Jack Cade, 'He need not fear the sword, for his coat is of proof' (*2 Hen. VI*, IV. ii. 67–8), and in the stage directions in the next scene Cade puts on the brigandine of the slain Sir Humphrey Stafford (IV. iii. 13).

Even the lighter kinds of armour were getting out of favour when Sir Richard Hawkins in 1593 wrote that 'he had great preparations of armours as well of proof as of light corselets, yet not a man would use them, but esteemed a pot of wine a better defence than an armour of proof'.

In the latter part of the sixteenth century we find the pauldrons, rerebraces, and vambraces, the defences respectively for the shoulders, the upper arm, and the lower arm, quite given up, except that the defences for the arms were either attached to the gorget and so carried like a milkman's yoke, or the rerebraces were fastened to the stout fustian or leather garment by 'points' which, passing through two holes in the top of the rerebrace, were then tied in a bow knot. The different methods had their advocates, but the system in which points or laces were used seems to have been very popular, and a picture said to be that of Marquis del Guasto, at Hampton Court, shows the attendant or squire fastening on the vambraces. These points were also the mark of a soldier, as we find in the *Satires* of Hall, who speaks of a man as

> Pointed on the shoulder for the nonce,
> As new come from the Belgian garrisons.

So Doll Tearsheet says to Pistol, 'with two points on your shoulder ?' *2 Hen. IV*, II. iv. 140. The Gorget is referred to in *Troilus and Cressida* (I. iii. 174–5), where Ulysses tells how Achilles is amused by Patroclus mimicking Nestor with his 'palsy-fumbling on his gorget', which shakes 'in and out the rivet'. In *Macbeth* (V. v. 52) we have armour called in the old way 'harness'. Breastplate occurs only once in the plays (*2 Hen. VI*, III. ii. 232). The Cuisses are mentioned in *1 Henry IV* (IV. i. 105), 'his cushes on his thighs'. Gauntlets, which were going out of use owing to the introduction of the complex hilts of the swords, which protected the hand more than the old fashioned cross-hilted swords, are mentioned in *King John* (v. ii. 154–6),

> For your own ladies and pale-visag'd maids,
> Like Amazons come tripping after drums,
> Their thimbles into armed gauntlets change;

and in *2 Henry IV* (I. i. 146–7), where we have

> A scaly gauntlet now, with joints of steel
> Must glove this hand.

When we come to the head-pieces of the time, we have the oft-discussed question of the use of the word 'beaver' in *Hamlet* (I. ii. 229). Now the beaver was only a part of a close helmet, and was the portion which protected the lower portion of the face, as the visor did the rest except the forehead, which was covered by the skull-piece or portion of the helmet. In some cases the beaver is used for the whole of the head-piece, as in 'I saw young Harry, with his beaver on' (*I Hen. IV*, IV. i. 104), and 'What, is my beaver easier than it was?' (*Rich. III*, v. iii. 50); also in 'I cleft his beaver with a downright blow' (*3 Hen. VI*, I. i. 12). Then again, the word is sometimes used for the visor, as in

> Big Mars seems bankrupt in their beggar'd host,
> And faintly through a rusty beaver peeps,
> *(Hen. V*, IV. ii. 43–4)

and in

> Their armed staves in charge, their beavers down,
> Their eyes of fire sparkling through sights of steel.
> *(2 Hen. IV*, IV. i. 120–1)

In only one passage does the beaver appear in its actual sense, when Nestor says, 'I'll hide my silver beard in a gold beaver' (*Troilus*, I. iii. 296). In *Hamlet* it is quite evident that the beaver means the visor :

Ham. Then saw you not his face?
Hor. O yes! my lord; he wore his beaver up. (*Haml.* I. ii. 228–9)

In Shakespeare's day the visor generally consisted of two parts working on one pair of pivots; the upper part might be raised independently of the lower part, and so it appears to have been in the combats at Barriers, when blows could only come from below, and the raising of the upper part gave air for the often heated combatants. There would be horizontal sights in the upper part of the visor and vertical in the lower.

As to casque, helm, and helmet, they are used as general

terms. The Burgonet, often mentioned, was an open-faced
head-piece with a ridged crest, and often worn in war and in
the tilt-yard with the Buffe, an arrangement of three or more
horizontal lames which could be raised or lowered as desired.
When raised, they protected the face, and were kept in position by staples fastening to the sides of the burgonet, and
small studs which sprang out as each lame was raised.
The burgonet was the defence for mounted men, while the
Morion was that for the infantry. Shakespeare, however,
never mentions the morion nor its congener, the cabasset.
Of older head-pieces, such as the Bascinet, there is no mention, and the Salade, which was also out of use in the poet's
day, only occurs in one play, where a weak pun is made on it.
Jack Cade says :

> I think this word 'sallet' was born to do me good ; for many
> a time, but for a sallet, my brain-pan had been cleft with a brown
> bill ; and many a time, when I have been dry, and bravely marching,
> it hath served me instead of a quart-pot to drink in ; and now the
> word 'sallet' must serve me to feed on. (2 *Hen. VI*, IV. x. 11–17)

Of Swords the only mention of the two-handed weapon is
in 2 *Henry VI* (II. i. 45), when Cardinal Beaufort says to
Gloucester, 'Come with thy two-hand sword'. But in the
Chorus (line 12) to *Henry V*, Act V, the 'mighty whiffler
'fore the king ' refers to a man with a two-hander clearing a
way in the crowds, as was done at Norwich.[1] Whiffler was
also a name for a player on the fife who marched at the
head of a procession, but who could not be reckoned as
clearing the way. In *Romeo and Juliet* (I. i. 81), when
Capulet calls, ' Give me my long sword, ho ! ' as also in *The
Merry Wives of Windsor*, when Shallow says, ' I have seen
the time with my long sword I would have made you four
tall fellows skip like rats ' (II. i. 235–6), we may suppose that
what is meant is the hand-and-a-half sword. In 2 *Henry IV*
(II. iv. 139) Doll Tearsheet calls Pistol ' you basket-hilt stale
juggler ', but though the Schiavona hilt, the original of the
basket-hilt, was in use in Shakespeare's day, it was not so
in the early fifteenth century.[2] In those days the Englishman's ordinary weapon in civil life was the backsword or
single-edged sword, which with the buckler was the national
weapon until the thrusting rapier was introduced (it is said

---

[1] For 'wyffelers' and 'slaughswords' see Hall's *Chronicle, Hen. VIII*, aº xxxi.
[2] Angelucci gives 1543 as the earliest Italian mention of the Schiavona.

by Rowland Yorke) in Queen Elizabeth's day, much to the disgust of the old-fashioned folk. Hotspur speaks of Prince Henry as 'that sword and buckler Prince of Wales', (*1 Hen. IV*, I. iii. 230), and the buckler as companion of the sword is anachronistically introduced in *Antony and Cleopatra* (I. iii. 82), when Cleopatra adds 'And target' to Antony's 'Now, by my sword'. In *Much Ado about Nothing* (v. ii. 17) the expression of Benedick, 'I give thee the bucklers,' indicates that he has got the worst of the encounter of wits with Margaret, bucklers being often given as prizes in sword and buckler fights. The bucklers or targets of Queen Elizabeth's day often had a spike projecting from the centre, and the length of this, as of the sword, was the subject of a proclamation in 1580. The spike was detachable, and in *Much Ado about Nothing* we have Benedick saying in reply to Margaret, who says 'we have bucklers of our own', 'If you use them, Margaret, you must put in the pikes with a vice' (v. ii. 18–21).

Spain was always famous for its sword-blades, and in *Romeo and Juliet* Mercutio tells of Queen Mab how

> Sometime she driveth o'er a soldier's neck,
> And then dreams he of cutting foreign throats,
> Of breaches, ambuscadoes, Spanish blades.   (I. iv. 83–5)

Bilboa seems to have been associated with the swords of that country, for we have Falstaff in *The Merry Wives of Windsor*, when describing his being in the buck-basket, say he was 'compassed, like a good bilbo, in the circumference of a peck, hilt to point, heel to head' (III. v. 114–16), and in the same play Pistol says to Parson Evans, 'I combat challenge of this latten bilbo' (I. i. 167). The 'latten bilbo' like the 'dagger of lath' (*Tw. N.* IV. ii. 140; *1 Hen. IV*, II. iv. 154) and the 'leaden dagger' (*1 Hen. IV*, II. iv. 424) refer to theatrical properties.

In *Othello* (v. ii. 252) we have 'It is a sword of Spain, the ice brook's temper'. So the modern version, but in the earliest printed edition, 1622, it was 'The Ise brokkes temper'. Isebrook was the English name for Innsbruck in the Tyrol, whence some of the best steel was imported into England from the early part of the sixteenth century until the Civil War. This steel was used for the manufacture of armour in England, and 'Isebrook' and other variants of spelling [1] can be found in documents quoted in the Calendars

---

[1] Isproka, Hysproka, Isprugk, &c.

of State Papers from April 1517 to April 1595. Moreover, warm water of various degrees of heat was used here, as in Japan, by the famous swordsmith Musamane,[1] for tempering the blades. Othello's expression merely means a Spanish blade of the best Innsbruck temper.

The Falchion, a single-edged sword, is mentioned several times, e.g. in *King Lear*, ' with my good biting falchion ' (v. iii. 278). The Scimitar occurs in *Titus Andronicus* (IV. ii. 92), in *Troilus and Cressida* (v. i. 2), and especially in *The Merchant of Venice*,

> By this scimitar,—
> That slew the Sophy, and a Persian prince.   (II. i. 24–5)

It was, however, an Eastern or African weapon, and no doubt the same as ' the hoked baslarde ', which Horman in his *Vulgaria*, 1519, says ' is a perelse (perilous) weapon with the Turks '.

The ' gallant curtle-axe ' of Rosalind (*A. Y. L.* I. iii. 120) and the curtle-axe of *Henry V* (IV. ii. 21) was the modern cutlass. Spenser calls it a ' curtaxe '.

We now come to the numerous notices of the Rapier, which name occurs in an inventory of the effects of King Henry VIII in 1547.[2] It was in those days not only a stabbing weapon, but also had a cutting edge. In *Twelfth Night* (III. iv. 260–1) we are told of a ' knight dubbed with unhatched (unhacked) rapier, and on carpet consideration '. In *Othello* (v. i. 72) Cassio says, ' My leg is cut in two '. Roderigo had a rapier and the thrust had failed, for Cassio had on a privy coat which protected the body only and left the legs defenceless. The stabbing rapier both by itself and in connexion with the Dagger or *maingauche,* held in the left hand point upwards to ward off or to hold the opponent's weapon, is of course mentioned very many times in *The Merry Wives of Windsor,* the two parts of *Henry IV*, in *Romeo and Juliet,* and in *Hamlet.* Stubbes, in his *Anatomie of Abuses*, inveighs strongly against the richness of the hilts and scabbards of the rapiers and daggers, and the hangers, as Hamlet preferred to call the carriages Osric spoke of—' very dear to fancy, very responsive to the hilts, most delicate carriages, and of very liberal conceit ' (*Haml.* v. ii. 158–60). In the plays the sword is in many instances connected with

---

[1] See *Tales of Old Japan.*   [2] *Archaeologia*, vol. vi, p. 245.

an emphatic statement : Pistol says, 'Sword is an oath, and oaths must have their course' (*Hen. V*, II. i. 106). All sorts of characters swear by their sword, Douglas, Falstaff, Richard Duke of York, Antony, &c., and it is on his sword that Hamlet swears to secrecy those who had seen his father's ghost. The old Passau swordsmith's stamp of a running wolf, known in Spain as the Perillo (or dog), and in England as the fox, gives numerous occasions for jokes on the subject. Pistol says 'thou diest on point of fox' (*Hen. V*, IV. iv. 9) ; Falstaff retorts upon Mrs. Quickly's asseveration of her truth and honesty, 'There's no more faith in thee than in a stewed prune, nor no more truth in thee than in a drawn fox' (*1 Hen. IV*, III. iii. 126–9). The contemporary poets and writers made much use of the term 'fox' for a sword.

Shakespeare makes no distinction between daggers and poniards, nor is it easy to say that there is any. In *Macbeth* daggers mental and physical are referred to, and the Scottish *skain* is not mentioned. The Dudgeon or box-wood hilt is referred to, and some writers have used the word for the whole weapon. The dagger or *maingauche* is in *Hamlet* sometimes called poniard, and is there generally mentioned as it was used in connexion with the rapier, point upward, for warding off or holding the opponent's weapon. In *Much Ado about Nothing* (II. i. 257) Beatrice 'speaks poniards, and every word stabs'; while Hamlet uses the same figure of speech but says 'I will speak daggers to her, but use none' (*Haml.* III. ii. 421).

The dagger was in Shakespeare's day generally worn behind the right hip. In *Romeo and Juliet*, Capulet, referring to the dagger with which Juliet has stabbed herself, says,

> This dagger hath mista'en !—for, lo, his house
> Is empty on the back of Montague.   (v. iii. 203–4)

In *Much Ado about Nothing* (v. i. 144–6), when Don Pedro says, 'I think he (Benedick) be angry indeed,' Claudio replies, 'If he be, he knows how to turn his girdle,' implying that Benedick can by so doing bring his dagger round to his hand. In *Henry V* (IV. i. 56) Pistol is warned by the king not to wear his 'dagger in his cap', but the reference is obscure, unless it refer to the threat of Pistol to knock Fluellen's leek about his pate.

In Derricke's *Image of Ireland* (1586), the English soldiers

Gard yor Selfe.

How to gard him selfe well, he must hold his Targett before him against his Left knee and shoulder firme & beare of the blowe downe rightly downe on the right syde by turne him selfe with the hilt of the sword till he may: ye it.

Put vp yor Sword.

How in sheathing his sword with the right hand he must beare the Buckler backeward on his body that he may do it without any impediment.

MOTIONS OF SWORD EXERCISE from *MARS HIS FEILD* 1595 (?)

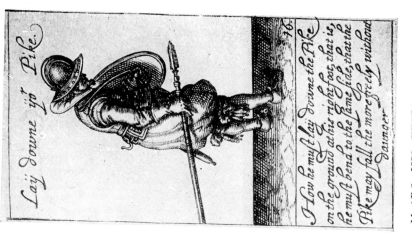

MOTIONS OF PIKE EXERCISE from *MARS HIS FEILD* 1595 (?)

are seen with their daggers at their backs, but Sir John Smythe says, 'they should wear their daggers not upon their girdles at their backs, but hanging down upon their right thighs before them, after the old English fashion'. Certainly Henry VIII and the Earl of Surrey are seen with their daggers in front, but Henry has his on his left side. That the dagger was worn aslant is shown by the expression in the *Complaynt of Scotland* (1549) of the ship's yards being daggerwise, or, as sailors called it, cock-billed, a custom in former years for showing mourning. Harrison in his *Description of England* says : ' Seldom shall you see any young countryman above eighteen or twenty years old, to go without a dagger at the least at his back, or by his side.' Thomas Becon, in *The Jewel of Joy* (c. 1550), says of our countrymen, ' Their dagger must be Scottish with a Venetian tassel of silk'.

The ' smoky muskets ' of *All's Well that Ends Well* (III. ii. 111) we may see at Penshurst, where are several of these weapons, as well as Calivers, and single examples of each, from the same house, are in the Tower of London. Some of these are dated 1595, and are heavy weapons. The Musket was five feet five and three-quarters over all, with a barrel of four feet two and a quarter, and in those days cost about twenty-seven shillings. Dutch muskets, however, were to be had at twenty-two shillings. The caliver was four feet ten over all, with a barrel of three feet five and a quarter, and cost, with its flask, touchbox (primer), laces, and mould, thirteen pounds six shillings. The musket took its name from the female of the sparrowhawk, which was so called. As to the caliver,[1] a lighter arm, we see its smaller weight distinctly referred to in the fact of its being put into the hands of Falstaff's wretched recruit Wart. That it was used also for sporting purposes we have evidence in Falstaff's remark that some of his men ' fear the report of a caliver worse than a struck fowl or a hurt wild-duck ' (*1 Hen. IV*, IV. ii. 20–1). A propos of sporting guns, we may note the habit referred to in *M. Wives*, IV.ii.57–60, of the home-returned sportsmen discharging their pieces up the chimney. It was evidently easier than drawing the charge. The Matchlock is

---

[1] In 1590 Sir John Smythe writes of ' Harquebuzes, by many miscalled Calivers '. In 1637 Hexham wrote, ' Forasmuch as of late there are no calivers in a foot company '.

never mentioned, nor is the Petronel, the arm in which the explosion of the charge was effected by sparks from a piece of iron pyrites, a system which, while an improvement on the matchlock, was itself superseded by the snaphance, the earliest form of the Flintlock. Of course, the petronel derived its name from the fact of a stone, not a match, being used, and not from its being, as some have supposed, fired from the breast (*poitrine*). The Dag, a smaller fire-arm, and the Tack, a variety of the pistol, are not to be found in any of the plays, though the pistol itself is the subject of many jokes, and is even introduced into the play of *Pericles* (I. i. 168–9), where Thaliard says :

> If I can get him within my pistol's length,
> I'll make him sure enough.

In *1 Henry IV* (II. iv. 385), Prince Henry scoffs at the story of Douglas killing a flying sparrow with a pistol. When in *Henry V* (II. i. 55–6) Pistol says,

> For I can take, and Pistol's cock is up,
> And flashing fire will follow,

we must consider that the class of pistol referred to was the wheel-lock, the flintlock being hardly introduced by 1600. With the wheel-lock, the cock which held the piece of pyrites was laid back towards the muzzle till it was time to use the weapon. Then it was brought up and back, to rest on the pan cover, which when the trigger was pressed slipped back, exposing the pyrites to the grooved edge of the quickly revolving wheel, and so generating the sparks necessary to inflame the priming in the pan and to cause the discharge of the weapon.

In *Love's Labour's Lost* (v. ii. 616), Dumaine speaks of ' The carved-bone face on a flask', referring to the carved ivory or bone flasks for holding the powder for military and sporting fire-arms. In *Romeo and Juliet* (III. iii. 129–32), Friar Laurence says to Romeo :

> Thy wit, that ornament to shape and love,
> Misshapen in the conduct of them both,
> Like powder in a skilless soldier's flask,
> To set a-fire by thine own ignorance.

In *1 Henry IV* (v. iii. 56), when Falstaff offers Prince Henry his pistol, saying ' There 's that will sack a city ', the Prince draws it out and finds it to be a bottle of sack. Evidently the slang term of pocket-pistol for a flask of wine is a joke of

THE MOTION *CHEEKE YOUR PIKE*

some antiquity. The Bandolier, although already in use in Shakespeare's day, is not mentioned.

The lance is often mentioned, and in *King Lear* (IV. vi. 171) 'the strong lance of justice' occurs. The more familiar figure of the sword of justice is used only in *The Winter's Tale* and *Othello*. The lance of Shakespeare's day as carried by cavalry appears in contemporary notices under various names, as chasing staves, Cullen staves, so called from being imported from Cologne. Northern staves also occur, but Shakespeare uses none of these terms. The lance was about twelve feet long, and was used by the English horse 'underhand', in contrast to the Irish who used it 'overhand', as shown by Derricke. The war-lances were of ash, and uniform in thickness so far as the head. The lance for the tilt-yard was made of deal and tapered to the point, with a swell in front and behind the grip. They were made to be broken, as in those days there was no instance of unhorsing an opponent in the lists, and the expression 'to break a lance' shows this. These tilt-yard lances were in general coloured as the plumes and scarves of the riders. The 'punching' staves were headless lances used in the encounters called Barriers, where the opponents on foot and on opposite sides of a waist-high barrier endeavoured to overthrow their *vis-à-vis*. The poet nowhere alludes to this sport, though it was common in his day. In *1 Henry VI* (III. ii. 50–1) the Pucelle says :

> What will you do, good grey-beard ? break a lance,
> And run a tilt at death within a chair ?

And in *Troilus and Cressida* (I. iii. 282–3), Æneas in his challenge says :

> The Grecian dames are sunburnt, and not worth
> The splinter of a lance.

Shakespeare uses the word 'to tilt' (*1 Hen. IV*, II. iii. 96–7) :

> This is no world
> To play with mammets and to tilt with lips.

The full and original expression was 'to run at the tilt' —that is, along the opposite sides of the tilt or barrier separating the jousters.

Of the staff weapons mentioned by Shakespeare we may note the Partisan, a spear with a broad head, the weapon of the guards, and at this day seen in the hands of the Yeomen of the Guard. Cotgrave gives 'Pertuisane—

partisan or leading staffe'. Such a weapon was carried
by officers, and Hentzner in 1598 mentions in the Tower
'hastae multae et splendidae quas *partisan* vulgo appellant'.
It was not so long as the infantry pike, but about nine feet
with a staff of stiff ash.   When Pistol asks,

> Art thou officer?
> Or art thou base, common, and popular? . . .
> Trail'st thou the puissant pike?   (*Hen. V*, iv. i. 37–40)

he evidently inquires whether the king carried a partisan
such as an officer would have.   The king replies that he 'is
a gentleman of a company'.   It must be remembered that
the pike was an honourable weapon, and in 1598 Sir William
Ward wrote in praise of it, and speaks of it as being 'put
into the hands of the skilful and experienced soldier'.
Markham, in his *Five Decades* (1622), says, 'The pike, for
that is accounted the gentleman's weapon'.   In *Hamlet*
(I. i. 140), Marcellus, who was an officer in the royal guard,
asks, 'Shall I strike at it with my partisan?' The pike
varied in length; those seen in Derricke's *Image of Ireland*
are about twelve feet; in the Sidney funeral procession
(1587) they appear about twelve to fourteen feet; and in
1590 Sir John Smythe advises that they be 'eighteen feet
with good and four square heads of good temper'.   In 1588
the pike cost three shillings and eight pence.

According to Markham, 'the lieutenant should carry a fair
gilt partisan, while the captain should have a fair feather
staff in time of peace, or for glory in a garrison, but in the
time of service and in the face of the enemy, a fair gilt
partisan richly trimmed, not being above twelve inches of
blade, sharp and well steeled'.   The feather staff was a sort
of swordstick, which, when held by the distal or lower end
and shaken, would project from the upper end a long central
blade and a shorter one on each side.   Shakespeare nowhere
mentions this weapon.

In *1 Henry IV* (II. iv. 376–8) we have, 'And swore the
devil his true liegeman upon the cross of a Welsh hook'.
This is the only mention of the weapon by Shakespeare, but
in Ben Jonson's *Honour of Wales* we find, 'As tall a man as
ever swagger with Welsh hook or long dagger'.   In the play
of *Sir John Oldcastle*, which was erroneously assigned by the
publisher to Shakespeare's pen, there appears the sentence,
'And that no man presumes to wear any weapon especially

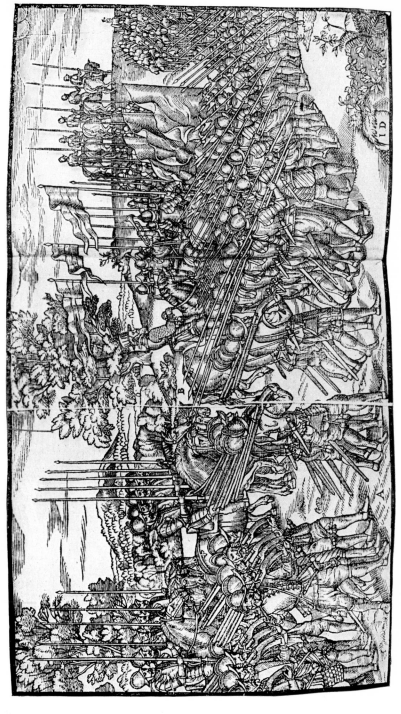

From DERRICKE'S *IMAGE OF IRELAND* 1586

AN ENGLISH ARMY ON THE MARCH

Welsh hooks and forest bills '. This play was acted in 1600. Cotgrave interprets the French word ' rancon ' as 'A Welsh hooke or hedging bill ; or (most properly) a triple forked weapon about the length of a Partisan'. It is difficult to say what it actually was, but it no doubt resembled a bill. In an inventory of arms of 1547 at Calais there is the entry ' Welche gloves (glaives) vii ᵐ '.

The Bills so often mentioned, and sometimes qualified by the prefix ' brown ', referring to the rusty condition of the weapon, were staff weapons with heads like a bill-hook of to-day, but furnished with spikes at the top and at back. They were essentially English weapons, and we are told that ' bills and bows ' was the alarm in camp when a sudden attack was expected. They were of simple make, and in peace time, when the staff was cut down, they were used for hedge and other work; hence the few survivals of the weapon. The bill, unlike the bow, was English made, whereas the best bows were in Henry the Eighth's time imported in a rough state from the Baltic and from Venice. English yew was hardly good enough for first-class bows, and many other woods were often used. The last appointment of bowmen for foreign service was in 1627, when a proportion of the troops levied for the relief of Rochelle were ordered to be archers. A later report from the counties stated that the requisite number of archers could not be obtained.

Artillery is referred to in many of the plays, and often regardless of chronology. In *The Winter's Tale* (I. ii. 388) we have the deadly gaze of the Basilisk referred to metaphorically, as also in *Cymbeline*, but in the history plays, *Henry IV*, *Henry V*, and *Henry VI*, it is the cannon of that name which is meant. It threw a shot of some forty pounds. The Culverine, with a shot of some seventeen and a half pounds, occurs in *1 Henry IV* (II. iii. 58). The general term 'cannon' is used in *Macbeth*, *Hamlet*, and *King John* quite anachronistically, while in many other plays it may not be considered out of place. The cannon of Shakespeare's day was, according to Sir William Monson, a sixty-pounder. In *Hamlet* (III. i. 58) we have possibly a reference to another piece of ordnance. When Hamlet speaks of ' the slings and arrows of outrageous fortune', to the audience of Shakespeare's day the 'slings' would have meant field guns. There were in those times whole, three-quarter, half, and quarter slings. The whole sling threw a shot of two and a half pounds ; it was earlier called a slang, a form derived from the Old Dutch or German 'Slange ', a snake, which gave its name to the gun, as also to the Culverine (from *Couleuvre*). The hand-sling, except in connexion with sacred history, was not a commonly known term till some thirty years after, when the wars

From *Webbe his travailes*, 1590.

of the Fronde ravaged France. In *Hamlet* (IV. v. 94–6) again,

> this,
> Like to a murdering-piece, in many places
> Gives me superfluous death,

may well refer to the cannon so called, which with others called Bases were used in the defence of fortresses. The detachable breech-pieces of the cannon of the day are meant by the ' chambers ' which are so often referred to in stage directions and in *2 Henry IV* (II. iv. 55–6), ' to venture upon the charged chambers bravely '.

BIBLIOGRAPHY.—The chief contemporary book on weapons and armour was Sir JOHN SMYTHE's *Certen Discourses concerning the formes and effects of divers sortes of weapons . . . and chieflie of the Mosquet, the Caliver, and the Long-Bowe*, 1590. The most important modern works are : F. GROSE's *Military Antiquities*, 1801 ; S. R. MEYRICK s *A Critical Inquiry into Antient Armour*, 1824 ; J. HEWITT's *Ancient Armour and Weapons in Europe*, 1855–60 ; C. FFOULKES's *Armour and Weapons*, 1909, and *European Arms and Armour in the University of Oxford*, 1912. *Archaeologia, The Archaeological Journal*, and the *Proceedings* of the Society of Antiquaries, contain many articles on the subject.

V

THE NAVY: SHIPS AND SAILORS

BY

L. G. CARR LAUGHTON

IT has been very generally conceded that Shakespeare's references to the sea and to sea-life are, almost without exception, accurate. Inasmuch as he had no known connexion with the sea, this feature of the plays has of late occasioned a good deal of comment. Some critics have found in this ready handling of a technical subject another proof of genius ; others have rushed to the conclusion that the poet must necessarily have invoked the assistance of a seaman ; others again have been inclined to carp, and to suggest that after all the sea references are not beyond criticism. It may be doubted, however, whether the subject has as yet been satisfactorily handled. It is not enough to have studied the plays and poems and to have extracted from them their wealth of sea phrases and allusions. To do so is of course an indispensable preliminary ; but a just opinion on the resulting collection cannot be framed from modern standards, nor even from a fairly wide reading of contemporary nautical literature.

The reasons that may be assigned for this are simple, though generally neglected. It is almost inconceivable to us nowadays that a man should know much of the sea and ships unless either by occupation or by interest he is brought into constant connexion with them. Sea-lore has become extraordinarily complicated, and the landsman's opportunities of acquiring it are scanty. If he makes a voyage by sea he learns little, for he travels in a special type of ship, and sees little or nothing of her working— even though the voyage be one of some weeks, for then the vessel is but a floating hotel, and the interests of the landsman lie chiefly with his fellow passengers. Nor does the landsman who lives in a great seaport stand much chance of acquiring any quantity of sea-knowledge. We have an excellent instance of this in London itself, still the greatest port in the world. Few Londoners know anything of the river east of London Bridge ; fewer still know anything of the shipping which crowds the Pool and lower reaches. The Londoner might by special observation in his leisure time learn something of the various types of sailing ships and steamers which frequent the Thames, but even so he would learn nothing of the men who sail in all these ships, for they are a class apart, and live a life apart in a distant quarter of the town. Finally, the landsman's task is made still more difficult by the modern complication of sea-life. The modern steamer hand has little in common with the sailor in a sailing-ship, and the Royal Navy is as widely different from each of these services, in ships, in men, even in speech, as is well conceivable. It follows that the modern man of letters, who has not followed the sea, can at the best pick up but a smattering of sea-knowledge, and that if he attempts to use technicalities he will at once betray himself.

In the Shakespearian era, there was, practically speaking, but one sea-service. Then, and for long afterwards, there was little difference, save in the matter of size, between men-of-war and merchant ships. Ships built to bear the brunt of war were bigger and more strongly armed and manned than any which the merchants found necessary; but the build was in essentials the same, the rig was the same, the men were the same, and the technicalities of the two professions were the same. Again, the dweller in a seaport, and more especially in London, was brought daily into touch with ships and sailors. The river then was London's main thoroughfare, which all must use, and sailors, instead of being confined, as they are now, to one distant quarter of the town, were commonly seen in all parts of it.

The spirit of oversea discovery and maritime expansion had permeated the national life. Exploration had become an integral part of maritime commerce at an early date ; the mere fact of it had helped to render the Spanish war inevitable. The merchants of London during Shakespeare's lifetime were men with whom ventures to the Levant, to the New World, to the far North, or to the distant East, were topics of daily conversation and debate ; and among

courtiers too, as long as Elizabeth lived, expeditions oversea were regarded as a sure way to royal favour, if not to
fame and fortune. Again, the long conflict with Spain
on the sea had made it clear once more to all thinking
men that the navy was the very 'wall and fence' of the
realm ; the national sentiment was echoed in the lines :

> Let us be back'd with God and with the seas
> Which he hath given for fence impregnable,
> And with their helps only defend ourselves :
> In them and in ourselves our safety lies.
>
> *(3 Hen. VI,* IV. i. 43–6)

Enough has been said to show that at the end of the
sixteenth century no man of intelligence could live in
London without having more than a superficial knowledge
of the sea ; nor could he avoid gaining some acquaintance
with the ships themselves, and, perhaps in a less degree,
with the sailors who manned them.

We should, accordingly, expect to find that Shakespeare
had some appreciation of what it is now the fashion to
call sea power ; that he was reasonably familiar with the
progress of oversea discovery, and was imbued with the
expansive spirit of the age ; and that he had at least as
much technical knowledge of the ships themselves and of
sailors as might readily be acquired by a man who could
see them almost daily. More abstruse technicalities, such
as would be met with only on board ships actually at sea,
we should not expect to find ; or, if we found them, we
should be likely to regard them as 'local colour' deliberately
acquired for a set purpose. Now this description of what we
might expect to find in Shakespeare is a very exact description of what we do find in him and in the authors of his time.
The same features are to be discovered in a marked degree in
the writings of contemporary dramatists and men of letters.
'Lyly has a mariner strongly emphasized in his *Galathea,* 1592 ;
Lodge, himself a sailor, wrote his *Rosalynde,* 1590, "in the
ocean, where every line was wet with a surge, and every
human passion counterchecked with a storm"; his *Margarite
of America,* 1596, was begun in the Strait of Magellan, on
board ship. The new spirit in literature is seen in the poems
of Spenser, and it had a profound influence upon Bacon.
Above all, it is reflected in the writings of Shakespeare.' [1]

---

[1] *Cambridge History of English Literature,* vol. iv, p. 77.

THE SHIPS AND THEIR USES

Although the ships of Shakespeare's time were, by comparison with the great complexity of modern times, simple and easy to understand, it must not be supposed either that a full knowledge of them was easy to a contemporary, or that modern students are satisfied that they have as yet recovered all that is to be known about them. On the contrary, there is much that is still obscure, though enough is known to show that Shakespeare's knowledge, as far as it went, was accurate. The terms in which nautical references are made in the plays are not always strictly technical, but none but a pedantic critic would refuse a poet the amount of licence which is taken with sea phrases, as in :

> Your breath of full consent bellied his sails.
>
> *(Troilus*, ii. ii. 74)

There are frequent mentions of ships and vessels of all classes, whether used for war, for piracy, for commerce, for passage, or for pageantry. The generic terms, Ship, Vessel, and Boat often occur. Bark, too, is used in the ordinary poetic fashion as a synonym for ' ship ' (*Com. of E*. iv. i. 86, *Lear* iv. vi. 19, *Oth*. ii. i. 48), though in strict language, then as now, the term had a narrower meaning. The particular application to a small ship does occur :

> A bark to brook no mighty sea,
>
> *(Rich. III*, iii. vii. 161)

and seems to be implied elsewhere :

> And I . . .
> Like a poor bark, of sails and tackling reft,
> Rush all to pieces.   *(Ibid.* iv. iv. 234)

Boat, among seamen of this period, was used exclusively for open boats and fishing-boats ; it never had the wider meaning of ' ship ' or ' vessel ', except in poetry, as in :

> . . . when the sea was calm all boats alike
> Show'd mastership in floating.   *(Cor.* iv. i. 6)

It is sometimes used by Shakespeare for ' ship ' in its narrow meaning of large ship, as the mention of a topmast shows in :

> . . . sands, that will not bear your enemies' boats,
> But suck them up to the topmast.   *(Cymb.* iii. i. 21)

On the other hand, he frequently makes very effective use of
the proper contrast between the ship and the boat, as in :—

> . . . the sea being smooth,
> How many shallow bauble boats dare sail
> Upon her patient breast, making their way
> With those of nobler bulk !
> But let the ruffian Boreas once enrage
> The gentle Thetis, and anon behold
> The strong-ribb'd bark through liquid mountains cut ;
> . . . Where's then the saucy boat
> Whose weak untimber'd sides but even now
> Co-rivall'd greatness ?   (*Troilus*, I. iii. 34–44)

In addition to these generic terms, many names of
specific classes of ships occur ; indeed few of the types
known and used in England at that period remain un-
mentioned. But almost all these terms are now obsolete,
or else have acquired different meanings.

In naval war the method of fighting with sailing ships
was still more or less haphazard. The need for the precise
term ' line-of-battleship ' had not arisen ; similarly, the
word ' frigate ' had not yet acquired its later meaning,
and the other types of the great wars had not yet come
into existence. For a fighting ship, Shakespeare uses
only the common generic term Man-of-war :—

> Leave you not a man-of-war unsearch'd.
>   (*Tit. Andr.* IV. iii. 22)

Men-of-war were divided into classes according to size,
irrespective of function. In the establishment of 1618
there were Ships Royal, Great ships, Middling ships, and
Small ships, all belonging to the Crown ; when Barks
occur at this period on the list of a naval expedition, they
are invariably ships hired from the merchants. Below
these categories the navy of the time included Pinnaces,
which were small and comparatively light ship-rigged
vessels, most, if not all, of which had auxiliary oar-power.
Their duty was to serve as scouts and advice-vessels ; but
they were in their degree effective men-of-war, carrying
a reasonable armament of heavy guns. These were the
official English categories ; but there were other terms,
both popular and technical, used to describe the same
ships. Thus a ship of importance was a ' tall ship ', whether
from the height of her masts or from the manner in which
parts of her hull were built up above the water. Shake-

speare uses the adjective ' tall ' five times with this connotation ; we find ' tall anchoring bark ' (*Lear*, IV. vi. 19),
and ' tall ships ' (*Rich. II*, II. i. 286) bound on a warlike
expedition.   Again, the ship of ' tall building ' is contrasted
with   the   ' shallow   worthless   boat '   (*Sonnet* lxxx.   12).
' Armada '   or   ' Armado '   was   the   ordinary   term   for   an
armed   fleet ;   less   frequently   it   meant   an   armed   ship.
Shakespeare uses it only in the first sense : ' whole armadoes
of carracks ' (*Com. of E.* III. ii. 11), ' a whole armado of
connected sail ' (*John*, III. iv. 2).   But in both senses the
term was obsolete in general use by the end of the seventeenth century.

The   terms   Galleon,   Galliass,   and   Galley   are   of   the
greatest   importance   in   the   history   of   naval   ship-build-
ing,   and   there   are   difficulties   still   unresolved   concerning
them,   but   Shakespeare   was   little   troubled   by   considerations   of   their   precise   technical   meaning.   The   galleon
existed   in   the   Royal   Navy,   but   was   not   often   officially   so
called.   The   term,   which   Shakespeare   ignores,   was   rather
a   ship-builder's   term,   and   seems   to   have   been   popularly
used   in   England   to   denote   the   Spanish   man-of-war.   Confusion   arises   from   this,   for   in   all   that   constitutes   a   galleon
the   English   ships   which   fought   against   the   Spanish   Armada
in   1588   were   as   much   galleons [1] as   their   adversaries.   This
important   type   was   developed   for   purposes   of   war   during
the   latter   part   of   the   sixteenth   century.   It   was   evolved
from   the   short   high   free-board   merchant   vessel,   was   armed
with   guns   on   the   broadside,   and   was   given   the   full   ship-
rig   of   the   period.   The   galleon's   essential   difference   from
the   merchantman   was   her   greater   proportionate   length.
The   keel   of   a   galleon   was   about   three   times   the   length   of
the   beam,   and   both   seaworthiness   and   speed   were   gained
thereby.   Though   the   technical   use   of   the   name   soon   fell
out   of   use,   the   type   continued,   for   its   proportions   were
such   as   to   keep   it   in   favour   for   men-of-war   to   the   very
end   of   the   sailing-ship   era.   The   term   ' galleon '   survived
until   the   beginning   of   the   nineteenth   century   in   the   restricted   sense   of   a   Spanish   treasure-ship.   This   carries   us
back   to   1565,   when   Spain   began   to   build   her   famous
' galleons   of   the   Indian   Guard ',   which   formed   a   private

---

[1] A few were officially described as such.   See Navy Records Society,
Armada Papers, vol. ii. p. 326.

'insurance squadron' owned by the Casa de Contratacion, and employed to convoy the 'Flota' of ships which annually brought to Spain the treasures of the New World. Later, Spain adopted the simpler plan of sending her American treasure home in men-of-war; and this was done throughout the eighteenth century, and till the trade came to an end. In this way 'galleon' came to mean a Spanish treasure-ship.

It is often implied by non-technical writers that the essential feature of the Spanish galleons of the Elizabethan

From title-page of Humphrey Mote. *The Primrose of London*, 1585.

era was what was then called their 'high-charging', that is to say, the loftiness of their upper works. Conversely, it is often popularly supposed that the English men-of-war of the period were not 'high-charged'. Neither opinion can be substantiated. It is true that the loftiest of the Spanish ships were higher built than the contemporary English ships, but the difference was merely one of degree. All alike would look immensely cumbersome and leewardly to a modern seaman. But the essential of the galleon type lay in its new ratio of length to breadth.

Shakespeare once mentions the galliass, but not as a man-of-war :

> . . . 'tis known my father hath no less
> Than three great argosies, besides two galliasses,
> And twelve tight galleys.   (*Tam. Sh.* II. i. 372)

It is obvious that merchant vessels are meant, and the application is correct, for the scene of the play lies in Italy, and the ' galeazza di mercantia ' was there a well-known type. But in Elizabeth's reign these galliasses no longer traded to England, and the only galliass ever used in

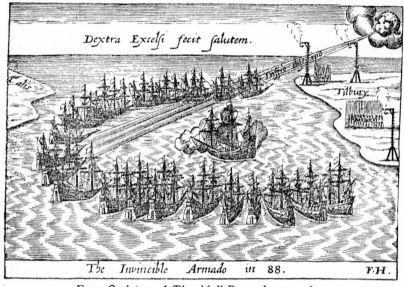

From Carleton, *A Thankfull Remembrance*, 1627.

England was a man-of-war. The term is a difficult one. It was used to describe certain ships of the navy of Henry VIII, but not any of Elizabeth's navy. The only men-of-war galliasses known to Shakespeare's generation were ships of the type that sailed in the Spanish Armada. These represented a compromise between the broadside sailing-ship, or galleon, and the row-galley, which could fire only ahead or astern. The first-named galliasses were such as fought with effect against the Turks at Lepanto in 1571 ; they had a tier of small guns on each broadside above their oars. They were, however, by comparison with galleons, very weakly armed, and the type was subse-

quently improved upon and more heavily armed, those
which came into English waters in 1588 being powerful
ships. They created a very favourable impression on
some observers ; being oared vessels they had great mobility
in calms and light winds, and they proved—unexpectedly—
as seaworthy as the galleons. Their exact proportions
do not seem to be definitely known, but the ' galeazza
di mercantia ' was 3⅔ times as long by the keel as she was
in beam, and it is probable that the war galliass was about
the same. The original galliasses were lateen-rigged, but
the Armada ships had the ordinary square rig.

The Galley, which is referred to by Shakespeare always
as a Mediterranean craft (*Tam. Sh.* II. i. 373, *Tw. N.* III. ii.
26, *Oth.* I. ii. 401, &c.), was at this date always an oared
vessel, long, low, and narrow, able to fire her guns only
ahead, the whole midship part of her being occupied
by rowers. She had little stowage, and therefore was used
chiefly for war and for carrying passengers, and not as
a regular trader. The galley proper never established
itself in England ; it was experimented with during
Elizabeth's reign for naval use, but was found unsuited
to English waters. Those which accompanied the Spanish
Armada came to grief from stress of weather. The cost
of manning them was for England an insuperable difficulty,
to which the Mediterranean powers were not subject, for
they found free labour in prisoners of war, infidels, criminals,
or ' like Venice, they bought surplus human stock by the
thousand from the Emperor '.[1] In England, slaves were
not to be had, and to keep a galley, manned with free
rowers, in commission, cost as much as a ship of 700 tons,
a much more efficient vessel. Sir John Hawkins did indeed
suggest using ' slaves ', by which he probably meant
negroes, though possibly ' slaves ' was his ' pleasant
Elizabethan way of describing criminals and vagrants '.
At any rate, though a statute of 1597 enacted that 'dangerous
rogues ' should be sent to the galleys, this was not done,
and the few galleys built for the navy were never used as
men-of-war, but only as tug-boats, or occasionally for
purposes of pageantry, when, it is believed, crews were
drafted to them from the men-of-war. Nor, other disadvantages apart, is it surprising that galleys were not used as

[1] Oppenheim, *Administration of the Royal Navy*, 126.

passenger vessels. Their scanty accommodation and the crowd of rowers made them, to say the least of it, extremely uncomfortable. In 1578 appeared a translation by Edward Hellowes of a Spanish tract by Antonio de Guevara, entitled *A book of the Invention of the Art of Navigation, and of the great travelles which they passe that saile in Gallies.* The author gives a humorous description in chap. v of the miseries of life in a galley, which may well be taken as a typical picture of the conditions of discomfort and insanitation in such craft:—

It is a privilege of the Gallie, that no man at dinner time shall there demaunde water that is either cleare, colde, whoalsome, or sweete; but of force must content himselfe to drinke troubled, grosse, warm, and unsavourie water: yet it is no lesse true, that unto such as be verie nice, the Captaine giveth licence, that all the while they shalbe a drinking, with one hande they may stoppe their nose, and with the other hande lift the pott unto their head.

It is a privilege of the Gallie, that the fleshe which they ordinarily shall eat, is joynts of Goats, quarters of Sheepe, salt Beefe, and rustie Bacon, not boyled, but parboilde: not roasted, but burnt: in such wise, that being sett on table it is lothesome to behold, hard as the divell to gnawe on, salt as broyne to feed on, and indigestible as a stone.

It is a privilege of the Gallie, that if any nice or curious passenger will needes washe any handkerchiefe or any shirte for his owne person, that it be in no freshe or sweete, but salt water. And as the salt water doeth breede ytch and scurffe, so the Capteine will give him licence, and the Boteswane will allow him place to rubbe his backe against the Mast, or seeke a Rower to scratch the same.

It is a privilege of the Gallie, that all fleas that leape uppon the hatches, and all lice that breede in seames, and all cheslockes (i.e. woodlice) that walk in chinkers (i.e. chinks), be common unto all men, and be divided and parted amongst all men: and if any person which is fine and nice shall appeale from this privilege, from thenceforth I prophesie, that if he make but a secrete inquirie, in his necke and bosome, and a privie searche in his breeches, he shall find more lice then money in his pursse.

The galley, however, was not the only type of oared vessel used for warfare in the sixteenth century. There was a regular descending scale of types—Galley, Foyst, Brigantine, Frigate—just as in the eighteenth century there were galleys, half-galleys, and quarter-galleys. As the type declined from the true galley type, the vessel became smaller, and was pulled by proportionately fewer oars, her oar-power becoming more and more an auxiliary to

Durch Ioseph Furttenbach.

A GALLEY from FURTTENBACH'S *ARCHITECTURA NAVALIS* 1629

her sails ; in the galley proper it was the sail-power that
was auxiliary. In England during the early Elizabethan
period all these types were tried in the royal navy, or at
least recommended for it. J. Montgomery, writing in his
Treatise concerning the Navie in 1570, held that the navy
should contain three gallies, three pinnaces, one galliota,
one brigantine, one foyst, and one frigate, all of which he
described as small light vessels to row. He had no doubt
the tradition of Henry VIII's 'row barges' before him. In
the second version written eighteen years later, however, he
had already abandoned his demand for these miscellaneous
small craft, thinking that the navy's oared pinnaces would
serve all needs.

The Pinnace has already been briefly referred to. These
vessels were square-rigged, and their oar-power was purely
auxiliary. They cannot have been fast under oars, for
they were of considerable beam in order to carry their
sails and armament to advantage. The usual proportion
of keel to beam seems to have been about $3\frac{1}{2}$ to 1, increasing latterly to 4 to 1, or slightly less than that of the much
larger galliasses. The weight of the rig was strictly in
proportion to that of the great ships, as was that of their
ordnance. The size of these craft varied very much,
usually from about 40 to 100 tons, though a few considerably larger are met with. The type, however, though
efficient, did not endure, and the last pinnace built for the
royal navy was launched in 1616. The British fleet sent
to the Mediterranean in 1620 found itself short of oared
vessels and hired brigantines on the spot. Of the Brigantine
Shakespeare has no instance, but Marlowe calls it the
' pilling brigantine ', the epithet being appropriate enough.
It has not been definitely established that the type took its
name directly from its being used for piracy, but it is clear
that etymologically the word is akin to ' brigand '. ' Pinnace ' occurs thrice in Shakespeare, once merely to suggest
speedy transit (*M. Wives*, I. iii. 87), and twice to designate
a pirate vessel (*2 Hen. VI*, IV. i. 9 and 107, where he attaches
a long-boat, line 68, to it). In assigning a pinnace to
Henry VI's reign, Shakespeare was guilty of an anachronism,
even as Marryat was when he sent Mr. Vanslyperken to
sea in a king's cutter under William III. Each of them
described the shipping of his own time, the seaman of

course in greater detail, but the poet without error, unless
perhaps it was an error for Shakespeare to give a long-
boat to the pinnace. The Long-boat was a very large
open boat used as a tender by ships of war ; it was so
large (though proportioned to the ship) that it was not
hoisted aboard, but was towed astern. It often happened
therefore that in bad weather ships lost their long-boats
at sea ; in the Armada campaign, for instance, nearly all
the ships did so. The ship's boat next largest to the long-
boat was the pinnace—not to be confused with the rigged
pinnace already described,[1] being of but 30 feet or little
more in length for a great ship, while the long-boat for
ships of the largest size was as much as 50 feet long ; it
was hoisted aboard. Next came the Jolywat, or Jollyboat,
as it is now called, a broad and heavy boat for rough work,
and last of all the Cock, corresponding roughly to the
modern punt or dinghy. Shallops, which were comparatively long and light boats, began to come in in James I's
reign. Of these various types, Shakespeare mentions only
the cock :—

> Yond tall anchoring bark
> Diminished to her cock,—her cock, a buoy
> Almost too small for sight.   (*Lear*, IV. vi. 20)

The Skiff, a small light boat, came into use on board
men-of-war early in the seventeenth century. It was no
new type, for Hellowes describes the galleys as carrying
it, but its name does not occur in the plays. The Wherry
was already a favourite waterman's boat on the Thames,
and one of the court messengers in 1590, for a bet, made
an adventurous passage from London to Bristol, round
the Land's End, in a boat of this type. Ferris described
the voyage in his *Most Dangerous and Memorable Adventure*.
A little time after Shakespeare's death, John Taylor, the
Water-poet, made many such journeys, and wrote rhyming
accounts of them.

Shakespeare ignores the wherry, but the Barge is mentioned more than once, and this name always means a large
river boat used for purposes of state or pageantry, as in
Henry VIII and *Antony and Cleopatra*. The barge as a cargo-
carrier did not then exist, though it had been in use up

---

[1] In the Establishment of 1618 the sizes of ship's boats were definitely
laid down.

to the end of the fifteenth century. The modern sailing-barge existed in embryo under another name; the ship's boat, called a barge, came later. The passage describing Cleopatra's barge (*Ant. & Cleop.* II. ii. 199 seq.), although borrowed almost literally from Plutarch, may be taken as describing, with some exaggeration, the type of barge in which Queen Elizabeth made her water progresses:—

> The barge she sat in, like a burnish'd throne,
> Burn'd on the water; the poop was beaten gold;
> Purple the sails, and so perfumed, that
> The winds were love-sick with them; the oars were silver,
> Which to the tune of flutes kept stroke.
> . . . she did lie
> In her pavilion,—cloth-of-gold of tissue, . . .
> A seeming mermaid steers; the silken tackle
> Swell with the touches of those flower-soft hands
> That yarely frame the office.

Coming to merchant-vessels, we find that Argosy[1] is the term that occurs most frequently in Shakespeare. The most striking instance is at the beginning of the *Merchant of Venice*:—

> There, where your argosies with portly sail,—
> Like signiors and rich burghers on the flood,
> Or, as it were, the pageants of the sea,—
> Do overpeer the petty traffickers.   (I. i. 9–12)

As to the type of these ships it is fairly certain that they were akin to, if not identical with, 'hulks' and 'carracks', or merchant-ships of the largest class. The 'wealthy Andrew' (*Merch. of V.* I. i. 27) must be supposed to be a ship of this class. 'Hulk' is used for a ship carrying a large cargo:—

> There's a whole merchant's venture of Bordeaux stuff in him; you have not seen a hulk better stuffed in the hold. (*2 Hen. IV*, II. iv. 69)

'Carrack' involved the additional implication of a rich cargo. This use was abundantly justified, for the most celebrated carracks of the Elizabethan age were the very large ships wherein the Portuguese brought home the wealth of the Spice Islands and the Far East:—

> He to-night hath boarded a land carrack:
> If it prove lawful prize, he's made for ever.   (*Oth.* I. ii. 50)

[1] As is indicated by the earliest recorded form ('Ragusye') and the known facts as to the prevalence of trade with Ragusa, this word is derived from the name of the Illyrian port.

The Carrack was a type of merchant-ship which had come down from the Middle Ages, and was used both in northern and southern Europe. With some addition to her fore and after castles she was frequently used for war. Her beam was very great, and her over-hangs were enormous. The celebrated *Madre de Dios* of Spain, for instance, was 100 feet by the keel, as were many other large ships of the period, but her beam was 46 feet 10 inches, and her length over all, 165 feet. The tonnage of this ship is given as about 1,500, while the contemporary man-of-war of the same length was not more than 600 or 700 tons. A carrack, by sheer inertia of her bulk and stout timbering, not infrequently beat off an enemy cruising to intercept her ; but the type was slow, and, as would be expected from the proportions, extremely unseaworthy ; many of them were lost at sea.

The Hulk, the ordinary large merchantman of Northern Europe, was also a ship of some two beams long. It was not till well into Elizabeth's reign that these proportions began to vary, and the merchant-ships to be made somewhat less broad and deep. It was from this slow and roomy type that the galleon was evolved, combining some of the qualities of the ' round ship ' with others from the ' long ship ' type. The term ' hulk ' has long since lost its old meaning, and signifies only a dismasted hull.

We know little of the details of most of the Elizabethan merchantmen, but it may be inferred that some at least had no bulwarks in the waist. This is important, for it helps to explain such passages as

I stood upon the hatches in the storm.   (*2 Hen. VI*, III. ii. 103)

and, again, in Clarence's vivid dream :—

> Methought that I had broken from the Tower,
> And was embarked to cross to Burgundy ;
> And in my company my brother Gloucester,
> Who from my cabin tempted me to walk
> Upon the hatches : . . .
>   As we pac'd along
> Upon the giddy footing of the hatches,
> Methought that Gloucester stumbled ; and, in falling,
> Struck me, that thought to stay him, overboard.
>   (*Rich. III*, I. iv. 9–19)

Other types of trading vessels were the Caravel, of Portuguese origin, rigged usually with four masts, the foremast carrying square sails and the others lateens (but the large lateen sail, though tried in England, never became a favourite); the Bilander, the Crumster, which it is hard to differentiate from the Hoy, the Crayer, and others. Of all these only the crayer and the hoy are mentioned in the plays. The crayer lasted on till the middle of the eighteenth century or later ; it was of no great size. Shakespeare speaks of a 'sluggish crare' (*Cymb.* IV. ii. 205 [1]), and to that unsatisfactory description there is little to add. The hoy, also once mentioned (*Com. of E.* IV. iii. 39), is a most interesting type. Essentially it was the same as the Thames barge of to-day, its lineal descendant, and still sometimes known by the same name. A flat-bottomed vessel, often of considerable size, and carrying as much as 300 tons, it had in the main the rig of the Thames barge—a large spritsail for a mainsail, and a fore and aft foresail ; but as fore and aft topsails and jibs were not yet invented, the hoy of Shakespeare's time had a square topsail and a square sail (spritsail) under the bowsprit. These hoys also set a square mainsail when before the wind, and some of them used studding sails even at this very early date ; the larger of them were fitted with a mizen, which was always a lateen, and they had leeboards.

It has been shown in the previous chapter that Shakespeare and his contemporaries knew nothing of a standing army. But there had long been in existence a royal navy or fleet, which was built and equipped at the royal expense, and was actively controlled by an admiral who owed his appointment to the Crown. During Elizabeth's reign and till past the middle of the seventeenth century, the royal navy proper was but a small force, forming merely the nucleus of the fighting fleets of the country, but its presence differentiated the organization of the naval from that of the military forces of the realm. Elizabeth at her accession had 22 men-of-war of 100 tons and over ; at her death she left 29 ; James left 30 men-of-war of all classes. Round these few men-of-war on occasion the effective armed merchantmen were gathered ; thus, during the Armada campaign, 197 ships in all took part, whereof only 34 belonged to the Crown.

---

[1] It is important to add that 'crare' in this passage is an emendation, the old editions reading 'care'.

The merchant-ships were recruited for war as a sort of naval militia by an impress service very similar to that by which men were raised : this was, and had for long been, the regular practice. It was therefore of interest for the Crown to be well informed of the number and size of merchant-ships in the kingdom, of which many lists are extant. A bounty of 5s. per ton was paid on the construction of the larger merchant-ships. That these could on occasion be used as men-of-war was due to the ordinary risks to which they were subject in their trading. Even the narrow seas were beset with pirates, in Elizabeth's reign chiefly by Englishmen, but in James's time by the rising Dunkirkers and by Moorish pirates from Sallee. The merchantmen, therefore, were always armed, often heavily. It is not possible to say what their number was. Harrison, who is no expert in nautical affairs, says ' there are 135 ships that exceed 100 tons ; topmen under 100 and above 40 tons, 656 ; hoies, 100 ; but of hulkes, catches, fisher-boats, and craiers it lieth not in me to deliver the just account '. He is obviously guessing, for, so far as can be known, no complete list was ever compiled. As to the size of English merchantmen at this period, it is clear that the ordinary large ship was of about 200 tons ; very few ran up to 300 and 350 tons, and scarcely any exceeded that figure. It was not until the East India Company showed the way that ships of 500 tons and more began to be regularly built in England for commerce, but even these were much smaller than the great Portuguese carracks.

It followed that if the Crown wanted heavy ships to bear the brunt of the fighting in fleet actions, it must provide them for itself. Thus it was that the greater part of the men-of-war built were much larger than the merchantmen of the time, a condition of things which continued as long as the sailing era. The dimensions of a few typical men-of-war can most readily be shown in tabular form :—

Ship.	Date.	Keel. ft.	Beam. ft.	Rake. Forward. ft.	Aft. ft.	Ton and tonnage.
Triumph . . .	1561	100	40	37	6	955
Ark Royal . .	1587	100	37	33·6	6	692
Vanguard . .	1586	108	32	32	5·8	561
Advice . . .	1586	50	14	12	2·6	52

The equipment and crews of the same ships were as follows:—

Ship.	Weight of masts and yards. tons.	Weight of ordnance. tons.	Mariners.	Gunners.	Soldiers.
Triumph	24·17	68	340	40	120
Ark Royal	18·4	50	268	32	100
Vanguard	14·14	40	150	30	70
Advice	1·4	3·5	30	5	5

The *Triumph* was a broad ship of pre-galleon days : the reduction of beam and of rake in the later ships, which were consequently faster and more seaworthy, is very noticeable. The *Advice* was a pinnace of the smaller class. The policy now pursued was in general followed during the subsequent reign, but not without throwbacks, for the famous *Prince Royal*, launched in 1610, a ship of about 1,200 tons, was much broader than the galleon proportion, having a beam of 43 feet to a keel length of only 115 feet.

The rig of all ships of importance was the same, whether for war or commerce, though it may be supposed that the man-of-war, having proportionately a far larger crew, was, as later, more heavily sparred than the trader. The chief characteristic of the Elizabethan rig was its simplicity. Even the largest ships carried only six or seven sails, to wit, mainsail, main topsail ; fore-sail, fore-topsail ; mizen ; and a spritsail under the bowsprit. The largest ships usually, if not always, had two mizen masts, named the main mizen, and bonaventure mizen. The sail set on each of these masts was a lateen ; all the others were square. The topgallant-sail was not in use in the early part of Elizabeth's reign. Experimented with under Henry VII and Henry VIII, it fell out of use for a time. By about 1588 it was beginning to come in again, and, it is to be supposed, gradually grew in favour, for in 1618 it was put on the establishment of the navy. Shakespeare, it will be seen, had kept pace with the times when he made Romeo speak of ' the high topgallant of my joy ' (*Rom. & Jul.* II. iv. 204, though the reference here is not to the sail, but to the ' top ', or platform on the mast, from which it was handled). At the same time two still newer sails were officially introduced, viz. a square mizen topsail and a spritsail topsail, to be set on a small mast planted on the end of the bowsprit. It has always been a mystery how such a peculiarly awkward and ineffective sail as this came to be introduced ; but the fact is certain, and Shakespeare in his later years must have seen it in the Thames.

Reefing did not exist at this period : the practice being to have a small sail, called a 'corse' (i. e. body), usually spelt 'course', and to add to the bottom of it in fine weather one or more strips called 'bonnets'. This was done to the lower sails only ; topsails very rarely had bonnets. Now in spite of the fact that a ship of the early seventeenth century had both topsails and topgallant-sails, it did not bear much resemblance to a modern ship using those sails. The most marked feature at this date was the shortness of the upper yards, each yard being about two-fifths as long as the yard immediately below it. This was the practice of Elizabeth's reign, and it was confirmed and extended by the establishment of 1618. At the same time the depth of the topsails was increasing, and that of the courses decreasing. A ship of 1618, even of 1588, was on this account very different to look at from a ship of 1558.

Other Shakespearian references to details of a ship's parts and equipment are more commonplace, indeed many of them are untechnical. Thus we have ' tackle ', used as a generic term for rigging, also ' tackling ', and the amplified phrase ' shrouds and tacklings ' (*3 Hen. VI*, v. iv. 18); the anchor, bowsprit, cable, hatches, hull, main-mast, main-sail, main-top, poop, ribs, top-mast, are all mentioned ; and there are numerous similes in which mast, anchors, tackles, and the like are introduced (e.g. *2 Hen. VI*, v. iv. 4 ; *John*, v. vii).

It is true that a very large proportion of Shakespeare's sea similes are drawn from the wind, waves, and, above all, the tide, from natural phenomena rather than from man's handicraft ; but even so, the residue of technicalities used is very considerable. Of these the most remarkable are :

Thou art our admiral ; thou bearest the lantern in the poop.
(*1 Hen. IV*, III. iii. 29)

a detail which many landsmen would not know. We find Bowlines mentioned (*Pericles* III. i. 4), ropes used to help the ship to sail closer to the wind ; but the passage is too short to show clearly whether Shakespeare fully understood their use. In the *Tempest* (I. ii. 196–200) Ariel flits from the Beak to the Waist, and to the Deck, in every

From T LANT'S engraving of SIR PHILIP SIDNEY'S FUNERAL 1588

THE SHIP IN WHICH SIR PHILIP SIDNEY'S BODY WAS BROUGHT TO ENGLAND

The Black Pynnes.

ANGLIA

Margt Tenet

cabin 'flaming amazement'. The reference is of course to St. Elmo's fire, occasionally seen at sea. The Beak, or Beak-head, was a projection at the bows of the ship under the bowsprit, and in this period was very long ; the Waist then was more marked than it is now, being that part of the deck which lies low between the high raised forecastle and the quarter-deck. And here it may be said that the nomenclature of decks in the Tudor period is a matter of great difficulty ; but, as Shakespeare does not use the term ' deck ' save in its generic sense, there is the less need here to attempt an explanation of the confused and conflicting evidence.

Before passing to the subject of seamanship, it is necessary to give a brief account of the naval ordnance of the period. There were three classes of fire-arms in use ; heavy guns of several calibres, quick-firers of various descriptions, and small arms. The fashion of the age was to designate each calibre of gun by a separate name ; the custom of describing guns by the weight of the shot which they threw came in later. At this period the heaviest gun was the Cannon, throwing perhaps a 42 lb. ball, but this was not in use in English ships. Next came the Demi-cannon, a 30-pounder, the Cannon-perrier, a light-made 24-pounder, and the Culverin, a long 18-pounder. The Spaniards had a 15-pounder, called a Basilisco, not used in English ships. The Demi-culverin was a long 9-pounder ; the Saker, a long 6-pounder; and below this calibre came in order the Minion, a 4-pounder ; the Falcon, a 3-pounder ; the Falconet, a 2-pounder ; and then a number of small pieces, such as Bases, Slings, Fowlers, Robinets, Hail-shot Pieces, Port Pieces, and so on. These last named threw some of them a small solid ball, some of them a handful of iron dice or slugs, and were used against men, not against the ship herself. The large guns were mounted on truck carriages, fitted with quoins, and fired through ports ; in the English Navy culverins and demi-culverins were most in favour for use on board ship. The small pieces, or many of them, were swivels mounted on the gunwale, or in the bulkheads of the forecastle and half-deck, in order to clear the waist of boarders if they should gain a footing there ; they were all quick-firers, each barrel having several Chambers, which were loaded first and then fitted into the guns, which were

in effect breech-loaders.   By the end of this period ships
with two complete covered decks of guns were normal ;   and
recent research has proved that not only the *Prince Royal*
of James I, but also three of the largest ships of Elizabeth's
reign, including the famous *Ark Royal,* were three-deckers.
English seamen learnt early to trust to the great gun, and
their experience with the Armada fully justified and confirmed their confidence in that arm.   The gunnery, however,
was not accurate, for the art was comparatively new on
shipboard, and the weapons were poor ;   nevertheless, there
can be no doubt that at this period the English seamen
gunners were the best in the world, or that English guns
were the finest that were to be had.   Shakespeare refers to
heavy ordnance only under the generic name of ' cannon '
(*Hen. V*, III. chor. 33) ;   he invents the abstract noun ' portage ' as a substitute for ' ports ' (*ibid.* III. i. 10) ;   he mentions
the ' linstock ' (*ibid.* chor. 33), with which guns were fired ;
and there are fairly frequent mentions of ' chambers ',
which were used in the theatre itself to counterfeit the
noise of heavy guns.   ' Gun-stones ' (*Hen. V*, I. ii. 282) was
a term still in use in the Elizabethan period, although
stone shot had almost ceased to be used ;   but in *Henry V*
Shakespeare employed it doubtless as an appropriate old
term, as indeed it was.   In *Othello* (II. i. 56) there is mention
of ' shot of courtesy ', that is, a salute.   The firing of pro-
miscuous salutes from a ship's ordnance was an old-
established practice, which continued down to the end of
the seventeenth century, by which time it had become such
a nuisance that, after many fruitless attempts, it was at last
put an end to by regulation.   The soldiers on board the ships
were employed in action as small-shot men, being armed with
muskets, a type of hand-gun recently introduced.

Shakespeare's references to the use of flags are unfortunately few.   He speaks of the white flag of truce (*Pericles*
I. iv. 72) ;   of the use of a black flag as a symbol of mourning (*ibid.* v, prol. 19), it would be interesting to know on
what authority ;   of streamers (*Hen. V*, III, chor. 6), which
were in common use at sea for decorative purposes, and of
a ' scarfed bark ' (*Merch. of V.* II. vi. 15), by which he
implies a bark decked with streamers ;   but he has no
mention of a national flag.   Flag signals did not exist at
that date.

The plays are very rich in examples of points of seamanship, by far the most ambitious being that with which *The
Tempest* opens. It must be described in detail. The ship
has been caught by a storm, and the boatswain, who was
then the master's chief officer in a merchantman, cries to
the crew to shorten sail. As reefs did not then exist, when
a ship could not bear her topsails they were either lowered
low on the mast, as a temporary measure, or furled. Here
the order was to furl the one topsail that was set. Con-
ceivably Shakespeare was contemplating a ship with but
one—a main—topmast and topsail; there were many such
even in his day. The ship is on a lee-shore, she has not
sea-room, and therein lies the greatest danger. In such
circumstances, with the stress of work and anxiety thrown
on him by the gale, the boatswain's irritation with the
troublesome passengers is most convincing. To ease the
ship the topmast is then struck.[1] This done, they lay the
ship to in the fashion then general, that is, by bringing
her as near to the wind as she would lie with only the
main-course (see p. 158) set. This was called ' trying ', or
' lying a-try '. A ship thus handled rode easily to the sea,
but drove bodily to leeward, away from the wind. If
the wind was very severe, a ship could not bear her main-
course, and this was now in Shakespeare's mind. The next
order, ' lay her a-hold,' as it stands, is meaningless ; there
was neither then, nor ever, such a term in use. It is in
all probability due to a mishearing on Shakespeare's part.
To ' lay a ship a-hull '[2] is to bring her as nearly as possible
to front the wind and sea and to make her lie in that
position with no sail set. In a severe storm this was always
done, but of course the ship drove to leeward. It soon
appears that if she continues to ' hull ', the ship must go
ashore ; the only hope lies in carrying a press of sail in
order to claw off the lee-shore, so the boatswain orders
the ' two courses', i.e. the equivalent of reefed main and
foresails, to be set. This heroic remedy, however, does not
succeed ; the ship does not gain sea-room, and presently
strikes. As the event proved, she did not ' split ' or go

---

[1] The date of the introduction of striking topmasts is unknown ; Ralegh
speaks of it as a recent invention, but on points of seamanship his evidence
is not convincing.
[2] Cf. the verb ' to hull ' = to lie a-hull, used in *Tw. N.* I. v. 217; *Rich. III*,
IV. iv. 439; *Hen. VIII*, II. iv. 197.

to pieces, as the passengers and crew feared, but her striking put an end to the boatswain's work for the present.
The whole scene is well thought out, and, with the single
verbal slip of ' a-hold ', is technically perfect.

Other references to seamanship are less elaborate, but
many are refreshingly technical; some, on the other hand,
as ' steer the helm ' (*2 Hen. VI*, I. iii. 103), ' My heart was
to thy rudder tied by the strings ' (*Ant. & Cleop.* III. ix. 57),
are erroneous. ' Loofed ' (*ibid.* III. viii. 27) is the modern
' luffed ' (brought with the head near to the wind) ; to
' bear away ' is to alter course away from the wind (*Com.
of E.* IV. i. 88) ; to ' bear up ' (*Temp.* III. ii. 3) is to put
the *helm* up so as to make the *ship* herself ' bear away ';
to ' yaw ' is to swerve from the course, but Hamlet, when
he uses the term, is deliberately talking nonsense (*Haml.*
v. ii. 121).   There is a true sea touch in

such a noise arose
As the shrouds make at sea in a stiff tempest,
As loud and to as many tunes.   (*Hen. VIII*, IV. i. 72)

' Weighed her anchorage ' (*Tit. Andr.* I. i. 73) is another
instance (like ' portage ') of the use of the abstract
for the concrete ; a similar invention is ' sternage ' in
Hen. V, III, chor. 18 ; in compensation, the mention of
an anchor ' holding ' and ' coming home ' (*Wint. Tale*,
I. ii. 213–14) are pure sea-speech; but ' holding-anchor '
(*3 Hen. VI*, v. iv. 4) is an unusual substitute for ' sheet-
anchor'.   For the rest, the word ' strike ', meaning to lower
a sail, occurs more than once : a sail may be struck for
stress of weather (*Rich. II*, II. i. 267), or in salute or sub-
mission, as 'must strike sail to spirits of vile sort' (*2 Hen. IV*,
v. ii. 18), and again, ' must strike her sail, and learn awhile
to serve ' (*3 Hen. VI*, III. iii. 5).   In

I had rather chop this hand off at a blow . . .
Than bear so low a sail to strike to thee.
(*3 Hen. VI*, v. i. 52)

there is some excess of metaphor.   Bearing a low sail is
in itself symbolical of humility; the striking is additional
to the sense.

There are frequent mentions, most of them inconsider-
able, of the many uses to which ships are put.   The references to ' the empire of the sea ' (*Ant. & Cleop.* I. ii. 198)
help us to realize that the Elizabethan age, like our own,

A GALLEON

was impregnated with the theory of Sea-Power. The
terms ' convoy ' and ' waftage ', the latter now obsolete,
occur several times ; references to sea-borne commerce
are frequent, to piracy still more so, and to sea-fighting
most frequent of all. Piracy in the Elizabethan age
still had almost the dignity of a recognized profession ;
but in James's reign, instead of remaining a source of
profit, and perhaps of illicit pride, to Englishmen, it grew
to be their bitter shame. English renegades went out to
the Moorish ports, and schooled the Moors in deep-sea
seamanship. In the sequel these southern pirates profited
by the naval weakness of the reign to scourge English
commerce, even in her own waters, heavily.

We have seen that in fighting at sea the Elizabethan
seamen learned to trust to off-fighting with the heavy
guns. The old, and still alternative method, was to ' grapple '
with the enemy, to ' board ' him, that is, to bring the two
ships into contact, and to ' enter ' a crowd of men. This
was the method in favour with those who, like the Spaniards,
crowded their ships with soldiers, and to this end they
carried hooked grappling irons at their yard-arms. It was
of this that Shakespeare was thinking when he wrote :

> Grapple him to thy heart with hooks of steel.
> (*Haml.* i. iii. 63 [1])

The metaphorical references to ' boarding ', usually in the
sense of accosting, are frequent. Mrs. Page and Mrs. Ford
use the same term with reference to Falstaff's attentions :

> *Mrs. Ford.* Boarding call you it ? I'll be sure to keep him above
> deck.
> *Mrs. Page.* So will I : if he come under my hatches, I'll never
> to sea again. (*M. Wives*, ii. i. 93–5)

The metaphor is well worked out. An enemy had not full
possession of a ship as long as he could not get below the
deck, or in other words, under the hatches.

> Clap on more sails ; pursue ; up with your fights !
> (*M. Wives*, ii. ii. 144)

describes a pursuit and the preparation for action. The
' fights ' were screens of cloth, usually coloured, laced on
above the bulwarks where they were low, in order that
the men on deck might be hidden from the enemy's fire.

Where Shakespeare's sea-language is so nearly faultless

Cf. Love's L. L. ii. i. 216.

it is natural that critics should be agog to seize upon the hint of a flaw. In two places the ' pilot's glass' (*All's W.* II. i. 168, *Merch. of V.* I. i. 25), that is, the sand-glass, is unmistakably described as an hour-glass; in *The Tempest* (I. ii. 240, v. i. 223) there are two further references to the glass, each of which is usually accepted as implying an hour-glass. It is objected that the glass in use at sea was a half-hour glass. Now it is true that Captain John Smith, writing eleven years after Shakespeare's death, described the nautical glass as being but of half an hour, which accords with later practice; but it must be said that the objection to Shakespeare's ' hour-glass' is by no means fully sustained, for no reference previous to Smith has yet been adduced in favour of the half-hour glass, which may very well have been a recent innovation, while a sea dictionary of less than one hundred years later definitely describes an hour-glass as being in use in the navy. But it is not necessary, even in this small matter, to defend Shakespeare's accuracy. Such an error would be no blemish, if error it could be proved to be. It must be decided that the poet has dealt very fairly by our sea language, and—what is of far greater importance—that he has assimilated and reproduced the splendid spirit of the great seamen who contributed so much to the glory of the Elizabethan age.

THE MEN

Not much of seamen, save the names of most of the different officers on board ship, could be learnt from Shakespeare's plays. Concerning their technical acquirements, with the one exception of seamanship, he says very little indeed; as to their victualling, he is content with a mention or two of biscuit; but of their life on board, their manners, customs, superstitions, dress, even of their moral qualities or their prospects, he tells little or nothing. Perhaps he had few opportunities of making a study of seamen until towards the end of his life; at all events, the sea characters in *The Tempest* mark a great advance on those of earlier plays. Elsewhere there is only one point as to which he shows intimate knowledge, the working of the impress service, and this only by accident, for the impress service which he describes is that used for raising land soldiers :

but the systems were so far identical that the picture he gives us is equally applicable to the navy.

No fuller description of the duties of naval officers is to be found than in the first of *Six Dialogues* (1634), by Captain Nathaniel Boteler. He goes through the list of officers from the bottom upwards, beginning with the Swabber (*Temp.* II. ii. 49, *Tw. N.* I. v. 217), whose office is 'to see the ship kept neat and clean, and that as well in the great cabin, as everywhere else betwixt the decks'. A man taken in a lie was rated 'a Liar' publicly, and was then sent to do duty under the Swabber, who employed him on the filthiest work of the ship. He held the post for a week only, but no doubt the supply of candidates for the office was steady and adequate. The Quartermaster was 'to rummage in the hold of the ship upon all occasions; to overlook the steward in delivery of victuals to the cook, and in his pumping and drawing of the beer'. These duties are now performed by the Captain of the Hold; but the Quartermaster also steered and conned the ship. The Purser was the accountant officer, with great opportunities of embezzlement, by which he not seldom profited. The Cockswain was 'to have an eye and care of the barge [1] or shallop, . . . with his whistle to cheer up and direct his gang of rowers; and this is the lowest officer in a ship who is allowed to carry a whistle'. The other officers who carry whistles are the master and the boatswain (see *Temp.* I. i. 8, *Pericles* IV. i. 63). The Boatswain had charge of all ropes, rigging, anchors, cables, sails, and flags. 'He is to take care also in especial of the long-boat; besides, he is to see all offenders punctually punished,' being thus the naval equivalent of the Provost Marshal of the army. Boteler then proceeds to describe in considerable detail the usual and customary punishments at sea, most of them sufficiently brutal, such as 'keel-raking' (better known as keel-hauling), ducking at the yard-arm, and so forth. The mildest is whipping: 'and the knaveries of the ship's boys are paid by the boatswain with the rod; and commonly this execution is done upon the Monday mornings, and is so frequently in use that some mere seamen believe in earnest that they shall not have a fair wind unless the poor boys be duly brought to the chest,

[1] In 1634 the term 'barge' had newly been applied to a ship's boat.

that is be whipped, every Monday morning '. The Master-
Gunner's office explains itself. It is observed that he and
his gang eat and sleep in the gun-room. ' The Master's
place and duty is to take the general conduction of the
way and sailing of the ship into his charge ; . . . he is to
appoint and order that some of the quartermasters be
always ready to cond her.' The Master was, in fact, the
navigating officer, using astrolabe, back-staff, cross-staff,
quadrant, and other navigating instruments.[1]

' A Lieutenant's place at sea is as on the shore ; for in
the Captain's absence he is to command in chief.' Many
of the ships employed in the 1588 campaign had lieutenants, but after that there was a break for some years,
until towards the close of James's reign they began to be
appointed again. It was recognized that the lieutenant's
office was a school for commanders, but until long afterwards no more than one lieutenant was appointed to
a ship.

' A Sea-Captain, commanding in chief in one of His
Majestie's Royal ships, hath as enlarged a charge under
his hand as any colonel at land.' He must be a man of
skill and experience.

So much for the ideal, and in Elizabeth's time such
a picture was, in the main, a true one ; but in James's
reign many worthless captains and dishonest pursers crept
in, the atmosphere was one of general neglect, and the
whole service degenerated. The men were raised by the
impress, that is, they were in theory ' prested' (or hired)
with the Queen's or King's shilling, which bound them
to their bargain. In practice they were, when need arose,
forced to serve ;[2] thus ' prest-money ' readily passed into
' press-money' (*Lear*, IV. vi. 88). The seamen class was
divided into Sailors, who were the elderly men employed
for the responsible but less active tasks ; Mariners, who

---

[1] It was noticed even early in the seventeenth century that masters of
merchant ships were in the habit of assuming the title of captain, which,
the navy thought, could be conferred only by a commission. A natural
result was that when a merchant ship was taken up for the navy, and her
master became subject to the captain commissioned to her, the master
underwent this command ' with a great deal of repining and sullenness '.
Here, of course, we have one of the causes which contributed to the inefficiency
and growing disorganization of the navy, which proceeded all through James's
reign, and reached its height about the time of his death.

[2] Cf. *Ant. & Cleop.* III. vii. 36, *Haml.* I. i. 75 ; but especially *1 Hen. IV*,
IV. ii. 13, *2 Hen. IV*, III. ii. 127.

were the able-bodied seamen ; Younkers, who were ordinary seamen ; Grommets, an intermediate rating ; and Boys.[1] The wage of the Mariner was in 1585, the year of the outbreak of war with Spain, raised from 6s. 8d. to 10s. per lunar month, and it stood uniformly at that figure till after our period closes. In addition the seaman had his victuals, which theoretically were good and abundant. He was allowed per day a gallon of beer and a pound of biscuit—Shakespeare makes a jest of its dryness at the end of a voyage (A. Y. L. II. vii. 39) ; on four days of the week he had two pounds of beef, or sometimes pork and pease ; on the remaining days he had fish, 2 oz. of butter, and ¼ lb. cheese. Boteler explains that the allowance is ' transcendent ', more than the men can eat, but that they are put off with short allowance, and complain bitterly. On long voyages the men were put at ' six upon four ', that is, six men were set to eat four men's allowance, in order to save provisions and consequently to lengthen the period during which the ship could keep the sea. But even so they would not necessarily have been badly off, unless the provisions had been bad in quality, as they very often were, and deficient in quantity, as was almost invariably the case. Dishonest victuallers ashore and equally dishonest pursers afloat took toll of them, and it too often happened that all that was left for the seaman was a shrunken ration of mouldy cheese, rancid butter, weevilly biscuit, putrid beef, and sour beer. In addition the officers were ignorant, and the men could not get their pay ; with the not unnatural result that the navy could not accomplish anything. It was almost impossible to get men during this reign. They deserted as soon as they were pressed, and such as could not succeed in deserting rapidly became sickly from semi-starvation, exposure, and want of clothes. It is almost impossible to exaggerate the picture. At the end of Elizabeth's reign the English were reputed to be ' good seamen and better pirates ' ; but under James ' they go with as great a grudging to serve in His Majestie's ships as if it were to be slaves in the galleys ', and it became necessary to fill up the ships with men who were not sea-men. The culminating point of inefficiency was exhibited by the Cadiz expedition in 1625, which in addition was so

---

[1] Shakespeare's term is ' ship-boys ', e.g. John, IV. iii. 4.

severely scourged by plague—due almost certainly to neglect of all sanitary precautions and aggravated by semi-starvation—that many of the ships returned with less than a quarter of their crew fit for duty. Boteler, who himself commanded a ship on the occasion, records that several of the ships were all but lost from sheer short-handedness. In order to conclude on a more cheerful note, let us try back to 1603, and quote a fair opinion [1] of the British seaman as he was when Fortune frowned less upon him. ' It speaks sufficiently for the courage of the Elizabethan sailor that during the whole of the reign only two English men-of-war were captured by Spain, and then only after desperate fighting against overwhelming superiority of force. The one was the *Jesus of Lubeck*, lost under the command of Sir John Hawkins at San Juan de Lua in 1568 ; the other, the famous *Revenge*, commanded by Sir Richard Grenville, in 1591, off the Azores. It speaks equally well for his seamanship afloat and the skill and good workmanship of shipwrights ashore, that, with the exception of the small *Lion's Whelp*, no dockyard-built ship was lost by stress of weather, by fire, or by running aground. During the same years, and sometimes during the same gales that English ships weathered successfully, whole Spanish fleets foundered at sea.'

[1] Oppenheim, *Administration of the Royal Navy*, p. 183.

BIBLIOGRAPHY.—During Shakespeare's lifetime there existed no English treatise on ships, their kinds, their equipment, the composition of their crews, the words of command, &c. The first English book of the kind was Captain JOHN SMITH'S *An Accidence, or the Path-way to Experience, Necessary for all Young Seamen*, 1626, a very slight performance ; it was expanded by another hand into the *Seaman's Grammar* of 1653. Sir HENRY MANWAYRING'S *The Sea-mans Dictionary*, written in or about 1625, was printed in 1644 ; and Captain NATHANIEL BOTELER'S *Six Dialogues about Sea-Services*, though written in 1634, was not published until 1685. The interest of J. MONTGOMERY'S *Treatise concerning the Navie of England* is strategical and political. It was written in 1570 (Brit. Mus., Addit. MSS. 18035), and revised in 1588 (*ibid.*, 20042), but was never printed. The best modern accounts of Tudor shipping, and especially of the navy, will be found in J. S. CORBETT'S *Drake and the Tudor Navy*, vol. i, cap. xii, and in M. OPPENHEIM'S *The Administration of the Royal Navy*. The *Mariner's Mirror*, 1911, in progress, also supplies much interesting detail.

Naval history in Shakespeare's time was represented by a few pamphlets describing particular campaigns and expeditions (see the Bibliography to vol. iii, cap. ix of the *Cambridge Modern History*); the *Naval Tracts* of Sir W. MONSON were indeed in part written, but were not published until 1732.

They have now been re-edited, by M. Oppenheim, for the Navy Records Society, 1902–14, 5 vols. The same Society's *State Papers relating to the Defeat of the Spanish Armada*, 2 vols., 1894, are also valuable.

In the latter half of the sixteenth century books on navigation and pilotage became numerous. The earliest practical treatises were not English. PEDRO DE MEDINA published his *Arte de Navegar* in 1545, and it was translated into English by J. Frampton in 1581. MARTIN CORTES's treatise on the Sphere and the Art of Navigation was translated by Richard Eden in 1561, and soon passed through several editions. Cortes's book was more popular than Medina's in England, and WILLIAM BOURNE's *Regiment of the Sea*, 1573, was designed as a supplement to it. Among English writers on navigation during this period the following must be mentioned : ROBERT NORMAN, EDWARD WRIGHT, THOMAS HOOD, and more particularly JOHN DAVIS, whose *Seaman's Secrets* appeared in 1594, followed by the *World's Hydrographical Description* in 1595. WAGENAAR's *Speculum Nauticum*, an important volume of charts, was issued in 1584, and the first English edition in 1588. (See also appendix to *Voyages and Works of John Davis*, edited by Captain A. H. MARKHAM, R.N., for the Hakluyt Society, 1880.)

Other technical works are TARTAGLIA's Colloquies concerning Artillery, which was translated into English by Cyprian Lucar in 1588. WILLIAM BOURNE's *Inventions and Devices*, 1578, is curious rather than important, and is evidence, perhaps, of acquisitiveness rather than of inventiveness in its author.

The introductory essay to MacLehose's reprint of Hakluyt by Sir WALTER RALEIGH deals with maritime enterprise and the struggle for sea-power during the era. The nautical literature of the period is well described by Commander C. N. ROBINSON, R.N., and JOHN LEYLAND in the *Cambridge History of English Literature*, vol. iv, caps. iv and v ; and in *The British Tar*. The nautical terms employed by Shakespeare are treated in W. B. WHALL's *Shakespeare's Sea Terms Explained*, 1910.

VI

VOYAGES AND EXPLORATION :
GEOGRAPHY : MAPS

BY

THE LATE J. D. ROGERS

SHAKESPEARE'S scenes are almost always laid inside what
the ancients called the civilized world, the Christians Christendom, and the geographers Europe. Africa is the centre
of interest in Greene's *Orlando*, Asia in Marlowe's *Tamburlaine*, Tunis in Massinger's *Renegado*, the Portuguese Spice
and Clove islands of Ternate and Tidore in Beaumont and
Fletcher's *Island Princess* ; but Europe is Shakespeare's
centre, and although things outside intrude now and
then, like spectres from another world, his plots, themes,
and scenes are almost exclusively European. The only
exception is *The Tempest*, which belongs partly to the
unsubstantial world of spirits and myths, partly to the
New World, but partly, too, to a fragment of Italy trans-
posed into the New World for a day or two. Although the
frontiers of Europe shift from time to time and are not the
same in the ancient and modern world, Shakespeare's plants,
so to speak, are always rooted in European soil : their
environment is invariably European.

To the ancient Greeks and Romans, Athens and Rome
were centres and the Eastern Mediterranean was part of
the civilized world ; therefore, of Shakespeare's old-
Mediterranean plays, some are identified with Rome,
others with Athens ; while Troilus hovers about Troy,
Pericles flits between Tyre, Tarsus, Ephesus, Pentapolis,
Mitylene, and Antioch, and *The Comedy of Errors* is enacted
at Ephesus, and the late tragedy of *Antony and Cleopatra*
at Alexandria. For the characters and events of old-
time plays, Shakespeare's Europe is concentrated upon
Athens and Rome, but is extended to the easternmost

recesses of the Mediterranean. In the Tudor period the Turks had pushed this frontier of Europe westward: Rhodes (1522) and Cyprus (1571) had fallen; Greece and its islands had already become Asiatic; and there was a redistribution of forces. Accordingly, in the modern-Mediterranean plays of Shakespeare—*All's Well, Much Ado, Two Gentlemen, The Winter's Tale, Twelfth Night, Othello, Romeo and Juliet,* and *The Merchant of Venice*—Athens is not named, and Rome is named only twice (*Tam. Sh.* IV. ii. 75, *Merch. of V.* IV. i. 153); and the scenes are laid in Verona, which is misdescribed as a tidal port (*Two Gent.* II. iii. 40), Venice, Padua, Milan, Mantua, Florence, Marseilles, Illyria, Sicily, or Messina; and of these only the last two figured in the old-Mediterranean plays. The eastern Mediterranean is only once to the fore. In *Othello*, Rhodes and Cyprus are physical and political storm-centres, where the Turks and Venetians would have fought had not all the Turks been drowned; and at Cyprus the Furies which watch over family life overwhelm all the leading characters in the play. With this exception—if it is an exception—the modern plays shun the eastern Mediterranean, Greece, middle Italy, and all the principal places in the old-Mediterranean plays. The sea is the same sea as of old, and swarms with pirates (*Merch. of V.* I. iii. 24), like those of which Pompey wanted to rid it (*Ant. & Cleop.* II. vi. 36); and Italy is still the place where Spaniards, Neapolitans, Frenchmen, Englishmen, Scotchmen, Germans, and Polish Counts Palatine meet (*Merch. of V.* I. i); and an occasional ' Moor ' (Mohammedan) lends an Asiatic or African tinge. Italy is still cosmopolitan and dominates the Mediterranean, but the centre of political gravity has shifted, and for Shakespeare, whose instincts draw him towards places where life is rich and full, Italy and the Mediterranean mean different things in ancient and modern times.

North of the Mediterranean the continental borders of Europe were differently defined by different writers, and even when defined by the same words, fluctuated from day to day. Richard Eden and Giles Fletcher held that the Don was its eastern boundary, and so did Robert Greene, who spoke of ' Tanais whose swift declining floods environ rich Europa to the *north* '.[1] The question

---

[1] *The History of Orlando Furioso*, 1594, ll. 8, 9.

how far Christendom extended was answered with equal vagueness.

Poland, whose frontiers varied perpetually, passed in popular estimation for the easternmost Christian power, because its king fought against the Turks, and it was in communion with Rome and used Latin as its official language. In 1569 Poland reached the Baltic on its north, followed, crossed, and recrossed the Dnieper on its east, and all but touched the Black Sea on its south. Of his three east-European plays, *Hamlet* is localized at Helsingör in Denmark, *Measure for Measure* at Vienna, and the ship in *The Winter's Tale* 'touched upon the deserts of Bohemia' [1]. Other countries are mentioned incidentally: in *Measure for Measure*, Hungary, where there are wars, and Poland, whither the Duke pretends to go; in *Hamlet*, Norway and Poland. The length of 'a Poland winter' is alluded to in *The Comedy of Errors* (III. ii. 101). Norway, which did not extend its civilization to its furthest bounds, was the northern or north-western frontier of Shakespeare's Europe. Like every Elizabethan, he was familiar with the 'Muscovites or Russians' (*Love's L. L.* v. ii. 121), however he may have placed them geographically.

Beyond these European limits lay the unknown, or hardly known, wonderland of discovery and romance, where monsters dwelt and miracles were common, and which Shakespeare regarded much as every instinctive geographer regards what lies half within and half without his intellectual horizon. These men look at their own country through the right end, and at other countries through the wrong end of the telescope. The Chinese point of view was described by a great Italian Jesuit traveller, Matteo Ricci, who traversed China from Canton to Peking, and from Nankin to Cheng-tu-fu (?), and sent messengers from Peking to Su-chau to greet another great Jesuit traveller, Benedictus Goes, who came from Lahore in India by Cabul, Badakshan, the Pamirs, Yarkand, Turfan, and Khamil to die at Su-chau in 1607. Between them Goes and Ricci learned more about China and the way thither than any one since the time of Marco Polo 300 years before, or any one until 260 years later. They announced for the first time

---

[1] Following R. Greene, *Pandosto*, 1588.

that China was really and indeed Marco Polo's Cathay; and Ricci studied amongst other things the geographical ideas of the Chinese. ' They had maps ', he wrote, ' pretending a description of the world, but presented only their fifteen provinces with the sea and a few islands, and the names of such kingdoms as they had heard of, all which kingdoms scarcely equalled one province of China. They now wondered to see themselves straitened in an eastern *corner* of the world. They have a conceit that the Heavens are round, the Earth square, and their empire to be seated in the midst thereof.' China was all but all the world : it was four-cornered, and beyond it there were unimportant seas and islands which might mend or mar the symmetry, but hardly altered the outline of the world, fifteen-sixteenths of which were Chinese. All imperfect instinctive geographers argue thus. One man compares the world to a circle, another to a triangle, another to a square, because the wide-awake world of which he knows something definite resembles a circle, triangle, or square; and the dreamland which surrounds it, as Oceanus surrounded the Homeric world, though dotted here and there with seas, islands, and great shadowy names, is a mere addendum. Shakespeare, too, wrote as if he thought thus. His real living and working world consisted of the fifteen or more kingdoms of Europe, which fronted Turks and Moors on its south, Turks and Tatars on its east, the polar regions on its north, and the Atlantic on its west. The British Isles were in one corner of the oblong, and

Come the three corners of the world in arms   (*John*, v. vii. 116)

against the British Isles, they would prevail. The misty region which encompassed Europe contained islands only, not continents ; and discoverers sailed from Europe merely in order to ' discover islands far away' (*Two Gent.* i. iii. 9); and as for the east and west Indies—that is to say, nearly all Asia and all America—they were little appendices to his book of life, which book was Europe.

In a passage which, like most of his passages referring to 'the beyond', is little more than an 'aside', and does not affect the main action of the play, he refers to ' the new map with the augmentation of the Indies' (*Tw. N.* iii. ii. 88). A peculiar interest is attached to this map, not because it includes the Indies—every map of the world published during the sixteenth century did that—but because we know its date (1600) and its authors. Edward Wright drew it, Richard Hakluyt and John Davis helped in its preparation, and it was the first English map that was drawn on what are called Mercator's principles of projection,—principles which were discovered, not by Mercator, it would appear, but by Edward Wright. Nor were these the only points of interest in the map, which made a great stir at the time.[1] It appealed, however, to Shakespeare because its rhumblines[2] illustrated Malvolio's smiles ; and it appeals to commentators on Shakespeare as showing that although Shakespeare knew something of Hakluyt, who dedicated himself to a study of what was outside Europe, yet in spite of maps Shakespeare did not write of the new-found new world and the new-found old world as momentous additions to the world in which his characters lived and moved. Being an idealist, he did not measure but weighed men and things, and he weighed them in the scales of destiny: his arithmetic was political ; places where ' Amurath an Amurath succeeds ' (*2 Hen. IV*, v. ii. 48) did not count for much ; and vast spaces full of emptiness or of vain things meant nothing to him. When he wrote of the stars and sun,

> Doubt thou the stars are fire,
> Doubt that the sun doth move, (*Haml.* ii. ii. 115-16)—

he wrote as a man for whom this world's joys and sorrows blotted out astronomy ; even so Europe fascinated him with so powerful a spell that what was not Europe was mere dust, possibly gold dust, but mere dust in the balance in comparison with Europe. Nevertheless some of this dust is scattered carelessly over his plays, sometimes as ornament, sometimes to catch the ear of the gallery with topical allusions, sometimes as part of the supernatural mysticism which hovers around his plays ; and it serves more serious uses in *The Tempest* and in the closing scene of *Henry VIII*.

---

[1] Hakluyt Society Publications, No. LIX, *Voyages of John Davis*, p. lxxxv; accompanied by *Map of the World, A.D. 1600*, reproduced here.

[2] Rhumb-lines were a set of straight lines drawn through a point on a map or chart to indicate the course of a ship sailing continuously in any direction.

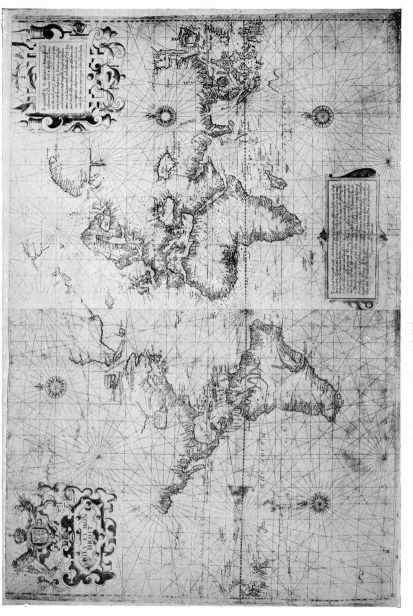

MAP OF THE WORLD 1600

To Hakluyt the non-European world was the region of heroic endeavours and sufferings, where men lived and made history, and won new worlds for humanity and England ; and accordingly to Hakluyt and to his predecessor Richard Eden, and his successor Samuel Purchas, we will now turn, for they alone among English writers have a connected story to tell of these parts.

Eden's *History of Travayle* was published in 1577, and in his history Spaniards and Portuguese bear the chief part. Hakluyt published the first edition of his *Principal Navigations* in 1589, and the second enlarged edition in 1598–1600. Down to the date of his death (1616) he went on collecting material which fell into the less skilful hands of Purchas, and was published by him under the title of *Hakluytus Posthumus, or Purchas his Pilgrimes* (1625); but some of it had already appeared in other forms. Both Hakluyt and Purchas emphasize the greatness of the English adventurers and of English initiative. Hakluyt died in the same year as Shakespeare, but he was some twelve years older. The collections of his ' great prose epic of the English nation ' are valuable for what they relate, and the directness with which things are related ; but the narrators, though often simple sailors, sometimes attained grandeur, as it were, by accident. John Hartop's narrative begins thus : ' Man being born of a woman, living a short time is replenished with many miseries, which some know by reading of histories, many by the view of others' calamities, and I by experience ' ; and he makes us feel what Shakespeare called 'sea-sorrow' (*Temp.* i. ii. 170). Francis Fletcher described a storm at sea thus : ' The seas were rolled up from the depths . . . as if it had been a scroll of parchment ; ' [1] and William Strachey thus : ' The sea swelled above the clouds and gave battle to Heaven. It could not be said to rain ; the waters like whole rivers did flood in the air ; ' and many other sea-scenes in Hakluyt bear comparison with those in *The Tempest* or *Othello*. But Hakluyt's volumes are primarily plain records of 'moving accidents by flood and field' (*Oth.* i. iii. 135), told by the men who did or suffered. These doings and sufferings were too tragic for tragedy, and on a gigantic scale ; and in them England bore the chief part.

[1] Hakl. Soc. Pub., No. XVI, *The World Encompassed*, p. 85.

The first volume in the epic of discovery had just closed when Hakluyt (1552 ?) and Shakespeare (1564) were born. In 1492 and onwards Columbus discovered islands and shores in the Caribbean Sea, which he mistook for India ; and then Cortes conquered Mexico and Pizarro Peru. The Indians whom Columbus saw were called 'Caribes Canibales', or in Italian ' Canibali ', and their land ' Caniba ' or ' Calibana '[1], and they were said to eat men. Their alleged habits added another word to the languages of western Europe, and this word amused Englishmen with its unwonted ending and its interchanges of ' l ', ' n ', and ' r ', so that Shakespeare's clowns confused it with ' Hannibal ' (Meas. for M. II. i. 188; 2 Hen. IV, II. iv. 179), and Shakespeare himself metamorphosed it into Caliban.[2] In 1500 Vicente Pinzon discovered Brazil and the river Amazon, and there ' wrote on the rinds of pine-trees the names of the king and queen', even as her lover carved the name of Rosalind on the barks of trees in As You Like It.[3]

In 1519 Magellan sailed from Spain through the Strait of Magellan—Terra Australis on his port and America on his starboard—into the ' South Sea of discovery ' (A. Y. L. III. ii. 208), and so to the Philippines, where he died; and one of his ships straggled on to Ternate and Timor, and came home by the Cape of Good Hope. In coasting along Patagonia he saw huge men clad in llama-skins—hair outside, and head, ears, and tail complete—and heard them bellowing like bulls to ' their great devil Setebos ', whose name lives as the name of Caliban's god and tormentor. In 1527 Alvaro de Saavedra sailed from West Mexico to the Portuguese Spice Islands, and those few who survived returned to Panama. In 1535-7 Pedro de Mendoça and Juan de Vadillo opened up ways from the mouth of the La Plata to Arica on the Pacific and to the Gulf of Uraba on the Caribbean Sea, this last being ' the greatest discovery that hath been heard of by land '—but a greater immediately followed. In 1540 Francisco de Orellana passed from Quito

---

[1] Hakl. Soc. Pub., No. II, Columbus, pp. 38, 114, and 124 ; No. LII, Magellan, p. 48 ; L. de Gomara, Hist. Gen., chaps. lvii and ccxviii.

[2] Christobal, Mogor, Argiers, and many other names familiar to travellers, exemplified the interchange of ' l ' and ' r ', so that there was ample precedent for the metathesis. The joke on Hannibal is also found in Ben Jonson : see Every Man in his Humour, III. iv.

[3] Cf. T. Lodge's Rosalynde.

on the Pacific coast over snow mountains, through tropical
forests, and down the Amazon and its tributaries the Coca
and Napo to the Atlantic—a land journey as long as a
traverse of the Atlantic, and as much exposed to the equa-
torial sun as Saavedra's sea journey. Well might José de
Acosta ridicule the old-world theorists who declared that
no one could live in the Torrid Zone ! In North America
Spaniards discovered the Bermudas, Florida, prairies where
' crookbacked oxen' browsed,[1] the mouth of the Mississippi,
and the Gulf of California. Gonzalo de Oviedo (1515)
mused as he watched flying fishes and cormorants pursuing and destroying one another off the shores of the
Bermudas, how ' in the self-same peril do men live '; or,
as Shakespeare's fishermen put it,—' Master,' said one,
' I marvel how the fishes live in the sea ' ; and the other
answered, ' Why, as men do a-land ; the great ones eat up
the little ones' (Pericles, II. i. 29–32). It is difficult to follow
the gist of Hakluyt's narrative without being turned aside
by Shakespearian echoes or echoes of echoes ; but the gist
was this : that before 1552 Spaniards or Portuguese had
discovered all that part of America which lay south of the
latitude of Europe, and which the map of 1600 outlines so
well ; and what they had discovered they had appropriated
and monopolized.

Similarly, the Portuguese had discovered the west and
east coasts of Africa and India, the entrances of the Red
Sea and Persian Gulf, Burma, Malacca, Siam, Sumatra—
where men ate men and many had ' tails like unto sheep'—
Abyssinia—where Prester John (Much Ado, II. i. 278),
after being hunted throughout the length and breadth of
Asia, had been located since the fourteenth century—
China, and Japan ; and these scenes of their discoveries
were dotted with forts upon the shore and visited by their
trading vessels year in and year out. Africa, however, is
a mere coast-line, and the Persian and Indian outlines
are botched in the map of 1600. The Portuguese, like
the Spaniards, claimed for their own exclusive use the
countries they discovered. Portuguese discoveries left their
mark on every shore of the eastern hemisphere, too ; and,
like Spanish discoveries, they never passed north of the
latitude of Africa except in the case of Japan, where the

---

[1] Gomara, op. cit., chap. ccxv.

Portuguese had no establishment until after the date of Hakluyt's birth.

'Discovery' in the sense which we have been using the word implied permanence as well as novelty. If discovery meant mere novelty, Italians were the great European discoverers of this period; but they came and went like Nicolo de Conti, who in the fifteenth century reached the Cambayan Gulf in India from Persia, and explored Socotra, the Ganges, and the coasts of Ceylon, Burma, Java, and Sumatra, which he and therefore his Portuguese successors wrongly identified with Taprobana; or like Lodovico di Barthema (1503), who went from Damascus to Mecca by land and thence to Aden Zeila and India by sea—for Italians had no country to back them; or else, like Columbus, Magellan's pilot, and the rest, they took service under the Portuguese and Spaniards to whose account their originality was credited. Italians found everything but founded nothing. They were cosmopolitan pioneers. And long before the Italians, Arabians roamed over the Indian Ocean, saw the 'oxfish' or dugong of Sumatra, the camphor trees of India, and the pearl-divers of Ceylon, and heard of giant birds in Madagascar, and giant tortoises in India, as may be read in the story of *Sinbad the Sailor*. Discovery implied something new, but also implied a permanent opening up of new lands by Europeans for Europeans. And in this sort of discovery Portugal was as supreme in the eastern as Spain was in the western hemisphere—south, that is to say, of a line which, with the one exception of Japan, coincided with the latitude of Gibraltar. And Portugal excluded other nations with a jealousy equal to, but not so effectual as, the jealousy of Spain.

What, then, was left for England to do? Robert Thorne answered thus (1527): Between them the Portuguese and Spaniards had proved 'no land uninhabitable nor sea unnavigable'; they had followed the equator round the world and had found human beings or calm seas from end to end. The finger of Fate pointed north: therefore let Englishmen boldly cross the North Pole to their far western or far eastern goal.

In 1497 Cabot had proved an English Columbus and had discovered for England Newfoundland and the neighbouring American continent. After him English fishermen had

MARTIN FROBISHER.
By CORNELIS KETEL

flocked to these new haunts of the codfish continuously; but French and, to a less extent, Spanish and Portuguese fishermen had followed in their wake. No new or great thing had been done by English discoverers except this, and this discovery pointed north-west. The new departure which Thorne advocated was not undertaken until 1553, or the year after Hakluyt was born, and then it was diverted to the north-east. Down to that date or thereabouts, English merchants like Richard Chancellor and Anthony Jenkinson were busy in the Mediterranean: after that date wars and pirates drove them from the Mediterranean for thirty years, and so, with the feeling that England was behindhand in the new European expansion, they began to look towards other points of the compass. First of all they attempted a north-eastern passage to Cathay. These attempts ushered in what may be called the second volume in the history of modern discoveries.

In 1553 Sir Hugh Willoughby, Chancellor, and others set out in three ships, rounded North Cape in Norway, sighted Nova Zembla, which they named Willoughby Land; and then a crowning tragedy and a strange success happened. Willoughby's two ships were frozen in at Arzina, near Kegor and Kola in Lapland, and every man on the ships died of starvation during the winter, but the ships survived. Chancellor, in the *Bonaventure*, reached Kholmogori, near where Archangel now is, and travelled up the frozen Dwina, and then overland to Moscow, which he reached in winter. He was received as an ambassador, and returned next year to Kholmogori and thence by sea to England with letters to his sovereign from ' the Duke of Moscovie and Emperor of Russia'. This exploit was described as the discovery of Russia and Moscovy; discovery being used in the sense in which Spaniards and Portuguese used it. The discovered country was thought to be in Asia, and was reached for the first time and for many years afterwards by the new English way from the Arctic Circle. In 1555 Chancellor set out for Moscow by the same route with the *Bonaventure* and another ship; and when in 1556 he retraced his course to England he was not alone. The first Russian ambassador to England accompanied him: so did Willoughby's two ships, which had been found, and which he now manned from his own. The *Bonaventure* was wrecked off Scotland, but the Russian ambassador was saved and reached London. Not so Chancellor, who was drowned with most of his crew. Willoughby's two ships and all their new crew were lost. Thus perished the ships and almost all the men who took part in the first new great thing which England did; but Stephen and William Burrough, Charles Pet, and some other unknown men were saved, and England was undaunted. The Muscovy Company was formed in 1555, and, in spite of all these losses, carried on what Chancellor began.

The work branched off in two directions. Anthony Jenkinson (1557–9) went from England to Kholmogori and Moscow, and thence passed by the Volga to the Caspian, which he was the first Englishman to see. From the Caspian he went by the Mangishlak Peninsula to Urgenj, the old capital of Khiva, and to Bokhara, which is half-way between Brindisi and Peking. He was not only the first, but, until 260 years afterwards, the last Englishman to enter Khiva and Bokhara, and at Bokhara Indian and Chinese merchants swarmed with their wares. War barred further progress, and he returned to Moscow with twenty-five freed Russian slaves and a yak's tail. His map (1562) showed Bokhara on the Jaxartes (wrongly) and the Jaxartes flowing into the Sea of Aral (rightly), which he called Lake Kitaia, and the Sea of Aral emptying into the Ob (wrongly); and men began to say that Lake Kitaia must be close by if not in Cathay, and that the Ob assuredly led to Cathay, though Jenkinson knew how wide Asia really was. Old illusions as to the width of Asia reasserted themselves in a new shape.

Jenkinson's later voyages led him from Kholmogori to the neighbourhood of Baku and the Caucasus, where he heard of a two-horned, horse-eared, cow-tailed giant, and to Tabriz and Kazvin, where he saw the Shah or, as he was more commonly called, the Sophy (*Merch. of V.* II. i. 25 ; *Tw. N.* II. v. 199) of Persia ; and English commercial agents soon travelled from Moscow to Persia and through western Persia by Tabriz, Kazvin, and Persepolis from north to south. In ' discovering ' Russia from the north, Englishmen got behind the Hanseatic leaguers, who kept on and near the Baltic : in 'discovering' Persia from Russia they got behind the Italians, who approached it from the Mediterranean. And if the journey

to Bokhara had borne fruit they would have established
communications with India and China behind the backs
of the Portuguese. Meanwhile, curious confusions between
the true Caucasus and the Himalayas, which were also
called the Caucasus, tended once more to contract Asia
and blur the geographical perspective.

Willoughby's and Chancellor's work was also continued
along the north shore of Asia. Stephen Burrough (1556),
Arthur Pet, and Charles Jackman (1580) passed Nova
Zembla and sailed into the Kara Sea, Jackman and his
crew dying an unknown death on their way back. Before
1584 an English ship reached the mouth of the Ob and was
wrecked and the wrecked men were murdered.

Valuable Arctic trade arose with the Lapps of Kegor and
Kola—near where Willoughby died—and with the Samoyeds
east of the White Sea,—in stockfish (dried cod), seals, whales,
walrus (which were often called unicorns, sea-oxen, sea-
horses, or by the Lapp word morse), furs, animal oil, and
blubber. But the Hollanders already plied this trade at
Kola in 1565, and reached the mouth of the Dwina in 1578;
and in 1586 Dutch, French, and English ships forgathered
at what was then the new fort of Archangel : so that
English discoveries could not be described as monopolies.
In 1596–7 William Barents, a Frieslander, passed round the
north of Nova Zembla, built a house on its north-east
coast, wintered there, but died on the journey home.
This house was marked on the map of 1600, but was
never seen by any human eye until 1871, when Captain
Carlsen landed there and searched and found among the
ruins a Dutch translation of the record of Pet's and Jackman's Voyage of 1580. Thus the principal original exploit
of the Dutchmen in these seas was to some extent inspired
and directed by Englishmen.

Ramusio regarded these expeditions as the one English
contribution to the history of discovery : although Shakespeare's references to ' an icicle on a Dutchman's beard '
(*Tw. N.* iii. ii. 30–1) implies that he associated polar expeditions not with Englishmen but with Dutchmen, who were
in some respects the pupils of the Englishmen.

Russian embassies reached London in 1567 and 1582, as
well as in 1556, by the Arctic highway, and ' frozen
Muscovits ', ' sea-sick from Muscovy ', figured in *Love's*

Labour 's Lost (v. ii. 266, 394), not indeed in the play, which
is European, but in a masque within the play. English
embassies to Moscow were frequent and continuous, and
one of the ambassadors, Giles Fletcher, wrote a classical
account of the strange country—*Of the Russe Common
Wealth* (1591). He says of the Lapps, much as others had
said, that 'for practice of witchcraft and sorcery they pass
all nations in the world', thereby justifying Antipholus's
reference to 'Lapland sorcerers' (*Com. of E.* IV. iii. II).
As for the Samoyeds, they were cannibals, and according to
some the word meant 'self-eaters' and not 'of themselves'
or indigenous. They resorted to the mouth of the Ob,
where invisible trumpets blared, and 'Slata Baba or
the Golden Hag' was supposed to utter oracles; but
Fletcher believed that winds made the music, and that
Slata Baba was really a rock which 'may seem to bear
the shape of a ragged woman with a child in her
arms', that their sorcerers drew the people there, pre-
tended to cut off their own heads and put them on
again, spoke oracles, and persuaded the people that the
'Golden Hag' was the speaker. Witches are common; but
the combination of one witch and one child is rare, so that
perhaps Sycorax and her 'hag-seed' Caliban may be far-
off reflections of the Golden Hag and her child. Giles
Fletcher heard, too, of 'men of prodigious shape—some
overgrown with hair like wild-beasts, others have heads
like dogs and their faces in their breasts without necks '—
and of 'fish with head, eyes, nose, mouth, hands, feet, and
other members utterly of human shape'. In Shakespeare
Caliban is a 'puppy-headed monster', 'a moon-calf', 'a
strange fish', 'half a fish and half a monster'.

> *Antonio.*   . . . Travellers ne'er did lie,
> Though fools at home condemn them.
> *Gonzalo.*   If in Naples
> I should report this now, would they believe me
> If I should say I saw such islanders?
>
>   . . . When we were boys,
> Who would believe that there were mountaineers
> Dew-lapp'd like bulls, whose throats had hanging at them
> Wallets of flesh? or that there were such men
> Whose heads stood in their breasts? which now we find
> Each putter-out of five for one will bring us
> Good warrant of.   (*Temp.* III. iii. 26–7, 43–9)

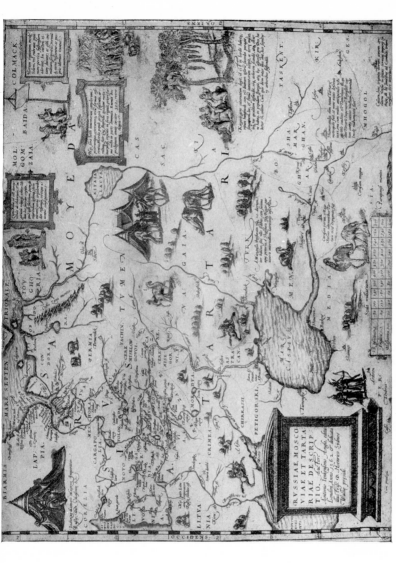

ANTHONY JENKINSON'S MAP OF RUSSIA

MUSCOVY AND TARTARY 1562

Othello, too, speaks of

> The Anthropophagi, and men whose heads
> Do grow beneath their shoulders.   (*Oth.* i. iii. 144–5)

If Shakespeare's monsters are of Asiatic origin, he keeps within dramatic probability in the treatment of his ox-like, fishy, goitred, dog-faced, headless models; and his pictures of cannibals, skin-clad savages, and the like are less grotesque than those in the prose writers and travellers of his day.

Our scene now shifts to the south.

When English merchants turned their backs upon the Mediterranean in 1550, they went to the Canaries (1550), Morocco (1551), and the Guinea Coast beyond Cape Verde (1553). In its wider sense the Guinea Coast included Gambia, Sierra Leone, and the Grain Coast, and even all the coast beyond Morocco to the equator; but in its narrower sense it included only the Ivory, Gold, and Slave Coasts, which lie due east and west of one another. Englishmen clung to the Grain, Ivory, Gold, and Slave Coasts, and the early voyagers used to take a few black men to England, who, after learning English, were restored to their kith and kin, between whom and their white teachers they proved useful intermediaries. The Portuguese, whose principal stronghold was on the Gold Coast at El Mina, tried to prevent Anglo-African trade by force, but the coast-line was long and they were few. French trade flourished for the most part near Cape Verde, but French ships obstructed or assisted English voyagers on their way to the Gold Coast in 1556. Spanish fleets while on their way to the West Indies were sometimes encountered in the Canaries, but not farther south; and Portuguese, Spaniards, and Frenchmen exchanged shots from time to time with their English rivals.

The arctic voyages had at least been free from the curse of war, from which these coasts were never quite free; and the climate was even more deadly than war. The first Guinea voyage of 1553 reached Benin on the west of the Slave Coast, and 'of seven score men came home to Plymouth scarcely forty and of them many died'; in the Guinea voyage of 1554, twenty-four died; in that of 1557 of three ships only one returned, and with only twelve sound men. Arctic 'sea-sorrows' were surpassed by those of tropical Africa.

In 1562 West Africa became the half-way house to the West Indies; and John Hawkins (knighted 1588) strengthened a fatal link between the old and new worlds, that link being the slave trade. In three vessels aggregating 260 tons, and with a crew of 100 men, he transported 300 African slaves, whom he had captured from their homes in Sierra Leone or wrested from Portuguese slave-dealers, to Hispaniola (Hayti), where he sold them to Spanish masters for the produce of sugar plantations and ranches, or else for indigenous West Indian spices and drugs. Hawkins did not himself create the trade, for there were negroes at Ulloa, the then port of Mexico, before his first voyage; but he followed a bad example. And these dark deeds in the history of the Atlantic had still darker sequels. In 1564–5 Hawkins repeated his exploit of 1562; and in 1567 he and Francis Drake (knighted 1581) were once more at Cape Verde with six ships, passed south-east, engaged in native wars against natives, and plundered Portuguese ships, by which means he obtained 500 negroes. After selling some of them in the West Indies or on the southern mainland at the Rio de la Hacha and Cartagena, he was caught by a hurricane and put in at Ulloa, to refit his ships and sell the rest of his living merchandise. His head was now in the lion's mouth. Hardly had he arrived when thirteen Spanish ships surprised, saluted, entertained, and treacherously attacked him. Only two of his ships, the *Minion* and the *Judith*, escaped. The *Minion* fled from Ulloa under Hawkins with 200 men, who were after a few days forced to feed on 'cats, dogs, mice, rats, parrots, and monkies', even as 'poor Tom' fed on

> Mice and rats and such small deer. (*Lear*, III. iv. 142)

Accordingly half the famished crew were landed, and the remainder, after many losses and with the help of fresh men, just reached home, Drake having returned home in the *Judith* a few days earlier.

The Englishmen who were captured by the Spaniards at Ulloa were slain or reserved for the calculated cruelties of the Inquisition. Men were hung up by the arms alive, stabbed, whipped, racked, mocked, burnt, made galley-slaves, or 'assigned' slaves, while they met with stray acts of kindness from friars. John Hartop was one of

Hawkins's men; and his cry of anguish which we have quoted (p. 175) was wrung from him by twenty-two years' experience of the Inquisition. The habit of torturing Indians and Africans had hardened Spanish hearts. Drake found a negro who had been sentenced to be whipped raw, set in the sun, and tortured to death by mosquitoes. An Indian was smeared with brimstone, fired, restored to health, anointed with honey, chained to a tree 'where mosquitoes flocked about him like moats in the sun and did pitifully sting him'—these mosquitoes being like wasps—'than which death had been better, as he said'. When Autolycus threatened the clown that he 'shall be flayed alive; then 'nointed over with honey, set on the head of a wasp's nest . . . recovered . . . then, raw as he is', exposed to the sun and 'with flies blown to death' (*Wint. Tale*, IV. iii. 816–25), some among the audience of Shakespeare's day must have shuddered, for they had seen it, or read of it, and knew that the Spaniards did these very things. Spanish hostility and cruelty entered like iron into Hawkins's and Drake's hearts, and thenceforth there was an unintermitting series of raids led by Englishmen against the West Indies, and, when Portugal became part of Spain (1580), against the East Indies. Whatever may be thought of Hawkins and Drake, or their methods, they discovered that freedom to sail the principal seas and oceans must be surrendered for ever or else fought for to the death; and they lived and died fighting for it. This fight in which they were protagonists gathered to a head in the attempted invasion of England by the Armada, which Hakluyt rightly treats as part of that world-drama which is his proper theme; it lasted on in the West Indies and elsewhere until Queen Elizabeth died, and raged in the Red Sea, the Indian Ocean, and the Persian Gulf until Sir Henry Middleton and John Saris blockaded the Strait of Bab-el-Mandib (1611), and Captain Thomas Best won the naval battle of Surat (1615), and Ormuz was taken from the Portuguese (1622); that is to say, it was not finished until after Shakespeare's death.

The fight for the dominion of the seas was world-wide; and it not only glanced off from West Africa to the West Indies, but from West Africa to the East Indies and the Pacific. West Africa, to which we will now return, was for Englishmen the starting-point for the Pacific Ocean before it became the starting-point for the Indian Ocean. In 1577 Drake reached West Africa with five ships, impressed a Portuguese pilot, crossed to the La Plata, coasted down south, saw Magellan's giants ' covered . . . to their buttocks ' with hair, heard them roar 'Setteboth', and entered the Strait of Magellan with three of his ships, one of which was lost there, and one returned. On emerging into the Pacific, he was driven south to 57° S. lat., and saw ' the Atlantic and the South Sea meet in a most large and free scope '. He declared that Magellan's ' Terra Australis ' was a myth, and the map of 1600 adopted his view. Thence, led by captive Spanish or Greek pilots, he raided the American coasts up to Guatulco in Mexico; then sailed west and north until he reached 48° N. lat. in what is now Washington State, then coasted south to 38° 30' (San Francisco ?), where he landed and made, or thought that he made, treaties with the Indians. All the coast north of the Gulf of California was new, and he named his landing-place Nova Albion. Returning south, but not far south, he crossed the Pacific—by a variant of what was then the Spanish trade route from the Philippines to Mexico—passed the Philippines, and made a lasting friendship with the people of Ternate in the Portuguese Spice and Clove Islands. He thought that America joined or all but joined Asia, a little north of 48°—a view which the map of 1600 corrected ; otherwise his geography, so far as it was new, was true. From Ternate he returned home by Java, the Cape of Good Hope, and Sierra Leone, having made the second circumnavigation of the world, and the first circumnavigation conducted throughout under the same command. The ship returned with ' gold, silver, silk, pearls, and precious stones ' (1580).

Immediately the Spanish Government dispatched Pedro Sarmiento (1581) to fortify and garrison the Strait of Magellan with over 400 men and women ; one of whom was rescued by Thomas Candish, or Cavendish, the third circum-navigator; but the rest were starved or slain by savages. Candish's voyage (1586–8) was a replica of Drake's, and he returned rich beyond the dreams of avarice. In trying to repeat his exploit (1591–2) Candish passed—but returned —through part of the Strait of Magellan, seeing 'men having vizors on their faces like dogs' faces, or else their faces are dogs' faces indeed ', and writing ' I lived hourly as he that expecteth death '. Mutiny, disease, defeat, and storm did their work. He made for St. Helena, 'either to make ourselves happy by mending or ending,' and died ; and a sailless ship with fifteen starved men returned, but ' on five only did the labour of the ship rely '. Allusions to Drake's ship which went round the world and was on view at Deptford [1] and to Candish's Golden Voyage [2] are numerous in contemporary poets and dramatists, but are conspicuous by their absence in Shakespeare, unless Setebos and dog-faced Indians came from them and not from the sources which have been mentioned.

The next circumnavigators were Dutch (1598–1601), with English pilots, William Adams and Captain Melis, and their goal was the Dutch East Indies, to which John Davis, the English pilot, conducted a Dutch squadron from the Cape of Good Hope at the same time. John Davis returned to England in 1600 and probably helped Wright in locating Achin, Bantam, and other East Indian towns upon his map of 1600. The Dutch object was colonization, but that was not yet the English object, although Dutchmen had been preceded by English travellers and privateers in the eastern hemisphere. The first English take-off for the East Indies was the Mediterranean, and the second was West Africa ; and as soon as colonial aims were entertained the second was substituted for the first.

Shortly after 1580 treaties were made with the Turkish authorities and English ships re-entered the Mediterranean ; and amongst these ships the *Tiger* of London, of which Alderman Martins was owner and Thomas Rickman was master, used to visit Tripoli in Syria and Alexandria in Egypt. This is the ship of which Shakespeare's witches sang—

Her husband 's to Aleppo gone, master o' the Tiger.

(*Macb.* I. iii. 7)

Tripoli was the port of Aleppo. In 1583 John Newbery and Ralph Fitch, of London, embarked on the *Tiger*, sailed to Tripoli, and travelled by Aleppo, Birejik on the Euphrates,

---

[1] Chapman, *Eastward Hoe*, III. iii ; Ben Jonson, *Every Man in his Humour*, I. iii ; Abraham Cowley, *Upon the Chair made out of the Reliques of Sir Francis Drake's Ship*, &c.   [2] Dekker, *Westward Hoe*, v. iii, &c.

and Bagdad to Bussora, and sailed thence to Ormuz and
Goa, Newbery having already been by that route as far
as Ormuz in 1580–2. There they were arrested by the
Portuguese, but escaped, and after an adventurous journey
overland by Bijapur, Golkonda, Sirpur, Burhanpur, Man-
dogarh, Ujjain, and Sironj, they reached Agra, where they
presented letters from Queen Elizabeth to the Great Mogul.
Newbery on his former journey had travelled from Ormuz
to Kazvin and Tabriz—which was already frequented by
Englishmen from Kholmogori and Moscow—and thence by
Erivan and Erzeroum in Armenia and by Tokat in Asia
Minor to the Bosphorus; and he now resolved to go overland
from Agra to Aleppo or Constantinople. He reached Lahore
and disappeared. John Mildenhall afterwards came from
Aleppo by Birejik, Bitlis in Kurdistan, Nakhichevan in
Armenia, Kazvin, Yazd, Seistan, Kandahar, and Lahore to
Agra (1599 et seq.), and Joseph Salbancke (1609), Richard
Steele and Thomas Coryat (1615) travelled over a similar
route with success ; in spite of which it proved, like Jenkin-
son's route to Bokhara, a failure. If it had proved a success,
it would have been the greatest original English achievement in overland enterprise that had yet been attained.
Fitch meanwhile descended the Jumna and Ganges, visited
Bassein and Pegu in Burma, reached Malacca, and after
revisiting the coasts of India, returned to England (1591).
Hakluyt published Fitch's account of the Portuguese East
Indies, which is the earliest first-hand account of India by
an Englishman ; and which, although it borrowed largely
from a translation of Caesar Frederick's descriptions, con-
tained shrewd original information—for instance, of a
Chinese trade route through Bhotan into India and by
Zimme into Burma.

The land-routes and partial land-routes to India were
foredoomed to failure, while the sea-route existed ; but the
sea-route was monopolized by Portugal. This monopoly
was attacked by Sir James Lancaster (1591–4) and Benjamin
Wood (1596–7). Both voyages belong to the history of
privateering rather than discovery; and both aimed not
at India but at Portuguese East Africa and Malacca.
Lancaster returned westward to the West Indies, from
which very few of his crew returned, owing to mutiny,
sickness, warfare, and storms off 'the still-vex'd Ber-

moothes' (*Temp*. I. ii. 229). In 1600 the English East
India Company was formed, and Sir James Lancaster, Sir
John Middleton, Sir Henry Middleton, and John Davys
led out to the East Indies, but not to India, the first expedition of the English East India Company, John Davys
having already performed the same service for the Dutch
Company. After this expedition Anglo-Indian history has
been continuous. The third voyage of the Company
(1606–10) reached Surat in India, left William Finch as
factor (1608) there, and sent William Hawkins to the Great
Mogul to obtain leave for a permanent English factory.
The fourth voyage (1607–9) ' discovered ' the Red Sea, one
century after the Portuguese ' discovered ' it. The ocean
was already made free to the ships of three nations ; and
when the Turks claimed the Red Sea as a close sea, Sir
Henry Middleton answered, 'To come into this sea I needed
no leave, but God's and my King's,' and followed up his
answer with cannon shot. In the eighth voyage John
Saris reached Japan (1613–14). Later still, Sir Thomas
Roe's embassy to the Great Mogul (1615–17) finally assured
the position of England in India. Sir Thomas Roe's ideal
was colonization, or what was then called plantation ; and
while naval battles were dissipating Portuguese dominion,
he upheld the peaceful character of his mission, and wrote :
' It has been the error of the Dutch, who seek plantation
here by the sword. . . . If you will seek profit, seek it at sea
and in quiet trade. . . . It is an error to affect garrisons
and land wars in India.' In these few years traffics and
discoveries had merged into colonization. The process
was rapid in the East, where England and Holland brought
strong unintermitting pressure to bear, and colonization
meant much less than it did in America ; and Anglo-
American colonial experiments, which we have hitherto
postponed, although a chronologist would have mentioned
them before, now claim our attention.

The third and last volume of the epic of discovery has
colonization for its theme. Voyages were not only sources
of wealth, schools of manhood, and means for winning the
new freedom of the seas, but they created new empires,
colonies, and nations. Continuous intercourse with Europe
gave birth in the old and crowded countries of the East to
empire by Europeans over natives and in the new and

empty countries of America to new European colonies and nations.

In America, Spain aimed at both ideals—imperial and colonial—worked, said Michael Lok, with a 'constant resolution of plantation . . . which may be exemplary unto us'; but built what was neither fortress nor home, but half one and half the other. And the building has crumbled into picturesque ruins haunted by half-breeds, who have grafted on the restless character of the Indian thin theories and institutions of European origin. The Portuguese resembled the Spaniards in their methods and results. Then France set to work. Jacques Cartier discovered the gulf and river of St. Lawrence (1534–5) and wintered at or near Quebec (1535–6) ; and he and Jean François de la Roche, Seigneur de Roberval, planted colonists there (1541–2) who returned or perished. The idea of building far away from the closely guarded Spanish and Portuguese zones was new and French. Frenchmen also inaugurated a new ideal, which they carried out far too near the Spanish and Portuguese settlements. Civil wars, based on religious differences, rent France. Why, it was asked, should not those who were weaker in number and stronger in spirit start a fresh life in a fresh world over which the spiritual clouds of the old world had never cast their shadow ? So the weary harassed Protestants, aided by Gaspard de Coligny, fled for peace to America. They went there not to fight or rule, but to live. One colony, led by Nicholas Durand, Seigneur de Villegagnon, settled in the bay of Rio de Janeiro, quarrelled with itself, and most of the colonists returned ; and those who remained were destroyed by their Portuguese neighbours (1555–8). The other, led by Jean Ribaut (1562), settled at Charles Fort on the coast of South Carolina, which was then called Florida. There a mutiny occurred, and the mutineers built a pinnace and set sail for France—'after they had eaten up their shoes and leather jerkins . . . they remained three days without eating or drinking, except it were of the sea water'—and were at last rescued by an English barque and were landed some in France and others in England, in order that the queen, 'which purposed at that time to, send into Florida,' might converse with them. René de Laudonnière, who succeeded Ribaut, led fresh colonists to

SIR WALTER RALEIGH

Charles Fort, and there Hawkins visited and succoured them (1565), and the Spaniards, egged on by the French king, visited and extirpated them (1565), a few only escaping to France and a few to England, among whom was Jacques Le Moyne, the artist.

The French example inspired Englishmen. In 1557 Englishmen had been offered, and in 1560 had proposed, a trade settlement on the African Gold Coast, but no English settlement was actually made in Africa before 1618.

Hardly had Jacques Le Moyne arrived in London when Humphrey Gilbert petitioned for a patent to discover and monopolize a north passage to Cathay (1566), and a book which he wrote shortly afterwards, but which was not published until 1576, advocated a north-west passage and a settlement in ' some part of those countries '. Martin Frobisher conducted three expeditions to Frobisher Bay, a few miles north of Hudson Strait (1576–8), in order to carry out this idea. He called his new country Meta Incognita (hopelessly misplaced on the map of 1600), built a house there, which was found by the American explorer, Captain Charles Hall in 1862, and meant to leave there a winter party, just as winter parties had already been left a few hundred miles farther north at Archangel in the eastern hemisphere. Like Cartier, he thought that he was on the threshold of Cathay, and exaggerated the delusion (which Cartier also shared) that North America, like South America, culminated in a short strait.

Frobisher's geographical discoveries were extended by John Davis (1585–7), Henry Hudson (1610–11), and William Baffin (1616), the discoverers of Davis Strait, Hudson Bay, and Baffin Bay respectively ; but Sir Humphrey Gilbert and Sir Walter Ralegh took up his colonizing task. Gilbert's object was to plant two colonies, one far away from and the other close to the West Indies, like Cartier's and Ribaut's colonies. In 1583 he led out a colony to St. John's, Newfoundland, annexed Newfoundland, and immediately returned homeward with his colony, he and most of his colonists being lost on the way home. In 1585–7 Sir Walter Ralegh sent out three batches of colonists to Roanoke Island, in North Carolina, or in what he called Virginia, between Cape Hatterack and Chesapeake Bay.

All the first batch (1586), and a few of the second and third batches—including John White, the artist—returned (1586-7), but the rest disappeared and left no trace behind. The Virginian settlements were safer than the Floridan settlements of Ribaut and Laudonnière, because they were farther from the Spanish zone. Ralegh now essayed a colony more exposed to danger from Spaniards and Portuguese than even the colony attempted by Villegagnon.

In 1594 Ralegh sent Captain Jacob Whiddon to 'discover' Guiana, 'the golden city of Manoa,' and 'the new El Dorado'; and he himself followed in the next year to 'conquer' and create a 'mighty empire', 'a better Indies for Her Majesty than the King of Spain hath any' (cf. *M. Wives*, I. iii. 77). He explored the Orinoco from its mouth to the Caroni, about 400 miles up-stream, but Antonio de Berreo had long ago descended the Orinoco and its affluents, the Meta and Cassanar, from near Santa Fé de Bogota, 1,400 miles or more up-stream, and Manoa and El Dorado remained as undiscoverable to Ralegh as they were to the Spaniards who had written of them sixty years before. In 1596 Ralegh sent out Lawrence Kemys on a third and last expedition, but no conquest, empire, or discovery ensued, and the splendid vision faded. Both Ralegh and Kemys wrote with poetic fervour about Guiana, besides adorning their narratives with the usual stories of 'headless' and 'dog-faced' men.

But before men knew it the founders of Greater Britain sowed their seed and a cluster of real colonies arose. These men were not credited with 'discoveries', 'conquests', or 'empires', but the colonies which they founded grew silently and permanently. The time of fret and ferment seemed past, and construction began, but not before the death of Queen Elizabeth. Virginia began to exist in 1606, two years before the first English factor stayed at Surat, and its capital, Jamestown, in 1607; Newfoundland was planted in 1610; and after a series of attempts at colonization by Bartholomew Gosnold (1602), George Popham and Raleigh Gilbert (1607-8), and others, New England was settled by the Pilgrim Fathers (1620) about the same time as the Portuguese were expelled from Ormuz. Even British Guiana began to grow. Charles Leigh (1604) and Robert Harcourt (1609) set to work at Wiapogo, between

the Orinoco and Amazon ; and, although Ralegh and
Kemys dashed once more to the Orinoco and failed disas-
trously (1617), Leigh's and Harcourt's work endured more
or less. The early seventeenth century is also the date when
New France was born. In the north, Pierre de Guast de
Monts, a Huguenot, founded St. Croix and Port Royal, now
Annapolis, in Acadia (1604), and Samuel Champlain Quebec
in Canada (1608), and in the south there was a temporary
colony at Cayenne (1613). All these occupations led to
more. Two West Indian examples may be given. One of
Charles Leigh's ships touched at Santa Lucia on the way
between Wiapogo and England (1605). Sixty-seven of the
crew chose to remain. They fed on tortoises and by net-
fishing, and the Caribs for a while brought them food, but
afterwards attacked them, burned their nets, and starved
them so that only nineteen survived, and they fled, and
were wrecked on an island opposite Tocuyo river in Vene-
zuela. 'There', wrote John Nicol, 'we continued fifteen
days having no kind of meat but wilks, salt water, and
tobacco, which did nothing at all nourish us,' until Spaniards
came to the rescue. This probably was the first brief
voluntary settlement by Englishmen on a West Indian
island.   There may well be a reminiscence of this episode in
Prospero's threat :

> Sea-water shalt thou drink ; thy food shall be
> The fresh-brook muscles,   (*Temp.* i. ii. 459–60)

and in Caliban's promise to his friends of ' young scamels
from the rock ' and to his foes of ' nought but brine '
(*Temp.* ii. ii. 185 ; iii. ii. 76).

The settlement of the Bermudas began involuntarily, but
proved permanent. Sir Thomas Gates and Sir George
Somers, who were on their way to Virginia (1609), appointed
the archipelago of the Bermudas as the trysting-place for
their fleet, although it was considered an ' enchanted place
affording nothing but gusts, storm, and foul weather ', and
because they wished to avoid the West Indies, where
storms of another kind were frequent. Most of the ships
went straight to Virginia, and only the Admiral's ship
reached the Bermudas, tempest-tossed, leaking, and with
some of its crew working heroically and others drunk.
There it was wrecked, but without loss of life. The islands
were uninhabited and, like other islands elsewhere, were

nicknamed Devil's Islands,[1] 'it being counted of most that they can be no habitations for men but rather given over to Devils'. But the castaways found to their surprise that the islands were 'habitable and commodious', the air temperate and 'sweet-smelling' though often afflicted with 'tempests, thunder, lightning and rain'; 'berries . . . made a pleasant drink' (cf. *Temp.* II. ii), and the noises in the islands came not from devils but from pigs, which the Spaniards had turned loose there long ago, and for which styes were built; and instead of being starved, like John Nicol, they fed sumptuously, built two pinnaces, one of 80 tons burden, and reached Virginia, which they saved— instead of Virginia saving them—from starvation.

Strike out Virginia, and William Strachey's story of Gates's and Somers's adventure reads like an epitome of Shakespeare's *Tempest*. But Shakespeare's *Tempest* has two notable additions—the supernatural, and Caliban. *The Tempest* is the only play in which Shakespeare leaves Europe and the Mediterranean. Elsewhere that which is beyond Europe is beyond knowledge, mere myth and vague atmosphere. Here he transplants himself into cloud-land, builds in air, and looks at solid Europe as something afar and less real. While crossing from Naples to Tunis, Italian dukes and their suite are transported in a moment and by magic into a region where space is annihilated and enchantment is the order of the day. The European characters in the play shrink into mere visitors and the principal interest is concentrated on two beings, both unique, the one aerial and dainty, and the other a fleshy amalgam of attributes drawn from anywhere or everywhere outside Europe and ascribed to every savage by every traveller of the day.

Caliban impersonates the savage. His religion has traces of that sun-worship which Shakespeare vaguely imputed to Indians (*All's W.* I. iii. 212–14) and travellers to Hindoos, Parsees, Chinamen, Mexicans, Guianans, and Patagonians. Even the Great Mogul is accused of sun-worship, because 'at the rising of the sun he adoreth [it] by the elevation of his hands'. Similarly, Floridans thought 'that we worshipped the sun because we always [during prayer] had our

---

[1] e. g. André Thevet's Demon Islands, so called 'pour autant que les Démons y font terrible tintamarre'.

MAP OF VIRGINIA by JOHN WHITE

eyes lifted up to Heaven '. Sun-worship, in Hakluyt, means that the worshipper does not belong to Christendom. Caliban's name proclaims him West Indian, and he is the dispossessed ' King ' of an island which is clearly West Indian. Many of his characteristics were noted for the first time among American Indians, though they belonged equally to every savage. According to Oviedo, 'when the devil intendeth to fear them [American Indians] he threateneth to send them great tempests'; according to Captain John Smith, ' All things that were able to do them hurt beyond their prevention they adore . . . as the fire, water, lightning, thunder, our ordnance, &c.'; and according to John Lerius they ' are wofully tormented by the devil ', who sometimes assumed ' the shape of a cruel beast ', so that they were heard ' crying out like frantic men, Hei, Hei, help us for Aygnan beateth us '. Even so Caliban was haunted, hunted, beaten, and persecuted by his ghosts. Like American Indians, Caliban fished with dams for his white master (*Temp.* II. ii. 193), who seemed able to inflict disease and death from afar ' without weapons '. But American Indians were familiar to Londoners,[1] Indians from Brazil (1530), Guiana (1595), Virginia (1584, 1605), and New England (1611) having visited England, as well as Eskimos (1502, 1578–9), Africans (1554), and others. Most French and English discoverers brought two or three natives home to learn the language and then return to their tribe. Sometimes they were brought as presents for the king, sometimes as commercial guest-friends, and once in order to be exhibited for money (1611). (Cf. *Temp.* II. ii. 30–35.) Londoners must therefore have known that that ignoble misshapen groveller Caliban was not to be taken as the physical and moral representative of an American Indian. Shakespeare, too, in isolating Caliban from his tribal and family relations must have felt that he was not painting a portrait, but blending an individualistic study in abstract savagery with pure poetic phantasy.

But, after all, the principal characters of *The Tempest* are Europeans who went out and came back like all those French and English colonists of the sixteenth century who did not go out to die. What, then, were they to the new world, or the new world to them ?

---

[1] Sidney Lee, 'Call of the West ' in *Scribner's Magazine*, 1907.

Almost at the first glance at the islands, good foolish
Gonzalo wished to plant Utopia here, and cried out—

Had I plantation of this isle, my lord;   (*Temp.* II. i. 150)

but his ideal state invited ridicule, because he would use
sovereignty to eradicate sovereignty, and to sow, maybe,
' nettle-seed, or docks, or mallows ' (*Temp.* II. i. 151).
Drayton's *Ode to the Virginian Voyage* lauded, *Eastward
Hoe* ridiculed, the colonization of Virginia ; but Shakespeare never even names Virginia, although he mentions both
Bermuda and Guiana once ; nor does he even write directly
of colonization, unless perhaps colonization is referred to in
Cranmer's prophetic vision of a future king of England :

Wherever the bright sun of heaven shall shine,
His honour and the greatness of his name
Shall be, and make new nations. (*Hen. VIII*, v. v. 51–3)

In the sixteenth century the Portuguese and Spanish
Empires were often described as empires on which the sun
never set ; but the idea of making new nations was rare.
Ralegh, too, said of Virginia, ' I shall yet live to see it an
English nation '[1] (1602) ; and perhaps this rare idea came
from him.   The passage continues :

He shall flourish,
And like a mountain cedar reach his branches
To all the plains about him.

And here, too, perhaps the poet had in his mind's eye
a philosophical reflection like that of John White, ' I deny
that such as are gone out from the State are cut off from the
State : the roots that issue out of the trunk of the tree
though they be dispersed yet they are not severed '[2] or like
that of Sir John Seeley, ' The ripe fruit dropping from the
tree and giving rise to another tree may be natural ; but
so is the acorn spreading into the huge oak that has hundreds
of branches and thousands of leaves '.[3]   John White and
Sir John Seeley were certainly thinking of colonies ; and
so perhaps was Shakespeare.   On the other hand, Shakespeare's prophecy of new nations, world-wide greatness, and
vast spreading branches may have been random metaphors
and nothing more.   But then, are not all prophecies random
metaphors ?

[1] *Life*, by W. Stebbing, p. 48 ; by Edward Edwards, vol. ii, p. 252.
[2] John White, *Planters' Plea*, 1630, p. 37.
[3] *Expansion of England* (1883), p. 56.

A cheife Herowan.

From a WATER-COLOUR DRAWING by JOHN WHITE

BIBLIOGRAPHY.—The chief authorities for exploration and sea voyages in early times down to Shakespeare's era are RICHARD HAKLUYT's *Principall Navigations, Voiages and Discoveries of the English nation, made by Sea or over Land, to the most remote and farthest distant Quarters of the earth at any time within the compasse of these 1500 yeeres*, which was originally published in 1589, and enlarged in 1598–1600; and SAMUEL PURCHAS's *Hakluytus Posthumus, or Purchas his Pilgrimes, contayning a History of the World in Sea Voyages and Land Trauells by Englishmen and others*, which was first published in 1625. Citation of these two great works has been made here from MacLehose's reprints, of which Hakluyt's ' Navigations ' appeared in twelve volumes in 1903–5, and Purchas's ' Pilgrimes ' in twenty volumes in 1905–7. The chief collection of voyages before Hakluyt's was Richard Eden's *The History of Travayle in the West and East Indies, and other countreys lying eyther way, towardes the fruitfull and ryche Moluccas. As Moscovia, Persia, Arabia, Syria, Ægypte, Ethiopia, Guinea, China in Cathayo, and Giapan : with a discourse of the Northwest passage.* It was ' set in order, augmented, and finished ' by Richard Willes, and published in 1577, the year after Eden's death.

Several of the Hakluyt Society publications deal with this period. Some important documents not in Hakluyt's and Purchas's collections are reprinted in *Voyages and Travels mainly during the 16th and 17th Centuries* (Arber's English Garner), edited by C. R. Beazley, 1903.

In the revision of this chapter, valuable help has been given by Professor C. R. Beazley.

VII

LAND TRAVEL

BY

CHARLES HUGHES

AT HOME

IN Shakespeare's time most of the motives which led
men to travel about the country were the same as to-day.
Education took the youths and young men to Oxford and
Cambridge, the lawyers followed the judges on circuit,
trade and business took merchants to buy and sell at every
market-town, companies of play-actors gave the provinces
a taste of their London successes, sick people sought health
at Bath or Buxton, and there was a general drift of the
enterprising and adventurous to seek a better fortune in
London. Wherever Queen Elizabeth's council happened
to be, courtiers flocked round, and couriers with news-
letters from home or abroad were continually arriving.
On the other hand, nobody went for health or holidays to
the seaside or the English lakes or the Welsh mountains.
Another source of travel that had been a most picturesque
addition to English roads before the Reformation was
missing. There were no pilgrims now to the holy shrines—
Canterbury, Walsingham, and Glastonbury. Probably the
only organized pilgrimage during the Shakespeare period
was that conducted by the Jesuit priest Garnett, which
took place in September 1605. A party consisting of
thirty Roman Catholics, ladies, gentlemen, priests, and
servants went from Sir Everard Digby's house, Gothurst,
on horseback to St. Winifred's shrine at Holywell in Flint-
shire, a distance of 150 miles, thus undertaking no less
than 300 miles of continuous riding. They stayed only one
night at Holywell, for the journey took about nine days
each way. It is not uncharitable to suppose that these
pious pilgrims (for they heard a mass every morning) were

urged on their journey by a wish to ask for St. Winifred's blessing on the Gunpowder Plot.

Shakespeare was not the only youth of Stratford-on-Avon who early in the reign of Queen Elizabeth wandered penniless to London and made in manhood there a rich competence. The records of Shakespeare's native place preserve accounts of expenses of numerous expeditions undertaken by municipal officers on legal business. The journey of some 120 miles, which was invariably accomplished on horseback, might be made in three days by two alternative routes ; one by Oxford and High Wycombe, and the other by Banbury and Aylesbury. The latter seems to have been the more frequented, although Shakespeare appears to have favoured the former. The long excursion was often repeated by his better-to-do fellow townsmen, chiefly in connexion with matters of litigation.

Roads intersected the country in all directions, but those connecting the smaller towns were mere tracks. The most frequented and broadest highways were the four passing from London respectively to Dover, Bristol, Chester, and Berwick-on-Tweed. That to Dover went through Gravesend, Rochester, Sittingbourne, and Canterbury ; foreigners usually entered England by way of Dover, and thither Englishmen often, but not invariably, journeyed when they went abroad. The road from London to Bristol, the usual port for South Ireland, lay through Reading, Marlborough, and Chippenham. Chester, whence boats regularly sailed to Dublin, was reached by Barnet, St. Albans, Dunstable, Stony Stratford, and Coventry. The great North Road to Berwick-on-Tweed passed through Huntingdon, Grantham, Doncaster, York, Durham, and Newcastle.

A subsidiary road of importance ran from Carlisle southwards, joining the Chester Road at Lichfield. It passed through Lancaster, Wigan, Warrington, and Newcastle-under-Lyme. But from Lancaster northwards the track which passed through Kendal, Grasmere, over Dunmail Raise and through Keswick, was only available for packhorse traffic. By this road the German miners who worked the mines of the Lake district in the interest of the Company of Mines Royal travelled up from London, and were regularly supplied by the carriers with wine, boxes of oranges, dress fabrics, and even pieces of German furniture.

The carriage rate from London to Keswick was one penny for each pound weight.

Road-making was in an elementary stage, and even the best thoroughfares were often impassable by reason of deep sloughs in bad weather. The smaller roads were always deeply rutted. Ineffectual legislation in the Middle Ages and in the reign of Henry VIII aimed at improving the roads. In 1555 Parliament passed an important Act requiring every parish to elect two surveyors to keep the highways in repair by forced labour. The preamble stated that ' highways are now both very noisome and tedious to travel in, and dangerous to all passengers and carriages '. But no genuine reform resulted. William Kemp, the actor, in his morris dance from London to Norwich in February 1600, had a common experience when he found that the road from Chelmsford to Braintree, which passed through a thick wood, was very ' foul ', ' full of deep holes ', and broken by broad plashes or pools of water and mud.

Many bridges had been erected in the fourteenth century and earlier across rivers where they ran through towns. The London Bridge that Shakespeare knew dated from 1209. The great stone bridge of fourteen arches over the Avon at Stratford, which a prosperous inhabitant, Sir Hugh Clopton, built at the end of the fifteenth century, replaced an old bridge of timber. There was little extension of bridge-building in Shakespeare's lifetime. The old bridges were, like the roads, often out of repair, and travel was thereby impeded. Stone to fill a hole in the bridge was a frequent item in the municipal expenses of Stratford-on-Avon in Shakespeare's epoch, and both ends were temporarily broken by a flood in 1588.

Towards the end of the sixteenth century maps and itineraries in which the mileage between the towns was recorded were available. Between 1574 and 1579 all the counties of England and Wales were carefully surveyed by Christopher Saxton, under the auspices of the Privy Council, and maps were engraved and published. The first road-book dates from 1577, when William Harrison inserted in his *Description of England* a list of ' the common ways ' of England and Scotland, indicating the thoroughfares and distances between all the chief towns. In 1579 a French traveller published in French at Paris *La Guide des Chemins d'Angleterre*, mainly for the help of foreigners passing through England to Scotland. Another Frenchman, Guillaume Paradin, had issued a guide-book in Latin, *Angliae descriptionis compendium*, as early as 1545.

Along all the main roads provision was made for travelling at the most rapid rate then known, by means of post-horses, relays of which stood ready for service at fixed stages. These posts or stages were usually the stable-yards of inns. They had been inaugurated early in the century along the great thoroughfares by officers of State for the purpose of accelerating communications between the King's Government in London and the provinces. As early as 1517 a Governor of the King's Posts had been appointed, and from 1572, when Thomas Randolph became Master of the Posts, or Queen's Postmaster, a posting or postal system on the high roads for official business, with a chief post office in London, became a permanent institution, which gradually underwent expansion and improvement. The Elizabethan postal system was solely designed for the conveyance of persons in the Government service and of official correspondence by official messengers. No provision was attempted by the Government for the carriage or delivery of private correspondence, which was left entirely to unofficial effort. But private travellers shared in the advantages of the regulated hire of post-horses. The cost of hire of post-horses by those engaged on public business was fixed by authority at 2½*d.* a mile, and private persons were charged 3*d.* a mile, with 6*d.* for a mounted postboy, who brought back the hired horse from stage to stage. Speed was encouraged, and ten miles an hour was the common rate when the roads were in good condition. From 70 to 150 miles could at need be accomplished in one day. Some very notable records of speed were made on the great roads on occasions of crisis. When Queen Elizabeth died in the early hours of the 25th of March, 1603, Sir Robert Carey, who had been Warden of the Middle Marches between Scotland and England, set out from London by the Great North Road between nine and ten o'clock, and the same night reached Doncaster, having ridden 162 miles. On the 26th he rode from Doncaster to his own house at Widdrington in Northumberland, another 136 miles. Next day, he had ridden by noon 49 miles to Norham Castle, but a fall from his horse gave him a severe wound in the head, so he had to ride 'softly' the last 50 miles to Edinburgh, which he reached the same night after King James had gone to bed. The same news was brought late the same night (March 27) to the Lord Deputy for Ireland, near Dundalk, by one who posted from London to Chester and had the benefit of a favourable wind across St. George's Channel. Another case of rapid travelling was the journey of Richard Boyle, afterwards Earl of Cork, in January 1601-2, who carried from Kinsale to London, by way of Bristol, the news of the Spanish surrender. Boyle writes in his Memoirs, 'I made speedy expedition to the Court : for I left my Lord President at Shandon Castle near Cork on the Monday morning about two of the clock, and the next day, being Tuesday, I delivered my packet and supped with Sir Robert Cecil at his house in the Strand'.

Shakespeare constantly refers to the speed of the messengers who ride ' post ', as in *King Lear* (II. iv. 30-3)—

> There came a reeking post,
> Stew'd in his haste, half breathless, panting forth
> From Goneril his mistress salutations ;
> Deliver'd letters,—

and frequently uses the term 'posting', the fastest-known method of travel, as an image of speed. Thus in *Richard III* (I. i. 145) Gloucester says that the king must not die

> Till George be pack'd with post-horse up to heaven,

referring to the impending murder of Clarence. Hamlet says of his mother's hasty marriage with his uncle :

> Most wicked speed, to post
> With such dexterity to incestuous sheets. (*Haml.* I. ii. 156-7)

And Antonio in *The Tempest* uses a still more remarkable phrase :

> She that from Naples
> Can have no note, unless the sun were post—
> The man i' th' moon 's too slow. (II. i. 255-7)

Post-horses were only in use for business of urgency. For ordinary travel, English gentlemen rode their own horses at a leisurely pace, and after twenty or thirty miles, according to the weather and the state of the roads, put up at an inn at nightfall :

The west yet glimmers with some streaks of day :
Now spurs the lated traveller apace
To gain the timely inn.   (*Macb.* III. iii. 5–7)

Persons who owned no horses and either could not afford
post-horses or were bound for places beyond the post-
roads might hire a horse for the whole journey at 12*d*. the
first day and 8*d*. a day afterwards, until it was delivered
back to the owner. At times a traveller would buy a horse
at the beginning of his journey and sell it at the end.

In spite of the prevalent use of horses, walking remained
the common means of travel for poor men, including
scholars, servants, and labourers. Students of humble
birth had much experience of walking in youth. Hooker,
as an undergraduate in 1570, went from Oxford to Exeter
on foot. On the way he visited Bishop Jewel at Salisbury.
His host gave him a walking staff, with which, according to
Walton, the Bishop ' professed he had travelled through
many parts of Germany '.

Most of the acting companies toured on foot, but some
rode horses and carried their baggage in a wagon. The
antiquary, John Stow, who visited ' divers cathedral
churches ' and other chief places of the land to search
records, ' could never ride but travelled on foot '. When
William Kemp danced from London to Norwich, the journey
took twenty-three days, of which only nine were spent
in actual dancing on the road. The route lay through
Romford, Chelmsford, Bury, and Burford Bridge. In
1618 two men of different note walked from London to
Edinburgh, Ben Jonson and John Taylor, the Water-poet.
Jonson started in June and reached his destination in
September. Both journeys were made at a leisurely pace,
and Jonson took the same time on the return journey,
between January and April of the following year. Taylor
extended his expedition to the highlands of Scotland. But
he seems to have diversified his pedestrian exercise with
much horse-riding after reaching Edinburgh, as well as on
his way back to his home in Islington.

Meanwhile wheeled vehicles, although they never superseded horse-riding or walking, supplemented the means of
locomotion and transport. Two-wheeled carts had been
employed for agricultural purposes from time immemorial,
and clumsy four-wheeled carriages had often conveyed, from

the fourteenth century onwards, the queens and princesses and women of the court, while two-wheeled wagons carried their baggage. Horse-litters, i.e. chairs or couches fixed to poles resting on horses' backs, were also used in the Middle Ages by great ladies and infirm persons. These contrivances survived to Elizabethan times. Occasionally horse-litters were exchanged for chairs of state, or sedan-chairs, the poles of which were carried by men. In one of these Queen Elizabeth now and then passed through London. But sedan-chairs were very rare in England before the reign of King Charles I. In Shakespeare's time, the practice of employing wheeled vehicles for the transport of both persons and goods steadily grew. Carts were taking the place of pack-horses, and coaches for the first time became part of the luxurious equipment of well-to-do women.

According to John Taylor, the Water-poet, 'William Boonen, a Dutchman, brought first the use of coaches hither' in 1564. Boonen became Queen Elizabeth's coachman. 'A coach was a strange monster in those days, and the sight of it put both horse and man into amazement.' But the 'new invention' made rapid progress among the rich. It proved for the nobility and gentry a cheaper mode of conveyance for country travel than the horse, besides being reckoned more fashionable for the gentler sex. The private travelling coach was large enough to accommodate, besides the mistress of the household, 'her gentlewomen, maid, and children, and what necessaries as they or any of them are to use'.

The male retinue for such expeditions might consist of only one or two horse attendants besides the coachman, instead of the troop of older days. Coaches could be hired for special journeys by middle-class people. Dr. John Dee, when appointed Warden of Manchester College in 1595, sent his wife and family as far as Coventry from Mortlake in a coach, himself following some days later on horseback. For town use there came into vogue a smaller carriage, which was known as a 'caroche', and in it the lady travelled alone. 'Coach' and 'caroche' mainly differed from one another in size, as may be seen in Hoefnagel's representation of the two vehicles in his view of Nonesuch. Both were four-wheeled, and the elaborately carved roof was often adorned with plumes of feathers. The sides were quite open. The interior might be upholstered in velvet or scarlet cloth, ornamented with gold or silver lace. The body rested solidly on the axles ; there were no springs. Queen Elizabeth at times complained of 'the aching pains ' she suffered from the fast driving of her coach. London streets in Shakespeare's later life were often inconveniently crowded with caroches. Coachmaking quickly 'became a substantial trade'. Mercutio talks familiarly of coachmakers (*Rom. & Jul.* I. iv. 70). In 1601 a bill was rejected on second reading in the House of Lords to restrain the excessive and superfluous use of coaches.

The baggage of the Court and rich noblemen and gentlemen was also transported in their visits about the country by wheeled vehicles, usually of a more antiquated pattern. According to a German visitor in 1592, ' When the Queen breaks up her court, with the intention of visiting another place, there commonly follow more than 300 carts (*Kärch*) laden with bag and baggage.' The writer adds, not quite accurately, that 'this service engaged only two-wheeled carts, which, however, are so large that they carry quite as much as wagons, and as many as five or six strong horses draw them'. Four-wheeled carts soon became as common as four-wheeled coaches or caroches.

A service of carriers to and from London from country places was also instituted in the sixteenth century. Thomas Hobson, the Cambridge carrier, who was born nearly twenty years before Shakespeare, was son of one of the same occupation who also let horses for hire on a large scale. Dr. Dee, in 1595, when removing his household from Mortlake to Manchester, sent on his furniture by ' Percival the Lancashire carrier'. Carriers travelled at first only with pack-horses. Shakespeare's carriers, who lodge in the inn at Rochester, and have much to say of their horses, carry in panniers their loads, which consisted of, besides turkeys, bacon and ginger destined for Charing Cross (*1 Hen. IV*, II. i. 1–51). The Stratford-on-Avon lad, John Sadler, who was Shakespeare's neighbour, and left his native place for London about the same time as the dramatist, after hiring a horse, ' joined himself to the carrier'. Throughout the country, especially in the north, there were many roads which could be traversed only by pack-horses and were inaccessible to wheeled traffic. But before the seventeenth century opened the carriers who went to and from populous places invariably employed carts or wagons for the greater part of their journeys. Hobson, the Cambridge carrier, 'died', according to his elegist Milton, 'for heaviness that his cart went light'.

The carrier's goods service was in Shakespeare's life well organized all over the country; and every town had its carriers who travelled to and from the capital at fixed intervals, varying from once a fortnight to three times a week according to the distance and population. Like the Cambridge carrier, Hobson, who put up each week at the Black Bull in Aldersgate Street, every carrier had a permanent office in a London inn, where he met his customers and received his commissions. Private correspondence was wholly in the hand of the carrier. Some carriers added the conveyance of passengers to that of goods. Fynes Moryson records that 'long covered wagons' carried passengers from place to place, but this innovation does not seem to have been generally welcome. 'This kind of journeying', Moryson remarks, 'is so tedious, by reason the passengers must take wagon very early and come very late to their inns, none but women and people of inferior condition travel in this sort.'

All travellers were greatly dependent on the inns, where frequent halts overnight could not be avoided by carriage folk, horsemen, or pedestrians on long journeys. Towns on the main roads, on which there was regular traffic, were well provided with 'great and sumptuous inns'. Fynes Moryson, who was acquainted with the inns of Germany, France, Italy, Poland, the Netherlands, and Switzerland, asserts:

The world affords not such Inns as England hath, either for good and cheap entertainments at the guest's own pleasure, or for humble attendance on passengers. . . . For as soon as a passenger comes to an Inn the servants run to him, and one takes his horse and walks him till he be cold, then rubs him and gives him meat, yet I must say they are not much to be trusted in this last point without the eye of the master or his servant to oversee them. Another servant gives the passenger his private chamber and kindles his fire, the third pulls off his boots and makes them clean. The Host or Hostess visits him, and if he will eat with the Host, or at a common table with others, his meal will cost him sixpence, or in some places but fourpence (yet this course is less honourable, and not used by gentlemen): but if he will eat in his chamber, he commands what meat he will according to his appetite, and as much as he thinks fit for him and his company, yea, the kitchen

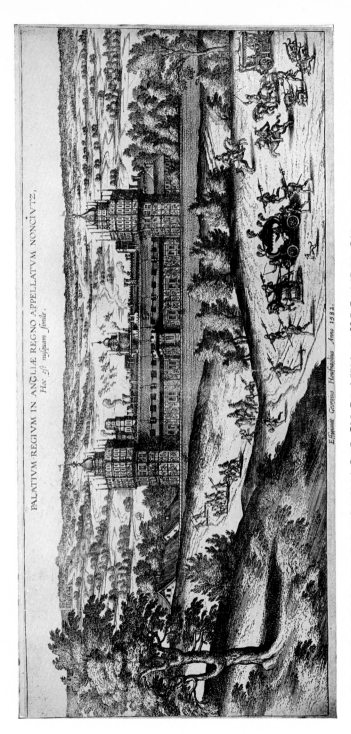

PALATIVM REGIVM IN ANGLIÆ REGNO APPELLATVM NONCIVTZ,
Huic & nusquam simile.

Effigiauit Georgius Houfnaglius Anno 1582.

NONESUCH PALACE BY HOEFNAGEL IN BRAUN & HOGENBERG'S *CIVITATES ORBIS TERRARUM*

(The royal coach is seen in the foreground)

is open to him to command the meat to be dressed as he best likes : and when he sits at table, the Host or Hostess will accompany him, or if they have many guests will at least visit him, taking it for courtesy to be bid sit down : while he eats, if he have company especially, he shall be offered music, which he may freely take or refuse and if he be solitary, the Musicians will give him the good day with music in the morning.

Harrison, in his *Description of England,* says that some inns could lodge two or three hundred people and their horses, and that with a very short warning they could make unexceptionable provision for their diet. Some towns had as many as twelve or more inns, and there was great competition among them to give the best accommodation to travellers, in beauty of rooms and furniture, of bedding, costliness of plate, excellence of the ale, and variety of wines. They also contended who should have the finest signboard hung out to attract travellers, and some would spend £30 or £40 on this piece of ostentation. Every traveller was given clean sheets ' wherein no man hath been lodged since they came from the laundress, or out of the water wherein they were last washed'.

Travellers were exposed to a variety of risks, which may be sometimes exaggerated, but were rarely absent altogether. Apart from the dangers incident to the state of the roads and bridges, there was the possibility of encountering highway robbers. The plundering of travellers was a well-known vocation, in which discharged soldiers or discarded serving-men engaged without scruple. They were occasionally joined by venturesome youths of the better classes, ' the which for sport sake are content to do the profession some grace ' (*1 Hen. IV*, II. i. 78).

Organized gangs infested exposed places, and Gadshill, near Rochester, Shooter's Hill, near Blackheath, Salisbury Plain, and Newmarket Heath, all enjoyed unenviable reputations. The scene in *1 Henry IV* (II. ii) in which Falstaff and his companions rob and bind travellers over Gadshill presents a common experience.

Often inn servants—the chamberlains (men who performed the functions of chambermaids), the ostlers, and the tapsters—gave the thieves the information of travellers' movements and property, on which they acted. It is the chamberlain of the Rochester Inn in *1 Henry IV* (II. i) who ' lays the plot ' for Falstaff's disreputable exploit on the road. The chamberlain in the play gives to Falstaff's highwayman-companion very helpful news :

It holds current that I told you yesternight : there's a franklin in the wild of Kent hath brought three hundred marks with him in gold : I heard him tell it to one of his company last night at supper ; a kind of auditor ; one that hath abundance of charge too, God knows what. They are up already and call for eggs and butter : they will away presently. (*1 Hen. IV*, II. i. 58–66)

Harrison states that 'by a general custom' innkeepers were answerable for losses which travellers sustained under their roof, 'so that there is no greater security anywhere for travellers than in the greatest inns of England'.

There were also occasional horse-stealers, and men who offered to hold travellers' horses by the wayside not infrequently made off with them.

Travellers who carried no great valuables were as liable to attack as the richly-laden. But highwaymen were commonly credited with merciful treatment of the very poor. As a rule the threatened travellers made little resistance, and the thieves were content with the delivery of their victims' purses. Murders by highwaymen seem to have been rare. But death on the gallows awaited all captured thieves, however gentle their procedure. The most notorious highwayman of Shakespeare's time was one Gamaliel Ratsey, who had fought in youth in Ireland, and early in the seventeenth century terrorized the eastern counties by his exploits on the road. He is said to have been always well mounted, to have worn a hideous mask, and to have combined rough humour with his daring. A Cambridge scholar who fell into his clutches was compelled to deliver a learned oration before being released. Once he gave an interesting lecture to a company of players whom he encountered and robbed on the road ; there is reason to believe Shakespeare himself was among his auditors. Ratsey was betrayed by his confederates and was hanged at Bedford on March 26, 1605. Long a hero of chapbook literature, he gave some catch phrases to the stage.

Native travellers through Elizabethan England were invariably bent on business of various kinds. Englishmen, who travelled for sight-seeing and pleasure, went abroad. Foreigners alone travelled in England on such errands, and many of these have left records of their experiences. Foreign tourists in Shakespeare's day often included Scotland in their journeys. The great scholar Scaliger explored the border country. The French poets Ronsard and Du Bartas travelled direct to Scotland by sea, and went home through England. The famous Huguenot general, the Duke de Rohan, wrote an account of a tour which he undertook in 1600 through both England and Scotland. German noblemen, who figured largely among foreign tourists, chiefly spent their time in the city of London inspecting the royal palaces of Whitehall and Greenwich, and making excursions to Richmond, Hampton Court, and Windsor. They rarely went further into the provinces than to the Universities of Oxford and Cambridge. Foreign tourists invariably travelled on horseback, and often complained that English saddles were too narrow and too hard for their comfort. The Government occasionally granted these foreign visitors special privileges of travel, which pressed hardly on inn-keepers. In 1592, Frederick, Duke of Wirtemberg, and his companions were officially permitted to requisition post-horses free of charge when travelling on the old Bristol Road to Windsor. It is in reference to this incident that Sir Hugh Evans in Shakespeare's *Merry Wives* (IV. v. 79 seq.) indignantly complains that 'there is three cozen-germans that has cozened all the hosts of Readins, of Maidenhead, of Colebrook, of horses and money'. Paul Hentzner of Brandenburg came in attendance on a young Silesian nobleman in 1598. The party made a sight-seeing tour from London. After visiting Lord Burghley's house at Theobalds, they went on to Cambridge, and thence to Oxford, and afterwards to Woodstock. On their way to Windsor and Eton they passed through Ewelme, Henley, and Maidenhead, and subsequently visited Hampton Court and the wonderful palace of Nonesuch at Cheam. Foreign visitors found much difficulty with the language, but in 1602 Philip Julius, Duke of Stettin in Pomerania, reports how a learned Englishman who spoke Latin obligingly acted as interpreter with a dense innkeeper, and helped him and his companions in settling their hotel-bill.

ABROAD

Travelling abroad was, for the English gentleman of Shakespeare's time, an education, a duty, and a romance.

When Valentine, in *The Two Gentlemen of Verona* (I. i. 5–8), says to Proteus—

> I rather would entreat thy company
> To see the wonders of the world abroad
> Than, living dully sluggardiz'd at home,
> Wear out thy youth with shapeless idleness

he bears witness to a widespread eagerness on the part of young Elizabethans of the upper and middle classes who were disinclined for soldiering or sea-fighting. The experience and knowledge of other countries was deemed necessary for the inspiring of the intellectual faculties. Proteus's father in *The Two Gentlemen of Verona* (I. iii. 6–21) is persuaded to take this view :

> Other men, of slender reputation,
> Put forth their sons to seek preferment out :
> Some to the wars, to try their fortune there ;
> Some to discover islands far away ;
> Some to the studious universities.
> For any or for all these exercises
> He said that Proteus your son was meet,
> And did request me to importune you
> To let him spend his time no more at home,
> Which would be great impeachment to his age,
> In having known no travel in his youth.

To which Antonio replies :

> I have consider'd well his loss of time,
> And how he cannot be a perfect man,
> Not being tried and tutor'd in the world.

Bacon was of the same opinion. 'Travel,' he wrote in his Essay of Travel, 'in the younger sort is a part of education, in the elder a part of experience.' He advised the traveller to study the foreign language, to visit all objects of interest in the towns—libraries, arsenals, warehouses, theatres, antiquities, and ruins—to change his residence often, and to keep a diary.

It was, on the other hand, often objected that the traveller acquired foreign affectations, foreign vices, and foreign diseases, and disabled his estate by his expenditure and extravagance. Voluble was the sarcasm levelled by Elizabethan dramatists and pamphleteers at travelled fops who dressed in the modes of France or Italy, substituted French wines for English beer, and contrived to speak English with a foreign accent. The popular view of the effect of foreign

travel on Englishmen is illustrated in the familiar dialogue
between Rosalind and Jacques in *As You Like It* (IV. i. 22–40):

> *Ros.* A traveller! By my faith, you have great reason to be sad.
> I fear you have sold your own lands to see other men's ; then, to have
> seen much and to have nothing, is to have rich eyes and poor hands.
> *Jaq.* Yes, I have gained my experience.
> *Ros.* And your experience makes you sad : I had rather have
> a fool to make me merry than experience to make me sad : and to
> travel for it too ! . . .
> *Ros.* Farewell, Monsieur Traveller : look you lisp, and wear
> strange suits, disable all the benefits of your own country, be out
> of love with your nativity, and almost chide God for making you
> that countenance you are ; or I will scarce think you have swam
> in a gondola.

But the wisest heads deemed, on the whole, a worse peril
the self-complacency and insularity which comes of home-
keeping. Shakespeare gave his countrymen a solemn
warning against the prejudices of the untravelled :

> Hath Britain all the sun that shines ? . . .
> There 's livers out of Britain. (*Cymb.* III. iv. 139–43)

Bacon, writing in the reign of James I, in his letter of
advice to Sir George Villiers, afterwards Duke of Bucking-
ham, says that it was Elizabeth's policy to encourage
educative journeys beyond the seas, and even to pay, in a
few cases, part of the expenses. ' There were always sent
forth into several parts beyond the seas some young men of
whom good hopes were conceived of their towardliness, to
be trained up, and made fit for such public employments,
and to learn the languages. This was at the charge of the
queen, which was not much ; for they travelled but as
private gentlemen, and as by their industry their deserts
did appear, so were they further employed or rewarded.'
The Oxford and Cambridge colleges sometimes gave their
Fellows liberty to travel for two or more years after taking
their degree. Fynes Moryson gratefully records his obligations to Peterhouse, Cambridge, for paying him his fellowship income of £20 per annum during his absence abroad.
He thus met about one-third of his travelling charges.

The following extract from Dallington's *Method for Travel*
(1605) indicates the expense of the continental journeys
of an English gentleman :

> If he travel without a servant, fourscore pounds sterling is a com-
> petent proportion, except he learne to ride : if he maintain both

these charges, he can be allowed no less than one hundred and fifty pounds : and to allow above two hundred were superfluous, and to his hurt. . . . The ordinary rate of his expence is this : ten gold crowns a month his own diet, eight for his man, two crowns a month his fencing, as much dancing, no less his reading, and fifteen crowns monethly his riding ; but this exercise he shall discontinue all the heate of the year. The remainder of his 150 pound I allow him for apparell, bookes, Travelling charges, tennis play, and other extra-ordinary expenses.

Moryson estimated that £50 to £60 a year was sufficient for a gentleman who travelled without a servant, and took his journeys in the spring and autumn, staying in one place for the winter and another for the summer ; but Moryson was an exceptionally studious person, who probably did not indulge in tennis-play, or have fencing or dancing lessons.

Opportunities for travel were only to a slight extent restricted by the inability of any English subject to cross the seas to foreign parts without a licence from the sovereign or the Privy Council. Travelling licences seem to have been readily procurable, and were essential passports to foreign countries. The documents commonly specified the length of time during which they were valid, together with the number of horses and servants and the amount of money which the traveller carried with him. Thus in 1598 the Earl of Southampton, who was then in some disgrace, was granted a licence to ' travel beyond seas and remain two years with ten servants, six horses, and two hundred pounds in money '. Next year Peregrine Bertie, younger son of Lord Willoughby of Eresby, was granted a licence to ' travel for three years with his tutor, two servants, two horses and sixty pounds in money'. Occasionally a sick man was granted a blank licence for ' travelling beyond seas for recovery of health '. Requests for extensions of time were granted unwillingly, and sometimes were answered by a summons from the Council to return home at once. There was a widespread suspicion that foreign travel weakened Protestant convictions and encouraged conversion to Roman Catholicism. Sometimes the licence expressly forbade its holder to visit Rome or St. Omer. But the prohibition as far as Rome was concerned was frequently evaded.

Not much hospitality was offered Elizabethan travellers, though the royal courts and noblemen gave them formal receptions and allowed the sights of the palaces to be seen. Travellers usually paid for their board and lodgings. Latin was still the universal language in educated circles, and few English travellers were unable to make themselves understood in that tongue.

Study at foreign universities was a chief object of the Elizabethan traveller. Paris, Montpellier, Padua, Bologna, all had many English or Scottish students. The University of Padua, 'the nursery of the arts', was in universal repute for its schools of medicine and law. The city was under the liberal rule of Venice. There William Harvey, the discoverer of the circulation of the blood, graduated M.D. in 1602. Horsemanship and fencing were also taught in the same city by experts of general fame. In most foreign universities students lodged in private houses. Residential colleges, as at Oxford and Cambridge, were unknown. Theodore Beza, the ruler of the theocratic state of Geneva during nearly the whole of Elizabeth's reign, entertained many young Englishmen or Scotchmen, who were studying theology. Among Beza's Elizabethan guests was Anthony Bacon, brother of Francis Bacon, who afterwards sojourned in the South of France for as long a period as twelve years (1579–91). Noblemen were wont to send their sons on long foreign tours in the company of governors and tutors, to hear lectures from distinguished professors at the chief universities, although as a rule they were not matriculated students. But many noblemen and gentlemen postponed foreign travel till the period of tutelage was past. Edward de Vere, Earl of Oxford, was twenty-five when he made his Italian tour, bringing home for the first time embroidered gloves and costly perfumes. Lord Herbert of Cherbury was the same age, and already had a wife and family before he made his first tour in France in 1608, and it was six years later before he visited Italy, going through Germany and returning through France by means of a *chaise à porteurs* over Mont Cenis.

A choice of routes lay at the free disposal of the Elizabethan traveller on landing at Dieppe or Hamburg, the favoured ports of debarkation. Germany was rich and peaceful, with active professors, scholars, and merchants scattered through the land. A religious truce prevailed in Germany before the storm of the Thirty Years' War. Sectarian bitterness, especially between Lutheran and Calvinist, was warm, but was held in check. Each German prince imposed his religion upon his subjects, and the sixty Free Cities were dominated by one or other of the three religious denominations, Catholics, Lutherans, and Calvinists. The Emperor himself, in his Austrian dominions, had proclaimed freedom of conscience, and most of his own guards were German Lutherans. Sir Thomas Overbury, who travelled in Germany in 1609, observed that the country, 'if it were subject to one monarchy would be terrible to all the rest', and he remarks that 'it only serves to balance itself'. The fortifications of the towns and the almost universal drunkenness of the men chiefly impressed the English traveller. German travellers were similarly struck by the absence of fortifications in England. English travellers, too, admired the way in which the peaceful citizens of towns were trained and practised in shooting, and commended 'the Germans, despite their lack of sobriety, for modesty, integrity, constancy, placability, equity, and for gravity, but somewhat inclining to the vice of dullness'.

The prestige of the imperial Court of Vienna, the flourishing city of Prague, and the independent kingdom of Poland, took many travellers further eastward. In Poland and Austria the intermittent attacks of the Turks were a standing menace. The high tide of the Sultan's power had passed, but the ebb was not yet perceived, and the slave-market of Constantinople was still plentifully supplied with Christian captives taken in war. The wealth and prosperity of Germany was increased by the misfortunes of her near neighbours. The war of the united provinces of the Low Countries and Spain was in spasmodic progress till 1609, and English soldiers had fought side by side with the Dutch. In France through near the whole of the time when Shakespeare was writing his plays, a national hero, Henry IV, occupied the throne, and ruled a gay Court. The civil wars of religion had cost France dear, but she showed her usual recuperative powers, and during Henry IV's reign was once more united and rejuvenated. Switzerland, as the seat of Calvinism, was to many congenial territory. Denmark, the country of 'Hamlet', excited Englishmen's interest. Fynes Moryson visited Denmark in 1593, and saw the castle of Cronberg at Elsinore, which commanded

Title-page of CORYAT'S *CRUDITIES* 1611 by WM HOLE

the entrance to the Baltic. The young king of Denmark, Christian IV, was brother of Anne, who married James VI of Scotland in 1589 and became Queen Anne of England in 1603. One of his governors was a grey-bearded old senator named 'Rosenkrantz', and his younger brother Ulric was a 'student in Wittenberg'.

From Spain, the arch-enemy of England, English travellers were excluded by the hostility of the Inquisition, even after the peace of 1604. If Englishmen respected without liking the Germans and Netherlanders, they hated the Spaniards; and if they found much to attract them in France, it was only the brightness and beauty of Italy, and of Italian art and literature, which inspired any romantic enthusiasm. The country was under divided rule, and offered varied receptions to the English travellers. The Pope's dominions formed a very substantial proportion of the country, while Lombardy and the kingdom of Naples were under the rule of Spain. The Papacy was still an aggressive power, and absorbed in 1598 the duchy of Ferrara with its traditions of Ariosto and Lucrezia Borgia, on the failure of heirs to the house of Este. The dukedoms of Mantua, Urbino, and Savoy, and the free cities of Lucca and Genoa were independent states, but the Grand Duchy of Florence and the Republic of Venice drew more foreign tourists than any other of the sovereign territories. Although Rome was regarded as the seat of Antichrist, English Protestants were suffered to see the sights and wonders of the Eternal City without much danger, and cardinals often gave them a friendly reception. The attraction of Italy steadily increased throughout the epoch. As early as 1574 Languet had written to Sir Philip Sidney, 'It seems to me quite absurd that your countrymen should make a point of speaking Italian well, since, as far as I know, you derive no advantage from them ; on the other hand, they derive the greatest from you, and therefore they ought rather to learn your language. Perhaps you are afraid you will not persuade them to take your money unless you speak with perfect fluency.' The Elizabethans were drawn to Italy by a predilection for culture, and all the varied allurements of an older and richer civilization. 'Some jay of Italy' (*Cymb.* III. iv. 51) proved a snare to many an Elizabethan tourist.

The most attractive town of all, not only to Englishmen, but to Frenchmen, Germans, and all the civilized world, was Venice, a little past the height of its greatest power, but perhaps at the greatest splendour of its decorative beauty and pictorial charm. Shakespeare makes the learned Holofernes say in *Love's Labour's Lost* (IV. ii. 98–101) :

I may speak of thee as the traveller doth of Venice:
—*Venetia, Venetia,*
Chi non te vede, non te pretia.

And the painstaking Moryson says that this most noble city is worthily called in Latin Venetia, as it were ' Veni etiam ', that is, ' Come again '. Tintoretto was living and working till 1594, and the new Rialto Bridge was commenced in 1588 and took three years to build, at a cost of two hundred and fifty thousand ducats. It was considered the latest and not the least of the glories of Venice. This great and powerful state and city of merchants—the greatest families had no scorn of commerce—was still the chief centre for trade and travel with the East, and, though losing ground steadily to the Turks, continued to do business with them even on the humiliating condition of paying a tribute. As the Jews did much of the business of the proud Turks, the ' Merchant of Venice ' was accustomed to deal with Shylock. The Venetians had lost Cyprus to the Turks in 1571, so the action of *Othello* must belong to an earlier period. Venice was also renowned throughout the world for the number and splendour of its courtesans, who surpassed in fame even those of Rome and Naples. English travellers report that if a man stepped into a gondola without giving particular directions the gondolier took him as a matter of course to the house of a courtesan. Except that she had to pay a tax to the state, she was free to live where she liked, to dress as finely as she could afford, and if any man refused her demands she could enforce a due payment by law. This solemn recognition of vice was always a surprise to Englishmen. Women of doubtful reputation were exposed at home to the capricious justice of constables and magistrates, as is reflected in *Measure for Measure*.

In 1572 Sir Philip Sidney went first to Paris, and when the St. Bartholomew's Massacre rendered the French capital unsafe for Protestants he passed through Strasburg into Germany, lodging at Frankfort with Wechel the printer.

A sojourn in Hungary and at Vienna preceded his visit to Venice, where his portrait was painted by Paolo Veronese. Subsequently he travelled to Genoa and Padua. On returning to Vienna he made a tour in both Poland and Bohemia, and came home to London in 1575 by way of Dresden, Heidelberg, and Antwerp, after an absence of three years.

In 1586, Edward la Zouche, Lord Zouche of Harringworth, went abroad at the age of thirty to qualify himself for the public service and to live cheaply. He was four years (1587–91) abroad, chiefly in Germany. Basle, Altdorf, Vienna, and Verona were the chief stopping-places in his tour.

Representative foreign travellers of the middle class in Shakespeare's era were Fynes Moryson and Sir Henry Wotton, the former two years and the latter four years younger than the dramatist. Both spent much time on the Continent after taking their degree at the university. Wotton's post-university tour lasted seven years, and Moryson's nearly six. Wotton went in 1589 from Oxford to the University of Altdorf. Thence he went to Linz to witness some experiments of the astronomer Kepler. Passing through Ingolstadt and Vienna he visited Rome, Naples, Genoa, Venice, Florence, Geneva, and Paris. Similarly, Moryson, on leaving Cambridge, went through Germany, Bohemia, and the Low Countries, where he matriculated at Leyden. Thence he passed through Denmark and Poland to Vienna, and afterwards into Italy. There he visited Naples, Rome, and many other cities, had an interview with Beza at Geneva, and came back through France.

The means and methods of travelling through Europe varied according to the rank of the traveller. Horse-riding was the usual manner. A nobleman or gentleman of position travelled with his own horses and servants. When Sir Philip Sidney set out on his continental travels in his eighteenth year in 1572, his licence authorized him to travel with three servants and four horses, but these numbers were often exceeded. Post-horses could also be had everywhere, but this was a somewhat expensive method of travel, as a footman had to be hired to bring the horse back every stage, and his expenses had to be paid, ' the footmen being as good and better drinkers than the horsemen '.

For a cheap and expeditious journey there was no better method than to buy a horse and sell him again at the journey's end. Fynes Moryson bought a horse at Cracow, in Galicia, and rode through Vienna and by Friuli into Italy, selling his horse with saddle and bridle at Padua. In another journey, when returning to England with all speed from Venice, Moryson bought two horses at Padua for himself and his servant, and rode over the Brenner and across Germany to Stade, at the mouth of the Elbe, whence there were regular sailings of English merchant ships to London. He was able to sell his horses with little or no loss.

Young Elizabethans who were travelling for study and experience were content to travel by public coaches and carriages, which were common in France, Holland, Germany, and Poland. In Germany the public coaches held six or eight people, and it was convenient to wait for a complement of travellers who were taking the same route, so as to have a full coach and lessened charges. A party of six paid fifty dollars—the dollar was worth about four shillings and fourpence—for a coach from Hamburg to Nuremberg, nine days' journey. In addition they paid for the coachman's food, but this was a matter of bargain. This long coach journey cost about two pounds a head. These coaches were sheltered at the top with hoops covered with leather or black cloth, which could be unbuckled and let down in fine weather. In the Low Countries most of the humbler travelling was done in long narrow wagons, 'the sides thereof being like racks for horses, and across over them short and somewhat narrow boards being fastened for passengers to sit upon, two in a rank, so as they hold some eight or ten passengers'. In Poland, being a flat country, coach travel was cheap, a coach from Dantzig to Cracow—ten days' journey—being hired for forty-four German gulden—the gulden being worth three shillings and fourpence. A coach which ran regularly from Paris through Dijon to Chalon-sur-Saône held ten persons, 'assez mal accommodez', paying six crowns each— about thirty-six shillings—for the journey.

Inns differed greatly in quality. Those in France were usually large and richly appointed; sometimes the sheets were of silk, and all the plate of silver. The inns of North Germany had a bad name. The discourtesy of the land-lords, and their arbitrary conduct, had been a by-word from the time of Erasmus, and probably throughout the Middle Ages. Travellers could have meals only at fixed times, and they often had to pay their share of what other visitors drank. The beds were below the English standard of comfort, and sometimes an undesirable bed-fellow was thrust upon the traveller. In South Germany better conditions prevailed. Montaigne compares the accommodation there very favourably with that offered in France. In Poland the inns were provided only with hard benches for sleeping, and travellers carried their bedding with them. Moryson complains that his horseman's coat lined with wolf's fur had to serve him for his mattress.

Diplomatic missions from England occasionally traversed parts of the Continent in imposing state. Sir Henry Wotton, who had been English Ambassador in Venice since the accession of James I, was dispatched in the spring of 1612 on a special mission to the Court of the Duke of Savoy at Turin to negotiate a marriage between Henry, Prince of Wales, and a daughter of Charles Emmanuel. The party consisted of fifty horsemen. Wotton carried as a present to the Duke a splendid sword mounted in gold and set with diamonds and valued at £16,000. Ten ambling horses with richly embroidered saddles and furniture were in charge of Sir Peter Saltonstall, one of the king's equerries, as a further gift. From Lyons the embassage rode over the Alps, and were received with splendid hospitality on their arrival in Turin.

An even more splendid embassy landed in the spring of 1605 at Corunna—which Englishmen called 'the Groyne' (a corruption of the French Corogne)—peace having been proclaimed between Spain and England the year before. A train of 600 Englishmen accompanied the English Ambassador, Sir Charles Cornwallis, and the special envoy, the Lord Admiral, the Earl of Nottingham, who was sent by King James as a compliment to King Philip in return for the recent visit to England of the Constable of Castile, who signed the treaty. The English cortège, after a toilsome journey through Galicia and across the mountains of Leon, arrived at Valladolid in Castile, where Philip III, under the tutelage of his all-powerful favourite, the Duke of Lerma, held his Court. But although the long war between Spain and England was ended, there was still no free travel in the land of the Inquisition for ordinary Englishmen.

English embassies of like size and magnificence visited most of the Courts of Europe from time to time in Shakespeare's epoch. Shakespeare's own profession also furnished organized bands of English travellers on a less splendid scale. Companies of English players made tours in Germany, France, Denmark, Austria, and the Low Countries. An English company invariably visited the great fairs held at Frankfort on the Main both in spring and autumn. They were also seen occasionally at the imperial Court at Gratz. Great interest was excited in them wherever they went, although they spoke their plays in English. England led the world in theatrical matters. Coryat, who was at Venice in 1608, went to a playhouse and saw a comedy acted. He deemed the building very inferior to the London standard, although he was impressed by the new experience of seeing women act.

It was chiefly commerce which drew Englishmen outside the limits of the European continent. There was a settlement at Aleppo of English merchants who belonged to the Levant Company, and the East India Company had its settlement at Agra. But overland travel in the East chiefly revolved round Aleppo. The city was reached from Turkey and the Levant, and long overland expeditions through Arabia and Persia were often organized there by Elizabethan visitors who sought the novel experiences of travel as well as the expansion of trade. Palestine and Egypt sometimes came within the tour.

Land travel in Eastern countries has not changed much since Shakespeare's time. The method was by caravan, which was formed of riding horses and mules and heavily laden camels. One Eastern traveller, John Cartwright, compares the means of transport to that of 'our carriers here in England'. Lodging was easily obtainable in the villages of Persia and Arabia, and good arrangements were made for camping in the deserts.

Laurence Aldersey, who made two journeys to the Levant in Shakespeare's youth, in 1581 and 1586 respectively, travelled overland to and from Venice and London in 1581. When in the East he spent a fortnight in Jerusalem and its neighbourhood. In his second journey he passed a fortnight in Egypt, visiting Alexandria and Cairo. The narrative of his travels, which is preserved by Hakluyt, is an interesting record.

Moryson's second tour, which lasted fully eighteen months (December 1595 to July 1597), brought him from Venice by sea to Joppa, whence he travelled by way of Tripoli, Aleppo, and Antioch, to Constantinople.

More adventurous and varied was Sir Anthony Sherley's journey to Persia in 1599. He left Venice with twenty-five English followers May 29, 1599. From Aleppo he sailed down the Euphrates to Babylon, and, after five months' stay in Persia, went by way of the Caspian Sea to Moscow. Thence he passed through the chief towns of Germany— Nuremberg, Augsburg, Munich, Innsbruck, and Trent—to Rome. The journey lasted nearly two years. The Sherleys were a family of travellers both in the East and South. Sir Anthony's brother, Robert, also spent much time in Persia in trading and diplomatic ventures. A third brother, Sir Thomas Sherley, obtained notoriety by his privateering expeditions in the Mediterranean, which led to a long imprisonment at Constantinople. The varied adventures of the three brothers in South and Eastern Europe formed the subject of a popular but illiterate play, *The Travailes of the Three English Brothers*, which was acted at the Curtain in 1607.

In 1600 four Englishmen, Jeffrey Kirby, Edward Abbot, merchants, John Elkin, gentleman, and Jasper Tyon, jeweller, travelled from Aleppo by Damascus to Jerusalem. They were accompanied by William Biddulph, minister to the company of English merchants resident in Aleppo, to whose letters we are indebted for the narrative. They hired a janizary for their protection, who was sufficient to secure them from insult and injury from Turks, but was small protection against bands of Arab thieves, for which they had to trust to their firearms and the help of other parties of travellers, with whom they joined whenever possible. The journey occupied twenty days, including two days' rest at Damascus. At Jerusalem they met Henry Tymberlake, an Englishman who had just made the journey by land from ' Grand Cairo in Egypt '. Biddulph relates how six Englishmen, when visiting Constantinople, had written their names on Pompey's Pillar.

In 1603 another English minister, John Cartwright, set out from Aleppo with an English merchant, John Mildenhall, for Ispahan, which he reached safely by caravan, returning in the like manner. His companion, Mildenhall, was bound for Lahore in India, and parted from him on the way.

But the most stirring exploit of all was the pedestrian tour of Thomas Coryat from Aleppo to India. He had already distinguished himself by a long walk through Europe. On May 11, 1608, he sailed from Dover to Calais, whence he made his way, chiefly on foot, through France and Italy to Venice. He reached that city on June 24 and left it on August 8, passing through Switzerland and Germany to London, where he arrived on October 3, after an absence of five months. Some part of the journey was made on cart, on horseback, and by boat. He crossed Mont Cenis on the outward journey on a *chaise à porteurs*, but he relied chiefly on his legs, and on his return home hung up his shoes,[1] in which he had covered a distance of 1,975 miles, in the church of his native place, Odcombe in Somerset. To a record of these experiences which he published in a strange book entitled *Coryats Crudities*, sixty wits of the day prefixed a generous series of mock-heroic eulogies.

For his Eastern journey, he sailed first to Constantinople (1612); thence he visited Greece and Asia Minor. From Smyrna he went by sea to Alexandria, and travelled up the Nile as far as Cairo and back. After a tour through Palestine he joined a caravan to Mesopotamia, passed through Persia to Candahar in Afghanistan, and thence reached Lahore and Agra (1616). He asserts: 'I spent in my ten months' travel between Aleppo and the Mogul's Court but three pounds sterling, yet fared reasonable well every day; victuals being so cheape in some countries where I travelled that I oftentimes lived competently for a penny sterling a day; yet of that three pounds I was cozened of no less than ten shillings by certain lewd Christians of the Armenian nation.' At the Mogul's Court he found a Mr. Peter Rogers, 'minister and preacher of our nation in this place', in the service of the East India Company. He addressed a special letter by this Mr. Peter Rogers in November 1615 to a club, '"The Worshipful Fraternity of

---

[1] These are depicted in one of the prefatory pages of his book, which is here reproduced, together with the title-page.

Incipit Henricus Peacham.

Memoriæ Sacrum.

Seu calcei Laureati THOMÆ CORYATI *Odcombiensis, Peregrinantium noſtri Seculi facile Principis.*

Ad Thomam noſtrum.

CVr Coryate *tibi calcem Phœbeia Daphne*
Cinxerit, & nudæ Laurea nulla comæ?
Inſanos mundi forſan contemnis honores,
Ignibus & Lauro es tutus ab Æmiliæ.
Veriùs at capitis pleni (Coryate) *miſerta*
In calces imos Muſa reiecit onus.

To

Sirenaical Gentlemen ", that meet the first Friday of every month at the sign of the Mermaid in Bread Street in London ', and his special remembrances to Ben Jonson and John Donne. Shakespeare did not belong to this Club, for he had then retired to Stratford.

BIBLIOGRAPHY.—I. Home Travel. WILLIAM HARRISON's *Description of England*, 1577–87, edited from HOLINSHED's *Chronicle* by F. J. Furnivall (New Shakspere Society), 1877, gives some interesting details which are supplemented in the notes to this edition. FYNES MORYSON'S *An Itinerary*: containing his ten yeeres travell through the twelve dominions of Germany . . . Italy, Turky, France, England, Scotland, and Ireland, 3 parts, 1617; WILLIAM KEMP's *Nine Daies Wonder : Performed in a Daunce from London to Norwich*, ed. Alexander Dyce (Camden Society), 1840; JOHN TAYLOR'S *The Pennyles Pilgrimage, or the Money-lesse Perambulation of John Taylor . . . How he travailed on foot from London to Edenborough*, 1618 (Spenser Society, 1868–9) and *The Carriers Cosmographia, or a briefe relation of the Innes . . . in or neare London*, 1637 (Spenser Society, 1873), are serviceable.

Useful modern works are : GEORGE ROBERTS'S *The Social History of the People of the Southern Countries*, 1856; WILLIAM LEWIN'S *Her Majesty's Mails : an historical account of the Post Office*, 1864 ; *England as seen by Foreigners in the days of Elizabeth and James I*, ed. W. Brenchley Rye, 1865; J. W. HALES'S *Notes and Essays on Shakespeare* (I. From Stratford on Avon to London), 1884; HALLIWELL-PHILLIPPS'S *Outlines of the Life of Shakespeare*, 1881, &c.; J. J. JUSSERAND'S *English Wayfaring Life in the Middle Ages* (fourteenth century), 1889.

II. Foreign Travel. A chief contemporary authority is FYNES MORYSON'S *Itinerary* (as above), together with his *Shakespeare's Europe : unpublished chapters of Fynes Moryson's 'Itinerary'*, ed. Charles Hughes, 1903. The *Calendars of State Papers* give many examples of licences for travel. See also ROBERT DALLINGTON'S *A Method for Travel—shewed by taking the view of France*, 1605, and JAMES HOWELL'S *Instructions for Forreine Travell*, 1642 (ed. Arber, 1869). For travel by Frenchmen in England and by English actors in France see J. J. JUSSERAND'S *Shakespeare in France*, 1899. For foreign tours of English players see ALBERT COHN'S *Shakespeare in Germany in the Sixteenth and Seventeenth Centuries, An account of English actors in Germany and the Netherlands*, 1865 ; JOHANNES MEISSNER'S *Die englischen Comödianten zur Zeit Shakespeares in Oesterreich*, 1884 ; and HERZ'S *Englische Schauspieler und englische Schauspiele zur Zeit Shakespeares in Deutschland*, 1903. For travel in the East see Sir *Anthony Sherley his relation of his travels into Persia*, London, 1613 ; *A True Report of Sir A. Shierlie's Journey overland to Venice . . . Antioch, Aleppo . . . Babilon . . . Persia*, &c., London, 1600 ; JOHN CARTWRIGHT'S *The Preachers Travels : Wherein is set down a true Journall to the confines of the East Indies*, &c., London, 1611, extracts from which are given by Purchas; LAURENCE ALDERSEY'S *Journal of his tour to Aleppo* in Hakluyt; THOMAS CORYAT'S *Coryats Crudities. Hastily gobled up in five Moneths travells in France, Savoy, Italy, . . . and the Netherlands*, 1611 ; and WILLIAM BIDDULPH'S Letters, published by Lavender, 1609.

VIII

EDUCATION

BY

SIR JOHN EDWIN SANDYS

SCHOOLS AND SCHOOL-BOOKS

IN our survey of the schools of England in the age of Shakespeare we may fitly begin with the two ancient and famous colleges of Winchester and Eton. Winchester, which had been founded in 1387, was still mainly governed by the statutes of William of Wykeham. Under Henry VI it had been the school of Grocyn and of Warham. Under Edward VI it had been threatened with dissolution by the Chantries Act of 1547, but the Royal Commission of that year did little more than require all the boys to read ' the New Testament in English and Latin ', adding that ' the Warden and schoolmaster in all lectures and lessons of prophane authors shall confute and refel by allegation of Scriptures all such sentences and opinions as seem contrary to the Word of God and Christian Religion '. Latin verses were composed by the school in honour of the visit of King Edward in 1552 ; of Queen Mary in 1554, on the occasion of her marriage with Philip in Winchester Cathedral ; and of Queen Elizabeth in 1570. The first and the last of these events must have aroused the keenest interest on the part of Christopher Johnson, head master from 1560 to 1571. He was a lad at Winchester (1549–53), and was the reputed author of a Latin poem (now ascribed to Robert Mathew, c. 1647) from which we learn that the boys rose at five and went to chapel at six, and, after prayers, devoted themselves to writing Latin verses, every one of them ' chained as closely to his desk as Prometheus to the crag on Caucasus '.

During the sixteenth century, Eton (which had been founded by Henry VI in 1441) passed under the rule of no fewer than twenty-one head-masters. One of them, Nicholas

Udall (1505–56), who published, in 1534, his *Floures for Latine spekynge, selected and gathered oute of Terence, and the same translated into Englysshe*, is described by his distinguished pupil, Walter Haddon, as 'the best Schoolmaster' and 'the greatest beater' of his time. He is still more famous as the author of the earliest known English comedy, *Ralph Roister Doister*. In 1542 he published an English version of Erasmus's *Apophthegms*, and he ultimately became play-writer to Queen Mary, and head-master of Westminster for the last two years of his life.

The first of English schools to be closely connected with the Revival of Learning was the New School of St. Paul's in London, founded about 1509 by Dean Colet,[1] the friend of Erasmus. In his Statutes of 1518 he enjoined that Christian writers of Latin, such as Lactantius, should be taught in preference to Caesar, Sallust, Virgil, and Terence, but these last were regarded as the ultimate standards of style, and the fact that Virgil, Terence, and Cicero were taught from the first is implied in the *Carmen de Moribus*, composed by the first high-master, William Lily or Lyly. Lily was among the earliest of the Greek students of his age ; Erasmus, in a Sapphic poem written for the school, confidently asserts that Lily's pupils will learn Greek as well as Latin ; while the Latin Grammar, originally com-

[1] The conditions on which boys were admitted to St. Paul's are detailed in Colet's *Aeditio* ; they are thus given in the edition of 1537 :

The master shal reherse these articles to them that offer their children, on this wise here folowinge.

If your childe can rede, and write latin, and englisshe sufficiently, so that he be able to rede and write his owne lessons, than he shal be admitted into the schole for a scholer.

If your childe after resonable season proued be founde here vnapte, and vnable to leringe, than ye warned therof shal take him awaye, that he occupye not here roume in vain.

If he be apte to lerne ye shal be content y^t he continue here tyl he haue some competent literature.

If he be absent 6 dayes, and in that meane season ye shewe not cause resonable (resonable cause is only sekenes) than his roume to be voyde, without he be admitted again and paye 4d.

Also after cause shewed, if he continue so absent tyl the weke of admission in the nexte quarter, and than ye shewe not the continuance of his sekenes : than his rowme to be voyde, and he none of the schole, til he be admitted again and paye 4d. for writing of his name.

Also if he fal thrise in absence, he shal be admitted no more.

Your childe shal on childermas daye waite vpon the Bishop at Pouwls and offer there.

Also ye shal finde him waxe in winter.

Also ye shal finde him convenient bokes to his lerninge.

If the offerer be content with these articles than let his childe be admitted.

posed for St. Paul's by Colet and Lily, was in its ultimate
form associated for no less than three and a half centuries
with the learning of Latin in almost all the schools of
England.

St. Paul's was soon followed by the Mercers' ' Chapel
School ', established in 1541 on the site of the ancient school
of St. Thomas of Acon ; and by Christ's Hospital, founded
in the former buildings of the Grey Friars in 1552, and soon
celebrated as the school of the historian Camden, who,
however, left it for St. Paul's, and, in 1593, became head
master of Westminster.

The ancient School of Westminster, which had been
founded anew under Henry VIII in 1540, was re-established
by Elizabeth in 1560. It owed much of its prosperity to the
fostering care of successive Deans of Westminster, one of
whom, the celebrated Lancelot Andrewes, towards the close
of the queen's reign, often ' sent for the uppermost scholars
to his lodgings at night and kept them with him from
eight to eleven, unfolding to them the best rudiments of the
Greek tongue and the elements of the Hebrew Grammar '.
Merchant Taylors' School, which was founded in 1561,
was described, in 1607, as ' a school for liberty most free,
being open especially for poore men's children, as well of
all nations, as for the marchauntailors themselves '.[1]

Among the country grammar schools connected with the
name of Henry VIII, a special interest attaches to that of
Warwick, which was founded afresh as ' the King's Newe
Scole of Warwyke ' in 1545. Under Elizabeth it was housed
in part of the picturesque buildings of the Earl of Leicester's
Hospital ; and, from about 1595 to 1620, its head-master
was John Owen, the most famous English writer of Latin
epigrams.

Of the schools described as the ' Grammar Schools of
King Edward VI ', many had existed in various forms long
before his time. The school originally founded by Roger
Lupton at Sedbergh, in 1523-5, was refounded in 1551.
This was partly due to Thomas Lever's public protest
against the spoliation of endowments, by which that school
' in the North countrey ' was ' now solde, decayed, and
lost '.[2] In the same year, on the banks of the Severn,

[1] H. Staunton's *Great Schools*, p. 177, ed. 1869.
[2] Lever's *Sermons*, p. 81, ed. Arber.

Shrewsbury School was refounded as a 'Free Grammar School', which soon acquired a more than local fame. Philip Sidney and his friend and future biographer, Fulke Greville, were entered on the books of that school on the same day in 1564.

At Stratford-on-Avon we read of a *rector scolarum* as early as 1295. In 1482 a chaplain of the Guild of the Holy Cross endowed it as a Free Grammar School; and in 1552, under Edward VI, the people of Stratford bought back from the Crown their Guild, their Almshouses, and their School, which thus, by the Charter of June 1553, gained a fresh lease of life under the name of 'The King's New School of Stratford upon Avon'. The square tower of the Chapel of the ancient Guild still looks down on the adjacent Grammar School, and a school erected in 1427, in the yard below the Chapel and the Almshouses, is part of the existing buildings. From 1568 to 1595 the school was held in the adjoining chapel. In *Twelfth Night*, a play assigned to 1600, Malvolio is compared to 'a pedant

A SCHOOLMASTER WITH SCHOLARS.
From the frontispiece of the comedy
Pedantius, 1631.

that keeps a school i' the church' (III. ii. 80); and it has been suggested that the poet is here recalling the chapel in which the school was held in the days of his own boyhood; but it is at least as likely that he was thinking of the school in St. Olave's, Southwark (near his theatre), or that of St. Michael's, Cornhill. In *As You Like It*

(II. vii. 145), the second of the seven ages of man is represented by

> the whining school-boy, with his satchel
> And shining morning face, creeping like snail
> Unwillingly to school;

while the boy's readiness to leave his books is noticed in *Romeo and Juliet* (II. ii. 156) and *The Taming of the Shrew* (III. ii. 152). In the latter play (III. i. 18 f.), Bianca, the daughter of a rich gentleman of Padua, is made to say,

> I am no breeching scholar [i. e. ' no novice '] in the schools;
> I'll not be tied to hours nor 'pointed times,
> But learn my lessons as I please myself.

Then follows a construing lesson in Ovid. We have also ' questions in accidence ' in *The Merry Wives of Windsor* (IV. i. 16 ff.).

Very few schools were founded during the brief reign of Queen Mary. Sir John Porte, who in 1556 had sat on a commission ' to search out heresies and to punish them ', made his will in March and died in June 1557. By this will he founded a school, which was to be placed either at Etwall or at Repton, in the south of Derbyshire, and he directed ' that the scholars of the said school should pray three times a day ' for the repose of his soul, and those of members of his family, and for all Christian souls. It is clear that the founder was thinking of a school of the old chantry type; but Queen Elizabeth had already been on the throne for more than six months before the school acquired ' a local habitation, and a name '. The executors fortunately chose for the site, not Etwall (where they placed the founder's hospital), but Repton, on the opposite bank of the river, where, on the twelfth day of June, 1559, they purchased the partially dismantled buildings of the ancient Priory. Repton soon became a prosperous school of the new type. Only a limited and local fame was then enjoyed by schools which are now the most widely known of the distinctively Elizabethan foundations. Among these are Rugby (1567), once a small school in comparison with the ancient school in the county town of Warwick; Uppingham (1584), in the bracing air of Rutlandshire; and the famous school founded in 1571 at Harrow-on-the-Hill. It was not until late in the life of Shakespeare and under the reign of James I that Charterhouse was founded, in 1611, by Thomas

Sutton, a man of ample means, who had travelled abroad, was familiar with foreign languages, and had seen service as a military officer in the reign of Elizabeth. Of all the other schools of that age we must here be content to say with the author of *A Description of England* : ' There are great number of Grammar Schools throughout the realm, and those very liberally endowed, for the better relief of poor scholars, so that there are not many corporate towns now under the Queen's dominion that have not one grammar school at the least with a sufficient living for a master and usher appointed to the same.' [1]

Two centuries before the boyhood of Shakespeare, the villeins led by Wat Tyler, in 1381, obliged ' teachers of children in grammar schooles to sweare never to instruct any in their art. . . . It was dangerous among them to be knowne for one that was lerned, and more dangerous, if any man were found with a penner and inkhorne at his side : for such seldome or never escaped from them with life.' Such is the language of Holinshed's *Chronicle*. Hence, in Shakespeare's version of the far later rising of the men of Kent, in 1450, when some of Jack Cade's followers bring forward the clerk of Chatham (who has been found ' setting of boys' copies ' and ' has a book in his possession with red letters in 't ', 'can write and read and cast accompt ', 'make obligations, and write courthand ', and, instead of making a mark ' like an honest plain-dealing man ', has been so well brought up that he can write his own name), Cade immediately declares him a conjurer, a villain, and a traitor, and sentences him to be hanged at once, ' with his pen and his ink-horne about his neck ' (2 *Hen. VI*, IV. ii. 92–117). In the same play, the poet is writing independently of the chronicler, when Cade, in summing up the offences for which Lord Say is to be beheaded, adds :

Thou hast most traitorously corrupted the youth of the realm in erecting a grammar school (IV. vii. 35–7).

At Stratford-on-Avon, Richard Fox, who has been identified with the founder of Corpus Christi College, Oxford, was the ' Master of Grammar ' in 1477–8. Walter Roche, who had been elected Fellow of Corpus in 1558, was master in 1571–3, and was succeeded by Hunt and (in 1577) by Jenkins, both of whom have been identified with Fellows

---

[1] W. Harrison, in Holinshed, ed. 1587, bk. ii, chap. 3, *prope finem*.

of colleges at Oxford. If Shakespeare went to school at the age of seven, in 1571, his first master was Walter Roche, and he may also have come under the care of Hunt and Jenkins. The better side of the ordinary rural schoolmaster is represented by the precise and pedantic Holofernes of *Love's Labour's Lost* (v. i), and the Welshman, Sir Hugh Evans, in *The Merry Wives of Windsor* (IV. i) ; and the worse by the conjurer and impostor, Pinch, in *The Comedy of Errors* (v. i. 238 ff.).

Before a boy could be admitted into Stratford School it was necessary for him to have attained the age of seven, and to be able to read. The elementary schoolmaster in *Love's Labour's Lost* (v. i. 49) 'teaches boys the horn-book'. This was a primer framed in wood and covered with a thin plate of transparent horn. It included the alphabet in small letters and in capitals, with combinations of the five vowels with *b*, *c*, and *d*, and the Lord's Prayer in English. The first of these alphabets, which ended with the abbreviation for 'and', began with the mark of the cross. Hence the alphabet was commonly known as the 'Christ cross row'—the 'cross-row' of *King Richard III*, I. i. 55. A short catechism was often included in the 'A-B-C book' (the 'absey-book' of *King John* I. i. 196).

The English grammar school of the Elizabethan age was primarily a school for learning Latin. The Latin Grammar in ordinary use was a composite work which owed its origin to Colet's Accidence of 1509, and Lily's Rudiments of Syntax. Both of these were written in English. They were followed by Lily's Latin Syntax, written in Latin, and first printed by Pynson in 1513. The editions of Lily's Latin Grammar, published in 1566, 1568, 1574, may well have been in use at Stratford in Shakespeare's boyhood.[1] The poet's familiarity with this Grammar is proved by the whole of the scene in *The Merry Wives of Windsor* (IV. i) where the Welsh schoolmaster asks the boy William 'some questions in his accidence'. As in that scene, so in the first two pages of the Grammar, we find *lapis* and *pulcher*,

---

[1] Reprinted from editions of 1527, 1566, 1574 in *Shakespeare Jahrbuch*, 1908-9. For edition of 1568 see *Notes and Queries*, December 11, 1880, p. 462 b. A copy of the edition of 1574 is preserved among Selden's books in the Bodleian. The title-page of the second (or Latin) part is reproduced on p. 231; that of the first (or English) part has the same design, with different lettering.

A HORNBOOK OF THE TIME OF CHARLES I
FOUND IN 1881 DURING EXCAVATION AT
BRASENOSE COLLEGE OXFORD AND NOW
IN THE BODLEIAN LIBRARY. THE UPPER
PART OF THE HORN AND SOME OF THE
PINS HAVE BEEN RESTORED

BREVISSIMA

INSTITVTIO
SEV RATIO GRAM-
matices cognoscendæ, ad
omnium puerorum vtilitatem
perscripta, quam solam Re-
gia Maiestas in omnibus
Scholis profitendam
præcipit.

EXCVSVM LON-
dini, per assignatio-
nem Francisci
Floræ.

M.D.LXXIIII.

Title-page of part 2 of Lily's Latin Grammar, 1574.

with the statement that 'articles are borrowed of the pro-
noune, and be thus declined', &c., and *vocativo caret*, as well as
vocativo ô musa. From the same source, '*homo* is a common
name to all men,' is quoted in *1 Henry IV* (II. i. 104). The
section on interjections has left its trace in *Much Ado
About Nothing* (IV. i. 22). The phrases 'diluculo surgere
saluberrimum' and 'vir sapit qui pauca loquitur' are
partly or fully quoted in *Twelfth Night* (II. iii. 2) and in
Love's Labour's Lost (IV. ii. 82) respectively. In *The Taming
of the Shrew* (I. i. 167) 'redime te captum quam queas minimo'
is literally copied from Lily's Latin syntax—of the ablative
after the verb, whereas the original line in the current Elizabethan (and other) editions of Terence runs : 'quid agas ?
nisi ut te redimas captum quam queas minimo' (*Eun.* I. i. 30).
The Grammar is the most obvious source of 'novi hominem
tanquam te' (*Love's L. L.* v. i. 10) and 'ad unguem' (*ib.* 84).
Twice in this text-book we find the Horatian lines 'Integer
vitae', &c. When the words are quoted in *Titus Andronicus* (IV. ii. 20–3), Chiron observes : 'O, 'tis a verse in
Horace ; I know it well : I read it in the grammar long ago.'
The use of some manual of short Latin phrases is implied
by passages in *Love's Labour's Lost* (IV. ii. 3–7 and v. i. 30–4),
especially in the question and answer : 'Videsne quis venit ?
Video, et gaudeo.' Aesop's fables were studied in Latin
versions, and seven of them are more or less distinctly
noticed in Shakespeare, e.g. 'The Fox and the Grapes' in
All's Well that Ends Well (II. i. 73 ff.).

One of the most popular school-books was the *Bucolica,*
or Eclogues, of Baptista Spagnolo (1448–1516), known as
Mantuanus, from the place of his birth, of whom it was said
that some would make him almost a second Maro.[1] The
earliest dated edition is that of Mantua, 1498. It was
translated into English by George Turbervile in 1567, and
the original text was published in London in 1573 and 1582.
The very first line is quoted by Holofernes in *Love's Labour's
Lost* (IV. ii. 96–103) :

Fauste, precor, gelida quando pecus omne sub umbra Ruminat,
and so forth.　Ah, good old Mantuan ! . . . Who understandeth thee
not, loves thee not.

Mantuanus is prescribed as a text-book in the original
statutes of St. Paul's, of St. Bees in 1583, and of Durham

---

[1] *Erasmi Epistolae*, ed. P. S. Allen. i. 163.

in 1593 ; as late as 1660, Charles Hoole elaborately explained the best method of giving lessons from the Eclogues.

Another favourite text-book was the *Zodiacus Vitae* of Marcellus Palingenius, a native of Stellata, not far from Ferrara, whose poem consists of more than 9,000 Latin hexameters. Written under the influence of Lucretius and Virgil, of Dante and Ariosto, it includes a survey of the life of man, and reflects the current thought of the day on morals and philosophy. It was prescribed as a text-book at St. Saviour's, Southwark (1562), as well as at St. Bees and Durham, and at Camberwell Grammar School in the year before Shakespeare's death. There were at least six editions printed in England between 1574 and 1616, and it had already been translated by Barnabe Googe in 1565.

In contrast with these importations from northern Italy, England could claim as her own the patriotic poems written in Latin hexameters by Christopher Ocland, a schoolmaster of Cheltenham and Greenwich. His *Anglorum Prælia* (1580) told the story of all the battles of the English from the beginning of the reign of Edward III to the end of that of Queen Mary. His *Elizabetha* (1582) was a panegyric on the peaceful rule of the queen. By an Act of the Privy Council of 21st April, 1582, the study of both poems was made compulsory in all the schools of the realm. ' The subject or matter of the saide Booke ' (say the Lords of the Privy Council) ' is such as is worthie to be read of all men, and especially in common schooles, where divers heathen Poets are ordinarily reade and taught, from the which the youth of the realme doth rather receive infection in manners than advauncement in vertue '. The matter of this book is doubtless ' heroical and of good instruction ', but it is only with the aid of a marginal note that we are enabled to identify the description of the battle of Agincourt, and it may well be doubted whether such a description was so likely to ' wake the hero in the boy ' as the patriotic passages of *Henry V*, which saw the light some fifteen years later.

The school-books of the Elizabethan age included the *Sententiae Pueriles* of Leonhard Culmann of Krailsheim, published at Leipzig in 1543 and entered on the Stationers' Register in 1569–70. It comprises a large number of short sentences from Latin authors. ' Belli incertus exitus ' finds its parallel in *Coriolanus* (v. iii. 141), and ' Doloris medicus tempus' in *The Two Gentlemen of Verona* (III. ii. 15), and in *Cymbeline* (III. v. 37).

The *Pueriles Confabulatiunculae* of Evaldus Gallus were prescribed at St. Bees in 1583. In tone and taste this conversation-book is inferior to those of the immediately preceding age. Foremost among these was the *Colloquia* of Erasmus, enlarged from time to time from the pamphlet of 1519 to the substantial volume of 1530. The vigour of its incidental attacks on the superstitions of the day led to its being widely read wherever the influence of the Reformation extended. Among other dialogues were the *Linguae Latinae Exercitatio* of Vives (1539), with its graphic touches of school-life and its dexterous introduction of Greek learning; the 'Sacred Dialogues' of Sébastien Castellion (1551); and the *Colloquia Scholastica* (1564) of Maturin Cordier (Corderius). These vivid pictures of the aims of the schoolmaster and the life of the schoolboy were translated by Brinsley and Hoole, and were still in use down to the end of the first third of the nineteenth century.

The vocabularies and dictionaries used in schools included Stanbridge's *Vocabula*, first printed by Wynkyn de Worde in 1507 and finally edited by Brinsley in 1630. The Latin-English Dictionary of Sir Thomas Elyot (1538) was improved and expanded by Thomas Cooper (1548, &c.), and finally published under the new title of *Thesaurus linguae Romanae et Britannicae* (1565, &c.). Cooper's Dictionary was recommended for general use by Queen Elizabeth, and its compiler, from being master of Magdalen College School rose to be Dean of Christ Church and of Gloucester, and Bishop of Lincoln and Winchester. His work was in part the source of the *Alvearie, or Triple Dictionarie in Englishe, Latin, and French*, prepared by John Baret, Fellow of Trinity, Cambridge (1573; Greek was added in 1580). These dictionaries were succeeded by the work of Thomas Thomas (Cambridge, 1587), and one of the subsequent editions of Thomas's book was supplemented by Philemon Holland (1615). For use in schools an English-Latin Dictionary was produced by John Withals in or before 1556 and repeatedly reissued down to 1634. It was arranged according to subjects, the aim being to aid the acquisition of Latin for purposes of speaking as well as writing. There were also various manuals for Latin verse composition.

In the plan of studies for Ipswich Grammar School prefixed to Wolsey's Latin Grammar (1529), the authors prescribed are to be read in the following order, the Latin Aesop and Terence, Virgil 'the prince of all poets', Cicero (*Select Letters*), Sallust or Caesar, Horace (*Epistles*), and Ovid (*Metamorphoses* or *Fasti*). The highest form studied the Grammar of Donatus and the *Elegantiae* of Valla. Instruction was to be given in an intelligent spirit, as is illustrated in some suggestions on the teaching of Terence.

The course of study followed in Elizabethan schools does not differ materially from that laid down by Wolsey, and (with the exception of Valla's *Elegantiae*) the curriculum at Ipswich may be accepted as approximately representing the curriculum at Stratford. Sallust was, in general, studied more than Caesar, but there is no proof that Shakespeare read either of these authors in the original. A knowledge of the text of Ovid's *Heroides* and *Metamorphoses* is implied in several passages. But it is not probable that Shakespeare found at school the couplet from the *Amores* (I. xv. 35 f.), which he places on the title-page of *Venus and Adonis*, or the reference to the *Ars Amatoria* (i. 633) in *Romeo and Juliet* (II. ii. 92 f.) :

> At lovers' perjuries, they say, Jove laughs.

Virgil's *Aeneid* (i. 11), 'Tantaene animis caelestibus irae ? ' is accurately quoted in *2 Henry VI*, II. i. 24 ; and a blend of *Aeneid* vii. 446, and Ovid's *Metamorphoses* iii. 40, has resulted in the less accurate reminiscence : 'gelidus timor occupat artus ' (*ib.* IV. i. 117).

It is not necessary to assume that Shakespeare read the *Menaechmi* of Plautus in the original, either at school or afterwards, but it seems simpler to suppose that he had some knowledge of the Latin text. Seneca's *Phaedra* (679, 1180) was known to the author of *Titus Andronicus* (IV. i. 81 f., II. i. 133 f.). Both dramatists are mentioned in a single sentence of *Hamlet* (II. ii. 419) :

> Seneca cannot be too heavy, nor Plautus too light.

We can only glance for one moment at the Elizabethan writers on the theory and practice of education. The Latin books recommended by Roger Ascham in *The Scholemaster* (posthumously published in 1570) are the *Letters* and *Speeches* of Cicero, with Terence, Plautus, Caesar, and

Livy; and translation and retranslation are prescribed as the best method for learning Latin. In opposing the opinion of a bishop that 'we have now no nede of the Greeke tonge, when all things be translated into Latin', Ascham pointedly urges that 'even the best translation is . . . but an evill imped wing to flie withall, or a hevie stompe leg of wood to go withall'.[1]

Richard Mulcaster, of Eton and Christ Church, Oxford, head master of Merchant Taylors' and of St. Paul's, sets forth the results of his long educational experiences in the *Positions* dedicated in 1581 to Queen Elizabeth. Like Ascham, he writes in English, but with a difference which is not in his favour. He is fully conscious of the merits of Latin as a means of education, but he strongly pleads that a place beside it should be found for English. In a sentence contrasting strangely with his ordinary cumbersome style he adds : 'I love Rome, but London better; I favour Italy, but England more; I honour Latin, but worship English.'

William Kemp, master of Plymouth Grammar School, was prompted to write his work on *The Education of Children* (1588) by the hope that the good town of Plymouth might 'bring forth some young imps and buds of learning'. He names logic and rhetoric as the appropriate subjects for a course of three years between 13 and 16 ; but only a sixth part of the boys' time is to be given to the formal side of these subjects ; all the rest is to be devoted to the study of Caesar and Cicero, Virgil and Horace, and Ovid's *Metamorphoses*.

Ascham had regarded the reading of Latin Grammar 'by itself' as 'tedious for the master, hard for the scholar, cold and uncomfortable for them both'; but many pages are devoted to the problems of parsing by John Brinsley, the Puritan master of Ashby-de-la-Zouch, whose *Ludus Literarius* provides us with a picture of the laborious life of the Elizabethan schoolboy of 1612. He recommends the reading of elementary Latin dialogues and maxims, Cato, Corderius, and the Latin Aesop, Cicero's *Letters* and *Offices*, with Ovid, Virgil, Horace, Persius, and Juvenal. But he also urges the importance of the study of English : 'there seems unto me to be a very main want in all our Grammar

---

[1] p. 151, ed. Mayor.

Schools generally, . . . that there is no care had in respect to train up scholars so as to express their minds purely and readily in our own tongue.'

Down to the year 1597 the Greek Grammar in general use was that of Clenardus (Louvain, 1530). At Westminster the corresponding text-book from 1575 to 1597 was the *Graecae Linguae Spicilegium*, a small catechism compiled by the head master, Edward Grant (1575). In 1597 both of these were superseded by the far briefer *Institutio Graecae Grammatices Compendiaria* of the next head master, the eminent historian, William Camden. The title-page of the first edition is reproduced on p. 239. It is practically certain that it was Savile (appointed provost in the following year) who promptly adopted Camden's Grammar at Eton. Hence, notwithstanding its Westminster origin, it was eventually known as the ' Eton Greek Grammar '. Meanwhile, in 1647–63, Westminster itself had given up the *Institutio* of Camden for the *Rudimenta* of that redoubtable head master, Richard Busby.

About 1647 the time-table at Winchester included Homer, Hesiod, and Musaeus (the poet of *Hero and Leander*) ; at Eton nothing higher is named than the Greek Grammar ; at Westminster we have Euripides and Isocrates, and at Shrewsbury, Isocrates *ad Demonicum*, and Xenophon's *Cyropaedeia*. At Harrow, in the first Statutes of 1590, the authors prescribed were Hesiod, Isocrates, Demosthenes, and (strange to say) Heliodorus, the author of the *Aethiopica*, and ' Dionysius of Halicarnassus '—probably the short treatise *De veterum scriptorum censura*, with its brief criticisms of Homer and Hesiod, Isocrates and Demosthenes, and other writers of verse or prose.

The teaching of Greek is briefly noticed in the *Ludus Literarius* of Brinsley. The author recommends ' Master Camden's Grammar, notwithstanding the many faults in the print '. He also names, but does not approve, the interlinear translation of the Greek Testament in the words of the Vulgate by Arias Montanus (last published in 1609). The authors mentioned are Aesop, Isocrates, Xenophon, Plato, and Demosthenes. Versifying in Greek is to be learnt from Theognis, and the other poets named are Phocylides, Hesiod, and Homer.

It may fairly be assumed that, in an ordinary English

grammar school, the teaching of Greek was rare. And yet the presence of the Greek alphabet, which was always printed (strange to say) at the beginning of the Latin Accidence, and again at the beginning of the Latin Syntax, must, at a very early stage, have brought home to the Elizabethan boy, as to backward boys in the Victorian era, 'a firm conviction that there are such languages'.[1] In the sixteenth century Greek was learnt by some of the highest ladies of the land. Roger Ascham has told us how, in 1550, before going abroad, he went to Bradgate Park, near Leicester, to take leave of Lady Jane Grey. While all the household were hunting in the park, he found her in her chamber reading the *Phaedo* of Plato.

Ascham, who had lectured on Greek in Cambridge, and was Public Orator from 1546 to 1554, probably exaggerates the proficiency of his pupil, the Princess Elizabeth. She began the day with a portion of the Greek Testament, and then studied some select orations of Isocrates and the tragedies of Sophocles. As princess, she read with him the *De Corona*, and, as queen, the *De Falsa Legatione* of Demosthenes, and the corresponding speeches of Aeschines. She translated a play of Euripides, as well as the *Hieron* of Xenophon and two orations of Isocrates. Before 1562, in a single day she answered three ambassadors in Italian, French, and Latin; and more than thirty-five years later, when the over-confident envoy from Poland had spoken in her presence, 'the Queen herself, not brooking to be braved by any power in the world', 'roundly and learnedly' delivered a prompt reply in Latin, and, in the spirited language of Speed,

thus Lion-like rising, daunted the malapert Orator, no less with her stately port and majesticall departure, then with the tartenesse of her princely checkes : and turning to the Traine of her Attendants thus said : God's death, my Lords, (for that was her oath ever in anger) I have been enforced this day to scowre up my old Latine, that hath laine so long in rusting.

UNIVERSITIES AND LEARNED SOCIETIES

William Harrison, in his *Description of England*, treats 'of Universities' in a separate chapter of his Second Book, and, as a graduate of Oxford and Cambridge, writes with a fair degree of impartiality on the merits of both.

---

[1] Bagehot's *Literary Studies* (1895), i. 82.

BACK OF THE GRAMMAR SCHOOL STRATFORD-ON-AVON

INSTITVTIO
GRAECAE
GRAMMA-
TICES
COMPENDIARIA,
Inuſum RegiæScholæWeſt-
monaſterienſis.

Scientiarum ianitrix Grammatica,

LONDINI,
Excudebat Edm. Bollifant **pro**
Simone Waterſon.

1595

Title-page of Camden's **Greek** Grammar.

Harrison's impartiality is rivalled by that of Ben Jonson, who dedicated his masterpiece, *Volpone*, to 'the most noble and equal sisters, the two famous universities' of Oxford and Cambridge.

Evidence as to University life in Cambridge may be found in the three comedies performed in the hall of St. John's at Christmastide 1598–1602, under the title of *The Pilgrimage to Parnassus* and *The Returne from Parnassus* (two parts). It is interesting to note that one of the earliest public quotations from *Romeo and Juliet* and from *Richard III* was made at Cambridge in the hall of St. John's.

While *The Returne from Parnassus* was being acted in the hall, the second court, one of the most beautiful of the Elizabethan buildings of Cambridge, was in course of erection (1599–1602). The greater part of the 187 feet of the first floor of the north side consisted of one long gallery, with an ornamental ceiling originally extending for 148 feet, which, even in its present dimensions of 93, is one of the finest rooms in Cambridge. Meanwhile, at Trinity, the chapel had been built in 1555–64, and the great court (the largest in either University) completed in 1597, when the statue of Queen Elizabeth was set up in the 'Queen's Gate' on the south side. The fountain was added in 1601. The hall was finished in 1605, and 'Nevile's Court' by 1612.

Of the colleges belonging to the reign of Elizabeth the first was the new foundation of Caius College, added in 1557 to the old foundation of Gonville Hall. In 1584 Sir Walter Mildmay, who had held the office of Chancellor of the Exchequer, received from Queen Elizabeth a charter for the founding of Emmanuel College. The only other Elizabethan college in Cambridge was that founded in 1596 by Frances, Countess of Sussex, the aunt of Sir Philip Sidney. Early in the next century her college was the first to open its fellowships to men of Scottish or of Irish birth.

At Cambridge, the accession of Queen Elizabeth in 1558 had put an end to the ten years of unrest during which that University had been under the government of four different constitutions. The new reign was ushered in by the appointment of a new Commission for the reformation of the University, with Cecil, the Chancellor, at its head. In August 1564 the queen gave the University a signal mark of her goodwill by a memorable visit. At the west door of King's College Chapel the Public Orator spoke in Latin, commending her virtues for nearly half an hour, while Her Majesty bit her lip and broke out into ' Non est veritas—et utinam ', adding that she would answer him in Latin but for fear she should ' speak falsely '. She marvelled at the beauty of the chapel, praising it above all others in her realm. On Sunday she heard her first Latin sermon, and, after evensong, saw the *Aulularia* of Plautus performed in the antechapel. On Monday she went to St. Mary's for the public disputations. On Tuesday she listened to a Greek oration at Trinity, while at Christ's she received some Greek verses, and replied in the same language. As she rode through the streets she conversed with divers scholars in Latin. At three o'clock the disputations were resumed in St. Mary's, when she was persuaded to make a Latin speech, in which she referred to Demosthenes and Alexander the Great, and expressed the hope that she might be able to follow the example of her ancestors and do something noble for the cause of learning.

Some information as to the subjects taught in the different departments of study may be derived from the Elizabethan Statutes of 1570. The duties of the University lecturers are there described in terms almost identical with those of the Edwardian Statutes of 1549. The praelector in Theology was to lecture on ' sound literature ' alone. Civil Law was to be studied in the Pandects, the Code, and ' the Ecclesiastical Laws of our Realm '. The lecturer on Philosophy was to expound the *Problems, Ethics,* and *Politics* of Aristotle, together with Plato or Pliny (the latter alternative implying that the physical science of the ancients was included in ' philosophy '). The text-books of the lectures in Medicine were to be Hippocrates or Galen. ' Mathematics ' was not confined to arithmetic (studied in Tunstall or Cardan), geometry (in Euclid), and astronomy (in Ptolemy). It included cosmography (studied in Pomponius Mela, Pliny, Strabo, or Plato). This last may possibly refer to the *Timaeus,* but it is more probably put by mistake for Ptolemy, who is named here (as well as under Astronomy) in the Edwardian Statute. The praelector in Dialectic was to expound the *Sophistici Elenchi* of Aristotle or the *Topica* of Cicero ; the praelector in Rhetoric, Quintilian and Hermogenes, or one of the rhetorical works of Cicero (this being a new item).

The professor of Greek was to lecture on Homer, Isocrates, Demosthenes, Euripides, or some other classical author, and also to give instruction in grammar and style (' linguae proprietas '). Lastly, the Hebrew lecturer was to confine himself to the Hebrew Scriptures and to the grammar of that language. The Oxford Statutes were almost identical.

At Oxford, the colleges of Trinity and of St. John the Baptist had come into being under Queen Mary, while the foundation of Jesus College in 1571 belongs to the reign of Elizabeth. The founder was a Welsh Oxonian, who from the beginning probably meant his foundation to be what it practically became—a Welsh college. The Tudors were always ready to own their connexion with Wales, and the Queen contributed to the endowment of the college, which still possesses three of her portraits, including the master-piece by Zuccaro. The front toward Turl Street dates from her time.

The colleges of Wadham (1610) and Pembroke (1624) belong to the reign of James I. The founders of Wadham, however, belonged, for the larger part of their lives, to the age of Elizabeth, and an Elizabethan spirit has been traced in its statutes and in its architecture. Pembroke was endowed ' at the cost and charges ' of Thomas Tesdale and Richard Wightwicke, but (by a singular arrangement) its nominal founder was King James I, while it received its name from the Chancellor of the University, William Herbert, third Earl of Pembroke, the 'noble patron of learning' and perhaps the friend of Shakespeare.

It was the age of Elizabeth that saw the founding of the famous Bodleian Library. To the ancient library of 1445–80, above the Divinity School, Sir Thomas Bodley added the east wing, begun in 1587 and finished by 1603, when the building was opened after a solemn procession from St. Mary's Church. When the adjacent schools of 1439 were rebuilt in 1613–18, a statue of King James was placed in the great gate (known as the 'Schools Tower'), which represents the five orders of Roman architecture, rising from Tuscan to Composite. In Merton College we have only to pass from the first quadrangle to the second (1610) to find a similar tower, minus the Tuscan stage. Among the greater glories, however, of Merton are the ancient library, partly altered under James I, and the chapel with its memorable monuments to Sir Thomas Bodley and his friend and adviser, Sir Henry Savile.

At Oxford, as at Cambridge, Queen Elizabeth appointed a body of Visitors to ' make a mild and gentle, not rigorous, reformation '. Protestant refugees gradually returned from the privations of their exile, but many Catholic scholars were lost to the University. The temporary confusion caused by religious controversies is illustrated by Wood's story of the Fellows of Merton singing the Psalms of Sternhold and Hopkins round a fire in the college hall, when the subwarden snatched the book out of the hands of a junior Fellow and declared that ' neither he nor the rest would dance after his pipe '. In 1563, when a plague was raging in Oxford, learning was so much decayed that there were only two preachers left—the Dean of Christ Church and the President of Magdalen. In their absence a layman, Richard Taverner, ' did several times preach in Oxford '. As high sheriff, he once came into St. Mary's Church with a golden chain about his neck and a damask gown, and, ascending the old stone pulpit, ' out of pure charity ' preached a lay sermon beginning with these remarkable words :—

Arriving at the Mount of St. Mary's in the stony stage where I now stand, I have brought you some fyne bisketts baked in the oven of charitie, carefully conserved for the chickens of the Church, the sparrows of the spirit, and the sweet swallowes of salvation.

From 1564 the office of Chancellor was held for twenty-four years by the Earl of Leicester. Under his influence the University was permanently ' incorporated ' by Act of Parliament, in 1571, and was thus relieved from ' the necessity of seeking a new charter from each succeeding king '. He also gave the University a new printing-press ; but his activity as Chancellor was marred by a certain degree of meddlesomeness. It is for this reason that one of the ablest historians of Oxford is compelled to confess that Leicester's administration of the University ' cannot be compared with the wise administration of Cambridge by the great Burleigh '.[1]

At Cambridge the office of Public Orator had been instituted in 1522. It was not until 1564 that the office was formally established at Oxford, ' upon a strong rumour that the learned Queen Elizabeth would visit the University '.

[1] G. C. Brodrick's *History of the University of Oxford*, p. 89.

At the Queen's first visit in September 1566 she was attended by Leicester (the Chancellor of Oxford), and by Cecil (the Chancellor of Cambridge) as Secretary of State. As at Cambridge, there was the regular round of festivals, orations, disputations, and dramatic entertainments. At the end of the third day, when, with some admirably acted hesitation, she rose to speak, few of her brief and clear-cut sentences could have given greater satisfaction to Oxford than the words of royal approval: ' ex quo primum Oxoniam veni, multa vidi ; multa audivi ; probavi omnia '. During the six days of her visit she won all hearts ' by her sweet, affable, and noble carriage ' ; and, on the last day, when she was escorted by the University authorities as far as the forest of Shotover, she listened to an eloquent oration in praise of learning and of her encouragement thereof. In September 1592, twenty-six years later, she revisited the University ' to behold ' (says Wood) ' the change and amendment of learning and manners that had been in her long absence made '. She went through the same round of ceremonies ; but on this occasion she heard Savile make ' a very good speech, though somewhat long '. The Queen herself addressed the authorities of the University in Latin, regretting at the outset the little use she had lately made of this language,—'sed fracta nunc est glacies; aut inhaerere aut evadere oportet '—and ending with an earnest exhortation to unanimity.

Giordano Bruno had visited Oxford in 1583, and had not been satisfied with the little he saw. In 1587 Alberigo Gentili happily came to stay as Regius Professor of Civil Law, and succeeded in reviving an interest in that subject. In August 1592 Oxford was visited by Frederick, Duke of Wirtemberg (who has been identified with the ' Duke de Jamany ' in The Merry Wives of Windsor IV. v. 90). In 1598 Paul Hentzner, a jurist of Brandenburg, describes Oxford as ' the famed Athens of England '. About 1610 Justus Zinzerling found Queen's College ' most hospitable '. In the same year the Prince of Wirtemberg visited Cambridge. He compares Trinity College to ' a superb princely house or royal palace ', and describes King's Chapel as ' without doubt one of the most beautiful chapels in Europe '.

When James I visited Oxford in 1605, the University was warned beforehand that all Commoners were to wear 'round caps', and that Dr. Parry was to preach in Latin for three-quarters of an hour. A full account of the ceremonies was drawn up by the Public Orator, Sir Isaac Wake, in his *Rex Platonicus*.

Anthony à Wood dates the increase of luxury and disorder at Oxford from this royal visit. But the king himself is hardly to be blamed for this result. He showed his goodwill to the University by entering at Magdalen his promising son, Prince Henry, who died prematurely in 1612. In 1606, after the discovery of the Gunpowder Plot, he conferred on the two Universities 'the right of presenting to all benefices in the gift of Roman Catholic patrons', a right which they still enjoy. Lastly, in 1611, he enlisted the services of divines and scholars of both Universities in the great and beneficent work of producing the Authorized Version of the Bible.

The study of logic is implied in Falstaff's phrase, ' I deny your major ' (*1 Hen. IV*, II. iv. 544), and in the use of *ergo* (*Com. of E.* IV. iii. 57, *Merch. of V.* II. ii. 59, *All's Well* I. iii. 53) and its vulgar equivalent, *argal* (*Haml.* V. i. 13, 20, 53). ' A figure of rhetoric ' is jocularly treated in *As You Like It* V. i. 45. Technical terms connected with the university course, such as ' commence ' and ' proceed ', ' act ' and ' degree ', are repeatedly used in close connexion with one another, as in *Timon of Athens*, IV. iii. 252 f., 268 ff., in *2 Henry IV*, Induction, line 5, and IV. iii. 24–6, and in *2 Henry VI*, III. ii. 118.

Shakespeare has a few references to seats of learning. Polonius ' played once i' the university ', when he ' did enact Julius Caesar ' (*Haml.* III. ii. 104–9), and ' a truant disposition ' brought Horatio from Wittenberg (*ib.* I. ii. 167). In *The Two Gentlemen of Verona* (II. iii. 1–27), Antonio sends his son to the emperor's court in Milan, instead of sending him to one of the ' studious universities ' ; and, in *The Taming of the Shrew*, Lucentio, who ' has been long studying at Rheims ' (II. i. 81), enters on ' a course of learning and ingenious studies ' at ' fair Padua, nursery of arts ' (I. i. 1–40), with the result that his father exclaims : ' O, I am undone ! I am undone ! while I play the good husband at home, my son and my servant spend all at the university ' (V. i. 69–71).

Harrison assumes the existence of ' three noble universities in England '. This third ' university ' is in London. It is the Inns of Court. In a curiously prophetic spirit, Sir George Buck, in *The Third Universitie of England* (1615), appended to most editions of Stow's *Chronicle*, describes all the colleges and schools of London as forming one University.

In London a bequest left by Sir Thomas Gresham led to the opening, in 1596, of the 'College of the Seven Liberal Sciences', which still bears his name. The Cambridge Orator of the day had in vain pressed upon the founder the prior claims of Cambridge, and had even suggested that, if established in London, the College would be the ruin of Oxford and Cambridge alike.

History was at that time studied with little intelligence at either University. It was, however, a hopeful sign when Giles Fletcher the elder resolved to write on the reign of Queen Elizabeth, and even applied to Lord Burghley for his advice and assistance. But his resolve remained in abeyance, and accordingly (in the language of a Cambridge writer of 1608) 'the Elizabethan age can boast of but one Camden'. 'Histories', wrote Bacon in 1597, 'make men wise', but, in this department of learning, neither of the Universities had so far added to the wisdom of the world.

The organization of academies for the promotion of a higher degree of intellectual life was a prominent feature of the Elizabethan age. Ralegh's step-brother, Humphrey Gilbert, who was educated at Eton and Oxford, produced, in the early part of his distinguished career, a scheme of liberal education for royal wards and others under the name of *Queene Elizabethes Achademy*. In this scheme, which belongs to about 1564, modern as well as ancient languages and mathematics and law are combined with technical and military exercises. The general aim is to place education on a broader basis and to bring it into closer contact with public life.

Whereas in the universities men study onely schole learninges, in this Achademy they shall study matters of accion meet for present practize, both of peace and warre. And yf they will not dispose themselves to *letters*, yet they may lerne languages or martiall activities for the service of their Cowntrey. Yf neither the one nor the other, Then may they exercize themselves in qualities meet for a gentleman. And also the other universities shall then better suffize to releive poore schollers, where now the youth of nobility and gentlemen, taking up their schollarshippes and fellowshippes do disapoinct the poore of their livinges and avauncementes.

The study and use of English is strongly urged.   There were also to be lectures on Civil Policy.   The boys were to learn riding, shooting, and marching, the art of navigation, elementary surgery and medicine, and natural philosophy. The teachers of these last subjects were ' to search and try out all the secrets of nature, as many ways as they possibly may '.   The Academy contemplated is in the main a school of liberal education, but there is also to be a Library, into which ' all printers in England shall be for ever charged to deliver at their own charges one copy, well bound, of every book . . . that they shall print ' : and every ' public reader of art and the common laws ' in the Academy shall publish a new book on his own subject once in six years, and every teacher of languages a translation once in three.

The next ' Academy ' which we must notice is solely and distinctly a society of learned men.   Matthew Parker, who produced, according to his lights, the earliest editions of the ancient chronicles of his country, kept up a correspondence with a number of persons interested in antiquarian studies, including Cecil, who possessed a goodly store of ancient manuscripts ; Stow, from whom Parker obtained his copies of Matthew Paris and other chronicles ; Lambarde, the author of the *Perambulation of Kent* ; and John Bale, the historian of English literature, several of whose manuscripts afterwards came into Parker's possession.

The year 1572 saw the definite foundation of a society for the study of English history and antiquities.   This antiquarian association drew its members from all classes, ' Peers and commoners, diplomatists and exchequer officials, heralds and city tradesmen, country gentlemen and town schoolmasters, lawyers and clergymen, all met together week by week, between 1572 and 1604, to discuss the archaeological and constitutional problems of English history '.[1]   Among the number were, besides Parker himself, Sir William Cecil and Sir Nicholas Bacon ; Thynne (one of the continuators of Holinshed's *Chronicle*) ; Camden and Cotton (who gave free use of his valuable library to Camden. Francis Bacon, Ralegh, Selden, Speed, Usher, and other scholars) ; and William Herbert, Earl of Pembroke.   They had also points of contact with the poets of the age.   Sir

---

[1] (Sir) Sidney Lee, in *New Shakspere Society's Publications*, p. 142 (1885).

John Davies and Arthur Golding were members of the
society ; Selden and Stow, Camden and Savile, counted
Ben Jonson and Michael Drayton among their intimate
friends. The learned Elizabethan Academy is the theme
of good-humoured allusions in the *Histriomastix* of 1610.
Among those who frequented its meetings were Anthony
Martin, keeper of the Royal Library at Westminster, and
John Hoskins, the lawyer and wit, who is said to have re-
vised Jonson's poems and Ralegh's *History of the World*.
Ralegh dropped out of the society for good reasons in 1603 ;
its private meetings were viewed with suspicion by the
Government, and it accordingly began to decline about 1604.
It is said that the meetings continued to 1614. In 1617 it
was regarded as extinct by the scholar and antiquary,
Edmund Bolton, who then formed a new scheme for a Royal
Academy of Letters and Sciences. This was formally
approved in 1624 by James I, who died in the following
year. The scheme was dropped in the early years of
Charles I, who, as prince, had described it as ' too good for
the times '.

In the year 1624, in which James I gave his first approval
to Bolton's Academy, Bacon was engaged on the composition
of his *New Atlantis*, in the course of which he described
the organization of a ' Solomon's House ' or academy, at
Bensalem, an imaginary island in the southern seas. The
old antiquarian association showed some signs of renewed
life in 1638 and 1659, and it was finally and effectively
restored by the foundation of the Society of Antiquaries
in 1717.

A satirical reference to the ' Academies ' of the age has
been traced in *Love's Labour's Lost* (*c.* 1591), where the
King of Navarre says :

Our court shall be a little Academe,

and his lords ' have vow'd to study ' and to live ' in
leaden contemplation ' (I. i. 13 ; IV. iii. 296, 321). It has
been suggested that the poet was partly referring to the
ninth Earl of Northumberland's, the ' Wizard Earl's ',
' Philosophical Academy ', satirized by Lodge and by
Greene.[1]

The love of discoursing on learned and philosophic topics
was one of the characteristics of serious society in the

[1] A. de Rothschild's *Shakespeare and his Day* (1906), p. 172 n. 2.

Elizabethan age. Though Giordano Bruno had formed an unfavourable opinion of the state of learning in Oxford, he found the very flower of both Universities in the persons of Sir Fulke Greville and of his schoolfellow and friend Sir Philip Sidney, when, at the London house of the former, he held high converse with them and their literary circle on themes not unworthy of a host who was afterwards the author of the thoughtful, though far from lucid, poem on *Human Learning*, who befriended Bacon and Camden, and who, as Lord Brooke, in 1628, in the last year of his life, established the first professorship of History in Cambridge.

BIBLIOGRAPHY.—*Schools and School life*:—NICHOLAS CARLISLE'S *Concise Description of the Endowed Grammar Schools in England and Wales*, two volumes, 1818, includes quotations from the original statutes, and notices of the course of study prescribed. The Report of the Schools Inquiry Commission, 1867, besides some historical matter, gives the ordinarily accepted dates for the foundation of the several schools. These dates are supplemented by those of the 'foundation' or 'first known mention' of a school in the same place, in the 'Chronological List' on pp. 321–7 of A. F. LEACH'S *English Schools at the Reformation, 1546–8* (1896). Mr. Leach also published, in the *Victoria Histories of Counties*, notices of schools, with quotations from original documents; special histories of *Winchester College*, 1899, and *Warwick School*, 1906, *Educational Charters*, 1911, *The Schools of Mediaeval England*, 1915, and a paper in *The Proceedings of the British Academy*, 1915. See also HOWARD STAUNTON'S *Great Schools*, 1869, T. F. KIRBY'S *Annals of Winchester College*, 1892, CHARLES WORDSWORTH, *The College of St. Mary Winton*, 1848, H. C. MAXWELL-LYTE'S *History of Eton College*, 1899, J. SARGEAUNT'S *Annals of Westminster School*, 1898, J. H. LUPTON'S *Life of Dean Cole*, ed. 2, 1909, F. J. MCDONNELL'S *History of St. Paul's School*, 1909, and A. K. COOK, *About Winchester College*, 1917; the histories of the Charterhouse (Tod, and Wilmot), Christ's Hospital (Johnson, and Pearce), Harrow (Howson and Warner, Thornton, and Williams), Merchant Taylors' (Wilson, and Robinson), Sedbergh (Platt), and Shrewsbury (Blakeway, and Fisher); and the bibliographies to the *Cambridge History of English Literature*, vol. iii, chap. xix (W. H. WOODWARD), and vol. vii, chap. xiv (J. B. MULLINGER).

As a popular illustrated monograph, founded on the best authorities, we may mention Dr. W. J. ROLFE'S *Shakespeare the Boy, with Sketches of the Home and School Life etc. of the Time*, 1897. See also A. W. TUER'S *History of the Horn-book*, 2 vols., 1896. Among works bearing on the theory and practice of education in the Elizabethan age, we have ROGER ASCHAM'S *Scholemaster*, 1570 (annotated by J. E. B. Mayor, 1863); Richard MULCASTER'S *Positions*, 1581 (edited by Quick, 1887); JOHN CONYBEARE'S *Latin Letters and Exercises*, 1580–94 (edited by F. C. Conybeare, 1905), and JOHN BRINSLEY'S *Ludus Literarius*, 1612 and 1627; also the memoranda on pp. xxii, lvi, lxii, &c., of Furnivall's edition of the *Babees Book*, &c. (E.E.T.S., 1868.)

School-books:—On the history of 'Lily's Latin Grammar', see THOMAS HAYNE'S preface to his *Grammatices Latinae Compendium*, 1640, and especially JOHN WARD'S preface to his standard edition of 'The Short Introduction to Grammar', 1732, &c.; also J. H. LUPTON, in *Notes and Queries*, December 4 and 11, 1880. Elizabethan text-books in general are noticed in FOSTER WATSON'S monograph on *The Curriculum and Text-books of English Schools* in 1600–50

(Bibliographical Society, February 1902; published February 1903), and in his *English Grammar Schools to 1660 : their Curriculum and Practice*, Cambridge, 1908 (reviewed by J. E. S. in *Cambridge Review*, December 3, 1908, p. 143 ff.). The same writer has described the *Zodiacus Vitae* of Palingenius (1908) and has translated the *Exercitatio* of Vives ('Tudor School-boy Life', 1908). School 'Colloquies' in general are discussed in Massebieau's *Les Colloques scolaires du seizième siècle*, 1878. The *Eclogues* of Baptista Mantuanus have been edited by W. P. Mustard, Baltimore, 1911.

Universities in the Elizabethan age.

Oxford. ANTHONY À WOOD, (1) *Historia et Antiquitates Universitatis Oxoniensis* (a Latin translation of Wood's original English) 2 volumes, folio, 1674; the original English of *The History and Antiquities of (a) the University* (1792–96) *and (b) the Colleges and Halls* (1786), with an Appendix of *Fasti* (1790), ed. John Gutch; (2) *Athenae Oxonienses*, with the *Fasti*, 2 volumes folio, 1691–2, ed. Philip Bliss, 1813–20; G. C. BRODRICK's *Short History of the University of Oxford*, 1886; ANDREW LANG's *Oxford*, 1890; CECIL HEADLAM's *Story of Oxford*, 1907, &c.; JOHN NICHOLS, *The Progresses . . . of Queen Elizabeth*, new edition, 3 volumes, 1823 (Oxford in vol. i, 206 ff., iii. 144 ff.); CHARLES PLUMMER's *Elizabethan Oxford*, Reprints of Rare Tracts, including Queen Elizabeth at Oxford (Oxford Historical Society, 1881). The four small volumes of *Oxoniana* (by the Rev. JOHN WALKER, of New College, 1806) include entertaining items on manners and customs at various periods.

Cambridge. THOMAS FULLER's *History of the University* (1655), ed. Prickett and Wright, 1840; C. H. COOPER's *Annals*, 5 volumes, 1842–1908; *Athenae*, 1858–61; J. B. MULLINGER's *University of Cambridge* vol. ii, from 1535 to 1625 (also his *Short History*, 1888); JOHN NICHOLS, *The Progresses . . . of Queen Elizabeth*, as above (Cambridge in vol. i, 149 ff.); *The Pilgrimage to Parnassus with the two parts of the Return from Parnassus*, 'performed in St. John's College, Cambridge, 1597–1601', edited from MSS. by W. D. Macray, Oxford, 1886; see also F. E. SCHELLING's *Elizabethan Drama*, 1908, ii. 64–70, 518.

For both Universities, cf. W. B. RYE, *England as Seen by Foreigners*, 1865.

Learned Societies in London : (1) Humphrey Gilbert's Scheme for *Queene Elizabeth's Achademy* (soon after 1562), printed by Sir Henry Ellis in *Archaeologia* xxi. 506 ff., and by Furnivall, E.E.T.S., Extra Series, viii (1869), pp. 1–12, with 'Forewords' pp. i–xii; (2) Matthew Parker's Society for the Study of English History and Antiquities (1592), *Archaeologia*, vol. i, pp. i–xli; HEARNE's *Collection of Curious Documents*, 1 volume (1720), 2 volumes (1771); (3) Edmund Bolton's Scheme for a Royal Academy, JOSEPH HUNTER in *Archaeologia*, vol. xxxii (1), 132–49, and Miss ETHEL M. PORTAL in the *Proceedings of the British Academy*, November 24, 1915. See also (Sir) SIDNEY LEE on 'The Elizabethan Literary Society' in New Shakspere Society's Publications, 1881–5, monthly abstract, pp. 142 ff. (March 13, 1885).

IX

SCHOLARSHIP

BY

SIR JOHN EDWIN SANDYS

CHRONICLERS AND HISTORIANS

To Matthew Parker we are indebted for the earliest (though not the best) editions of some of the ancient chronicles of our country—the *Flores Historiarum* of ' Matthew of Westminster ', Asser's *Life of Alfred*, Matthew Paris, and Thomas Walsingham. In the next generation the *Scriptores post Bedam* were meritoriously, but somewhat inaccurately and uncritically, edited by Savile (1596).

Among the immediate precursors of the Elizabethan chroniclers, we may note the name of Robert Fabyan, whose work extends from the fabulous advent of Brutus (the invention of Geoffrey of Monmouth) to the year 1485. It was printed in 1516 as *The New Chronicles of England and France*.

In the next generation, a friend of Linacre, More, and Erasmus, named Polydore Vergil, lived for nearly half a century in England (1502–51), and wrote his *Historia Anglicana* (1534) at the request of Henry VIII. It ' required the brain of an Italian ' [1] to unravel the real significance of the reign of Henry VII, and, as an authority for that reign, Polydore ' surpasses all native writers '.[2] Down to the death of the seventh Henry, he is faithfully followed in the *Chronicles of the Union of the Houses of Lancaster and York*, written by Edward Hall, of Eton and King's, who, with the accession of his hero, Henry VIII, throws off his pompous style, and writes with vivid directness about the events which had passed before his own eyes. While he is a first-hand authority on an important part of the career of Wolsey, he is at his best when he is describing a procession or

---

[1] Gairdner, *Early Chroniclers*, p. 307.
[2] Gardiner and Mullinger's *Introduction*, p. 302.

pageant, such as that of the coronation of Anne Boleyn, or of the Field of the Cloth of Gold.

Purity and vigour of diction marked the account of Edward V and Richard III by Sir Thomas More, who probably derived his facts from his patron, Archbishop Morton.

The substance of large portions of Polydore Vergil and Edward Hall was absorbed into the comprehensive *Chronicles of England, Scotland, and Ireland*, written by many hands under the general editorship of Raphael Holinshed. They begin with the Flood, and the *History of England* is brought down to within four years of the date of publication (1577).

The *Description of England* is contributed by William Harrison. Holinshed himself compiled the *Historie of England*, with the aid of all the earlier Chronicles. For the primitive times we find passages from Caesar and Tacitus interwoven with the late and untrustworthy *Historia Britonum* of Geoffrey of Monmouth. Geoffrey is the source of the story of King Lear, and is (with Matthew of Westminster) one of the sources of *Cymbeline*. In Holinshed's *Historie of Scotland*, the few facts recorded of the real Macbeth by the Irishmen of the eleventh century, Marianus Scotus and Tighearnach, and by the Ulster Annals and the Saxon Chronicle, are buried beneath the elaborate romance composed by Hector Boece. The stories of the three 'weird sisters', and of Birnam Wood, and of Macbeth's fate at the hand of a foe 'of no woman born', were first told in Andrew Wyntoun's *Cronykil of Scotland* (c. 1424).

In compiling all these histories, Holinshed professes to have had 'more regard to the matter than the apt penning '. The language, however, was easy for all to understand ; it aroused the patriotic enthusiasm of the people; and it even proved a source of inspiration to Spenser, as well as to Shakespeare.

In the second edition of Holinshed the first 250 folio pages are about equally divided between the *Description of Britaine* and the *Description of England* by William Harrison. Harrison had an almost unrivalled knowledge of the topography of England, thanks to 'letters and pamphlets from sundry places and shires ', and to Leland's notes and the 'cardes' or maps of Thomas Sackford. He discourses on degrees of people in the English commonwealth, on cities and towns, on gardens and orchards, on fairs and markets, on the laws and the Church of England, on food and diet, apparel and attire, on the building and the furnishing of houses, on provision for the poor, on the air and soil and commodities of the island, the minerals and metals, cattle and fowls, savage beasts and vermin; on the qualities of English dogs, on the fish of our coasts, on quarries of stone, woods and marshes, parks and warrens, and royal palaces; on armour and munition, on the navy, on sundry kinds of punishment, and, lastly, on universities and schools.

The next two in our series, John Stow and John Speed, had much in common. Both alike were learned antiquaries and freemen of the Merchant Taylors Company. In middle life Stow lost ' his own peculiar gains ', and he died a poor man. ' His only paine and care ' (as his friend tells us) ' was to write truth.' In the church of St. Andrew Undershaft, in the heart of the London that he loved, he is commemorated by a monument in which he is represented seated at a table with a book and a pen, and with other books on either side. Besides publishing an edition of Chaucer, and a *Summarie of English Chronicles*, he produced in 1580 *The Chronicles of England*, known in later editions as *The Annales*. Like the earlier chroniclers, he is uncritical, but he surpasses them in a love of literature which leads him to notice the death of Chaucer and of Langland. Stow was also the author of the oft-edited and oft-quoted *Survay of the Cities of London and Westminster* (1598, 1603), in which the accurate description of the topography of the great city is varied with notices of many points of interest in connexion with the history of education and learning.

In contrast with the precise and pedestrian style of Stow, we have in Speed a master of all the resources of rhetoric. He tells us that even foreign writers have termed our country ' the Court of Queen Ceres, the Granary of the Westerne World, the fortunate Island, the Paradise of Pleasure and Garden of God ', and he exults in describing the ' admirable and glorious sight that both armies made ' at the battle of Agincourt. He uses seals and coins to illustrate his work, and he surpasses his predecessors in the careful use of manuscript authorities. Thus he founds his character of Henry VII on the *Life* by Bacon, which was still unpublished ; and he handsomely acknowledges his obligations to the *Life of Wolsey*, definitely assigning it to George Cavendish.

A loftier level is attained by William Camden in his *Annals of England and Ireland during the Reign of Elizabeth*. He wrote the work in Latin, and his preliminary chapter, with its brief and vivid account of the fate of the successive wives of Henry VIII, loses nothing by his vigorous use of that language. In the work in general, Polybius is his model, and truth his only aim. He acknowledges the aid derived from the public documents lent him by Lord Burghley, and from his access to the great library of Sir Robert Cotton. The first part was published in 1615 ; the second (posthumously) in 1627. These two parts were translated into English by Abraham Darcie and Thomas Browne respectively. The former relied on a French rendering of the original, but the fact that he was fully alive to the grand motive of the work is clearly revealed in the English title, which is all his own : *The True and Royall History of the famous Impresse Elizabeth Queene of England, France and Ireland . . . True Faith's Defendresse of Divine renowne and happy Memorie.* Camden celebrates the prowess of Drake and the other heroic navigators, or founders of new colonies beyond the seas, while in the world of letters he laments the death of Spenser, but is completely silent about Shakespeare.

Shakespeare was, in fact, still living at the date of the publication of the first part of Camden's *Annals* (1615), and he was only at the outset of his public career in 1586, when Camden, in his *Britannia*, stated that Stratford owed all its *dignity* to an Archbishop of Canterbury who built the church, and to a Lord Mayor of London who built the bridge, —' emporiolum non inelegans, quod duobus suis alumnis omnem dignitatem debet.' In 1610, Philemon Holland, in his translation of the *Britannia*, rendered these words thus,— ' a proper little mercate town, beholden for all the beauty that it hath to two men there bred and brought up '; and the rendering reappears unaltered in the edition of 1637. Camden was appointed usher of Westminster School in 1575 and head-master in 1593. During the school vacations of 1578–1600 he pursued his antiquarian researches throughout

From the painting at LAMBETH PALACE

MATTHEW PARKER by RICHARD LYNE

the length and breadth of England with a view to his first great work, which found a sequel in his *Remaines* (1605). For the larger part of his life he was best known as the author of the *Britannia*, which, in the spirit of a scholar and a schoolmaster, he wrote in Latin. Throughout his work, he is inspired with the keenest patriotism. Proud of the land that he loves, he leads his fellow countrymen along its high-roads and through all its towns and cities, faithfully guiding them amid the hills and dales and rivers and the monuments of bygone ages, and thus meriting the name of ' the Pausanias of the British Isles '.

' A Chart or Map of England as she standeth and is governed' on May 28, 1565, is provided in a clear and concise and practical and popular work on the *Common Wealth of England*, first printed in 1584. Its author, Sir Thomas Smith, was one of the most versatile of men. He was not only a Member of Parliament, a diplomatist and a Secretary of State, but also an alchemist and an astrologer, and Public Orator and Professor of Greek at Cambridge.

The briefest mention must here suffice for the vast but uncritical work of that keen Protestant, John Foxe, whose *Actes and Monuments* is better known as the 'Book of Martyrs ', one of the authorities followed in *King Henry the Eighth*.

The lawyer, Sir John Hayward, who was educated at Pembroke College, Cambridge, differs from the chroniclers and others whom we have briefly reviewed in being a distinctly professional historian. His earliest work, the *First Part of the Life and Raigne of Henrie the IIII*, incurred the displeasure of Elizabeth and led to his languishing in prison for several years. After his first unfortunate experience, he found in a far earlier age the theme of his second work —the *Lives of the Three Normans, Kings of England* (1613). His real interest, however, lay in his own times, but he never actually came down to that date in his works on Edward VI and on the first part of the reign of Elizabeth. His portrait of the Queen at her accession has been recognized as ' almost a masterpiece '.

We are hardly surprised to learn that our next historian, Sir Walter Ralegh, was a great reader. ' He studied most in his sea-voyages' (says Aubrey), ' where he carried always a trunk of books along with him, and had nothing to divert him.' Nor indeed had he much to 'divert him' during the thirteen years of his imprisonment in the Tower (December 1603–16), which were mainly devoted to the composition of his *History of the World* (1614). The result is not exactly a history of the normal type : it is rather a series of dissertations on theology and law, on mythology and magic, and on war and the ideal form of government, intermingled with an ample narrative of the rise and fall of ancient empires. The historian begins with chaos and ends with the successors of Alexander. The opening and the closing pages of this vast fragment of a universal history are its most remarkable portions. In the preface, the author moralizes on the lessons to be learnt from the history of England, and of the world. On the last page, like Hamlet musing in the churchyard on the fortunes of Alexander and of Caesar, he sums up his meditations on the fate of fallen empires :

All is vanity and vexation of Spirit : but who believes it till Death tells it us ? . . . O Eloquent, Just and Mighty Death ! whom none could advise, thou hast perswaded ; what none hath dared, thou hast done ; and whom all the World hath flattered, thou only hast cast out of the World and despised : thou hast drawn together all the far stretched Greatness, all the Pride, Cruelty and Ambition of Man, and covered it all over with these two narrow Words, *Hic jacet*.

Bacon had published the first edition of his *Essays* in 1597, but it was not until 1622 (six years after the death of Shakespeare) that he gave the world his *History of the Reign of King Henry the Seventh*, a work characterized by a severely judicial impartiality, a constant consciousness of the relation between cause and effect, and a generally uniform and unbroken majesty of style. His faculty of clear discrimination forms a vivid contrast to the uncritical compilations of his predecessors ; and we are fully conscious of the greatness of the finished work, when we compare it with the rude material out of which it was composed —the Chronicles of Fabyan and Polydore Vergil, and of Hall, Holinshed, and Stow.

CLASSICAL SCHOLARS

Henry Savile (1549–1622), in dedicating to Queen Elizabeth his edition of the *Scriptores post Bedam* (1596), has some severe remarks on Polydore Vergil and the subsequent historians of England, 'the summ whereof' (says Edmund Bolton) 'is the common wish : That the Majesty of Handling our History might once equal the Majesty of the Argument'.

Savile's translation of the *Histories* and *Agricola* of Tacitus (1591) was eulogized in verse by Ben Jonson, and, within fifty years, passed through six editions. In 1598 Bodley's plan for his Library was prepared in concert with Savile. In 1604 Savile was knighted after a banquet given to James I at Eton. As a Greek scholar, he took part in the preparation of the Authorised Version of the Bible (1611), and, with the aid of men of learning at home and abroad, he produced in 1613 a magnificent edition of Chrysostom in eight folio volumes, printed at his own press at Eton.

Among those associated with Savile in his edition of Chrysostom was a Cambridge scholar, Andrew Downes (*c.* 1549–1628), professor of Greek for more than forty years. He was one of the six final revisers of the Authorised Version. Another of the final revisers was Downes's pupil, John Bois (1561–1644), who could read and write Hebrew before he was six and who learnt Greek from his father before being sent to the Grammar School at Hadleigh ; there he was a friend of Overall, the future Bishop of Norwich, who was also associated with the Authorised Version.

Among the contemporaries of Downes at Cambridge was that eccentric genius, Gabriel Harvey (*c.* 1550–1630), a scholar of Christ's, who became a Fellow of Pembroke and afterwards of Trinity Hall, and was most persistent in pressing a junior member of that college, Edmund Spenser, to adopt the old classical metres in writing English poetry. He also had some reputation as a Latin scholar. His favourite Latin phrases were attacked in *Pedantius*, which was acted in Trinity College in February *circa* 1581.[1]

Savile and Camden are repeatedly mentioned together as the leading Greek scholars of their time in England. Savile is also associated with the later years of Casaubon, who spent the evening of his days in the land that he had once regarded as 'the island of the blest'. It was as the guest of Savile that Casaubon visited Oxford in May 1613.

[1] The frontispiece picture of *Pedantius* is reproduced on p. 227.

He was hospitably entertained, and was taken to see all the sights of the University. As he gazed on the ancient buildings, he admired what he describes as 'the piety and magnificence of our ancestors '. He also viewed the fine frontage towards the meadow which Savile was then finishing at Merton. He spent many hours of each day in the Bodleian. Next year, the martyr of learning, the editor of Strabo and Polybius, was buried on the west side of the south transept of Westminster Abbey. His tomb was the first of a new series, that of the historians, and the monument to Camden came next. Across the same transept is ' poets' corner ', with the tomb of Jonson and the monument to Shakespeare.

Among the editors of Latin Classics we may here mention John Bond (1550–1612), an editor of Horace (1606) and Persius. A diminutive edition of the *Satires* of Juvenal and Persius, with an expurgated text and with marginal notes, was published in 1612 by Thomas Farnaby (1575–1647), who in his youth left Merton for a college of the Jesuits in Spain, sailed in the last voyage of Drake and Hawkins, and settled down as a schoolmaster in Goldsmiths' Alley for the larger part of his life. Among other classical authors edited by him were Seneca (tragedies 1613), Martial (1615), Lucan (1618), Virgil (1634), and Ovid (*Metamorphoses* 1637). His merits are thus summed up in the *Athenae Oxonienses* :

He was the chief grammarian, rhetorician, poet, Latinist and Grecian, of his time ; and his school was so much frequented, that more churchmen and statesmen issued thence than from any school taught by one man in England.

Farnaby's great contemporary, Francis Bacon (1561–1629), declared in a letter to Lord Burghley, 'I have taken all knowledge to be my province '. Aristotle and Plato, Xenophon and Demosthenes, Cicero and Seneca, Livy and Tacitus, are the principal classical authors quoted in *The Advancement of Learning* (1605). These quotations give proof of first-hand familiarity with the authors quoted, being in this respect very different from Shakespeare's quotation of a line in Terence, not from the original text, but from the form which it assumed in the Latin Grammar.[1] Similarly, in *The Wisdom of the Ancients*

[1] p. 232, *supra.*

(1609), the fables of Greek mythology are interpreted by Bacon in the spirit of a moralist or a politician, while in Shakespeare the same mythology is utilized in the spirit of a poet.

TRANSLATORS

At the close of the reign of Queen Mary, the first seven books of the *Aeneid* were 'converted in Englishe meter' by Thomas Phaer, a lawyer and physician of Oxford, who began his work with a view to showing that the English language was not incapable of elegance and propriety. He claims to be a pioneer. His metre is the line of seven feet commonly employed by the early translators.

Two more books were posthumously published in 1562, and the work was completed by another physician, Thomas Twyne, in 1573. The first four *Aeneids* were rendered in rude but vigorous hexameters by Richard Stanyhurst of University College, Oxford, whose work was printed at Leyden in 1582 and in London in 1583. Bald and literal translations of the *Eclogues* (1575) and the *Eclogues* and *Georgics* (1589) were published by Abraham Fleming of Peterhouse. Both of these are in lines of seven feet, with rhyme in the former work, and without it in the latter.

Horace's *Satires* were 'Englished' in 1566 by Thomas Drant, a grave divine of St. John's College, Cambridge, who in the following year reprinted this version at the end of his rendering of the *Ars Poetica* and the *Epistles*. Selections from the *Odes* were apparently first translated by Sir Thomas Hawkins in 1625. It has been suggested that Shakespeare's 55th Sonnet was founded on Horace's 'Exegi monumentum' (iii. 30), but something similar had already appeared in Spenser's sonnet to Lord Charles Howard, and elsewhere.

It was not until 1598 that a complete rendering of Terence was produced by R(ichard) B(ernard), a puritan of Christ's College, whose work was often reprinted.

Nine tragedies of Seneca were paraphrased by Jasper Heywood, John Studley, and others in 1559–66, and were collected and completed in the *Tenne Tragedies* of 1581 by the poet, physician, and divine, Thomas Newton, of Trinity, Oxford, and of Queens', Cambridge. In the induction to *A Warning for Faire Women* (1599), the three most striking features of Seneca's plays, the ghost, the chorus, and the presentation of sensational horrors on the stage, are all noticed as the leading characteristics of Elizabethan tragedy. In particular, 'the Ghost, imported from Seneca into English tragedy, had a long and brilliant career'.[1] Sackville's *Gorboduc*, exhibited early in 1561, after the publication of Jasper Heywood's translation of the *Troades* and *Thyestes*, is described in Sir Philip Sidney's *Apologie for Poetrie* as ' full of stately speeches, and well-sounding phrases, clyming to the height of Seneca his stile '. Marlowe, Jonson, Chapman, Marston, and Massinger 'read Seneca and reproduced their reading in their tragedies'. Middleton and Thomas Heywood were indirectly indebted to him. There is no proof that Shakespeare had ever read Seneca. In *Titus Andronicus*, a play of doubtful or divided authorship, we have one or two direct quotations from Seneca's *Phaedra* ; and another passage from the latter, 'quis eluet me Tanais', &c., has long been noticed as a parallel to the famous phrase in *Macbeth* (II. ii. 60):

> Will all great Neptune's ocean wash this blood
> Clean from my hand?

It is of the translation of 1581 that Thomas Nashe said in his preface to Greene's *Menaphon* (1589):

> English *Seneca* read by Candle-light yeeldes many good sentences ...; and ... hee will affoord you whole Hamlets, I should say handfuls of Tragicall speeches. But ... *Seneca*, let blood line by line and page by page, at length must needes die to our Stage.

Nashe is here, apparently, referring to the earlier *Hamlet* (ascribed to Kyd), on which Shakespeare founded his *Hamlet*. The ' undiscover'd country from whose bourn no traveller returns ' has much in common with two passages in Seneca, in the *Hercules Oetaeus* and the *Hercules Furens*,[2] and the original text of the latter play[3] is closer than the translation is to the lines in *King John* (III. iv. 135) beginning

> A sceptre snatch'd with an unruly hand
> Must be as boisterously maintain'd as gain'd.

There is undoubtedly a general resemblance between Lady Macbeth's speech (*Macb.* I. v. 41–55) and the first monologue

---

[1] See J. W. Cunliffe, *The Influence of Seneca on Elizabethan Tragedy*, 44–6.
[2] *H. Oet.* 1531, *H. Fur.* 869 f. Cp. Munro in *Journal of Philology*, vi. 71.
[3] *H. Fur.* 345 f.

in Seneca's *Medea*, but there is apparently no borrowing of the language of the translation.

The only translation from Plautus that was actually published in the Elizabethan age was that of the *Menaechmi* by W(illiam) W(arner). The work was not licensed for publication until June 10, 1594, nor published until 1595. Shakespeare's *Comedy of Errors* was certainly founded, directly or indirectly, on the *Menaechmi*, and it may have owed something to a lost play called *The Historie of Error* (1576). *The Comedy of Errors* was produced about 1591, and the author may have read the *Menaechmi* in Latin, or seen the translation in manuscript. The printer's advertisement of the latter states that the translator had some time previously ' Englished ' the *Menaechmi* and ' divers ' other comedies of Plautus, and had circulated them ' for the use of and delight of his private friends, who, in Plautus's own words, are not able to understand them '. The scene in which Antipholus of Ephesus is kept out of his house (III. i) resembles a scene in the first act of the *Amphitruo*.

Ovid was the favourite poet of the Elizabethan translators. Arthur Golding (*c.* 1536–*c.* 1605), a friend of Sir Philip Sidney, and a member of Parker's Society of Antiquaries, completed in 1567 his celebrated version of the *Metamorphoses*. It was written in the same metre as Phaer's *Aeneid*, but it is far superior to that work in poetic spirit. One of the best-known passages is the rendering of Medea's incantation in the seventh book :

Ye Ayres and Windes: ye Elves of Hilles, of Brookes, of Woods
    alone,
Of standing Lakes, and of the Night approche ye everychone.
Through helpe of whom (the crooked bankes much wondring at
    the thing)
I have compelled streames to run cleane backward to their spring.

It was first pointed out by Richard Farmer, Master of Emmanuel, that Golding's translation rather than the original Latin was the source of certain phrases in the first line of Prospero's farewell to his magic art in *The Tempest* :

Ye elves of hills, brooks, standing lakes, and groves. (v. i. 33)

Golding's rendering of the tempest in the *Metamorphoses* (xi. 480 ff.) finds a close parallel in *Othello* (II. i. 188 ff.).

Elsewhere the translator describes the Calydonian boar, with ' his brawned back ' :

> And like a front of armed pikes, set close in battle ray,
> The sturdy bristles on his back stand staring up alway.

This is echoed in *Venus and Adonis*, where the boar 'hath a battle set of bristly pikes', and 'brawny sides, with hairy bristles arm'd'. In Golding, one of Actaeon's dogs 'was a hound of Crete, the other was of Spart'; there were ' other twaine that had a sire of Crete, and dam of Sparta', ' a great and large flew'd hound', and another called ' Ringwood ' (Golding's rendering of Ovid's *Hylactor*). Crete and Sparta are similarly mentioned in *A Midsummer-Night's Dream* (IV. i. 107 ff.), and Ringwood in *The Merry Wives of Windsor* (II. i. 122).

Venus and Adonis was inspired by Ovid's version of the same story, and by Ovid's myth of Hermaphroditus. The author's earliest ambition was apparently to be known as the ' English Ovid '. He is so regarded by Francis Meres in 1598 :

> As the soule of Euphorbus was thought to live in Pythagoras, so the sweete wittie soule of Ovid lives in mellifluous and hony-tongued Shakespeare.

In *Love's Labour's Lost* (IV. ii) Holofernes implies that, for elegancy, facility, and golden cadence of poesy, ' Ovidius Naso was the man'. In *Titus Andronicus*, Titus asks, ' Lucius, what book is that she tosseth so ? ' and Lucius answers, ' Grandsire, 'tis *Ovid's Metamorphoses* '; then follows the fable of Philomela and Tereus, which is also recalled in *Lucrece*, in *Cymbeline*, and in *A Midsummer-Night's Dream*. In this last we have the story of Pyramus and Thisbe, which appears once more in the moonlight scene at Belmont in *The Merchant of Venice* (v. i. 6 ff.). In general we may assume that the larger part of the poet's mythology came directly or indirectly from the *Metamorphoses*. A copy of the text printed by Aldus in 1502 is preserved in the Bodleian, bearing on its title-page the signature Wm She [1], and, opposite this, the inscription : ' This little Booke of Ovid was given to me by W Hall who sayd it was once Will Shaksperes T N 1682.' John Hall married the poet's daughter.

[1] See Chapter X, p. 308, foot-note.

In the year in which Golding completed the *Metamorphoses* (1567), the *Heroides* were translated by George Turbervile of New College, Oxford. The *Ibis* was translated by Underdowne (1569); and the first three books of the *Tristia* by Churchyard, 1572.[1] Marlowe's rendering of the *Amores*, posthumously published about 1597, was burnt at Stationers' Hall by command of the Archbishop of Canterbury and the Bishop of London in 1599. In the following year a corrective was supplied in the rendering of the *Remedia Amoris*, dedicated by F. L. 'to the youth of England'.

Select epigrams translated freely from Martial and from Ausonius were included in the *Flowers of Epigrammes*, published in 1577 by Timothy Kendall, of Eton and Oxford. The sixteenth *Idyll* of Ausonius was translated by Sir John Beaumont (1629). The first book of Lucan was rendered 'line for line' by Marlowe (1593), and the whole by Sir Arthur Gorges (1614), whose version was superseded by that of Thomas May (1627).

Turning from the Latin poets to the writers in prose, we note that the *De Officiis* of Cicero had been translated by Robert Whyttington, 'laureate in grammar' at Magdalen College, Oxford (ed. 1533). Whyttington had also rendered the *De Senectute*, and in 1550 the *De Amicitia* had found a translator in John (father of Sir John) Harington, who was imprisoned in the Tower with the Princess Elizabeth. Shortly after Elizabeth's accession, the *Tusculan Disputations* were translated by John Dolman (1561), and the *De Senectute* and *Paradoxa* by Thomas Newton (1569), the editor of Seneca's *Tenne Tragedies*. Of the letters, an 'Epistle to Quintus' (I. i) was translated by G. Gilby (1561), the 'Familiar Epistles' by J. Webbe, while 'Select Epistles' formed part of the *Panoplie* provided by Abraham Fleming (1576). Our list ends, as it began, with the *De Officiis*. A translation of that work, in or before 1556, was made by the poet Nicholas Grimald, of Christ's College, Cambridge.[2]

The first important English version of any of the genuine prose works of Seneca was Arthur Golding's rendering of

---

[1] Warton, *History of English Poetry*, iv. 241, adds, 'I learn from Coxeter's notes that the *Fasti* were translated into English verse before 1570'.

[2] A version by Queen Elizabeth of the *Pro Marcello* has recently been discovered in the Bodleian; see *English Historical Review*, 1914, pp. 721-3.

the treatise *De Beneficiis* (1577). A complete translation appeared in the monumental work of Thomas Lodge, which was not published until 1614. Sir Thomas Elyot in *The Governour* (1531) found in Seneca's treatise *De Clementia* a long discourse on mercy, in which he says : ' Suerly nothing more entierly and fastly ioyneth the hartes of subiectes to their prince or soueraygne than mercy'; and three passages from that treatise are the ultimate source of part of Portia's speech on mercy in *The Merchant of Venice*. The Roman historians were a favourite field for the efforts of English translators. The *Jugurtha* of Sallust had been rendered about 1521 by Alexander Barclay, whose work was edited in 1557 by Thomas Paynell. The *Jugurtha* and *Catilina* were translated in 1608 by Thomas Heywood the dramatist. *The Actes of the great Alexander*, as related by Quintus Curtius, were rendered into English by John Brende (1553). Arthur Golding translated Justin in 1564, Caesar in 1565, Pomponius Mela in 1585, and Solinus in 1587. The most interesting of these is the Caesar. It has been assumed that the passage in *The Second Part of Henry VI* (IV. vii. 65)—

> Kent, in the Commentaries Caesar writ,
> Is term'd the civil'st place of all this isle—

is a school-reminiscence of Caesar, *De Bello Gallico*, v. 14 ' ex his omnibus longe sunt humanissimi qui Cantium incolunt'; but to find the immediate English source of the passage we have only to turn to Golding's rendering :

> Of all the inhabitantes of thys Ile the civilest are the Kentysh folke.

The treatise on the art of war by Vegetius was translated in 1572 by John Sadler of Corpus Christi, one of the original Fellows of Trinity College, Cambridge. The first four books of the *Histories*, and the *Agricola*, of Tacitus were translated and annotated in 1591 by Sir Henry Savile, and the *Annals* and *Germania* were rendered in 1598 by Richard Grenewey. Early renderings of limited portions of Livy were superseded in 1600 by the complete translation achieved by Philemon Holland (1552–1637), ' Doctor in Physicke', Fellow of Trinity, Cambridge, and ultimately head master of Coventry grammar-school. He is well described by Fuller as ' the Translator Generall of his age'; and he earned that honourable title, not by his Livy alone, but also by his translations of the Elder Pliny (1601), Suetonius (1606), and Ammianus Marcellinus (1609); of the *Moralia* of Plutarch (1603) and the *Cyropaedia* of Xenophon (1632); and of Camden's *Britannia* (1610). A passage in the translation of Pliny (II. 97)—'The sea Pontus evermore floweth and runneth into Propontis, but the sea never retireth backe again within Pontus'—is apparently the source of the allusion to 'the Pontic sea' in *Othello* (III. iii. 454–7); and there is a coincidence between the description of the infant whom nature 'hath laid all naked upon the bare earth, even on his birth-day, to *cry and wraule* presently from the very first houre that he is borne into this world' (VII Proeme), and *King Lear*, IV. vi. 183–5.

Justin had been translated by Golding in 1564, and was translated anew by G. W. in the same volume as Aurelius Victor (1606). Florus was translated by the historian and poet, Edmund Bolton, of Trinity Hall, in 1618; the *metamorphoses* of Apuleius, by William Adlington in 1566.

The Greek dramatists were translated into Latin abroad, before any English rendering had been published in this country. It was suggested by Lowell that Shakespeare may have laid hold of an edition of the Greek tragedians, *Graece et Latine*[1]; and it was independently suggested by the late Mr. Churton Collins in 1904 that 'through the medium of the Latin language', he was 'more or less familiar' with the Greek dramatists. Parallels from Shakespeare had previously been quoted by Boyes in the course of his *Illustrations of the Tragedies of Aeschylus and Sophocles* (1841–4). But these parallels, however interesting they may be, have failed to carry conviction with calm and cautious critics. They have been justly regarded either as 'no more than curious accidents—proofs of consanguinity of spirit, not of any indebtedness on Shakespeare's part'; or as due to the 'general literary and theatrical tradition' that had reached the Elizabethan dramatists 'through Seneca'.

While, thus far, there was no English translation of Aeschylus or Sophocles, we possess what is 'partly a paraphrase, and partly an abridgement' of a single play of Euripides, the *Phoenissae*, in the *Jocasta* of George Gascoigne and Francis Kinwelmarsh 'of Grayes Inne, and there by them

---

[1] *Among my Books* (1870), reprinted in *The English Poets* (Camelot Series), 1888, p. 115 ff.

presented' in 1566. This was an adaptation from the Italian
of Lodovico Dolce. The chorus, characters, and substance
of the story are retained, but the greatest liberties are taken
with the language of the choral odes. In 1581 Thomas
Watson, the poet (d. 1592), produced a Latin verse translation of the *Antigone* of Sophocles, which gives proof of
a direct study of the Greek text.

Among the translations of the Elizabethan age, the name
of Homer is associated with the *Battle of the Frogs and Mice*,
rendered by W(illiam) F(owldes) in 1603, and finally, as 'the
Crown of all Homer's Works', by George Chapman in 1624.
The first ten books of the *Iliad* were translated in 1581,
not from the original Greek, but from the French version of
Hugues Salel (1545), by a turbulent M.P., Arthur Hall, who
had been encouraged to attempt the task by Ascham.
Hall's dull and lame attempt was entirely superseded by
the splendid and vigorous work of George Chapman (*c.* 1559–
1634), who, after producing in 1598 the *Shield of Achilles*
and books I, II, VII–XI, completed in 1611 '*The Iliads of
Homer*, Prince of Poets, never before in any language truly
translated'. The completed *Iliad* of 1611 was followed by
the *Odyssey* of 1615 in heroic verse. In his commentary,
which is only incidental, he has no first-hand knowledge of
Eustathius ; he relies mainly on the two folio volumes of
Spondanus, Jean de Sponde (1583), while he often quotes
the current Latin translations. In his preface to the *Iliad*
he describes the aim of a translator as follows :

> The work of a skilfull and worthy translator is to observe the
> sentences, figures and formes of speech proposed in his author, his
> true sence and height, and to adorn them with figures and formes of
> oration fitted to the originall in the same tongue to which they are
> translated.

But Chapman introduces conceits of his own, which are *not*
'fitted to the originall', as in the well-known line :

> When sacred Troy shall *shed her towers, with tears of overthrow.*

He has, however, much that is truly Homeric. Waller
could never read his *Iliad* without a feeling of transport ;
and it was in this rendering that Keats discovered Homer.
In 1618 Chapman 'translated elaborately out of the Greek'
the *Georgicks* of Hesiod, and in 1624 added to his *Iliad*
and *Odyssey* his version of *The Battle of the Frogs and Mice*
and the Homeric *Hymns and Epigrams*.

Six idylls of Theocritus were anonymously translated at Oxford in 1588. A poetic paraphase of the *Hero and Leander* of Musaeus was begun by Marlowe and completed by Chapman (1598). Marlowe's poem (l. 76) is quoted in *As You Like It* (III. v. 82) :

> Who ever loved that loved not at first sight ?

In the province of Greek prose, there was a special interest in the minor works of Isocrates. These were repeatedly translated. In 1531 Sir Thomas Elyot had described him in *The Governour* as ' so swete and delectable to rede, that, after him, almost all other seme unsavory and tedious ' ; and, three years later, he had published, under the title of *The Doctrinal of Princes*, a rendering of the exhortation by Isocrates to Nicocles, King of Cyprus. The ' admonition ' *Ad Demonicum* was translated by John Bury in 1557, and by Richard Nuttall in 1585 ; and Hieronymus Wolf's complete edition in Greek and Latin (Augsburg, 1570) was followed by English translations of Select Epistles in Abraham Fleming's *Panoplie* (1576), of the *Ad Demonicum*, *Ad Nicoclem* and *Nicocles* by Thomas Forrest (1580), and of the *Archidamus* by Thomas Barnes (1624).

Latin editions of *Aesop's Fables* had been printed in England in and after 1502 ; they were translated into English by William Bullokar (1585), and others.

The manual of Epictetus was translated (from a French rendering) by James Sanford (1567), and was combined with the ' Table ' of Cebes and the ' Characters ' of Theophrastus by John Healey (1616).

The first complete edition of Diogenes Laërtius was published in 1533, and the *Life of Plato* in that work was the basis of Elyot's treatise *Of the Knowledge which maketh a wise man*, published in the same year in the form of a dialogue between Plato and Aristippus. Diogenes fills the greater part of the ' treatise of Morall Phylosophye contayning the sayings of the wyse, gathered and Englyshed ' by William Baldwin in 1550. Plato himself is but poorly represented by two translations of the spurious dialogue on the immortality of the soul, known as the *Axiochus*. The whole of Plato was accessible in the Latin translation by Ficino (1551, &c.), and the *First Alcibiades* in particular (with Ficino's translation) in a separate Paris edition of

1560. It has been suggested that the above dialogue is the source of a passage in *Troilus and Cressida* (III. iii. 95–117); but it seems more probable that one at least of the sources is Dolman's translation of Cicero's *Tusculans*.[1]

A rendering of Aristotle's *Ethics* by J(ohn) W(ilkinson) was made in 1547, not from the original Greek, but from an Italian translation. Similarly, a rendering of the *Politics* by J. D. (1598) was confessedly taken from the French of 'Loys le Roy, called Regius'.

Shakespeare has sometimes been credited with a knowledge of Aristotle. In *Troilus and Cressida* (II. ii. 166) Hector, by an amusing anachronism, is made to refer to 'young men whom Aristotle thought unfit to hear moral philosophy'. Bacon, in *The Advancement of Learning* (1605), writes: '(Aristotle) saith that young men are not fit auditors of moral philosophy.' Both, it is alleged, make the same mistake, for, in the *Ethics* (i. 8), it is *political* philosophy for which Aristotle deemed young men unfitted. We may rest content with supposing that Bacon and Shakespeare alike may have been thinking of a passage on the first page of the last item in Erasmus's widely current *Colloquia*: 'Velut irrepens in animos adolescentium, quos recte scripsit Aristoteles inidoneos auditores Ethicae Philosophiae' (1527)[2]. It has even been suggested that Shakespeare was acquainted with Aristotle's treatise on poetry, but it is in the highest degree improbable that Shakespeare was in any way familiar with Aristotle's theory of tragedy, when a classical scholar such as Ben Jonson contented himself with borrowing largely from Daniel Heinsius, *De Tragoediae Constitutione* (1611), in the common-place book known as his *Discoveries* (posthumously published in 1641).

The common reliance on French translations is shown in 1550, when Thomas Nicolls, 'citezeine and goldesmyth of London', translated Thucydides from the French of Claude de Seyssel, who, in his turn, had followed the Latin of Laurentius Valla.

Xenophon's *Cyropaedia* was rendered by W. Bercker (or Barker) in 1567, by John Bingham in 1623, and by Philemon Holland in 1632; the *Oeconomicus* by Gentian Hervet in 1532.

---

[1] i. 28; J. M. Robertson, *Montaigne and Shakespeare* (1909), p. 100.
[2] For *moralis* as an Elizabethan rendering of πολιτικῆς see *Pedantius*, ed, Moore Smith, p. 107, note on l. 327.

'The most famous and worthy Chronographer', Polybius, was translated in 1568 by a clerical graduate of Cambridge, C(hristopher) W(atson); and the *History of the Successors of Alexander*, &c. out of Diodorus Siculus and Plutarch, by Thomas Stocker in 1569. Thomas Wilson, of Eton and King's, D.C.L. of Ferrara, was inspired by a patriotic purpose in publishing his translation of the *Three Olynthiacs* and *Four Philippics* of Demosthenes (1570). Dionysius's *Surveye of the World* was 'Englished' by Thomas Twyne (1572); the *Various Histories* of Aelian by Abraham Fleming (1576), and Aelianus Tacticus by J. B(ingham) in 1616; while Appian's 'exquisite chronicle' of the Roman wars was published by Henrie Bynneman in 1578. The latter was apparently the source of Shakespeare's account of Sextus Pompeius in *Antony and Cleopatra*, and it may have suggested some points for Antony's orations in *Julius Cæsar*.

A far higher interest and importance belong to the translations of Plutarch. Jacques Amyot had (in Montaigne's phrase) made Plutarch speak the French language. Amyot's translation was practically a new and original work, in which all the rough places in Plutarch had been made plain, and the simple and natural spirit of the dweller in Chaeronea had been made to emerge from the disguise of an artificial and straggling style. Amyot had completed the *Lives* in 1559, and the *Moralia* in 1572. In 1579 his version of the *Lives* was translated into English by Sir Thomas North. If Amyot had practically made Plutarch a Frenchman, North, by his command of a vigorous and highly idiomatic type of English prose, made Plutarch an Englishman, while he also transformed the 'noble Grecians and Romans' into heroes of the Elizabethan age. North's version is celebrated as the authority followed by Shakespeare in *Coriolanus*, *Julius Cæsar*, and *Antony and Cleopatra*. *Julius Cæsar* is founded on the Lives of Caesar and Brutus; *Antony and Cleopatra* on the Life of Marcus Antonius, while the latter and the Life of Alcibiades are among the sources of *Timon of Athens*. Not merely the plots of these plays, but their very words are either closely copied from North, or else transformed into a still nobler language. In the case, however, of *Julius Cæsar*, it may be mentioned in passing that the finest passage in the play, the funeral oration over the dead body of Caesar, is also the most original.[1] The sentence in North's Plutarch (*Life of Julius Cæsar*, c. 50), ' *veni, vidi, vici* : to wit, "I came, I saw, I overcame ' ", is the source of the quotation and of the rendering of these three words in *Love's Labour's Lost*, IV. i. 70, and in *2 Henry IV*, IV. iii. 46.

While the *Lives* of Plutarch had been rendered by North from the French of Amyot, the *Moralia* (or ' the Philosophy ') of Plutarch were translated from the original Greek by a more distinctly scholarly translator, Philemon Holland (1603). The first two books of Herodotus were rendered by B. R. (possibly Barnabe Rich) in 1584 ; and ' the famous and memorable workes ' of Josephus were 'translated out of the Latin and French' (not, be it observed, out of Greek) by Thomas Lodge (1602).

The *Toxaris* of Lucian was ' translated out of Greek into English' by A. O. in 1565. His dialogues in general were not published in English until 1711, but *Certain Select Dialogues together with his True History* were translated by Francis Hickes in 1634, and fifteen were included in T. Heywood's *Pleasant Dialogues and Drammas* (1637). Lucian's *Timon* is the principal ultimate source of *Timon of Athens*, produced by Shakespeare in 1607 with the aid of another dramatist ; but it is uncertain whether the authors had a direct knowledge of Lucian's dialogue.

Thomas Underdowne opened to England a new field of Greek romance by his rendering of the ' very wittie and pleasaunt' Aethiopian History of Heliodorus (*c.* 1569), and in 1591 (the year after it had been prescribed by the founder of Harrow) its opening portion was translated into English hexameters by Abraham Fraunce in *The Countesse of Pembrokes Yvychurch*. The heroes are Theagenes and Chariclea, and a dramatic rendering of their romance was performed at court as early as 1572-3.[2] The episode in which the robber Thyamis purposes to kill Chariclea is recalled in *Twelfth Night*, v. i. 121-3 :

> Why should I not, had I the heart to do it,
> Like to the Egyptian thief at point of death,
> Kill what I love ?

---

[1] See, in general, *Shakespeare's Plutarch*, ed. Skeat, 1875, and ed. C. F. Tucker Brooke, 2 vols., 1909 ; and especially M. W. MacCallum, *Shakespeare's Roman Plays and their Background*, 1910.

[2] See *Revels at Court*, ed. Peter Cunningham (Shakespeare Society, 1842), p. 34, last lines.

The *Daphnis and Chloe* of Longus was translated by Angell Daye in 1587, and ten years later 'the most delectable and plesant historye of Clitophon and Leucippe' was translated by W. B(urton) from the Greek of Achilles Tatius.

The Elizabethan translators of the classics are animated by a spirit of bold adventure that aims at winning new conquests for England in the world of letters. They are diffuse and redundant, and far from being scrupulously accurate. Few of them have any serious pretensions to being regarded as scholars in the highest sense of the term. Golding is a fluent and lucid translator of Latin verse, who has also a large experience as an interpreter of historical prose. North transforms the French of Amyot into his own noble English, untrammelled by any fear of the Greek original, yet sometimes proving more faithful to the Greek than his immediate model. Savile is a professional scholar, but he is 'unidiomatic' in his English. Holland is also a scholar, but he is a man of much wider range, and he has not allowed his scholarship to cramp the expansive energy of his English style. Chapman is a scholar as well as a poet. but he relies largely on a recent Latin commentary on Homer. North's translation of Plutarch's *Lives* is in general two degrees removed from the original ; the 'citizen and goldsmith of London' who translated Thucydides is still further removed, for he relied entirely on a French rendering of a Latin version of the Greek original. In such a version it is not the letter, or the literal sense, that survives. The spirit of ancient Greece may sometimes survive, but more often it is a new spirit that has supervened and suppressed the old, the spirit of 'the spacious days of great Elizabeth'.

We may add a brief notice of some of the more important English translations from modern authors belonging to Spain, Italy, and France.

Marcus Aurelius was the theme of a didactic novel published in Spanish by Don Antonio de Guevara, bishop of Mondoñedo, in 1528, under the title *Libro aureo de Marco Aurelio*. This was translated into French by René Bertaut de la Grise, and into English by Lord Berners, as *The Golden Boke of Marcus Aurelius* (1534). The original

Spanish rendering was also recast and expanded by Guevara under the title *Relox de principes* (1529). In 1540 this was translated by the French translator above mentioned, as *Lorloge des Princes*, and the French translation was rendered into English in Sir Thomas North's *Diall of Princes* (1557). The translator, however, was acquainted with Spanish, for he adds from the original Spanish edition certain letters 'which are not in the French copye'. *Amadis de Gaule* was translated from the Spanish of Montalvo by Thomas Paynel (1568) and by Anthony Munday (1589), who in the preceding year had translated the French version of an unknown Spaniard's *Palmerin of England*. Montemayor's pastoral romance of *Diana*, partially rendered by Thomas Wilson, was completely translated by Bartholomew Yong in 1598. The latter version had existed in manuscript as early as 1582-3, and part of the romance had been dramatized in 1584. It was this romance that supplied the materials for the adventures of Julia and Proteus in *The Two Gentlemen of Verona* (1591). Thomas Shelton's translation of *Don Quixote* did not appear until 1612-20.

In William Painter's *Palace of Pleasure* (1566-7, authorized edition, 1575) we have an encyclopaedic repertory of stories ultimately derived from Greek and Latin and from French and Italian authors. It includes stories from Herodotus, Livy, and Gellius ; from the *Heptameron* of Margaret, Queen of Navarre, and from Boccaccio and Bandello. Bandello was the source of Arthur Brooke's *Tragical Historye of Romeus and Juliet* (1562), on which Shakespeare founded the earliest of his tragedies (1591). The story is also told in Painter's *Palace*, from which Webster, Marston, and Massinger borrowed some of their plots. The date of the second volume of Painter's *Palace* (1567) is also that of Fenton's translation of the *Tragicall Discourses* of Bandello. These were 'written out of French and Latin', and not out of the original Italian ; Boccaccio's *Filocopo* was translated by H. G. in 1567, and his *Fiammetta* by Bartholomew Yong in 1587. The original source of the plot of *All's Well that Ends Well* is Boccaccio's *Decameron* (III. ix), but Shakespeare had it ready to hand in Painter's *Palace* (No. 38). A story from Boccaccio (II. ix) is interwoven in *Cymbeline* ; but the *Decameron*, which had been repeatedly translated into French, was not translated into English until 1620. Hoby's version of Castiglione's *Cortegiano* appeared in 1561, and its high moral tone was approved by Roger Ascham, who deplored the influence of certain other books (plainly those of Painter and Fenton) 'made in Italie and translated in England'. Machiavelli's *Art of War* was translated by Peter Whitehorne of Gray's Inn (1560), and his *Florentine History* by Thomas Bedingfield (1595), while his *Prince*, which remained untranslated until 1640, was known to English dramatists mainly from the fact that in 1602 Simon Patricke produced an English version of the attack on *The Prince*, written by the French Huguenot, Gentillet. Ariosto's *I Suppositi* had been translated by Gascoigne in 1566, and is the source of the story of Bianca and her lovers in *The Taming of the Shrew*. *Orlando Furioso* was translated into 'English heroical verse' by Sir John Harington in 1591; the first three books of Boiardo's *Orlando Innamorato*, by R(obert) T(ofte) in 1598; and Tasso's *Gerusalemme Liberata*, by Richard Carew (1594) and Edward Fairfax (1600).

The works of Du Bartas were translated by Joshua Sylvester (1590–1605), and the History of Philippe de Commines by Thomas Danett (1596), while Montaigne's *Essayes* were 'done into English' by John Florio in 1603. Florio was an irrepressible personality. His work is full of flowers of speech that are all his own, and of proverbial phrases which are apt and idiomatic equivalents of the original. As early as 1595 a copy of Montaigne's *Essayes* was entered in the Stationers' Registers. It may be assumed that this refers to Florio's translation, which was licensed for a second time in 1600, and first printed in 1603. It was seen in manuscript by Sir William Cornwallis in 1600–1, and, as Florio was a friend of Ben Jonson, and was under the patronage of the Earl of Southampton, his translation may well have been known to Shakespeare before it was published. Certain parallels have been noticed between Florio and *Hamlet*, which was probably written in 1600–1. But none of them are so close as that between Gonzalo's speech in *The Tempest*, II. i. 147–54 (*c.* 1611), and a long passage in the description 'of the Caniballes' in the thirtieth chapter of

Florio's Montaigne. Ben Jonson, referring to Pastor Fido
in his *Volpone* (1605), tells us that all our English writers

> Will deigne to steale out of this author, mainely ;
> Almost as much, as from Montagnie.

Shakespeare's signature in a copy of Florio, now in
the British Museum, is generally held to be a forgery.[1]
It may be added that the poet's debt to Montaigne
has been much discussed. Thus it was held by M. Phila-
rète Chasles that Shakespeare's study of Montaigne may
be traced in *Hamlet*, *Othello*, and *Coriolanus*, and that
it transformed the poet into the 'thinker' and the philosopher.[2] In the opinion of Herr Stedefeld, the poet wrote
Hamlet to counteract the scepticism and the cosmopoli-
tanism of the essayist.[3] According to Mr. Jacob Feis,
Shakespeare was deeply indebted to Montaigne, and nevertheless wrote *Hamlet* to discredit the essayist's opinions.[4]
The poet's indebtedness has since been maintained with
greater moderation by Mr. John Mackinnon Robertson.[5]

All discussions as to the 'learning' of Shakespeare begin
with the phrase from the long poem by Ben Jonson prefixed to the First Folio of 1623 : 'though thou hadst
small Latine, and lesse Greeke'. We have only to compare
Jonson and Shakespeare to see the difference between
a dramatist who was distinctively a classical scholar and
one who was not. Jonson is constantly hampered by his
learning. If, in the course of his plays, he ventures to
introduce anything marvellous or unexpected, he feels
himself compelled to quote the Classics as a justification
of his audacity. In his *Catiline* and his *Sejanus* we find
elaborate notes from Sallust and from Tacitus respectively,
to prove he had good authority for every detail in his
drama, and to make it perfectly plain that 'Fancy had
no part in his work'. While Jonson thus preserves the
outer garb of the Roman world and allows the soul to
escape him, Shakespeare makes his men true Romans
simply because he takes his models from living Englishmen who had much in common with the ancient Romans.
'Shakespeare' (says Goethe) 'turns his Romans into

---

[1] See chap. x, p. 308.
[2] *L'Angleterre au seizième siècle* (1846), pp. 115–39 (ed. 1879).
[3] *Hamlet : ein Tendenz-Drama* (1871).
[4] *Shakspere and Montaigne* (1884).
[5] *Montaigne and Shakespeare* (1897 and 1909).

THE
ESSAYES

Or

Morall, Politike and Millitarie Difcourfes

of

Lo: Michaell de Montaigne,

Knight

*Of the noble Order of S*ᵗ· *Michaell, and one of the Gentlemen in Ordinary of the French king,* Henry *the third his Chamber.*

The firft Booke.
(*ₓ*)

Firft written by him in French.

And

now done into Englifh

By

By him that hath inviolably vowed his labors to the Æternitie of their Honors, whose names he hath severally inscribed on these his consecrated Altares.

The first Booke.

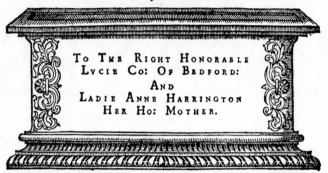

TO THE RIGHT HONORABLE
LVCIE CO: OF BEDFORD:
AND
LADIE ANNE HARRINGTON
HER HO: MOTHER.

The second Booke.

TO THE RIGHT HONORABLE
ELIZABETH CO: OF RVTLAND,
AND
LADIE PENELOPE RICHE.

The third Booke.

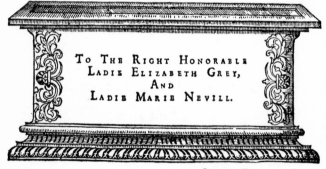

TO THE RIGHT HONORABLE
LADIE ELIZABETH GREY,
AND
LADIE MARIE NEVILL.

IOHN FLORIO

¶ Printed at London by Val. Sims for Edward Blount dwelling in Paules churchyard. 1603.

Englishmen, and he does right, for otherwise his nation would not have understood him.'

In some lines prefixed to the poems in the duodecimo edition of 1640, Leonard Digges, who had been a wit of the town in the poet's lifetime, boldly declares

> he doth not borrow
> One phrase from Greekes, nor Latines imitate,
> Nor once from vulgar Languages translate.

In the presence of Ben Jonson, John Hales of Eton, 'hearing Ben frequently reproaching (Shakespeare) with the want of Learning, and Ignorance of the Antients, told him at last, " That if Mr. Shakespear had not read the Antients, he had likewise not stollen any thing from 'em ".' Fuller, who was eight years of age at Shakespeare's death, and was for thirty years a contemporary of Jonson, says of Shakespeare that 'his learning was very little'; Jonson 'was built far higher in Learning', while Shakespeare excelled 'by the quickness of his Wit and Invention'. Milton, born in the same year as Fuller, contrasts the 'learned sock' of Jonson with the 'native wood-notes wild' of 'sweetest Shakespear, Fancy's child'. Dryden asks:

> Has not great Johnson's learning often fail'd,
> But Shakespear's greater Genius still prevail'd ? [1]

It was Dryden, too, who happily said that Shakespeare 'was naturally learned ; he needed not the spectacles of books to read Nature'.[2]   John Dennis emphatically declared that ' he who allows that Shakespear had Learning, and a familiar Acquaintance with the Ancients, ought to be look'd upon as a Detractor from . . . the Glory of Great Britain'.[3]   On the other hand, among Shakespearian editors of the eighteenth century, Pope supposed there was little ground for ' the common opinion of his want of learning', and similarly moderate language was held by Theobald and Warburton.   Upton, in his *Critical Observations* of 1746, attempted, by the accumulation of 'parallel passages', to prove the poet's profound acquaintance with Greek and Latin.

It was reserved for Richard Farmer to show, in his *Essay on the Learning of Shakespeare* (Cambridge, 1767), that this ' learning ' (or a very large part of it) was acquired in the

---

[1] Prologue to *Mistakes* (1690).   [2] *Of Dramatick Poesie.*
[3] *On the Genius and Writings of Shakespear* (1711), letter iii.

most natural way in the world—from translations. When Cleopatra is described as ' Queen ' of Lower Syria, Cyprus, *Lydia*, Upton quotes Plutarch and writes *Libya*, while Farmer finds the source of the poet's mistake in North's translation ; and similarly with two other ' corrections ' of the same type. He also points out that the plot of *Timon of Athens* comes, not from the Greek of Lucian, but from the English Plutarch and from Painter's *Palace of Pleasure*, and that Prospero's farewell-speech in *The Tempest* is drawn from Golding's translation of the *Metamorphoses* and not from the original (p. 261, *supra*). Towards the close, he sums up his opinion of Shakespeare thus :

> He remembered perhaps enough of his school-boy learning to put the *Hig, hag, hog*, into the mouth of Sir Hugh Evans ; and might pick up in the Writers of the time, or the course of his conversation, a familiar phrase or two of French or Italian : but his Studies were most demonstratively confined to Nature and his own Language.

Farmer's *Essay* did not cover the whole ground, but Johnson and Warton held that it ' put an end for ever to the dispute concerning the learning of Shakespeare '. It is more important, however, to have Warton's detailed opinion :

> It is remarkable that Shakespeare has borrowed nothing from the English Seneca. Perhaps a copy might not fall in his way. Shakespeare was only a reader by accident. Hollinshed and translated Italian novels supplied most of his plots or stories. His storehouse of learned history was North's Plutarch. The only poetical fable of antiquity, which he has worked into a play, is *Troilus*. But this he borrowed from the romance of Troy. Modern fiction and English history were his principal resources. These perhaps were more suitable to his taste : at least he found that they produced the most popular subjects. Shakespeare was above the bondage of the classics.[1]

Farmer's *Essay* met with protests from Colman, and with faint demurs from Capell and Malone. In 1839, William Maginn, in the course of three articles in *Fraser's Magazine*, urged that there was more evidence of the poet's knowledge of the text of Ovid than had been admitted by Farmer.[2] Charles Knight used language implying ' that, if Dr. Farmer were right in alleging Shakespeare's ignorance of languages, the poet would be a mere pretender to the crown of fame '. One of the German commentators,

---

[1] *History of English Poetry*, Section 57 *prope finem*.
[2] Reprinted in Maginn's *Miscellanies* (1885), ii, pp. 1-116.

Gervinus (1848–9), has maintained that the poet was deeply versed in Seneca and Plautus. M. Paul Stapfer protests against this view. He holds that ' Shakespeare's feelings towards classical antiquity were those of complete indifference ', but he adds : ' if we take the word " learning " in its large and liberal sense, and no longer reduce the question to a miserable pedantic wrangling over his more or less of Greek and Latin, then, of all men that ever lived, Shakespeare is one of the most learned '. Sir A. W. Ward in his *History of English Dramatic Literature,* holds ' that the vexed question as to Shakespeare's classical attainments is in reality not worth discussing'. The school-learning of Shakespeare was discussed by Mr. T. S. Baynes in *Fraser* in 1879–80, but his evidence as to the school-curriculum is taken from treatises written from forty to sixty-five years later than the poet's boyhood. He contended ' that Shakespeare was a fair Latin scholar, and in his earlier life a diligent student of Ovid'. Mr. John Fiske suggests that Jonson's phrase ' can hardly imply less than ability to read Homer at sight, and perhaps Euripides less fluently'.[1] The late Mr. Churton Collins ' suggests and marshals many new arguments in favour of the hypothesis that the poet was not merely a fair Latin scholar, but that his knowledge of the classics both of Greece and Rome was remarkably extensive '; and he 'supports these arguments' with numerous illustrations.[2] It has since been shown by Mr. J. M. Robertson that 'much of Mr. Collins's " case " turns upon classical quotations and allusions found in plays long held ' (like *Titus Andronicus*) ' to contain much that is not Shakespeare's work '.

In our account of the Schools of the Elizabethan age, we have already said all that seems necessary on the school-boy learning of Shakespeare, and, in dealing with the translations of that age, we have incidentally noticed the poet's debt to the current renderings of the Greek and Latin Classics and of the modern literature of Spain, Italy, and France. We may now sum up the subject by adding a conjectural list of the works which, from time to time,

---

[1] *Atlantic Monthly,* Nov. 1897, p. 640.
[2] *Studies in Shakespeare* (1904), pp. 1–95.

T

may have formed part of the poet's library. Not that we ever hear of that library. Ben Jonson was constantly buying books and selling them again out of sheer poverty. Shakespeare's son-in-law, John Hall, leaves to his own son his 'study of books', and his apparently worthless papers ; Shakespeare himself, in his will, bequeathes his sword, his 'broad silver-gilt bole', and even his 'second-best bedstead', but not a word is said about his books.

We must here distinguish between the books used for the plots of his plays, and those which were the sources of the general learning incidentally reflected in his works.

For his plots he must have used Thomas North's rendering of Amyot's French translation of Plutarch's *Lives* (for *Julius Cæsar, Coriolanus, Antony and Cleopatra*, and a small part of *Timon of Athens*) ; Holinshed's *Chronicles* (for *Cymbeline, Macbeth*, and perhaps *King Lear*, for *King John, Richard II, Richard III, Henry IV, Henry V, Henry VI, Henry VIII*), Hall's *Chronicle*, in Grafton (for *Henry VI, Richard III*, and *Henry VIII*), and Foxe's *Actes and Monuments* (for *Henry VIII*).

Some form of the *Menaechmi* of Plautus was used for *The Comedy of Errors* ; old plays, still extant, for *Henry IV* and *Henry V, King John, King Lear, The Taming of the Shrew*, and *Measure for Measure* ; old plays, now lost, probably for *Cymbeline, Twelfth Night* (mainly founded on Barnabe Riche's *Apolonius and Silla*, from Bandello), and *The Two Gentlemen of Verona*, and, certainly, for *Hamlet, The Merchant of Venice*, and *Timon of Athens*; Bartholomew Yong's translation of Montemayor for *The Two Gentlemen of Verona* ; a work founded on Bandello's *Novelle* for *Much Ado about Nothing*; an old play founded on Cinthio's *Hecatommithi* (iii. 7) for *Othello* ; old versions of Italian tales, such as Giovanni Fiorentino's *Pecorone*, and Straparola's *Piacevole Notti*, for *The Merry Wives of Windsor* ; a tale from Boccaccio in Painter's *Palace of Pleasure*, for *All's Well that Ends Well* ; Lodge's *Rosalynde*, for *As You Like It* ; Greene's *Pandosto*, for *The Winter's Tale* ; Arthur Brooke's poem for *Romeo and Juliet* ; Chaucer and Caxton, for *Troilus and Cressida* ; John Gower's *Confessio Amantis* and Lawrence Twyne's *Painful Adventures*, for *Pericles* (only in part by Shakespeare). *Titus Andronicus*, of doubtful authorship, is perhaps a rehandling of the lost *Titus and*

Vespasian. There is no known source for the plot of *Love's Labour's Lost.* Chaucer's *Knight's Tale,* Plutarch's *Theseus,* Ovid's *Metamorphoses* (IV), Lord Berners's rendering of *Huon of Bordeaux,* and Lyly's *Euphues* have supplied some hints for *A Midsummer-Night's Dream.* Some lost novel may have suggested the plot of *The Tempest.*

From incidental allusions in the text of the poet's works, it may be inferred that at one time or another he had possessed, or at any rate used, the following books :

SCHOOL-BOOKS AND CLASSICAL AUTHORS. A horn-book, an A B C-book with the Catechism, Lily's Latin Grammar (in two parts, English and Latin), a Latin version of Aesop, Mantuan's *Eclogues,* Cooper's Latin *Thesaurus* and Withal's Latin Dictionary, Golding's translation of Caesar, and of Ovid's *Metamorphoses* (with a Latin text of the latter and of the *Heroides*); Virgil, but probably not Horace ; possibly some plays of Plautus and Seneca, in Latin or English ; and possibly Philemon Holland's translation of the Elder Pliny, and Underdowne's translation of Heliodorus.

RELIGIOUS BOOKS. The Bible, with the Apocrypha ; the Book of Common Prayer, with the metrical Psalms.

TRANSLATIONS, &c. FROM MODERN LANGUAGES. *French*: Florio's Montaigne (1603), an Elizabethan version of part of Rabelais (now lost), Ronsard's *Odes,* and a French Dictionary. *Spanish* : Montemayor's *Diana,* translated by Yong. *Italian* : translations from Boccaccio in Painter's *Palace of Pleasure* ; Ariosto's *I Suppositi,* translated by Gascoigne ; Florio's Italian-English Dictionary, *A Worlde of Wordes.*

ENGLISH WORKS. Prose Writings of Lyly, Samuel Harsnett's *Declaration of . . . Popish Impostures* (1603), Ralegh's *Discovery of Guiana* ; sundry 'books on good manners' (*A. Y. L.* v. iv. 95) ; also books on sport.

Romantic Stories of Arthur, Guy, Bevis, &c.

Poems of Chaucer, Sidney, Marlowe, Daniel, &c.

Plays of Marlowe, Lyly, Kyd, Peele, Greene, Gascoigne, &c.

Ballads of Robin Hood, Cophetua, Susanna, Jephthah, &c., and many Songs, Popular Rhymes, and Popular Tales.[1]

---

[1] List revised and rearranged from *Synopsis* on pp. 1, 2 of Anders, *Shakespeare's Books* (1904) ; see also Jusserand, iii, pp. 169 ff., and J. M. Robertson, *The Baconian Heresy,* pp. 554 ff.

BIBLIOGRAPHY.—*Chroniclers and Historians.* The English chroniclers were criticized by SAVILE in the epistle dedicatory addressed to Queen Elizabeth in his edition of the *Scriptores post Bedam* (1596) and by EDMUND BOLTON in his *Hypercritica* (1618 ?). They are reviewed by JAMES GAIRDNER, *Early Chronicles (England)*, 1879 ; by J. B. MULLINGER in Part II of GARDINER and MULLINGER's *Introduction to the Study of English History*, 1881 ; and (for the present period) by CHARLES WHIBLEY, in the *Cambridge History of English Literature*, vol. iii, chap. xv, pp. 313–38, with full bibliography on pp. 527–32. On Elizabethan Plays founded on the History of England, compare F. E. SCHELLING's *English Chronicle Play*, 1902, and *Elizabethan Drama*, 1908, i. 247–308, ' The National Historical Drama,' and the literature there quoted in the bibliography, ii. 470–2, 477–81. On the popular historical sentiment of Elizabeth's day, compare pp. xxiii–xxx of Introduction to *The Chronicle History of King Leir*, ed. (Sir) Sidney Lee, 1909.

Classical Scholars. Savile, Downes, and Bacon are the theme of pp. 333–40 in (Sir) J. E. SANDYS' *History of Classical Scholarship*, vol. ii (1908). On Casaubon's sojourn in England (1610–14), and on his relations with English scholars, see MARK PATTISON's *Life of Casaubon*, ed. 2, 1892.

Translators. A general survey in WARTON's *History of English Poetry*, sections 57 to 60 ; a rapid sketch in JUSSERAND's *Literary History of the English People*, iii. 368–77 ; also in SECCOMBE and ALLEN's *Age of Shakespeare*, i. 81–4, 210–23 ; a brief conspectus in (Sir) J. E. SANDYS' *History of Classical Scholarship*, ii. 239–43 ; and an admirable essay by CHARLES WHIBLEY in *Cambridge History of English Literature*, IV (1909), 1–25, with bibliography of Translations from ' the Classics ', 435–41, and from ' Medieval and Contemporaneous Authors ', 441–9. See also STEEVENS on ' Ancient Translations from Classic Authors ' in MALONE's *Prolegomena to Shakespeare*, 1790 ; M. A. SCOTT's *Elizabethan Translations from the Italian* in Mod. Lang. Ass. of America, vols. x, xi, xiii, xiv ; W. J. HARRIS's *The First Printed Translations into English of the Great Foreign Classics*, 1909 ; and HENRIETTA R. PALMER's *List of English Editions of Greek and Latin Classics printed before 1641*, printed for the Bibliographical Society, 1911 ; also T. G. TUCKER's *Foreign Debt of English Literature*, 1907 ; A. H. UPHAM's *French Influence in English Literature*, 1909 ; and (Sir) SIDNEY LEE's *French Renaissance in England*, 1910.

' Shakespeare's Books.' The sources of the poet's plots were first investigated by GERARD LANGBAINE, in *Momus Triumphans*, 1688, and *The English Dramatick Poets*, 1691 (part on Shakespeare reprinted by New Shakspere Society, IV, 3, 318–31). Mrs. CHARLOTTE LENNOX collected and translated *The Novels and Histories on which the Plays are founded*, 3 vols., 1753–4. This was followed by COLLIER's *Shakespeare's Library*, 1843, edited by Hazlitt, 1875. The *Six Old Plays* of 1779 had their sequel in Part II of Hazlitt's collection. The *Romances, Histories, Plays, and Poems* used by Shakespeare form the 20 vols. of ' the Shakespeare Classics ', general ed. Prof. Gollancz, 1908–9, ending with *Shakespeare's Plutarch*. All the passages in HOLINSHED's *Chronicle* used by Shakespeare have been reprinted, annotated, and indexed in *Shakspere's Holinshed*, ed. by W. G. Boswell-Stone, 1896. *Shakespeare's Books* by H. R. D. ANDERS (Berlin, 1904) is an excellent ' Dissertation on Shakespeare's Reading and the immediate Sources of his Works '. A list of a collection of books ' studied by or referring to the poet in the seventeenth century ' is contained in *A Catalogue of Shakespeareana*, with a prefatory Essay by (Sir) SIDNEY LEE, 100 copies for presentation only, Chiswick Press, 1899. The latest ed. of *The Shakspere Allusion-Book* is that of JOHN MUNRO, 2 vols., 1909.

Shakespeare's ' learning ' is discussed in the following works : RICHARD FARMER's *Essay on the Learning of Shakespeare*, 1767, 2nd ed. 1767, reprinted 1789, 1821, &c. ; PAUL STAPFER's *Shakespeare et l'Antiquité*, 2 parts, 1880 ; the first part republished in two vols.—*Drames et Poèmes antiques* (ed. 1884), and *Les Tragédies romaines* (ed. 1883), and translated by E. J. Carey, *Shake-*

speare and Classical Antiquity (1880) ; the second part, on ' Shakespeare and the Greek Tragedians ', not yet translated ; THOMAS SPENCER BAYNES's articles in *Fraser's Magazine*, Dec. 1879, and January–May, 1880, reprinted in *Shakespeare Studies*, 1894 ; WILLIAM MAGINN's *Miscellanies* (1885), vol. ii, reprinted from *Fraser's Magazine*, Sept., Oct., Dec., 1839 ; D. NICHOL SMITH's *Eighteenth Century Essays on Shakespeare*, 1903 ; JOHN CHURTON COLLINS's *Studies in Shakespeare*, pp. 1–95, 1904 ; W. THEOBALD's *The Classical Element in the Shakespeare Plays*, 1909 ; G. G. GREENWOOD's *The Shakespeare Problem restated*, 1908 ; J. M. ROBERTSON's *Montaigne and Shakespeare*, 2nd ed. 1909, and *The Baconian Heresy* (a confutation), 1913 ; and G. G. GREENWOOD's *Is there a Shakespeare Problem?* ('the learning of Shakespeare', pp. 111–67), 1915. See also R. K. ROOT's *Classical Mythology in Shakespeare*, New York, 1903.

X

HANDWRITING

BY

Sir Edward Maunde Thompson

In the course of the sixteenth century the handwriting
of the English was subjected to a foreign influence which,
becoming more potent as time progressed, ultimately succeeded in suppressing the native style. This influence
was the humanist influence of the Italian renaissance.
The national cursive hand in everyday use, taught in
the schools and practised through life by the inhabitants
of this country, was the development of the mediaeval
current writing which had been introduced after the Norman
Conquest, and which had at that time superseded the
characters previously employed in the Anglo-Saxon period.
It is not necessary here to follow the course of that development ; it is enough to state the fact that the English
generally of the late fifteenth and early sixteenth centuries
wrote a style which, in the forms of its letters, bore to the
more formal characters found in contemporaneous literary
MSS. (inappropriately termed ' gothic '), and to the printing
type which has been called ' black letter ', the same relation
as our modern writing does to the Roman type of the
printed books of the present day. In many respects the
indigenous script resembled the handwriting of Germany,
which within our own memory has been giving way to an
influence similar to that which wrought the change in our
native handwriting of the sixteenth century.

It was the artistic sentiment fostered in Italy by the
renaissance of learning in the fifteenth century that brought
about reform in the handwriting of that country, and
subsequently in the handwritings of the other countries of
Western Europe which came under the sway of the humanist
movement. Since the twelfth century, handwriting in Italy,
as in all western countries, had much deteriorated. Seeking

for the most beautiful model of writing in which to embody the texts of the exquisite manuscripts which they produced for their wealthy patrons, the skilled scribes of Italy in the fifteenth century found it in the fine script of Italian codices of the early twelfth century. On this basis the Italian humanists formed that simple and noble lettering which is conspicuous in so many of the masterpieces of the calligraphy of the renaissance, and which was soon to be the source of the Roman type of the early presses. Concurrently with the development of this new literary hand, there was evolved in Italy a class of cursive handwriting suited to the requirements of daily life, but of a refined and stately character, the counterpart of which in printed books is that form of type which is to the present day known as *Italic*. It was this newly modelled Italian cursive handwriting which was destined to revolutionize the handwritings of other countries, and notably the handwriting of Shakespeare's England.

In the early days of its introduction into this country the new style was naturally restricted in its acceptance. To learn to write it was an accomplishment, not a necessary detail of education. A native style of writing could only be displaced when its foreign competitor had proved itself to be not only more beautiful in appearance but also more convenient in practice. The new style had to overcome the naturally conservative resistance of the national hand ; and it could only accomplish such a feat by the force of inherent superiority, when once that superiority had been recognized. How stubborn the resistance could be is proved by the fact that the national cursive handwriting of Germany and the cognate cursive handwritings of the Scandinavian countries have survived to our own day, and that only in comparatively recent times has the Italian, or, as we should now rather style it, the Roman, hand made rapid progress in general adoption in those countries.

A change affecting so widely the habits of the English nation as the acceptance of a new form of handwriting could only be initiated by a movement among the higher and better educated ranks of society. As in the case of other domestic changes, the first impetus to its adoption came from foreigners who visited England under influential auspices. There was settled in the Court of Henry VII an Italian cleric holding an appointment, the very duties of which implied the recognition of the new style for official purposes. This Italian was Pietro Carmeliano, a native of Brescia, who appears to have migrated to England as early as the reign of Edward IV. A literary man and a poet, he was attached to the Court and secured preferment in the English Church. He was one of Henry's chaplains, and also held the important post of the king's Latin Secretary. In this office it was his duty to compose and write with his own hand, in the Italian calligraphy of which he was a master, the royal letters addressed to foreign courts. A specimen of such correspondence is the letter addressed to Ferdinand and Isabella of Spain, a facsimile of which is here given: the text is in the handwriting of Carmeliano, with the king's signature appended (Facsimile No. 1).

Serenissimis ac potentissimis principibus Dominis ferdinando et hellizabeth, Dei gratia regi atque reginę Castellę, legionis, aragonum, Sicilię, granatę, &c., Consanguineis et germanis nostris carissimis, Henricus, eadem gratia Rex anglię et francię ac dominus Hybernię, Salutem et prospera successuum incrementa. Intelleximus ex clarissimo oratore uestro, domino doctore de puebla, circa conclusionem uestrarum Maiestatum cum Serenissimo francorum rege factam, articulum quemdam in nostrum fauorem per uestras Maiestates initum, quod sane, si ita res sese habuerit, non potuit nisi ab optimo animo uestrarum Maiestatum erga nos proficisci et ingentes gratias de nobis benemereri, quamquam nostra communis necessitudo et uinculum, quibus inuicem astringimur, id genus officii de se postulare uideatur. Cęterum ad noticiam nostram peruenit Vestras Maiestates de negociis nostris et Scoticis sinistre informatas esse et longe aliter quidem quam ueritas habeat. Hinc est quod nos, licet singularis uestra sapientia sit nobis perspecta persuadeamusque nobis uestras Serenitates quę intelligenda sunt omnia intelligere, presertim hęc nostra et Scotica, quę omnibus ferme patent et sunt cognita, habuimus cum prefato Domino oratore uestro longam de his rebus collocutionem, qui et ipse ex sese satis hęc omnia intelligit, quem non dubitamus ueram uestris Maiestatibus facturum relationem ; quę fęlices semper ualeant ad uota. Ex Castello nostro de Shena, die xv. Iunii, M°cccclxxxxviiii°. HENRICUS R.

Henceforward such State letters addressed to sovereign princes were issued in the style here followed, the Italian hand being adopted for the text and acquiring, as time passed, the impress of English character, resulting in the beautiful and simple writing which is seen in perfection in the 'script' or 'copper-plate' writing of the seventeenth and eighteenth centuries.

S.mus
Serᵉ ac potentissimis principibus Dnis ferdinãdo et Isabeeth De gnᵃ rege atq̃ regine Castelle legõis aragonũ
Sicilie granateq̃ &c Cõsanguineis et amantiss̃ nr̃is car̃ Henricus eadᵉ gra Rex anglie et francie ac dñs hybernie
Sal·et p̃pᵉm successuũ Incrementa. Intelleximus ex claro oratore urᵒ dño doctore deputabla Orta Coclusione ... mo
urãq̃ m̃tes, eu sero p̃ncep rege facta, nõtculã illã ... mus fauoᵉ p urãs m̃tes imbum: quod sane, si ita res se se
habuerue nõ potuit nisi ab optimo ano urãq̃ m̃tes erga nos p̃fecisci et ingꝰtes grãs de nob benemer̃ quãq̃ iṃal
Cõmunis necessitudo ... uewlu quibus tuiẽ astringemur id genus officij de se postulare uidebaꝰ Cæeꝰ ad noticiã
urãs p̃uenie Urãs m̃tes de negoꝰijs nr̃is et sotaeis simptre, simafeere, formatus et ee lope deiter quidꝗ quas uitas habeae:
hine est ꝗ nos licet singularis urã sap̃ia sic nob p̃spectca persuadamus p nob urãs scire ꝗ intelligedꝰ sunt
oia itellige p̃sertim hec nr̃a et sotaeia, quas obꝗ ferme patet et sue cognitu, habuimus cu p̃fato Dno oratore urᵒ pro
urᵃ m̃tibus. Vogᵃ, de his rebꝗ collocutione qui et ipe ex sese satis hec oia itelligit quem nõ dubitamus urãa urᵒ m̃tibus
facturuꝰ relationeꝰ quas felices semp̃ ualeat ad uota· Ex castello nᵒ deshena die xv Junij M·cccc·Lxxxxviiij·

Shakespeare himself seems to have had in mind this style of State letter when composing a well-known scene in *Hamlet*. It will be remembered that the Prince of Denmark contrived to steal from the two envoys, Guildenstern and Rosencrantz, their 'grand commission'—that is, the letter sent by their hands from the king to his English brother-sovereign requiring Hamlet's immediate execution on his arrival in England—and that he substituted for it a false one of his own composition and written in his own hand :

> I sat me down,
> Devis'd a new commission, wrote it fair :
> I once did hold it, as our statists do,
> A baseness to write fair, and labour'd much
> How to forget that learning ; but, sir, now
> It did me yeoman's service . . .
> Folded the writ up in form of the other ;
> Subscribed it ; gave't th' impression ; placed it safely,
> The changeling never known.   (*Haml.* v. ii. 31–53)

Such a 'grand commission' in Shakespeare's days would have been drawn up in the formal Italian calligraphy which an English prince of that time would have been taught in his youth, and in which the poet accordingly represents Hamlet as sufficiently versed to enable him to counterfeit the original, in spite of his past 'labour' to forget his learning in fair penmanship. The Prince of Denmark must indeed have been well skilled to have succeeded not only in writing the false document itself in the proper style, but also the superscription so dexterously as to deceive the unsuspecting envoys, 'the changeling never known'. Hamlet's words are a half-apology for 'writing fair', and it is not obvious why the poet should have dragged in the 'statists'' supposed contempt for good handwriting. Nothing could be more contrary to the fact than a wholesale condemnation of the handwriting of Elizabethan statesmen as essentially bad. The handwriting of educated men of that period was no worse than that of our own day ; in some respects it was far better. It is probable that Shakespeare was merely giving expression to the common view among men in public life, which has not been confined to those of his own time, that to 'write fair' is the mark of a trained clerk and not of a gentleman.[1]

---

[1] Samuel Rowlands, in *The Letting of Humours Blood in the Head-Vaine,*

Early in the sixteenth century it had become the practice to teach the Italian style of writing to children at least in the higher classes. The letter of Henry VII shows that that monarch used his native English hand in his signature ; and, indeed, there is no reason to suppose that he could write in any other style. His son, the eighth Henry, followed the same course, and wrote a strong heavy English hand, characteristic of the man. But when the time came for the education of his children the new fashion had set in; and the faculty of writing in the Italian style was now regarded as a necessary accomplishment in a young prince. As might be expected, the new handwriting was early practised by English scholars of the new learning ; and thus we find that many of those who were rising into distinction in the universities were skilful masters of Italian penmanship. From among such the teachers of the young Tudor princes were selected, and thus it came to pass that the Royal children were taught writing in the new style, apparently to the entire exclusion of the old native hand. Edward VI habitually wrote the Italian hand, and wrote it well. Indeed, on special occasions he could write like a professional calligrapher. Mary Tudor was mistress of a good handwriting in the same style ; and, in her youth, Elizabeth was equally versed in Italian calligraphy, and could, when required, produce a very handsome letter so written, although her handwriting in later years degenerated into the well-known straggling scrawl that confronts us in her letters written as queen. Among other members of Henry's family Queen Katharine Parr was famous for her fine Italian handwriting, in which she is said to have been trained by the scholar, Dr. Richard Croke, who also instructed Prince Edward in the use of the pen ; Lady Jane Grey's Italian handwriting was again of the most beautiful kind.

It came to be the fashion for tutors and their scholars to write out in their best calligraphy some small work as a memorial of their skill in handwriting ; and examples of

1600, repeats the sentiment in some lines addressed ' To Poets ' :—

> You see some strive for faire handwriting fame,
> As Peeter Bales his signe can prove the same,
> Gracing his credite with a golden Pen :
> I would have Poets prove more taller men :
> In perfect Letters rested his contention,
> But yours consists in wits choyce rare inuention.

As to Peter Bales and his golden pen, see p. 290.

etio spiritus

7Z Igitur da mihi domine prudentī:
am cœlestem, vt discam querere, et
inuenire te, et amare te super oña

77 Da mihi gratiam abducereⱭ
me ab illis qui me adulantur, et
patienter illos ferre qui me adu-
vexant

74. Quando tentatio, et tribulatio ⁊
veniunt, digneris succurrere mihi
domine, vt omnia vertentur mihi
in spirituale solatium et semper
feram patienter, ac dicam: bene
dictum sit nomen tuum.

fragilite laquelle tu congnois le
mieulx

74 Ayes mercy de moy, et me
deliure de tout peche et iniqui-
te acellefin que ie ne soye acca-
ble dieeux

75 Il m'est souuentesfois fort grī
ef, et cela quasi me confond, de
ce que ie suis sy instable, sy fer-
ble et fragile, pour resister aux
motions iniques lesquelles, cō-
bien quelles ne me causent de
confentir, ce nonobstant me sōt
leurs assaulx tresgriefz.

No 2   PRAYERS IN THE AUTOGRAPH OF PRINCESS ELIZABETH 1545

the penmanship of young English princes of the sixteenth century and later have thus descended to us. Among the Royal MSS. in the British Museum is an interesting little volume, written fair in the Italian book-hand by the Princess Elizabeth in her twelfth year, and dedicated to her father King Henry VIII, and sent to him presumably as a Christmas gift in December 1545. It contains versions by the Princess, in Latin, French and Italian, of prayers and meditations composed by Queen Katharine Parr ; and is bound in crimson silk embroidered with the initial H and a monogram of the name Katharina, the dutiful handiwork no doubt of the future queen. Two pages are selected as an illustration (Facsimile No. 2).

Of scholars of the time, Roger Ascham, who was also tutor to Prince Edward and his sister Elizabeth, was distinguished for his fine writing, and owed his advancement in a great measure to that accomplishment. He was appointed Latin Secretary by Edward VI, and again by Mary and Elizabeth. Letter-books containing the drafts of the Secretary's official letters during the later reign are still in existence ; and from one of them is selected a page as a specimen of the handwriting of an English scholar in the middle of the century. This style exhibits nothing of the English character ; it is altogether Italian ; and the letter might have come from the hand of a native of Italy : a complete demonstration of the firm position which the new handwriting had established for itself in this country (Facsimile No. 3).

Cardinali Mantuano.
Pro Petro Vannes.

Reuerendissime Pater et Illustrissime Princeps. Intelligimus, et id quidem libenter, quanta cum humanitate Vestra Reverendissima Dominatio nuper Mantuæ acceperat nostrum, ad Senatum Venetum, Oratorem, Petrum Vannes. Itaque non potuimus committere quin, quod erat tam humaniter factum nostra caussa, comprobaretur libenter et quam primum nostris litteris. Et cum alia atque alia indies nouaque vestra in nos constent officia, has etiam alteras nostras nouasque litteras Vestræ Dominationi scribendas esse duximus : non ut vestram nunc humanitatem compensent, sed ut nostram in posterum voluntatem solum significent. Mens enim nostra non est, ut verba respondeant factis, nec ut litteræ satisfaciant officiis, sed ut nos, studio iam pares, beneficiis aliquando superiores existamus, cum idonea nobis ad id occasio data fuerit. Nam si Vestra Humanitas in benemerendo tantum de nostro Oratore constitisset, de gratiis, Vestrae Dominationi agendis, deque officiis, vestris vicissim hominibus opportunè referendis, solummodo laborassemus. Sed cum vestra ipsius probe nobis cognita atque perspecta sint, non dicta solum honorificè, sed facta etiam officiosissimè, pro nostromet tuendo nomine atque Dignitate, quantum nos merito Vestræ Reverendissimæ Dominationi debemus, litteris nunc quidem libenter significare, sed debitis vicissim officiis cumulatè aliquando repræsentare aliquando cogitamus. Hamptoniæ, 26 Augusti, 1554.

During Shakespeare's lifetime teachers of handwriting filled a prominent place in social life and gave exhibitions of skill which excited general public interest. Peter Bales, who is said to have transcribed the Bible within the limits of a walnut, taught 'all manner of hands', and in 1595 had a public competition with a rival calligrapher, Daniel Johnson, wherein he won a golden pen. He published in 1590 *The Writing Schoolemaster*, of which a second edition came out seven years later. A more eminent teacher of writing, who was reported equally efficient in ' Secretary, Roman, Court, and Text ', was John Davies of Hereford, who was well known as a poet. His pupils were drawn from the noblest families in the country, and among them was Prince Henry. Although he died in 1618, no earlier edition than that of 1633 is known of his *Writing Schoolemaster*; but this was an improvement on Bales's book, as it gave engraved specimens of various styles of handwriting. Bales, however, was not the first to instruct the English in the art of handwriting. Jehan de Beauchesne, a French writing-master who had already, in 1550, printed at Paris his *Thresor d'Escripture*, produced, in 1571, with the help of John Baildon, an English edition of it : *A Booke containing Divers Sortes of Hands* (viz. English and French Secretary, and Italian, Roman, Chancery, and Court hands), which served generally as a model for most of the English writing-books for the next hundred years. As the output of such books increased, the number of styles affected by the writing-masters likewise multiplied. The professional pen-man, like other skilled craftsmen, was not above magnifying his office ; and the writing-books soon abound in specimens of calligraphy which experts alone, in different professions, would have any need to practise and which could only have been objects of curiosity to the general. Setting aside the later creations of the writing-masters,

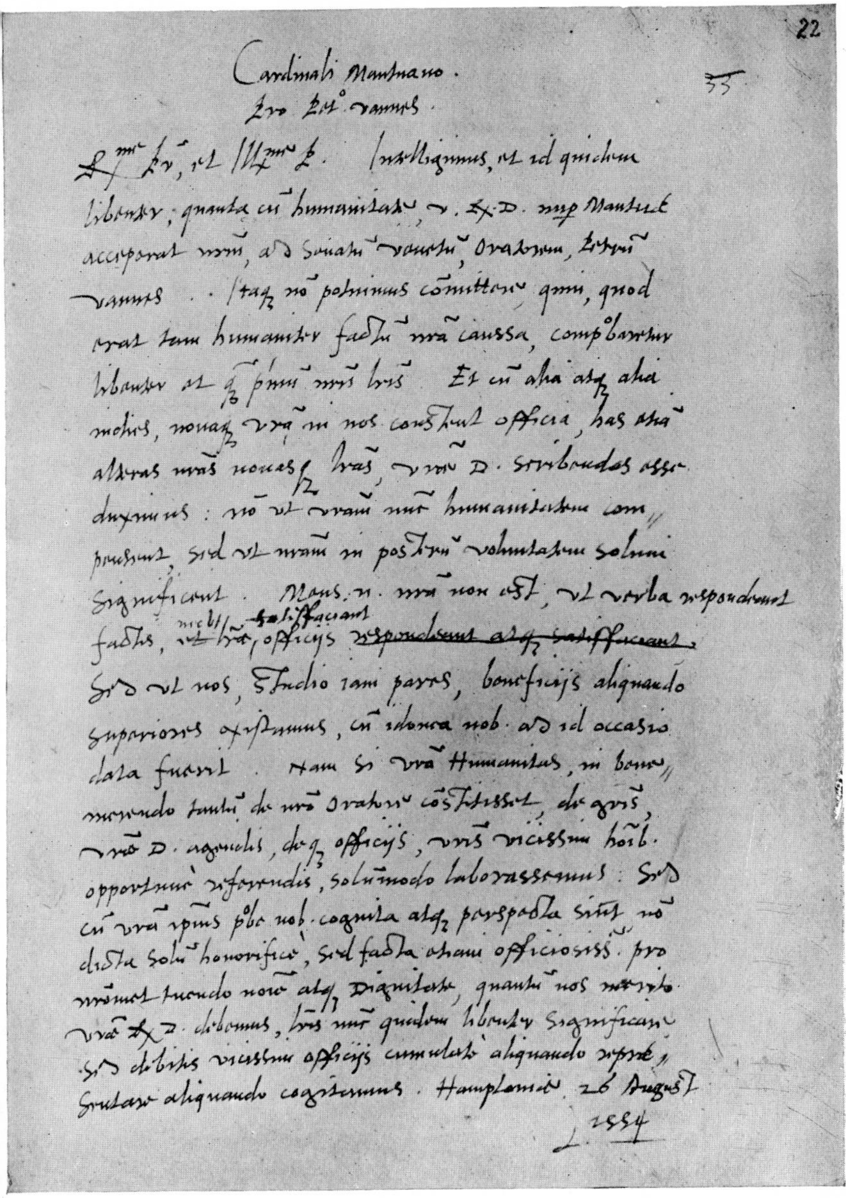
22
33

Cardinali Mantuano.
Pro Rege et Reginis.

Rme Pr, et Illme D. Intelligimus, et id quidem
libenter, quanta cum humanitate V. R. D. nuper Mantue
acceperat virum, ad Senatum Venetum, Oratorem, nostrum
Vannes. Itaque non potuimus committere quin, quod
erat tam humaniter factum nostra caussa, comprobaretur
libenter et quam primum nostris literis. Et cum alia atque alia
nobis, nouaque vestra in nos conferat officia, has alias
alteras nostras nouasque literas, vestrae D. scribendas esse
duximus: non ut vestram nunc humanitatem com-
prehendant, sed ut nostram in posterum voluntatem solum
significent. Nam. n. nostrum non est, ut verba respondeant
factis, ut literae officijs ~~respondeant atque satisfaciant~~.
Sed ut nos, studio iam pares, beneficijs aliquando
superiores existamus, cum idonea nobis ad id occasio
data fuerit. Nam si vestra Humanitas, in bene
merendo tantum de nostro Oratore constitisset, de gratiis
vestrae D. agendis, deque officijs, vestris vicissim hominibus
opportune referendis, solummodo laborassemus: Sed
cum vestra ipsius probe nobis cognita atque perspecta sint, non
dicta solum honorifice, sed facta etiam officiosissime pro
nomine tuendo nostro atque dignitate, quantum nos merito
vestrae R. D. debemus, literis nunc quidem libenter significamus
sed debitis vicissim officijs cumulate aliquando exprimere,
gratareque aliquando cogitemus. Hamptoniae. 26 Augusti
1554

No 3 DRAFT LETTER OF ROGER ASCHAM 1554

BRITISH MUSEUM ADD MS 35840 f 22

we have the following : Secretary, Italian, Roman, Chancery, Court, and Text, which call for some explanation. Of these styles the Italian and Roman alone are of foreign origin ; the other four are developed from the native English script. Unfortunately the writing-masters are not altogether in agreement in their descriptions ; and their engraved plates do not in all instances afford full assistance in identification. To begin with the Italian and Roman hands, there seems to have been little to choose between them, either in the writing-books or in popular estimation. When Malvolio commends Olivia's ' sweet Roman hand ' (*Tw. N.* III. iv. 32), he bears testimony to the fashionable vogue of the new script—the imported Italian hand. Beauchesne, however, seems to have in his mind, as the true Roman hand, the calligraphic upright lettering which followed the pattern of the book-hand of the Italian humanists and the thence derived Roman type of the printers, and which was in favour particularly with the French calligraphers of the sixteenth century in the production of their pretty little pocket volumes.

Of the styles of native English origin, the first is the ' secretary ' hand, by far the most practical and widely employed style of English cursive writing in Shakespeare's days, the principal business hand of the time. In Facsimile No. 8 we have a good example of it. The Chancery hand was one of the official styles which, elaborated by the skill of the scriveners of the different Courts of Law, have served for the engrossment of departmental legal records in a form sufficiently artificial to satisfy the jealousy of official experts, while at the same time proving difficult reading to the uninitiated. Court hand is a general term for the scripts employed in drawing up charters and other formal legal documents, with which lawyers would be generally familiar. The unhappy Clerk of Chatham, whom we shall have to cite again in another place, probably had enough knowledge of domestic legal records to give colour to the accusation by Jack Cade's rabble of ability to ' make obligations and write court-hand ' (*2 Hen. VI*, IV. ii. 104–5). Lastly, there is ' text ' hand—a rather vague term. It has been generally defined as one of the larger and more formal hands in which the text of a book would be written, as distinct from the smaller hand appro-

priate to the gloss. It seems that in the sixteenth century
it indicated a clear upright lettering of the book-hand type,
as distinguished from the epistolary style, which under the
pens of the writing-masters took the form of a simplified
black-letter. But the authorities differ. For example,
Billingsley, in his *Pens Excellencie*, classes ' text ' with
' bastard secretary ', a style which he informs us is so
named ' because it is gotten of the secretary ' and continues that ' it is a hand of great validitie and for divers
purposes exceeding gracefull, as for engrossments, epi-
taphs for tombes, titles of bookes,' &c. However, we
may be content that the general aim of ' text ' was to be
a clear, handsome, and distinguished style. Assuredly
Schoolmaster Holofernes (*Love's L. L.* v. ii. 42) would
count it for a worthy compliment that Biron's verses
should be thought to make Rosaline ' fair as a text B in
a copy book '.

The handwriting of Shakespeare's contemporaries naturally has a special interest for us. In the first instance two
examples of literary value deserve study. The one comes from
the hand of the poet, George Peele, who may have had a hand
in the first draft of the play of *Henry VI*, the other from that
of Shakespeare's close friend, Ben Jonson, who, to quote his
own well-known words, 'loved the man and honoured his
memory, on this side idolatry, as much as any '. Peele's
letter was addressed to Lord Burghley, in 1595. In the
high-flown complimentary language of the day the poet
presents to Lord Burghley his *History of Troy in 500 Verses*,
sending the book by the hand of ' this simple messenger
my eldest daughter and necessities servant '. The poor
scholar pathetically adds, ' Longe sicknes, havinge so
enfeebled me, maketh bashfullnes allmost become impudency '. Peele wrote in the Italian hand, with the beautiful
flow of a ready writer, which continual practice had made
perfect. Special attention should be paid to the peculiar
way in which he here signed his name, in two lines, the surname below the Christian name. The mechanical reason
for this arrangement is obvious : he had inscribed his
Christian name so close to the margin of the paper that
there was no room left to complete the signature in one
line (Facsimile No. 4).

The main interest of Peele's manner of signature is that

Salue Parens Patriæ, tibj plebs, tibj curia nomen
hoc dedit, hoc dedimus nos tibj nomen æquès.

In these tearmes (r. honorable) am I bolde
to salute yr Lordeship whose highe desertes in &
Englandes greate designes haue earned Large praises
euen from Indies mowthes. Pardon greate Patrone of
Learninge & Virtue / this rude encounter, in that I
presume, A Scholler of so meane merit to present yr
wisdome with this small manuell / by this simple Messenger
my eldest Daughter & necessities seruant. Longe
sicknes hauinge so enfeebled me maketh bashfulnes,
allmost become impudency. Sed quæ Psitaco suæ
Expediut / Magister artis ingenij Largitor Venter
The subiect whereon I presume to greete yr honor
is the history of Troy in soo Verses set downe &
memorable accidents thereof. Receiue it (noble Senator of
Englandes Counsell-howse) as A schollers dutie signifiacon
& Liue Longe in honor & prosperitie as happie as
Queene Elizabeths gracious comtenance can make ye

Hæc tibj nihilum magno pro munere mitto /
Esse botest aliquid (te capiete) nihil.

                                        Yr honor most
                                        bownden George
                                                Peele

No 4 LETTER OF THE POET GEORGE PEELE
     TO LORD BURGHLEY 1595
BRITISH MUSEUM LANSDOWNE MS 991 f 554

two of the six extant signatures of Shakespeare himself are written in exactly the same way and from the same cause, namely, lack of marginal space.

Our other example is a page from Ben Jonson's *Masque of Queenes*, which was represented at Whitehall on February 2, 1609. This beautiful MS. was dedicated to Prince Henry, and forms part of the Royal Library in the British Museum (Facsimile No. 5).

It is a wonderful piece of calligraphy which in its neatness does not lose its individual character. Ben Jonson had an astonishing command of the pen to be able to write thus faultlessly page after page without wearying or failing in precision. It will be seen that the character of the writing is of a mixed nature : neither altogether Italian, nor yet true English, but partaking of both styles, in fact a fanciful hand, which betrays the writer's intimate knowledge both of his native handwriting and of the fashionable foreign script. Had he not been well skilled in both the one and the other, he could never have formed the mould in which he has cast this delicate example of literary calligraphy. The actual forms of the individual letters are mainly Italian, but, besides here and there a trick or catch of the English style, purely English forms, as the double-stemmed *r*, the reversed *e*, and the long-tailed *h* (following a *g*), are also intermingled.

Of other Elizabethan men of letters, it may be noticed that John Lyly wrote far less neatly in a style somewhat similar to that of Jonson. He combined on no regular plan English and Italian lettering (Hatfield MS. letter to Sir Robert Cecil, Feb. 4, 1602–3). On the other hand, Thomas Kyd was faithful to the English hand, which he wrote with great efficiency. His autograph signature is, however, in the Italian script, and when he quotes Latin he carefully copies out the words in that style (Harleian MS. 6849, f. 218).

As a favourable example of the kind of handwriting which was at the command of the ' statists ' or public men who were supposed, in Hamlet's phrase, to hold it ' a baseness to write fair ', a letter is selected (written to Sir Julius Caesar) which has the advantage of coming from the pen of Shakespeare's friend and patron, Henry Wriothesley, Earl of Southampton. It is a good easy hand, in flowing Italian style, written without effort, though, at the same time, without pretence to clerical exactitude (Facsimile No. 6).

Leaving the Court and men of letters, we turn to Shakespeare's native countryside and see what the documents of his own provincial town have to tell us in regard to the handwriting of friends and of members of his family, who belonged to the smaller mercantile class.

The style of handwriting then taught in Stratford-upon-Avon was the native English hand; apparently the new Italian style was practically unknown there until quite late in the century. Neither of the poet's parents appears to have been able to write at all; they simply made their marks in execution of deeds. Of Shakespeare's two surviving children, the eldest, Susanna Hall, wrote a painfully formed signature, which was probably the most that she was capable of doing with the pen; the second, Judith Quiney, we conclude could not write at all, for she signed with a mark. We have to descend to the next generation to find a well-educated female member of the family in the poet's granddaughter, Elizabeth Hall, who was born in 1608, and was married successively to Thomas Nash of Stratford, and to Sir John Barnard of Northamptonshire. In her day the native English hand was disappearing from ordinary correspondence; and the lady wrote a good signature in the Italian style.[1]

Few men and fewer women of the poorer class in Shakespeare's England could use the pen; but still some discredit attached to the disability. Jack Cade asks the Clerk of Chatham, who is charged with 'setting of boys' copies', 'Dost thou use to write thy name? or hast thou a mark to thyself, like an honest plain-dealing man?' The Clerk replies: 'Sir, I thank God I have been so well brought up that I can write my name' (*2 Hen. VI*, iv. ii. 80 seq.). At Stratford the art, despite the apparent inability of Shakespeare's father, was in common practice.

Some very favourable specimens are extant of the handwriting of Shakespeare's fellow townsmen and contemporaries. There is, for example, a letter of his friend Richard Quiney, a mercer of Stratford, the father of Thomas Quiney, who afterwards married the poet's younger daughter Judith. By good fortune this letter has the peculiar interest of being actually addressed to Shakespeare himself: the solitary item that has survived of all his correspondence. The writer was evidently a man of better education, who could express

---

[1] *Birthplace Catalogue*, Nos. 122, 124.

THE MASQVE OF QVEENES

Penthesilea, the braue Amazon,
Swift=foote Camilla, Queene of Volscia,
Victorious Thomyris of Scythia,
Chast Artemisia, the Carian Dame,
And fayre=hayr'd Beronice, Ægipts fame,
Hypsicratea, Glory' of Asia,
Candace, pride of Æthiopia
The Britaine honor, Voadicea,
The vertuous Palmyrene Zenobia,
The wise, and warlike Goth, Amalasunta,
And bold Valasca of Bohemia.
These (in theyr liues, as fortunes) crown'd the choyse
of Woman=kind) and 'gaynst all opposite voyce
Made good to Time, had after death the clayme
To liue æternis'd in the House of Fame.
Where howrely hearing (as what there is old?)
The Glories of Bel-anna so well told,
Queene of the Ocean; How that shee, alone,
Possest all vertues, for wch One by One,
They were so fam'd; And wanting then a head,
To forme that sweete, and gracious Pyramide,
Wherein they sit, it being the soueraigne place
of all that Palace, and reserud to grace
The Worthiest Queene: These, whom enuy'on her
Jn life desir'd that honor to confer,
Wch, wth theyr death, no other should enioy.
She then embracing, wth a vertuous ioy,
Farre from selfe=loue, as humbling all her Worth
To him that gaue it, hath agayne brought forth
Theyr Names to Memory, and meanes this night
To make her, once more, visible to light;
And to that light, from whence her truth of Spirit
Confesseth all the lustre of her Merit.

himself well with business-like brevity and at the same time
with clearness and dispatch. The letter is written off, as
he himself says, in haste ; but one is struck with the excellence of the small but legible, though somewhat cramped,
handwriting in the English style, of which Shakespeare's
friend was palpably a master. He was one of the leading men
of business in his native town, was twice bailiff or mayor, and,
at the time of writing the letter, he was engaged in London
on important municipal affairs. The handwriting is quite
that of a lawyer. It will be observed that the writer fills in
blank spaces at the end of the third and eighth lines of the
letter with a flourished stroke, just as a careful lawyer
would do in a legal draft, or as an official clerk would do
in an official document, in order to prevent the improper
insertion of words into the text. A careful and exact man,
in any case, with a natural gift for writing with speed
(Facsimile No. 7).

Loveinge Contreyman, I am bolde of yow as of a Frende, craveinge
yowr helpe with xxx*ll.* vppon Mr. Bushells and my securytee, or
Mr. Myttons with me. Mr. Rosswell is nott come to London as
yeate, and I have especiall cawse. Yow shall Frende me muche in
helpeing me out of all the debettes I owe in London, I thanck God,
and muche quiet my mynde, which wolde nott be indebeted. I am
nowe towardes the Cowrte, in hope of answer for the dispatche of my
Buysenes. Yow shall nether loase creddytt nor monney by me, the
Lorde wyllinge ; and nowe butt perswade yowr selfe soe as I hope,
and yow shall nott need to feare, butt, with all hartie thanckefullnes,
I wyll holde my tyme and content yowr Frende, and yf we Bargaine
farther yow shalbe the paiemaster yowr selfe. My tyme biddes me
hasten to an ende, and soe I committ thys [to] yowr care and hope of
yowr helpe. I feare I shall nott be backe thys night From the
Cowrte. Haste. The Lorde be with yow and with vs all, amen.
From the Bell in Carter Lane, the 25 October, 1596.

Yowrs in all kyndenes
RYC. QUYNEY.

Address :
To my Loveinge good Frend
and contreyman Mr. Wm.
Shackespere deliver thees.

Richard Quiney's faculty for writing well was inherited by
his son Thomas, who was born in 1589 and was therefore
under education towards the end of the century. He wrote
a very fine hand in the Italian style, which he seems to have
been proud of showing off, gracing his signature with all the

flourishes of a writing-master.[1] We may, perhaps, date the
first practice of the Italian style among the teachers of
Stratford as contemporaneous with the rising generation succeeding that of Shakespeare; and, whoever he may have been,
the writing-master of young Thomas Quiney was assuredly
a very skilful penman. A Stratford deed of March 5,
1609–10, bears three admirable signatures of Shakespeare's
fellow townsmen, one of which, in a well-formed Italian handwriting, is that of Gilbert Shakespeare. This signatory has
been identified with the dramatist's brother of that name,
who was born in 1566. But the signature appears to belong
to the period of a younger generation, and may be that of a
young man of the name who was buried at Stratford in the
year 1612, and who was doubtless a son of the elder Gilbert
and nephew of the poet.[2]

While the native English style of writing thus at the close
of the sixteenth century was practically abandoned in
general education in favour of the foreign style, it still
continued in official use, as we have already noticed, under
various forms and for various purposes. The general business
hand of this type was the 'secretary' of the writing-masters
and professional calligraphers of the sixteenth and seventeenth
centuries ; and it was in this hand that plays were transcribed for theatrical uses, as may be seen from the fragments
of Greene's *Historie of Orlando Furioso* (*c.* 1591), which are
preserved among Alleyn's papers at Dulwich. As an example
of the 'secretary' hand we have selected an official letter of
William Herbert, Earl of Pembroke, addressed, as Lord Chamberlain, to Viscount Mandeville, President of the Council, with
reference to the relief of the prohibition imposed, at the instance of the Spanish Ambassador, upon the King's Company
of Comedians, for having performed Middleton's *Game at Chess*.
The subject-matter has an interest of its own. Our concern
for the moment is the style in which the letter is composed :
the text is in the neatly written 'secretary' of the official
clerk ; the Lord Chamberlain's signature is, as usual, in
the Italian style (Facsimile No. 8).

My very good Lord,
　　Complaynt being made vnto his Majesty against y^e Company
of his Comedians for Acteing publiquely a Play knowne by the name

---

[1] Facsimiles in Halliwell-Phillipps, *Outlines*, ed. 1887, i. 256.
[2] *Birthplace Catalogue*, No. 115.

of a Game at Chesse contayning some passages in it reflecting in
matter of scorne and ignominy vpon yᵉ King of Spaine, some of his
Ministers, and others of good note and quality, His Majesty, out of
yᵉ tender regard hee had of that Kinges honnour and those his
Ministers who weare conceived to bee wounded thereby, caused his
letters to bee addressed to my Lords and yᵉ rest of his most honnourable Privy Counsell, thereby requireing them to convent those his
Comedians before them, and to take such course with them for this
offence as might give best satisfaccion to yᵉ Spanish Ambassadour
and to Their owne Honnors.   After examinacion, that honnourable
Board thought fitt not onely to interdict them yᵉ playing of that
play, but of any other also vntill his Majesty should give way vnto
them, and for their obedience herevnto they weare bound in 300*l.*
bondes.   Which punishment when they had suffered (as his Majesty
conceives) a competent tyme, upon their peticion delivered heere
vnto hym, it pleased his Majesty to comaund mee to lett your
Lordship vnderstand (which I pray your Lordship to impart
to yᵉ rest of that honnourable Board), That his Majesty nowe
conceives yᵉ punishment, if not satisfactory for that their Insolency,
yet such as, since it stopps yᵉ current of their poore livelyhood and
maintenaunce, without much prejudice they cannot longer vndergoe.
In commiseracion therefore of those his poore servantes his Majesty
would have their Lordships connive at any common play lycenced
by authority, that they shall act as before ; As for this of ye Game
at Chesse, that it bee not onely antiquated and sylenced, but yᵉ
Players bound, as formerly they weare, and in that poynt onely
never to act it agayne ; Yet notwithstanding that my Lords proceed
in their disquisicion to fynd out yᵉ originall roote of this offence,
whether it sprang from yᵉ Poet, Players, or both, and to certefy his
Majesty accordingly.   And so desireing your Lordship to take this
into your consideracion and them into your care, I rest

Your Lordship's most affectionate Cousin to serve you

PEMBROKE.

Court at Woodstock
the 27th of August
1624.

The question of the character of Shakespeare's own handwriting must always remain a subject of particular interest
from many points of view.   The tradition of his extraordinary facility in literary composition, as conveyed to us
by Ben Jonson and by the editors of the First Folio of his
works, demands a corresponding fluency in actual handwriting.   It is intolerable to imagine the utterance of his
thoughts being checked by mere physical difficulties in
committing his ideas to paper ; and therefore on this ground
alone, and even though every vestige of his handwriting had

vanished, we should reject any fanciful theory of Shakespeare's inability to write with adequate expertness.

In the 'Analysis of Shakespeare's Autograph Signatures' which accompanies this chapter, an attempt has been made to offer, from a survey of the scanty material at our command, a reasonable solution of this interesting question; and it is hoped that the conclusion arrived at, viz. that the poet, when in the vigour of life, was master of a good working hand, may gain acceptance. But the subject of his capacity for physical use of the pen leads on to another of more enduring interest and importance.

In the minds of those who have given attention to the subject of the handwriting, curiosity naturally arises regarding the extent to which the obscurities and errors in the text of his plays that have been transmitted to us from the earliest printed collection may be due to misreadings of his autograph MSS. Although the editors of the First Folio of 1623 announced in their preface, with perhaps intentional vagueness, that they had 'scarce received from him a blot in his papers', and thereby may have intended to lead their readers to believe that they had had access to Shakespeare's originals (would that they had!), we may be extremely doubtful whether they had a single shred of the poet's own MSS. before them. The autographs of the plays would have ceased to have any practical value after they had been transcribed for the acting copies, and were probably thrown aside; and we should have to seek the first origin of obscurities and errors in those transcripts. But it must not be forgotten that Shakespeare was not only the author of his plays, but that he was also an actor and took part in the performance of at least some of them, and therefore it is to be assumed that he would at once have detected and amended any blunders made by the copyists. It does not then seem likely that many of the existing difficulties in the text of the plays in which he acted are due to defects in the first theatrical transcripts—errors which, having escaped the author's ear or eye, have been transmitted to later copies. The case would, however, be different in regard to the few plays which he composed after he had severed connexion with the stage; and the corruptions to be found in those plays might perhaps offer a field for emendation by the reconstruction of phrases

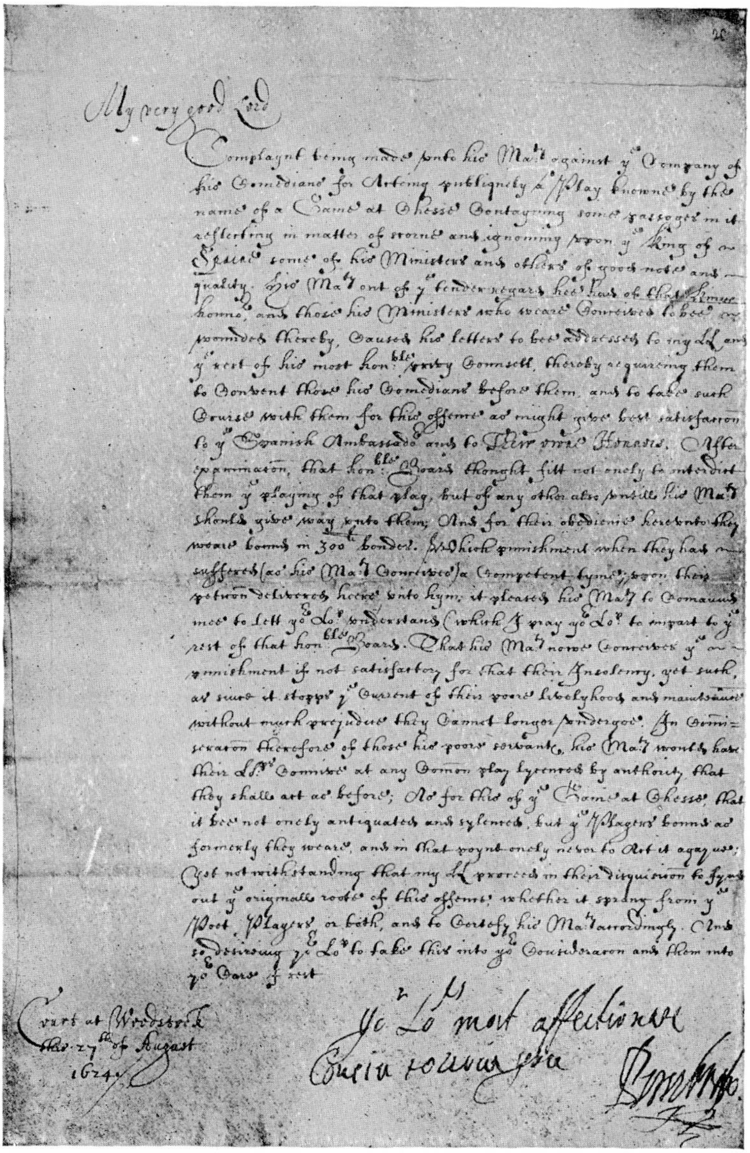

20

My very good Lord

Complaynt being made unto his Matie against ye Company of his Comedians for Acting publiquely a Play knowne by the name of a Game at Chesse Contayning some passages in it reflecting in matter of scorne and ignominy upon ye King of Spaine some of his Ministers and others of good note and quality. His Maty out of ye tender regard hee hath of that Princes honnor, and those his Ministers who weare Conceived to bee wounded thereby, Caused his letters to bee addressed to my LL and ye rest of his most honble privy Counsell, thereby requiring them to Convent those his Comedians before them, and to take such Course with them for this offence as might give best satisfaction to ye Spanish Ambassador and to their owne Honours. After examination, that honble Board thought fitt not onely to interdict them ye playing of that play, but of any other also untill his Maty should give way unto them; And for their obedience hereunto they weare bound in 300li bondes. Which punishment when they had suffered (as his Maty Conceived) a Competent tyme, upon their petition delivered heere unto hym, it pleased his Maty to Comaund mee to lett yor Lop understand (which I pray yor Lop to impart to ye rest of that honble Board) That his Maty nowe Conceives ye punishment if not satisfactory for that their Insolency, yet such, as since it stopps ye Current of their poore livelyhood and maintenance without much prejudice they Cannot longer undergoe. In Comiseration therefore of those his poore servants, his Maty would have their LLps Connive at any Comon play lycenced by authority, that they shalle act as before; As for this of ye Game at Chesse, that it bee not onely antiquated and sylenced, but ye Players bound as formerly they weare, and in that poynt onely never to Act it agayne; Yet notwithstanding that my LL proceed in their disquisition to fynd out ye originall roote of this offence, whether it sprang from ye Poet, Players or both, and to Certefy his Maty accordingly. And so desiring yor Lop to take this into yor Consideration and them into yor Care I rest

Court at Woodstock the 27th of August 1624

Yor Lops most affectionate Cousin to serve you

Pembroke.

No 8 LETTER OF WILLIAM HERBERT EARL OF PEMBROKE TO THE PRESIDENT OF THE COUNCIL 1624

BRITISH MUSEUM EGERTON MS 2623 f 28

in the old English hand which Shakespeare wrote. But,
taking the plays as a whole, it is not probable that any
large proportions of the obscure passages are immediately
due to misreadings of the original MSS. It is, however,
allowable to regard the question of emendation from another
point of view in connexion with the handwriting of the time.
The early transcripts would have been written according to
custom in the common clerical hand, the 'secretary' hand
of the scriveners, which has been already described. Few,
if any, would have been copied in the more legible Italian
style. It is therefore not improbable that many errors may
have crept into the pages of the First Folio from the com-
positors' misreadings of the transcripts; and we believe
that there is still room for emendation of not a few of the
doubtful passages in the printed text of Shakespeare by
bringing to bear upon them, more systematically than has
been done, exact and practical knowledge of the construction of the English handwriting of his time.

An Analysis of Shakespeare's Autograph Signatures

The facts, as far as they have been recorded, of Shakespeare's
school education and early life are of primary importance in an
inquiry into the character of his handwriting. To begin with, it
must always be borne in mind that, as the result of an imperfect
education, he would naturally write only in one style of hand, the
native English hand which he had been taught in the Free School
of Stratford, and that he probably never had any practical experience
in the fashionable Italian style of writing, although he saw it in
constant use among his noble and literary contemporaries in the
metropolis. We know that he was withdrawn from school when
probably only about thirteen years of age, at a period of youth
when the handwriting is still unformed; and there is no reason to
suppose that during the next decade he had occasion to use his pen
as a special means of livelihood, if we are to accept the tradition of
his occupations in his native town before seeking his fortune in
London. Therefore when the period of regular authorship arrived,
and the call for constant occupation at the desk, we may reasonably
imagine the young man of some seven-and-twenty years equipped
with a handwriting casually developed from that of his schooldays,
rough and untrained, though capable of being worked by practice
into a fluent and useful style of writing; but one always wanting in
the calligraphic finish which a more thorough education would have
imparted.

But we are not altogether dependent on conjecture. We still
possess actual specimens of Shakespeare's handwriting, but so

scanty that it might appear almost hopeless, nay, presumptuous, to essay to form from them any just idea of the general character of the great dramatist's writing. Yet an attempt may be made to ascertain whether they afford any clue to the writer's methods in the mechanical use of the pen.

The only known examples, of undisputed authenticity, of Shakespeare's handwriting are six signatures attached to the following documents :

1. The poet's deposition in a suit brought by Stephen Bellott against his father-in-law, Christopher Montjoy, of Silver Street, Wood Street, in the city of London, recently discovered by Dr. C. W. Wallace in the Public Record Office ; May 11, 1612.

2. The conveyance of a house in Blackfriars, London, purchased by Shakespeare ; March 10, 1613 (now in the Guildhall Library).

3. A mortgage-deed of the same property ; March 11, 1613 (now in the British Museum).

4. The poet's will, written on three sheets of paper, with his signature at the foot of each one ; executed March 25, 1616 (now in Somerset House).

That there should have survived so little of Shakespeare's handwriting may seem surprising ; but this is not a singular instance of the practically total disappearance of the papers of even a prolific author. In Shakespeare's days men set little store by autographs ; and the idea of preserving his writings for the inspection of posterity, we may be certain, never entered his head.

The six signatures may be divided into two groups, viz. three appended severally to the deposition of 1612 and to the two deeds concerning the Blackfriars property of the following year, which were written when the poet was presumably in ordinary health ; and three subscribed to the three sheets of his will when he was already stricken with his mortal sickness. All of us are conscious how subject the handwriting is to variation under the influence of changes in our bodily health ; and it will presently be shown that the reason for this grouping is not merely fanciful.

We here submit facsimiles of the three signatures forming the first group (Facsimiles Nos. 9–11).

Of the three signatures before us, written, as we may assume, under conditions of ordinary bodily health, by far the best is that attached to the deposition (No. 9). It is dashed off with freedom, and it conveys the impression of coming from the hand of a ready writer. The other two, attached to the Blackfriars deeds, are constrained, and therefore not quite natural, owing to the writer's apparent desire to keep within the limits of the seal-labels : that of the purchase-deed (No. 10) being rather feeble ; the other (No. 11) being somewhat laboriously written down in disconnected letters and thereby losing the natural run of the hand. It seems then that the deposition signature is the only one that can be wholly relied on as a true standard for our inquiry. But we must not omit to note in this place the value of the third subscription to the will (No. 14), as including the only two words ' By me ', besides the actual words comprising his name, that have come down to us in Shakespeare's handwriting. These two words happen to be fairly well written, and therefore may be added to the deposition signature to help us to our conclusion.

We believe that all will agree that the hand which could write the signature to the deposition must have been capable of wielding the pen with dexterity and speed. The firm control of the pen in forming the sweeping curves in the surname is indeed remarkable. The style also of the two initial words in the third subscription to the will, after due allowance made for the conditions under which they were written, shows readiness in writing. On the other hand, the awkwardness and constraint of the two Blackfriars signatures mark the writer's inability to adapt his hand neatly to a limited space. We therefore conclude that, under ordinary conditions, Shakespeare wrote a free and rapid, though careless, hand, sufficiently legible and business-like for practical purposes, and at the same time, perhaps, manifesting impatience in a tendency to a liberal use of abbreviations ; but that he made no pretence to be an elegant penman.

We turn again to the three signatures forming our first group. It will be at once observed that in all three instances the surname is written in an abbreviated form, although the deeds to which they are attached are legal instruments.

The two Blackfriars deeds first claim attention. The signature to the purchase-deed (No. 10) is WILLIAM SHAKSPĒR, that to the mortgage-deed (No. 11) is Wᵐ SHAKSPĒ, the concluding letter or letters of the full name being omitted, and their omission being indicated by a flourish above the line.[1] It has been suggested that the writer curtailed his name in each instance with the mistaken idea that he was obliged to keep within the limits of the label or strip of parchment inserted into the foot of the deed for the purpose of carrying the seal. This view has certainly received support from the fact of the signature in the purchase-deed being written in two lines, the surname below the Christian name ; just as we have seen above the signature of George Peele subscribed for want of space. And, indeed, it seems that Shakespeare, from whim or fancy, did intend to confine his name to the labels. But the supposition that he was fortuitously compelled to shorten his name is altogether erroneous. In both instances he could easily have written his surname in full within the labels by a more careful economy of the space at his command ; and if in the purchase-deed he had accidentally, by miscalculation, found himself under the necessity of

---

[1] The mark of abbreviation in No. 11 has been sometimes read as an over-written open *a*. But that it is nothing more than a double-curve flourish, here written, like the individual letters of the signature, rather carefully, is shown by the similar formation of the mark in the purchase-deed, written hurriedly and palpably only as a flourish.

using a shortened form, he would hardly have repeated his mistake in the mortgage-deed executed on the following day. A close scrutiny of these two signatures casts some further light upon the problem.

It has been stated above that the signature to the purchase-deed (No. 10) is to be read WILLIAM SHAKSPER; and special attention must be directed to the last two letters, *er*. When he had written the *e*, Shakespeare had reached the extreme edge of the label; and there, as in the case of No. 11, he might have stopped, the flourish above the *e* being enough to indicate abbreviation. But, instead of doing so, he added the *r*; and still, as it seems, trying to cling to the label, he squeezed the letter, but not without passing, with its upper part, over the label's edge, on to the parchment of the deed, although he succeeded in bringing back the lower half of the letter into the label. The ink of the *r* is fainter than that of the rest of the name; and this would suggest that the letter was added by Shakespeare, perhaps after only a moment's hesitation, but, for some reason now beyond conjecture, after the rest of the signature had been subscribed. This suggestion received support from the fact that the mark of abbreviation is distinctly placed above the *e*—its correct position, if that were the concluding letter.[1]

When we turn to the mortgage-deed (No. 11), we naturally expect to find a signature uniform with that of the purchase-deed executed only a day earlier. It is therefore surprising to find a difference. The final *r* of No. 10 is here omitted, and the signature stands Wm SHAKSPĒ, although there is room for the missing letter within the limit of the label. Here, then, is a curious instance of a man signing his name in two different forms in two connected documents within a period of a few hours. But, though different in form, the signatures are alike in the important particular that they are abbreviated; and it is clear that the abbreviation was intentional. On the evidence of the Blackfriars deeds we can affirm that the employment of shortened signatures in subscriptions to legal documents, in business of such importance as the conveyance of property, demonstrates that Shakespeare must have made a practice of using them so commonly that they had come to be accepted as his legal subscription.

This view has now received unexpected confirmation by the discovery of the signature to the deposition of May 11, 1612, the first on our list (No. 9). In this instance we have again a signature in an abbreviated shape. It is true that the abbreviation is not

---

[1] The photograph from which our facsimile is produced has been very successful in bringing out clearly the faintly written *r*; it has even intensified it. Other facsimiles have not always been so fortunate. For example, in those given in Sir S. Lee's *Life of Shakespeare* and in his pamphlet *Shakespeare's Handwriting* (1899), by one of the freaks to which photography is susceptible, the upper part of the letter has disappeared; but the existence of the *r* is noticed on p. 522 (1925 ed.).

No 9

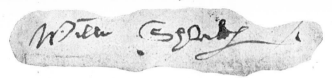

No 10

No 11

SHAKESPEARE'S SIGNATURES TO THREE
LEGAL DOCUMENTS 1612 1613
PUBLIC RECORD OFFICE GUILDHALL LIBRARY
BRITISH MUSEUM

the same as that of either of the two signatures which have been discussed ; but the remarkable fact remains that here Shakespeare has written his name in shortened form without any mechanical obligation for doing so, such as that of keeping within the confined limits of a label. Briefly, then, there is now still more absolute proof that he was in the habit of cutting short his signature, though not always in the same form.

The signature to the deposition is WILLM SHAKP with a sweeping stroke dashed through the tail of the *p*. If we were to apply the rules of mediaeval abbreviation to this signature we might determine the final letter *p* with its added stroke to be read as *per* ; and, had Shakespeare been a lawyer accustomed to write with legal abbreviations, we might reasonably accept this interpretation. But the poet was not a lawyer, nor is there any reason for supposing that he had in his mind any thought of exact and methodical abbreviation according to rule, when he thus subscribed his name. We should prefer to regard the under-written flourish in this instance as serving the same purpose as the over-written flourish in the Blackfriars deeds, that is as simply indicating that the name was shortened and nothing more. At the same time it must be granted that Shakespeare was certainly familiar with the abbreviated form of *per*, which was then, as it is now, in common use in trade and commerce ; and he must also have seen the symbol introduced into his own name by at least one of his correspondents. In the sole surviving letter addressed to him, a facsimile of which has already been given (No. 7), written by his friend Richard Quiney, one certainly conversant with the shortened words and symbols employed in trade, the poet's name in the address appears with this commercial abbreviation introduced into it.

It is to be noticed that in this deposition signature Shakespeare goes beyond simple abbreviation, the mere curtailment of his surname by omitting the ending ; he also drops out the second *s* from the middle. This may have been only an act of carelessness, or he may have deemed that the emphatic *p* of the second syllable was enough to identify the signature as that of William Shakespeare. But, however that may be, the difference in form of this abbreviated signature from the abbreviated signatures of the Blackfriars deeds (Nos. 10, 11) calls for some attempt at explanation. The surname in each of the latter subscriptions, as we have seen, is shortened to the letters SHAKSPER and SHAKSPE ; in the deposition it is SHAKP. Of these varieties which one probably would Shakespeare himself and his contemporaries have acknowledged as his more usual subscription ? We are disposed to decide in favour of the form adopted in the mortgage-deed (No. 11). This subscription is penned with a certain formality, the letters written disconnectedly and therefore with deliberation. The deed is a formal document, carefully drawn up, and connected with the conveyance of property ; and the signatures of the parties are formally attested by witnesses. There was every reason therefore why Shakespeare should here employ a form of signature which would be legally and indubitably recognized as his. Most of what has just been said would equally apply to the signature of the purchase-deed (No. 10), were it not for the difficulty caused by the existence of the final *r* in the surname. But it has already been shown that there are cogent reasons for suspecting that the signature was in this instance also written originally in the form that appears in the mortgage-deed, and that the addition of the *r* was an afterthought. A further reason for proposing the selection of the abbreviated form of signature in No. 11 as the one most commonly used by Shakespeare will appear when we come to examine the subscriptions to the will. Unlike the Blackfriars signatures, the subscription to the deposition is dashed off with a careless freedom which would seem to indicate that, in the mind of the signatory, the document, although a legal document, was not of such high importance as an attested deed, and that a hasty signature was sufficient.

Keeping before us these important discoveries in regard to the habits of the poet in his penmanship, we will now pass on to the consideration of the second group of signatures, viz. the three subscriptions to the three sheets of his will (Facsimiles Nos. 12–14). This document is a draft, originally dated January 25, 1616; but it was not executed until two months later. It is to be noted that the testator was certified to be ' in perfect health '. But by the time of the execution something of urgent moment must have meanwhile occurred—so urgent, indeed, as to necessitate the immediate use of the draft without waiting for a fair engrossment. The draft in all its roughness, with corrections and interlineations, received the signatures of Shakespeare and the witnesses on March 25. The only adequate reason for so sudden an execution of a will would be the dangerous illness of the testator ; and the traditional account of Shakespeare's last illness is that he was seized with a fever following on a carouse with his friends Drayton and Ben Jonson. But, while the poet did not expire until April 23, nearly a month after the execution of the will, the hurried action of the business indicates that the seizure must have been very unexpected and alarming, and rather suggests that something more critical than the traditional fever had fastened on the stricken man. In the hurry of things the words ' in perfect health ' were left unaltered.

The three subscriptions present difficulties which are almost beyond explanation. In the first place, they differ from one another to such a degree that it is not going too far to declare that, were they met with on three independent documents, they might not unreasonably be taken, at first sight, for the signatures of three different persons. And, besides their intrinsic dissimilarity, the methods of writing them also vary.

With regard to the first signature, it is written in two lines, the surname standing beneath the Christian name : the method adopted, as we have seen, in the subscription to the Blackfriars purchase-deed.

The name is, in this instance, inscribed at the foot of the sheet, in the margin, where there was not sufficient space to write it in one line. The survival of two instances of Shakespeare's signature written thus in an abnormal fashion is interesting as a further indication of his carelessness in signing his name.

The signature to the second sheet of the will is written in the normal manner, in one line. The third signature, again, is in one line; but it differs from the other two in having the words ' By me ' prefixed.

As an explanation of these varieties both in handwriting and in form it would be hardly reasonable to propose that the three consecutive sheets of the will were signed on different days. We must conclude that Shakespeare executed the will in its entirety at one and the same time, just as any other testator would have been legally required to do. Both the variations in the handwriting of the three subscriptions and the differences in the method of writing them can, we believe, only be attributed to the weakened bodily condition to which the poet had been reduced by his mortal illness. All of them bear on their face, more or less, indications of the unsteady action of a tremulous hand ; but it will be observed that the third signature is the best of the three. It is most probable that this one was written first ; indeed it is the subscription to the will as an entire document, and therefore would naturally be the first to be affixed, being formally introduced by the words ' By me '. In what order the other two signatures would be subscribed to the first two sheets is of no great concern. By a strong effort, as we may believe, the sick man braced himself to subscribe the important signature (No. 14) at the foot of the third sheet, and succeeded fairly well. Then, when he was required to sign the other sheets, we may surmise that, knowing these signatures to be in the nature of mere subscriptions of verification and therefore of secondary importance, he was careless how he wrote ; he relaxed his effort and, in the weariness of sickness, scrawled the two ill-formed specimens of his autograph with a failing hand.

If this explanation of the manner in which the signatures to the will were subscribed may be accepted, we have still to account for their intrinsic differences, which have been so perplexing that even the spelling of the surname, at least in two of them, has been matter of dispute. We will first examine the third signature, which, as already stated, may be regarded as the most important of the three. In this instance the first three words ' By me William ' are written with a firmness which, as we think, justifies the suggestion that the invalid braced himself to the task. But the hand then begins to fail : the first three letters of the surname are still clearly legible, but are somewhat deformed ; then ensues almost a breakdown, an imperfect *k*, and a long *s* ending in a tremulous finial ; after which come the letters *pe* linked together. To this letter *e* we would direct particular attention. It is of the type with reversed loop, which was common in English writing of the time. In this signature

Shakespeare has not formed the loop (he has done so in his signature to the deed of March 10, 1613, No. 10) but has finished the letter with a mere thickening (in fact making a blind letter) and has attached to it a long flourish, as though the signature were completed. Having regard to the abbreviated signatures to the two Blackfriars deeds put forward above (Nos. 10, 11), this flourish is very significant; for in construction it is a double-curve flourish, formed on the same lines as the abbreviating flourish used in those deeds. Therefore in the signature so far written we are disposed to see another instance (badly written, it is true) of the shortened form of his surname which we have suggested was employed by Shakespeare in important legal transactions. But in the present instance, if we are correct in our view that the abbreviated surname was at first intended, for some reason (perhaps the lawyer required him to sign absolutely in full; perhaps the testator himself deemed it better to do so in the case of so solemn a document as his last will) it was thought more expedient that the name should be in full and the final letters added. Hence it may be seen, on close inspection, that the full signature is completed by the addition of the letters *are*, the *a* (blotted) being brought close up to follow the preceding *e* and to stand under the flourish. Assuming that this reading of the signature is correct, it is to be noticed that in this instance at least the poet has written his name WILLIAM SHAKSPEARE, with the letter *a* in the last syllable.[1]

The subscription to the first sheet of the will (No. 12) has now become indistinct; but we are personally satisfied that the signature is to be read WILLIAM SHAKSPERE, a reading which is supported by the facsimiles of it made when the document was in better condition. The signature to the second sheet (No. 13) is certainly WILLM SHAKSPERE. That the surname has been read 'Shakspeare' (with *a* in the last syllable) is owing to its being entangled with the pendent bow of the letter *h* of the word 'the' in the last line of the text beneath which the signature is written. It will be seen that the signature proceeds as far as 'Shakspe', when, coming to the bow, the pen is lifted and jumps the obstruction before completing the name with the letters *re*. The fact that the surname in these two signatures is written in full may be regarded as supporting the suggestion that they were added after the main signature (No. 14) had been subscribed in expanded form.

We here have an unusual instance of a writer spelling his name in two different ways. It is well known that in Shakespeare's time

---

[1] The existence of the *a* has been disputed by Malone, *An Inquiry*, 1796, p. 117 (supported by Madden, *Observations*, 1838), who sees in it only a random blot due to the tremor of the hand. But this view can hardly be maintained. The letter is badly formed; it is a blotted or blind letter; but the fact that it is linked with the following *r* by a decided connecting stroke proves that the writer intended it for a letter. He would not have linked a smudge.

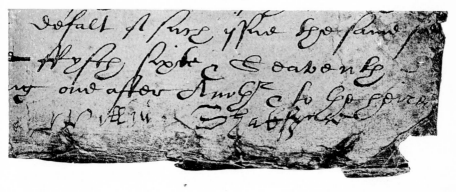

SHAKESPEARE'S SIGNATURES TO THE THREE
SHEETS OF HIS WILL 1616

SOMERSET HOUSE

people were not consistent in their signatures and that they exercised considerable freedom of spelling in subscribing their names. But it is remarkable that two differently spelt signatures should be employed in one and the same document. The inconsistency may be attributable to the writer's state of health; or it may even be taken as further evidence that Shakespeare was so much in the habit of abbreviating his signature, that he was indifferent to the form of the conclusion of the name when he was required to write it in full.

It would occupy more space than could be afforded in these pages to analyse the construction of the individual letters of the few words which we have in Shakespeare's handwriting; we will confine our remarks on this point to the initial letters of his name, which in certain particulars have proved a stumbling-block to Shakespearian forgers through misconception of the system of their formation. Shakespeare makes use of two forms of the capital W : the one, which resembles the ordinary modern cursive letter, is seen in the signature to the deposition (No. 9), in that to the Blackfriars mortgage-deed (No. 11), and in the subscription to the third sheet of the will (No. 14) ; the other, which is the more fully developed English letter of the time, having the final limb attached to the middle stroke by a base-curve, as in the modern German cursive letter, appears in the other three signatures. In most instances also a dot (merely an ornament) is inserted within the curve of the final limb.

The initial S of the surname was formed from the centre, the pen first making an incipient curve to the left, then a full one to the right, thus tracing a rather imperfect S, and then sweeping round in an external curve embracing the letter. In the two constrained signatures to the Blackfriars deeds (Nos. 10, 11) the S has been written slowly, and the result is, in each case, a rather clumsy and characterless letter, but complete in outline. On the other hand, the letter in the signature to the deposition (No. 9) is an excellent, symmetrical example, dashed off with a free hand and a light touch, the pen skimming the paper and leaving only a thin trace of the ink in the base of the encircling curve as the hand moved in the retrograde direction from right to left, and ending in a well-formed semicircular stroke topping the letter. Turning to the signatures of the will, we see that in the main signature (No. 14) the sick man has managed fairly well to form first the small incipient curve of the S to the left (inside the letter), then the full curve to the right ; but, when he attempted to carry out the retrograde movement of the hand in order to accomplish the outer encircling curve, he failed: the curve becoming angular, then passing upwards and skirting the back of the small incipient curve of the S, and then finishing off, rather better than might have been expected (the hand now moving in easier action, from left to right), with the upper arch covering the letter ; the little tag at the extremity being no doubt an accidental touch of the trembling hand. After this experience of the difficulty of turning the corner, so to say, in forming a retrograde curve, it will be seen that, when required to write the second signature (No. 13), Shakespeare did not attempt to make the encircling curve in a continuous stroke, but was content to indicate it by two sectional strokes with a gap between them.[1]

We may also draw attention to the manner in which the letters *ha* of the surname, as it appears in the deposition signature (No. 9), are linked together by a particularly free action of the hand. It will be seen that the final stroke of the pendent bow of the *h* is continued from below the line and carried up high above the line in a bold arched curve merging into the *a*, which, as a consequence of this form of linking, is left open at the top like a *u*. It is probable that at this period of his life, when in normal health, Shakespeare was in the habit of connecting in this fashion these two letters in his signature. We find them thus linked in the constrained signature to the Guildhall deed (No. 10), in which instance, however, it is to be observed that the ink has partially failed in the formation of the arched curve ; they are not linked in the British Museum deed (No. 11), because the signature there is designedly written in detached letters. But we must be careful to guard against an assumption that this elaborate form of linking the two letters is a personal peculiarity of Shakespeare's handwriting. In all cursive scripts various methods of linking the letters are naturally developed, at first invented by individual caprice and afterwards adopted and

[1] With regard to the signature purporting to be that of Shakespeare, in the British Museum copy of Florio's translation of Montaigne's *Essays* (1603), the malformation of the two capital letters *W* and *S* affords sufficient reason for its condemnation as an authentic signature of the poet. The tall straggling *W*, formed on a scale out of all proportion to the rest of the signature and written with a light hand and a fine-pointed pen, bears no resemblance to the letter as written by Shakespeare in any of the genuine documents subscribed by him. The fabricator has also failed to comprehend the construction of Shakespeare's *S* with its encircling curve, which he ignores ; merely finishing off the top of the letter with an independent head-stroke. The letters generally of the signature are irregular, and in some details they are feeble. They appear to have been imitated from letters in the signatures to the will, and rather from memory than by direct copying. There is, however, a certain facility in the execution of the signature, indicating a practised hand and one more expert than is usually to be found in such Shakespearian curiosities.

Nor is it possible to give a higher character to the signature (' W^m Sh^e ') in the Aldine Ovid's *Metamorphoses*, 1502, in the Bodleian Library. This again is a forgery. The letters *W* and *S* are copied from those letters in the principal signature to Shakespeare's will (No. 14 above). The *W* differs slightly from its prototype in having the minute loop at the end of the long initial stroke rather exaggerated, and in omitting the ornamental dot within the final curve. But in the case of the *S* the forger has come to grief completely. Not understanding the formation of Shakespeare's Old English *S*, he has mistaken the ending of the encircling curve for an initial limb, and has thus converted the letter into a roman capital. Perhaps he may have relied too confidently on the facsimiles of the genuine signatures given in Johnson and Steevens's *Shakespeare*, which are not beyond reproach.

It is a grotesque idea to imagine Shakespeare writing his name in his books in his death-bed hand.

systematically taught by the writing-masters in the schools. This linked *ha* was a not uncommon form in the native English hand of the time ; and the straggling letters of that hand, and among them prominently the letter *h* with its pendent bow sweeping under the line of writing, seem to invite a free style of linking. But this was not the only form of the linked *ha*. There was also employed a less bold and more common way of joining the two letters by a simple connecting stroke, just as we should link them in our modern hand ; and often they were left unlinked. Shakespeare would have been taught at school the different styles of linking his letters ; and it is significant, as a practical proof of readiness with his pen, that he should have adopted the more elaborate and bolder style of the linked *ha* in signing his name. Whether he continued to employ this link in his signature down to the end of his life may be open to doubt. The two legible signatures to his will (Nos. 13, 14) do not exhibit it. In No. 13 the two letters are not connected ; but yet it is curious that, in No. 14, the final stroke of the *h* is carried up, as if the writer had been about to continue it above the line of writing, with the intention of linking it in that position with the following *a*, and had then feebly broken off, as though the effort were beyond his strength. It is interesting to see that Richard Quiney, who presumably was educated at Stratford, also shows a preference for the more complicated link of *ha* in several instances in the body of his letter to Shakespeare (No. 7), as well as in the name ' Shackespere ' in the address : a fact which, owing to the small scale of his writing, might escape observation.

Lastly, it seems that when Shakespeare wrote his Christian name in the shortened form WILLM, he indicated the abbreviation by a dash above the word. This dash is seen in the deposition signature (No. 9), and it appears to be painfully attempted (above the *m*) in the second subscription to the will (No. 13).

BIBLIOGRAPHY.—The acceptance in Western Europe, in the sixteenth century, of the Italian hand as a new style of writing for correspondence, in substitution for the old national styles, naturally inspired a wider interest in the art of handwriting and led to the first publication of educational writing-books. There was a steady flow of these ephemeral publications during the sixteenth, seventeenth, and eighteenth centuries. The writing-books published in England during Shakespeare's lifetime are not numerous ; but some, if not all, passed through many editions. An article was contributed to *Bibliographica* (1895–7), iii. 156–72, by E. J. STRANGE, *The Early English Writing-Masters* ; and was supplemented by the same writer in the Transactions of the Bibliographical Society, iii. (1895), 41–69 : *The Writing-Books of the Sixteenth Century*, noticing those published in Italy, Spain, and France. The following were published or recorded in England between 1571 and 1619 : JOHN DE BEAUCHESNE and JOHN BAILDON. *A Booke containing divers sortes of hands, as well the English as French Secretarie with the Italian, Roman, Chancelry & court hands. Also the true and iust proportion of the Capitall Romane*, London, 1571 ; *A New Booke containing all sortes of handes vsually written at this daie in Christendom, as the English and French Secretarie, the Roman, Italian, French, Spanish, high and low Dutch, Court and Chancerie handes* (&c.), London, 1590, published anonymously; the plates are chiefly copied from de Beauchesne, with additions illustrating foreign styles; THOMAS SCARLETT, *A newe copie booke conteyninge theis handes followinge, viz. Englishe and Frenche, Secretarie, with the Italian, Roman, Chancerie and Courte handes, and the Spanishe, Jerman and Duche handes* [entered by Scarlett in the Stationers' Register (Arber, ii. 264), under date of September 20, 1590]; PETER BALES, *The Writing Schoolemaster, conteining three Bookes in one, the first teaching Swift writing, the second, True writing, the third Faire writing. . . . The third Booke is the Key of Calygraphie, opening the readie waie to write faire in verie short time* [&c.], London, 1590; only the third part of the work is devoted to handwriting proper; JOHN DAVIES, of Hereford, *The Writing Schoolemaster or the Anatomie of Faire Writing, wherein is exactlie expressed each severall character,* London; the first extant edition is of 1633; MARTIN BILLINGSLEY, *The Pens Excellencie or The Secretaries Delight,* London, 1618; RICHARD GETHINGE, *Calligraphotechnia, or The Art of faire writing sett forth, and newly enlarged,* London, 1619; Gethinge was a scholar of John Davies of Hereford. On the subject of the handwriting of Shakespeare and of members of his family, the following works may be referred to :—E. MALONE, *An Inquiry into the authenticity of certain miscellaneous papers and legal instruments published* [by S. W. H. Ireland], *Dec.* 24, 1795, London, 1796. In the course of remarks on Shakespeare's autograph signatures, Malone states that the mortgage-deed of the Blackfriars property (purchased by the British Museum in 1858) was found in 1768 among the title-deeds of Mr. Fetherstonhaugh, of Oxted, Surrey, and was presented by him to David Garrick. The Blackfriars purchase-deed (acquired by the Guildhall Library in 1843) also belonged to Fetherstonhaugh, and had, when Malone wrote, been recently rediscovered. He draws attention to the letter *r* written at the end of the surname, ' though on the very edge of the label '.—Sir F. MADDEN, *Observations on an Autograph of Shakspere and the orthography of his name, Archaeologia,* 1838, xxvii. 113–23. Madden upholds the genuineness of the so-called autograph signature of Shakespeare inscribed in a copy of Florio's translation of Montaigne's Essays. This led to subsequent correspondence and controversy in *The Gentleman's Magazine,* N.S. xiii, xiv. —J. O. HALLIWELL-PHILLIPPS, *Outlines of the Life of Shakespeare,* 1887. Besides the general value of this work, the facsimiles of various autographs and documents, although drawn by hand, are carefully executed.—Sir SIDNEY LEE, *A Life of William Shakespeare,* 1925; the subject of Shakespeare's handwriting is dealt with in chapter xxii, 518–23. From an earlier edition the author extracted and issued, in pamphlet form, *Shakespeare's Handwriting,* 1899, with facsimiles.—*Catalogue of the Books, Manuscripts, Works of Art, Antiquities and Relics, at present exhibited in Shakespeare's Birthplace: with 61 Illustrations,* Stratford-upon-Avon, 1910, contains many photographic facsimiles of the autograph signatures of the Shakespeare family.—C. W. WALLACE, *New Shakespeare Discoveries,* contributed to *Harper's Monthly Magazine,* March 1910; describing his discovery in the Public Record Office of the papers concerning a suit brought in 1612 by Stephen Bellott against his father-in-law, Christopher Montjoy, with whom Shakespeare lodged. Among the papers is the deposition of Shakespeare, bearing his signature. —J. F. NISBET, *The Insanity of Genius,* 1891. The writer examines (pp. 151–9) the signatures to Shakespeare's will, and concludes that the poet's ' ailment was a prostration of the nervous system ', and that ' in his later days Shakespeare was a victim to nerve disorder '.

[The whole subject has been critically handled in *Shakespeare's Handwriting,* by Sir EDWARD MAUNDE THOMPSON, 1916; *English Literary Autographs 1550–1650,* edited by W. W. GREG (1925, 1928, and in progress); and *The Later Court Hands in England,* 1927, by HILARY JENKINSON.]

XI

COMMERCE AND COINAGE

BY

GEORGE UNWIN

§ 1. TRADE AND MANUFACTURES

IT was a mediaeval tradition of trade and industry that first impressed itself on the boyish imagination of Shakespeare in the quiet life of market towns like Stratford and Warwick, or in the wider activities of a manufacturing centre like Coventry. Later on as an adventurous youth he may have gazed upon the glowing forges of Birmingham, or peeped down the colliery shafts of Bedworth, or stolen an admiring glimpse at the new Flemish looms at Barcheston, where an enterprising fellow-countryman was designing on tapestry the map of his native county. Lastly, in his mature years he came into prolonged and intimate contact with the life of the capital, which was not only the centre of national industry and commerce, but was already before Shakespeare's death showing promise of that cosmopolitan pre-eminence which it has since attained. We cannot do better than adopt in our survey the natural order of the poet's experience.

The most primitive form of trade, and at the same time the most striking to the childish imagination, is the fair. As an institution the fair preceded the town, and could not be wholly displaced by it, since it satisfied wider needs. It long remained, in fact, the great bulwark of free trade against the monopolizing policy of the local trader. The great fairs of Winchester, Stourbridge, Boston, and St. Ives had been throughout the Middle Ages the main centres of national and international trade. Here the Genoese with silks and spices, the Hanse merchant with skins and tar, the Dinandier with copper ware, the Gascon with wine, met the Lincolnshire wool-grower, the Suffolk or Wiltshire clothier, and the Cornish tinner. Goods bargained for at

x

one fair might be delivered at a second, and paid for at a third, and disputes were speedily and equitably settled by a jury of merchants in a court of Pie-Powders (*pieds poudreux*=dusty feet). In Shakespeare's time the development of the more regular operations of trade had robbed the fairs of much of their pre-eminence, yet there were still several, Harrison tells us, not inferior to the greatest marts in Europe. Amongst these, Stourbridge Fair, held in a large field near Cambridge during the three weeks following September 8, claimed the first place. No sooner was the crop cleared than a miniature London sprang up as if by magic—a new Cheapside of grocers and mercers, a Soper's Lane confined to the goldsmiths, a great Cloth Exchange known as the Duddery, a Pewterers' Row, a Braziers' Row, a Fishmongers' Row. The London Livery Companies, having long and vainly resisted this migration of trade, appointed delegates to ride down and inspect it. From the city itself Hackney coaches (after 1613) regularly plied for hire to the fair, and from all the country round, stewards of great households, bursars of colleges, farmers, and small traders came to lay in their stores for a twelvemonth. The provision of food and drink, rest and entertainment, for such an assemblage required a legion of bakers and butchers, innkeepers and cooks, carriers and colliers, musicians and players. The Vice-Chancellor's Court had much ado to keep order.

Many fairs had their specialities. A yearly fair was held at Yarmouth during the herring season, which claimed to monopolize the market in that commodity. Cheese-fairs and sheep-fairs must have been common then as they were later. Harrison tells us that the fairs at Ripon, Newport Pond, Wolfpit, Harborough, and Malton were notable for great plenty of horses and colts. At such gatherings a price was set on live stock that remained current in the country round till the next fair. Hence the anxious inquiries with which Justice Shallow interrupts his communings on human mortality. ' How a good yoke of bullocks at Stamford fair ? ' ' How a score of ewes now ? ' (*2 Hen. IV,* III. ii. 42–55).

At most fairs, however, the business was not so serious. Harrison gives a selected list of several hundred (eighty of which were held in the month of May alone), and adds that

of the rest ' some . . . be scarce comparable to Lowse faire[1]
and little else bought or sold in them than good drinke, pies
and some pedlerie trash: wherefore it were no losse if
diverse of them were abolished. Neither doo I see whereunto this number of paltrie fairs tendeth, so much as to the
corruption of youth.'

The youth of the period thought differently, and in spite
of Parson Harrison, who would fain see them clad in sober
English kersies, of Puritan Stubbes, who denounced looking-
glasses as the Devil's spectacles, of economists who lamented
the decline of home industries, and of legislators who obliged
them to wear woollen caps on Sunday, looked forward to
the next fair as their only chance of seeing London fashions,
the latest cut of ' gally hosen ', or of French hoods. There
would Mopsa receive ' the tawdry lace and the pair of sweet
gloves ' which her swain had promised her, and Dorcas pick
up the new ballad to the tune of ' Two men wooing a maid '
that was all the rage in the West country. For it must have
been at one of the four Stratford fairs (all of them apparently in the category denounced by Harrison) that Shakespeare first met Autolycus celebrating in song his ribands
and smocks, points, cambrics, and lawns (*Wint. Tale*, IV. iii.
220 seq.). There were fairs enough in Warwickshire during
May to keep Autolycus on the move. He might be at
Coventry on the 2nd, at Coleshill on the 6th, at Warwick
on the 12th, at Stratford on the 14th, at Rugby on the 15th,
and then if Whitsun were early he could find a welcome at
Henley-in-Arden and Birmingham.[2]

Bartholomew Fair, immortalized by Ben Jonson, was a
distracting mixture of quaint ceremonial, serious business,
and such frivolity as only a great capital can descend to.
Before the mayor and aldermen, who rode in scarlet robes
and gold chains to open it, the mob wrestled in pairs for
prizes, and rabbits were loosed amongst the boys. The
Merchant Taylors, fortified with a good dinner, carried
round their silver yard-stick to test the measures of the
country clothiers, whose transactions served as a pretext
for the rest of the fair. But to the majority of Londoners,
Bartholomew Fair already wore the aspect depicted by
Ben Jonson—of a noisy gathering of toyshops and ginger-

---

[1] Later ' Rag Fair ' in London.
[2] *Report of Commission on Market Rights and Tolls*, vol. i, 211–12.

bread-stalls, of pig-women, and quack-doctors, of showmen
and balladmongers, of horse-dealers and pickpockets.[1]

Every considerable town had one or two annual fairs
(some had half a dozen) to serve as a kind of inoculation

Der Krämer.

Ich bin ein Krämer lange jar/
Kompt/vnd kaufft hie mancherley Wahr/
Als Brüch/Pfeiffen/vnd Schlötterlein/
Item/Würtz/Zucker vnd Brenten Wein/
Spiegel/Schelln/Käm/nadl vñ Harbät/
Leckkuchn/Nestel vnd Brillen gnannt/
Die Krämerey mancherley Wahrn/
Erfand lieber Pater vor jarn.

The Pedlar, by Jost Amman.

with the dreaded virus of free trade. The host of pedlars,
of foreigners from the next county, of Londoners and aliens,
who were allowed direct access to the consumer on these
occasions, were strictly excluded on all others. No traders,

[1] Morley, *Memoirs of Bartholomew Fair*, chap. **x.**

save from the near neighbourhood, came to the weekly markets, of which all market-towns had one, and many two or three. On these days not only the farmers of the district, but also the butchers and bakers, the tanners and weavers, and sometimes other craftsmen of the adjoining towns and country, were admitted to sell their wares. Partly for the convenience of the buyer, but still more for the purposes of toll-gathering and inspection, each kind of produce was appointed to be sold at a separate stand, so that many of the main streets of the town were occupied by the market. The amount of freedom that was to be thus allowed to the outside trader was the most disputed point of Elizabethan municipal policy, and each new set of market regulations was contested with the same eagerness and from much the same motives as a modern American tariff. The local consumer demanded a restriction on the free export of tallow and hides, and insisted upon a free import of bread, beef, and other victuals. The local producer claimed protection against the unfair competition of outside traders, who did not help to bear the town's burdens. The Stratford council employed men armed with cudgels to keep out the traders of Coventry.[1] The Leicester glovers strove with might and main to prevent the glovers of Ashby and Loughborough from buying skins in their market.[2] Between many neighbouring towns there raged an animosity almost as fierce as the feud between Ephesus and Syracuse.

> If any born at Ephesus
> Be seen at any Syracusian marts and fairs;
> Again, if any Syracusian born
> Come to the bay of Ephesus, he dies. (*Com. of E.* i. i. 16–19)

This conflict of local interests was no new development. It was essentially a heritage from the Middle Ages, though modified in its details by the special conditions of the Tudor period. To understand how these conditions were destroying the stability of the local market we must have recourse again to honest Parson Harrison, whose guidance is none the less helpful because he failed to see that the changes of which he complains were an inevitable consequence of the economic expansion of the nation. Harrison's sympathies are entirely with the small producer and the local consumer.

[1] *Coventry Leet Book*, edited by Miss M. D. Harris for Early Eng. Text Soc., pp. 683–5, 717, 723, 739, 789.
[2] *Records of Leicester*, edited by Miss Bateson, vol. iii, Introd. xxxviii.

His ideal is a mediaeval one. In his view the market exists for 'the ease and benefit of the country round about'. Of such a market we get a vivid glimpse in Shakespeare's version of the stratagem by which Joan of Arc captured Rouen.

> [*Enter Joan La Pucelle, disguised, and Soldiers dressed like countrymen, with sacks upon their backs.*]
> *Guard* (*within*). Qui est là ?
> *Pucelle.* Paisans, pauvres gens de France :
> Poor market-folks that come to sell their corn.
> *Guard.* Enter, go in ; the market-bell is rung. (*1 Hen. VI*, III. ii. 1–4)

The ringing of the bell, which announced the opening of business, was intended to give all buyers and sellers an equal chance, and to prevent wholesale buyers cornering the market. In the mediaeval corn-markets of London the whole of the first day was reserved to the retail purchaser. Harvests fluctuated terribly in the Middle Ages, yet any reservation of supply by private enterprise, with a view to balancing the inequality, was severely repressed. Hence in all large cities, public provision for times of scarcity became an absolute necessity. Municipal granaries, mills, and bakehouses were built, and the city companies were obliged to provide each their quota of corn. This system still survived in Shakespeare's time, but the limitations of the local market, out of which it had arisen, had already been largely broken down in the interests of both producers and consumers. The production of corn, wool, and meat was coming to be specialized in the districts where the conditions of soil and transport were favourable, and the services of enterprising middlemen were needed to keep the supply level over the country, and even to carry any surplus across the sea. Harrison describes the activity of this agency. ' To say the truth,' he says, ' these bodgers are fair chapmen, for there are no more words with them but Let me see it ! What shall I give you ? Knit it up ! I will have it . . . and if you bring in twenty seme more . . . I will have it. . . . Thus the bodger beareth away all.' ' It is a world also,' he adds, ' to see how many places of the realm are pestered with purveyors who take up eggs, butter, cheese, pigs, capons, hens, chickens, hogs, bacon, etc. in one market . . . to sell the same in another or to poulterers in London.' When it is remembered that Harrison's observations were made in Essex—then, as now, one of the main sources of the London food supply—it will be easily realized that his proposal for limiting the producer to the local market was impracticable.   As a rule the Government, when called upon to interfere, contented itself with confining the trade to holders of licences.   The Privy Council records of Elizabeth's reign are full of special licences to London bakers to import corn from Kent to Suffolk, to cheese and butter factors to export supplies to London, and to court favourites to carry wool, corn, or beer beyond the seas.   The effect of this method was to raise prices by conferring a monopoly on a few middlemen.

The only effective remedy for the grievances of the small producer lay in that co-operative organization by which the peasant population of most European countries is now learning to get in touch with a larger market.   Amongst the city craftsmen, as will be seen later, efforts were not wanting in this direction, but in rural districts the conditions were not yet favourable to organization, whilst the guilds of small producers in the towns spent all their energies in endeavouring to ward off the competition of the country round about them.   To the majority of the town craftsmen this policy was natural enough.   To the baker and the butcher, the carpenter and the plasterer of the town, the town itself offered the only possible market.   But, on the other hand, it was equally natural that the main body of consumers should resist the formation of any monopoly in the first necessaries of life.   For this purpose the local authorities had been entrusted with the Assize of Bread and Ale.   The promise made by Jack Cade to his followers that ' there shall be in England seven halfpenny loaves sold for a penny ;   the three-hooped pot shall have ten hoops ' (*2 Hen. VI*, iv. ii. 73–6), is not a mad absurdity, but merely represents the exaggerated view taken by an enthusiastic reformer of the regulative powers of government.   By the Assize the weight of the penny loaf was altered from time to time in accordance with the price of wheat, and the number of gallons of beer to be sold for a penny was fixed with reference to the price of barley.

The Assize of Bread was based on a careful calculation of a living wage for the baker.   In the year 1618, as the price of wheat fell steadily, the Lord Mayor and Aldermen of London raised the weight of the penny loaf four times, adding an ounce each time till it reached seventeen ounces. The bakers then protested that this only allowed them six shillings a quarter for baking, and to prove that it could not be done for the money, they drew up a list of a week's expenses, a brief version of which is worth recording [1]:

House rent at £30 per annum		11	6
Diet of man and wife, 10/; of three children, 7/ . .		17	0
„ „ 4 journeymen, 2 apprentices, 2 maids @ 4/ .	1	12	0
Clothing of man, wife, and apprentices at £20 per ann. .		7	8
Clothing and schooling of 3 children		3	0
Wages of 4 journeymen at 2/6 ; of 2 maids at 10d. .		11	8
Yeast 10/, wood 12/, coal 1/4, sacks 1/, salt 1/; Boulters 1/, garner rent 2/, baskets 3d., water 8d. . .	1	9	3
Miller's Toll 15/, porters' fees 2/		17	0
Parson, Poor rate, Scavenger, Watch		1	0
Total expense of baking 6 quarters £6		10	1

Disputes of this fundamental character between the municipal authorities and the bakers, butchers, brewers, fishmongers, poulterers, fruiterers, and other victuallers were universal and incessant during Shakespeare's lifetime. As a rule, the Mayor could put sufficient pressure on the recalcitrant town traders by admitting outsiders to the market more freely, but not unfrequently he had to proceed to disfranchisement and imprisonment. The butchers, brewers, and bakers of London were all at different periods temporarily deprived of their political rights. In 1587 the Mayor of Chester committed the whole of the Butchers' Company to prison.

Apart from the special cases of bread, beer, wine, and candles, the proclamation of definite price-lists by authority was becoming obsolete. The Act of Parliament of 1533, under the authority of which the prices of beef and mutton were fixed in London at a halfpenny and three-farthings a pound respectively, had to be repealed in 1541, and the price of meat steadily rose to twopence and twopence farthing in Shakespeare's time. The Lord Mayor attempted once more to curb the greediness of poulterers in 1572 by an official price-list, in which the best fat swan was rated at six shillings and eightpence, the stork at four shillings, the heron at half-a-crown, the large fat goose at fourteen pence, chickens from twopence halfpenny to fourpence, blackbirds

[1] Analytical index to *Remembrancia*, p. 386.

at a shilling a dozen, larks at eightpence a dozen, and eggs
at five a penny. The Lord Mayor continued to receive as
a perquisite, samples not only of corn, grain, and salt, but
of all apples, pears, and plums, and of all edible roots and
onions brought into London long after he had ceased to fix
the price.

But the most remarkable regulation affecting the food-
supply was one which attained its full rigour during Shakespeare's youth, and which, in view of his early familiarity
with the slaughter-house,[1] must have been brought particularly to his notice. This was the law, first enacted in
1549 and extended in 1563, enforcing abstinence from flesh
for political and economic reasons, not only in Lent and on
Ember days, Vigils and Fridays, but also on Saturdays, and
even on Wednesdays. The object aimed at in this legislation was the strengthening of the navy through the encouragement of the fisheries—the North Sea fisheries being
regarded as a gold-mine, which the Dutch were exploiting
on our freehold estate. In 1563, four women who had
a meal of meat in a London tavern during Lent were set in
the stocks all night, and the woman who supplied them was
set in the pillory. The licences granted to butchers to meet
the case of invalids were naturally much sought after, and
hence the significance of the grant with which Shakespeare,
by an anachronism, makes Jack Cade reward the prowess of
Dick, the butcher of Ashford :

Cade. They fell before thee like sheep and oxen . . . therefore
thus will I reward thee, the Lent shall be as long again as it is ;
and thou shalt have a licence to kill for a hundred lacking one.
Dick. I desire no more.   (*2 Hen. VI*, IV. iii. 3–8)

The other important group of craftsmen who were, like
the victuallers, confined to a local market, was composed of
those engaged in the building trades—the carpenter, the
joiner, the wright, the plasterer, the bricklayer, the mason,
the tiler and slater. After food and drink, houses and clothing are the prime necessities of life, and houses cannot, like
clothing, be imported from a distance. Builders, however,
may be imported. In the case of the mediaeval mason, the
wandering life, which was almost a necessity of his vocation, had led to a widespread organization of labour, which

---

[1] There are seventeen references to the butcher's trade in the historical
plays.

called forth the denunciation of Parliament in 1425 (3 Hen. VI, c. 1). But in other branches of the building trades the local organization retained its predominance, and did its best to prevent the wandering plasterer or bricklayer from taking employment directly from the householder at reduced terms. The town councils everywhere resisted this interference with liberty of contract, for the most part in vain. An Act embodying their views, which was passed in 1549, roused such a protest from the building trades that it was repealed the next year (2 & 3 Edw. VI, c. 15, and 3 & 4 Edw. VI, c. 20), a fact which proves that the craft guilds did not, as is sometimes asserted, perish with the Reformation.

Many of the weaker guilds, no doubt, especially those of journeymen, disappeared about this time, having been extinguished or absorbed by more powerful organizations. This process had been long going on, and though hastened by the religious changes, was largely independent of them. The Elizabethan 'Company', therefore, though it had generally grown out of a guild, presented a more consolidated structure, and was not infrequently an amalgamation representing a certain amount of dependence of one trade or one class within a trade on another. This tendency was often characteristic of the building crafts. In Chester there was one Company of Wrights, Carpenters, Slaters, and Sawyers, and another of Joiners, Turners, and Carvers.[1] At Hull, the Bricklayers were united with the Tilers, Wallers, Plasterers, and Paviors.[2] These Companies contained small contractors, independent masters, and journeymen ; but the master-craftsman, who was the predominant figure, was no longer a mere worker on the materials of others, but a tradesman who supplied timber, bricks, or lime for the building on which he worked, though, like the small builder of the present day, he often bargained to receive an advance when the job was half completed. A considerable portion of the old gang spirit of equality survived amongst the builders. The Hull bricklayers inserted at the head of their ordinances, after the opening verses of St. John's Gospel, the following sentiment, which they ascribe to Plato : ' All men are by nature equal, made all by one workman of like mire.' The builders made some attempt

---

[1] Harleian MSS. 2054, 2 and 17.
[2] Lambert, *Two Thousand Years of Guild Life*, p. 269.

to live up to their principles. Their rules often required that a master should share a bargain of timber or other material with his fellows, or even that he should share a job with another master, rather than increase the number of his journeymen.

The craftsmen working in metals frequently formed themselves into a group (sometimes under the name of hammermen, as in Scotland) like the builders. But between the goldsmith, the pewterer, or the cutler, who retailed wares made in London or Sheffield, the wiredrawer or pinner, who sometimes produced for a distant market, and the blacksmith or plumber, who worked for the local consumer, there could be no such bond of union as there was between the bricklayer, the plasterer, the carpenter, and the tiler, who were often working together on the same house.

One other important group of crafts remains to be considered—those concerned with dress. Doublets and hose, hats and caps, boots and shoes, girdles and gloves, are light in proportion to their value, and the gain in fashion may easily counterbalance the cost of transport. Throughout the Middle Ages the shops of the London mercer, haberdasher, and draper were full of the fashions of Paris and of Milan, the silks of Venice, and the fine fabrics of Flanders. But the common man went clad and shod in the handiwork of the local craftsman, and every considerable town with the country round it furnished sufficient employment for a complete set of the crafts connected with dress. The sixteenth century saw a twofold change. Not only did foreign fashions penetrate the country in the pack of Autolycus and his fellows ; there began also that concentration of native manufactures into special localities, with which we are familiar to-day. From both causes the calling of the local craftsman, the capper, the glover, the girdler, the pointmaker, and the hosier, suffered decay, and was displaced by that of the retail dealer in imported native or foreign wares.[1]

The hard lot of the capper was a typical one. In vain had Parliament decreed in 1511 that none below the degree of a knight might wear a foreign hat or cap (3 Hen. VIII,

---

[1] *A discourse of the commonweal of this realm of England* (1550-81). edited by Elizabeth Lamond, Cambridge Press, p. 125.

c. 15), in vain had it forbidden (in 1529) even the upper classes to spend more than two shillings on an imported cap or bonnet (21 Hen. VIII, c. 9), and commanded (in 1570) every person over six of the lower classes to wear an English woollen cap on the Sabbath (13 Eliz., c. 19). More fashionable headgear still poured in, 'some', says Stubbes, ' of silk, some of velvet, some of taffeta, some of sarcenet,' some 'pearking up' like a steeple, some broad and flat like the battlements of a house. When Petruchio wooed Katherine another extreme ruled the fashion.

> *Haberdasher.* Here is the cap your worship did bespeak.
> *Petruchio.* Why, this was moulded on a porringer ;
> A velvet dish : fie, fie ! 'tis lewd and filthy :
> Why, 'tis a cockle or a walnut-shell,
> A knack, a toy, a trick, a baby's cap :
> Away with it ! come, let me have a bigger.
>   (*Tam. Sh.* IV. iii. 63–8)

But the most dangerous rival of the woollen cap was not the millinery imported by the haberdasher. The more substantial felts which we associate with costumes of the seventeenth century had already come into vogue, and were now largely made in England. Great numbers of Norman, Dutch, and Flemish feltmakers settled in this country during the Reformation period. To some extent, as at Bristol, Chester, and Newcastle, the new industry occupied the ground left vacant by the old, but more generally it made a new start on a larger scale, the more fashionable trade going to swell the new suburbs of South London, whilst the manufacture of the cheaper hats made a new settlement in the rural districts of the north and midlands.

The two crafts least affected by these changes were those of the tailor and the shoemaker, and both are uncommonly well represented in the literature of the time. All the bitter diatribes of Stubbes are not more convincing evidence of the extravagance of the age on dress than Touchstone's laconic proof of his assumed character of courtier, ' I have undone three tailors ' (*A. Y. L.* V. iv. 48). And this implies that the tailor often combined with his vocation as a skilled artist that of a dealer in rich materials. Ben Jonson has shown us such a combination in Fashioner :

> *Pennyboy, jun.* I pray thee tell me, Fashioner, what authors
> Thou read'st to help thy invention : Italian prints ?
> Or Arras hangings ? they are tailors' libraries.

Fashioner. I scorn such helps.
Pennyboy, jun. Oh, though thou art a silkworm,
And deal'st in satins and velvets, and rich plushes,
Thou canst not spin all forms out of thyself.   (*The Staple of News*, I. ii)

Yet even here the artist predominated over the trader, and it was still quite common in Shakespeare's time for the customer to supply his own materials as Petruchio had done for Katherine's gown.   Hence perhaps the degree of insult which, in his assumed wrath, he allowed himself to use to the poor craftsman, who was, moreover, only a journeyman :

Petruchio. I tell thee, I, that thou hast marr'd her gown.
Tailor. Your worship is deceiv'd ; the gown is made
Just as my master had direction.
Grumio gave order how it should be done.
Grumio. I gave him no order ; I gave him the stuff.
                    (*Tam. Sh.* IV. iii. 115-19)

Literature has dealt more kindly with the shoemaker than with the tailor.   Dekker's *Shoemakers' Holiday* gives us the best picture in the Elizabethan drama of the everyday life of the mediaeval craftsman as it survived in the sixteenth century.   We see the master rousing his household betimes to their work and observe the blunt but hearty domestic relations that subsist between the journeymen and the shrewish mistress of the household, their jealousy for the honour of St. Hugh, and their readiness to strike work at a moment's notice.   We witness the reception of a Dutch journeyman with the customary 'drinks round' to the workshop, and learn the number of tools he is required to bring, ' a good rubbing pin, a good stopper, a good dresser, four sorts of awls, two balls of wax, a paring knife, your hand and thumb leathers, and good Sir Hugh's bones to smooth up your work '.   We watch a pair of shoes being ordered, and hear of their being sent home and smoothed on by the journeyman.   But the most striking feature of the picture is the mercantile transaction quite outside the limits of his craft, by which the master shoemaker acquires a fortune and becomes Lord Mayor.   This incident, which might naturally be attributed to the poetical licence of the dramatist, is a representative fact embodying an essential truth.

In mediaeval England no sharp line had been drawn, as a rule, between craftsman and shopkeeper, or between shopkeeper and wholesale merchant.   This indeed had been one of the main secrets of progress, just as in Scotland the maintenance of such distinctions by the burghs had been one of the causes of the relative backwardness of their commerce

Der Kauffmann.

Ich aber bin ein Handelsmann/
Hab mancherley Wahr bey mir stan/
Würtz/Atlas/Thuch/Wolln vñ Flachß.
Sammat/Seiden/Honig vñd Wachß/
Vnd ander Wahr hie vngenannt/
Die führ ich eyn vñd auß dem Land/
Mit grosser sorg vnd gfehrlichkeit
Wann mich auch offt das vnglück reit.

The Merchant, by Jost Amman.

and industry.   But the freedom thus enjoyed was secured merely by custom and compromise, and was directly opposed to the mediaeval doctrine that every one should restrict himself within the limits of his own calling.   In the sixteenth century a distinct revival of this doctrine is observable.

The shopkeepers of the towns attempted to limit the retailing operations of the craftsmen. The new-fledged companies of Merchant Adventurers in ports like Exeter, York, Newcastle, and Chester tried to prevent the shopkeepers from sharing in foreign trade. The craftsmen of the metropolis struggled hard for the abolition of the 'custom of London', which enabled an enterprising citizen to pass freely from one occupation to another. This reactionary movement in the towns was part of the resistance of the older industrial and commercial England to the gathering forces of that newer England which still remains to be described.

Throughout almost all the social legislation of the Tudor period we may see the England of the past erecting vain barriers against the England of the future. To a large extent it was a struggle between town and country, but, strange as it may seem to us, the country was often on the side of freedom and progress, whilst the towns represented stagnation and privilege. For two centuries the mediaeval manor had been steadily decaying. Serfdom was already a thing of the past, and the rigid and wasteful routine of the village community, though still largely prevalent, was resented by every resourceful agriculturist as an antiquated survival. The dominant social type in rural England was no longer the peasant rooted to his thirty acres, and engaged in producing wheat and barley mainly for the consumption of his own family, but the prosperous yeoman or tenant farmer, owning or holding a hundred or more acres, who furnished wool to the distant clothier, and whose butter, cheese, and meat fed the markets of the industrial districts or of the rapidly expanding metropolis. This method of farming produced more wealth. The higher rents it yielded built the mansions of the Elizabethan gentry, and furnished customers to the goldsmiths and haberdashers of Cheapside, whilst the profits 'garnished the cupboards' of the yeoman with pewter, 'their joined beds with tapestry and silk hangings, and their tables with carpets and fine napery'.

The enriched shepherd of *The Winter's Tale*, who sends to market the fleeces of fifteen hundred wethers, and is able to regale his servants and neighbours on 'warden pies, coloured with saffron', and to treat them to such foreign fruits and spices as raisins and currants, mace, dates, and sugar, is a typical representative of this phase of rural economy.

But the four-and-twenty shearers for whom Perdita made nosegays cannot have been in the regular employment of the shepherd. Sheep-farming and grazing required little labour. With improving methods of husbandry, even tillage required less than before. The surplus of a steadily increasing population was therefore constantly seeking other means of livelihood and shifting its locality in the search. This was not in itself a new development. The outflow from the villages had been going on for more than two centuries. But in the Middle Ages it had served to feed the growth of the towns, and in the sixteenth century many of the towns themselves—the old privileged corporations —were in a condition of arrest or decay. The guilds, which had formerly assisted the expansion of trade and industry, had now become the organs of vested interests and of antiquated ideas, and the towns were no longer willing, even when they were able, to receive the surplus population of the country. They had, in fact, a surplus of their own. They would not find room for the enterprise of their own young men. In their exclusiveness they checked the growth of their own suburbs.

To this rule London afforded the one important exception. The influences that favoured its expansion were too powerful to be resisted, and the ring of industrial suburbs which had already formed around the city from Clerkenwell to Whitechapel was being rapidly filled during Shakespeare's lifetime with aliens bringing new trades, and with countrymen who supplied a reinforcement of labour to those already established. Elsewhere the stream of migratory labour was not directed towards the old centres of industry. In part it went to swell the population of certain industrial villages which, unhampered by civic traditions, were beginning to make a prophetic show of future greatness—Birmingham, which Camden found full of inhabitants, and resounding with hammers and anvils, Sheffield, 'a town of great name for the smiths therein,' Halifax, Wakefield, and Leeds, famous for clothing, and Manchester, whose 'cottons' (made as yet of wool) were already in great request. But the greater part of it spread itself more widely over the open country, and settled in thousands of wayside cottages where

GOLD COINS OF MARY AND ELIZABETH   SOVEREIGN   RYALS   ANGELS   HALF ANGEL

a great number of home industries were combined with the cultivation of a small allotment.

In most cases the immigration of skilled aliens provided a nucleus for this development. The introduction of felt-making, already mentioned, was followed by that of straw-plaiting, and Shakespeare, in his journeys between Strat-ford and London may well have seen the cottagers of Bedford, Buckingham, or Hertfordshire busied in plaiting the rye-straw hats worn by the sunburnt sicklemen of the masque in *The Tempest* (IV. i. 136), and by 'the fickle maid full pale' in *A Lover's Complaint* (line 8). On such journeys also he must have heard the song of

> The spinsters and the knitters in the sun,
> And the free maids that weave their thread with bones.
>
> (Tw. N. II. iv. 44–5)

The alien introduction of pillow-lace making (called also bone-lace, from the bone bobbins used in the manufacture) has taken popular form in the story that good Queen Katherine of Arragon taught this art to the people of Ampthill whilst awaiting her trial there. Early in the seventeenth century it spread through Bedford, Bucking-ham, and Northampton shires. If the poet's route lay through Oxfordshire or Worcestershire he could scarcely have failed to notice the glovemaking, which had already become an important cottage industry, and is still carried on in these counties.

But the most widespread, and by far the most important, of the village industries—the cloth manufacture—was of long standing. Its earliest seat had been in the eastern counties, from Norfolk to Kent. That region of small free-holders, whose numbers were steadily reinforced, and whose ideas were constantly invigorated by contact with the busiest and most democratic people of the Continent, was the Lancashire and Yorkshire of mediaeval England, and had in Shakespeare's time only just begun to lose its industrial supremacy to the West and the North. It was the manu-facturing district of eastern England that had risen behind Wat Tyler and John Ball, had bred the Protestant martyrs, and was to prove the stronghold of the Puritan Revolution, and there the visitor may still admire the village guildhall or the cathedral-like church built out of the profits of weaving. Norwich was the centre of one great group of industrial villages, Bury St. Edmunds of another ; a third spread along the valleys of the Colne and the Blackwater in Essex, and a fourth covered the weald of Kent. Each region had its own special product, and the names of Worstead, of Ayleham, and of Coggeshall were known and respected in the fairs of Novgorod and the bazaars of Constantinople.

For two generations before Shakespeare's time the cloth manufacture had been rapidly spreading through the country districts of the West and North, to the great alarm of the older urban centres of the industry. The town craftsmen complained bitterly of the competition. The town employers, though they could not prevent, and perhaps did not desire to prevent, the multiplication of country weavers, wished to retain the control of the manufacture and the disposal of its products in their own hands. Acts of Parliament were procured by Norwich, Shrewsbury, York, the five chief towns of Worcester, and the three leading cloth centres of Somerset, for the purpose of hindering capitalists from settling in the country immediately around them, and of excluding London merchants and foreigners from driving a direct bargain with the country weavers (25 Hen. VIII, c. 18, 26 Hen. VIII, c. 16, 2 & 3 P. and M. c. 12). Chartered corporations were erected and municipal regulations framed with the same object. But the expansive tendency was too strong to be thus controlled, and in the Weavers' Acts of 1555–7, in which this legislation for the protection of towns had been consolidated, it had been found necessary to exempt from such restrictions the whole of the Northern counties and of Wales, Cornwall, Suffolk, Kent, and the Stroud valley (2 & 3 P. and M. c. 11, 4 & 5 P. and M. c. 5). A little later the cloth districts of Essex, Wiltshire, Somerset, and Gloucestershire were added to the free area (1 Eliz. c. 14, 18 Eliz. c. 16), and in 1623 the restrictions were abolished altogether (21 Jac. I, c. 28). By that time, though there were few counties in England in which some branch of clothmaking was not carried on, the industry was mainly centred in the south-eastern counties, in Wiltshire, Gloucester, Somerset, and Devon, on the Lancashire and Yorkshire slopes of the Pennine chain, and along the Welsh border.

Into this outer ring of clothmaking districts the midland

SILVER COINS OF ELIZABETH   CROWN   HALF CROWNS   SHILLINGS   SIXPENCES
HALF GROAT   PENNY   HALFPENNY

counties poured a constantly increasing surplus of wool. Warwickshire was one of these counties; the Clown in *The Winter's Tale*, reckoning up the produce of his master's flocks, may well have been seen by Shakespeare on the way to Stratford market.

Clown. Let me see : Every 'leven wether tods ; every tod yields pound and odd shilling : fifteen hundred shorn, what comes the wool to ? (*Wint. Tale*, IV. ii. 33–5) [1]

There was another reason for the poet's exact knowledge of the price of wool. The various occupations attributed to his father—those of butcher, glover, and woolstapler—were not inconsistent, but were on the contrary often combined. In fact, the licensed wool-brokers, who were always asking the Government for the suppression of outsiders, made special complaints about the competition of the glovers. The services of many kinds of middlemen were needed to keep the producer and the consumer of wool in touch with each other. Indeed, without their assistance the class of independent small manufacturers who were to contribute very largely to England's industrial prosperity could scarcely have come into existence. From Halifax market scores of purchasers were to be seen week by week carrying off a stone or two of wool on their backs to their hill-side cottages, four or five miles distant, whence they would return later with the woven cloth for sale.[2] In Devonshire we have the same picture of independence. The comber or spinster bought the wool and sold the yarn to the weaver, and he disposed of the cloth at the next market to an Exeter merchant, who had it dyed before exporting it. Besides these there were the numerous makers of the new draperies. The manufacture of these lighter fabrics of coarser wool, the 'bays', 'says', &c., had been introduced by the Dutch and Walloon immigrants, who came after the Reformation and settled in thousands at Norwich, Colchester, Canterbury, and elsewhere, and by whose agency the industry spread along the coast counties from Yarmouth to Plymouth. 'All sorts of these people', we are told, 'are masters in their trade, and work for themselves.' [3]

---

[1] The average price of wool at Eton for the years 1572–82 (when Shakespeare was a boy at Stratford) was 20s. 9d. the tod of 28 lb. Eleven sheep to a tod would give a fleece of 2½ lb. (Rogers, *Hist. of Agriculture*, vol. v, p. 408). [2] 2 & 3 Phil. and Mary, c. 13.
[3] *State Papers Domestic, Jas. I*, vol. lxxx. 13.

The existence of this large body of independent small masters contributed very largely to preserve the status of the English working-class at a period when the effective organization of large masses of wage-earners for self-protection was impossible. In the older branches of the industry the development of a more capitalistic system led to social crises of a serious character at every temporary dislocation of foreign trade. The situation described in *Henry the Eighth* was, in fact, repeating itself in the last months of the poet's life.

> The clothiers all, not able to maintain
> The many to them 'longing, have put off
> The spinsters, carders, fullers, weavers, who,
> Unfit for other life, compell'd by hunger
> And lack of other means, in desperate manner
> Daring the event to the teeth, are all in uproar,
> And danger serves among them. (*Hen. VIII*, I. ii. 31-7)

This system of employment had produced some famous capitalists in the early sixteenth century, such as Thomas Spring of Lavenham, whose daughter married a de Vere, and whose son was the lord of eleven manors, and 'Jack of Newbury', who is said to have marched at the head of a hundred workmen to Flodden Field. Under it the workers received a pittance of fourpence or sixpence a day, or worked in their own homes at a low piece-work rate. As in either case they were liable to have their wages assessed by the magistrates, and had neither the skill nor the bargaining power of other craftsmen, they were reduced to nearly the same level of dependence as the agricultural labourer.

The helpless condition of the mere wage-earner was due in part to the unexampled rise of prices produced by the influx of precious metals from America. Although during the Middle Ages the price of food fluctuated widely, with good or bad harvests, the average had been remarkably steady. The average price of wheat for three centuries before 1540 had been about six shillings a quarter. At the time Shakespeare was producing his earliest plays, a price of twenty shillings betokened a good year. For the few years before his death the average price was about thirty-five shillings. Most other food prices, except that of herrings, went up in like proportion. These changes rendered the old machinery for fixing the wages of labourers

obsolete, and in the great industrial code of 1563 a new
scheme was devised, under which the justices received
powers to adjust wages from time to time, so that they
might bear a 'reasonable' proportion to prices. Whatever
may have been meant by a reasonable proportion, it is clear
that wages were not raised in the same proportion as prices.
In the closing years of the sixteenth century, when the price
of wheat was always at least three or four times as high as
the average of the previous century, the wages of the skilled
workman were little more than double, and those of the un-
skilled labourer considerably less than double those of the
earlier period.   In the year of the Armada the wages of the
'best and most skillful' journeymen of the London crafts
were assessed at rates varying from £3 6s. 8d. to £6 13s. 4d.
by the year, or from sixpence to ninepence by the day with
meat and drink.   For those who provided their own meat
and drink the rates were from tenpence to fourteenpence
per day;[1] and the highest of these rates was about double
that of the highest paid to a country weaver or farm labourer
at the same period.

Even with butter at fivepence a pound, beef at twopence,
and bread at a penny, the wage-earner would find it hard
to keep a house over his head and bring up a family on sixpence a day.   And this was no doubt the main reason why
in Shakespeare's time so large a proportion of the working-
class were not content to be mere wage-earners.   The typical
working-man of the period was the small master, who
worked not for a wage, but for a profit, and who was at the
same time a small-holder, producing part of his own food.
He was not only a worker but a trader, the smallest link in
a chain of traders who maintained the connexions between
production and consumption.   He was a small capitalist,
who needed the co-operation of larger capitalists, in order
to keep in touch with supply and demand.   When this dependence became oppressive it took the form of debt—of
an advance made on extortionate terms.   In itself an
advance of capital was not an abnormal or oppressive act.
It represented, in fact, merely the beginnings of that system
of basing industrial enterprise on credit, which has since
then been so enormously developed.   Already in Shakespeare's time the giving and the taking of credit was part of

[1] *City of London Letter Book, &c.*, 256 (MS. in City Records).

the daily business of all classes engaged in the larger forms of industry and commerce. The wool-broker paid in advance for fleeces not yet grown, so that the farmer might increase his flock. The clothier entrusted his goods to the merchant; as much as £30,000 is said to have been lost by Suffolk clothiers in 1622 by the failure of London merchants. When so many people were working and trading on borrowed capital, and the importance of time as a factor in value was so practically obvious, the mediaeval condemnation of interest had become an anachronism, and Parliament, after a prolonged struggle with popular and clerical prejudice, had finally, in 1571, legalized the payment of interest up to 10 per cent.

If, when Shakespeare produced *The Merchant of Venice*, in 1594, interest was still a word of such ill omen that the popular Antonio could find no stronger term with which to stigmatize the ' bargains and the well-won thrift ' of Shylock, this was not because the practice of taking it was uncommon, but because in one form or other it was becoming universal. In the social problems of that period the question of interest occupied the same central position as the question of wages occupies in the social problems of to-day. There was a wages question then, too. At the very time when Shakespeare drew the character of Shylock, an Act was being drafted (which never passed) to raise the wages of poor spinners and weavers, and to fix a minimum, and the Privy Council later on attempted a similar policy. But the class whose condition it was sought to improve was one of semi-paupers. What the independent worker complained of was not low wages, but usury.

The condition of the Cornish miner affords an illustration of this. Like the lead-miner of Derby or of Cumberland and the iron-miner of the Forest of Dean, the tinner of Cornwall was originally an independent small capitalist. As the metal lay on the surface he needed at most only the co-operation of one or two fellow-workers in order to retain his hold on the claim he had staked out. But in the sixteenth century the surface metal was fast disappearing. Shafts had to be sunk and mines drained, and the capitalist shareholder came to dominate the fellowship of working miners. The development of the tin trade introduced further complications. From the earliest times Cornish tin

SILVER COINS OF ELIZABETH CROWN SHILLING SIXPENCES HALF GROAT PENNY HALFPENNY

had found its way to the far east, but now the London pewterers, whose wares had attained a European reputation, were eagerly seeking a monopoly of the chief material of their craft. Capital, therefore, flowed readily into tin-mining, but the application of capital took a form which was stigmatized as usury. The London merchant advanced money to the tin-masters on condition of their delivering certain quantities of tin at the next coinage, and the tin-masters in their turn furnished capital to the working miners on similar conditions. Though there were thousands of labourers receiving a low wage, and often paid in truck, the typical Cornish miner of Shakespeare's time was in transition from the status of an independent adventurer like the Californian or Australian gold-digger, to that of a 'tributer', who, along with a group of his fellows, contracts to work a section of a mine for a percentage of the produce. The tributer, who is still far from extinct in Cornwall, is a small capitalist, and takes part of the risk of the enterprise, but he usually receives advances of capital from the owners of the mine. On a similar footing was the salter of Northumberland and Durham, who paid four-fifths of the salt he produced to the owner of the pan, who also supplied the coals. From this condition to that of piece-workers like the colliers of Warwickshire and Staffordshire, who were paid so much the chaldron with bounties, was but a step.

On the other hand, a small step upwards made the working master an independent capitalist. With so fluctuating a market it was difficult to achieve this unless the industrialist had some other resource to tide him over bad times. And just as the cottagers and small farmers of Yorkshire and Devon were developing into clothiers, so the yeomen in a dozen counties were serving as pioneers to the later industrial triumphs of England. When we learn, for instance, that in the early part of the seventeenth century there were about twenty thousand smiths and ironworkers producing nails, horseshoes, keys, locks, and agricultural implements within a circuit of ten miles of Dudley Castle, the number seems incredible, till we discover that in this country every farm had one forge or more at which the farmers worked when not employed in the fields.[1] It was

---

[1] S. Smiles, *Industrial Biography*, p. 69.

in this way that many yeoman families were founding
fortunes in the Weald of Kent and Sussex, which in Elizabeth's time, and till the woods were exhausted, was the
leading centre of the iron industry.   In Warwickshire the
yeomanry and smaller gentry sank coal-pits, in Worcestershire they opened salt-springs, in Stafford they made pot-
tery, in Lancashire and Yorkshire they dug for alum, in
Buckinghamshire they set up paper-mills, in Northamptonshire they opened stone and slate quarries, and supplied
the growing leather trade from their tan-yards.

When one contemplates this widespread activity, one is
tempted to ask why so little is heard of it in the annals of
the time, and why the industrial revolution did not happen
a century earlier.   The answer to both questions is the
same.   The triumph of honest enterprise was overshadowed
by the feverish delusions of speculation and the selfish greed
of monopoly.   A lively mood of adventure pervaded all
classes, but the sound elements were counteracted by the
unsound.   The habit of wagering or gambling on difficult
and dangerous voyages of exploration, which was laying in
a paradoxical fashion the foundations of the insurance
system of the country, was a conspicuous sign of the rising
tide of reckless speculation.   When Gonzalo in *The Tempest*
(III. iii. 47–9) tells of the strange prodigies

> which now we find
> Each putter-out of five for one will bring us
> Good warrant of,

he is referring to those merchant voyagers in unknown seas
who pledged a sum of money with the capitalist at home
on the strange condition that the premium should be for-
feited in case nothing further was heard of them, but that
five times as much should be paid them on their safe return.
Ben Jonson expressed himself more scornfully of the
practice when he wrote rather elliptically

> Of those, that put out monies, on return
> From Venice, Paris, or some inland passage
> Of six times to and fro.   (*Epigrams*, No. cxxxiii)

The courts of Elizabeth and of James were crowded by
a medley of projectors and suitors, compared with the best
of whom the most self-helpful of Mr. Smiles's heroes shines
as a disinterested enthusiast.   Some of these, no doubt, had
practical qualifications.   Such, for instance, were the German

GOLD COINS OF JAMES I   UNITES   DOUBLE CROWN   THISTLE CROWN
BRITISH CROWN

experts who directed the search for gold, silver, copper, and quicksilver in the northern and western counties, and in Wales, and whose operations at Keswick for thirty-seven years resulted in a loss of £27,000. Such, too, were the Dutchman Vermuyden, who began the draining of the Fens, and the Italians who wished to introduce new mechanical or chemical inventions, or the finer industrial arts of their native land.

But the great majority of those interested in projects were courtiers and their dependants or agents. These were the titled directors and company promoters of that age, but their activities were less honourable to themselves and more prejudicial to the commonwealth than those of their modern representatives, inasmuch as they openly exploited the power of the State. Manifold opportunity for this was afforded by the financial needs of the Government, and by the demand for State regulation, which could easily be elicited from an ill-informed public, prompted by vested interests. The most sympathetic view that can be taken of the patents and monopolies granted by Elizabeth and her successors is to regard them as an attempt to build up a Civil Service on a system resembling that of privateering in warfare. The patentees and monopolists undertook—for a consideration—to perform the functions now entrusted to the Home Office, the Board of Trade, the departments of Customs and Inland Revenue. They devised and collected a great variety of new indirect taxation, they inspected and penalized trade abuses, they sold dispensations from impracticable laws, and licensed forbidden pleasures. These grants brought little or no direct profit to the Government, but they served the purpose of a Civil List; they satisfied the claims of the family connexions, the favourites, and the servants of the sovereign.

The picture drawn in *Mother Hubbard's Tale* by Edmund Spenser—himself a suitor—of the fierce scramble that went on amongst courtiers, great and small, for these favours, is fully borne out by the State Papers. In 1595 the Earl of Oxford and Lord Buckhurst were bidding eagerly against each other for a monopoly of tin, which Sir Walter Ralegh afterwards secured, and which he defended in the great debate on monopolies in the House of Commons, as having raised the wages of the tinner. At the court of James we find the Duke of Lennox struggling with Lord Harington for a share in the monopoly of brass farthings, and the rising Hay snatching from the falling Northampton the profits of a monopoly in starch.

But the spirit of industrial and commercial monopoly was far too widespread to be accounted for by the greed of those in high places or by the intrigue and fraud of their allies. Broader social abuses were behind it. In part, it was a survival from the past. The mustard-seed of guild monopoly had often grown into a flourishing tree. The Society of Hoastmen, which comprised the leading burgesses of Newcastle, contrived at the end of Elizabeth's reign to acquire a monopoly of the coal supply of London. The cost of Mrs. Quickly's 'sea-coal fire' went up steadily, while Shakespeare was in London, from four shillings the chaldron to nine. It was in vain that the Lord Mayor complained to the Privy Council. The Crown had authorized the monopoly on condition of receiving a tax on the exportation; and the coal trade of Newcastle retained till the time of the Commonwealth most of the characteristics of an American Trust, with the additional immunity that would be conferred by a favourable decision of the Supreme Court. The output was restricted, and prices continued to rise, whilst the quality of coal put on the market declined. A similar natural monopoly was exploited by the burgesses of Droitwich, who resisted the opening of new salt-springs in the neighbourhood of those owned by the shareholders of the town.

Nor were the newer enterprises in which the age was so fertile any less exclusive in their methods. As the bounds of the known earth and of the navigable seas were continually expanded by the daring of Elizabethan explorers, the monopoly which had been acquired of the export trade in cloth by the guild of Merchant Adventurers was encroached upon by half a dozen younger companies, each of which endeavoured to monopolize a region of its own. The Muscovy Company, which claimed as its sphere of influence the whole of Russia, Armenia, Media, Hyrcania, Persia, and the Caspian Sea, though nominally composed of some eight score members, was entirely managed by fifteen directors, who limited to every man the proportion of stock he should trade for, and placed the whole capital thus subscribed in the hands of a single agent in Russia. They made a 'corner' in Russian cordage, and by restricting the supply, raised the price 150 per cent. 'This', said an indignant Committee of the Commons in 1604, 'is a strong and shameful monopoly.' A similar control was sought by the Eastland Company, which traded to the Baltic, over the exportation of cloth thither, and the importation of timber and tar; by the Levant Company over the supply of currants from Turkey; by the East India Company over the trade in spices; and by the Virginia Company over the tobacco trade. A brief glimpse at one of these spheres of trade will serve to give us the environment in which Shakespeare studied Antonio. Some three years before *The Merchant of Venice* was produced, a lively controversy was started on the Levant trade. A small group of wealthy London merchants urged the necessity of a joint stock. A fleet of eight or ten big ships (i.e. not less than 180 or 200 tons) was required for security against 'water rats'. An ambassador must be kept at Constantinople, and large presents made to the Grand Seigneur and the Bashaw. Having already invested £40,000 in the trade, they asked for exclusive rights in it. A chorus of protests arose from independent traders, who repudiated the notion that the proposed monopolists had discovered the Levant. Colthurst & Co., for instance, said they had been in the trade fourteen years, and found the risks less than those of the Spanish trade. Their ship *Dolphin*, with a cargo of £2,000 to the Straits, had lately been sunk by the Spaniards, but their ship *Eagle* had made a good voyage the year before to Zante and Scio, and was at that moment in Venice, hoping to find a good market for English tin, lead, and cloth. This dispute between the Companies and the 'free traders' rapidly acquired national dimensions, and kept the first Parliament of James I debating for a fortnight. Not only the merchants of the lesser ports, but also three-fourths of the London merchants were arrayed against the privileges of the London Companies, and each company, whilst stoutly defending its own monopoly, 'repined' at the restrictions imposed by the others. The Commons passed the Free Trade Bill, but it was thrown out by the Lords. The Crown continued to grant charters to companies, and most of the trade continued to be done by 'interlopers'.

Closely connected with the history of the privileged companies is a phase of commercial development which links the age of Shakespeare to our own—the rise of joint-stock enterprise and the growth of the investing public. Shareholding is in itself one of the most primitive devices of mankind, and there appears to be some mystical reason for division by sixteenths. Sixteen Celtic households within a tribe shared the use of the land ; sixteen German miners in the thirteenth century formed a working fellowship; sixteen Scottish traders in the seventeenth century owned a ship in common ; and the shares in the Blackfriars Theatre, which raised Shakespeare to affluence, were likewise sixteenths. But these earlier shareholders, as a rule, knew something of the business they engaged in. The typically modern form of shareholding, by which the capital of the outside public is made to fertilize enterprises which are beyond the resources of individuals, may almost be said to have had its beginnings in Shakespeare's time.

During the last ten years of the poet's life the air was full of projects of this kind. The king was urging the London Livery Companies to take up shares in the schemes for the colonization of Ulster and Virginia, and he himself became the leading shareholder in the New River Company for supplying London with water, whose works were opened in 1613. But it was the success of the East India Company that gave the main impetus to joint-stock enterprise. The profit of $87\frac{1}{2}$ per cent. realized on the first joint-stock voyage caused a rush of subscribers to the second. Over a million and a half was raised from nearly a thousand shareholders. Courtiers and titled ladies, Privy Councillors and judges, led the way, and a crowd of knights and clergymen, widows and spinsters, merchants and tradesmen followed their example.

A new and incalculable source of capital was thus revealed, and fresh projects were continually forthcoming to find a use for it. The most interesting of these schemes were those of the London craftsmen for delivering themselves from that dependence on the middleman which has already been described, and which in varying degrees characterized the silk-weavers, the feltmakers, the pinners, the glovers, the skinners, the printers, &c., who crowded in thousands the poor tenements of Southwark and White·

GOLD COINS OF JAMES I   THIRTY SHILLINGS   ROSE RYAL   SPUR RYAL

FIFTEEN SHILLINGS   HALF ANGEL

chapel, of Shoreditch and Clerkenwell. The Feltmakers'
Company proposed to raise a capital of £15,000 to form the
basis of a Hat Trust. They would take all hats from the
makers at a fair price, and thus oblige all dealers to come
to their warehouse for a supply. The scheme fell through,
but others like it were floated. The Prospectus became a
familiar form of popular literature. Its cant phrases are
parodied by Ben Jonson in *The Staple of News*. All the news
of the day is to be brought from the four cardinal quarters—
the Court, Paul's, the Exchange, and Westminster-hall—by
four emissaries to the Governor of the Staple, who with
the help of an examiner, a register, and two clerks will
classify it as authentical, apocryphal, barber's news, tailor's
news, &c., and then proceed to stamp it and give it currency
(*The Staple of News*, I. i, ii).

Still more amusing is the scheme propounded by Meercraft, the projector, to Lady Tailbush 'for serving the whole
state with toothpicks', so as to prevent the putrefactions
that are bred in the gums by those 'made of adulterate and
false wood'.

> To have all toothpicks brought unto an office,
> There sealed ; and such as counterfeit them mulcted !
> And last, for venting them, to have a book
> Printed to teach their use, which every child
> Shall have throughout the kingdom that can read
> And learn to pick his teeth by. (*The Devil is an Ass*, IV. i)

No one who knows the records of the time will charge Ben
Jonson with wild exaggeration. He seems rather to err in
the direction of pedantic realism. The list of Meercraft's
other projects is almost dull in its actuality, and Meercraft's
account of his methods of flotation—

> We'll take in citizens, commoners and aldermen
> To bear the charge, and blow them off again
> Like so many dead flies when it is carried
>   (*The Devil is an Ass*, II. i)

—is a sufficiently accurate description of the methods that
were then being followed by Sir Arthur Ingram, Comptroller
of Customs and M.P. for Stafford, in floating the alum
monopoly. Indeed, a study of the leading characters in
The Devil is an Ass—the Projector himself ; Fitzdottrell his
dupe, who is prepared to mortgage his broad acres in
Norfolk that he may become the Duke of Drowned Land,

and devote himself to the Devil ; Gilthead, the city usurer, who supplies the money for the mortgage, since ' he lives by finding fools out to be trusted'; and Lady Tailbush, the woman of fashion who intrigues at court for monopolies and talks her projects into social acceptance—would be by far the best introduction to the economic history of the period when Shakespeare had laid down his pen and was living quietly at Stratford.

§ 2. COINAGE, CURRENCY, AND TOKENS

If we judged of the coinage of Shakespeare's time merely by its denominations, it would appear to differ from that of our own only by its greater variety. It included all the denominations with which we are familiar to-day except the four-shilling piece and the two-shilling piece, and the want of these was more than balanced by the existence of the noble and the half-noble, the angel, half-angel, and quarter-angel, the unite, the ryal, the groat, the half-groat, and the three-farthing piece. But the actual differences are much greater than this seems to imply. In the first place, nearly all the coins above the value of a shilling were of gold, whilst the shilling and all of less value were of silver. In the second place, there were two distinct standards of gold coined. Fine gold of the old English standard, 23 carats 3½ grains, was used for the older coins—the noble, the ryal or rose noble, the angel, the angelet, and for sovereigns weighing twice as much as our own ; whilst the 22 carat gold which we now use was coined into sovereigns half as heavy again as ours, into half-sovereigns, crowns, and half-crowns. In addition to all these there were in constant circulation a considerable number of foreign gold coins of various standards, French crowns, Spanish ducats, Dutch florins, Burgundians, kaisers, and pistolets. And finally, to complicate matters still more, there was a double standard ; either metal was legal tender, and as the relative values of gold and silver then, as now, continually changed, the Government found itself obliged from time to time to re-state the value of its own gold coins and of the foreign coins in circulation in terms of the silver coinage. Thus the lighter sovereign of 22 carat gold was called down from 20s. to 13s. 4d. in 1561, and raised again to 20s. in 1592.

GOLD COINS OF JAMES I SOVEREIGNS HALF SOVEREIGN DOUBLE CROWN
CROWN HALF CROWN

A generation earlier than Shakespeare a far worse element of confusion had been introduced by the debasement of the coinage, which began in 1545–6, and lasted till the accession of Elizabeth. During this period the amount of silver in a pound weight of coin fell from 11 oz. 2 dwt. to 3 oz. The gold coinage was less affected, but the last sovereigns coined by Henry VIII were of the lowest standard ever coined in England, i.e. 20 carat. Though the debased coins were called in by Elizabeth, many remained in circulation, as is evident from the following passage in Ben Jonson's *Alchemist*:

Face. Have you provided for her grace's servants ?
Dapper. Yes ; here are six score Edward shillings.
Face. Good !
Dapper. And an old Harry's sovereign.
Face. Very good !
Dapper. And three James shillings, and an Elizabeth groat,
Just twenty nobles.
Face. Oh, you are too just.
I would you had had the other noble in Maries.
Dapper. I have some Philip and Maries.
Face. Ah, those same are best of all.   (*The Alchemist*, III. ii)

The sovereign of the old standard (weight 240 grains, value 30s.) was not coined after 1601, and was replaced in James I's reign by the rose ryal (weight $213\frac{1}{3}$–216 grs., value 30s.–33s.). The ryals of Elizabeth (120 grs., 15s.) had been equivalent to half-sovereigns of the old standard, and were replaced under James by spur ryals (108–98 grs., 15s.–16s. 6d.). The only other coins of the old gold standard were the angel, the angelet, or half-angel, and the quarter-angel (weights 80, 40, and 20 grs., values 10s., 5s., and 2s. 6d.), the two former of which were coined by James I, with the weight diminished to 72 grs. and 36 grs., and the value raised to 11s. and 5s. 6d. respectively.

The same tendency to a diminution of weight and an increase of value was shown by the coins of 22 carat gold. The sovereign ($174\frac{6}{11}$ grs., 20s.), the half-sovereign ($87\frac{3}{11}$ grs., 10s.), and the crown ($43\frac{7}{11}$ grs., 5s.) of Elizabeth were replaced in 1604 by the unite ($154\frac{26}{31}$ grs.), the half-unite or double crown ($77\frac{13}{31}$ grs.), and the Britain crown ($38\frac{22}{31}$ grs.), whose names commemorate the union of the kingdoms ; and the values of the Jacobean coins were raised in 1611 to 22s., 11s., and 5s. 6d. respectively. Both these changes were necessitated by the rise in the relative value of gold, which was causing gold coin to be exported.

It is significant that we hear hardly anything of the larger gold coins in Shakespeare. The name of the angel, indeed, afforded opportunities that no poet could afford to neglect. Dromio brings angels to deliver his master (*Com. of E.* IV. iii. 12 seq.). Falstaff speaks of 'a legion of angels' that are at the bidding of Mrs. Ford (*M. Wives*, I. iii. 57), and Benedick in his demand that his mistress shall be 'noble, or not I for an angel' (*Much Ado*, II. iii. 35), puns upon the noble as the earlier name of the angel. But the coin in which the Shakespearian character most naturally expresses large sums is the crown. Not only Adam's thrifty savings (*A. Y. L.* II. iii. 38) and Orlando's poor inheritance (*ibid.* I. i. 3), but the rich dowry Petruchio is to receive with Katherine (*Tam. Sh.* II. i. 123) and the debt of the King of France to the King of Navarre are reckoned in crowns (*Love's L. L.* II. i. 128 seq.). Petruchio himself boasts of his wealth as crowns in his purse, and offers to stake a hundred of them on Katherine's obedience (*Tam. Sh.* I. ii. 57; V. ii. 74). It is with crowns that Poins promises to stuff the purses of Prince Hal and Falstaff by their exploit at Gadshill (*1 Hen. IV*, I. ii. 145), and that King Henry actually fills the glove of the soldier Williams after Agincourt (*Hen. V*, IV. viii. 61). The crown was originally derived from France, and French crowns (worth 6s. to 6s. 4d.) would seem from the frequent references to them in literature to have been almost as familiar as the English coin. The ducat, immortalized by Antonio's negotiations with Shylock, was a Spanish coin, valued under Philip and Mary at 6s. 8d., the 'double ducat' being worth 13s. 4d.

Silver crowns and half-crowns had been struck only in the last coinage of Henry VIII and in one coinage of Edward VI, and were not repeated till the closing years of Elizabeth. In size and weight they were not unlike their modern equivalents; but the shilling, sixpence, and three-penny-piece being much thinner, were larger than our own; and the groat was almost exactly the size of the modern shilling. There were also in circulation silver pieces of the value of twopence, three halfpence, a penny, three farthings, and a halfpenny. Confusion between coins of the same type so near in value was very easy, and a rose was accordingly

TRADESMEN'S TOKENS

placed behind the Queen's head on the sixpence, three-pence, three halfpence, and three farthings to distinguish them from the groat, the twopenny piece, the penny, and the halfpenny. It is to the spare profile of Elizabeth on a coin of this type and also to the contemporary habit of wearing a rose behind the ear that we owe the lively figure of the Bastard :

> my face so thin
> That in mine ear I durst not stick a rose,
> Lest men should say, ' Look, where three-farthings goes !'
>   (*John*, I. i. 141–3)

The sixpence was popularly known as a ' tester '—

> *Pistol.* Tester I'll have in pouch when thou shalt lack ;
>   (*M. Wives*, I. iii. 94)

and the ' mill sixpences ' in Slender's purse (*M. Wives*, I. i. 160) were the result of an attempt—only very partially successful in Shakespeare's time—to replace the irregular products of hammering by machine-made coins with hard clear edges, and so to make the offence of clipping easier of detection.

Even this abundance of small silver could not satisfy the needs of the retail trader and his poorer customers. The purchasing power of a silver halfpenny in many commodities (meat, for instance) was as great as that of our threepenny piece, yet a halfpenny purse was proverbial for smallness. Falstaff, we are told, could not creep into a halfpenny purse (*M. Wives*, III. v. 152). But the silver halfpenny was not coined till 1582, and long before this the need for small change had led the shopkeepers of London and other large towns to issue halfpenny and farthing tokens of brass, tin, lead, or even leather, which they undertook to redeem or receive in payment for goods. The evils that might arise from counterfeiting or from the bankruptcy of the issuer, and the profit that the Crown might make out of issuing brass farthings, were too obvious to be overlooked by the projectors that swarmed in the court of Elizabeth. Proposals were made in 1576 to coin a pound weight of copper worth eightpence into ten or twelve shillings worth of halfpennies and farthings, which were to displace private tokens and be legal tender to the value of a groat. A proclamation was issued and some coins were struck, but the repugnance to a debased coinage seems to have prevented the scheme from being carried further. The city of Bristol was, however, authorized in 1594 to issue copper farthings, and its example was followed by Worcester and Oxford. The London tradesmen continued to issue their tokens; Sir Robert Cotton says that as many as 3,000 did so.

In the reign of James I the proposal for a royal issue was renewed, and in 1613 the scheme was carried out for the benefit of Lord Harington, who had incurred large debts as tutor to the Princess Elizabeth. A farthing became known as a 'Harrington', but the gain expected from the coinage was not realized either by the Crown, the patentee, or the contractor, who, after vainly endeavouring to force his farthings into circulation, was literally paid in his own coin. The patent farthings, however, continued in use till the Civil War, when they were displaced once more by tokens issued by tradesmen and by corporations; and most of the early tokens preserved belong to this period (1648–72). The interesting collection of Stratford tokens at Shakespeare's birthplace serves excellently to illustrate the small change used in the poet's own lifetime, most of which had passed before the 'Harrington' came into circulation.

BIBLIOGRAPHY.—Much of the most valuable material for the economic history of Shakespeare's time is still in MSS., e. g. the State Papers, the Lansdowne and Harleian MSS., the records of the City Companies and of the Corporation of London.

Contemporary authorities and printed records : FRANCIS BACON'S *Letters*, ed. J. Spedding, 1861–8; W. CAMDEN'S *Britannia*, translated by P. Holland, 1610; *Memorials of Goldsmiths' Company*, ed. Sir W. S. Prideaux, 1896; R. HAKLUYT'S *The Principal Navigations ... of the English Nation*, 1598–1600; W. S. [John Hales of Coventry ?] *A Discourse of the Common Weal*, 1581, ed. Eliz. Lamond, 1893; W. HARRISON'S *Description of England*, ed. by F. J. Furnivall, for New Shakspere Society, 1877 ; *Henslowe's Diary*, ed. by W. W. Greg, 1904; *Historical MSS. Commission*—Hatfield Papers, House of Lords Papers, and Calendars of records of many towns, e. g. Yarmouth, Canterbury, Ipswich ; *House of Commons Journals*, vol. i ; B. JONSON, *Dramatic Works* ; *Records of Leicester*, ed. by Mary Bateson, vol. iii, 1905 ; *Memorials of the Guild of Merchant Taylors*, by C. M. Clode, 1875 ; *History of Pewterers' Company*, by C. Welch, 1903; *Acts of Privy Council*, ed. J. R. Dasent ; *Calendars of State Papers Domestic, Elizabeth and James I* ; *Transcript of Register of Stationers' Company*, by E. Arber ; PHILIP STUBBES'S *Anatomie of Abuses*, 1583 (New Shakspere Society, 1877–9) ; JOHN STOW'S *Survey of the Cities of London and Westminster*, ed. Strype, 1720.

Modern works are : W. J. ASHLEY, *Introduction to Economic History* ; A. E. BLAND, P. A. BROWN, and R. H. TAWNEY, *English Economic History : Select Documents*, 1914 ; J. W. BURGON, *Life and Times of Sir Thomas Gresham*, 1839 ; W. CUNNINGHAM, *Growth of English Industry and Commerce, Modern Times*, 1907 ; *Dictionary of National Biography* (arts. on Ralegh, Philip Henslowe, Arthur Ingram, Thomas Knyvett, Th. Gresham); F. H. DURHAM, *Relations of the Crown to Trade under James I*, in Royal Hist. Soc. Trans., N. S. XIII, 1899; T. FULLER, *Church History of Britain*, ed. by J. S. Brewer, 1845; R. L. GALLOWAY, *Annals of Coal Mining and the Coal Trade*, 1898; S. R. GARDINER, *History of England, 1603–25*; N. S. B. GRAS, *The Evolution of the English Cornmarket*, 1915; A. H. JOHNSON, *History of the Worshipful Company of Drapers*, 1915; HUBERT HALL, *Society in the Elizabethan Age*, 1901; S. LEE, *Life of Shakespeare*, 1925; S. LEE, *Stratford-on-Avon*, 1907; G. R. LEWIS, *The Stannaries*, 1908; D. MACPHERSON, *Annals of Commerce*, 1805; R. H. MORRIS, *Chester in the Plantagenet and Tudor Reigns* [1893]; W. H. PRICE, *English Patents of Monopoly*, 1906; J. E. T. ROGERS, *History of Agriculture and Prices in England, 1886–7*; R. RUDING, *Annals of the Coinage of Great Britain and its Dependencies*, 1840; W. R. SCOTT, *The Constitution and Finance of English, Scottish, and Irish Joint Stock Companies to 1720*, 1910–13; S. SMILES, *The Huguenots in England and Ireland*, 1889; T. SNELLING, *View of the Copper Coinage of England*; R. H. TAWNEY, *The Agrarian Problem in the Sixteenth Century*, 1912; G. UNWIN, *Industrial Organization in the Sixteenth and Seventeenth Centuries*, 1904; G. UNWIN, *Gilds and Companies of London*, 1908; *Victoria County History of England* (the articles on Industries are generally in the second volume dealing with each county); C. WALFORD, *Fairs Past and Present*, 1883.

XII

AGRICULTURE AND GARDENING

BY

R. E. PROTHERO

§ 1. AGRICULTURE

SHAKESPEARE'S knowledge of the country and of country pursuits differs from the literary stock-in-trade acquired by writers in order to surround their various actors with the details appropriate to their respective callings. The background to his delineations of human nature, and the atmosphere in which they are steeped, are English rural life ; from it also are drawn the images by which he illustrates human character, conduct, and fortunes. The creations of his fancy, whether their home is Athens or Messina, live and move on the barren keen-aired uplands of the Cotswolds, or among the woodlands, rich meadows, and scented pastures of Warwickshire.

But Shakespeare is rather a sportsman than a farmer. He uses the technical language of woodcraft and venery with that natural accuracy which is the despair of book-students, because it is only bred by lifelong familiarity. The traditions that he was a deer-stealer, or that he earned his livelihood by holding horses, may be false in fact ; but if they are fables, they are true to life. He is the poet of sunrise rather than of sunset, and he paints the ' vaward of the day' (*Mid. N. D.* IV. i. 111) as few poets have painted it, because, before the sun is fully up, he has harboured the stag by the light of the moon and the seven stars. Though he contrasts human faithlessness with canine fidelity (*Timon*, IV. iii. 317), his enthusiasm is for the hound as an adjunct of the chase, and the horse, not the dog, is his loved companion. Had longer life been granted to him in his country retirement, he would have been less likely to experiment in arable farming than to turn horse-master, keep a stud of mares, and breed a 'rage' of colts by a Barbary roan or a stallion of the new Arabian breed.

In Shakespeare's allusions to horses and to sport are suggested some broad features of agricultural conditions and of the changes through which Tudor society was passing. Feudalism gave place to trade; rent-paying tenants supplanted baronial retainers; new needs created new markets, enclosed open spaces, and required new communications with growing centres of commerce. To meet the fresh demands new types of horses were bred. The spirit of the change can scarcely be better summarized than in the fate of the 'Great Horse'. The courser which in time of war had endured the 'shock of wrathful iron arms' (*Rich. II*, I. iii. 136), and in peace was the 'foot-cloth horse' (*2 Hen. VI*, IV. vii. 52) which carried Lord Say and three times stumbled under Lord Hastings (*Rich. III*, III. iv. 83), has passed into the shire horse or Clydesdale of a commercial age. As highways improved, travellers no longer journeyed only on horseback. The ambling roadster, whose artificial gait was easier than the motion of the hard-trotting hackney, and the laden pack-horse of our Elizabethan ancestors began to give way to the carriage-horse, the hack, and the cart-horse, as well as the hunter and the race-horse. Shakespeare's standard of horseflesh changes with the times and approximates to the modern ideal. It passes from the heavy, powerful courser (*Ven. & Ad.* 293) to the 'prince of palfreys', who 'trots the air', and causes the earth to sing when he touches it with his elastic tread (*Hen. V*, III. vii. 17).

Sport also adapts its forms to the changing conditions of society and physical features of farming. The race-horse was nothing to Shakespeare, though he had heard

> of riding wagers,
> Where horses have been nimbler than the sands
> That run i' the clock's behalf,   (*Cymb.* III. ii. 72–4)

and knew that 'switch and spurs' (*Rom. & Jul.* II. iv. 75) were plied in a 'wild-goose chase' on the Cotswold Hills. But even for hunting, pace was little needed in Tudor times. A 'good continuer' (*Much Ado*, I. i. 149), or, as we might say, a good stayer, was more useful. For coursing the hare, the greyhounds alone must be fleeter than 'poor Wat'. The red deer was followed by hounds 'slow in

pursuit' (*Mid. N. D.* IV. i. 129), and by men on foot, armed
with leaping-poles, except on those rare occasions when the
great hart was hunted 'at force'. Unless the long-winged
peregrine fled down wind, horsemen were not pushed to
a gallop, and the humbler art of the 'astringer' (*All's W.*
v. i. 7), with his short-winged goshawk, exacted no turn
of speed. But as agriculture advanced, the red deer's
covert was destroyed, and his extermination was demanded
as an inveterate foe to crops. So too the sport of falconry
was doomed when hedgerows and enclosures displaced the
broad expanses of village farms, and the partridge no longer
cowered in the stubble by the edge of the turf-balk on a
common field under the tinkling bells of the 'towering'
falcon (*Macb.* II. iv. 12). Another beast of the chase and
other means of capture were needed. Shakespeare had
stood on 'no quillets how to slay' a fox with snares and
gins (*2 Hen. VI*, III. i. 261). But the fox is an enemy only
to the game-preserver and the poultry-farmer, he destroyed
no crops ; hedgerows only added zest to his pursuit ; the
new sport satisfied the changed agricultural conditions,
and to meet its needs were created the modern hound and
the modern hunter.

Shakespeare was too familiar with rural life to describe
in direct and deliberate detail the contemporary methods of
English farming. Some evidence of its conditions is, as has
been shown, afforded by his allusions to sport. Incidentally
also his plays illustrate many of the broad features of Elizabethan agriculture, and one of his rare appearances on the
stage of local history associates him personally with the
great agricultural revolution which the sixteenth century
was witnessing. That revolution is summed up in the
change from farming in common to farming by individuals.
Twice Shakespeare contrasts the two methods. In *Love's
Labour's Lost* (II. i. 221) he puns on the technical terms of
land-tenure 'common' and 'several'; in the *Sonnets*
(cxxxvii. 9–10) he distinguishes between 'a several plot'
and 'a common place'.

Land in the fourteenth century was, in most parishes,
divided into three parts: the lord's demesne, the village farm,
and the commons, wastes, and woodlands, which ministered
to the agricultural needs of both the other portions.

The lord's demesne, a compact block, held in individual

ownership and cultivated as a separate holding, has left its mark on the field nomenclature of rural districts in the frequent occurrence of such names as the Court, Hall, or Manor Farm. Originally the demesne was cultivated by the labour services of the manorial tenants. But gradually these labour rents were commuted into money payments, and from their proceeds servants in husbandry and farm labourers were hired, with or without food, at yearly or daily wages. The Black Death upset the advantages of these arrangements, because it doubled the wages of labour by halving its supply. Feudal lords, whose huge households necessitated large supplies of agricultural produce, found that farming grew daily more expensive. They vainly endeavoured to revive the old labour services, or to fix the scale of wages at the old rates by statute. Foiled in both attempts, they adopted a new plan. Owners of land, both lay and ecclesiastical, cut up the demesne into smaller holdings, and let them to tenants for varying terms of years at money rents. Tenancies of this modern type continually increased in number from other sources, as landlords improved, enclosed, and let portions of the waste in separate farms ; or broke up the common-field system by withdrawing their land from the association and leasing it in individual occupations, or by encouraging all the partners to exchange, consolidate, enclose, and rent their scattered strips as compact wholes.

At the beginning of the Tudor period there thus existed a considerable number of tenants who, in the broad features of their tenure, resembled the tenants of to-day. Side by side with these modern farmers were the tenants of the village farm, holding and cultivating their land under a system of immemorial antiquity, which has now almost entirely disappeared. With every variety of tenure and interest, but for the most part paying money rents for the use of the land, occupiers of common-field farms were associated in a common venture for the supply of their own food and drink. In this agrarian association each partner, whether lord of the manor, parson, yeoman, freeholder, copyholder, tenant at will, on lease, and for life, or the occupier of a cottage to which common-field rights were attached, contributed, according to his stake in the common venture, to the cost and maintenance of the plough teams or helped with hand and tool in the operations of the farm. As with the tenure, so with the interest. The holdings varied widely in extent. But a share of average size would be eighteen acres of arable land, two acres of meadow land, and common rights for as much live-stock as the tenant could fodder in winter.

Out of a bare, hedgeless expanse rose the cluster of timber-framed, mud-built, reed-thatched cottages, which formed the *tûn*, ' town ' or village, marked, as at Berkeley, by its ' tuft of trees ' (*Rich. II*, II. iii. 53). Round it lay a few small enclosures of permanent pasture, held in private occupation and highly prized. Sometimes a similar but larger piece of pasture was reserved for the stinted use of the commoners. In enclosures of these kinds calves were reared, beasts fattened, and field-oxen, which could not endure ' his warke to labour all daye, and then to be put to the commons or before the herdsman ', were main-tained in comparative luxury :

> It is the pasture lards the rother's sides,
> The want that makes him lean.   (*Timon*, IV. iii. 12–13)

The permanent meadows, often called ' ings ', lay in the lowest part of the land—if possible, as in the common-fields of Stratford-on-Avon, along the banks of the stream. Every year, from Candlemas (February 2) or St. Gregory's Day (March 12) to hay harvest, they were put up for hay, fenced off into strips, and distributed by lot among the partners. After the hay was cut and carried, they reverted to common occupation, and were grazed indiscriminately by the village live-stock from harvest-time, till they were again fenced off and drawn for by lot. Some puzzling field-names, such as the ' Pell ' or the ' Crane's foot ', may be often explained by the marks which indicated the various strips in these annual drawings. Bottom could distinguish between the ill-saved hay which satisfied oxen and the ' good hay, sweet hay ', that ' hath no fellow ' (*Mid. N. D.* IV. i. 39), a ' bottell ' of which was the feed prescribed for a horse by Elizabethan horse-keepers.

Beyond the meadows lay the arable land and the rough pasture. Here were the lands of Ceres :

> Thy rich leas
> Of wheat, rye, barley, vetches, oats, and peas ;
> Thy turfy mountains, where live nibbling sheep.
> (*Temp.* IV. i. 60–2)

BRITANNVS.

At quem Romanis stadus, nostrisque trahens / Tegula it nostro que trahitur undique potnos. / Natrix equans placidus, gratus, gratifaque liquitis / Dexter, haud dori storum urribus iequat.

THE ENGLISH GREAT HORSE

Instead of hedges, narrow, unploughed, bush-grown strips or 'balks' of turf marked the lines of division between the three great fields and their component parts. These fields were usually cultivated on a three-course, more rarely on a two-course, sometimes on a four-course system. Every year one field lay fallow; one was under wheat or rye; the other under barley, oats, vetches, beans or pease. A third of each man's holding lay in each of the three fields. Thus, if a man occupied eighteen acres, six were under each of the three courses. But the six acres, though in the same field, did not lie together. They were scattered in acre or half-acre strips all over its extent, so that in each field every partner had his share of good, bad, and indifferent land. From seed-time to harvest the arable land was held in separate occupation, fenced and guarded against trespassers by the village hayward, and, from seed-time till the blade showed above the soil, was protected from crows and pigeons by the crow-keeper, whose clumsy handling of his bow provoked Shakespeare's gibes (*Lear*, IV. vi. 89; *Rom. & Jul.* I. iv. 6). On Lammas Day (August 12)—ten days later in the year then than now—common rights recommenced; and when once the crops were cleared and the fences removed, the live-stock of the village, tended by the common neat-herd, shepherd, and swineherd, grazed over the land from harvest to seed-time.

Beyond the three arable fields lay the cow and sheep downs of the farm, bounded by acres of 'long heath, brown furze' (*Temp.* I. i. 71), or 'tooth'd briers, sharp furzes, pricking goss and thorns' (*Temp.* IV. i. 180), which fringed the edges of the woodlands. These wastes and woods supplied many village wants. They provided heather and fern for thatching, or bedding for the cattle, or light fuel for brewing or baking; they fed the swine with beech-mast or acorns; in winter their trimmings and loppings helped to keep the half-starved stock alive; they furnished bushes to stop gaps as well as wood for movable fences, hop poles, and implements of husbandry.

The ordinary crops grown on arable land are enumerated in Shakespeare's line, and the more abundant resources of the modern farmer are at once apparent. Red or white rivet wheat was recommended for light land, red or white pollard for heavy soils, grey wheat for clay. The best practice was to sow wheat on a thrice-ploughed fallow. The sowing, which was broadcast by hand, generally began at the end of September or in October and was completed at latest by Hallowmas (November 1). Shakespeare mentions both red and white wheat (*Lear*, III. iv. 121), and if the summer evening, when Justice Shallow ordered the headland to be sown with red wheat (*2 Hen. IV*, v. i. 17), was in August, he may be alluding to the August sowings of red wheat on the Cotswold Hills, which astonished agricultural writers at the end of the eighteenth century. But in Tudor times rye, sown early in September, and not wheat, was the bread-corn of the country. Bread made from rye, ' brown as a nut ', or from a mixture of wheat and rye, was considered by those who defeated the Armada and founded our empire to be more sustaining than bread made from wheat alone. Rye was a slower crop than wheat to ripen. It was therefore sown earlier. But it was also more hardy, and when Shakespeare speaks of ' rye-straw hats ' (*Temp.* IV. i. 136) he alludes to another of its useful qualities—the toughness of its straw. Barley, sown on light land in March or April—and the later, say Elizabethan writers, the better—or a mixture of barley and oats (drage), was the drink-corn, as rye and wheat was the bread-corn, of the country. Its malting was an important part of the house-wife's duties. Beer was scarcely ever brewed with hops till the reign of Henry VIII. But in Shakespeare's life-time the importation of hops from the Netherlands diminished, and on enclosed land their home cultivation rapidly increased. Harrison speaks of the ' corruptions used by the Flemings and forgerie dailie practised in the kind of ware', and tells us that already there were ' few farmers or occupiers in the countrie which have not gardens and hop-growing of their owne and these farre better than doe come from Flanders unto us '. Oats (best sown in ' the dust of March ') were regarded as an exhausting crop, and suspected of encouraging twitch. But in the north, from which, as Shakespeare notes (*Hen. VIII*, II. ii. 4), came the best breeds of horses, they were extensively grown as food for man and horse. Common-field farmers, however, preferred oxen for the plough. Oxen cost less to keep, to harness, and to shoe. They required less attendance. They were not subject to the many diseases of the horse (*Tam. Sh.* III. ii.

50–8).   Horseflesh in England was regarded as carrion.   But an ox, when lame or aged, might be made into human food. It was, therefore, the farmer of enclosed or ' several ' land who profited by the growing demand for ' good dry oats ' (*Mid. N. D.* IV. i. 37), and by the rise in their price which in Elizabethan times caused the death of Robin Ostler of Rochester (*1 Hen. IV*, II. i. 12–14).

The only variations in cropping which the limited resources of the Elizabethan farmer could command were the various kinds of ' codware ', the beans, pease, and vetches, which produced a pod or cod.   Shakespeare knew the danger to sheep from too much ' honey-stalk ' (*Tit. Andr.* IV. iv. 90), but neither clovers nor artificial grasses found a place in a farmer's routine.   In Tudor gardens new sources of agricultural wealth were accumulating.   Cabbage (*M. Wives* I. i. 125) was already known, but when Shakespeare makes potatoes rain from the sky (*ibid.* V. v. 21) he means the sweet or Spanish potato.   Anne Page would rather

be set quick i' the garden,
And bowl'd to death with turnips
(*M. Wives* III. iv. 90–1)

than marry the wrong man.   It was not till the middle of the seventeenth century that turnips were introduced into field cultivation by Sir Richard Weston, who had observed the practice in Brabant.   No greater impediment existed to the introduction of winter crops than the common occupation of the fallows and of arable land from harvest to seed-time, which prevailed on village farms.   So long as the tillage was Lammas-land, and subjected to common rights of pasture, it was financial suicide for any individual member of the association to grow turnips for the benefit of his neighbour.

On enclosed lands some crops were grown which now are forgotten or have become entirely local.   Hops have been already mentioned.   At one time vineyards were not uncommon.   They are frequently mentioned in Domesday. Few monasteries had been without them, and those of Ely were among the wonders of the city :

Quattuor sunt Elie, Lanterna, Capella Mariae,
Et Molendinum nec non dans Vinea vinum.

Nor is it possible to ignore the evidence of the frequent occurrence of ' vineyards ' and ' vinefields ' in local nomenclature. If it is remembered that wine was generally sweetened with honey and flavoured with spices, a change of taste will account for their disappearance without the necessity of supposing a change of climate. Saffron is another forgotten crop. Tusser advises every housewife to set aside a plot, and Harrison in a long passage dilates on its cultivation. Since the reign of Edward III it had spread from Walden in Essex over many parts of the country, and in Kett's rebellion (1549) one of the grievances put forward by the rebels is the enclosure of saffron grounds. In spite of the great expenses of its cultivation, it remained a profitable crop, so extensive was its use in medicine, in the linen chest, and in the kitchen. It was one of the ingredients which the clown was to buy for the sheep-shearing feast 'to colour the warden pies' (*Wint. Tale* IV. ii. 49). Flax, necessarily a local crop, and hemp (both sown in May), were also extensively grown. Flaxen linen for board-cloths, sheets, shirts or smocks, and towels, as the napkins were called on which, before the use of forks, the hands were wiped, was only used in the houses of the rich and on special occasions. Hemp in ordinary households supplied the same and other necessary articles, such as candle-wicks (*2 Hen. VI*, IV. vii. 94), in coarser materials. Shoe-thread, halters, stirrup-thongs, girths, and ropes were woven from the 'carle' hemp: the finer kind, or 'fimble' hemp, supplied the coarse linen for domestic use, and 'hempen homespun' (*Mid. N. D.* III. i. 82) passes into a proverb for a countryman. Nettles were also extensively used in the manufacture of linen, and nettle sheets and table-cloths were to be found in many homes at the end of the eighteenth century.

To the live-stock of a common-field farm little or no attention could be paid. The scab was rarely absent from the common-fold, or the rot from the ill-drained land. No individual owner could improve his live-stock, when all cattle and sheep of the village grazed promiscuously on the commons. Local breeds were numerous and capable of development; but under the haphazard mating of nobody's son with everybody's daughter they were dwindling in size and quality. Then as now cows were kept for milk and pigs for bacon. But the cow, a smaller animal than modern science and feeding have made her, was scarcely worth more than half the price of an ox, and, according to Tusser, was less profitable than a sow. Dairy produce was increased from another source. Ewes were often milked, and six ewes gave the yield of one cow. Other animals were valued for different purposes then than at the present day. Oxen were judged by their power of draught and not by their fattening precocity. Sheep were prized for their fleeces and their leather, not for their mutton. Farmers in Elizabethan times took their seats on the wool-sack, and the wool of the Ryelands and Cotswold sheep (shorn in June) commanded the highest prices. It would be useless to attempt to do the Clown's sum—' fifteen hundred shorn, what comes the wool to ? ' (*Wint. Tale* IV. ii. 34–5). But according to a contemporary estimate (1602) a wether weighed from 40 lb. to 60 lb. ; the fleece weighed from 4 lb. to 6 lb., and wool was worth about twelve pence a pound.[1] Valued for such objects, no true standard of shape, from a grazier's point of view, was recognized in cattle or sheep. Large bones and frames were prized, and long legs were necessary in animals which wandered miles in search of food.

Except in a salted state, little meat was eaten. The rule of eating fish twice a week was continued by Elizabeth from Catholic times, and a third day was added from motives of ' civile policy '. ' Accounting the Lent Season, and all fasting daies in the yeare together with Wednesday and Friday and Saturday, you shall see that the one-halfe of the yeare is ordeined to eate fish in.' [2] Strictly speaking, therefore, fresh fish, or salted fish bought at the August fairs and stored, was eaten three days in the week. At Easter, so Tusser tells us, veal and bacon were in season, and John the Baptist's Day (June 24) was the time for ' grasse beef and pease ', probably because the pastures were at that time at the height of their feeding capacity. Half-starved in winter, and tortured, as Shakespeare observes, by the ' breese ' (*Troilus* I. iii. 48 ; *Ant. & Cleop.* III. viii. 24), or gadfly, in summer, cattle had little flesh on their bones except in early autumn. Then they had had the aftermath of the mowing meadows and the eddish of the stubble. Cattle were therefore slaughtered at Martinmas (November 11), and the beef, salted and smoke-dried in the

---

[1] Cf. p. 329 for another estimate.
[2] Cogan, *Haven of Helthe*, ed. 1612, p. 138.

chimney, was preserved for winter use. For the same reason pigs were in best condition when they had fattened on the shack of the corn, the acorns, and the beech-mast, and were killed from Hallowmas (November 1) up to Candlemas. Very little of the animal, however, was eaten fresh; only the 'souse' fell to the lot of the 'lower messes' (*Wint. Tale* I. ii. 227), and the greater part was salted for winter consumption. It was at Michaelmas also that the 'crones' (that is, sheep whose teeth were too worn to feed on the sheep walks), bought in August and fattened, were killed and eaten.

Numerous feast-days varied the Spartan fare of the agricultural population. Such violent alternations were characteristic of the lives of our ancestors. As in farming routine excessive cropping alternated with fallows, so, in the consumption of food, feasting trod on the heels of famine. The festivities of Christmas were carried on to Twelfth Night, and ceased only at the dawn of Distaff's Day (January 7). Plough Monday followed on the first Monday after the 6th. Lent was ushered in by 'Merry Shrovetide', by 'Collop' Monday and 'Pancake' Tuesday. 'May Day morrises', 'Whitsun Pastorals', 'Church Ales', and the wake or feast-day kept on the day of the patron saint of the parish church, were occasions for better fare. Sheep-shearing, harvest home at the end of the corn harvest, the 'seed cake' at the end of the wheat sowing, were rural feasts, and to Shakespeare's mind the prodigious plenty of Martlemas suggested Falstaff in its proportions (*2 Hen. IV*, II. ii. 112). But in everyday life, till after the middle of the sixteenth century, white-meat, by which was meant milk, butter, eggs, and cheese, was the staple food of all classes in country districts. The importance of cheese-making is shown by Tusser's frequent references to the subject. 'Now what cheese is well made or otherwise', says Cogan, 'may partly be perceived by this old Latine verse:

Non nix, non Argos, Methusalem, Magdaleneve,
Esaus, non Lazarus, caseus ille bonus.

That is to say, Cheese should not be white as Snowe is, nor full of eyes as Argos was, nor old as Methusalem was, nor full of whey or weeping as Mary Magdalen was, nor rough as Esau was, nor full of spots as Lazarus.' According to the same authority, Banbury cheese was the best. But he admits that some preferred 'Cheshire cheese made about

Nantwich '.   Banbury cheese is the only sort mentioned by
Shakespeare, though it is used as a term of contempt when
applied by Bardolph to Slender (*M. Wives* I. i. 133).   The
choice of the best kind of cheese as an opprobrious epithet
suggests the fact noticed by Harrison that white-meat was
beginning to be regarded as 'appertinent onelie to the
inferior sort', in spite of its great rise in price, and that
the more wealthy had begun to feed on flesh and fowl.
The increased demand for butcher's meat and the high
prices of dairy produce probably strengthened the tendency
towards separate enclosed holdings.   It was only on 'several',
not on 'champion', land that beasts were fattened

> at a stall,
> The better cherish'd still the nearer death.
>
> (*1 Hen. IV*, v. ii. 14–15)

It was no partner in a village farm who could say with
Gremio :

> I have a hundred milch-kine to the pail,
> Six score fat oxen standing in my stalls.
>
> (*Tam. Sh.* II. i. 351–2)

If village farmers had been obliged to buy the necessaries
of life or of their profession, they would have been forced
to farm for profit and sell their produce.   But their industry
was singularly self-sufficing.   Even rent was sometimes
paid in corn, though much to the disadvantage of the
tenants.   Harrison describes how one quarter in ten was
lost through 'the iniquitie of the bushell', how the receivers
complained of the 'goodnesse and cleannesse of the graine'
unless 'some peece of monie' passed into their purses ;
how, if the market price of corn fell below the rate allowed
for it in their rent, they were obliged to pay money.   Except
for the payment of rent, it is surprising how little coin was
used or needed in rural districts.   Parishes were isolated and
self-supporting.   Between large towns good highways existed :
but off the main lines wheeled carriages were rarely used ;
the drift-lanes, which led from the village to the cultivated
land, ceased when the bounds of the parish were reached,
and could only be called roads by an improbable courtesy.
The inhabitants had little need of communication with their
neighbours, still less with the outside world.   The fields and
the live-stock provided their necessary food and clothing.
Whatever wood was required for building, fencing, and

fuel was supplied from the wastes. Each village had its mill, and nearly every house had its oven and brewing kettle. Women spun wool into coarse cloth, and hemp into linen ; men tanned their own leather. The rough tools required for cultivation of the soil, and the rude household utensils needed for the comforts of daily life, were made at home. In the long winter evenings, farmers, their sons, and their servants carved the wooden spoons, the platters, and the beechen bowls, though Harrison notices the increased use of pewter among the farming aristocracy. They fitted and riveted the bottoms to the horn mugs, or closed, in coarse fashion, the leaks in the leathern jugs. They plaited the osiers and reeds into baskets and into ' weeles ' for catching fish ; they fixed handles to the scythes, rakes, and other tools ; cut the flails from holly or thorn, and fastened them with thongs to the staves ; shaped the teeth for rakes and harrows from ash or willow, and hardened them in the fire ; cut out the wooden shovels for casting the corn in the granary ; fashioned ox yokes and bows, forks, racks, and rack-staves : twisted willows into scythe-cradles, or into traces and other harness gear. Travelling carpenters, smiths, and tinkers visited farmhouses and remoter villages at rare intervals to perform those parts of the work which needed their professional skill. But every village of any size found employment for such trades as those of the smith and the carpenter, and the frequency with which ' Smiths Ham ' appears among field names suggests the value which the inhabitants attached to the forge and the anvil. Meanwhile the women plaited straw or reeds for neck-collars, stitched and stuffed sheepskin bags for cart-saddles, peeled rushes for wicks and made candles. Thread was made from nettles. Spinning wheels, distaffs, and needles were never idle. Home-made cloth and linen supplied all wants. The formation of words like spinster, webster, lyster, shepster, maltster, brewster, and baxter, indicated that the occupations were feminine, and show that women spun, wove, dyed and cut out the cloth, as well as malted the barley, brewed the ale, and baked the bread for the family.

Evidence is not wanting that, in the early part of the sixteenth century, the general level of arable farming had deteriorated. The monks, who had been the pioneers of agricultural improvement, were gone. Lay landlords had reduced their great households, and no longer needed so large a supply of agricultural produce ; they had withdrawn their own holdings from the village farm and let them as separate farms ; they had encouraged the more enterprising of the common-field farmers to consolidate, enclose, and rent their scattered strips as separate occupations ; they had cut up their own demesnes into smaller tenancies. They were therefore less directly and personally interested in maintaining the standard of farming. The strict supervision which their reeve had exercised was a thing of the past. He had enforced a proper rotation of crops ; even if he did not always sow the seed with his own hand, he had carefully regulated the quantity sown, taken care that the heaviest grain was used, and insisted that every second or third year vale corn was exchanged for upland corn and *vice versâ*. Now, left to their own devices, farmers impoverished the land by taking too many grain crops in succession ; the skuttle, or casting shovel, lay disused in the granary ; weeds were too often sown with the grain ; or the corn was too thinly scattered to check the growth of weeds. The crowd of 'sarclers', or weeders, armed with weed-hook, knife, and glove, who mustered in early June on the lord's demesne, no longer assembled to do their labour services. Much of the arable land was crowded

with rank fumiter and furrow weeds,
With burdocks, hemlock, nettles, cuckoo-flowers,
Darnel, and all the idle weeds that grow
In our sustaining corn.   (*Lear* IV. iv. 3–6)

Except by fallowing, 'un véritable Dimanche accordé à la terre', little was done to restore fertility. The value of 'compas' or manure was imperfectly understood. Everywhere the 'gilded puddle' (*Ant. & Cleop.* I. iv. 62), of which Shakespeare speaks, told its tale of wasted wealth. On many farms the dung was collected, dried, and consumed as fuel. Straw, often burned on the ground (*Tit. Andr.* II. iii. 123), or ploughed in, was chiefly used as winter food for cattle ; but its value as bedding, to be thrown in the yards and eventually become farmyard manure, was beginning to be understood, if only as litter for men and pigs. 'Wast thou fain, poor father,' asks Cordelia,

To hovel thee with swine and rogues forlorn,
In short and musty straw ?   (*Lear* IV. vii. 39–40)

Many of these defects were not peculiar to village farms. But it is not the least of the charges which may be brought by practical agriculturists against the common-field system that it discouraged and impeded the liberal use of manure. The droppings of the cattle were wasted over too large an area, and the labour of each individual was quadrupled in carting the dung on to his scattered strips. Fitzherbert (1523-5) notices that many useful practices, known to a previous generation, like that of marling, had been discontinued ; that husbandry had grown more slovenly ; and that the yield of the land per acre was smaller. In the same direction point Tusser's warnings (1573) against the barbarous cropping practised by 'champion', that is, common-field, farmers. Shakespeare was probably not drawing entirely from imagination, but in a great measure from his own observation of actual conditions in England, when he painted the war-wasted fields of France :

> her fallow leas
> The darnel, hemlock and rank fumitory
> Doth root upon, while that the coulter rusts
> That should deracinate such savagery ;
> The even mead, that erst brought sweetly forth
> The freckled cowslip, burnet, and green clover,
> Wanting the scythe, all uncorrected, rank,
> Conceives by idleness, and nothing teems
> But hateful docks, rough thistles, kecksies, burs,
> Losing both beauty and utility.   (*Hen. V*, v. ii. 44-53)

Some of the practical defects of village farms have already been noticed, though these were less apparent than they afterwards became with the rapid progress of agricultural skill and resources. The most enterprising farmer on enclosed land then embarked no capital in improved breeds of live-stock, knew nothing of winter crops, was ignorant of the science of drainage, and commanded no chemical aids to fertility. Here, therefore, in Elizabethan times the country suffered no great economic loss from the prevalence of village farms. But some of the disadvantages of the older system were already obvious. Unless the whole body of partners agreed together, no individual could swerve a hairbreadth from the routine of the association. The apathy of one man might ruin the enterprise of twenty. Land was wasted in innumerable footpaths and balks. Farmers spent their whole day in visiting the different parcels of which their holdings were composed, and their labour of manuring, reaping, and carting was indefinitely increased by the remoteness of their scattered strips. Systematic drainage was difficult, for if one man drained his land or scoured his courses, his neighbour might choke his outfall. The land was often, therefore, pitted with wet places, and overrun with rushes. Clean farming was discouraged when the occupier of the next strip might be a sloven. Disputes and litigation were perpetual when it was easy to poach land by a turn of the plough, or filch another man's crops when reaping. Agricultural writers of the day agree that enclosed land was more profitable to the tenant than a holding in a common-field farm. Fitz-herbert argues strenuously in favour of enclosure. Tusser states that there is more profit in one acre of 'several' land than in three of 'champion'. 'W. S. Gentleman', in his *Examination of Complaints* (1581), says : ' Experience showeth that Tenaunts in common be not so good husbandes, as when every man hath his parte in severalty.' The early prevalence of enclosures in Kent had made the wealth of its farmers proverbial, and it was not rare for ' a franklin in the wild of Kent ' to be a rich prize to highway robbers. Such evidence might be multiplied. Already there is that strong antagonism between the economic and the social advantages of the system, which at the end of the eighteenth century and the beginning of the nineteenth eventually destroyed the old village farms. It is beyond dispute that economically common-fields were unsound ; it can scarcely be denied that socially they kept the men on the land, and saved their occupiers from the worst hardships of the agricultural revolution of the sixteenth century. It was on the tenant of the enclosed land that the storm fell with the greatest severity; the village partners, there is reason to believe, escaped comparatively free.

The agricultural changes which the sixteenth century witnessed were due partly to causes already at work, partly to the introduction of a new spirit. The Black Death, as has already been said, had led to a considerable increase in the number of free tenants, renting separate enclosed holdings. The long series of labour statutes, beginning with the reign of Edward III and continuing into that of Elizabeth, not only testify to the break-up of the old manorial system, but had assisted its progress. The local dependence of villeins on their feudal lord was weakened. Their rates of wages were to be fixed by Justices of the Peace, and they were emancipated from his exclusive right to their agricultural services. The way was thus paved for the creation of a free labouring class—free, that is, to sell their labour in the open market. The break-up of the old manorial system was further accelerated by the introduction of a new spirit. Feudalism had burnt itself out in the Wars of the Roses, and from its ashes rose a new social structure, based on trade and the influence of the middle classes. Land was regarded as an instrument less of power than of wealth. To the mediaeval baron the value of an estate lay in the number of retainers it sent to his banner ; to the Tudor landlord it consisted in the amount of revenue it paid into his pocket. Fresh incentives stimulated individual enterprise ; new markets sprang up for agricultural produce. Mediaeval farmers had been, for the most part, satisfied to raise the food they themselves required ; Tudor rent-paying tenants farmed rather for profit than for their own food. Both the old and the new movement tended in the same direction. But the new influences extended into districts which the Black Death or the Statutes of Labourers had left comparatively unaffected.

Lancastrian legislation had given an artificial stimulus to corn-growing by laws regulating the export and import of grain according to a sliding scale. This policy was now reversed. The trading classes demanded cheap provisions and a cheap supply of raw material. Violent fluctuations in the price of corn made its cultivation a risky trade, as the area under corn alternately contracted or expanded, to the loss now of the consumer, now of the producer. The new landlords needed a smaller supply of food from their estates, when feudal households and monastic institutions, with their lavish hospitality, were either reduced or secularized. They were therefore the more ready to make their land pay by other means. From a practical point of view, wool enjoyed advantages over other forms of agricultural produce. It was more durable, and therefore could be more easily held over for better prices ; it was also more easily transported on the pack-saddle, a consideration of serious importance when roads were always bad and often impassable for wheeled traffic. Since 1464 the importation of manufactured woollen goods from Flanders had been prohibited, and there was a steady demand for English wool, though prices do not seem to have risen till the second half of the sixteenth century. Thus commercial reasons prompted the development of pasture farming, and, in the damper climates, encouraged the adoption of a convertible husbandry which could readily adjust itself to changing needs.

To meet these new requirements landlords sought the command of larger areas of land, and they obtained it by evictions and enclosures. Numbers of small farmers, cottiers, and rural handicraftsmen lost their hold upon the land; others found themselves unable to subsist when their harvest earnings were cut off and their commons restricted. Numerous farm-servants, who boarded in the farmhouses and performed the regular work of the farm, lost their employment. Their ranks were swelled by the discharge of feudal retainers and monastic dependants. The effect on the rural population was deplorable. Historians like Bacon, thinkers like Sir Thomas More, agriculturists like Fitzherbert, preachers like Latimer or Tyndale, satirists like Stubbes, ballad-writers and pamphleteers by the score, lament the consequences of the change. Statute after statute endeavoured to control the tendency and limit the development of large farms. On the other hand, no practical statesman or farmer could deny that consolidation meant progress. The problem which Henry VII had to solve was the exact compromise between agricultural advance and social welfare. He and his successors tried to draw the line at the point where progress caused rural depopulation. To a great extent their efforts failed. Still the process continued. Villages were pulled down; ploughlands which had supported twenty men and their teams were turned into pasture where the shepherd was the only sign of human life. Goaded by hunger, the people rose in repeated insurrection. Two years before the close of the sixteenth century the bitterness of feeling is cradled into rude verse:

> Sheep have eat up our Meadows and our Downs,
> Our Corn, our Woods, whole Villages and Towns;
> Yea, they have eat up many wealthy Men,
> Besides Widowes and Orphane Children;

Besides our Statutes and our Iron Lawes,
Which they swallowed down into their Mawes ;—
Till now I thought the Proverbe did but jest
Which said a black Sheep was a biting beast.

The mass of legislation which endeavoured to check the conversion of pasture into tillage shows that the usual methods by which enclosure was effected were within the limits of the existing law. The Government tried its best to create new offences by new Statutes, and the novelty of the experiment partially explains the ease with which the new legislation was set aside. Landlords acted within their strict legal rights in evicting from the demesne, when occasion offered, tenants at will, or for terms of years, or for lives ; or, if any of their land lay within the common-fields, in withdrawing them at will from the association, or in effecting an agreement by which all the partners divided the commons and consolidated their scattered holdings in separate farms ; or by enclosing the wastes which had never been arable, if those who claimed rights of common claimed them as tenants of their land ; or in overstocking their commons with their own sheep to the exclusion or injury of other commoners ; or in refusing to renew copyholds which were not hereditary, and, where the renewal fine was not fixed, in demanding a prohibitory sum. Nor, again, is it certain that the new landlords of monastic lands were not justified by law in their contention, that, with the rights of the church, were extinguished all the customary rights of copyholders and tenants. The size of the area which this interpretation of the law placed at their disposal may be estimated when it is remembered that one-fifth of the cultivated land is said to have been held by monastic institutions. In many cases also the land was doubtless cleared by force, or fear, or fraud :

Good Landlord, who findeth, is blessed of God,
A cumbersome Landlord is husbandman's rod.

So says Tusser, speaking from his experience. Spread over England there must have been many lawyers like ' John of Ludlow alias Mason ' of Essex, who, in Harrison's opinion, excelled all others of his profession in shaving the beard of the tenant.

Whether Shakespeare regarded the victims with any sympathy is a question which cannot be answered from the plays. It would be fanciful to find an allusion to the break-up of the feudal system and the enforcement of legal rights over land in Gaunt's lament over England ' leas'd out '—

> Like to a tenement, or pelting farm ;
> . . . bound in with shame,
> With inky blots, and rotten parchment bonds.
>
> *(Rich. II*, II. i. 60–4)

No argument can be based on his reference to the Duke of Suffolk's ' enclosing the commons of Melford ' (*2 Hen. VI*, I. iii. 23–5) as one of the grievances which stirred Jack Cade to rebellion, though enclosures were not among the complaints of Cade and were, on the other hand, in the forefront among the causes of the insurrection of Kett (1549). Nothing more definite can be inferred, though the lines are appropriate enough to the circumstances of his time, from the lament of the shepherd :

> But I am shepherd to another man,
> And do not shear the fleeces that I graze :
> My master is of churlish disposition
> And little recks to find the way to heaven
> By doing deeds of hospitality. (*A. Y. L.* II. iv. 79–83)

But when we pass from the movement itself to some of its effects, the references are clear enough. The mass of ' vagrom men ' was a real social danger, which, in the sixteenth century, exercised the wits of wiser men than Dogberry. All the fifteen characters enumerated by Harman in *A Caveat or Warening for Commen Cursetors, vulgarely called Vagabones* (1567) are not depicted. But several of the types of beggars in Harman's pages or in Awdelay's *Fraternitye of Vacabondes* (1565) reappear in Shakespeare. There is Harman's ' Rufflar ', ' the worthiest of this unruly rabblement ',

> fit to bandy with thy lawless sons,
> To ruffle in the commonwealth of Rome.
>
> (*Tit. Andr.* I. i. 312–3)

There is the ' pedlar ', the aristocracy of the profession, a clever, plausible rascal like Autolycus. ' The droncken tyncker ' is represented by Christopher Sly—' by birth a pedlar . . . by present profession a tinker '—drunk on the heath, and in debt for ale to Marian Hacket (*Tam. Sh.* Ind. ii. 19–22). There is the ' prygger ', or ' prygman ', who 'haunts wakes, fairs, and bear-baitings' (*Wint. Tale* IV. ii. 109). There is 'chop-logyke', who gives 'xx wordes for one', to whom Capulet likens his daughter Juliet (*Rom. & Jul.* III. v. 150). There is Harman's 'Rogue', or 'Wild Rogue', in the 'rogue forlorn' who shares the hovel and the straw with King Lear and the swine (*Lear* IV. vii. 39). Edgar, disguised as a madman and calling himself 'poor Tom' (*Lear* III. iv. 37), is Awdelay's 'Abraham man', who 'walketh bare armed and bare legged, and fayneth hymselfe mad, and . . . nameth himselfe "poore Tom"'. 'Whipped from tithing to tithing', he had only received the punishment to which an Elizabethan Statute (39 Eliz. c. 4) sentenced 'all fencers, bearwards, common players, and minstrels ; all jugglers, tinkers and petty chapmen', and other vagrants who were adjudged to be rogues, vagabonds, and sturdy beggars.

Of all the contemporary treatises which deal with the subject of Tudor enclosures, the most remarkable is *A compendious or briefe examination of certayne ordinary complaints, of divers of our country men in these our dayes*, by 'W. S. Gentleman', published in 1581, though probably written at an earlier date. The authorship is disputed, though it has been attributed, on the initials only, to William Shakespeare as well as to William Smith and William Stafford. Most probably the treatise was written by John Hales. In form the work is a discussion between a Merchantman, a Knight, and a Husbandman, with a summary of results and a suggestion of remedies by a Doctor. 'Many of us', says the husbandman, 'saw long ago that our profit was but small by the plough and therefore divers of my neighbours that had in time past some two, some three, some four ploughs of their own have laid down some of them part and some of them all their teams, and turned either part or all of their arable land to pasture; and thereby have waxed very rich men. And every day some of us encloseth some part of his ground to pasture, and *were it not that our ground lieth in the common-fields intermingled one with another, I think also our fields had been enclosed of common agreement of all the township long or this time.*' The italicized passage is important. It confirms the view, already stated, that common-field farms weathered the storm, and were not, as some historians have

W. Sempson fecit

The Second booke of Flowers Fruicts Beasties
Birds and Flies exactly drawne

And are to bee sold by George Humble
at ye white horse in Popes head Ally

argued, swept away by the Tudor enclosures.   Their number was probably diminished : but in the eighteenth century more than half the arable land of England was still cultivated on this ancient system.

The difficulty of breaking up a common-field, except by mutual agreement, is forcibly illustrated by the story of the Welcombe common-fields at Stratford-on-Avon, a story in which Shakespeare was a considerable figure, though the part which he actually played is somewhat obscure.

In 1614 William Combe, of Stratford-on-Avon, tenant under the Crown of the College, wished to withdraw his arable land from the common-field farm of Welcombe, enclose it, and lay it down to pasture.   He also wished to enclose so much of the ancient greensward or pasture as his rights of pasturage represented.   To his scheme he had obtained the consent of Lord Chancellor Ellesmere, as representative of the Crown, and the active co-operation of the Chancellor's steward.   Shakespeare, however, was in a position to be a formidable opponent, for he not only owned land adjoining, but also held the unexpired term of a lease of half the tithes of the common-fields.   But a deed, dated October 28, 1614, secured him from any loss of tithe through the conversion of tillage into pasture, and his consent was obtained.   Combe had now only to deal with the Corporation of Stratford, who offered a strenuous resistance.   Strong language did not move them ; in the Corporation MS. the witnesses are duly noted who heard him call them ' Purtan knaves ', ' doggs and curres '. Tempting offers were refused, though Combe proposed to compensate them in more than the value of the tithe, to undertake the perpetual repair of the highways passing over the land, and to increase the value of the rights of freeholders and tenants by waiving part of his claim to turn out sheep and cattle on the commons.   Then Combe took matters into his own hands and prepared to enclose his land by surrounding it with a ditch.   This brought the dispute to a crisis.   Not, apparently, without the knowledge of the Town Clerk, the townspeople filled it in.   A breach of the peace seemed imminent.   The matter was, therefore, referred to the law-courts, and at Warwick Assizes, on March 27, 1615, Lord Chief Justice Coke made an order that 'noe inclosure shalbe made within the parish of Stratforde'. The Dingles, which formed part of the common-fields of Welcombe, remain unenclosed to this day.

BIBLIOGRAPHY.—The principal contemporary authorities are : JOHN FITZ-HERBERT's *The Boke of Husbandrie*, 1523, and *The Boke of Surveyinge and Improvements*, 1523, ed. for English Dialect Society, 1870; ANDREW BOORDE's *Fyrst Boke of the Introduction of Knowledge, Dyetary*, and *Breuyary of Health* (1542-7), Early English Text Society, 1870; JOHN AWDELAY's *The Fraternitye of Vacabondes*, 1561, and THOMAS HARMAN's *A Caueat . . . for Commen Cursetors*, &c., 1567, E.E.T.S., 1869; THOMAS BLUNDEVILLE's *The fower Chiefyst Offices belonging to Horsmanshippe*, &c., 1565-6; THOMAS TUSSER's *Five hundredth Pointes of good Husbandry*, 1573, English Dialect Society, 1878; WILLIAM HARRISON's *A Description of England* (1577-87), ed. for New Shakspere Society, 1877; W. S. [John Hales of Coventry ?], *A Discourse of the Common Weal*, 1581, ed. E. Lamond, 1893 ; THOMAS COGAN's *The Haven of Helthe*, 1584 ; GERVASE MARKHAM's *The English Husbandman*, &c., 1613, *Farewell to Husbandry*, 1620, *The whole Art of Husbandry, by C. Heresbach*, translated by B. Googe, enlarged by Gervase Markham, 1631 ; Sir RICHARD WESTON's *A Discourse of Husbandrie used in Brabant and Flanders* (ed. Samuel Hartlib), 1650.

Among modern books the following should be consulted: C. ROACH SMITH's *The Rural Life of Shakespeare*, 2nd ed., 1874; J. E. THOROLD ROGERS's *History of Agriculture and Prices in England* (1259-1582), 4 vols., 1866-82 ; FREDERICK SEEBOHM's *The English Village Community*, 1883; C. M. INGLEBY's *Shakespeare and the Enclosure of Common Fields at Welcombe*, &c., 1885 ; T. E. SCRUTTON's *Commons and Common Fields*, 1887; D. H. MADDEN's *The Diary of Master William Silence*, 1897 ; Sir WALTER GILBEY's *The Great Horse; or the war-horse till its development into the shire horse*, 1899 ; W. HASBACH's *A History of the English Agricultural Labourer*, translated from the German by Ruth Kenyon, 1908.

§ 2. GARDENING

Gardening in the time of Shakespeare is a title which covers much ground and opens up many tempting by-paths. Here the subject will be treated under the three headings of the orchard, the kitchen-garden, and the flower-garden. When all medicine was herbal, and mostly home-made, and when meat was rarely eaten except in salted form, the cultivation of herbs, vegetables, and fruit for physic or for food had always been a necessity of existence. But flower-gardens were a new luxury rendered possible in Tudor times by new conditions of wealth and security. Thus for orchards and kitchen-gardens the question to be asked is, what was the progress made during the Elizabethan period ; while for flower-gardens the question rather is, what was the special form in which they were introduced by Tudor gardeners.

Shakespeare's plays show, incidentally and unintentionally, that he was a lover of sport and an observer of country life.

In the same natural fashion they also prove that he loved flowers, and noted, with watchful eyes, the plants and trees with which an Englishman, in the days of Elizabeth, would be familiar in English woods, hedgerows, orchards, and gardens. He who could write

> the ripest mulberry
> That will not hold the handling   (*Cor.* III. ii. 79–80)

knew the fruit well. There was, therefore, no confusion in his mind between two different kinds of fruits when he embroidered Desdemona's handkerchief with strawberries (*Oth.* III. iii. 435) instead of with the three mulberries of Otello el Moro. He makes no effort to describe gardens; he does not pretend to be a botanist; he decorates his verse with little or none of the artificialities of classical allusion. Every reference to a flower arises in a natural way out of the subject which he is treating, and the simple force of the true epithet gives his slightest pictures the vividness and reality of those which are directly drawn from outdoor life. Passages might, indeed, be quoted to show that he had a practical knowledge of the gardener's art, that he was no novice with the pruning-knife (*Rich. II*, III. iv. 29), and that he had mastered the different ways of propagating plants by grafts and slips, and artificial impregnation (*Wint. Tale* IV. iii. 85; *Hen. V*, III. v. 5). But the proof that Shakespeare was a lover of gardens is to be drawn rather from the general impression left by the plays than from any instances of professional knowledge.

Many of the periods of history which are fullest of romance and meaning are also the periods when gardening, like other arts, has been most interesting and significant. It is certainly true of Shakespeare's time. Full and crowded as was the Elizabethan age, it yet found space, not only to develop the art of gardening, but to lay out gardens. Adventurers, mariners, and merchants brought back new plants. Protestant refugees introduced improved methods of cultivation from the Continent. The literature of the garden grew rich. Nurseries were established. Gardening became a pursuit of sovereigns like Elizabeth, philosophers like Bacon, statesmen like Burghley and Walsingham. Throughout the country magnificent houses were built by architects of genius, who themselves planned the pleasure grounds, where they translated the ideas of the Italian Renaissance into English forms moulded on English patterns. No longer planted only for practical purposes, gardens were designed also to enhance the beauty and enjoyments of the home, and to minister to every social pleasure of domestic life.

The love of flowers is old as time and universal as the elements. In mediaeval England it had shown itself in the use of flowers in Church services, in monastic legends, in early garden literature, in the poetry of Chaucer. The taste was there; it wanted only the opportunity, which the wars and tumults of the Middle Ages denied. Feudal strongholds, standing on sites chosen for strategic strength, offered little scope for gardeners within or without their battlements. Kings might lay out bowers and mazes at Woodstock or at Windsor; collegiate students might plan pleasure-grounds in which their 'retired leisure' might take delight; and dwellers in cities might follow in comparative security the peaceful pursuit of rearing fruit and flowers, as in the Bishop of Ely's garden at Holborn, famous for its roses, its saffron crocuses, and its strawberries. But it was mainly in the fertile valleys where the inmates of monastery and convent felt the need for gardens, and by their skill supplied the want, that the art of horticulture, as well ornamental as practical, was studied and advanced. Now, with the downfall of feudalism, the increase of wealth, and the establishment of more settled government, dawned a different era.

In Tudor times the flower-garden assumed a new importance. Hitherto, except as an adjunct to royal palaces, great houses, or cloisters, it had counted for little as compared with the fruit and kitchen garden. The change came slowly. Tusser, writing in 1575 for mistresses of manor-houses and farm-houses, has nothing to say on flower-gardens. Among 'seedes and herbes for the kitchen' he gives marigolds, primroses, and violets; he includes violets among the 'herbes and rootes for sallets'; he mentions the plants most suitable for 'strewing'; but his only flower-garden is that which can be made in windows and in 'pots'. It had become the custom to strew the floor with sweet-scented flowers and herbs as well as rushes, to appropriate particular kinds, like rue and rosemary, to special occasions, to gather flowers and place them in 'pots', or vases, for domestic decoration, and to grow them in rooms and in window-boxes.

But there is a changed world of meaning in Parkinson's advice to banish the kitchen-garden from the front to the side of the house, ' for the many different sents that arise from the herbes, as cabbages, onions, &c., are scarce well-pleasing to perfume the lodgings of any house'. This pro-motion of the flower-garden to the pride of place is the great gardening innovation of the period. Arranged in the dis-tinctive style of the Elizabethans, it occupied the central position in full view of the house, and on either side were placed the orchard and the kitchen-garden.

Side-gates led from the enclosure of the formal flower-garden into the orchard and the kitchen-garden. If there was a vineyard—and under both the Tudors and the Stuarts attempts were made to revive the culture of the vine— Barnaby Googe advises that it should be on the western side. Shakespeare expresses the same opinion (*Meas. for M.* IV. i. 31). But an orchard seems to have been generally placed on the north-east, because of the shelter its trees afforded to the flowers : ' it standeth north-north-east . . . from thy curious-knotted garden' (*Love's L. L.* I. i. 246–8). In small manor-houses and farm-houses the orchard served the purpose both of pleasure-garden and fruit-garden. Lawson (*A New Orchard*, 1618) says that its ' principal end ' is ' the honest delight of one wearied with the workes of his lawful calling ', and finds that it removes ' the tediousness and heavie load of three or four score years '. The orchard had this double use in Shakespeare's time. Here covered alleys were formed from the arches of pleached cherry or apple trees (*Much Ado* I. ii. 11), and for dryness the paths beneath were paved with gravel, sand, or, in humbler gardens, with sawdust, ashes, or brickdust. Here also were arbours, like that to which Justice Shallow invited Falstaff.

The range of fruit which was grown differed little from that of the present day. Modern observers would probably have been most struck by the fact that scarcely any trees were trained against the walls. This practice was as yet a novelty, and did not become at all common till the seventeenth century. Even apricots were grown only as standards ; otherwise Shakespeare's epithet of ' dangling ' (*Rich. II*, III. iv. 29) would have been misplaced. ' Our orchards', writes Holinshed, ' were never furnished with such good fruit nor with such varietie as at the present.' In Shakespeare's plays are mentioned apples, pears, plums, medlars, mulberries, quinces, apricots, pomegranates, and almonds, ' purple ' figs and ' rubied ' cherries, walnuts, chestnuts, hazel nuts, and ' clustering ' filberts, strawberries and gooseberries, as well as blackberries, dewberries, and ' blue ' bilberries. Though peaches came into England with the Romans, he does not refer to the peach except as a colour. Of comparatively recent introduction were apricots, almonds, gooseberries, raspberries, melons, and currants, which only appeared in English gardens in Tudor times. Shakespeare does not mention either melons or raspberries, though the latter appear in Tusser's poems as ' respes ', and ' respies '. He makes no reference to currants except to the dried imported fruit. Both orange and lemon trees were brought to England before the close of the century. But though the fruit of both is mentioned by Shakespeare, it is not likely that he saw either of them growing on the tree.

The different sorts of pears and apples were already too numerous to be counted by Elizabethan gardeners. To attempt to enumerate them would be to ' send an owle to Athens, or to number those things that are without number '. Only two varieties of pear are mentioned by Shakespeare, the Poperin pear (*Rom. & Jul.* II. i. 38), of which there was a summer as well as a winter sort, and the Warden pear (*Wint. Tale* IV. ii. 49) (so called after the Cistercian Abbey of Warden in Bedfordshire), which seems to have become a generic name for stewing pears. That Shakespeare's ' warden pies ' were made of this well-known pear seems to be accepted as certain. But there were also Warden apples. Andrew Boorde in his *Dyetary* recommends ' Warden appulles rosted, stued, or baken ' as ' nutrytyue ', and also, baked or stewed, as a remedy for the Pestilence. If the invalid could not get the Warden apple, he might ' eate stued or baken peers, with comfettes '. Pears in a pie are, to our ideas, less familiar than apples. But lovers of apples need not grudge the pear the possible reference, since the apple is much more often and less contemptuously mentioned. One forgotten use of the fruit is not referred to by Shakespeare. Mixed with hog's lard and rosemary, the pulp made pomatum. The reference which he most frequently makes is to an apple that now is rarely seen except in preserves. Crabs, roasted, and hissing in a Christmas bowl of ale, or, in spite of their sourness (*Tam. Sh.* II. i. 228), eaten raw, were popular favourites. He also speaks of Pomewaters, Bitter Sweetings, Golden and Easter Pippins, and Leathercoats. In picking and storing apples the utmost care was taken : it was a ' last year's ' pippin that Justice Shallow set before his guest (*2 Hen. IV*, v. iii. 2). Between the bush fruit-trees and the paths it was the practice to ' powder ' the ground with strawberries. Strawberries thrive well, says Tusser, under gooseberry, raspberry, and rose bushes. These were then almost always raised from the wild strawberry. Tusser advises his housewife to choose her roots where she found them growing under the thorn-trees in the woods, to set them in a garden plot in September, and in December to cover them with straw. In *Henry V* (I. i. 60–6) the Bishop of Ely compares the luxuriant growth of the young King's virtues under the shadow of his youthful vices to the strawberry thriving under the nettle. The comparison is apt enough on the lips of a celebrated strawberry-grower, and the strawberry's independence has pointed the teaching of other moralists. Elizabethan gardeners believed that a plant derived from its neighbours the good or evil qualities they possessed : but the strawberry was an exception. Although it crept along the ground exposed to every sort of contamination, yet no evil companionship could taint its purity.

Banished out of the sight of great houses, the kitchen-garden was by no means forgotten. If Holinshed can be believed, the raising of vegetable produce had been neglected since the early years of the fourteenth century, and had only revived since Elizabeth's father had ascended the throne. Such evidence as exists does not confirm so extreme a statement, which may be the flattery of a courtly historian. But great progress had undoubtedly been made in the early years of the century. The modern observer in the Elizabethan kitchen-garden would probably have been most struck by the absence of glass, by the different proportions in which the vegetables were grown, and by the preponderance of medicinal herbs. In 1580 he might have found there artichokes, cabbages, turnips, broad beans, 'Rounceval' peas, pumpkins, cucumbers, skirrets, radishes, carrots, parsnips, onions, garlick, leeks, endive, spinach, common— not French—sorrel, lettuce, parsley, mustard, cress, sage, tarragon, fennel, thyme, mint, savory, rhubarb, and numerous herbs used in the still-room or for medicine. Rhubarb, generally supposed to be known to Shakespeare only as a drug, was not as yet used in cookery ; it appears in Tusser's list among herbs to be grown for ' physicke '. Other plants, like artichokes and peas, were still garden novelties. But the modern observer would not, even then, have found asparagus, kidney beans, scarlet runners, cardoons, horse-radish, and, above all, potatoes. All these had come into use by the beginning of the seventeenth century. Potatoes were, of course, the most important introduction. Brought back from the Pacific slopes of South America about 1580, they made their way very slowly into English gardens. As was said before, the potato mentioned by Shakespeare is the sweet potato, which was known in Europe nearly a century earlier. On the other hand, some of the plants formerly grown in kitchen-gardens have now almost disappeared. Skirrets have fallen into undeserved neglect. Neither cowslips, violets, primroses, longwort, liverwort, nor purslane, once valued for its antiscorbutic properties, find a place in our salads. Harefoot, blood-wort or bloody-dock, pennyroyal, marigolds, sea-blite, burnet, cat-mint, and tansy have disappeared from kitchen-garden and cookery-book. Sea-holie, as Tusser spells it, the 'eringoe' (*eryngium maritimum*) of Shakespeare (*M. Wives* v. v. 23), has gone from the still-room and the physic border, together with the mysterious mandrake, *carduus benedictus*, or the Blessed Thistle, worm-wood, plantains, and valerian.

Vegetables can rarely be subjects for poetical treatment. Shakespeare mentions a considerable variety, such as cabbages, turnips, radishes, potatoes, garlick, onions, leeks, cucumbers (' pumpions '), parsley, lettuce, mint, and savory. But all the allusions are of a humorous kind. He also adds largely to the list of culinary material which Tusser gives under the heading—

> These buie with the penie,
> Or looke not for anie.

Tusser's list includes only capers, lemons, olives, oranges,

THE GARDEN MOUNT ROCKINGHAM CASTLE

rice, and samphire.   With the exception of capers, and the fruit of the olive-tree, all these are referred to by Shakespeare.   He adds sugar, pepper, nutmeg, cloves, mace, dates, currants, and raisins.   He also mentions ginger ; but, in doing so, he may refer to dittany or garden ginger. Another condiment, certainly home-made, often alluded to and probably very necessary as an aid to the digestion of the hung beef of Elizabethan times, was mustard.   It was made by our Anglo-Saxon ancestors from mustard seeds ground between two stones and liquefied with vinegar.   The Rev. H. N. Ellacombe quotes a passage showing that 'Tewksbury mustard' (2 *Hen. IV*, II. iv. 262), ground and made into balls, was then sold as 'the best that the world affords'.

Full in view of the principal windows of the house was the flower-garden.   The high ' embatailled ' walls of early Tudor gardens, which preserved the traditions of recent insecurity, now sheltered the growth of tender plants. At Hampton Court, Wolsey and Henry VIII had laid out their figured flower-beds, edged with trellises of painted woodwork.   Here they had planned their arbours, formed their trellised galleries, carried their water-conduits, built their fountains, raised their terraced mounds, trimmed their yew and box into strange monsters, and adorned their open spaces with multitudes of beasts made of wood, gilded and painted.   Working on these native foundations, Elizabethan designers of gardens developed a national style, adapting to their own needs and materials the ideas of the Italian Renaissance.   Like the Italians, they designed their gardens for use and pleasure at all hours of the day and for the different purposes of social enjoyment ;   they did not plan them, like the subsequent French School, for spectacular effect, or, like the later Dutch gardeners, for the restful privacy of the citizen's life.

The Italian gardens were essentially architectural.   The same principles were followed both in the dwelling and the pleasure-grounds ;   the garden was not a mere adjunct, it was rather a setting, to the house.   So also the Elizabethans in their pleasure-grounds adopted an architectural plan which harmonized with the building and continued its lines. In shape the flower-garden was usually square, because, as Parkinson says, that form ' doth best agree with any man's dwelling '.   It was surrounded by a fence, either a paling of 'sawen wood', a thick hedge of holly or hornbeam, or a wall of stone or brick.

>He hath a garden circummured with brick,

says Isabella in *Measure for Measure* (IV. i. 30). On the side facing the house was the principal gate of the garden, often made of elaborately wrought iron and sup-

Certaine inſtructions moꝛe curious to be learned of euery ſkilfull Gardener, in the beſtowing of ſeedes and daintie hearbes in a well dꝛeſſed earth. Chap. 21.

The learned Plinie woꝛthy of memoꝛie, vttereth a ſpeciall note and rule of the auncient obſeruers, to be learned of euery carefull Gardener, in the beſtowing of ſeedes: that if he bee occaſioned to commit ſeedes into a moyſt earth, oꝛ the ſeedes to be beſtowed are of a greate moyſture, then ſhall the Gardener commodiouſly chooſe the ende of the Moones decreaſe oꝛ wafne, and neare to hir chaunge.

From Thomas Hill's *The Gardeners Labyrinth*, 1577.

ported on stone pillars. Other and simpler means of egress, like Shakespeare's 'planched gate' or wooden door, pierced the fence on either side, and gave access to the orchard or the 'cook's garden'.

The garden square thus formed an enclosed yard. It was laid out with the utmost stiffness and formality in paths and flower-beds. Except on the bowling-green or in the wilderness beyond, turf was little used, though Shakespeare recognized, as did Bacon, the beauty of close-shorn grass. The garden proper was cut into sections by broad paths, running away from the house, straight through, and also straight across, its extent. Underfoot, these paths, the 'forth-rights' of the *Tempest*, were paved for the sake of dryness with gravel, sand, or shells, and in humbler gardens, or in orchards, as has been mentioned before, with brickdust, ashes, or even sawdust. Overhead, they were either open, sheltered between tall hedges, or arched with the boughs of trees planted at intervals along the sides, either plashed and closely interwoven or carried on trellises of 'carpenter's work'. For these 'thick-pleached alleys' (*Much Ado* I. ii. 11) a variety of trees were used, such as willows, cornel-plums, maples, limes, privet, wych-elms, yew, box, juniper or white-thorn, interspersed with sweetbriars, honeysuckle, roses, or rosemary. For the trellises, vines and clematis, or Lady's Bower, were often employed. Parallel with the house ran narrower paths. These were open overhead and at the sides, and were either turfed, or planted with sweet-smelling herbs such as thyme, burnet, water-mint, or camomile (*1 Hen. IV*, II. iv. 446). The spaces between these paths and the 'forth-rights' were entirely filled with flower-beds, formed of earth, either raised above the level of the paths and kept in place by supports of wood, or tiles, or lead, or else kept at the same level and edged with box, thrift, ivy, marjoram, or savory. In the designs of these beds Elizabethan gardeners exercised their ingenuity. Often the 'curious-knotted garden' (*Love's L. L.* I. i. 247) repeated the geometrical design which surmounted the brickwork of the house. But however 'odd-conceited' might be the knots, they were carried out with mathematical precision and regularity.

In 'prince-like' gardens, such as that which Bacon de-signed, many embellishments appear. Along the front of the house ran a broad terrace from which flights of steps led to the main pathways of the garden. Often a second terrace ran along another side of the garden square, raised high enough to command a view over the enclosure, and over the adjoining country. This terrace also communi-cated with the pathways by flights of steps, and terminated at either end with an arbour, often placed upon a terraced mound. In every garden arbours were a prominent feature. Sometimes they were really magnificent buildings, fitted for the centre of a pageant or a masque; sometimes they were turfed seats, set in the recesses of the wall or hedge; sometimes they were simple shelters, formed of upright and horizontal poles over which were trained roses or climbing plants like clematis,—bowers

> Where honey-suckles, ripen'd by the sun,
> Forbid the sun to enter.   (*Much Ado* III. i. 8-9)

Between the flower-beds, or at intervals along the terraces, were placed vases of lead and stone, or, more rarely, figures; rows of cypresses, or yews, box-trees, rosemary, and privets, cut into quaint shapes, were symmetrically distributed to form vistas or open avenues: sundials, and sometimes fountains, were set in the open spaces where the main pathways intersected. Where the opportunity occurred, water in running stream or open sheets was introduced, but its artificial use became a more prominent feature under the later influence of Le Nôtre and the French School.

The flowers with which the knots were planted were for the most part hardy perennials in all the variety that horticulture could then command. No attempt was made to mass the blooms in modern fashion. The flowers were arranged so as to secure some uniformity of height and some balance of their supposed sympathies and antipathies. But the chief aim was to secure as much colour as possible at every season of the year. Here grew the flowers and plants that Shakespeare loved: the 'faint ', ' pale ' primrose, ' first-born child of Spring '; crocuses with their ' saffron wings '; daffodils ' that come before the swallow dares '; the ' azured ' harebell or wild hyacinth; the ' pied ', ' April ' daisy; ' freckled ' cowslips; orchids, or ' long purples ', that maids call ' dead men's fingers '; ' lady-smocks ' or cuckoo-flowers; ' purple ' violets; flower-de-luces or irises; ' crow-flowers ' or ragged-robins; ' cuckoo-cups ', or buttercups, of ' yellow hue '; broom; columbines; pinks; carnations, or ' streak'd gillivors which some call Nature's bastards '; peonies; ' larks-heels ' or larkspurs; ' sweet ' marjoram and ' sweet ' balm; poppies; ' bold oxlips, and the crown-imperial ' both orange and yellow; marigolds, that close and ' ope their golden eyes ' with the sun; anemones; aconites or monkshood; tall white lilies; ' hot ' lavender; rosemary; the ' luscious woodbine ' and its ' sweet honeysuckle ' flower; the eglantine, or sweet-brier, with its flower and scent ; pansies 'for thoughts', or 'love-in-idleness', or 'Cupid's flower'; the 'soft' myrtle ; and roses in rich profusion, white, red, and crimson and of varied sorts—the damask rose, the musk rose, the canker or dog rose, the rose of Provence (or as it should

A proper knotte to be cast in the quarter of a Garden, or other= wise, as there is sufficient roomth.

From Thomas Hill's *The Gardeners Labyrinth*, 1577.

be of Provins), the rose of York and Lancaster. Neither foxgloves nor snapdragons are mentioned, and it is strange that Shakespeare makes no allusion to some of the common flowers which appear in Tusser's list of flowers for ' windowes and pots ', such as hollyhocks, sweet-william, love-lies-bleeding, love-in-a-mist, and lilies of the valley. Tulips, though grown in Holland as early as 1560, did not reach England till the close of the century.

The formal artificial garden of Elizabethan times has disappeared ; the enclosed yard, with its straight paths and curious knots, has vanished. Few traces remain of the shape in which a picturesque and brilliant age expressed its taste in gardening. But those traces strike our imagination with all the force of relics of a stately yet simple world which has changed almost beyond recognition ; they appeal to us also with all the added charm of the memories that they evoke of the men and women who planned and used and loved them. Our modern gardeners are rich in resources beyond the dreams of a Gerarde or a Parkinson, a Burghley or a Shakespeare. Yet Bacon's words remain true : ' A man shall ever see, that when ages grow to civility and elegance, men come to build stately sooner than to garden finely.'

BIBLIOGRAPHY.—The principal contemporary authorities are : WILLIAM TURNER'S *The names of herbes in Greke, Latin, Englishe, Duche, and Frenche,* &c., 1548, English Dialect Society, 1881 ; THOMAS TUSSER'S *Five hundreth Pointes of good Husbandry,* &c., 1573, English Dialect Society, 1878 ; DIDYMUS MOUNTAIN [i. e. Thomas Hill], *The proffitable Arte of Gardening,* 1568, &c., and *The Gardeners Labyrinth,* 1577 ; BARNABY GOOGE'S *Foure Bookes of Husbandry, collected by M. Conradus Heresbachius. . . . Newely Englished, and increased, by Barnabe Googe,* 1577 ; RAPHAEL HOLINSHED'S *Chronicles of England, Scotlande, and Irelande,* 2 vols., folio (1577); JOHN GERARDE'S *The Herball, or, Generall Historie of Plantes,* 1597 ; WILLIAM LAWSON'S *A new Orchard and Garden,* 1618; FRANCIS BACON'S ' Of Gardens ', essay, 1625 ; JOHN PARKINSON'S *Paradisi in sole, Paradisus terrestris,* &c., 1629.

Among modern books the following should be consulted : The Rev. H. N. ELLACOMBE'S *The Plant-lore and Garden-craft of Shakespeare,* 1878 ; The Hon. Mrs. EVELYN CECIL'S *A History of Gardening in England,* 3rd ed., 1910.

XIII

LAW

BY

ARTHUR UNDERHILL

DESPITE Shakespeare's frequent use of legal phrases and allusions his knowledge of law was neither profound nor accurate, and it is unnecessary to explain such knowledge as he had by assuming that he enjoyed even a legal education as clerk in a lawyer's office. In Shakespeare's England the Inns of Court were not, as now, merely inhabited by practising barristers for business purposes. Their members formed a real and very lively community, dwelt in the Inns, dined habitually in their halls, and regarded them much as University men still regard their colleges. They were the intellectual as well as the geographical centre of London. The Inns of Court men, as we know, delighted in ' masques and revels ' and dramatic performances, and at least three of Shakespeare's plays were acted in the Halls of the Middle Temple and Gray's Inn. Many authors of that age beside Shakespeare made free use of legal phrases and allusions. The writings of Ben Jonson, Spenser, Webster, Beaumont and Fletcher, and others are full of them.

It seems probable, therefore, that both dramatists and actors were much in legal society, and picked up the technical phraseology and legal slang of the day. The dramatist and his father, like most of their contemporaries, were prone to litigation, and not infrequently figured in suits in the local Court of Record at Stratford-upon-Avon. The dramatist's purchases of houses and land in his later life must also have brought him into professional contact with lawyers and legal procedure.

Many of Shakespeare's allusions (such as those referring

to fines and recoveries, which seemed to Lord Campbell to infer profound knowledge of the abstruse law of real property) related to picturesque and grotesque proceedings which were in Shakespeare's time of constant occurrence in the Westminster Courts, and only seem profound and difficult to lawyers of the nineteenth and twentieth centuries because they have become archaic and unfamiliar. Possibly their solemn absurdities tickled Shakespeare's sense of humour. In addition to these considerations it must not be forgotten that the connotation of many words once in general use has, like the forensic wig, survived only in the Courts. For instance, the word 'determine', in the sense of 'put an end to', is now only used by lawyers, whereas in Shakespeare's time it was in common use. Thus in the *Sonnets* (xiii) Shakespeare writes as a lawyer might still write:

> So should that beauty which you hold in lease
> Find no determination.

But, on the other hand, in *Antony and Cleopatra* (IV. iv. 36–7) we find

> That he and Cæsar might
> Determine this great war in single fight!

where the word is used in precisely the same sense without any legal allusion whatever.

The following passage in *Love's Labour's Lost* (II. i. 220–1) no doubt seems at first sight marvellously technical :

> *Boyet.* So you grant pasture for me.
> *Maria.*   Not so, gentle beast.
> My lips are no common, though several they be.

This alludes to the distinction, familiar to real property lawyers, between a right to take something from another's land (e.g. fish, game, or pasture) to the exclusion of all others (in which case it is called a 'several', i.e severed, right), and a similar right exercisable in common with others (in which case it is called a 'profit in common'). Maria doubtless meant that her lips were not to be enjoyed in common, though they were intended for the several (i.e. exclusive) use of one favoured man. That Shakespeare borrowed this 'quaint conceit' from one of his legal friends is all the more probable because the allusion is not technically accurate, for it attributes the 'several' and 'common' to the lips rather than to the right to kiss them, and uses the word 'though' incorrectly, in place of 'but', which rather suggests that he considered common rights to be in some way connected with, instead of opposed to, several ones.

However, whether Shakespeare received any legal training or not, his numerous legal allusions and those of other contemporary English authors afford interesting illustrations of the English law of the sixteenth and seventeenth centuries. The broad general principles of the Common Law with regard to civil matters still remain unchanged. The principal alterations have taken place rather in the region of criminal than of private law, and in the procedure and tone of thought of the Courts. What we call ' Equity ', too (considered as a scheme of law founded on definite principles), is mainly the growth of the later seventeenth and subsequent centuries, and in Shakespeare's time the Court of Chancery was almost as unfettered by precedent as the typical Cadi under the Palm Tree. Of chief pertinence here are those branches of law and procedure with regard to which there is a strong contrast between past and present, together with the life of the Inns of Court in Elizabethan times.

THE COURTS

At the end of the sixteenth century the Superior Courts were much the same as they were in the latter half of the nineteenth, when, by the Judicature Acts 1873 and 1875 they were consolidated into one Supreme Court of Judicature. The High Court of Chancery was there, the Queen's Bench was there, so were the Courts of Exchequer and Common Pleas. The Judges also from time to time went on circuit, as they still do, and with much the same pomp and circumstance ; Justices of the Peace then, as now, held petty and quarter sessions ; and in the latter they had power of life and death. But there was also another powerful Court, hated and feared, owning no obedience to law or precedent, which has long since ceased to exist, viz. the Star Chamber. There has been much speculation as to the origin of the Star Chamber, but the best opinion seems to be that it was a remnant of the judicial side of the King's Council, of which the other Courts were offshoots. All the King's Courts were, and indeed still are, supposed to be emanations of the King himself as the fountain of justice ;

the judges being merely his delegates.   This theory is alluded
to both in *Measure for Measure* (I. i. 43), where the Duke
says to Angelo :

> In our remove be thou at full ourself,

and also in *2 Henry IV* (**v.** ii. 73–9), where Chief Justice
Gascoyne says :

> I *then did use the person of your father ;*
> The image of his power lay then in me:
> And, in the administration of his law,
> Whiles I was busy for the commonwealth,
> Your highness pleased to forget my place,
> The majesty and power of law and justice,
> *The image of the King whom I presented.*

In virtue of the King's delegated justice, suitors were entitled
to appeal to the King in Parliament (whence the judicial
duties of the House of Lords), or to the King in Council (now
represented by the Judicial Committee of the Privy Council),
or to the Keeper of the King's conscience (the Lord Chancellor), when the ordinary law afforded no adequate relief.
Apparently on similar grounds there appears to have been
reserved to the Council a jurisdiction over criminal or quasi-
criminal matters for which the ordinary law made no
adequate provision, and this jurisdiction was exercised in
the Star Chamber.   Its particular function was the correction of such offences as riots, slanders, and libels, or even
criticisms on magistrates or great officers, cozenage or
embracery (i.e. corrupting or menacing juries), bribery of
officers of justice, and the like, against which the Common
Law then afforded no adequate protection.   It was a kind
of criminal Court of Equity, limited by no settled rules, and
exercising jurisdiction at the discretion of the Executive in
the alleged interests of good government, much as in days not
very remote the Russian Government imprisoned, transported, or executed political offenders by ‘ administrative
order ’ without trial.   In theory it supplemented the shortcomings of the Common Law in criminal matters, just as the
Court of Chancery was supposed to supplement or control
it in civil proceedings.   In point of fact, however, it became
the servant of a tyrannical Executive.   Shakespeare was well
aware (as probably were most of his contemporaries) of its
peculiar jurisdiction.   Thus we find in *The Merry Wives*
(I. i. 1–7) :

> *Shallow.*   Sir Hugh, persuade me not ; I will make a Star-chamber

matter of it ; if he were twenty Sir John Falstaffs he shall not abuse Robert Shallow, esquire.

> *Slender.* In the county of Gloster, justice of the peace, and *coram.*
> *Shallow.* Ay, cousin Slender, and *cust-alorum.*

And again, later on (I. i. 35) :

> *Shallow.* The Council shall hear it ; it is a riot.

Other contemporary authors also frequently refer to the Star Chamber. Thus Ben Jonson, in *The Magnetic Lady* (III. iii) :

> Sir, you forget
> There is a Court above, of the Star Chamber,
> To punish routs and riots.

And again, Barry, in *Ram Alley* :

> I will Star Chamber you all for cozenage.

The point in all these passages is the peculiar jurisdiction of the Court.

The punishments inflicted by the Star Chamber varied from heavy fines to the pillory, ear-cropping, and branding (as in Prynne's case) or whipping, but not death. They became, however, outrageously and increasingly severe and out of all proportion to the offence ; and the Court's unpopularity was probably owing partly to this and partly to its practice of interrogating the accused and hearing witnesses *in camera*.

In his learned and interesting work on *English Legal Institutions* Dr. Carter gives several amazing instances of the severity of this Court. Thus, Sir John Hollis and Sir John Wentworth were in 1615 prosecuted by Bacon, then Attorney-General, for traducing public justice. Their offence was that they went to the execution of a man named Weston, who was hanged for poisoning Sir Thomas Overbury. Wentworth merely asked Weston if he really did it ; and Hollis desired him to discharge his conscience by confessing and so 'satisfying the world'. Hollis had also said when the verdict was given that if he had been on the jury he should have had his doubts. For these mild observations Sir John Hollis was fined £1,000 and Wentworth 1,000 marks (£666), and each of them got a year's imprisonment in the Tower.

In another case, a London merchant was fined £2,000 and imprisoned for six years for saying that the merchants are 'in no part of the world so screwed and wrung as in England, and that they had more encouragement in Turkey'.

The case of Prynne in 1634 completed these outrageous and vindictive punishments. For political libel he was disbarred, deprived of his degrees, ordered to be placed twice in the pillory, to have one ear cut off on each occasion, to be fined £5,000, and to be perpetually imprisoned without books, pen, ink, or paper. After this it is a relief to read the sentence on a fanatic who, objecting to pork on religious grounds, was ordered by the Star Chamber to be imprisoned and fed on nothing but pig's flesh. It is not surprising that the Star Chamber was destroyed by the Long Parliament in 1641.

The Star Chamber gained additional odium from its use of torture, which was quite illegal in the other English Courts. So late as 1614, a Somerset clergyman, Edmond Peacham, was interrogated on the rack before the Star Chamber in the presence of Coke, then Attorney-General.

Another Court that existed in Shakespeare's time was the Court of Wards and Liveries, created by two statutes of Henry VIII to deal with the estates of infant wards of the King, and also apparently with lunatics and idiots. This Court was presided over by the Lord Treasurer, who had, as his associates, the two Chief Justices, the Chief Baron, the King's Serjeant, and divers Surveyors and an Attorney of the Court. The Lord of a vassal who held by military tenure was guardian of the vassal's orphan, infant heir, or heiress without any liability to account for the profits of the infant's lands until, in the case of males, the ward attained twenty-one, or in the case of females, sixteen years. On attaining these ages the infant could 'sue out livery' on payment of half a year's profits. During the infancy the guardian had the right of marrying the ward to any one he pleased of equal rank. Wardship had become odious in Shakespeare's time, and was abolished along with military tenures by 12 Charles II, c. 24.

There is no specific mention of this Court in Shakespeare's works, but he alludes (although incorrectly) to the right of the Lord as guardian in *All's Well that Ends Well*, where the King of France insists upon his highborn ward Bertram marrying Helena, a poor physician's daughter, who was of inferior rank to him. The King parades all his male wards and says:

> Fair maid, send forth thine eyes: this youthful parcel
> Of noble bachelors stand at my bestowing;   (II. iii. 58–9)

and when Bertram, whom Helena chooses, protests, the King informs him peremptorily that

> It is in us to plant thine honour where
> We please to have it grow. Check thy contempt:
> Obey our will, which travails in thy good. (*ibid.* 163–5)

Other writers of the time also mention this right. For instance, Wilkins, in his *Miseries of Inforst Marriage*, published in 1607, writes:

> You are his Ward; being so, the law intends,
> He is to have your duty, and in his rule
> Is both your marriage, and your heritage;
> If you rebel 'gainst these injunctions,
> The penalty takes hold on you; which for himself
> He straight thus prosecutes; he wastes your land,
> Weds you where he thinks fit, Sir.

So in Ben Jonson's *Bartholomew Fair* (III. v):

> *Grace.* Now he will marry me to his wife's brother, this wise gentleman that you see; or else I must pay the value o' my land.
> *Quar.* 'Slid, is there no device of disparagement or so?

an allusion to the condition that the spouse must be of equal rank with the ward, which Shakespeare had ignored.

The suing of livery by the ward is frequently mentioned by Elizabethan and Jacobean writers. Thus:

> Our little Cupid hath sued livery
> And is no more in his Minority. (Donne, *Ecl.*, 1613)

In *Richard II* the Duke of York, referring to the consequences of seizing upon the rights of 'banished Hereford', says:

> If you ...
> Call in the letters-patent that he hath
> By his attorneys-general to sue
> His livery, and deny his offer'd homage,
> You pluck a thousand dangers on your head.
> (*Rich. II*, II. i. 202–6)

And again in the same play Bolingbroke is made to say:

> I am denied to sue my livery here. (II. iii. 129)

Si parva licet componere magnis, another ancient Court still existing in Shakespeare's day has long become obsolete, viz. the Court Leet. It was the predecessor of the modern Police Court, and like it could present for trial or indict for all crimes, and could summarily punish trivial ones. It was shorn of much of its jurisdiction by a statute of Edward IV, and is now obsolete, except in some few manors, where it survives rather as an ancient ceremonial than as a practical court of law.

Shakespeare mentions it in *Othello* (III. iii. 140) thus :

> Keep leets and law days, and in session sit ;

and again in *The Taming of the Shrew* (Ind. ii. 87–90) :

> Yet would you say ye were beaten out of door,
> And rail upon the hostess of the house,
> And say you would present her at the leet,
> Because she brought stone jugs and no seal'd quarts.

But probably even in Shakespeare's time the Leet was but little used.

Another obsolete Court of record which flourished in Shakespeare's time was that which bore the strange name of the Court of Pie-Poudres. It and the Court of the Clerk of the Market were incident to every market. The one decided all civil disputes arising in the market (but not in any preceding one), the owner's steward acting as Judge, and the other dealt with criminal matters, mainly questions of false weights and measures. The Court of Pie-Poudres is said by Lord Coke to have gained its name from its speedy justice, which was dispensed as fast as dust could fall from the foot. Blackstone, however, gives it a more prosaic derivation from *pied puldreaux*, a pedlar. This picturesque Court is not mentioned by Shakespeare, but Ben Jonson speaks of it in *Bartholomew Fair* (II. i), where one of the characters says, ' In whose Courts of Pie-poudres I have had the honour during the three days sometimes to sit as Judge '.

Other Courts there were not mentioned by Shakespeare. The Court of Requests (not to be confounded with the local Courts of the same name which lasted down to our times and were replaced by the modern County Courts) was a kind of relief Court of Chancery, specially devoted to dispensing Equity to poor suitors. It was in the Court of Requests that one Stephen Bellott in Easter term 1612 sued his father-in-law, Christopher Montjoy, a tiremaker, of Silver Street in the city of London, for the fulfilment of certain promises alleged to be made on the plaintiff's marriage with defendant's daughter eight years before. Shakespeare had lodged in Montjoy's house when the plaintiff Bellott, who had been Montjoy's apprentice, proposed marriage to Montjoy's daughter. The dramatist was accordingly one of Bellott's witnesses, and his signed depositions are in the

Public Record Office. In the result the Court remitted the dispute to the French Huguenot Church in Threadneedle Street, of which both parties to the suit were members, and the consistory upheld Bellott's plaint, severely reprimanding Montjoy and suspending him from membership of the church. In 1598 the Common Law Courts refused to recognise the authority of the Court of Requests, but it lingered on until the Civil War, when, its legal machinery being lost, it died a natural death.

LEGAL PROCEDURE

Although the Courts of Chancery, King's Bench, Common Pleas, and Exchequer, survived to the latter part of the nineteenth century, when, by the Judicature Acts,

> The Courts that were manifold dwindled
> To divers divisions of one,

yet the contrast between the procedure and the tone of those Courts in Shakespeare's day and ours is profound. Their procedure and atmosphere were pedantic, unyielding, even puerile. The respect paid to forms and fictions, and the verbal quibbles solemnly discussed without regard to the obvious reality of things, suggest to a modern mind that the whole administration of justice was regarded as an elaborate intellectual game in the course of which justice itself was entirely lost sight of. The very language of the profession was a mysterious jargon compounded of Latin, French, and English, calculated to prevent any but the initiated from having the least notion of what was meant. For instance, we read of refined but futile distinctions between 'writs of entry sur disseisin in the per, in the post, in the per and cui, and in the quibus', distinctions which we may be quite sure had but little relation to 'the merits'. The use of French and Latin in the actual proceedings had, it is true, long been forbidden by statute ; nevertheless, the Records were kept in Latin, and the Reports still continued to be written in Norman French, much as physicians still veil their prescriptions in Latin. But it had become a doggerel language, and some of the reports of that date furnish amusing instances of the unfamiliarity of the reporter with the tongue as an instrument of thought. The Law reporters, who were a highly conservative class of men, strongly opposed the substitution of English. Thomas

Style, in the Preface to his Reports in the year 1658, excuses himself for writing them in English in the following quaint words :

I have been always and yet am of opinion, that that part of the Common Law which is in English hath only occasioned the making of unquiet spirits contentiously knowing, and more apt to offend others than to defend themselves. I have done it in obedience to authority and to stop the mouths of such of this English age, who, though they be confessedly different in their minds and judgements, as the builders of Babel were in their language, yet do think it vain if not impious to speak or understand more than their own mother tongue.

Even now a few words and phrases survive in common use, such as ' semble ', ' aliter ', ' quia timet ', ' in fieri ', ' cestui que trust ', ' alibi ', &c., and all the old prerogative writs retain their Latin names, e. g. 'mandamus', 'certiorari', and ' quo warranto '.

Trial by battle still survived, and was occasionally resorted to with regard to the title to land, or in cases of felony, or in the Court of Chivalry. But it was evidently dying out, as there seems to be no recorded instance of it between 13th Elizabeth and 1639. It remained, however, part of our law so late as 1819, when it was abolished by 59 George III, c. 46.

But perhaps the most interesting item of procedure of those days was the different manner in which an action for the same cause had to be commenced according as it was in the King's Bench, the Common Pleas, or the Exchequer. The Common Pleas was from the time of Magna Charta settled at Westminster to do justice between subject and subject. For some time its jurisdiction was limited to certain fixed causes of action, for each of which a specific writ was issued. If the facts of a case could not be brought within one of these writs, there was no remedy. This of course led to frequent denials of justice, and by 1 Edward I, c. 24, a new writ was ordered to be issued in any case which could not be met by the old fixed forms. Actions commenced by these new writs became known as actions of ' trespass on the case ' (or, shortly, ' actions on the case '), because the special facts of each case were stated in a writ framed as near as possible by analogy to the old writ of trespass. There was an immense amount of ' lean and wasteful learning ' expended on the distinction between

THE COURT OF WARDS AND LIVERIES ABOUT 1585
From the painting in the Collection of the
DUKE OF RICHMOND AND GORDON

trespass and trespass on the case, which lasted down to our own time, and even now fine distinctions are sometimes traceable to the question whether a wrong would formerly have been remediable by 'trespass' or 'case'.

The King's Bench, however, had originally no general jurisdiction as between subject and subject, but only between King and subject. As, however, the judges in those early days were paid by suitors' fees, they had every inducement to widen their jurisdiction, and this they did in a most ingenious but disingenuous way. Having original jurisdiction over all trespasses committed in the county in which the Court was held, as being breaches of the King's peace, the Judges invented the theory that once a man got within the jurisdiction for trespass committed in that county the Court could also deal with all other wrongs which he had committed against any of the King's subjects. It accordingly became the regular procedure in the King's Bench to issue a writ directing the Sheriff of Middlesex to arrest the defendant to answer a fictitious trespass committed there, *and also* to answer whatever the true cause of action might be. This writ was called a Bill of Middlesex, and the clause stating the true cause of action was called the *ac etiam* clause. If, as frequently happened, the defendant was not in Middlesex, the Sheriff made return that he was not to be found there. Thereupon a fresh writ, called a *latitat*, was issued to the Sheriff of the County where the defendant resided, setting forth the issue of the Bill of Middlesex, and stating that 'it is sufficiently attested that the aforesaid William lurks (*latitat*) and runs about in your county', and the writ then commanded the Sheriff to arrest him. It thus came about that civil actions in the King's Bench were commenced by Bill of Middlesex, followed, if necessary, by a writ of *latitat*, and in either case by the arrest of the defendant, who had to give bail for his appearance. This roundabout process, strange as it may seem, lasted for centuries, until it was abolished by the Common Law Procedure Act, 1854. It is frequently alluded to by Shakespeare and his contemporaries. Thus in *The Comedy of Errors* (IV. ii. 41–3) :

Adriana. Why, man, what is the matter ?
Dromio of S. I do not know the matter : he is 'rested on the case.
Adriana. What, is he arrested ? tell me at whose suit.

And again, in Webster's *Cure for a Cuckold* (IV. i) :

Pettifog. The defendant was arrested first by latitat, in an action for trespass.

Compass. And a lawyer told me it should have been an action of the case.

And in Jonson's *Magnetic Lady* (v. iii) :

> Sue him at Common Law ;
> Arrest him on an action of choke-bail,
> Five hundred thousand pound ; it will affright him
> And all his sureties.

And in Massinger's *Fatal Dowry* (I. ii) :

> He was arrested, and for want of bail
> Imprisoned at their suit.

The Court of Exchequer, whose jurisdiction was originally confined to cases affecting the revenue, usurped jurisdiction in civil actions by a similar fiction, viz. that by reason of the defendant's wrongful conduct the plaintiff was less able to pay his taxes.   This was called a writ of *quo minus*, and also lasted down to the middle of the last century.   This usurpation is all the more singular as, down to the time of Elizabeth, the Exchequer judges were not trained lawyers, but promoted clerks, and the Court was scarcely accounted a superior Court, nor were its judges accorded equality with those of the King's Bench and Common Pleas.   In Elizabeth's reign, however, Serjeant Shute was appointed a Baron of the Exchequer with the same rank as the judges of the other Courts, and thenceforward serjeants only were appointed with the like rank.

This make-believe tone of the Courts was carried into the consideration of questions of fact or intention, the most puerile distinctions being made where no sane person could have had the least doubt of the truth.   It is impossible, for instance, to imagine the businesslike judges of to-day taking such extraordinarily fine, not to say childish, distinctions as the following : It was held slander to say of an Attorney that ' he hath no more law than Master Cheyney's Bull even though Master Cheyney hath no Bull, for in that case the scandal is greater ' (1 Siderfin's Reports, 327).   On the other hand, to say that ' he hath *as much* law as a monkey ' was not slanderous, because ' he hath as much law *and more also* ' (1 March, pl. 93 ; 1 Rolle, Ab. 58).   It is scarcely surprising after this to find the sapient reporter in one case thoughtfully adding ' quaere whether it be not actionable to say an attorney hath no more law than the man in the moon ' (1 Siderfin, 424).

This topsy-turvy tone of mind is also apparent in the judgements in the leading case of Manby *v.* Scott, decided in 1602, where Wyndham J., discussing the question whether a husband should be bound by his wife's contracts, thus describes the fancied dangers :

The husband will be accounted the common enemy ; and the mercer and the gallant will unite with the wife, and they will combine their strength against the husband. Wives will be their own carvers and, like hawks, will fly abroad and find their own prey (1 Siderfin, 109).

Shakespeare parodied the quibbling prevarications which infested all legal argument when he made the First Gravedigger in *Hamlet* (v. i. 15 seq.) discourse on the legal meaning of suicide :

First Clown. Here lies the water : good ; here stands the man : good ; if the man go to this water, and drown himself, it is, will he, nill he, he goes ; mark you that ? but if the water come to him, and drown him, he drowns not himself : argal, he that is not guilty of his own death shortens not his own life.
Second Clown. But is this law ?
First Clown. Ay, marry, is 't ; crowner's quest law.

There is little doubt that Shakespeare here had in mind the argument concerning the suicide by drowning of Sir James Hales, which was used in the case Hales *v.* Petite in 1561, and is fully reported in Plowden's Reports : ' As Sir James Hales, being alive, caused Sir James Hales to die, therefore the act of the living man was the death of the dead man, for which the living man must be punished.' The legal argument of the Gravedigger is no more obvious a ' reductio ad absurdum '.

The technicalities of the written pleadings, too, were monstrous. As an instance one may take the report of a case decided in 1651.[1]

Trespass. Plaintiff declares that the defendant did break his close and eat his grass etc *cum averiis suis* to wit oxen sheep hogs *avibus anglice* turkies. And the judge did hold that turkies are not comprised within the general word *averia* which is an old law word, and these fowls came but lately into England. And upon this it was directed to sever the damages ; for otherwise, if the damages be joyntly given, and it be ill for this of the turkies, for the reason above-said, *it will overthrow all the verdict.*

[1] Usley's Case (Clayton's Reports, 50).

With justice stifled by these formal futilities it is not surprising to find the Court of Chancery stepping in as a Court of Equity to set matters right. It could not interfere directly by reversing the decisions of the Common Law Courts, but it effected the same object by granting an injunction prohibiting a plaintiff who had obtained judgement from proceeding to enforce it, on pain of imprisonment for contempt. This gave great offence to the Common Law judges, and the granting of these injunctions by Wolsey was one of the chief charges against him. In Shakespeare's time, however, this battle was fought to a finish. At first the Common Law Courts had the better of it, for by an Act of 27 Elizabeth it was made a *praemunire* to apply to other jurisdictions to impeach or impede the execution of judgements given in the King's Courts. The Chancellors seem to have ignored this; but the matter came to a head in 1616 in the historical encounter between Lord Chief Justice Coke and Lord Chancellor Ellesmere, the latter of whom issued an injunction perpetually restraining a plaintiff who had obtained a judgement in the King's Bench under circumstances of gross fraud. Thereupon the King's Bench preferred indictments against everybody concerned—counsel, solicitors, and suitors— for a *praemunire* for daring to question in the Chancery a judgement of the King's Bench. The matter was so serious that the King himself stepped in and supported the Chancellor, and thenceforth the power of the Court of Chancery to issue injunctions against proceedings at Common Law was never questioned until it was finally abolished by the Judicature Act, 1873, by which every branch of the High Court was enabled to give equitable as well as legal relief. Curiously enough no allusion to this distinctive process of the old Court of Chancery occurs in Shakespeare's writings. Perhaps it was too burning a question to be safely touched on. Donne, however, refers to it in his *Second Satire* :

> I have been
> In love e'er since tricesimo of the Queen.
> Continual claims I have made, injunctions got
> To stay my rivals suit, that he should not
> Proceed.

And Jonson, in *An Execration upon Vulcan*, says :

Lies there no writ out of the Chancery
Against this Vulcan ? No injunction,
No order, no decree ? Though we be gone
At Common Law, methinks in his despite
A Court of Equity should do us right.

The foundation of the Chancery jurisdiction was *in personam,* and the peculiarity of its procedure was that it got at the truth by putting searching interrogatories to the defendant himself, which he had to answer on oath, and by clapping him in prison if he disobeyed the Chancellor's orders. This power of interrogating a defendant (which was quite contrary to the spirit of the Common Law) became known as 'scraping the conscience', and was a most effective, although often a costly and dilatory, process. Shakespeare refers to interrogatories of this kind in *The Merchant of Venice* (v. i. 300–3) :

Let it be so : the first interrogatory
That my Nerissa shall be sworn on is,
Whether till the next night she had rather stay,
Or go to bed now, being two hours of day.

The main Chancery work of Elizabethan days was founded on fraud or on the unconscientious enforcement of strict legal rights. The law now administered by the Chancery Division was practically non-existent. The law of trusts, for instance, as we know it, was the work of Lord Chancellor Nottingham (1673–82). But for the following passage, Shakespeare gives no hint that he knew of the existence of Courts of Equity as distinguished from Courts of Law :

Thou robed man of justice, take thy place ;
And thou, his yoke-fellow of equity,
Bench by his side. (*Lear* III. vi. 39–41)

Of the aspect of the Law Courts in Shakespeare's day, much information survives. First, then, with regard to the building in which they were held, the Common Law Courts and the Court of Chancery were not, as now, held in separate chambers, but in different parts of Westminster Hall ; and this practice continued till late in the reign of the Georges.[1]

Next, as to the costume of the judges and counsel. It is not perhaps generally known that the present wig and sombre black gown date only from the funeral of Queen

[1] An old print, showing the interior of the Hall with several of the Courts actually sitting, is reproduced in the late Mr. Inderwick's interesting little book, *The King's Peace.*

Anne. As the late Chief Baron Pollock is said to have re-marked, the Bar then went into mourning, and has never gone out of it again. In Elizabeth's time the costumes were much more picturesque. Counsel below the rank of ser-jeant wore no head-gear. The ancient order of Serjeants at Law, which was abolished some quarter of a century ago, answered in the sixteenth century to the present K.C.'s. They wore a head-dress of white taffeta (somewhat similar in shape to the ordinary barrister's wig), called ' the coif ', the origin of which is lost in extreme antiquity. Over the coif (when not actually engaged in a cause) the serjeant, and apparently the judge when actually sitting on the bench, usually wore a black velvet or silk skull-cap of the same shape, but slightly smaller, so as to leave the white coif showing as an edging or border. When, after another century, wigs became general, the judges and other serjeants had small round holes cut in the top of their wigs, through which the coif was supposed to be seen ; but in reality there was a small black patch edged with white inserted to cover the hole and suggest the coif.

With regard to robes, those of the judges were not very different from those used by the King's Bench judges at the present day, the colour varying according to the days of the calendar from scarlet to violet, and the lining according to the season from silk to minever.

The serjeants' robes were similar, viz. a robe some-what like a modern dressing-gown, with a small cape just covering the shoulders, over which was a hood, similar to but not so full or long as the ordinary academic hood, and in front ' two white labels ' (now the white bands or tabs worn by all counsel). The colour of the robes seems to have been left much to fancy, but in Shakespeare's time, and for some centuries before, they were parti-coloured—the right-hand side one colour, and the left another. There is in the Inner Temple Library a very interesting illumination of the four Courts in the time of Henry VI, showing the serjeants in parti-coloured robes of blue and green, with white coifs. In the painting of the Court of Wards and Liveries, done in the reign of Elizabeth, and now the property of the Duke of Richmond and Gordon at Goodwood, the serjeants who are pleading wear parti-coloured robes. In an address delivered to some newly-created serjeants in the thirty-sixth year of Elizabeth's reign the Lord Chief Justice said, ' by the parti-coloured garments *being both of deep colours,* and such as the judges themselves in ancient times used (for so we receive it by tradition), is signified soundness and depth of judgement, an ability to discerne of causes, what colour soever be cast over them, and under or with what vail or shadow soever they be disguised'. Fortescue, writing in the fifteenth century, describes the serjeant's robe as parti-coloured, and differentiates it from that of a judge, partly by that fact, and also (in his quaint language) by the fact that the judge's cape is furred with minever, ' whereas the serjeant's is ever furred with lamb '.

The Elizabethan costume of counsel who were not serjeants is extremely obscure. That they wore a gown of some sort seems certain from the records of the four Inns of Court, the Benchers of which were very particular as to the wearing of gowns, even in ordinary life. Moreover, Webster, writing in the early part of the seventeenth century, says, ' My forehead has more crumples in it than the back part of a Counsellor's gown ' ;[1] which is suggestive of the numerous pleats in the present gown of a junior barrister. What the colour was seems very questionable, but it was probably sombre, as the wearing of gowns of a ' sad colour ' by members of the Bar was enjoined by Philip and Mary ; and, by an order of the judges in the time of Elizabeth, no fellow of any of the Inns of Court was to go into the city or suburbs ' otherwise than in his gown, according to the ancient usage of the gentlemen of the Inns of Court '. By the same order, the wearing of ' swords and bucklers and great ruffs and silk and fur ' was forbidden.

However, if the Bar has changed its dress, it still retains that old spirit of comradeship which so annoyed Mr. Pickwick, and which Shakespeare has immortalized in *The Taming of the Shrew* (I. ii. 281–2) :

> And do as adversaries do in law,
> Strive mightily, but eat and drink as friends.

It will be seen from the above sketch that the appearance of the Courts in Shakespeare's day must have differed widely from that which they present nowadays. To realize the full extent of the change one has but to go into Westminster Hall, and divide it up mentally into three open

[1] *Westward Hoe* II. i.

Courts, somewhat like the stalls of a modern fancy fair, and people them with judges in scarlet or purple, with the black and white coif, serjeants in parti-coloured robes of blue and green pleading in their white coifs, and junior counsel bare-headed in sad-coloured robes ; while lookers-on, in all the varied costumes in which that age delighted, wandered from Court to Court.

CRIMINAL LAW

With regard to substantive law, the greatest changes that have been made are in the department of criminal law. From the beginning of Elizabeth's reign to the end of the seventeenth century high treason and all felonies, except petty larceny (i. e. the theft of goods under the value of twelve pence), were punishable with death, subject to ' benefit of clergy ', where it applied. In the time of Shakespeare, statutory felonies had become somewhat numerous, and included all thefts of goods or money exceeding twelve pence in value, and the death penalty was carried out in an appalling number of cases. It has been calculated that at the end of the sixteenth century over 800 persons were annually hanged in England, the population of which at that date scarcely reached five millions. At one Assize for Exeter in 1598, 134 prisoners were indicted. Of these 17 were condemned to the gallows, 20 were ordered to be flogged, 15 were pardoned, and 11 claimed benefit of clergy, and were branded and set free. Quite half of the persons condemned to death in England were tried before magistrates at Quarter Sessions without the attendance of a judge.

This wholesale slaughter even moved Coke (who was no sentimentalist) to write at the end of his third Institute : ' What a lamentable case it is to see so many Christian men and women strangled on that cursed tree of the gallows ; insomuch as if in a *large field* a man might see together all the Christians that, but in one year, throughout England, came to that untimely and ignominious death, if there were any spark of grace or charity in him, it would make his heart bleed for pity and compassion.'

Treason was, of course, the highest of all crimes, and was punishable with hanging, drawing, and quartering, the barbarous process to which Shakespeare makes familiar

SIR EDWARD COKE

from the painting by

CORNELIUS JANSEN VAN CEULEN

reference in *King John*, where Philip the Bastard, mocking the love-lorn Dauphin, says:

> Drawn in the flattering table of her eye!
> Hang'd in the frowning wrinkle of her brow!
> And quarter'd in her heart! he doth espy
> Himself love's traitor: this is pity now,
> That hang'd and drawn and quarter'd, there should be
> In such a love so vile a lout as he. (II. i. 504–9)

By a curious begging of the question the unfortunate person who was *accused* of treason was not even allowed the assistance of counsel. Persons accused of even ordinary felonies were not allowed counsel to address the jury on their behalf, but merely to examine and cross-examine witnesses and argue points of law, until the early part of the nineteenth century, when, in spite of strong protests from several of the Common Law judges, the privilege was granted.

In cases of high treason or petty treason by women (i. e. murder, or conniving at the murder, of a husband or master) the sentence was death by burning, which Blackstone (apparently without conscious irony) attributes to the regard of our ancestors ' for the decency due to the sex ' (4 Bl. Comm. 93).

The same terrible fate was awarded freely to the unfortunate women who were found guilty of the imaginary offence of witchcraft, and occasionally (notwithstanding the statute 1 Elizabeth, c. 1, which repealed all the statutes relating to heresy) the writ *de comburendo heretico* was issued (probably illegally) for the burning of a ' contumacious ' or ' relapsed ' heretic. Two Anabaptists, for instance, were sent to the fire in 17 Elizabeth, and two Arians in 9 James I.

Shakespeare refers to the burning of heretics in several passages. For instance :

> When the devout religion of mine eye
> Maintains such falsehood, then turn tears to fires !
> And these, who often drown'd could never die,
> Transparent heretics, be burnt for liars !
>
> (*Rom. & Jul.* I. ii. 93–6)

And again in *King Lear* (III. ii. 84) the Fool predicts the confusion of England when, among other follies, no heretics are burned.

Probably Shakespeare, like the rest of his contemporaries, had a firm belief in the reality of witchcraft ; for at the trial of the Suffolk witches in 1664 (nearly fifty years after Shakespeare's death) we find the presiding judge, Sir Matthew Hale, directing the jury that ' it was undoubted that there were such creatures as witches, for the Scripture affirmed it, and the wisdom of nations had provided laws against such persons ' (*State Trials*, vi. 647).

In *2 Henry VI* (II. iii. 5–7) the King is made to say :

> You four, from hence to prison back again ;
> From thence, unto the place of execution :
> The witch in Smithfield shall be burn'd to ashes.

Statutes against witchcraft were passed in the reigns of Henry VIII and Elizabeth. James I wrote a tract on it, and nearly all the writers and playwrights of the period are full of allusions to it.

Other barbarous punishments were also common for misdemeanours, such as amputation of the hand, the stump being thrust into boiling pitch or tar (when the mutilation was not intended to be merely preliminary to the execution of a death-sentence), not to speak of the pillory for political offenders, the ducking-stool for women with too free a tongue, and whipping ' at the cart's tail ' for both sexes.

Here is an ' impressionist ' picture of the fierce tone of the criminal courts of the seventeenth century set in a grotesque frame of the barbarous law French of the day.[1]

Richardson C. J. de C. B., at Salisbury in summer 1631 fuit assault per prisoner condemne pur felony, que puis son condemnation ject un brickbat a le dit justice que narrowly mist. Et pur ceo immediately fuit indictment drawn pur Noy enver le prisoner, et son dexter manus ampute et fixe al gibbet, sur que luy mesme immediatement hange in presence de Court.

One peculiar brutality must be mentioned, the *peine forte et dure*. When a prisoner accused of felony refused to plead he could not be tried, and as conviction of felony involved forfeiture of property, many bold men refused to plead, in order that their possessions might be preserved for their families. But they well knew the consequences. They were laid on their backs, and heavy weights piled on their breasts until they either gave way and consented to plead or died. This *peine forte et dure*, which Shakespeare calls ' pressing to death' in *Measure for Measure* (V. i. 525), was not abolished until the reign of George II.

---

[1] Note per Treby, C.J., on the margin of his copy of Dyer's Reports, quoted in *Curiosities of the Law Reporters*.

Another drastic punishment of Shakespeare's day was the writ of *praemunire* for giving obedience to papal encroachments on the royal power. It was a statutory offence and punishment, dating back to 16 Richard II, c. 5, and the effect of the writ is correctly described in *Henry VIII* III. ii. 338–45), thus :

> Lord Cardinal, the king's further pleasure is,
> Because all those things you have done of late,
> By your power legatine, within this kingdom,
> Fall into the compass of a *praemunire*,
> That therefore such a writ be sued against you ;
> To forfeit all your goods, lands, tenements,
> Chattels, and whatsoever, and to be
> Out of the king's protection.

Another peculiarity still extant in Shakespeare's day, which only gradually died out some centuries later, was the extraordinary class privilege known as ' benefit of clergy '. Originally a privilege from temporal jurisdiction claimed by the Catholic Church for its ordained clergy, it was ultimately extended to all clerks, whether secular or religious, and its effect was, after the Reformation, to substitute imprisonment, and in some cases branding on the hand, for death, in the case of convicted felons who could read. This is referred to in *2 Henry VI* (IV. ii. 69–71) :

> But methinks he should stand in fear of fire, being burnt i' the hand for stealing of sheep.

By Elizabeth's time the benefit had by a series of statutes been disallowed in cases of petty treason, piracy, homicide, burglary, housebreaking with violence, highway robbery, horse-stealing, robbing of churches, theft from the person, rape, and abduction ; but the fact that eleven persons claimed benefit of clergy at Exeter Assizes in 1598, and were branded and released, instead of being hanged, shows how valuable the privilege was. Women (except originally professed nuns) were denied the privilege until 1692. In 1827 benefit of clergy was abolished generally, but, by a slip, peers were not included in that statute. The privilege was, however, taken from them in 1841.

Benefit of clergy is alluded to in *2 Henry VI* (IV. vii. 39–51), where Jack Cade says :

> Thou hast caused printing to be used ; and, contrary to the king, his crown, and dignity, thou hast built a paper-mill. It will be proved to thy face that thou hast men about thee that usually talk

of a noun and a verb, and such abominable words as no Christian ear can endure to hear. Thou hast appointed justices of peace, to call poor men before them about matters they were not able to answer. Moreover, thou hast put them in prison; *and because they could not read*, thou hast hanged them; when indeed only for that cause they have been most worthy to live.

One cannot help feeling some sympathy with Jack Cade in this impeachment of benefit of clergy, but Shakespeare himself gives no sign that it was any more obnoxious to him than the other matters denounced by Cade.

But perhaps the worst feature of the Criminal Courts in Shakespeare's time was the subservience of the judges to the executive. They were then appointed *durante bene placito*—removable at the sovereign's pleasure. It was not until early in the eighteenth century (12 & 13 Will. III, c. 2) that the judges were made independent of government influence, since when they have been appointed *quamdiu se bene gesserint*, and can only be dismissed on an address by both Houses of Parliament.

This subservience was not only shown in the conduct of trials, but in the withholding of the writ of Habeas Corpus when persons were imprisoned by order of the King or the Privy Council; and it was not until 16 Car. I, c. 10, that an attempt was made to remedy this, which was subsequently clinched by the famous Habeas Corpus Act, 1679, which still governs the subject, and imposes heavy penalties on judges who refuse to issue the writ.

The Elizabethan age was pitiless, and 'the way of the transgressor' was certainly made as hard as it could be.

LAND LAW AND OTHER BRANCHES OF PRIVATE LAW

The main principles of the law relating to land were much the same in Shakespeare's time as they are now, with the following exceptions: (1) Military tenures still existed; but actual military service had been, practically in all cases, commuted for a money payment called 'escuage'. Nevertheless the other burdensome incidents of the tenure, such as wardship, relief, &c., remained, and this had made them hateful. They were, however, not abolished until 1646. (2) The various ingenious purposes to which the Statute of Uses and the Statute of Wills of Henry VIII could be perverted had not yet been discovered; and (as a corollary) the modern system of strict settlement had not been invented. (3) The methods of conveying land, and of barring entails, dower, &c., were entirely different from what they are now, and were extremely quaint.

The first of these subjects was too technical for notice either by Shakespeare or other lay writers of that age. But the third is frequently referred to in popular Elizabethan literature. The common method of conveying land to a purchaser in fee simple was by ' feoffment with livery of seisin '. This is the most ancient form of assurance known to the law, and similar methods are still practised in communities whose civilization has not progressed so far as ours. The 'livery', i. e. delivery of possession, was either 'livery in deed', i. e. actual delivery, or 'livery in law '. In the case of livery in deed the owner (feoffor) and the donee or purchaser (the feoffee) met on the land itself, and the feoffor there and then delivered possession of it to the feoffee, at the same time stating by apt words that he enfeoffed him for whatever estate (i. e. interest) he was intended to take, e. g. if the fee simple were to be taken, the words would be, ' I deliver these lands to you and your heirs for ever '. No writing was at that date required for a valid feoffment to persons other than corporations, but in practice it was not unusual to have a ' charter of feoffment ' recording the transaction and the nature of the estate conferred. Very generally, too, some symbolical act was added, such as the delivery of a key, a twig, or a clod of earth.

' Livery in law' took place *in sight of* but not *on* the land, and was not complete unless and until the feoffee, in the joint lives of himself and the feoffor, actually took possession or attempted to do so but was stopped by force.

Feoffments gradually died out owing to the invention after Shakespeare's day of the lease and release operating under the Statute of Uses ; but instances of feoffments were not infrequent in the early part of last century.

References to this ancient method of conveying land are to be found in Elizabethan literature :

> Therefore inclyning to his goodly reason,
> Agreeing well both with the place and season,
> She gladly did of that same babe accept,
> As of her owne by liverey and seisin.
>
> (Spenser, *Faerie Queene*, VI. iv. 37)

Keep your possession, you have the door by th' ring;
That 's livery and seisin in England.
(Webster, *Devil's Law Case*, I. ii)

Shakespeare himself, however, never mentions the subject, although he was not only a considerable purchaser of real estate, but seems to have been involved in litigation in relation to it. In 1597 he purchased ' New Place ', Stratford-on-Avon, from a collateral ancestor of the present writer (one William Underhill), the property consisting of ' one messuage two barns and two gardens with their appurtenances ' ; but apparently owing to the sudden death of the vendor by poison in July 1597, the conveyance was not completed until 1602, when Shakespeare was enfeoffed by Hercules Underhill, the heir of William, on attaining his majority.

Shakespeare subsequently purchased other lands in the neighbourhood, including 107 acres of arable land in 1602, and 20 acres more in 1610. He also became a copyhold tenant of the Manor of Rowington in 1602. Last of all, in 1613 he bought a house and shops in Blackfriars.

With regard to the barring of estates tail and the prospective dower of married women, the method was very curious. For about two hundred years after the passing of the celebrated statute *de donis conditionalibus* (13 Edw. I, c. 1), estates tail (i. e. estates descendible only to the heirs or heirs male *of the body* of the original feoffee) were incapable of alienation either by gift or sale. But in the reign of Edward IV, an old device known as a Common Recovery (which had at one time been used to enable ecclesiastical corporations to acquire lands, notwithstanding the laws against mortmain) was applied to defeat the heirs in tail and persons claiming in remainder (i. e. in default of heirs of the body). This common recovery was a collusive action commenced by a friendly plaintiff (called the demandant) against the person in possession (tenant in tail, or sometimes tenant for life in possession and tenant in tail in remainder). asserting that the defendant claimed through some third person who had wrongfully deprived the demandant of the possession. The defendant pleaded that he derived his title from the crier of the Court who had warranted it, and demanded that the crier should be ' vouched to warranty ', i. e. called upon to defend the action. The crier (the ' com-

mon vouchee ') at once admitted the warranty, and craved
leave to 'imparl' (i.e. to negotiate outside the Court). He
then failed to return until judgement was given that the
demandant should recover the lands and that the common
vouchee should provide other lands for the defendant of
equal value, which of course he was quite incapable of
doing. Thus, by this fictitious judgement, the plaintiff
acquired an estate in fee simple, and forthwith conveyed it
to the defendant or his nominee, so defeating not only the
entail, but all remainders to take effect in the event of failure
of heirs of the body. Sometimes single vouching was
sufficient ; in other cases (for technical reasons) a double
vouching was necessary for a complete bar. In all cases the
whole proceeding was a solemn and costly farce. It seems
scarcely credible that this grotesque fooling should have
been enacted many times every year from the time of
Edward IV until that of William IV, when it was abolished
in favour of a simple enrolled deed.

A ' fine ' was somewhat similar to a recovery, but the
action was stopped before judgement by a collusive compromise. It was used mainly to enable married women to
join with their husbands in selling the fee-simple property of
either. Except by means of a fine, a husband could not
sell his own property free from his wife's contingent right
to dower ; and she, on the other hand, could not sell her
own property at all, being under coverture.

The impossibility of selling freehold land free from the
widow's right to dower without going to the expense of
a fine, led to various devices intended to prevent the right
ever attaching. In later times this barring of dower was
effected by an elaborate and highly technical system of
uses and powers operating under the Statute of Uses, and
this method lasted down to the reign of William IV. But
in Shakespeare's time the usual method was for a purchaser of land to take the conveyance not to himself alone,
but to himself and several friends (as trustees for him) in
joint tenancy, dower only attaching to lands held by one
person solely. When one of these joint tenants died, his
place was filled up by another person, and so the property
never became vested in a sole owner. This plan was
adopted when Shakespeare purchased his Blackfriars
property. Sir Sidney Lee conjectures that this was

done for the purpose of depriving Shakespeare's wife of dower, but to a conveyancer it is clear that it was necessary in order to enable him to mortgage the property (as he did the next day) without the expense and delay of a fine.

Fines and recoveries seem to have specially appealed to Shakespeare, who doubtless witnessed the process at Westminster Hall. Thus in the grave scene, Hamlet says:

This fellow might be in 's time a great buyer of land, with his statutes, his recognizances,[1] his fines, his double vouchers, his recoveries; is this the fine of his fines, and the recovery of his recoveries, to have his fine pate full of fine dirt? Will his vouchers vouch him no more of his purchases, and double ones too, than the length and breadth of a pair of indentures? (*Haml.* v. i. 110–18)

And again in *The Merry Wives of Windsor* (IV. ii. 227–30):

Mrs. Page. The spirit of wantonness is, sure, scared out of him: if the devil have him not in fee-simple, with fine and recovery, he will never, I think, in the way of waste, attempt us again.

So in *The Comedy of Errors* (II. ii. 74–9):

Dro. S. There's no time for a man to recover his hair that grows bald by nature.
Ant. S. May he not do it by fine and recovery?
Dro. S. Yes, to pay a fine for a periwig and recover the lost hair of another man.

The cutting off of entails was considered a desirable thing by Edward IV and his judges, otherwise the audacious common recovery could scarcely have been invented; but the question of fettering the free alienation of land has always been a burning one. A member of Lincoln's Inn in 1641 gravely treated the question as depending on the laws of God, and declared that to abstain from disentailing an estate in tail male was contrary to those laws, as the result might be to cut out daughters for the benefit of remote cousins, issue of the first tenant in tail; ' oneley ', he added sententiously, ' I must note by the way, that such as avoyd and cut off these estates to none other purpose but to enlarge their wanton expences, and to give them more scope to live licentiously, as they unjustly spoile their heires of their due inheritances, so shall not this my

---

[1] What ' statutes and recognizances ' had to do with the buying of land is not evident to a lawyer, and may suggest that Shakespeare's knowledge of the law of property was neither accurate nor extensive.

FRANCIS BACON by WILLIAM MARSHALL

defence extend unto them ; since my purpose onely is to
reduce estates taile to the most proper conveyance of the
Common Law ' ; and he concluded, ' I could never (after
long observation) find any family continue in the heires
male three descents after an entaile made and continued to
the heires male, by which I ghesse they are not watered
with heavenly blessings '.

Mortgages were on a very different footing from what they
are now. Shakespeare never mentions them, although, as
above mentioned, he mortgaged the house which he bought
in Blackfriars the day after the purchase.

Deeds (which were then usually called Specialties [1]) were
for the most part written in Latin ; in the case of bonds,
the actual bond was sometimes in Latin, and the condition
on which it was to become void in English. Deeds between
two or more parties were indented, i. e. after being written
in duplicate or triplicate on one skin of parchment, the
parts were severed by being cut in a wavy or indented line
so as to guard against forgery when the parts were fitted
together, whence the technical word 'indenture'. As
Hamlet says :

> Will his vouchers vouch him no more of his purchases, and double
> ones too, than the length and breadth of a pair of indentures ?
> (*Haml.* v. i. 115–18)

Marriage required no religious ceremony for its validity,
although the omission of it was an offence. The only essential was *verba de praesenti* (as distinguished from a promise
to marry at a future date), the man and woman saying to
each other, ' I receive you as mine '. No ceremony, no priest,
no physical consummation was required ; so that after such
a pre-contract (as it was called) neither party could marry
any other person. If either of them purported to do so, the
second marriage was bigamous and voidable, and the issue
of it bastards. Shakespeare clearly refers to this in *Measure
for Measure* (I. ii. 157–9), where Claudio insists, after his
condemnation to death for cohabitation with Juliet without
the previous sanction of the Church,

> She is fast my wife,
> Save that we do the denunciation lack
> Of outward order.

---

[1] Let specialties be therefore drawn between us,
That covenants may be kept on either hand. (*Tam. Sh.* II. i. 127–8

And again, where the Duke, urging Mariana to simulate Isabella and accept the embraces of Angelo, says :

> Gentle daughter, fear you not at all.
> He is your husband on a pre-contract :
> To bring you thus together, 'tis no sin.
>
> (*Meas. for M*. IV. i. 72–4)

In short, Angelo's condemnation of Claudio for alleged fornication was, and was intended by Shakespeare to be, absolutely tyrannical and illegal.

It was quite common form in Shakespeare's day for a bridegroom to give a bond that no pre-contract existed. Shakespeare himself gave one on the occasion of his marriage.[1] Curiously enough, too, Lord Coke married his second wife, Lady Hatton, in a private room, as she refused to go to church with so old a man. For this offence he was prosecuted, but got off by pleading ' ignorance of the law ', a plea which must have given great joy in legal circles. But no one suggested that the marriage was invalid.

The capacity of making a will of lands was, in the time of Shakespeare, as ample as it is now; except that where lands were held by military tenure the power was confined to two-thirds of them. It would seem, however, that with regard to personal property the ancient law restricted the owner to the disposal of one-third only if he left wife and child, or one-half if he left a wife only, the wife and children having (as in Scotland at the present day) a right to the rest. This was clearly enunciated as still existing law by Sir Harry Finch in the reign of Charles I, although Coke doubted it. But apparently it was considered a moot point and practically obsolete in Shakespeare's day, and was certainly ignored in his own will. It also seems that in cases of intestacy the wife and children took in the same shares as above, but that, subject to their claims, the residue went to the person to whom the Ordinary granted administration. Nominally he took it for *pios usus*, but practically he could keep it for himself, until the Statute of Distributions (22 & 23 Car. II, c. 10) deprived him of the right.

THE INNS OF COURT AND OF CHANCERY

The four Inns of Court—the Middle Temple, the Inner Temple, Lincoln's Inn, Gray's Inn—were at the height of

---

[1] Halliwell-Phillipps, 7th ed. (1887), vol. ii, p. 55.

their glory in Elizabeth's reign. Whatever their true origin, it is certain that at that date they formed, along with the more humble Inns of Chancery, a set of colleges for the study of the law, linked together (in imitation of the colleges at Oxford and Cambridge) into what would have been a University if they had been incorporated. The Benchers represented the Master and Fellows of a college, the Utter or Outer Barristers (the Junior Bar of to-day) the Masters of Arts, and the Inner Barristers (now the students) the Bachelors and undergraduates. To make the analogy with Oxford and Cambridge more complete, each Inn of Court had its dining hall, its library, and its chapel ; except that the two Temples shared the beautiful old church of the Templars between them. Like a college, too, each Inn was enclosed, and had its garden. All these features survive to the present day, except that the halls and libraries of Lincoln's Inn and the Inner Temple, and the libraries of the Middle Temple and Gray's Inn, were rebuilt during the last century. The Middle Temple Hall dates from 1572, and that of Gray's Inn from 1556.

Legal education seems to have been without much method, consisting of readings and moots, and the period of proba-tion was extraordinarily long. ' For the space of seven years or thereabouts ', says Stow, ' they frequent readings, mootings, boltinges, and other learned exercises, whereby, growing ripe in the knowledge of the lawes, and approved withal to be of honest conversation, they are selected and called to the degree of Utter Barristers.'

Every year the Benchers chose from among their own number two ' Readers ' whose election was the occasion of a mighty feast. These learned persons occasionally delivered a reading—a lecture as we should call it now—on some single point, after which the Utter Barristers would debate it, and finally some of the Bench would give their views.

This does not seem to be a very hopeful system of teaching the law. Coke lamented the inferiority of the ' Readings ' in his day to those of the past, saying (1 Inst. 280 h) :

But now readings have lost the said former qualities, have lost also their former authorities : for now the cases are long, obscure, and intricate, full of new conceits, like rather to riddles than lectures, which, when they are opened, they vanish away like smoke ; and the Readers are like to lapwings, who seem to be nearest their nests when they are farthest from them.

Dugdale, in his *Origines*, mentioned that some of the Utter Barristers were also appointed to assist the younger students, much as is done now by the Council of Legal Education ; and one may make a shrewd guess that it was (as it is still) by the labour of these gentlemen, coupled with invaluable practical experience in the chambers of counsel in good practice as pleaders and conveyancers, and by attendance at the Courts, that the young barrister of Shakespeare's day got his real professional education. Textbooks were few and invariably in Latin.

The Inns were very exclusive in those days, admitting none except 'gentlemen of blood', and this was enjoined by a royal command of James I. There were numerous sumptuary and disciplinary regulations enforced by fines, putting out of commons, and even apparently by imprisonment. Thus, attendance at chapel, shaving 'at least once in three weeks', the wearing of gowns even outside the Inns, the renunciation of swords and bucklers, boots and spurs, great hose, great ruffs, silks and furs, were all insisted on.

On certain feast days there were revels. At Christmas, for instance, according to Dugdale, there were revels and dancing every night from Christmas Day to Twelfth Night, even the Justices, Serjeants, and Benchers (the two former must have been guests) dancing apparently *pas seuls*. But the world was younger then than now, when such performances by the sages of the law are scarcely imaginable.

The early Elizabethan drama owed much stimulus to the performance by barristers of plays in their halls at festive seasons. It was in the Hall of the Inner Temple on Twelfth Night, 1561, that the first English tragedy, *Gorboduc*, which was written by two members of the Inn, was first acted. Again, the first regular English comedy, *Supposes*, was first acted in Gray's Inn Hall, five years later, the authors, George Gascoigne and Francis Kilwelmershe, being both students of the Society ; in both these plays the actors as well as the authors belonged to the legal profession. Instances of like procedure abound throughout the period of Shakespeare's professional career, although the pieces which were presented in the halls of the Inns were not always from lawyers' pens. It was for a Christmas revel at the Middle Temple that Shakespeare wrote *Twelfth Night* ; and *The Comedy of Errors* was certainly played in Gray's Inn Hall in 1594 in the intervals of ' dancing and revelry with gentlewomen '.

The origin of the eight lesser Inns of Chancery—Thavies', Furnival's, Barnard's, Staple, Clifford's, Clement's, New, Lyon's—is even more obscure than that of the four Inns of Court. They appear, however, to have been resorted to by the clerks in Chancery, and by students who were unable to gain access to the Inns of Court, and, at all events at one time, were considered as preparatory schools. When, however, in 1557 the Inner Temple refused admission to attorneys and solicitors, and in 1574 expelled such as still remained on their books, they seem to have taken refuge in the Inns of Chancery, which, by the middle of the seventeenth century, had been abandoned to them. Shakespeare makes no mention of them collectively, although he mentions individual Inns such as Clement's Inn, to which Justice Shallow belonged :

Shallow. A' must, then, to the inns o' court shortly. I was once of Clement's Inn ; where I think they will talk of mad Shallow yet. (*2 Hen. IV*, III. ii. 14–16)

And later on, in the same scene (24–5) :

You had not four such swinge-bucklers in all the inns of court.

And still further (34–7) :

The very same day did I fight with one Sampson Stockfish, a fruiterer, behind Gray's Inn. Jesu! Jesu! the mad days that I have spent.

The Serjeants had Inns of their own, and were with much ceremonial dismissed from their Inn of Court upon being promoted to the coif. This was a most expensive proceeding, involving the presentation of gold rings to all the other Serjeants and divers other great persons, and a feast at the Inn of Court to which the newly made Serjeant belonged, which is said to have cost sometimes over £600. With the virtual abolition of the Order in the last quarter of the nineteenth century, all this of course came to an end, and Serjeants' Inn in Chancery Lane was sold and demolished.

On the whole the constitution of the Inns of Court remains much what it was in the year 1600 ; but the readings, the revellings, the ' boltinges ', even (with the exception of Gray's Inn) the moots, the dancings of Lord Chancellors and judges round the hall fire at Christmas time, nay, even the social life, have for the most part vanished.

BIBLIOGRAPHY.—The chief legal work by a contemporary of Shakespeare is COKE's *Institutes of the Laws of England*, in four parts (1628, 1642, 1644). FERDINANDO PULTON's *Statutes at Large* (1618) is the standard authority for the text of the statutes in force at the time of publication. A special branch of legal procedure is fully treated in WILLIAM LAMBARDE's *Eirenarcha, or Of the Office of the Justice of Peace* (1581-8, 1610). A more popular account of the common law is ABRAHAM FRAUNCE's *Lawiers Logike* (1588).

The chief law reports of the period are those by EDMUND PLOWDEN, of which the first part came out in 1571 and the second part in 1579; by SIR EDMUND ANDERSON, whose work, covering the period 1574-1603, was first published in 1664; COKE's *Reports*, in thirteen parts, 1600-15. An elaborate account of all the Inns of Court of the time in London is given in Sir GEORGE BUCK's *The Third Universitie of England* (London, 1631)—an appendix to STOW's *Annales*.

The chief works on the history of law and law-courts of Shakespeare's day are: POLLOCK and MAITLAND's *History of English Law*; STEPHEN's *History of the Criminal Law*; CARTER's *English Legal Institutions*; DUGDALE's *Origines Judiciales*; FORTESCUE's *De Laudibus legum Angliae*; INDERWICK's *The King's Peace*; PULLING's *Order of the Coif*; HEARD's *Curiosities of the Law Reporters*; BLACKSTONE's *Commentaries*; *Select Legal Essays*, published by the Association of Law Schools of the United States of America.

The chief works on Shakespeare's knowledge of law are: Lord CAMPBELL's *Shakespeare's Legal Acquirements Considered*, 1859; C. K. DAVIS's *The Law in Shakespeare*, New York, 1884; F. F. HEARD's *Shakespeare as a Lawyer*, New York, 1883; and CHARLES ALLEN's *Notes on the Bacon-Shakespeare Question*, Boston, 1900.

XIV

MEDICINE

BY

ALBAN H. G. DORAN

THE PHYSICIAN

At the outset of the tragedy that bears his name, Richard II, anxious to preserve the peace between his nobles, exhorts them to ' purge this choler without letting blood '.

> This we prescribe though no physician . . .
> Our doctors say this is no month to bleed. (*Rich. II*, I. i. 154)

Lafeu talks of ' Doctor She ' (*All's W*. II. i. 82), and Cymbeline asks—

> Whom worse than a physician
> Would this report become ? . . .
> . . . yet death
> Will seize the doctor too.   (*Cymb.* v. v. 27–8)

Thus in Shakespeare's England ' physician ' and ' doctor ' were already understood, as now, to be almost synonymous. Lafeu also speaks of Helena as a ' medicine' (*All's W*. II. i. 75), a word likewise used by Caithness (*Macb.* v. ii. 27) and Florizel (*Wint. Tale*, IV. iii. 600) to signify ' doctor '. ' Leech ' occurs only once, namely, where Alcibiades closes *Timon of Athens* with his speech on peace and war. This, the native word, was first replaced by the French-derived ' medicine', which was in its turn ousted by ' doctor'.

The Saxon ' leeches ' were succeeded by monk physicians who came over with the Normans. Notwithstanding papal prohibitions (1163 and 1215) which were directed against surgery, that is, the shedding of blood, several eminent ecclesiastics practised in the fifteenth century, and the servants of the clergy, especially the barbers, were sent out to the laity to bleed and to draw teeth. In Shakespeare's own days the College of Physicians refused to allow any man in orders to practise. Dr. Alexander Leighton, who afterwards lost his ears for his attack on episcopacy, was inhibited in 1617 because he was a clergyman, but proved contumacious. The Church, on the other hand, granted licences

Der Doctor.

Ich bin ein Doctor der Artzney/
An dem Harn kan ich sehen frey
Was kranckheit ein Menschn thut beladn
Dem kan ich helffen mit Gotts gnadn
Durch ein Syrup oder Recept
Das seiner kranckheit widerstrebt/
Daß der Mensch wider werd gesund/
Arabo die Artzney erfund.

The Doctor, by Jost Amman.

to practise medicine and surgery, a custom made law in 1511.[1] The licentiates were 'first examined, approved, and

[1] The Act of 1511 is distinct from that passed twenty years later whereby the Archbishop of Canterbury was empowered to grant degrees in medicine as well as in other faculties. (The Lambeth M.D. was abolished by the Medical Act of 1858.)

admitted by the Bishop of London or the Dean of St. Paul's calling to him or them four Doctors of Physick, and for Surgery other expert persons in that faculty'. These practitioners 'in nomine Domini' were, nevertheless, distrusted.

Friar Laurence is represented as a doctor and a medical botanist (*Rom. & Jul.* II. iii. 7). When interrupted by Romeo, he was about to collect baleful weeds and precious-juiced flowers. The qualified laymen in Shakespeare's time were sometimes botanists as well. This was the case with Gerarde, who tells us in his *Herbal* that he found a variety of the woody nightshade with white flowers 'in a ditch side against the garden wall of the right honourable the Earle of Sussex his house in Bermondsey streete by London'.

In 1546 Regius Professorships of medicine or physic were founded at both the Universities of Oxford and Cambridge; and when Gresham College was established in 1597 a professorship was instituted there, a flourishing practitioner, Dr. Matthew Gwinne, being its first holder.

Two qualifying bodies, the College of Physicians and the Company of Barber-Surgeons, were in full swing when Shakespeare was born. The mighty College of Physicians was founded in 1518, on the prayer of Linacre joined to that of three other physicians, and Cardinal Wolsey. Its original home was Linacre's own house in Knightrider Street, bequeathed to the institution, but from 1560 until its removal to Warwick Lane in 1674, it occupied premises at Amen Corner. In Queen Elizabeth's time its authority was fully recognized, and Shakespeare mentions it with respect as 'the congregated college' (*All's W.* II. i. 120). It was at first a qualifying body only and provided no medical education, but in 1582-3 Lord Lumley, together with Richard Caldwell, M.D., founded the Lumleian lecture in Surgery at the College with a stipend of £40. The great Harvey, when he held the chair, had much trouble about the salary.

The physicians were men of good education, and their degrees were generally taken abroad, at Padua, Heidelberg, Leyden, Basle, or Montpellier, for example, and they were incorporated afterwards at Oxford or Cambridge. Linacre, Caius, and Harvey all graduated at Padua. This habit of seeking medical education abroad raised adverse criticism in England. Harrison insisted that medical and legal education was as well conducted at Oxford and Cambridge as elsewhere, and expressed strong objections to sending youths on their travels. He quoted Peter Turner, a well-known physician of the day, in evidence that Italy was a perilous place for the student 'because of the licentious and corrupt behaviour of the people'. A low standard of morality prevailed in the medical profession in Italy to the great hurt of English students, who learnt, as Harrison declares, 'the framing of such compositions [i. e. poisons] as were better known than practised'. Stubbes was even more plain-spoken. He felt assured that some physicians 'if they hope for any preferment by their patients' deaths, will give them such medicines, such potions and drinks, as will soon make an end of them'. Qualified English physicians may be held quite guiltless of such crimes, but a 'mortal mineral' was easily purchasable from struggling doctors by unqualified persons (*Cymb.* v. v. 50), and it cannot be doubted that recipes for subtle poisoning freely circulated in Shakespeare's England outside medical circles. Shakespeare was alive when Sir Thomas Overbury was poisoned in the Tower (1613). The victim was drugged by slow poisons prepared by an apothecary and mixed by his enemies with his food. An apothecary's assistant provided the poison which ultimately proved fatal. None of the physicians in attendance were suspected of complicity. The apothecaries and the humbler among those who employed them suffered capital punishment.

From its inauguration in 1518, the College of Physicians held examinations for the licentiate, conducted by officials known as Censors. The candidate must have graduated at a university. No previous apprenticeship was required, but most young men who intended to become doctors began their careers by work under a qualified physician. The College was especially strict about its admissions to practise in London and the suburbs. A very rigorous examination had to be passed before licences were granted for practising in the metropolitan area, and the metropolitan licentiates were known specifically as 'candidates' and were of a standing equivalent to that of the 'Members' of the Royal College of Physicians of the present day. The title signified that they were candidates for the Fellowship of the College, which was conferred on those who proved of good repute after a probationary period. The College was less severe about licences to practise in the country.

The College undertook the selection of a medical officer to attend generals and admirals during their campaigns. In 1591 Dr. Moffett accompanied Essex's troops in Normandy, while Dr. Marbeck was present when Essex, in 1596, sacked Cadiz, being physician to the Lord High Admiral Lord Howard of Effingham. He wrote *A Brief and True Discourse of the Late Honourable Voyage into Spaine.* Dr. Atkins was selected physician ' ad nobilissimum comitem Essex ' for the ill-fated ' Islands Voyage ' in 1597, leaving Plymouth with the fleet.[1] He apparently did not know of Pisanio's prescription—

> if you are sick at sea,
> . . . a dram of this
> Will drive away distemper,   (*Cymb.* III. iv. 192-4)

for he suffered so badly ' ex jactitatione maris ' that he was put ashore and Dr. Mountford was appointed in his place. It is not clear that the substitute ever sailed. Atkins's prospects were not ruined, for he was deputed in 1604 by James I to bring the infant Charles Stuart from Scotland to England, and died in 1635 a very wealthy man. The physician or surgeon appointed to the Army or the Fleet was his general's or admiral's officer. Thus Clowes, who served in the Earl of Warwick's army, had the lid of his case of surgical instruments stamped with the bear and ragged staff as well as with the royal cipher or arms.

In 1565, when Shakespeare was an infant, Queen Elizabeth granted the College permission to dissect human subjects on its premises. The Fellows were called on, under fine for refusal, to give in turn a public demonstration and to deliver anatomical lectures.

The greatest man of science among English physicians in Shakespeare's days was William Harvey, born at Folkestone in 1578, the son of a Kentish yeoman. When sixteen years of age he became a pensioner of Gonville and Caius College. In 1598 he went abroad and studied under

---

[1] For another instance, cf. Sidney Young, *Annals of the Barber Surgeons*, p. 321 : December 7, 1598. ' This daye commaundmt cam from the lordes of her mats most ho: privie councell for to presse a sufficient Surgeon for her mats s'vice in Ireland under the conduct of Captayne Windsor.' We trust that the surgeon came off better than the Commander Essex, who did not bring back ' rebellion broached on his sword ' (*Hen. V*, v. Chor. 32).

Fabricius ab Aquapendente at Padua. This distinguished anatomist found that the valves of the veins opened towards the heart, a truth which led Harvey to a greater discovery. Unlike most students of medicine of that time, master and pupil studied from the 'subject' and not merely from books and plates. In 1602 Harvey received the degree of M.D. of Padua, in 1604 he incorporated at Cambridge, and five years later was elected physician to St. Bartholomew's Hospital, where he carefully attended patients. In 1615 he was made Lumleian Lecturer at the College of Physicians. The second lecture was delivered on April 17, 1616, just six days before Shakespeare died. From this lecture it is clear that Harvey had already completed his discovery of the circulation of the blood, and disproved the existing notion that the heart was merely a fountain of supply. For the first time, Harvey lucidly demonstrated the real action of the heart and the course which the blood took through the arteries. Others had already made the suggestion conjecturally and without demonstration; Caesalpinus had advanced a correct theory in his *Quaestiones Peripateticae* published in Florence in 1569 ; Servetus had described the pulmonary circulation in *Christianismi Restitutio*, a religious book which was printed at Vienne in 1553 ; but Harvey was the first to indicate by experiment the true nature of the facts. His great discovery was first published at Frankfort in 1628, in his *Exercitatio Anatomica de Motu Cordis et Sanguinis*, but he had completed his investigations twelve years earlier. Harvey lived till 1657, and saw his great discovery established all over Europe.

Theodore Touquet de Mayerne, Baron d'Aubonne (1573–1655), became a famous London doctor. When physician to Henri Quatre he was persecuted by the Faculty of Medicine of Paris because he was an anti-Galenist, Quercetanus suffering with him. Lafeu and Parolles relate (*All's W.* II. iii. 10–12) how the King, when cured by Helena, had been 'relinquish'd of the artists . . . both of Galen and Paracelsus '.[1] Mayerne, a Protestant born in Geneva, did not think Paris well worth a mass, and was much disliked by Marie de Médicis. The Faculty boycotted him in 1606, and as its members were forbidden

---

[1] The Paracelsians, as against the Galenists, laid stress upon chemical principles.

to consult with him, he came to England a year later. The College of Physicians admitted him into its circle, his Montpellier degree was accepted at Oxford, James I knighted him, and as Sir Theodore de Mayerne he rose to the highest position among the doctors at Court. It was Mayerne who introduced calomel into practice. He had many distinguished patients and attended in his early days the Earl of Salisbury, Lord Rochester, Prince Henry, and Isaac Casaubon. He wrote a history of Prince Henry's fatal illness, which was almost certainly typhoid fever.

Sir William Paddy (1554–1634), an excellent doctor, was appointed physician to James I on his accession. The profession occasionally attracted men of letters. The poet and dramatist Thomas Lodge took to medicine when over forty, and graduated M.D., at Avignon, it is said, in 1600. He practised for over twenty years in London, and wrote a *Treatise on the Plague* in 1603, when there was an epidemic of that terrible malady in England. While denouncing astrology, he believed in Avicenna's theory that the disease could be warded off by the wearing of an Eastern 'hyacinth', too often a 'counterfeit stone' (*Wint. Tale*, IV. iii. 610). Lodge's prescriptions did not rise above the empiric standards of the time. He prescribed the application of a fowl, after the plucking out of its tail feathers, to a plague carbuncle, which was still orthodox treatment in the great visitation of 1665. Lodge, who passed unscathed through the epidemic, was persecuted in his latter days as a Roman Catholic, and died in 1625. Like Caius the physician, and the majority of the surgeons in Shakespeare's days, Lodge wrote his medical works in the 'vulgar tongue'.

Many distinguished physicians practised in the provinces, Caius for a time in Shrewsbury, and afterwards in Norwich; and Moffett in Ipswich about 1588. John Hall, Shakespeare's son-in-law, was a country doctor from the date of his marriage in 1607 till his death in 1635, and he left interesting notes about his patients. He was only eleven years younger than his father-in-law. Hall held no medical degree, and though he called himself Master of Arts, his university is not known. His practice extended far, and among his patients were Lord Compton and the Earl of Warwick, who lived at Ludlow, forty miles from Stratford. The parish register described him on his death as 'medicus

peritissimus'.   Eight years after Hall's death, a detachment
of the parliamentary army visited his widow at New Place.
Its surgeon was James Cooke, of Warwick, author of *The
Marrow of Chirurgery*, and she showed him a packet of
manuscript notes in Latin made during the last thirteen
years of her husband's life, and now preserved in the British
Museum (Egerton MS. 2065).   Cooke 'put into English for
common benefit' these notes which were published in London
in 1657 with the title *Select Observations on English Bodies :
or, Cures both Empericall and Historicall, performed upon very
eminent Persons in desperate Diseases.   First, written in Latine
by Mr. John Hall Physician, living at Stratford upon Avon . . .
where he was very famous.*   These notes, we must remember,
were meant to be private, so that their publication under
ordinary circumstances would be indefensible.   Hall records
how he himself was seized with a bad attack of a painful
malady.   He physicked himself and was already getting
better when two other doctors, summoned by the faithful
Susannah, attended him at New Place.   Hall's treatment
was very active, and his prescriptions were highly complicated.   He doctored his wife successfully for acute dyspepsia
and proudly records how by similar means 'i delivered
the Earl of Northampton from a grievous cholick'.   Hall's
only daughter, Elizabeth, had two bad attacks of face-ache.
Her ' Neck was fomented with Aqua Vitae in which was
infused Nutmegs, Cinnamon, Cloves, Pepper.   She eat
Nutmegs often.'   He also attended her for an ' Erratick
Feaver'.   After his usual polypharmacy, 'she was delivered
from death and deadly diseases and was well for many
years.   To God be praise.'   His wife took the scurvy with
disagreeable complications, including ' melancholie ' and
'laziness'; the prescription of the medicine which she took
fills an octavo page in small print, and ' by these she was
cured '.   A ' new Feaver ' from which ' the Lady Beaufou,
godly honest, being of noble extract ', recovered under
Hall's treatment, appears to have been small-pox.   Drayton,
author of the *Poly-Olbion*, was treated when suffering from
a ' Tertian ' with an ' Emetick Infusion ' mixed with syrup
of violets, which quickly brought him into the way of
convalescence.

The physician's fee seems to have been one angel
a visit, and he was apt to overdo his visits.   He often

gained more than a competence. The word 'fee' in the
sense of a doctor's honorarium only occurs once in the
plays—when Kent exclaims to King Lear,

> Kill thy physician and the fee bestow
> Upon the foul disease. (*Lear*, I. i. 166–7)

The physician arranged with a chirurgeon and an apothecary to be at his service, as Nicholas Breton notes in *The
Good and the Bad* (1616).

Shakespeare's plays show that he had heard much about
the teaching of practical anatomy and understood certain
theories about the movement of the blood. He wrote of

> the ruddy drops
> That visit my sad heart; (*Jul. Cæs.* II. i. 289–90)

and described the belly as sending 'the general food . . .
which you do live upon'

> through the rivers of your blood,
> Even to the court, the heart. (*Cor.* I. i. 137–42)

Such language, however, is perhaps merely figurative, and
the poet died before Harvey's views were made public,
and doubtless held the old notion that the blood flowed in
the veins, and that the arteries held, besides blood, the
vital spirits. 'Why,' says Biron—

> universal plodding prisons up
> The nimble spirits in the arteries. (*L. L. L.* IV. iii. 305–6)

The direct filling of the veins by nourishment was another
error which Shakespeare accepted. Menenius says

> The veins unfilled, our blood is cold . . .
> . . . but when we have stuff'd
> These pipes and these conveyances of our blood
> With wine and feeding, we have suppler souls. (*Cor.* V. i. 52–6)

Space will not allow any full criticism of anatomical
references in the plays. 'Pia mater', a membrane immediately investing the brain, is used in *Troilus and Cressida*
(II. i. 77) to mean the brain itself, whilst in other plays (*Love's
L. L.* IV. ii. 71, &c.) references to the pia mater are based on
false theories then in vogue. The 'ventricle of memory'
(*ibid.*)—*ventriculus* or *cellula memorativa*—in mediaeval
nomenclature was the third ventricle of the brain, the first
and second being the seat of imagination and reason.

Gratiano, Sir Toby Belch, and Falstaff allude to the
bloodless liver of the coward (*Merch. of V.* III. ii. 86, *Tw. N.*

III. ii. 69, *2 Hen. IV*, IV. iii. 113) and to the warming of the liver by wine (*Merch. of V.* I. i. 81), a popular idea based on a theory of Hippocrates.

Perhaps the most arresting, from the modern point of view, of the old medical theories represented in Shakespeare is the theory of the humours, which survived well into the seventeenth century.   It was held that four humours or fluids entered into the composition of a man[1] —blood, phlegm, choler (or yellow bile), and melancholy (or black bile) ; that the predominance of one or other of them determined the temperament as sanguine, phlegmatic, choleric, or melancholy; that an excess or morbid condition of any of them caused disease, and that the cure lay in purging or avoiding the peccant humour, as by reducing the amount of blood by cupping or reducing the bile by means of drugs.   The theory is illustrated in many passages. Melancholy is called ' the black oppressing humour ' (*Love's L.L.*I.i.233); Falstaff is 'that trunk of humours' (*I Hen.IV*, II. iv. 501) ; Ajax is a man into whom Nature has ' crowded humours ' (*Troilus*, I. ii. 23).   A morbid condition is signified in the following passages :

> *D. Pedro.* What ! sigh for the tooth-ache ?
> *Leon.*   Where is but a humour or a worm ?
>
> <div align="right">(<i>Much Ado</i>, III. ii. 26–7)</div>
>
> through all thy veins shall run
> A cold and drowsy humour.   (*Rom. & Jul.* IV. i. 95–6)
>
> This inundation of mistemper'd humour
> Rests by you only to be qualified :
> Then pause not ; for the present time 's so sick,
> That present medicine must be minister'd ; (*John*, V. i. 12–15)

and the form of cure is referred to in the well-known lines of *Richard II* with which this chapter opens.

THE SURGEON

Although surgery is mentioned more than once in Shakespeare's plays, there is no surgeon among his dramatis personae, no counterpart to the physicians of *Macbeth, King Lear, Cymbeline,* and *Pericles.*   Contemporary references

---

[1] This notion was so familiar that it is the basis of many metaphors and allusions in Elizabethan literature ; and it gave rise to the use of ' humour ' in the successive senses of temperament, constitutional tendency, mood, temper, disposition, fancy, caprice, and finally (long after Shakespeare's death) the current modern acceptation.

From an engraving after a picture by HOLBEIN

HENRY VIII CONFERRING A CHARTER UPON THE SURGEONS COMPANY

to the surgeon are on the whole uncomplimentary. The Clown informs Sir Toby Belch that ' Dick Surgeon ' is too intoxicated to attend to his duties (*Tw. N.* v. i. 202). Sir Thomas Overbury (1581–1613), in his *Characters*, contrasts the surgeon very unfavourably with the physician. Nashe, inveighing against the vice of London in *Pierce Penilesse*, couples him with the apothecary in his censure: ' Surgeons and Apothecaries, you know what I speake is true, for you live (like Sumners[1]) upon the sinnes of the people.' Allusions to bleeding are frequent in the plays. Biron, with direct reference to receptacles employed for measuring with accuracy the amount of blood removed, talks about letting out the fever in Dumain's blood in saucers (*Love's L. L.* IV. iii. 98). They are recommended in *The Surgeon's Mate*, written by Woodall, medical officer in the army of ' brave Lord Willoughby ' in the Low Countries in 1591. Richard II, when hearing Hereford's ' boisterous appeal ', proposes to ' purge this choler without letting blood ' (*Rich. II*, I. i. 153), and Ajax offers to let Achilles' 'humours blood' (*Troilus*, II. iii. 226). The Saxon ' leech ' had used the *ǽdderseax* (vein-knife or lancet) long before Shakespeare's days.

In 1308 Richard le Barber was sworn first master of the Barbers' Company, and in 1493 there was an informal alliance between the Barber Surgeons and a Fellowship of Surgeons which had developed early in the fifteenth century. In 1540 they were formally united (Act 32 Henry VIII), and opened a common hall in Monkwell Street. Holbein's picture (here reproduced) of the presentation of the charter by the King is still the chief treasure of the Company, while the preliminary design for the original picture is to be seen at the Royal College of Surgeons. The Barbers and Surgeons remained united until 1745. In 1569 the Company received a grant of arms, and in 1605 a new charter.

This union gave the surgeon the benefit of great municipal and corporate privileges, whilst his barber-colleagues were precluded from all surgical work except bleeding and dentistry. The surgical department of the Company did admirable work in Shakespeare's days. The apprentice was as well cared for physically and morally as he was

---

[1] Summoners for ecclesiastical courts.

well educated. In 1556 his master was required to forbid him 'to weare a bearde past xv dayes growing'. If he were rightly corrected 'for pleaing at dice', he could on the

Der Zanbrecher.

Wolher/wer hat ein bösen Zan/
Denselben ich außbrechen kan/
On wehtagn / wie man gbiert die Kinder/
Auch hab ich Kramschatz nicht destmindr/
Petrolium vnd Wurmsamen/
Thriacks vnd viel Mückenschwamen/
Hab auch gut Salbn / für Flöhe vñ Leuß/
Auch Puluer für Ratzen vnd Meuß.

The Barber-Dentist, by Jost Amman.

other hand charge his master 'for lack of vittuals' and the master was bound to 'kepe him as an app'ntice ought to be kept'. Even a youth that had no 'skyll of the Latin tonge' might become a 'prentice. After his 'examynation' the apprentice, if he passed, was 'made free', paying a very moderate fee.

The Company enforced strict rules for consultation between the Fellows about any case 'in perill of mayme or dethe'. In June 1568 John Frende was 'committed to ward for a pacient dying under his hand and not presented', and many other Fellows were prosecuted. The 'profitt' of a consultation or 'presentation' was divided by 'even porcions among the Master Governors and Deputies'.

In addition, this enlightened corporation held what is now called a post-graduate course, and attendance at demonstrations of anatomy were made compulsory on the Fellows in 1572. Two Masters and two Stewards 'of the anatomies' were chosen annually. The professors received the corpses of convicts, but there is no evidence that even on one single occasion did a living person come under the scalpel of the anatomist excepting when in 1587 the corpse of a malefactor came to life. This misadventure is recorded in Stow's *Annals* in 1592, and an article had to be framed to meet such a case in future. The demonstrations were conducted with perfect decency about four times a year, corresponding to the supply of the bodies of four executed felons [1] granted yearly according to the charter of 1540. A member could obtain permission to perform a 'private anatomy' at the Hall.

Thus the study of anatomy from the human subject had become generalized in the poet's day. The great leader in the new movement was Andreas Witing of Wesel, known as Vesalius, who died at Zante in 1564 when Shakespeare was an infant. Vesalius set up his first articulated skeleton in 1535, and in 1568 there was at least one 'skellyton' in Barbers' Hall. When Antipholus speaks of Pinch as a 'mere anatomy' (*Com. of E.* v. i. 239), 'skeleton' (a word not found in the plays) would be the modern equivalent. Caius, a very different man from his namesake in *The Merry Wives of Windsor*, was a pupil of Vesalius, and obtained from the Crown a grant like that accorded to the Barber Surgeons, so that one subject was annually dissected at Gonville and Caius College. Vicary, Surgeon to St. Bartholomew's Hospital, who died three years before the birth of Shakespeare, wrote *A Profitable Treatise of the Anatomie of a Man's Bodie*, not published until 1577. It was, how-

---

[1] The granting of a felon's body to teachers of anatomy was not abolished until the passing of the Anatomy Act in 1832.

ever, highly inaccurate, being merely a reproduction of
a fourteenth-century manuscript, devoid of any reference
to Vesalius or any other sixteenth-century writer.

As the Barber Surgeons' demonstrations were well known
it is not surprising that, while we find no mention of
the theories and experiments of Caesalpinus and Harvey,
Shakespeare's plays include numerous allusions to dissections. Oliver, speaking of Orlando to the wrestler, says
'should I anatomize him to thee as he is, I must blush and
weep' (*A. Y. L.* I. i. 165), and Touchstone speaks of how

> The wise man's folly is anatomized. (*ib.* II. vii. 56)

A French lord would gladly see Bertram's 'company
anatomized' (*All's W.* IV. iii. 37). Elsewhere a morbid
condition is implied, such as is sought for at a post-mortem
rather than at a demonstration of normal anatomy. 'Let
them anatomize Regan, see what breeds about her heart'
(*Lear*, III. vi. 80–1). 'For Andrew,' observes Sir Toby
Belch, 'if he were opened, and you find so much blood in
his liver as will clog the foot of a flea, I'll eat the rest of the
anatomy' (*Tw. N.* III. ii. 68–70), alluding to the old patho-
logical theory that the veins arose from the liver. The
relation of the material to the spiritual man is questioned
by Romeo:

> In what vile part of this anatomy
> Does my name lodge? (*Rom. & Jul.* III. iii. 105–6)

whilst Isabella speaks of man's 'glassy essence' (*Meas.
for M.* II. ii. 120), and Prince Henry observes that some
suppose the brain to be 'the soul's frail dwelling-house'
(*John*, V. vii. 3).

Shakespeare gives no hint that the study of anatomy from
dissections was held to be impious in England. Cymbeline's
queen suggests that Cornelius should try his poisons

> on such creatures as
> We count not worth the hanging,—but none human;

and Cornelius (who bears the name of a physician to
Charles V) replies—

> Your highness
> Shall from this practice but make hard your heart.
> (*Cymb.* I. v. 19–24)

But anthropotomy is nowhere censured by Shakespeare,
nor by Marlowe in his *Doctor Faustus*, who practised 'more
than heavenly power permits'.

Shakespeare, we may assume, never witnessed a demonstration of anatomy, but he was familiar with gibbets and neglected burial-grounds, whilst in order to stay men 'from the fall of vanity' (*Rich. III*, III. vii. 97) religious art often depicted decomposition in pictures as graphically as the Lady Constance described it in her frenzy (*John*, III. iv. 25).

The greatest surgeon of the Elizabethan age was William Clowes, senior (1540 ?–1604). He was of good family and saw active service, first in France with the Earl of Warwick's army in 1563, then in the Low Countries with Leicester in 1585, and lastly in the fleet opposed to the Armada in 1588. Like Vicary, he was on the staff of St. Bartholomew's Hospital. Clowes wrote freely in the vernacular. His *Proved Practice for all Young Chirurgions* was the prototype of numerous text-books still familiar to the medical student. Another work, published in 1602, *A Right Frutefull and Approved Treatise for the Artificial Cure of the Struma or Evill, cured by the Kinges and Queenes of England*, recalls Malcolm's speech about 'the evil' which afflicted

> strangely-visited people,
> All swoln and ulcerous, pitiful to the eye,
> The mere despair of surgery. (*Macb.* IV. iii. 150–2)

William Clowes, junior (1582–1648), Sergeant-Surgeon to James I, was deputed specially to examine all persons who were brought to be cured by the royal touch, for, as Malcolm says of Edward the Confessor,

> To the succeeding royalty he leaves
> The healing benediction. (*ib.* 155–6)

The younger Clowes assisted in the prosecution of a quack who professed to cure 'the evil' by the Touch, being a seventh son,[1] but it was discovered that his father had had only six children.

Banester (1540–1610) was a distinguished military surgeon. After returning from the wars and studying at Oxford, he practised as a physician and surgeon at Nottingham. The College of Physicians, after much wrangling, granted him a conditional licence in 1593. His friend, George Baker (1540–1600), was a scholarly man. He translated a foreign work into English, but retained the Latin

---

[1] Cf. the seven vials of Edward's sacred blood in *Rich. II*, I. ii. 12, and 'William of Windsor was the seventh and last' (*2 Hen. VI*, II. ii. 17).

titles of the simples, holding that it would do his readers good to look up the English names, for he ' would not have every ignorant asse to be made a chirurgion by my booke '. The two great lights of the Barber Surgeons, Vicary and Ferris, both died within a few years of Shakespeare's birth, and both were Sergeant-Surgeons to the sovereign.   Arris and Gale, who founded the now united lectureship at the Royal College of Surgeons, were both contemporaries of the poet.

The College of Physicians vexed the surgeons by vexatious rules and by-laws.   The surgeon was forbidden, for example, to prescribe internal remedies.   Though, as a rule, socially inferior to the physicians, the Elizabethan surgeons by their talents and the truly scientific methods of their corporation set going those influences to which we owe the achievements of Wiseman, Cheselden, Hunter, Paget, and Lister.

The surgeons, unlike the physicians, were irregular in the matter of fees.   A Robert Money was committed ' to the Compter [1] for his Contempt ' by the Court, for his ' evill practize ' in supplanting a colleague.   Fees were taken, in part at least, in gownes, lace, &c.   A certain Thomas Adams once ' complained against John Padice who had receyved certayn money in hand, and a gowne in pawne for the remainder, to cure the daughter of the sayed Thomas, which daughter died'.   The Master and Governors ordered that ' the gown should be redelivered to the father ', who in return was to ' geve unto Jo. Padice for his boat [i. e. hire] which he spent in going to the mayde at Putney, v s.'

THE APOTHECARY

'I do remember an apothecary,' says Romeo when in search of a poison, the sale of which in Mantua was prohibited on pain of capital punishment.   He proceeds to a description of the shop and the wares of the thin poverty-stricken wretch:

> And in his needy shop a tortoise hung,
> An alligator stuff'd, and other skins
> Of ill-shaped fishes ; and about his shelves
> A beggarly account of empty boxes,
> Green earthen pots, bladders, and musty seeds,
> Remnants of packthread, and old cakes of roses,
> Were thinly scatter'd, to make up a show.
>
> (*Rom. & Jul.* v. i. 42–8)

[1] i. e. the debtors' prison.

The occupation was of long standing, but the English apothecaries did not receive a charter until 1607. This charter included the grocers, to whom Shakespeare makes

Der Apotecker.

Ich hab in meiner Apoteckn
Viel Matery die lieblich schmeckn/
Zucker mit Würtzen ich conficier
Mach auch Purgatzen vnd Clistier/
Auch zu stercken den francken schwachn
Kan ich mancherley Labung machn/
Das alles nach der Artzte raht
Der seinen Brunn gesehen hat.

The Apothecary, by Jost Amman.

no reference, but in the year of the poet's death James I granted a separate charter to the apothecaries—to their great satisfaction, as it gave them the right of controlling the purchase and sale of drugs and of searching grocers' shops. The charter thus mitigated the annoyance to which they were subjected by the special powers already conferred

on the College of Physicians to overhaul the apothecaries'
own stores for ' evil and fawty stuffe '. These powers and
Romeo's speech show that the ' evil stuffe ' was that
of which Harrison and Stubbes spoke in reference to the
experiences of students in Italy. The apothecary had
already been exhorted by Bullein [1] ' that he doe remember
his office is onely to be the Physician's Coke' (Cook) ; and
Cymbeline's queen puts herself in the apothecary's place
when she says to Cornelius—

> Hast thou not learn'd me how
> To make perfumes ? distil ? preserve ?
>
> (*Cymb.* I. v. 12–13)

After the charter of 1616, trade disputes between the then
separated apothecaries and grocers grew very frequent.
Grocers might sell perfumes, but as they were excluded
from the sale of drugs, it seemed hard that the apothecaries should be permitted to supply perfumes to their
customers. It is to an apothecary that Lear appeals
(*Lear*, IV. vi. 133), not to a grocer, for an ounce of civet,
which he required as a scent and not as a drug.

Romeo's speech implies that many English sellers of
drugs were starvelings and something worse, yet the apothecary in this country was as a rule a worthy man,[2] though
apt to make exorbitant charges. There were several distinguished foreigners among the members of the ' art and
mystery ' in London, such as Paul de Lobel, but unfortunately it was one of his assistants who, bribed by the
jailer, administered to Sir Thomas Overbury the dose
that killed him. There was no pharmacopoeia in Shakespeare's lifetime ; but the first *London Pharmacopoeia*
was in preparation, for it appeared in 1618. Among the
physicians whose names are to be found in its pages is
Harvey, styled ' medicus regius iuratus '.

QUACKERY AND EMPIRICAL PRACTICE

Two pernicious influences specially encouraged quackery
in Shakespeare's days : interference by ministers of state

---

[1] *The Booke of Compoundes and the Apotecaries Rules.* Bullein died in 1576.

[2] Gerarde entrusted the preparation of that very powerful drug elaterium
to ' Master *William Wright* in Bucklers Burie my louing friend [who) hath
taken more paines in curious composing of it, and hath more exactly performed the same then any other whatsoeuer, that I haue had any knowledge
of ' (*Herball*, p. 766).

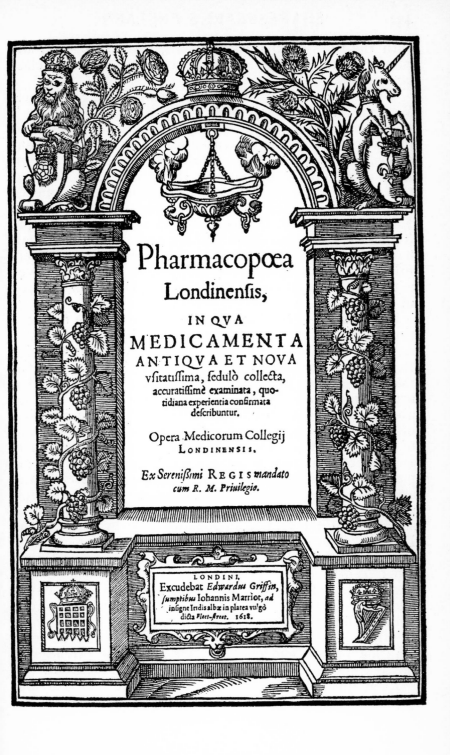

Pharmacopœa Londinensis,

IN QVA MEDICAMENTA ANTIQVA ET NOVA

vſitatiſſima, ſedulò collecta,
accuratiſſimè examinata, quo-
tidiana experientia confirmata
deſcribuntur.

Opera Medicorum Collegij
LONDINENSIS.

Ex Sereniſſimi REGIS mandato
cum R. M. Priuilegio.

LONDINI,
Excudebat *Edwardus Griffin*,
ſumptibus Iohannis Marriot, ad
inſigne Iridis albæ in platea vu'gò
dicta *Fleet-ſtreet*. 1618.

with the rules of the corporations, and a clause in the charter of the Barber Surgeons favouring a certain class of empirics.

The College of Physicians most nobly defied Sir Francis Walsingham, the layer of plots and 'inductions dangerous', the man who hunted down Mary Queen of Scots, and it worsted him on three occasions. The first dispute concerned a herbalist, Margaret Kenwix, favoured by Queen Elizabeth, and the upshot was that the College declared that it was 'willing and content to abide any inconvenience whatever might ensue' rather than cease to restrain Mistress Kenwix from practice. One Not, a quack pure and simple (though Walsingham's own doctor), and another charlatan named Buck, were similarly restrained, and then the powerful minister apologized, promising that he would never act again in anything contrary to the benefit or dignity of the College.

The Charter of the Barber Surgeons bound the corporation to allow persons supposed to be experienced in the nature of herbs and waters to apply outward remedies and to administer drinks for the alleviation of certain internal maladies. The Barber Surgeons deeply resented this arrangement, and endeavoured to check 'the beastlie abusses both of Chirurgie and Physike' by the granting of licences for a stated time only, not renewable at the end of the period if the holder acted in any objectionable manner. In 1609 one Mathias Jenkinson was 'dischardged from his practize in surgery for that he hath not observed the articles of his tolleracion, and for his evell and unskilfull practize'. The Barber Surgeons, however, were not so successful as the College in resisting men in power. One Esthorpe from Lincolnshire was recommended for his 'well Doyinges in Surgery' by 'the earle of Lyncolne with Divers other gentlemen'. The corporation compromised the matter, for Esthorpe was admitted as a brother 'but not allowed as examined and approved thereunto'. Empirics with the limited licence could only hang out their banners or other signs at the 'howse' where they dwelt. The corporation put an end once and for all to the privilege of practice allowed to ignorant parish clerks and sextons.

Even qualified doctors employed secret remedies and kept them secret. During the plague of 1603 Woodall made use of a compound, the nature of which he never divulged. The family of Lawrent Colot kept the use of certain instruments for lithotomy entirely to themselves. In 1569 William Chamberlen, a French Huguenot refugee, came over to England. His descendants held secret for many years their truly great invention, the obstetric forceps; but it is doubtful whether that instrument was devised till some years after Shakespeare's death.

In Shakespeare's time there appear to have been many flourishing empirics who succeeded in keeping clear of prosecution by the College and the Company. *All's Well that Ends Well* is based on a triumph of empiricism, and Shakespeare distinctly sympathized with Helena. The King, probably Charles V of France, who suffered from a thoracic fistula,[1] is not

> so credulous of cure,
> When our most learned doctors leave us, and
> The congregated College have concluded
> That labouring art can never ransom nature
> From her inaidable estate. (*All's W.* II. i. 118–22)

MALPRAXIS AND UNPROFESSIONAL CONDUCT

The scientific doctor is not always skilful, while the most practical and dexterous man may make mistakes. Gideon Harvey (1640–1700) speaks with some acrimony of his great namesake as ' felicissimus anatomicus licet medicus nequaquam insignissimus ' and refers to the case of Lord Rainton, to whom the discoverer of the circulation gave an overdose of medicine, of which fortunately only half was taken. George Baker in his treatise *Proved Practice* wrote of the army surgeons of his day in highly depreciatory terms, declaring that they ' slew more than the enemy did '. William Clowes (p. 427) was for a time in trouble about a Master William Goodness who complained before a court of the Barber Surgeons that Clowes had not cured his wife. The decision of the court was remarkable : ' Yt was awarded that the said Clowes sholde either geve the said Goodness XXs, or else cure his saied wief, which Clowes agreed to pay the XXs. And so they were agreed and

[1] ' Nel petto ' (in the chest) according to the original tale in Boccaccio's *Decameron*, Giorn. 3, Nov. 9.

eche of them made acquittance to other', which was certainly prudent on Clowes's part.

Unprofessional conduct was frequently condemned by the Barber Surgeons in open court. Clowes himself, a man of a difficult temper, was made to apologize in 1576 for using 'scoffing words and jests' concerning not only 'one Goodinge', but also 'most of the Masters of the Company'; and he and his distinguished colleague Baker were summoned, in 1577, 'for that they bothe contrary to order and the good and holsome rules of this howse misused eche other and fought in the fields together'. However, they were pardoned 'this great offence'. In 1573 a surgeon having called a colleague a knave, 'he paid his fyne xiid, and they toke hands and were frends', while a year later a Master Brode complained of Mr. Saunders 'for lykening him to Esoppes dogge'—in the manger—'and they were appoynted to be frends'. The Worshipful Company was sorely tried by trumpery charges of this kind.

DISEASES AND TREATMENT

All Shakespeare's plays contain passages referring to medical matters. Even in *Titus Andronicus*, which J. C. Bucknill expressly excludes from discussion, we find in Act IV, Scene iii, that Titus fits letters on to arrows, to be aimed at the heavens 'and move the gods', and Marcus thinks it a 'heavy case' to see Titus 'thus distract'. Shakespeare's physicians and apothecaries do not act and talk so professionally as But and Tim Iten in Ben Jonson's *Magnetic Lady*, yet the plays afford us a fair general view of prevalent ailments and the treatment in fashion in his time.

'Distemper' and 'distemperature' alike are used for disease or indisposition in general (*Com. of E.* v. i. 82, *John* III. iv. 154, *1 Hen. IV*, III. i. 34, *2 Hen. IV*, III. i. 41, *Haml.* II. ii. 55). The word 'patient', well established by this time in the medical sense, occurs no less than fourteen times in the works; it provides the motive in a striking simile in *Sonnet* cxi:

> Pity me, then, and wish I were renew'd;
> Whilst, like a willing patient, I will drink
> Potions of eisel 'gainst my strong infection.

Ague was extremely common, since fields were badly drained and its germs were probably distributed by gnats[1] which bred in millions in stagnant pools, and in puddles in badly kept roads. Macbeth hopes that famine and the ague may eat up the foe (v. v. 4), Richard II exclaims ' this ague-fit of fear is over-blown (III. ii. 190), and Rosalind speaks of ' the quotidian of love ' (*A. Y. L.* III. ii. 389). Mistress Quickly says confusedly that Falstaff was ' shaked of a burning quotidian tertian ' (*Hen. V*, II. i. 124). The quotidian and the tertian were intermittent fevers, the paroxysm of the one recurring every day, of the other every other day. Continued fevers were yet more prevalent. Shakespeare correctly ascribes them, under certain circumstances, to the effect of putrefaction. The bodies of those who fall in battle may ' breed a plague ' (*Hen. V*, IV. iii. 103). Troilus speaks of ' a feverous pulse ' (*Troilus*, III. ii. 38). The signification of ' measles ' (*Cor.* III. i. 77) is doubtful ; it most probably meant leprosy, certainly not the febrile disease with a rash now known by that name. The sweating sickness was the subject of a monograph by Caius published in 1552 ; it is alluded to in *Measure for Measure* (I. ii. 89),[2] and possibly in the description of Falstaff's death,[3] but the name ' sweat ' is also applied to the profuse perspirations which appear to have been common in agues in those days. The hostess of the Boar's Head believed that the knight was ' rheumatic ' when he muttered in his swan-song that women were fiends (*Hen. V*, II. iii. 40). She meant ' lunatic ', but the mistake implies that ' rheumatic ' (subject to ' rheums ' or defluxions) was a word already in popular use.

The city of London was rarely free from bubonic plague,[4] and there were serious outbreaks in 1582 and 1603. In *Remembrancia* it is noted that the Privy Council, when ordering precautions against it, expressed surprise that London lacked a special plague hospital such as existed in smaller foreign cities. ' Red plague ' (*Temp.* I. ii. 364,

---

[1] Malarial diseases in Italy and yellow fever in West Africa and America seem without doubt to be propagated by mosquitoes, which begin their existence in stagnant water.

[2] ' What with the war, what with the *sweat*, what with the gallows.' The word clearly signifies a deadly epidemic, not an endemic disease.

[3] Creighton, *History of Epidemics in Britain*.

[4] The rat flea is now held to be the conveyer of the plague germ.

not erysipelas), 'red murrain' (*Troilus*, II. i. 13), and 'red pestilence' (*Cor.* IV. i. 13) all signified bubonic plague, the name arising from the coloured swelling, sometimes red, which was one of its earlier signs. 'Carbuncle' (*Lear*, II. iv. 227) also meant a plague sore, and not, as now, simple *anthrax*. 'The Lord's tokens' (*Love's L. L.* v. ii. 424), 'the tokened pestilence' (*Ant. & Cleop.* III. viii. 19), and the 'death tokens' of Achilles 'so plaguy proud' (*Troilus*, II. iii. 189) were marks or spots which appeared in the later stages. Woodall, however, showed that they were by no means certain tokens of death, in contradiction of the popular notion implied in the 'No recovery' of *Troilus* II. iii. 190.

Gout is repeatedly mentioned, especially by Falstaff, who confounds it with another malady (*2 Hen. IV*, I. ii. 262 and 277), but, as he complains that 'it plays the rogue with my great toe', gout was the correct diagnosis. Chronic gout with irritation of the skin from 'serpigo' (most probably eczema or else herpes circinatus) and cough with expectoration ('the rheum') make an elderly man so miserable that he curses them for not ending him sooner (*Meas. for M.* III. i. 31). 'Salt rheum', according to Sir Dyce Duckworth, is the chronic naso-pharyngeal and tracheal catarrh of elderly folks (*Oth.* III. iv. 52); the dramatist also applies the term to the running from the nostrils in a neglected cold (*Com. of E.* III. ii. 132).

When Lord Say talks of 'palsy' (*2 Hen. VI*, IV. vii. 98) he means shaking palsy, paralysis agitans, while York appears to be suffering from a true paralytic stroke, or hemiplegia, when he regrets that his arm is 'prisoner to the palsy' (*Rich. II*, II. iii. 104). A bad apoplectic stroke causes unconsciousness as well as loss of power. 'This apoplexy is, as I take it, a kind of lethargy,' observes Falstaff (*2 Hen. IV*, I. ii. 126). The true relation of brain disease to paralysis, however, was not recognized in Shakespeare's England.

Phthisis was common then as now. The faint odour of the breath of a confirmed consumptive, and the sour smells common in a fen, are compared by Sebastian, Adrian, and Antonio to the air which breathes upon them 'most sweetly' in Prospero's island (*Temp.* II. i. 48–50). The influence of worry and bad news on the digestion is noted more than once in the plays:

Unquiet meals make ill digestions;
(Com. of E. v. i. 74)

and Shakespeare knew that jaundice was associated with depression of spirits. Gratiano wonders why a man should

creep into the jaundice
By being peevish. *(Merch. of V.* i. i. 85)

Agamemnon asks the heroes

What grief hath set the jaundice on your cheeks?
(Troilus, i. iii. 2)

Beatrice remarks to Antonio that Count John looks so tartly that

I never can see him but I am heart-burned an hour after.
(Much Ado, ii. i. 4)

A five-o'clock tea not rarely causes that symptom, at a similar interval. Colic is alluded to in several plays, and it seems strange that a high-tragedy character, Hotspur, should introduce it as a simile when Glendower talks about the portents at his birth (*i Hen. IV,* iii. i. 29).

Nervous disorders are largely worked into the dialogue and plots in the plays. Lear experiences the globus hystericus:

O! how this mother swells up toward my heart;
Hysterica passio! *(Lear,* ii. iv. 56–7)

Mental disease is more skilfully handled than any other medical subject. Numerous passages in *Hamlet* and the cross-examination of Malvolio by a self-constituted commission of lunacy (*Tw. N.* iv. ii) come readily to the mind, but the abbess's remarkable speech about Antipholus—

And thereof came it that the man was mad!
(Com. of E. v. i. 68)

is less familiar.

In cursing 'preposterous discoveries' Thersites makes mention of fifteen diseases, for the most part under their popular names—an instructive catalogue, the complete interpretation of which has baffled medical commentators.

Now, the rotten diseases of the south, the guts-griping, ruptures, catarrhs, loads o' gravel i' the back, lethargies, cold palsies, raw eyes, dirt-rotten livers, wheezing lungs, bladders full of imposthume, sciaticas, lime-kilns i' the palm, incurable bone-ache, and the rivelled fee-simple of the tetter, take and take again such preposterous discoveries! *(Troilus,* v. i. 19–28)

The names of the diseases in modern language would be 'syphilis, colic, hernias, catarrhs, pain in the loins ascribed rightly or wrongly to gravel or stone in the kidneys, apoplectic stroke with unconsciousness, permanent paralysis of the limbs, chronic inflammation of the lids with inverted lashes, obscure diseases ascribed to the liver, asthma, chronic cystitis, lumbago or sciatica (possibly a euphemism), psoriasis of the palm,[1] bone-ache from any cause, and chronic ringworm (?)'.[2] Thersites also compares Patroclus to a ' green sarsenet flap for a sore eye '. Blindness is often mentioned ; the allusion to cataract, called the ' pin and web' (*Wint. Tale*, I. ii. 291) or the ' web and the pin ' (*Lear*, III. iv. 120) is clear, as Florio in his *New World of Words* interprets the Italian *catarátta* as ' a cataract or a pin and a web'. Edgar, when he mentions the ' web and pin ' adds ' the squint ', both ascribed to Flibbertigibbet's fiendish malevolence. Small-pox is referred to in *Love's Labour's Lost* :

> Ros. O that your face were not so full of O's !
> Kath. A pox on that jest ! (v. ii. 45–6)

The term ' small pokkes' for variola is found as early as 1518. In 1593 Simon Kellwaye (or Kelling) wrote the first English work on the subject.

The England of Shakespeare was well acquainted with the scourge of contagious disease, and a truly dramatic summary of its complications is included in Timon's address to Phrynia and Timandra (*Timon*, IV. iii. 152–67). The popular name [3] is frequently introduced as a mere vulgar curse or exclamation (e.g. *Rom. & Jul.* II. iv. 29) equivalent to ' a plague ! ' (compare *Temp.* I. i. 39 and 43). References to its foreign origin are common, *mal de Naples* being signified in two passages (*Oth.* III. i. 4, and *Troilus*, II. iii. 20), while there are numerous allusions to its association with France.[4] ' Winchester goose ' (*1 Hen. VI*, I. iii, and *Troilus*, V. x. 55) is another euphemism.[5] Several familiar symptoms, such as ' sciatica ' (*Meas. for M.* I. ii. 63, *Troilus* V. i. 25, and *Timon* IV. i. 23), are mentioned. Treatment by a course

---

[1] A source of great discomfort.

[2] Bucknill, p. 235 ; ' rivell'd ' means wrinkled, and ' tetter ' was applied to several skin diseases.

[3] Originally the plural of ' pock ' applied to a protruding pimple.

[4] In Hanmer's edition of the plays, 1743-4, it is stated that a ' French crown ' signifies the scab on the head called corona veneris. It may mean baldness, another symptom. (Compare *Meas. for M.* I. ii. 55, and *Mid. N. D.* I. ii. 100, with *Timon* IV. iii. 116.)

[5] The Bishop of Winchester owned the stews in Southwark.

of suffumigation with cinnabar in a meat-pickling vat, practised by Paré and popular in England at the time, is signified by 'the powdering tub of infamy' (*Hen. V*, II. i. 79) and 'herself in the tub' (*Meas. for M.* III. ii. 59). The patient was kept on a low diet ('tub-fast', *Timon* IV. iii. 87) during the course. The sweating treatment is meant by 'till then I'll sweat' (*Troilus*, V. x. 56). 'Burning' is used euphemistically for a less severe malady of the same class (*Com. of E.* IV. iii. 57, *Troilus* V. ii. 194, *Lear* III. ii. 84).

Heatstroke ('calenture'), yellow fever ('tabardillo'), prickly heat ('las espinas'), tropical dysentery ('cámaras de sangre', fatal to Drake in 1595), erysipelas, and scurvy are well described in the first treatise on tropical medicine published in English, 1598, *The Cures of the Diseased, in remote Regions : Preventing Mortalitie, incident in Forraine Attempts of the English Nation,*[1] by G. W. (probably George Whetstone), who states that he suffered from the 'tabardilla' himself when a prisoner in Spain, and wished to let men know of remedies for tropical diseases, 'not that I purpose practitioner-like in Phisick or Chirurgerie, to assume unto me anie knowledge in those Sciences and Faculties'.

There is some obscurity about the precise meaning of the names of minor diseases that occur in the plays. Since Bucknill's work appeared, the researches of the compilers of the Oxford English Dictionary have thrown light on much that is doubtful. 'Blain' is very freely applied:

> Itches, blains,
> Sow all the Athenian bosoms, and their crop
> Be general leprosy !   (*Timon*, IV. i. 28–30)

Woodall writes of a 'pestilential blain' in his *Surgeon's Mate* (1612). More (1529) and Ascham (1544) speak of their fingers suffering from a 'hoate blane' and a 'little blane' (? chilblain). The epithet 'hoate' (hot) suggests a whitlow, which causes general constitutional disturbance, and possibly Desdemona had this complication in mind in her reference to finger ache (*Oth.* III. iv. 145). 'Imposthume' certainly means an abscess, a circumscribed collection of pus, in *Hamlet* (IV. iv. 27), as it 'inward breaks', but even Paré applied the term to other morbid conditions.

---

[1] Reprinted in facsimile by the Clarendon Press, 1915, under the editorship of Dr. Charles Singer ; see 'Notes on Text', pp. 9–13, for *Tabardill-a* or *-o*.

' Boil ' (or ' byle ', ' bile ', as in old editions), on the other
hand, did not exclusively signify furunculus, the common
hard painful boil which softens and breaks, though boils
and abscesses both ' gather to a head ' (*Temp.* v. i. 1), while
lancing (*Rich. II*, I. iii. 303) is much more practised on an
abscess than on a boil ; and neither is now called a sore.
A ' botchy core ' is the piece of slough which comes away
from a boil (*Troilus*, II. i. 6), but ' botch' was used so
loosely, even by authorities, that it is never clear what is
meant where it occurs in the plays.   Boorde in his *Breviary
of Health*, 1547, vii. 9, states that ' in English it (*ulcera*) is
named byles or botches '.   This adds to the confusion, as
an ulcer is not a boil but a diseased open surface, as recognized in *Macbeth*, where the patients with the ' king's evil '
are ' all swoln and ulcerous ' (IV. iii. 151), bearing, in fact,
the ulcers which leave unsightly scars on the necks of
tuberculous or scrofulous subjects.   Bardolph's ' bubukles '
(*Hen. V*, III. vi. 111), a confusion of ' bubo ' with ' carbuncle ', meant big pimples, acne rosacea, or acne pustulata.
' Embossed ' when applied to ' sores ' (*A. Y. L.* II. vii.
67) or to a carbuncle (*Lear*, II. iv. 227) means simply
swollen.   ' Plurisy ' was not our pleurisy, but plethora
(*Haml.* IV. vii. 117).   ' Side-stitches ' (*Temp.* I. ii. 325)
perhaps signified muscular pains between the ribs, or else
intercostal neuralgia.   ' Cramp ' is used vaguely in *The
Tempest* (*ib.* 325 and v. i. 286) for rheumatic or other pains
all over the body.   Prospero punishes Caliban with ' cramps '
and ' convulsions ' (*ib.* IV. i. 262), which are probably the
shivering fits of ague.   Leontes's ' tremor cordis ' (*Wint. Tale*,
I. ii. 111) was ' psychical ' and not due to heart disease.
Falstaff's ' never spit white again ' (*2 Hen. IV*, I. ii. 241)
refers to a supposed sign of intemperance.   ' Hectic ' (*Haml.*
IV. iii. 69) was not restricted, as now, to the fever of advanced consumption.   ' Green sickness ' (*Pericles*, IV. vi. 14)
is chlorosis, the anaemia very frequent in maidens.   Dropsy
(*Temp.* IV. i. 231) was very common in Shakespeare's
England, but its causes were not understood.

Three hospitals were in existence in London in Shakespeare's days, all formed out of religious houses dissolved
at the Reformation, and all still flourishing at the present
time. St. Bartholomew's was from the first, when founded
in connexion with the Priory in 1123, a hospital for the

sick. It was refounded in 1544, and a new charter two years later restored the greater part of its revenues for the benefit of 'an hundred sore and diseased people'. St. Thomas's Hospital, originally an almonry, was purchased by the citizens of London in 1552 as a hospital for the relief of the poor and the impotent. Bethlehem Hospital, or Bedlam, originally the Hospital of St. Mary of Bethlehem, a priory before the dissolution, was granted by Henry VIII to the citizens of London, who converted it into a hospital for lunatics. In 1557 the management was handed over to the governors of Bridewell, a 'hospital' presented by Edward VI to the city as a house of correction. Bedlam became the organized asylum for the insane (*2 Hen. VI*, v. i. 131). Shakespeare was familiar with the half-witted vagrants, discharged from Bedlam, roaming through the country in search of alms (Tom o' Bedlam, *Lear* I. ii. 152; Bedlam beggars, *ib.* II. iii. 14).

The word 'hospital' occurs only once in the plays, when Biron declares himself prepared to 'jest a twelvemonth in a hospital' (*Love's L. L.* V. ii. 879). 'Spital' is to be found twice and in the same play (*Hen. V*, II. i. 78 and V. i. 86), and in both passages means a 'lock hospital'. This form of the word, as distinguished from 'hospital', denoted institutions reserved for the treatment of the poorer people and the more loathsome diseases.

Many drugs are mentioned in the plays, such as rhubarb and senna (*Macb.* V. iii. 55) and bitter apple, colocynth, or coloquintida (*Oth.* I. iii. 356). Poppy (never laudanum or opium) is named with mandragora and 'drowsy syrups' (*ibid.* III. iii. 331–2, and *Com. of E.* V. i. 104). Syrups were popular vehicles for unpalatable drugs. Narcotics and poisons enter into the plots of *Romeo and Juliet, Cymbeline, King Lear*, and other plays; but the toxicology is usually incorrect, and it is not always clear what poison is meant. Thus 'cursed hebenon' (*Haml.* I. v. 62) may mean henbane, 'the insane root'[1] (*Macb.* I. iii. 84), or heben, 'the double fatal yew' (*Rich. II*, III. ii. 117). Lear's physician rightly recommends 'many simples' as narcotics for the king's insomnia (*Lear*, IV. iv. 14).

[1] An unspecified poison, first mentioned, according to Sir Thomas Browne, in Plutarch's Life of Antonius.

Shakespeare fully recognized the medicinal value of

> Sleep that knits up the ravell'd sleave of care,
> The death of each day's life, sore labour's bath,
> Balm of hurt minds, great nature's second course,
> Chief nourisher in life's feast,   (*Macb.* II. ii. 38–41)

and of repose, the ' foster-nurse of nature ', as the physician calls it in *King Lear* (IV. iv. 12) ; the wise abbess in *The Comedy of Errors* declares that

> In food, in sport, and life-preserving rest
> To be disturb'd, would mad a man or beast.   (v. i. 83–4)

The King and Polonius, prescribing for Hamlet's mental disturbance, agree that change of scene may provide a speedy remedy :

> Haply the seas and countries different
> With variable objects shall expel
> This something settled matter in his heart. (*Haml.* III. i. 180–2)

The homely remedy of the plaster is mentioned three times by Shakespeare, in one instance to point a contemptuous reference to the incompetence of the contemporary surgeon :

> *Gon.*   you rub the sore,
> When you should bring the plaster.
> *Seb.*   Very well.
> *Ant.* And most chirurgeonly.   (*Temp.* II. i. 145–7)

'Cataplasm ', often synonymous with 'plaster', is found once (*Haml.* IV. vii. 143).

The painful cautery or red-hot iron which was in use for checking bleeding of the tongue is perhaps referred to when Timon speaks of 'cauterizing' a liar's tongue (*Timon,* v. i. 138)—if that be the right reading ; unless he intends by it the action of the caustic or ' corrosive ' (*2 Hen. VI,* III. ii. 403) so much in vogue in his time. The surgical ' tent ', a roll of lint with which wounds were commonly searched and cleansed at this period, is introduced for the sake of a pun in *Troilus* V. i. 11 :

> *Patr.* Who keeps the tent now ?
> *Ther.* The surgeon's box, or the patient's wound.

The corresponding verb occurs several times either in metaphorical use (*Haml.* II. ii. 634) or with the derived sense of ' cure ' (*Cor.* I. ix. 31). The climax of Lear's indignation against Goneril is reached in the words—

> Th' untented woundings of a father's curse
> Pierce every sense about thee !   (*Lear,* I. iv. 324–5)

BIBLIOGRAPHY.—The important contemporary English treatises on the various departments of medicine are set down in the course of this chapter. Something may be gleaned of the popular estimate of the profession from the ' Characters ' of ' A worthy physician ' and ' An unworthy physician ' in NICHOLAS BRETON's *The Good and the Bad*, 1616, and the ' Character ' of a ' quack salver ' in OVERBURY's *Characters*, 1614, and from the ' Character ' of ' A Surgeon ' in EARLE's *Microcosmographie*, 1628.

For the College of Physicians and the state and progress of medical science the chief authorities are Sir WILLIAM MUNK's *Roll of the College of Physicians* (1518–1700), 3 vols., 1878, and NORMAN MOORE's *The Physicians and Surgeons of St. Bartholomew's Hospital before the time of Harvey*, in St. Bartholomew's Hospital Reports, vol. xviii, 1882, page 333. For the Barber Surgeons and Surgery, J. FLINT SOUTH and D'ARCY POWER's *Memorials of the Craft of Surgery in England*, 1886, and SIDNEY YOUNG's *Annals of the Barber Surgeons of London*, 1890. For the advance of anatomical science in the sixteenth century, MORITZ ROTH's *Andreas Vesalius Bruxellensis*, Berlin, 1892, and FRANK BAKER's *The Two Sylviuses : An Historical Study*, in Bulletin of the Johns Hopkins Hospital (Baltimore, U.S.A.), November 1909, p. 329, should be consulted. For the founders of scientific obstetrics, see J. H. AVELING's *The Chamberlens and the Midwifery Forceps*, 1882. For Shakespeare in relation to medicine, the chief authorities are J. C. BUCKNILL's *The Medical Knowledge of Shakespeare* and *The Psychology of Shakespeare*, and MOYES's *Medicine and Kindred Arts in the Plays of Shakespeare*, all out of print.

[F. P. WILSON's edition of *The Plague Pamphlets of Thomas Dekker*, 1925, and his work on *The Plague in Shakespeare's London*, 1927, are valuable studies.]

XV

THE SCIENCES

§ 1. ASTRONOMY AND ASTROLOGY

BY

E. B. KNOBEL

FROM the time of Ptolemy in the second century to the middle of the sixteenth century, all astronomy in Europe was based upon the system which he enunciated in Greek in his *magnum opus* known as the Almagest. That treatise in a Latin version enjoyed a world-wide circulation and authority. Ptolemy is responsible for the general belief that the earth was the fixed centre of the system, round which sun, moon, planets, and stars all revolved in separate spheres. The view of the ancient Greeks that the sun, the moon, the planets, and the firmament of stars, were all severally attached to material, transparent, and concentric spheres, and that the friction of one sphere revolving on another created, according to Pythagoras, ' the music of the spheres', lent itself peculiarly to poetic imagination, and is reflected in many expressions current in literature even down to the present day. Shakespeare echoed them in his phrases ' the music of the spheres' (*Pericles*, v. i. 231) and ' the tuned spheres' (*Ant. & Cleop.* v. ii. 84). Cleopatra talks of the great sphere in which the sun moves (*Ant. & Cleop.* IV. xiii. 10). The King in *Hamlet* asserts : ' The star moves not but in his sphere' (IV. vii. 15). Often does the dramatist liken disaster to the straying of the stars from their ' spheres ' or ' orbs '.[1]

The Ptolemaic system, which was accepted with little demur throughout the Elizabethan period, harmonized with ocular observation. A fairly adequate description of the system was supplied by Marlowe in *Doctor Faustus* (lines 644–78) :

[1] Cf. *Mid. N. D.* II. i. 153 : ' And certain stars shot madly from their spheres ' : so in *Haml.* I. v. 17 and *Ant. & Cleop.* III. xi. 145-6.

Faust. Come, Mephistophiles, let us dispute again,
And argue of divine Astrology.
Tell me, are there many heavens above the moon ?
Are all celestial bodies but one globe,
As is the substance of this centric earth ?
Meph. As are the elements, such are the spheres,
Mutually folded in each other's orb,
And, Faustus,
All jointly move upon one axle-tree,
Whose terminine is termed the world's wide pole ;
Nor are the names of Saturn, Mars, or Jupiter
Feign'd, but are erring stars.
Faust. But, tell me, have they all one motion, both *situ et
tempore* ?
Meph. All jointly move from east to west in twenty-four hours
upon the poles of the world ; but differ in their motion upon the
poles of the zodiac.
Faust. . . . Who knows not the double motion of the planets ?
The first is finish'd in a natural day ;
The second thus ; as Saturn in thirty years, Jupiter in twelve,
Mars in four, the Sun, Venus, and Mercury in a year, the Moon
in twenty-eight days. . . . But tell me, hath every sphere a dominion
or *intelligentia* ?
Meph. Ay.
Faust. How many heavens or spheres are there ?
Meph. Nine ; the seven planets, the firmament, and the empyreal
heaven.
Faust. Well, resolve me in this question ; why have we not
conjunctions, oppositions, aspects, eclipses, all at one time, but
in some years we have more, in some less ?
Meph. *Per inaequalem motum respectu totius.*
Faust. Well, I am answered.

In agreement with the Ptolemaic theory Shakespeare
once calls the earth ' this centre ' (*Troilus*, I. iii. 85).

Meanwhile Ptolemy's theories had become obsolete in
the sight of men of science. The renaissance of Astronomy
took place in the year 1543 when Copernicus, a student
of Polish nationality, sent to press from his death-bed his
great work—*De revolutionibus orbium coelestium*, and
therein laid the foundation of the new Solar system of
astronomy.

Copernicus regarded his system as no more than an
hypothesis. ' It is ', he declared, ' not necessary that hypotheses should be true, or even probable : it suffices that
they lead to calculations which agree with observations.'
His theory very gradually won acceptance. It could hardly

be said to be established until the publication (by Kepler in his *De Motibus Stellae Martis* in 1609) of the laws of planetary motion, or until Galileo reported his corroborative

Der Aſtronomus.

So bin ich ein Aſtronomus/
Erkenn zukünfftig Finſternuß/
An Sonn vnd Mond/durch das Geſtirn
Darauß kan ich denn practiciern/
Ob künfftig komm ein fruchtbar ſar
Oder Theuwrung vnd Kriegßgefahr/
Vnd ſonſt manicherley Kranckheit/
Milleſius den anfang geit.

The Astronomer, by Jost Amman.

observations in his *Sidereus Nuncius* of 1610. The discovery of Newton's law of gravitation was necessary to render Copernicus's position irresistible.

Copernicus's hypothesis quickly spread through Europe. In England it attracted the notice of the learned some thirty years before Shakespeare's working career began. In *The Castle of Knowledge,* which was published in September 1556, Robert Recorde, a distinguished astronomer and mathematician, called attention to the Copernican theory at the same time as he described the Ptolemaic system. His work was written in the popular form of dialogue between master and scholar. After a brief description of the Copernican theory (p. 165), Recorde continues his dialogue thus :

Scholar. Nay syr in good faith, I desire not to heare such vaine phantasies, so farre againste common reason, and repugnante to the consente of all the learned multitude of Wryters, and therefore lette it passe for euer, and a daye longer.

Master. You are to yonge to be a good iudge in so great a matter : it passeth farre your learninge, and theirs also that are muche better learned then you, to improue [to disprove] his supposition by good argumentes, and therefore you were best to condemne no thinge that you do not well vnderstand : but an other time, as I sayd, I will so declare his supposition, that you shall not only wonder to hear it, but also peraduenture be as earnest then to credite it, as you are now to condemne it.

A year later another astronomical student, John Feild, expressed in his *Ephemeris anni 1557 currentis juxta Copernici et Reinhaldi canones* his conviction of the truth of the Copernican theory. A like attitude was taken by a third writer, John Dee, one of the acutest scientific inquirers of the age. Dee, in the preface to Feild's *Ephemeris,* ranged himself with the supporters of Copernicus. To the same category belongs Thomas Digges, who, in his encyclopaedic *Geometrical Practise* of 1571, remarked upon the excessive complexity and diversity of the Ptolemaic system; ' like a set of hands, head, and feet, taken off different men '. Digges saw in the confusion ' the principal reason why Copernicus, a man of admirable ability and singular industry, used another hypothesis '.

Towards the close of the century the Copernican theory found an even abler English champion in William Gilbert, the author of *De Magnete,* the greatest English contribution which had yet been made to physical science.

Throughout Shakespeare's lifetime, the continued activity

of astronomical speculation on the Continent stimulated the pursuit of the science at home. The ablest English students of astronomy and mathematics read eagerly the books of the great foreign astronomers, corresponded with them, and at times visited them. Tycho Brahe, the Danish astronomer who propounded a new and valuable theory of comets, learned of Digges's researches and commended them warmly. With Kepler, the most eminent of astronomical observers and calculators of the era, several English men of science were in close touch. Thomas Harriot, the friend of Marlowe and of Sir Walter Ralegh, was on intimate terms with Kepler and helped him in his calculations. The foreign astronomer was warmly appreciative of Harriot's powers. Galileo's discoveries, too, were followed by Harriot with close attention. To Kepler's lecture-room an amateur student of optics, Sir Henry Wotton, at times made his way in 1590. In optics, indeed, Elizabethan Englishmen anticipated in notable directions the triumphs of their continental guides. Digges, Harriot, and Dee all used instruments, which may have been of the nature of telescopes, more than a decade before the invention was claimed by Hans Lippershey of Middleburg (in 1608) or by Galileo (in 1609). The Englishmen called their instrument 'perspective glasses'. Shakespeare makes many references to 'perspectives', but it is questionable whether he had in mind anything beyond a fashionable toy for producing optical illusions (cf. *All's W.* **v.** iii. 48; *Tw. N.* v. i. 227; *Rich. II*, ii. ii. 18).

The current progress in astronomical research was clearly little known outside a small circle of specialists. Yet of some of the problems which were inviting solution there would seem to have been popular knowledge. The author of *The First Part of Henry VI* wrote (i. ii. 1–2) of the perplexity attaching at the time to the motion of the planet Mars:

> Mars his true moving, even as in the heavens,
> So in the earth, to this day is not known.

Owing to the eccentricity of the orbit of Mars, and the consequent variation in the rate of its orbital motion, the actual intervals between successive oppositions of the planet are very unequal. The acknowledged difficulty of understanding the 'true moving' of Mars owing to these conditions led Kepler to make exhaustive investigation of the planet's orbit, and to discover the laws of planetary motion, which he gave to the world in 1609 in his *De Motibus Stellae Martis.*

IMAGINES CONSTELLATIONVM
BOREALIVM.

From Ptolemy's *Almagest*, 1541 : after Dürer.

The need of revising Ptolemy's results could not be ignored altogether. Spenser would seem to have been familiar with the change that had taken place since Ptolemy's calculations in the longitude of the stars by reason of what is called the precession of the equinoxes.

In *The Faerie Queene*, Book V, Introd., stanzas v–vi, the poet directs attention to the subject :

> For who so list into the heavens looke,
> And search the courses of the rowling spheares,
> Shall find that from the point, where they first tooke
> Their setting forth, in these few thousand yeares
> They all are wandred much ; that plaine appeares.
> For that same golden fleecy Ram, which bore
> Phrixus and Helle from their stepdames feares,
> Hath now forgot, where he was plast of yore,
> And shouldred hath the Bull, which fayre Europa bore.
>
> And eke the Bull hath with his bow-bent horne
> So hardly butted those two twinnes of Jove,
> That they have crusht the Crab, and quite him borne
> Into the great Nemæan lion's grove.
> So now all range, and doe at randon rove
> Out of their proper places farre away,
> And all this world with them amisse doe move,
> And all his creatures from their course astray,
> Till they arrive at their last ruinous decay.

The principal star of the *constellation* of the Ram, which in the time of Ptolemy was in the Zodiacal *sign* of the Ram, had in the Elizabethan period according to Spenser's verse 'wandred' to the *sign* of the Bull. Again, when Spenser says that Castor and Pollux 'have crusht the Crab and quite him borne into the great Nemæan lion's grove', the explanation is that Praesepe, the principal feature of the *constellation* of the Crab, which was in the *sign* of the Crab in the second century, had moved to the *sign* of the Lion in the sixteenth century. Spenser no doubt had compared Ptolemy with the catalogues of stars in current use in his own time. There the Almagest would be reduced to the sixteenth century by a fixed addition to the longitude.

The common attitude of mind to pending astronomical theory and investigation is best illustrated by Bacon's treatment of the topic. In his *Advancement of Learning* (1605), as well as in his *De Augmentis* (1623), Bacon fully acknowledged the importance of the study. He was impatient of the subtleties and arbitrary hypotheses of Ptolemy and his disciples, but he found no satisfaction in contemporary research on the Continent. He rejected the conclusions of Copernicus and his followers, whom he called derisively 'new carmen which drive the world about'

(*Praise of Knowledge,* 1592 ; *Works,* ed. Spedding, i. 124).
Finally in 1612, after reading Galileo's *Sidereus Nuncius,*
which came out two years earlier, Bacon devised an abstruse
astronomical system of his own wherein he insisted on the
fixity of the earth and on the revolution of the heavenly
bodies about it ; the mobility of the planets increased (he
thought) with their distance from the globe's surface.
Bacon's strange theory was mere futility and does no
credit to his scientific intuition. A surer glimpse of the
truth—that the sun and not the earth was the central feature
of the heavenly bodies—is visible in the impressive speeches
of Shakespeare's Ulysses (*Troilus,* I. iii. 85–91) :

> The heavens themselves, the planets, and this centre
> Observe degree, priority, and place,
> Insisture, course, proportion, season, form,
> Office, and custom, in all line of order : [1]
> And therefore is the glorious planet Sol
> In noble eminence enthron'd and spher'd
> Amidst the other.

Not that Shakespeare narrowly considered the competing
theories of professed astronomers. He preferred a less
rigorous method of observing sun and stars than they
practised :

> Study is like the heaven's glorious sun,
>   That will not be deep-search'd with saucy looks ;
> Small have continual plodders ever won,
>   Save base authority from others' books.
> These earthly godfathers of heaven's lights,
>   That give a name to every fixed star,
> Have no more profit of their shining nights
>   Than those that walk and wot not what they are.
>   (*Love's L. L.* I. i. 84–91)

In Shakespeare's England a mass of folklore and superstition clung about the heavenly bodies and gave the
phenomena curious shapes to the popular eye. 'The man
in the moon' (cf. *Mid. N. D.* v. i. 251 ; *Temp.* II. ii. 149)
embodies one of many popular hallucinations. Eclipses
were regarded solely as portents of evil : 'though the
wisdom of nature can reason it thus and thus, yet nature
finds itself scourged by the sequent effects [of eclipses]'

---

[1] A similar idea is found in Hooker's *Ecclesiastical Polity,* Book I, ch. iii :
'If celestial spheres should forget their wonted motions ... what would become
of man himself, whom these things now do all serve ? '

(*Lear*, I. ii. 116 ff.).   Comets, which were also designated meteors, were credited with as direful a significance, and were invariably associated with the deaths of kings. ' Comets ', exclaims Bedford at the opening of *1 Henry VI* (I. i. 2–5),

> importing change of times and states,
> Brandish your crystal tresses in the sky,
> And with them scourge the bad revolting stars,
> That have consented unto Henry's death !

Popular belief in the comet's evil boding was universal and irremovable.   Justly might Pandulph say :

> No natural exhalation in the sky,
> No scope of nature, no distemper'd day,
> No common wind, no customed event,
> But they will pluck away his natural cause
> And call them meteors, prodigies, and signs,
> Abortives, presages, and tongues of heaven,
> Plainly denouncing vengeance upon John.
>
> (*John*, III. iv. 153–9)

So in *Julius Cæsar* (II. ii. 30–1) Calphurnia says :

> When beggars die there are no comets seen ;
> The heavens themselves blaze forth the death of princes.

The twelve signs of the Zodiac attracted no less general attention.   They figured prominently in allegorical poetry through the Middle Ages.   Following in the path of a long succession of poets, Spenser in *The Faerie Queene*, Book VII, Canto vii, gave the signs an elaborate figurative interpretation which accorded with popular fancy.   Shakespeare makes a more literal use of them when the Princess bids Ferdinand

> There stay, until the twelve celestial signs
> Have brought about their annual reckoning.
>
> (*Love's L. L.* v. ii. 805–6)

That the sun should gallop each day through the Zodiac was an almost universal belief.

> As when the golden sun salutes the morn,
> And, having gilt the ocean with his beams,
> Gallops the zodiac in his glistering coach,
> And overlooks the highest-peering hills.
>
> (*Tit. Andr.* II. i. 5–8)

Yet the popular observations were not always delusive. Many, although at first sight difficult, bear witness to an accurate habit of vision.

All navigation was directed by close observation of the

stars. It is with expert knowledge that the Gentleman in
Othello (II. i. 13–15) describes how

> The wind-shak'd surge, with high and monstrous mane,
> Seems to cast water on the burning bear,
> And quench the guards of the ever-fixed pole.

The constellation of the 'burning bear' is Ursa Minor, and
the so-called 'guards' are the two stars β and γ Ursae
Minoris. Recorde wrote : ' The most northerly constellation
is the lesser Beare, called Vrsa Minor. . . . This is the chiefe
marke whereby mariners gouerne their course in saylings
by nyghte, and namely 2 starres in it which many do call
"the shafte", and other do name the "Guardas" [or signals],
after the Spanish tonge.' [1]

Shakespeare probably took his information from Richard
Eden's *Arte of Navigation*, 1561, which gives rules for
observing the 'guards' and speaks of 'the two starres
called the *Guardians*'. In Tapp's *Seamans Kalender*, 1602,
the 'guards' are similarly noticed.

At the same time it was no uncommon practice on land to
tell the time of night by the position of stars over buildings.
'Heigh-ho!' cries the Carrier in *1 Henry IV* (II. i. 1–3).
'An't be not four by the day I'll be hanged : Charles' Wain
is over the new chimney, and yet our horse not packed.'
'Charles' Wain' is, of course, the popular name for the
principal stars of Ursa Major.

But observations of rarer phenomena were also made by
untrained eyes. Shakespeare read in Holinshed an account
of a strange apparition of 'three suns' 'sodaynely joyned
altogether into one'. He vividly works out the suggestion
thus :

> *Edward.*   Dazzle mine eyes, or do I see three suns ?
> *Richard.*   Three glorious suns, each one a perfect sun ;
> Not separated with the racking clouds,
> But sever'd in a pale clear-shining sky.
> See, see ! they join, embrace, and seem to kiss;
> As if they vow'd some league inviolable :
> Now are they but one lamp, one light, one sun.
> In this the heaven figures some event.
>   (*3 Hen. VI*, II. i. 25–32)

---

[1] The word ' guards ' in this connexion is often misunderstood. A writer
of repute on navigation, Thomas Hood, rightly speaks in his *Marriners
Guide*, 1596, of the guards, from ' the Spanish word *guardare*, which is to
beholde, because they are diligently to be looked into in regard of the
singular use which they have in navigation '.

This is evidently the phenomenon of Parhelia. The context shows that it was in the morning, and it is to be noted that mock suns are generally seen when the sun is at a low altitude.

Less easy is it to explain a like phenomenon of mock moons which is noticed in *King John* :

> My lord, they say five moons were seen to-night :
> Four fixed, and the fifth did whirl about
> The other four in wondrous motion.
>
> (IV. ii. 182–4)

A scientific explanation is possible of the complimentary language of the King of Navarre in *Love's Labour's Lost* :

> My love, her mistress, is a gracious moon ;
> She, an attending star, scarce seen a light.
>
> (IV. iii. 230–1)

The maritime explorer Sir Richard Hawkins (Hakluyt Society, *The Hawkins Voyages*, p. 128) reported that he had both heard talk and read of ' a starre which never separateth it self from the Moone, but a small distance'. Molina (*Fables and Rites of the Incas*) likewise declared that ' the Incas worshipped several of the stars which they regarded as attendants on the Moon'. Scientific observers have satisfactorily accounted for this unfamiliar belief. Sir William Herschel records that he observed in 1783 on the dark part of the young moon a visible disk of luminous matter as bright as a star of the fourth magnitude (*Phil. Trans.* 1787). Wilkins in 1794 saw with the naked eye a light speck which appeared like a small star on the dark part of the moon, and says, ' I believed a star was passing over the moon'. ' Two strangers saw it and said it was a star' (*ibid.* 1794). This was investigated by Maskelyne, and considered as equal to a star of the third magnitude (*ibid.* 1821). Captain Kater in 1821 made a similar observation,—' like a small star of the sixth or seventh magnitude'; and William Henry Smyth in his *Cycle of Celestial Objects* (1844, vol. i) gave a drawing of what he saw. The cause of the appearance is clearly the power of the lunar mountain Aristarchus to reflect light.

Eclipses, however popular fancy interpreted them, are as a rule accurately reported by the Elizabethan dramatists.

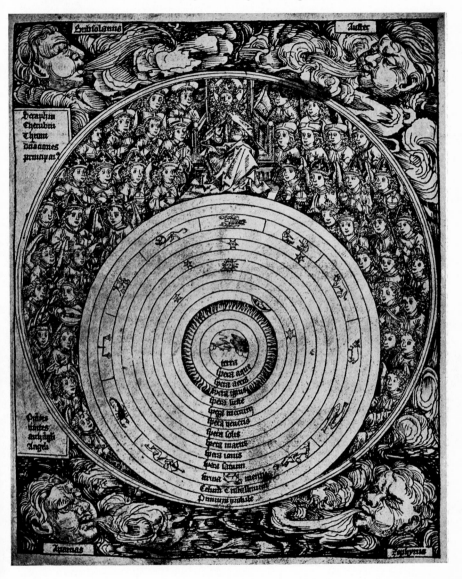

THE PTOLEMAIC SYSTEM

A remarkable example is to be noted in *King Lear*, the first performance of which took place in the presence of James I at Whitehall on St. Stephen's Night, Christmas, 1606. When Gloucester (*King Lear* I. ii. 115) speaks of 'these late eclipses in the sun and moon' he refers to the important solar eclipse of October 2, 1605, O.S. (October 12, Gregorian date), and to the lunar eclipse of September 27, 1605 (Gregorian date). This solar eclipse was total. The line of totality, shown in Oppolzer's *Canon der Finsternisse*, passed south of the British Isles, but though the sun would probably be not completely eclipsed in England, the eclipse would be a very striking event. The lunar eclipse was partial.

Ben Jonson supplies an equally precise notice of a strange phenomenon. 'Now Heaven!' says Sir Politic in *Volpone* (II. i),

> What prodigies be these?   The fires at Berwick!
> And the new star!

Volpone was written in 1605. On October 17, 1604, Kepler had discovered the new star which had burst out in the constellation *Serpentarius*, and which surpassed Jupiter in brightness. The great interest which was excited obviously finds reflection in Jonson's words.

From an epoch far more remote than that of Ptolemy, the study of the celestial bodies was coloured by the conviction that they exerted a direct and definable influence on human and terrestrial affairs, and that an examination of their movements enabled a skilled observer to foretell the future. Men were indeed blind puppets of the stars. Astrology and astronomy had little in common, yet Elizabethan writers often treated 'astrology' and 'astrologer' and 'astronomy' and 'astronomer' as synonyms. Astrology was strongly condemned in the fourteenth century by the Church of Rome, and by Calvin in the sixteenth century.

Imogen exclaims of Posthumus's handwriting:

> O! learn'd indeed were that astronomer
> That knew the stars as I his characters;
> He'd lay the future open.   (*Cymb.* III. ii. 27–9)

The astrological observation of the skies was popularly rated of higher interest than the scientific. Its death was long delayed, and during the sixteenth century it stubbornly resisted attack.

At every court of Europe during Shakespeare's lifetime astrology had its eager votaries, and in the ranks of the learned were found both champions and practitioners. Shakespeare's fellow-countryman John Dee enjoyed high repute at home and abroad as an astrologer as well as an alchemist, and Queen Elizabeth showed an active interest in the practice of his art.

Astrology, which had a recondite jargon, was professionally divided into three branches, called respectively horary, judicial, and natural. The heavens were in each case examined by a different method and for a different purpose. By means of horary astrology questions about business of the moment were answered ; judicial astrology foretold human affairs ; natural astrology, in which the horoscope was cast, disclosed the destiny of persons from the configuration of the planets at their birth.

Some of the serious astronomers were not disposed to deal too harshly with the vain pretensions of astrology. 'Astrology', wrote Kepler, 'is the foolish daughter of a wise mother, and for one hundred years past, this wise mother could not have lived without the help of her foolish daughter.' Kepler thought that the study of astronomy had been neglected since men ceased to apply themselves to astrology. But in Shakespeare's England the cry against the bastard science gathered volume as the years passed.

Philip Stubbes, the exposer of current abuses (*Anatomie*, pt. ii, 56–66), denounces the brood of 'astrologers, astronomers and prognosticators'. 'It is the wickedness of our own hearts', he declared, 'that draweth us to evil, and not the stars or planets.' Shakespeare tilted with equal frankness against the astrological principle of starry domination :

> The fault, dear Brutus, is not in our stars,
> But in ourselves, that we are underlings.
>
> > (*Jul. Cæs.* I. ii. 139–140)

Edmund, in *King Lear*, speaks with bitterer irony to the same effect :

This is the excellent foppery of the world, that, when we are sick in fortune,—often the surfeit of our own behaviour,—we make guilty of our disasters the sun, the moon, and the stars : as if we were villains by necessity, fools by heavenly compulsion, knaves,

ASTROLOGASTER,
OR,
THE FIGVRE-CASTER.

ather the Arraignment of Artleſſe Aſtrologers, and Fortune-tellers,
that cheat many ignorant people vnder the pretence of foretelling things to
come, *of telling things that are paſt, finding out things that are loſt, ex-*
pounding Dreames, calculating Deaths and Natiuities,
once againe brought to the Barre.

By Iohn Melton.

Cicero. *Stultorum plena funt omnia.*

Imprinted at London by *Barnard Alſop,* for *Edward Blackmore,* and are
to be fold in *Paules* Churchyard, at the Signe of the
Blazing-Starre. 1620.

thieves, and treachers by spherical predominance, drunkards, liars, and adulterers by an enforced obedience of planetary influence; and all that we are evil in, by a divine thrusting on.

(I. ii. 132-41)

To each heavenly body was allotted by popular super-stition a special influence on human existence. To the moon were ascribed very wide powers: she produced moisture, and controlled the tides (*Wint. Tale,* I. ii. 426-9). According to Titania:

> the moon, the governess of floods,
> Pale in her anger, washes all the air,
> That rheumatic diseases do abound.

(*Mid. N. D.* II. i. 103-5)

Edward IV's widow, Queen Elizabeth, declares:

> All springs reduce their currents to mine eyes,
> That I, being govern'd by the wat'ry moon,
> May send forth plenteous tears to drown the world!

(*Rich. III*, II. ii. 68-70)

Polixenes calls the moon 'the wat'ry star' (*Wint. Tale,* I. ii. 1-3), and Horatio calls it 'the moist star' (*Haml.* I. i. 118). It was a natural corollary that vegetation should depend on alleged lunar moisture for its sustenance: 'plantage' was inseparable from the moon (*Troilus,* III. ii. 184). Prince Henry describes himself and his riotous followers as 'the moon's men', whose fortune 'doth ebb and flow like the sea; being governed as the sea is, by the moon' (*I Hen. IV,* I. ii. 35 ff.).

Further, the moon was generally regarded as the cause of madness. Othello says:

> It is the very error of the moon;
> She comes more nearer earth than she was wont,
> And makes men mad.   (*Oth.* V. ii. 107-9)

The moon was, moreover, regarded as the ruling planet over thieves. 'We that take purses', cries Falstaff, 'go by the moon and the seven stars, and not by Phoebus ... we be men of good government, being governed as the sea is, by our noble and chaste mistress the moon, under whose countenance we steal' (*I Hen. IV,* I. ii. 15 ff.).

The moon was therefore the planet whose position was first to be considered in all questions relating to thieves and stealing. The aspect of the moon with the planets had to be determined. If 'evil aspects were found between the

Moon, Mars, and Mercury, the native is inclined to dis-
honesty '. The ' seven stars ', which Falstaff links to the
Moon, was an ordinary synonym for the Pleiades (cf. Recorde,
Castle of Knowledge, p. 101). ' The reason ', says the Fool
in *King Lear*, ' why the seven stars are no more than seven
is a pretty reason ' (I. v. 38–40). The brightest star in the
Pleiades, according to astrologers, was dominated by, or
had the significance of ' Mars and the Moon ', and when
Mars was ill-dignified the native was ' a lover of thieving '
and ' a highway thief '.

According to the astrological theory, the disposition of
men and women was determined by the planet or star under
which they were born and by the relations of the planet
or star to other planets or stars at the time. If at one's
birth ' good stars were opposite ' (i.e. in opposition), no good
fortune could result (*Rich. III*, IV. iv. 216). ' Planets of
good luck ' in opposition shed evil influence.

Parolles, who would be known as a soldier, disclaims the
suggestion that he was ' born under a charitable star '; he
asserts that he was born ' under Mars ' (*All's W*. I. i.
208–9).

Similarly, Autolycus asserts that he was ' littered under
Mercury ' (*Wint. Tale*, IV. ii. 25). Mercury was the ' author
of subtlety, tricks, devices, perjury, &c.'

A like technical knowledge of astrological formulae is
betrayed in Edmund's ironical account of his own birth :

My father compounded with my mother under the dragon's tail
and my nativity was under *Ursa Major*; so that it follows I am rough
and lecherous. (*Lear*, I. ii. 144–7)

The ' Dragon's tail ' was the descending node in the Moon's
orbit, and it had an evil significance : ' when joined with
the evil planets, their malice, or the evil intended thereby,
was doubled, and trebled, or extremely augmented '. All
the stars in Ursa Major were reckoned to be of the nature
of Mars, who was ' choleric and fiery, a lover of slaughter
and quarrels, murder, a traitor of turbulent spirit, perjured,
and obscene '. The astrological influence of the fixed stars
was according as they were ruled or dominated by the
planets.

The twelve signs of the Zodiac were reckoned to control
strictly various organs of the human body. ' Shall we set
about some revels ? ' asks Sir Andrew Aguecheek.

Sir Toby Belch. What shall we do else ? were we not born under
Taurus ?
Sir And. Taurus ? that 's sides and heart.
Sir Toby. No, sir, it is legs and thighs. (*Tw. N.* I. iii. 146–51)

Sir Andrew makes a mistake. It is Leo that governs
' sides and heart '. Leo rules ' all diseases in the ribs and
sides . . . trembling or passion of the heart '. Sir Toby
corrects his friend ; Taurus is ' legs and thighs '. The
quality of Taurus is ' nocturnal and bestial '. In the
authoritative astrological treatise *Liber Novem Iudicum,*
Taurus is stated to govern ' crura et pedes ', almost the very
words Sir Toby uses. All is in harmony with the character
of the two knights.

Astrological terminology has lost much of its point since
Shakespeare wrote *2 Henry IV.* When Prince Henry sees
Falstaff and Doll Tearsheet together, he cries out, ' Saturn
and Venus this year in conjunction ! What says the
almanack to that ? ' Poins carries on the jest and pointing
to Bardolph adds, ' And, look, whether the fiery Trigon, his
man, be not lisping to his master's old tables, his note-book,
his counsel-keeper ' (II. iv. 286 ff.). ' The fiery Trigon ' is
a term technically applied to the triple combination of the
three signs of the Zodiac,—Aries, Leo, and Sagittarius,—all
of the same hot and dry quality.

The technical language of astrology was familiar to the
Elizabethan playgoer, and the forgotten knowledge must
needs be studied afresh before the meaning of many
passages in Elizabethan drama grows intelligible.

BIBLIOGRAPHY.—The chief sources of astronomical knowledge in Shakespeare's time were CLAUDIUS PTOLEMY'S *Almagest,* Venice, 1515, 1528, and
Basle, 1541 ; his *Omnia quae extant opera praeter geographiam,* Basle, 1551,
fol. ; his *De praedicationibus astronomicis* (Greek text with Melanchthon's
later translation), Basle, 1533, 8vo (and other editions) ; and his *Plani-
sphaerium,* Venice, 1558, 4to. *The Compost of Ptholomeus, Prynce of
Astronomye, translated out of French in to Englysshe,* was published in
London about 1535 and several times reprinted down to 1600. The works
of other Greek astronomers were accessible in *Astronomica veterum scripta
isagogica,* Heidelberg, 1589. Besides the great publications of Kepler and
Galileo, already mentioned, astronomical treatises of importance by foreign
writers included BAYER'S *Uranometria,* 1603.

In English books the progress in astronomical knowledge can be traced in
ROBERT RECORDE'S *The Castle of Knowledge,* 1551 ; in RICHARD EDEN'S *The
Arte of Navigation,* 1561 ; in THOMAS HOOD'S *The Marriners Guide,* 1596 ; in
JOHN BLAGRAVE'S *Astrolabium Uranicum Generale,* 1596 ; in JOHN TAPP'S *The
Seamans Kalender,* 1602. Bacon's astronomical views are fully explained
by R. L. Ellis in his preface to BACON'S *Descriptio Globi Intellectualis,* in

Spedding's edition of the *Works*, iii. 715 ff. See also ABBOTT'S *Francis Bacon*, pp. 373 ff. DE MORGAN in *Companion to the Almanac*, 1831–57, describes astronomical and mathematical literature of the period. See also HALLIWELL'S *Letters Illustrative of the Progress of Science in England*, and RIGAUD'S *Correspondence of Scientific Men of the Seventeenth Century*, 1841. The *Dictionary of National Biography* has a useful notice of Thomas Harriot. The main text-book of astrology of the day was *Liber Novem Iudicum in Iudiciis Astrorum*, 1509; the writings of Dr. John Dee throw light on the professional practice (cf. *John Dee*, by Miss Fell Smith, 1909). Of contemporary tricks of humble astrologers a good account is given in GREENE'S *Third Part of Conny Catching*, 1592; see Greene's *Works*, ed. Grosart. A credulous *Astrological Discourse*, 1582, by RICHARD HARVEY (brother of Gabriel Harvey), was supplemented by ' an astrological addition ' by another brother, John (1583); in 1591 appeared *A Wonderful strange and miraculous Astrologicall Prognostication*. In 1601 JOHN CHAMBER issued *A Treatise against Judicial Astrologie*, to which Sir CHRISTOPHER HEYDON replied in *A Defence of Judiciall Astrologie* in 1603.

§ 2. ALCHEMY

BY

ROBERT STEELE

with contributions by Percy Simpson and C. T. Onions

THE science of chemistry was not in being in Shakespeare's days, but the chemical or alchemical art [1] had been carried far and had made such progress as was possible in the absence of securely based theories. The art of metallurgy, in particular, had been brought to a very high state of excellence in Germany, and the properties of the principal metals and alloys were well known. No one in everyday life was mistaken in the recognition of gold, silver, tin, iron, lead, and brass, and in the case of chemical compounds such as nitre or tartar, where one name connoted three or four distinct substances, any one who desired to use them was well enough acquainted with the rough tests of their suitability for his purpose. These tests were mainly trade secrets, and remained so till the end of the eighteenth century, but the technical knowledge of the time, though purely empirical, was fully abreast of its needs. Further advance awaited only the development of a new scientific system. All chemical changes met with in nature are complex, and in most of those that occur in everyday life air and other gases bear a considerable part ; but, till the existence of these bodies as ponderable substances was clearly recognized, it was impossible to direct at will or to predict the results of any chemical operation outside the very narrow limit of experience.

The distinction between chemistry and alchemy is basic : chemistry is founded on the principle of the indestructibility of matter, derived from the experimental evidence of the balance ; alchemy rested on the theory of the essential unity of matter—a pure assumption of the schools. Primary matter was supposed to fill all space, and to be capable of taking upon it diverse forms, which were classified by the

---

[1] The Latin *ars chemica* seems to have reacted upon the term *alchemia*, and produced a new form, *archemia* (cf. *archemie* in the title of Ripley's book, 1591), just as *ars metrica*, the art of measurement, contaminated *arithmetice*, and produced *ars metice*.

impressions they produced. The school classification of
these impressions was Hot or Cold, Dry or Moist. These
qualities may co-exist two at a time in the same substance, which may therefore be either Hot and Dry, Hot
and Moist, Cold and Dry, or Cold and Moist. Thus four
classes of matter came to be distinguished, which were named
Fire, Air, Earth, and Water. These are the four elements.
'Does not our life', asks Sir Toby Belch, 'consist of the
four elements ? ' (*Tw. N.* II. iii. 10). These elements were
not necessarily the substances bearing those names in
ordinary language, though they were confounded with them
in popular parlance, as in *Troilus and Cressida* (I. iii. 41),
where air and sea are called ' the two moist elements ', or
as in *Hamlet* (I. i. 153), where the enumeration of all four is
meant to cover ' the universal world '. Nor were they what
we now understand by chemical elements, into which any
body can be resolved ; they were only conditions in which
universal matter existed. The action of these four elements
can be traced in all bodies, and it is only when they are in
due proportion that the resulting body is perfect.

All substances were divided into imperfect or perfect compounds. In imperfect compounds—'meteors'—one element
or another predominated, as that of fire in the rainbow
or in lightning, of water in dew. In perfect compounds,
those which have assumed substantial forms, the elemental
character is entirely masked. Such bodies may be animate
or inanimate. Inanimate or earthy bodies are either metals
or fossils—fossils or minerals being taken to mean all inanimate bodies, such as stones or clay, that may be dug out
of the earth. Mediaeval alchemists, following Avicenna,
recognized 145 of these distinct bodies, which were compounds of mixed elements.

Metals were said to be composed of earth, water, and air
in varying proportions, the composition determining their
comparative readiness to melt or volatilize. They were also
said to contain Sulphur, Mercury, and Salt. These again
are not to be understood as the common substances so
named, but as qualities which these substances possess in a
high degree. For example, if a piece of wood is heated,
a certain amount of moisture is first given off ; this fluid
portion is its mercury : if it is further heated, the wood
burns ; this is due to its sulphur : when the sulphur is

all consumed, an ash is left; this is its salt. In metals, sulphur represented their combustibility, salt their solidity, and mercury their weight, malleability, lustre, and power of becoming fluid. This theory was based upon certain chemical facts. Many ores of metals are sulphides (or, in the older nomenclature, 'sulphurs'), that is, they contain sulphur in large quantities, either obtainable from them in a pure form or recognizable by its smell when the ore is burnt. Mercury was no doubt suggested by the resemblance of molten metals to quicksilver. The theory of the salt was suggested by the fact that when certain substances were calcined, the resulting ash, being lixiviated with water, yielded a crystalline matter resembling common salt when the solution was evaporated.

The recognized metals were : lead (Saturn), tin (Jupiter), iron (Mars), gold (the Sun), copper (Venus), quicksilver (Mercury), and silver (the Moon). They were all regarded as being compounded of sulphur and mercury in a state of greater or less perfection. In gold, the perfect metal, all the qualities were compounded in a state of equality.

Mediaeval science was founded almost entirely on analogy. Man, the microcosm,[1] was compared to the great universe, the macrocosm, and, as his body was thought to be formed and secreted from the blood in its interior, so the stones and metals were formed in the interior ' veins o' th' earth ' (*Temp*. I. ii. 255) ; but, as the life of the earth was incalculably longer than the life of a man, so the time taken in the formation of a metal was thousands of years. This analogy was carried further in the use of ' generation ' and ' corruption ' for the coming into being and the ceasing to exist of any substance as such ; thus, when wood is burnt, the wood is corrupted and flame and smoke are generated. Shakespeare does not use these words in their technical sense, though they were familiar to him and his contemporaries as terms of the schools in current use, and are reflected in literature. So in Jonson's masque *Mercury Vindicated* :

Out o' the corruption of a Lawyer was the best generation of a Broker in suits ;

and in Middleton and Dekker's *Roaring Girle* :

Would you have a catchpoole rightly deriv'd, the corruption of a Citizen is the generation of a serjeant.

[1] ' If you see this in the map of my microcosm ' (*Cor.* II. i. 69–70).

The ordinary explanation of nourishment by food was that food was digested and concocted and turned into a vapour by the internal heat of the body; the vapour passed along the veins and was concreted in various parts of the body as blood, fat, and flesh, each substance being able to impress its own form on the vapour. In the same way all minerals were conceived to be begotten of subterranean vapours, generated and perpetually distilled by subterranean fires. Metals partook of the nature of water and fire; stones, of earth and fire.

Analogy was pushed further and carried to sublime heights. Since the perfect proportion of the elements in the human body resulted in health, and in a metal made it gold, it followed that the less perfect proportion in other metals was a kind of disease, which could be remedied by an appropriate medicine. In this theory the two main streams of alchemy met—the search for the art of making gold, coming from Egypt; the search for the elixir of life, the universal medicine, rising in China. The ' medicine ', which by its strong attractive power could impose the form of gold —that is, of perfect proportion—on the purified substance of metals in contact with it, was called, in this connexion, the Philosophers' Stone (*lapis philosophorum*); [1] when used as a medicine for the body it was called the Elixir, *elixir vitae*, and lastly, *aurum potabile*—a term which no doubt suggested the ' grand liquor ' of Alonso's question in *The Tempest*:

> And Trinculo is reeling ripe : where should they
> Find this grand liquor that hath gilded them? (v. i. 279–80)

and is more directly represented in :

> Other [gold], less fine in carat, is more precious,
> Preserving life in medicine potable. (*2 Hen. IV*, iv. v. 160–1)

The sources from which it was prepared were various ; their nature and scope may be gathered from a licence granted in 1456 for making the elixir of life and the philosophers' stone :

In former times wise and famous philosophers in their writings and books have left on record and taught under figures and coverings that from wine, precious stones, oils, vegetables, animals, metals, and minerals [2] can be made many glorious and notable medicines,

---

[1] Shakespearian allusions are in *2 Hen. IV* (iii. ii. 359) and *Timon* (ii. ii. 117).

[2]   the blest infusions
That dwell in vegetives, in metals, stones. (*Pericles* iii. ii. 35–6)

and chiefly that most precious medicine which some philosophers have called the mother and Empress of medicines, others the priceless glory, others the quintessence, others the Philosophers' Stone and Elixir of Life. Of which potion the efficacy is so certain and so wonderful that by it all infirmities whatsoever are easily curable, human life is prolonged to its natural limit, and man wonderfully preserved in health and manly strength both of body and mind, in vigour of limbs, clearness of memory, and perspicacity of intellect to the same period. All kinds of wounds too which are curable, are healed without difficulty, and in addition it is the best and surest remedy against all kinds of poisons. By it too, many other advantages most useful to . . . the Commonwealth . . . can be wrought, such as the transmutation of metals into actual gold and the finest silver. (*Rot. Pat.* 34 Hen. VI, m. 7, May 31, 1456.)

It was the alchemist's claim to the power of 'multiplying' the precious metals, especially gold, by the transmutation of the baser metals, that naturally appealed to the popular imagination and brought to the alchemist's study clients eager to repair their broken fortunes or willing to gamble on the chance of making a rich haul. It is this gold-making side of alchemy—dependent on the use of the sovereign philosophers' stone, the ' multiplying medicine ' (*All's W.* v. iii. 102)—to which all Shakespeare's sparse allusions to the practice of the art are made. King Philip, blessing the day on which Lewis and Blanch are to be joined in marriage, says :

> The glorious sun
> Stays in his course and plays the alchemist,
> Turning with splendour of his precious eye
> The meagre cloddy earth to glittering gold.
>
> (*John* III. i. 77–80)

To this we have a close parallel in :

> Full many a glorious morning have I seen
> Flatter the mountain-tops with sovereign eye,
> Kissing with golden face the meadows green,
> Gilding pale streams with heavenly alchemy.
>
> (*Sonnet* xxxiii)

Timon employs a pungent metaphor when he beats the painter and the poet from his presence :

> Hence ! pack ! there 's gold ; ye came for gold, ye slaves :
> You have done work for me, there 's payment : hence !
> You are an alchemist, make gold of that ; (*Timon* v. i. 117–19)

and the point of Henry V's reproach to Lord Scroop is similar :

> That almost mightst have coin'd me into gold,
> Wouldst thou have practis'd on me for thy use !
>
> (*Hen. V*, II. ii. 98–9)

Sometimes the reference goes deeper, to the transmutation of the base into the sublime, as in Casca's estimate of the character of Brutus:

> And that which would appear offence in us,
> His countenance, like richest alchemy,
> Will change to virtue and to worthiness;
>
> (*Jul. Caes.* I. iii. 158–60)

or in the subtle turn of *Sonnet* cxiv, where alchemy is the magic influence of love:

> Or whether shall I say, mine eye saith true,
> And that your love taught it this alchemy,
> To make of monsters and things indigest
> Such cherubins as your sweet self resemble,
> Creating every bad a perfect best,
> As fast as objects to his beams assemble?

The stories that were popularly circulated about the 'multiplication' of gold were not all without a substratum of truth. For instance, a piece of copper might be made to appear converted half into gold. In this trick a piece of gold-copper alloy had some of the surface copper removed by cementation. Another artist had a powder which turned silver to gold; but the powder was a salt of gold, and the silver was not converted into gold, but burnt away in the process.

The two critical processes in the production of gold were multiplication and projection, which are the last of the twelve processes or 'gates' of the art, as they are classified and defined in Ripley's treatise, *The Compound of Alchymy*, which, originally presented to Edward IV, was printed in 1591 and dedicated to the Queen. A brief account of these must suffice in this place.[1] The first gate, Calcination,

> is the purgation of our stone,
> Restoring also of his naturall heate.

The second, Dissolution,

> maketh intenuate things that were thicke also,
> By vertue of our first menstrue cleare and bright,
> In which our bodies eclipsed been of light,
> And of their hard and drye compaction subtilate,
> Into their owne first matter kindly retrogradate.

---

[1] There is a large body of jargon, for the mention of which no space is here available. Much of it will be found (as far as the general literature of the period is concerned) in Jonson's *Alchemist* and his masque *Mercurie Vindicated from the Alchemists*, and in Lyly's *Gallathea*, 1592, II. iii (the source of which is Reginald Scot's *Discoverie of Witchcraft*, 1584, bk. xiv, chap. i).

The third, Separation, divides

> The subtile from the grosse, the thick from the thinn.

The fourth, Conjunction,

> is nothing els
> But of dissevered qualities a copulation,
> Or of principles a coequation.

The fifth gate is Putrefaction, without which 'no seed may multiply'. The sixth, Congelation, is the induration of soft white things and the confixation of flying spirits. The seventh, Cibation, is

> a feeding of our matter drie,
> With milke and meate, which moderately thou doe,
> Untile it be brought the third order unto.

Of Sublimation, the eighth gate, Ripley says that fools sublime, but the true practitioner must not imitate them. Its object is threefold, to make the body spiritual, the spirit corporeal so that it may become 'fixt with it and consubstantiall', and finally that 'he may be cleansed' from his 'filthie originall' and that his sulphurous saltness may be diminished. Few workers understand the ninth process, Fermentation, he says; it was held to be an internal change in the nature of metals, wrought by a ferment comparable to the leaven that works in dough. The next gate is Exaltation, differing 'full little' from Sublimation. The final stages are Multiplication and Projection, the first consisting in the 'augmentation' of the elixir, the second in the penetration and transfiguration of metals in fusion by casting upon them the powder of the philosophers' stone, which is then called the 'powder of projection'.

Just as the witch was almost invariably a poisoner, the alchemist was as a rule either a charlatan or a maker of base coin. Here and there alchemy might be pursued in a spirit of honest inquiry, but usually the practitioner experimented only on other people's purses. Chaucer in *The Canterbury Tales*, and Ben Jonson in *The Alchemist*, acted in 1610, show marked agreement in depicting this type of rogue. He affected the strictest virtue; he employed an elaborate and high-sounding jargon of technical terms; and he could always explain away the failure of experiments, so as to lure his dupes on to further outlay. The second act of Jonson's play opens with the triumphant entry of Sir Epicure Mammon, who has been steadily fleeced for ten

ALCHEMY 469

months by the alchemist Subtle, and has been led to expect
on that very day the complete success of a costly series of experiments. 'This night', he tells his sceptical friend, Surly,

> I'll change
> All that is metal in thy house to gold.
> And early in the morning will I send
> To all the plumbers and the pewterers
> And buy their tin and lead up ; and to Lothbury
> For all the copper . . .
> Yes, and I'll purchase Devonshire and Cornwall
> And make them perfect Indies!

The magical qualities of the Stone—'the perfect ruby,
which we call Elixir'—endow its possessor with a wide range
of gifts. He

> Can confer honour, love, respect, long life,
> Give safety, valure—yea, and victory,
> To whom he will. In eight and twenty days,
> I'll make an old man of fourscore a child.

The patriarchs before the Flood attained their longevity

> By taking once a week, on a knive's point,
> The quantity of a grain of mustard

of the elixir. Mammon has even secured some of their
literature on the subject.

> I'll show you a book where Moses and his sister
> And Solomon have written of the art ;
> Ay, and a treatise penn'd by Adam. *Surly.* How ?
> *Mammon.* O' the Philosophers' Stone, and in High-dutch.
> *Surly.* Did Adam write, sir, in High-dutch ? *Mammon.* He did :
> Which proves it was the primitive tongue. *Surly.* What paper ?
> *Mammon.* On cedar board. *Surly.* Oh that indeed, they say,
> Will last 'gainst worms.

Face, masquerading as the drudge who attends to the
furnace, enters to announce the signs of coming success,
ensured by his own careful labour :

> I have blown, sir,
> Hard for your worship ; thrown by many a coal
> When 'twas not beech ; weigh'd those I put in, just,
> To keep your heat still even. These blear'd eyes
> Have waked to read your several colours, sir,
> Of the pale citron, the green lion, the crow,
> The peacock's tail, the plumed swan. *Mammon.* And lastly
> Thou hast descried the flower, the *sanguis agni* ?
> *Face.* Yes, sir. *Mam.* Where's master? *Face.* At's prayers, sir, he,
> Good man, he's doing his devotions,
> For the success.

Intoxicated with hope, Mammon rhapsodizes on the life of exquisite sensuality which he will lead when the honest wretch, Subtle, worn out with prayer and fasting, has achieved the Stone for him. After this adroit preparation Subtle enters :

The work is done: bright Sol is in his robe ;
We have a med'cine of the Triple Soul,
The Glorified Spirit. Thanks be to heaven,
And make us worthy of it !

He turns to practical matters.

Look well to the register,
And let your heart still lessen by degrees
To the aludels. *Face.* Yes, sir. *Subtle.* Did you look
O' the bolt's-head yet ? *Face.* Which ? on D, sir ? *Subtle.* Ay.
What's the complexion ? *Face.* Whitish. *Subtle.* Infuse vinegar,
To draw his volatile substance and his tincture ;
And let the water in glass E be filter'd
And put into the Gripe's Egg. Lute him well,
And leave him closed *in balneo.*

Unfortunately an experiment is not perfect ; Subtle satisfies himself by cross-examining Face that the process was right ; they might have ' a new amalgama ', but it is really unimportant ; the other experiments are so promising. But Face is superstitious : he objects that one failure might bring them bad luck. Mammon swallows the bait greedily.

What is some three ounces
Of fresh materials ? . . .
Away, here 's money. What will serve ? *Face.* Ask him, sir.
Mammon. How much ? *Subtle.* Give him nine pound—you may
gi' him ten.

Finally Mammon puts the crucial question : ' When do you make projection ? ' Subtle manœuvres with consummate skill :

Son, be not hasty, I exalt our med'cine
By hanging him *in balneo vaporoso*
And giving him solution ; then congeal him ;
And then dissolve him ; then again congeal him ;
For look, how oft I iterate the work,
So many times I add unto his virtue.
As if at first one ounce convert a hundred,
After his second loose he'll turn a thousand ;
His third solution ten ; his fourth a hundred ;
After his fifth a thousand thousand ounces
Of any imperfect metal into pure
Silver or gold, in all examinations,

AN ALCHEMIST AT WORK by PIETER BREUGHEL 1558

As good as any of the natural mine.
Get you your stuff here against afternoon,
Your brass, your pewter, and your andirons.
  Mammon. Not those of iron? *Subtle.* Yes, you may bring
    them too ;
We'll change all metals.

Before the goods arrive, Subtle has already disposed of
them to a Puritan deacon, whose congregation covet the
Stone for the prospect it affords them of ' rooting out the
bishops '. Mammon is trapped into an intrigue, the im-
moral character of which causes the furnace to blow up at
the critical moment timed for the ' projection '. Little will
be saved, Face tells him, except a peck of coals, and advises
him to go home and repent.

The golden age of alchemy in England was during the
Wars of the Roses. In Tudor times it flourished in the
smaller Hanse towns, such as Emden and Lubeck, at
Brunswick, and at the court of the Holy Roman Emperor.
The Duke of Brunswick and the Emperor kept alchemists
in their pay, and welcomed all comers who professed a
knowledge of the art.

In Elizabeth's reign a good deal of encouragement was
given in England to alchemy, or at least to alchemists, by
personages in high places, even by the Queen herself. The
most prominent of the practitioners was John Dee, a learned
mathematician (1527–1608), to whom are ascribed no fewer
than 79 learned works. Under the patronage of Dudley and
the Earl of Pembroke he made an astrological computation
for the Queen's coronation day. This brought him to
Elizabeth's notice, and from about 1564 onwards we find
him installed as her instructor in mystic secrets, and the
Queen paying him visits from time to time. All this appears
to have brought him little reward, and he finally settled
down to alchemical studies and to intercourse with supernatural beings. In 1582 he became connected with one
Edward Kelly, alias Talbot (1555–95), who had already had
his ears cropped for forging or coining and was an out-and-
out impostor, though undoubtedly a man of considerable
abilities. Dee possessed a magic crystal, and Kelly acted
as his ' skryer ', seer, or crystal-gazer. These two were
joined by Albert Laski, Palatine of Siradz in Bohemia, who,
broken in fortune, had given himself up to the discovery of

the great elixir, and in 1583 was visiting England. At first
the trio received some recognition from the Earl of Leicester,
but, their means of support becoming less and less sufficient,
Laski bethought himself of providing for their needs in his
own country. They all three accordingly left for Prague,
where, however, they were disappointed of a cordial reception at the hands of Rudolph II. They were at length
expelled the country, and by 1589 Dee had broken with
Kelly. Some years later the latter revisited the Emperor's
court and was forthwith imprisoned. He lost his life in
attempting to escape. The many references to him in
contemporary and later writings testify to the widespread
notoriety to which he had attained. There are allusions to
him in Gabriel Harvey, Jonson, Dekker, and in the dramatist Fletcher. The following passage from Nashe's *Have
with you to Saffron-Walden* bears witness at the same time
to the alchemist's tyranny over the spirits of the departed
and to his power over the purses of the living :

Carnead. Let him call uppon Kelly, who is better than them
both [*scil.* Lully and Paracelsus] ; and for the spirites and soules of
the ancient Alchumists, he hath them so close emprisoned in the
firie purgatorie of his fornace, that for the welth of the King of
Spaines Indies, it is not possible to release or get the third part of
a nit of anie one of them, to helpe anie but himselfe.

Import. Whether you call his fire Purgatorie or no, the fire of
Alchumie hath wrought such a purgation or purgatory in a great
number of mens purses in England that it hath clean fir'd them out
of al they have.

To relate the achievements of other adventurers in this
line is, by comparison with the romantic story of Kelly, to
' chronicle small beer '. But they are not without interest
in their bearing upon the credulity of such as had money to
spare for the furtherance of their designs.

Among the more easily understood treatises of the
Theatrum Chemicum is one by ' Cornelius Alvetanus ' ' de
conficiendo divino Elixire sive lapide philosophico ', dedicated to Queen Elizabeth and dated July 14, 1565. Its
author is Cornelius de Alneto, or de Lannoy, and a long
correspondence with him is preserved in the Public Record
Office, in the British Museum, and at Hatfield. The earliest
notice of him is a letter, dated February 7, 1565, in which
he offers his services to the Queen and engages to produce
for her 50,000 marks of pure gold annually at a moderate

JOHN DEE

charge. His offer seems to have been accepted, and he was given rooms in Somerset House, where he set to work, first to write his treatise and secondly to make the gold. The Princess Cecilia, daughter of Gustavus I of Sweden, was at this time an exile in England and was lodged near de Lannoy. She was in debt, and the alchemist who was doing such great things for the Queen could surely help her. Negotiations were entered into, as a result of which de Lannoy signed a bond on January 20, 1566, to lend the princess £10,000 on the following May 1, to be repaid in thirteen yearly instalments of £1,000 each, in consideration of a payment of £300 to de Lannoy. Rumours of this agreement soon got abroad, and the Queen, angry to find others reaping the benefit of her protection (for alchemy was forbidden by statute), forbade de Lannoy to hold any communication with the princess. The alchemist was put under observation. He writes to the Queen to complain of the suspicion around him, and to Cecil that ' our great and glorious design has fallen into suspicion ', and swears on the holy gospels that he will carry it through successfully. He promises to hold no communication with the princess. But he did not keep faith. Cecil was warned that de Lannoy was preparing to leave England with the princess, and he was immediately arrested and called to account. In January 1567 Cecil's diary records his committal to the Tower ' for abusing the Queen's majesty in Somerset House in promising to make the elixir ', and again on February 10 tells how he ' abused many in promising to convert any metal into gold'. The last mention of him is on March 13, 1567, when he writes again to Cecil, promising if he is released and supported, to make unlimited quantities of gold and gems.

Such stories are typical of the lives of the alchemist adventurers, which, though sometimes meteoric in their brilliance, ended for the most part in poverty or the jail. A fitting epilogue to all such records is to hand in Ben Jonson's epigram addressed to the fraternity :

> If all you boast of your great art be true,
> Sure, willing poverty lives most in you.

BIBLIOGRAPHY.—There are no good modern works on Alchemy, and students of the Alchemy of our period cannot do better than refer to the writers in one of the collections below—Manget, for example, which is arranged chronologically. As Alchemy was illegal in this country until the end of the Stuarts, no English treatises on it can be expected. A. Collections of Alchemical works and translations. (1) in Latin :—*Artis auriferae quam chemiam vocant volumen primum*, &c., 3 vols., 1593–1610, *Theatrum Chemicum*, 6 vols., 1659–61, J. J. MANGET'S *Bibliotheca Chemica Curiosa*, 2 vols., 1702 ; (2) in English :—E. ASHMOLE'S *Theatrum Chemicum Britannicum*, 1652, W. SALMON'S *Medicina Practica*, 1691 ; (3) in Greek :—M. P. E. BERTHELOT'S *Collection des anciens Alchimistes grecs*, 3 vols., 1888 ; (4) in Arabic and Syriac :—M. P. E. BERTHELOT'S *La Chimie au moyen âge*, 3 vols., 1893. B. Mediaeval accounts of Alchemy by non-alchemists. VINCENTIUS BELLO- VACENSIS (*c.* 1190–*c.* 1264), *Speculum doctrinale*, lib. xi, *De arte mechanica*, caps. 105–13 ; BARTHOLOMAEUS ANGLICUS (fl. 1230–50), *De proprietatibus rerum*, lib. xvi ; see also R. STEELE'S *Medieval Lore*, 1905, for a popular selection from this work. An exposition in plain language of Alchemical terms is given by ROGER BACON : see *Part of the Opus tertium*, ed. A. G. Little, 1912. C. History of Alchemy and Alchemists. T. THOMSON'S *The History of Chemistry*, 2 vols., 1830–1, J. C. F. HOEFER'S *Histoire de la Chimie*, 1866–9, M. P. E. BERTHELOT'S *Les Origines de l'Alchimie*, 1885, H. KOPP'S *Die Alchemie*, 2 vols., 1886, G. F. RODWELL'S *The Birth of Chemistry*, 1874, H. C. BOLTON'S *The Literature of Alchemy*, 1901, M. M. P. MUIR'S *The Story of Alchemy*, 1902. D. Bibliography, &c. H. C. BOLTON, *A Select Bibliography of Chemistry*, 1492–1892, &c. 1893, &c., M. RULAND'S *Lexicon Alchemiae*, 1612, translated into English 1892 (six copies printed), J. FERGUSON'S *Bibliotheca Chemica*, 2 vols., 1906 (a storehouse of materials for the history of the subject).

§ 3. NATURAL HISTORY

I. ANIMALS

BY

C. T. Onions

To the Englishman of Shakespeare's day, whether learned or simple, the animal kingdom meant, not vertebrates and invertebrates, not mammalia, insecta, crustacea, and the like, but beasts and fowls (both wild and tame), fishes, and creeping things or worms. *Insecta*, which is the literal Latin for Aristotle's *entoma*, was, it is true, already a recognized term—William Harrison is at pains to translate it by ' cut or girt-waisted '—and ultimately took a place in the terminology of Linnaeus (1707–78), the creator of systematic nomenclature as we know it now ;[1] but the idea of a general arrangement of the animal creation on the basis of natural affinities had barely taken hold even among the most advanced students of the time. The starting-point of modern zoology was the revival of the Aristotelian classification, and is associated with the name of Edward Wotton, who did little more than expound Aristotle's *Historia Animalium* in his *De Differentiis Animalium* of 1552. The first great name is that of the German-Swiss Conrad Gesner (1516–65), eminent in his own day not only as a naturalist, but as a physician and a bibliographer. His is the greatest name among those who worked in the ' collecting ' stage of zoology, which had succeeded to the ' credulous ' stage, and preceded the ' anatomical and microscopic ' stage. Advance in the direction of this third stage, that is towards modern zoological classification, was not possible until the practice of dissection, which at the close of the Elizabethan age

---

[1] Of the other classes enumerated above, it is interesting to note that Mammalia is not earlier than Linnaeus, and that, while Sir Thomas Browne in 1646 could speak of lobsters, shrimps, and crayfishes as crustaceous, following Aristotle's division, the class Crustacea was not recognized till 1801 by Lamarck. When Lamarck defined the groups Vertebrata and Invertebrata, it was virtually a reversion to Aristotle's two great classes of Enaima and Anaima, blooded and bloodless animals, with which his own are approximately coextensive.

was yet in its infancy, was extended from the human subject to the bodies of the lower animals.

Side by side with the critical researches of men who followed in Gesner's path, ran traditional natural history, full of errors of observation, inventions, myths, and false etymologies.

In 1567 appeared the first book in the English language in which the term Natural History is known to occur. Its author was John Maplet, and its long title begins, *A Greene Forest or a Naturall Historie.* It is divided into three books, dealing with stones and metals, trees, herbs, and shrubs, and beasts, fishes, fowls, &c., in that order. To each book is prefixed a preface of general observations on the kingdom of which it treats. The preface to the third book lays down the characters of male and female, distinguishes mild animals from fierce, the strong from the subtle, those that ' be full of blood ', as the hart, the hind, and the roe, from those that ' in stead thereof have their natural humor ', as the bee, the beetle, the fly, the eaters of flesh from those that ' will none of it ', those ' of good memorie ', as the dog, the lion, and the camel, from the forgetful, as the ostrich and the dove.

The substance of Maplet's duodecimo is taken out of the 16th, 17th, and 18th books of the *De Proprietatibus Rerum* of Bartholomaeus Anglicus, the great mediaeval encyclopaedia. The books treated respectively of the mineral, vegetable, and animal kingdoms, and Maplet's books, as we have said, take the subjects in the same order. Bartholomaeus draws his facts about animals largely from Aristotle[1] and Pliny, but he is careful at the same time to give the etymologies of their names—usually some fancies of Isidore's—and to explain their bearing on the habits or appearance of the animals in question. Two editions of the English translation of Bartholomaeus were issued in the sixteenth century, one in 1535 and another, a revision by Batman, in 1582. At the time that Shakespeare began to write, one or other of these editions would probably be accessible in the house of any one who possessed a library, however small.

Maplet's order of treatment follows the alphabet—not

---

[1] Hence, the prefatory matter to Maplet's 3rd book is an abstract of the introduction of Aristotle's *Historia Animalium.*

even the scientific Gesner arrived at a classification more zoological. ' Let us begin Alphabetically,' he says, ' (as in the residue of our work before) with the Adder.' We take two articles as illustrations of his style :

Of the Cat.

The Cat in Latin is called *Catus*, as if you woulde say *Cautus*, warie or wise. In Greeke she is named *Galiootes*, with the Germans *Katz*. She is to the Mouse a continuall enimie : verie like to the Lyon in tooth and clawe ; and useth to pastime or play with the Mouse ere she devoureth hir. She is in hir trade and maner of living very shamefast : always loving clenlinesse. There is also a kind hereof called the wild Cat, which of all things is annoyed with the smell of Rue, and the Almond leafe, and is driven away with that sooner then with any other thing.

Of the Parret.

The Parret hath all hir whole bodie greene, saving that onely about hir necke she hath a Coller or Chaine naturally wrought like to Sinople or Vermelon. Indie hath of this kinde such as will counterfaite redily a mans speach : what wordes they heare, those commonly they pronounce. There have bene found of these that have saluted Emperours : give them Wine and they will be wanton inough : they are as hard in their head as in their Beak or Bill : When they learne to speak they must be beaten with an Iron Rod, or else they feele it not : Plinie saith that in a certaine Wood called Gagandes, this kinde was first founde : of all other Foules she and the Turtle Dove have greatest friendship.

Perhaps no writings of this period contain such an abundance of animal lore as Shakespeare's, unless it be Lyly's *Euphues*, in which every few pages yield some fable or comparison drawn from animal life. If we are to set down the sources of the knowledge of animals exhibited by Shakespeare [1] and his fellow writers, we shall say roughly that they were the experience of everyday life, especially in the country, the meagre resources of the Tower or other menageries, books of travel and of natural history, and, above all, the traditional stock of fact and fable derived from ancient sources. In the later years of Shakespeare's life books on natural history received two notable English additions in Philemon Holland's translation of Pliny (1601) and Topsell's abridgement (1607-8) of the voluminous works of Gesner.

---

[1] It is not the purpose of this article to enumerate all the errors and misconceptions of which Shakespeare is guilty ; this has been done in many places elsewhere, for instance, by a writer in *The Quarterly Review*, April, 1894.

The animals familiar in the ordinary life of the time are those of which William Harrison was concerned to give some account in his *Description of England* (1577–87)— namely, the English animals that he himself knew or knew of ; and he frankly confesses the imperfectness of his knowledge. He begins with cattle kept for profit, of which all that need be said here is that they were the same as they are now : oxen, of which he says that ours ' are such as the like are not to be found in anie countrie in Europe, both for greatnesse of bodie and sweetnesse of flesh ', horses, sheep, goats, swine. ' Our land dooth yeeld no asses,' he says, ' and therefore we want the generation of mules or somers [i. e. sumpter-mules] ; and therefore the most part of our cariage is made by these [horses], which remaining stoned, are either reserved for the cart, or appointed to beare such burdens as are convenient for them '. ' Asses are made to bear,' says Katherine in *The Taming of the Shrew* (II. i. 200), and Shylock classes mules with asses and dogs as being used ' in abject and in slavish parts ' (*Merch. of V.* IV. i. 92).

Of horses Harrison says that ours, though not so large as some others, are of an easy pace, and altogether hard to beat. He speaks of the importation of ' outlandish ' horses : the Spanish jennet, the Neapolitan courser, the Irish hobby, the Flemish roil, and the Scottish nag. More is said about these horses in Chapter XXVII, § 6.

We pass on to dogs. The standard work of the century on dogs was the treatise of the physician, John Kaye or Caius (1510–73), co-founder of Gonville and Caius College, Cambridge. It was made accessible in an English translation in 1576, and Harrison gave an abstract of it the next year in his contribution to Holinshed's work. Caius made three chief classes of dogs—game-dogs, house-dogs, and toy-dogs. Of the first class there are spaniels and hounds, and of hounds there are eight kinds, harriers, terriers, bloodhounds, gazehounds, greyhounds, lymers, tumblers,[1] and thieves. There are also the water-spaniel and land-spaniel for falconry. Of these Shakespeare has the bloodhound, the greyhound, and the lym, and outside them, the beagle and the brach. The further treatment of these falls into the appropriate sections of Chapter XXVII. ' Dogs

---

[1] A kind of lurcher which tumbled about and played antics in order to deceive rabbits as to his intentions.

Iohannes Stradanus inuentor

Strution insequitur celeri greis Maura molosso, Et Gabos plumas apiat greftamen bonorum.

HUNTING OSTRICHES WITH MOLOSSIAN DOGS by JOANNES STRADANUS

of the homelie kind', says Harrison, 'are either shepherdes curs, or mastifes.' These were also called ban-dogs (*2 Hen. VI*, I. iv. 21) and tie-dogs. It will be observed that 'cur' in the sixteenth century was not always a term of derogation; the watch-dog and the mastiff were curs. But it was already on the down-grade, as its abusive application to human beings bears witness; and Harrison calls toy-dogs, for which Caius expressed great contempt—with much rhetoric against the mincing ladies who allowed them to lick their lips in their coaches—dogs of the currish kind or toyish curs. In Shakespeare there are 'village curs', that 'bark when their fellows do' (*Hen. VIII*, II. iv. 157–8); and ''tis a foul thing', as Launce says, 'when a cur cannot keep himself in all companies'. 'Tike' is another word of much the same status. 'Base tike,' exclaims Pistol to Bardolph, 'call'st thou me host?' (*Hen. V*, II. i. 31).

The English mastiff was famous; says the French Lord Rambures:

That island of England breeds very valiant creatures: their mastiffs are of unmatchable courage. (*Hen. V*, III. vii. 155–7)

Three were considered a match for a bear, four for a lion. Our Harrison devotes many lines to a discourse upon the mastiff and he lets us know why. He himself once had one that would not suffer any man to bring his weapon in further than his gate and even tried to prevent him beating his own children by seizing the rod or pulling their clothes down.

Nearly all the important kinds of dogs are included in Macbeth's rapid catalogue and the jingle recited by Edgar in *King Lear*:

> Ay, in the catalogue ye go for men;
> As hounds, and greyhounds, mongrels, spaniels, curs,
> Shoughs, water-rugs, and demi-wolves, are clept
> All by the name of dogs: the valu'd file
> Distinguishes the swift, the slow, the subtle,
> The housekeeper, the hunter. (*Macb.* III. i. 92–7)

> Mastiff, greyhound, mongrel grim,
> Hound or spaniel, brach or lym,
> Or bobtail tike, or trundletail. (*Lear* III. vi. 71–3)

Shakespeare's water-rugs are perhaps the same as water-spaniels; his demi-wolves are presumably such as

those which are bred betweene a bitch and a woolfe, and called *Lycisca*, a thing verie often seene in France . . . also betweene a bitch and a fox, or a beare and a mastiffe.

To Spartan hounds he has three references (*Mid. N. D.* IV. i. 120, 125; *Oth.* v. ii. 361); these are apparently bloodhounds of some kind.[1] For a fuller treatment of hunting and coursing dogs the reader is referred to Chapter XXVII, §§ 1, 2, and 3.

The lapdogs remain to be mentioned ; the chief of them is the spaniel, spaniel-gentle, Maltese dog, or comforter. The fawning habits of the spaniel are several times alluded to by Shakespeare. Henry VIII snubs Bishop Gardiner with

> You play the spaniel,
> And think with wagging of your tongue to win me.
> *(Hen. VIII*, v. iii. 126–7)

The Iceland shough or sholt, the Iceland cur, or simply the Iceland (as Drayton calls it), was a great favourite with ladies. They were imported daily from Iceland, if we may believe Harrison. Pistol's contempt for Nym could find no stronger expression than

> Pish for thee, Iceland dog ! thou prick-eared cur of Iceland !
> *(Hen. V*, II. i. 44)

Another kind, the wap or wappet, by some called a warner, is not mentioned by Shakespeare. When Launce is telling how he lost the pet dog intended by Proteus for Sylvia he can summon up no more complimentary term than ' squirrel ' *(Two Gent.* IV. iv. 60).

Of the ' harmless necessary cat ' (*Merch. of V.* IV. i. 55) little need be said ; Shakespeare does not find occasion to attribute much virtue to it. A gib-cat is a tom-cat (*1 Hen. IV*, I. ii. 83 ; *Haml.* III. iv. 190).

The kinds of wild animals in England seem to have been the same as now. Wolves still roamed at large in Scotland, and in *As You Like It* (v. ii. 121) we read of ' the howling of Irish wolves against the moon ', but in England they were to be found only in shows. Wild boars and wild bulls had disappeared long ago from the whole island.

The boar appears to have no good side to his character ; certainly Shakespeare gives him none. Even his physical aspect must be described in horrid terms like these :

> this foul, grim, and urchin-snouted boar. (*Ven. & Ad.* 1105)

In another place it is

> The wretched, bloody, and usurping boar,
> That spoil'd your summer fields and fruitful vines.
> *(Rich. III*, v. ii. 7–8)

---

[1] In Virgil they are coupled with the hounds of Molossus. Perhaps we have a reminiscence of the classics in these Shakespearian passages.

Alcibiades, in his wild onrushes,
> like a boar too savage, doth root up
> His country's peace.   (*Timon* v. i. 170–1)

Of red and fallow deer the country had plenty, but of roe deer not so many. These and the hare, the other chief beast of the chase, are dealt with in Chapter XXVII, § 1.

The rest of the English wild quadrupeds are usually classed as vermin ; four of them are the object of sport in one form or another : the fox, ' which lives by subtilty ' (*Ven. & Ad.* 675), the badger or brock, the rabbit—the ' earth-delving ' cony (ibid. 687), ' that you see dwell where she is kindled' (*A. Y. L.* III. ii. 361–2)—and the otter, which is abused as being ' neither fish nor flesh ' (*1 Hen. IV*, III. iii. 143). Besides the badger and otter there are several members of the weasel family, as the marten, the polecat, fitchew, or foumart,[1] the miniver, the stoat, the ferret, and the weasel itself. Many allusions could be quoted from contemporary writings to the weasel's supposed propensity for sucking eggs ; Shakespeare has two :

> I can suck melancholy out of a song as a weasel sucks eggs.
>   (*A. Y. L.* II. v. 12–14)

> For once the eagle England being in prey,
> To her unguarded nest the weasel Scot
> Comes sneaking and so sucks her princely eggs.
>   (*Hen. V*, I. ii. 169–71)

Its fierceness is also well known :

> A weasel hath not such a deal of spleen
> As you are toss'd with.   (*1 Hen. IV*, II. iii. 43–4)

Its nocturnal habits are introduced with sinister significance in the line :

> Night-wandering weasels shriek to see him there.
>   (*Lucr.* 307)

Many of these names of animals are susceptible of being applied to men and women with an unfavourable connotation ; for instance, brock (*Tw. N.* II. v. 115), ferret (*Jul. Caes.* I. ii. 185), polecat (*M. Wives* IV. ii. 199).

The beaver was once widely distributed over Europe, and Harrison declares him to have been found in this country in his own day, ' but onelie in the Teifie in Wales ',

---

[1] Etymologically equivalent to ' foul marten '. The marten differs from its allies in not possessing a strong smell.

and he doubts whether the number 'of our bevers or marterns may be thought to be the lesse'. The beaver is not mentioned by Shakespeare, nor the marten either. Among the more common rodents he has the rat, the mouse, the 'joiner' squirrel (*Rom. & Jul.* I. iv. 69), and the dormouse. Among insectivorous quadrupeds he has the 'thorny' hedgehog [1] (*Mid. N. D.* II. ii. 10), for which the old name was 'urchin' (occurring in *Temp.* I. ii. 326, II. ii. 5, and *Tit. Andr.* II. iii. 101), and the mole, Hamlet's 'worthy pioner' (*Haml.* I. v. 163), called also by the still dialectal name of moldwarp (*1 Hen. IV*, III. i. 148). It is strange that he has no allusion to the shrewmouse, whose supposed evil

The Badger.   From Turbervile's *Noble Arte of Venerie*, 1575.

influence upon cattle had been for centuries a favourite subject of allusion, and may well have been the origin of the application of the word 'shrew' to human beings of ill-grained disposition. The eye of the mole, which

casts
Copp'd hills towards heaven,   (*Pericles* I. i. 100–1)

is so minute that it always has been and still is, popularly, supposed to be non-existent; to this belief there are no less than three references (*Temp.* IV. i. 194; *Wint. Tale* IV. iii. 873; *Pericles* I. i. 100).

Of animals nearly related to these there remains only the bat or rearmouse, with its 'leathern wings' (*Mid. N. D.* II. ii. 4) and woolly body (*Macb.* IV. i. 15), whose nocturnal habits and uncanny appearance caused it to be much associated with dark deeds and malefic influences (*Temp.*

---

[1] Called hedge-pig by one of the witches in *Macbeth* (IV. i. 2).

I. ii. 340 ; *Macb.* III. ii. 40–3). The only other native wild animal is the wild cat ; its habit of sleeping by day supplies Shylock with one of the items in his characterization of Launcelot (*Merch. of V.* II. v. 47–8), and its proverbial fierceness provides Gremio with an uncomplimentary name for Katherine in *The Taming of the Shrew* (I. ii. 200).

The wild cat links naturally with the exotic feline animals, of which several were familiar by tradition and pictorial representation, if not by actual sight, to the people of the sixteenth century. Since the twelfth century at least England seems never to have been long without some specimen of these creatures, whether in the private domain of the sovereign or of some nobleman,—as in Woodstock Park, where Henry I kept lions, leopards, lynxes, and

The Otter. From Turbervile's *Noble Arte of Venerie*, 1575.

porcupines—or in the Tower of London, where, in 1485, the collection occupied a part that had come to be known as the Lion Tower, under the custody of the Earl of Oxford as Constable.[1] In a ballad of the sixteenth century, a ' cittie maide ', describing the attractions of London life to a ' countrey maide ', includes a visit to the Tower ; she says :

> Ile take thee to the Tower soone,
> and lyons in their cages.

Shakespeare's references to the lion and lioness speak for the most part of their fierceness, especially when excited by hunger ; there is nothing more ravenous than a ' lion in prey ' (*Lear* III. iv. 94). The leopard was acknowledged to be ' german to the lion ' and its spotted

---

[1] Stow, in his record for the year 1604, tells of the birth on the 5th August of ' A Lions whelpe ' of the lioness named Elizabeth, ' which Lions whelpe lived not longer then till the next day.' Such a birth was considered ominous : see Ben Jonson's *Volpone* II. i.

skin (*Timon* IV. iii. 345) was a matter of common knowledge probably apart from any biblical reference. It was
of old said to be generated between a lioness and a pard.
The pard, to which Shakespeare applies the epithets
'pinch-spotted' (*Temp.* IV. i. 263) and 'bearded' (*A. Y. L.*
II. vii. 150), is, says Bartholomaeus Anglicus (quoting
Isidore and Pliny),

the most swyfte beste, with many dyvers colours and rounde speckes,
as the panthera . . . and varieth not fro the panthera, but the pantera
hath no white speckes.

It was otherwise named 'pardal', as by Spenser in :

> The spotted Panther, and the tusked Bore,
> The Pardale swift, and the Tigre cruell.

This attempted distinction between the pard and the
panther followed the usage of the ancients, who, by a
fanciful analysis of the latter word into Greek *pan* 'all'
and *ther* 'a beast', attributed to the panther a friendliness
for all animals (except the dragon),—a friendliness which
they held was especially induced by the alluring odour
which it possessed. The result was a difference of application of the words 'leopard' (ultimately supplanting
'pard') and 'panther', which cannot be scientifically
maintained, but which survives even to the present day,
when the variety specifically known as the black leopard
is by some called the panther. The only work of Shakespeare's in which the name occurs is *Titus Andronicus*.
Another old synonym was 'catamountain' (*Temp.* IV.
i. 264, *M. Wives* II. ii. 28), which in more recent times has
been applied both to the ocelot and the tiger-cat.

The fierce and inexorable tiger,[1] 'that doth live by
slaughter' (*Lucr.* 955), needs no more than a passing
mention. The name 'jaguar' was only just becoming
known to Europeans at the beginning of the seventeenth
century, and 'cougar', the early name of the puma, is
of still later date. 'Lynx' and 'ounce' were synonymous
terms, but in the sixteenth century and later the latter
name was applied without definite identification, and so
it may very well be in the following lines :

> Be it ounce, or cat, or bear,
> Pard, or boar with bristled hair.
>
> (*Mid. N. D.* II. ii. 30–31)

[1] Cf. *3 Hen. VI.* I. iv. 154-5, *Rom. & Jul.* v. iii. 38-9, *Sonnet* xix.

Other ' cats ' that an Elizabethan would recognize are the civet cat (*A. Y. L.* III. ii. 71 ; *Lear* III. iv. 108), differing in some particulars from the cats proper and yielding the perfume after which it is named, and the musk-cat (*All's Well* v. ii. 21), by which was probably intended the musk-deer, not a cat at all, but a small ruminant of the deer kind, from which the musk of commerce is obtained.

The hyena is an animal of which various fables had been current from ancient times. It was supposed to be hermaphrodite or to change sex every year ; but Aristotle denies that, as Bartholomaeus rightly notes. The belief in its alleged habit of imitating the human voice is preserved in the popular name—Laughing Hyena—of one of the species. One of Rosalind's promised waywardnesses is that she ' will laugh like a hyen, and that when ' Orlando is ' inclined to sleep ' (*A. Y. L.* IV. i. 162–3).

With the bear we come to the end of the carnivorous mammals. It was associated in Shakespeare's age chiefly with the popular sport of bear-baiting and the street performances of the ' muzzled bear ' (*John* II. i. 249), ' led by the nose ' (*Wint. Tale* IV. iv. 836). Harrison knew of the white bears of ' the Goths ', which were killed for their skins. The age-old superstition that the bear brought forth its young in an unformed state and licked them into shape—another fable which Aristotle does not countenance—is to this day perpetuated in a familiar metaphor, and is enshrined in the following lines :

> Like to a chaos, or an unlick'd bear-whelp
> That carries no impression like the dam.
> (*3 Hen. VI*, III. ii. 161–2)

Caesar, says Decius,
> loves to hear
> That unicorns may be betray'd with trees,
> And bears with glasses. (*Jul. Cæs.* II. i. 203–5)

The allusion is obscure ; but it has been plausibly conjectured that Shakespeare had read and imperfectly remembered Pliny's story about tigers (not bears), how they were sometimes beguiled by the scattering of glass on the ground, in which seeing their own reflection and supposing it to be a cub, they were hindered in the pursuit of their human prey.

As examples of ferocity Shakespeare couples together ' the rugged Russian bear ', ' the arm'd rhinoceros ', and 'the Hyrcan tiger' (*Macb.* III. iv. 100–1). The tigers of Hyrcania, a country south of the Caspian or Hyrcanian Sea, were known from Pliny, who, says Bartholomaeus, describes them as 'beastes of dreadful swyftenes'. The other foreign mammals mentioned by him are the camel, the elephant, the rodent porcupine, and the monkey. The camel is the type of the beast of burden (*Troilus* I. ii. 269), but is unfit for warfare (*Cor.* II. i. 269–70). The 'slow' elephant, which was supposed to have no joints in its legs, is described by Shakespeare as having joints, 'but none for courtesy' (*Troilus* I. ii. 21, II. iii. 114–15); it is caught 'with holes' (*Jul. Caes.* II. i. 205), that is, by means of pitfalls, an ancient method of capture. The only form in which the name 'porcupine' occurs in the old editions is familiar to all from Hamlet's 'fretful porpentine' (*Haml.* I. v. 20). The hippopotamus is not found in Shakespeare, nor the dromedary, nor the giraffe, which was beginning to be known by that name in his day—a name which was to succeed to the old 'camelopard'.

What is loosely called the simian group of animals is represented by the ape, the monkey, the baboon, and the marmoset. 'Ape' was still the generic name; 'monkey' was a word of comparatively recent introduction; the first is about twice as frequent as the second in Shakespeare's works, but they are employed without any discernible difference of meaning. In a few passages there seems to be some sort of implication that the monkey was simply a degraded form of man; as when Apemantus, the churlish philosopher, girding at the courtesies exchanged by Alcibiades and Timon, exclaims:

> The strain of man's bred out
> Into baboon and monkey.   (*Timon* I. i. 260–1)

'The nimble marmozet' occurs once (*Temp.* II. ii. 183).

When Shakespeare was born, the most comprehensive work on birds that had been produced by an Englishman was the small treatise of William Turner, published in Latin in 1544. This is a real contribution to zoology, and is worthy to take rank with Gesner's work.

In English birds, wild and tame, William Harrison confesses 'small skill'; it is all the more interesting to compare his lists with those that can be extracted from Shakespeare.

The Camel. From Topsell's *Foure-footed Beastes*, 1607.

If Shakespeare's predilection for any particular class of
creatures can be inferred from the number of his allusions
to them, the first place must be given to birds. We at
least know what his thoughts were when he saw a bird
wounded. 'Alas! poor hurt fowl,' says Benedick of
the stricken Claudio; 'now will he creep into sedges'
(*Much Ado* II. i. 211–12).

Of tame fowl Harrison says there are cocks, hens, geese
(which in Essex, it appears, were kept chiefly for their
feathers), ducks, peacocks, and pigeons (the number of
which had grown to be a plague). He has an incidental
reference to the 'turkie hen', which at his date could
mean either the guinea fowl or the female of the turkey.
The turkey was already a feature of Christmas fare, having
been introduced into Europe shortly after its discovery
as a domesticated bird in Mexico in 1518. Its appearance
in the farmyard must have been familiar; Pistol is described as 'swelling like a turkey-cock' as he advances
(*Hen. V*, v. i. 16).

Among wild birds Harrison has some strange omissions,
as of the sparrow, the swallow, the cuckoo, the owl, and
the wren. All of these are favourites with Shakespeare.
His one special mention of the hedge-sparrow is in connexion with one of many myths concerning the breeding
habits of the cuckoo. It

> fed the cuckoo so long,
> That it had it head bit off by it young.   (*Lear* I. iv. 238–9)

The owl, otherwise the howlet (*Macb.* IV. i. 17), is several
times more particularly called the 'night-owl' (*Lucr.*
360) and is perhaps meant by 'night-crow' (*3 Hen. VI*,
v. vi. 45) and 'night-raven'[1] (*Much Ado* II. iii. 90); and
the screech-owl (or, to use the old form, scritch-owl) is
found in five passages (*Mid. N. D.* v. ii. 6, *2 Hen. VI*, I. iv.
21, III. ii. 327, *3 Hen. VI*, II. vi. 56, *Troilus* v. x. 16). It
is 'the obscure bird' which 'clamour'd the livelong night'
when Duncan was murdered (*Macb.* II. iii. 65–6).

Shakespeare calls the wren 'the most diminutive of
birds', and says that she is so plucky that she

> will fight—
> Her young ones in her nest—against the owl. (*Macb.* IV. ii. 9–11)

---

[1] These are both old names for nightbirds; the nightjar may possibly be
meant.

A woman's pleading is compared to 'the chirping of a wren ' (*2 Hen. VI*, III. ii. 42).

Of the wild birds that are commonly used for food Shakespeare has the mallard, the snipe, the plover,[1] the quail, the woodcock, the partridge, and the pheasant, but not the teal or the widgeon. Other members of the duck family, such as the sheldrake, the shoveler, or the scaup-duck—Harrison's dunbird—are not referred to. Nor has he any instance, among wading birds, of the bittern, the curlew, the heron, the stork, or the sand-piper.[2]

All of his four allusions to the cormorant have reference to its voraciousness : ' cormorant devouring Time ' (*Love's L. L.* I. i. 4), ' Light vanity, insatiate cormorant ' (*Rich. II*, II. i. 38), ' the cormorant belly ' (*Cor.* I. i. 126), and

> All damage else,
> As honour, loss of time, travail, expense,
> Wounds, friends, and what else dear that is consum'd
> In hot digestion of this cormorant war. (*Troilus* II. ii. 3–6)

The swan, which in ancient mythology was sacred to Venus, is by Shakespeare associated with Juno (*A. Y. L.* I. iii. 78). The legend of its dying song is beautifully expressed in the lines :

> And now this pale swan in her watery nest
> Begins the sad dirge of her certain ending. (*Lucr.* 1611–12)

The little grebe or dabchick appears once as the dive-dapper, a name which has various older forms—dive-dopple, divedap, and dive dop. Adonis

> did raise his chin
> Like a dive-dapper peering through a wave,
> Who being look'd on, ducks as quickly in.
> (*Ven. & Ad.* 85–7)

Shakespeare's singing-birds include the nightingale, the thrush or throstle (*Mid. N. D.* III. i. 132), the blackbird—not called by this name, but by the name of ousel (*Mid. N. D.* III. i. 131, *2 Hen. IV*, III. ii. 9)—the lark, and the robin redbreast or ruddock (*Cymb.* IV. ii. 224) ; the linnet and the finches are ignored by him.

The wagtail is once introduced as a term of contempt

---

[1] The name ' lapwing ' is applied to a species of plover and is specially associated with the bird's habit of drawing away visitors from the neighbourhood of its nest (*Com. of E.* IV. ii. 27), and with the belief that the newly-hatched bird runs about with the shell on its head (*Haml.* V. ii. 193).

[2] One species was called the knot—Harrison spells it ' notte '.

for an obsequious fellow (*Lear* II. ii. 72). An old name was washtail; the bird is still called locally dishwasher, and one of its French names is 'lavandière'.

Still following Harrison's divisions, we come to the 'unclean' birds, the raven, the crow, the magpie or maggot-pie (*Macb.* III. iv. 125), the rook, the kite or puttock (*2 Hen. VI*, III. ii. 191, &c.), the jay, the jackdaw, known also as chough (*Mid. N. D.* III. ii. 21, &c.) or chewet (*1 Hen. IV*, v. i. 29), and daw (only as a type of foolishness in *1 Hen. VI*, II. iv. 18, *Cor.* IV. v. 48), and the starling. To these Harrison would add woodpeckers and ringtails.

The larger birds of prey, the eagle (formerly called 'erne')—which is 'Jove's bird' (*Cymb.* IV. ii. 348), as the oak is 'Jove's tree'—the vulture or gripe (*Lucr.* 543), and the osprey (*Cor.* v. vii. 34) are all in Shakespeare. He has several species of hawks; these are dealt with in the article on Falconry in Chapter XXVII, vol. ii, pp. 351 ff.

The ostrich and the parrot, paraquito, or popinjay, are the only two foreign birds with which Shakespeare shows acquaintance.

Passing to aquatic creatures, we find that Shakespeare has only some thirty specimens. There are fishes, such as the carp, the cod, the dace, the dogfish or shark, the eel, the gudgeon, the herring, the ling, the loach, which 'breeds fleas' (*1 Hen. IV*, II. i. 23), the pike,[1] the mackerel, the minnow, the pilchard, the salmon, the sprat, the tench, which was said to be afflicted like the loach (*1 Hen. IV*, II. i. 16–17), the trout 'that must be caught with tickling' (*Tw. N.* II. v. 25–6). There are also the three common molluscs, the cockle, the mussel, and the oyster, and the crustacean crab, prawn, and shrimp.[2] The anchovy, the gurnet, and the conger are introduced as articles of food; there are also poor-John, which is salted hake—typical poor man's fare (*Rom. & Jul.* I. i. 36)—and stockfish, which is dried codfish and is beaten before it is cooked (cf. *Temp.* III. ii. 81).[3]

---

[1] The term 'luce' is used in *The Merry Wives of Windsor* (I. i. 16) for the heraldic charge representing a pike. It was properly used for the pike when full grown, the terms, in ascending order of age, being fry, gilthead, pod, jack, pickerel, pike, luce.

[2] Used only to connote a puny creature (*Love's L. L.* v. ii. 591, *1 Hen. VI*, II. ii. 23).

[3] In *1 Hen. IV*, II. iv. 275 it is a term of contempt for a thin person.

Shakespeare has many instances of the three well-known cetaceans, the whale, the dolphin, and the porpoise. His references to the whale, in his time often called 'whirlpool', 'hurlpool', and 'thirlpool', are either to its feeding on small fry (*All's Well* IV. iii. 248–50, *Pericles* II. i. 34–5), its proneness to run aground (*M. Wives* II. i. 64–5, *2 Hen. IV*, IV. iv. 40), or its spouting water (*Troilus* V. v. 23). The huge monster of the sea, called leviathan in ancient Hebrew poetry, is a favourite theme for metaphor and simile, and it would have been surprising if Shakespeare had given us no instance of it. In *The Two Gentlemen of Verona* Proteus says that Orpheus' lute could

> Make tigers tame and huge leviathans
> Forsake unsounded deeps to dance on sands.
>
> (III. ii. 80–1)

Puck is commanded by Oberon to fetch the flower of love-in-idleness and to be back again

> Ere the leviathan can swim a league.
>
> (*Mid. N. D.* II. i. 174)

We come now to creeping things. At this period the words 'worm' and 'serpent' could be applied to any and every creature that crept or crawled; 'reptile' had not yet come into general use. Shakespeare's use of 'worm' is representative. For example, it denotes the earthworm, which 'will turn being trodden on' (*3 Hen. VI*, II. ii. 17), feeds on dead bodies, and is used for bait (*Haml.* IV. iii. 29–31); it signifies the larva of the clothes-moth in 'worm-eaten tapestry' (*Much Ado* III. iii. 145), and of the silk-moth in

> The worms were hallow'd that did breed the silk.
>
> (*Oth.* III. iv. 74)

Its application to snakes and other venomous creatures is frequent. The serpent with which Cleopatra made away with herself is 'the pretty worm of Nilus' (*Ant. & Cleop.* V. ii. 242). The current belief that a snake 'stung' with its tongue is expressed in 'the soft and tender fork of a poor worm' (*Meas. for M.* III. i. 17). The canker was a sort of worm that infested roses and caused plants to waste away (*Two Gent.* I. iii. 43, *1 Hen. IV*, I. iii. 176, *Rom. & Jul.* II. iii. 30).

Topsell's employment of the word 'serpent' follows

'the warrant of the best ancient Latinists', but rather goes beyond contemporary usage : he understands by it

all venomous Beasts, whether creeping without legges, as Adders and Snakes, or with legges, as Crocodiles and Lizards, or more neerely compacted bodies, as Toades, Spiders, and Bees.

'Adder' and 'viper', which are now synonymous and denote the only British venomous reptile, were generally differentiated.[1] The adder was commonly said to be deaf (cf. *2 Hen. VI*, III. ii. 76, *Troilus* II. ii. 172), as in the Bible ; 'it is reported,' says Maplet,

to envie and hate the Hart, to kill the Lyon, and by all maner of meanes to flee from the Herbe Rue. . . . It loveth to live among hollow trees, to seeke his food in Pasture and Groave : to set muche store by Milke : to hurt both with tooth and mouth, and also with his hinder part or taile ; to suck fleshe.

The viper meant the viviparous snake, and it was supposed that the young gnawed their way out of their mother's side, a belief referred to in

I am no viper, yet I feed
On mother's flesh which did me breed. (*Pericles* I. i. 64–5)

Other reptiles mentioned by Shakespeare are the blind-worm, the slug, and the snail.   He has also the frog and the tadpole, the toad or paddock, supposed to be venomous (*A. Y. L.* II. i. 13), the lizard, the 'gilded newt' (*Timon* IV. iii. 183), and the wall-newt.   Of exotic reptiles there are the alligator—only a stuffed specimen in an apothecary's shop (*Rom. & Jul.* v. i. 43)—Cleopatra's 'aspic', 'the mournful crocodile' (*2 Hen. VI*, III. i. 226), the chameleon, which was fabled to feed on air (*Two Gent.* II. i. 181, *Haml.* III. ii. 97–100), and the tortoise.

Insects form the most abundant class of land animals, and the works of Shakespeare contain examples of a considerable number of them.   There is the 'painted' or 'gilded' butterfly with its 'mealy wings' (*Troilus* III. iii. 79), together with its larva, the grub (*Cor.* v. iv. 12) or caterpillar, which gnaws 'the tender leaves' (*Ven. & Ad.* 798) ; and there is the moth, which often singes itself in the candle (*Merch. of V.* II. ix. 79).   He has much to say concerning the bee, of whose generation, according to Aristotle, there were many hypotheses, the most favoured

---

[1] Harrison is disposed to regard them as names for the same creature.

in later times being that it took place in the carcass of a
bullock ; but

> 'Tis seldom when the bee doth leave her comb
> In the dead carrion.   (*2 Hen. IV*, IV. iv. 79–80)

The fury of the mob is likened to the anger of bees disturbed
when swarming :

> The commons, like an angry hive of bees
> That want their leader, scatter up and down,
> And care not who they sting in his revenge.
>   (*2 Hen. VI*, III. ii. 125–7)

The details of their polity were very imperfectly understood ; they are made the basis of a discourse on state
government by the Archbishop of Canterbury in *Henry V*.
Each man has his function in the state, and

> so work the honey-bees,
> Creatures that by a rule in nature teach
> The act of order to a peopled kingdom.
> They have a king and officers of sorts ;
> Where some, like magistrates, correct at home,
> Others, like merchants, venture trade abroad,
> Others, like soldiers, armed in their stings,
> Make boot upon the summer's velvet buds ;
> Which pillage they with merry march bring home
> To the tent-royal of their emperor :
> Who, busied in his majesty, surveys
> The singing masons building roofs of gold,
> The civil citizens kneading up the honey,
> The poor mechanic porters crowding in
> Their heavy burdens at his narrow gate,
> The sad-ey'd justice, with his surly hum,
> Delivering o'er to executors pale
> The lazy yawning drone.   (I. ii. 187–204)

There are many references to the ' red-hipped humble-
bee ' (*Mid. N. D.* IV. i. 11–12) with its ' waxen thighs '
(ibid. III. i. 176). The drone is frequently used as a type of
the lazy good-for-nothing, and the wasp of the spiteful or
injurious character.

There are various kinds of flies, the house-fly, the blue-
bottle, the carrion or flesh-fly, the water-fly, and the breese
or gad-fly, which pesters cattle (*Ant. & Cleop.* III. viii.
24–5). There are also the grasshopper, the ant or pismire,
the merry cricket which sings ' at the oven's mouth '
(*Pericles* III. Gower 7), the flea, the louse, and the sheep-
tick. To beetles there are several references without precise

recognition of species; the dung-beetle or dor-beetle is called 'the shard-born beetle' (*Macb.* III. ii. 42), an appellation which has given rise to much controversy.[1] The glow-worm, which is the wingless female of a species of beetle, was and is still popularly regarded as a worm. The Ghost in *Hamlet*, as he bids farewell, says :

> The glow-worm shows the matin to be near,
> And gins to pale his uneffectual fire. (I. v. 89–90)

Shakespeare has the spider or spinner, the venomous scorpion, and the cheese-mite, which are classed in modern zoology as arachnids. He does not mention the tarantula, or 'Neapolitane spider', as Harrison calls it. This creature was becoming known by the Italian name 'tarantula' in the later years of the sixteenth century; the name occurs in Lyly, but it was often vaguely applied.

Not only were many beliefs current that had no basis of fact concerning the animals of everyday life, but there existed a large body of legend concerning animals now known, or with good reason presumed, to be entirely mythical. Some of the names of these fabulous animals have come to be applied to animals whose identity and habits are facts of science; such are pelican, salamander, and siren. Other names have long ceased to appear in works on natural history; such are basilisk, cockatrice, phoenix, dragon, griffin, and unicorn.

The barnacle goose stands in a category by itself. A wild goose of the northern regions, it was for several centuries believed to have its origin in the fruit of a tree or a shell-fish attached to a tree—hence its name of tree-goose—or else to be generated from timber rotting in water. In the natural history of the sixteenth century, therefore, it might call for treatment in a book on plants—Gerarde's *Herball* contains an excursus on the subject—or in an account of birds, or of shell-fish.[2] Caliban fears that he and his evil company may 'be turn'd to barnacles' (*Temp.* IV. i. 251); this is Shakespeare's only instance of the word.

---

[1] See *The Oxford Dictionary*, s.vv. Shard *sb.*[2] and Shard-born.

[2] Turner is disposed to accept the current belief. Gesner is sceptical, and relates how he once paid a visit to Scotland, where he had learnt that the barnacle was to be seen growing on a tree; but he found that the miracle drew further and further away, for he was told that the famous tree grew not on the mainland, but in the Orkneys.

AN ELEPHANT ATTACKED BY A DRAGON

THE PHOENIX

The name survives in our day for the goose and for the shell-fish from which it was once supposed to be produced.

The pelican, ' a bird in Egypt, dwelling among the deserts of Nilus ', was said to revive or to feed its young with its own blood which poured from self-made wounds. In Shakespeare it is ' the kind life-rendering pelican ' (*Haml.* IV. v. 145), and rapacious children are likened to its young (*Rich. II*, II. i. 126–7, *Lear* III. iv. 74).

The Pelican. From Epiphanius, *Physiologus*, 1587.

The salamander was a kind of lizard capable of living in or enduring fire. It became the emblem of all things that had to do with fire—a soldier exposed to the fire of battle, a fire-eating juggler, and a poker. Falstaff says he has ' maintained ' Bardolph's ' salamander ', meaning his red face, ' with fire any time this two-and-thirty years ' (*I Hen. IV*, III. iii. 52–5).

The siren or mermaid and the griffin were seriously catalogued as late as 1675 among the animals of Noah's Ark by the learned Jesuit Athanasius Kircherus. They are both composite creatures. In classical mythology the siren was a compound of a woman and a bird ; in mediaeval times the name was applied to the mermaid, half woman and half fish. The habits attributed to both were much the same ; sirens lured sailors to destruction by their singing or distressful weeping (*3 Hen. VI*, III. ii. 186, *Com. of E.* III. ii. 45–6, *Mid. N. D.* II. i. 150–1, &c.). The griffin had a lion's head and the body and claws of an eagle.

The basilisk or cockatrice was hatched by a serpent from a cock's egg. The virtue of weasels (it was said) was death to the cockatrice.[1] Wherever the beast occurs in Shakespeare,

The Unicorn.　From Topsell, after Gesner.

the reference is to the belief that the mere glance of its eye brought immediate death. The King in *2 Henry VI* says to the Duke of Suffolk :

> Look not upon me, for thine eyes are wounding :
> Yet do not go away ; come, basilisk,
> And kill the innocent gazer with thy sight. (III. ii. 51–3)

Juliet, when the Nurse suggests that Romeo is dead, wails :

> Hath Romeo slain himself ? say thou but 'I',
> And that bare vowel, 'I', shall poison more
> Than the death-darting eye of cockatrice.
>
> (*Rom. & Jul.* III. ii. 45–7)

The phoenix, the 'Arabian bird' (*Ant. & Cleop.* III. ii. 12,

---

[1] It was an axiom that God and nature will not suffer anything to be without his match.

Cymb. I. vi. 17), 'the bird of wonder' (*Hen. VIII*, v. v. 41), was the proverbial type of singularity, for there was but one of the kind, inhabiting Arabian deserts. It lived for hundreds of years (cf. *Sonnet* xix), and at the end of the time it gathered together twigs of extremely hot and odoriferous trees into its nest, which was laid in the top of the highest fir-tree ; there it sat and was finally consumed to ashes, and from these ashes a new phoenix arose. Sebastian, amazed at the wonders of Prospero's island, is ready to believe all manner of travellers' tales, even

> That there are unicorns ; that in Arabia
> There is one tree, the phoenix' throne ; one phoenix
> At this hour reigning there.　　　　(*Temp.* III. iii. 22–4)

Dragons. From Topsell, after Gesner.

In our own day the unicorn and the dragon are the most familiar of all the fabulous animals. The unicorn or monoceros is among the least tameable of beasts (*Lucr.* 956), his pride is excessive (*Timon* IV. iii. 339–41), but his own horn is often the means of his destruction. Spenser in a single stanza describes how 'unicorns may be betray'd with trees' (*Jul. Caes.* II. i. 204) :

> Like as a Lyon, whose imperiall powre
> A prowd rebellious Unicorne defies,
> T'avoide the rash assault and wrathfull stowre
> Of his fiers foe, him to a tree applies,
> And when him running in full course he spies,
> He slips aside ; the whiles that furious beast
> His precious horne, sought of his enemies,
> Stikes in the stocke, ne thence can be releast,
> But to the mighty victour yields a bounteous feast.

The dragon rivalled the basilisk for the kingship among serpents. His lair was in a cave (*Rom. & Jul.* III. ii. 74). There was an unwinged and a winged kind, ' one curiously reminiscent ', as Dr. Shipley says, ' of the fossil plesiosaurs, the other of the pterodactyls '. Pliny says that there is a natural war between him and the elephant, and describes the different ways in which they encounter and destroy each other.

This by no means exhausts the catalogue of fabulous beasts. One might relate the marvels of the mantichore, the ' manslayer ' of India, with its triple row of teeth, of which Aristotle gives a detailed account derived from Ctesias; or of the lamia, a deadly monster of composite form, of which Gesner tells the whole legend, leaving it to the judgement of his critical readers; or again of the scolopendra, a sea-fish mentioned by Spenser, which, ' feeling himselfe taken with a hooke, casteth out his bowels, untill hee hath unloosed the hooke, and then swalloweth them up againe '. But in all these Shakespeare manifests no interest.

BIBLIOGRAPHY.—The most important work of the sixteenth century from a scientific point of view is the series of volumes produced by CONRAD GESNER (1516–65), in which he claimed to give not only a plain account of animals, but also comments upon and corrections of ancient and recent writers, but especially Aristotle, Pliny, Aelian, Oppian, and Albertus Magnus : *Conradi Gesneri medici Tigurini Historiae Animalium Lib. I de Quadrupedibus viviparis, Liber II. de Quadrupedibus oviparis, Liber III. qui est de Avium natura, Liber IIII qui est de Piscium & Aquatilium animantium natura,* fol. 1551–8, *Liber V qui est de Serpentium natura,* fol. 1587. The five books contain more than 3,500 large folio pages. The first Englishman to produce a treatise ' in anything like a modern scientific spirit and not from the medical point of view adopted by nearly all his predecessors ' was WILLIAM TURNER, who in 1544 published his book on birds entitled *Avium Praecipuarum, quarum apud Plinium et Aristotelem mentio est, brevis et succincta historia* ; a scholarly edition of this work has been made by A. H. EVANS, *Turner on Birds,* 1903. Dogs received particular treatment in JOHN CAIUS's *De Canibus Britannicis liber unus,* with which was issued *De rariorum animalium et stirpium historia liber unus,* 1570. Traditional natural history was available in English in two sixteenth-century reissues of TREVISA's translation of the *De Proprietatibus Rerum* of BARTHOLOMAEUS ANGLICUS,of which book xvii treats of animals; the second of these came out as *Batman uppon Bartholome, His Booke De Proprietatibus Rerum, Newly corrected, enlarged and amended,* 1582. From this JOHN MAPLET drew the material for the third part of *A Greene Forest, or a Naturall Historie, Wherein may bee seene first the most Sufferaigne Vertues in all the whole Kinde of Stones & Mettals : next of Plantes, as of Herbes, Trees & Shrubs, lastly of Brute Beastes, Foules, Fishes, creeping Wormes & Serpents, and that Alphabetically, so that a Table shall not neede,* 1567. In 1601 PHILEMON HOLLAND's translation of Pliny's Natural History appeared with the title *The Historie of the World. Commonly called, The Naturall Historie of C. Plinius Secundus* ; the 8th book deals with ' land beasts ', the 9th with ' water creatures ', the 10th with ' birds and foules ', the 11th with ' insects ' ; Holland owed much to the French translation of Antoine du Pinet, 1562, to which many of his amplifications of Pliny are traceable. EDWARD TOPSELL popularized the researches of Gesner in *The Historie of Foure-footed Beastes. Describing the true and lively figure of every Beast, with a discourse of their severall Names, Conditions* [&c.] . . . *Collected out of all the Volumes of Conradus Gesner, and all other Writers to this present day,* 1607, to which a second book was added, *The Historie of Serpents . . . Wherein is contained their Divine, Naturall, and Morall descriptions,* 1608. Caius's treatise on dogs was put into English by ABRAHAM FLEMING with the title *Of Englishe Dogges, the diversities, the names, the natures, the properties,* 1576 ; reprinted by Arber in *An English Garner,* vol. iii, 1870. GEORGE TURBERVILE's *The Noble Arte of Venerie,* 1575, gives detailed descriptions of the forms and habits of deer, dogs, badgers, otters, &c., and his *Booke of Faulconrie,* 1575, of the several kinds of hawks. A metrical account of silkworms, *The Silkewormes, and their Flies : Lively described in verse, by T. M., a Countrie Farmar,* 1599, is attributed, to THOMAS MOUFET, whose *Insectorum . . . theatrum* (1634) was issued in English in an appendix to the 1658 edition of Topsell's book. A succinct history of zoology is to be found in the article ' Zoology ', by E. RAY LANKESTER, in *The Encyclopaedia Britannica,* 12th ed.

Books dealing particularly with, or throwing light upon, Shakespeare's knowledge of animals are : H. W. SEAGER's *Natural History in Shakespeare's Time,* 1896, which is a collection of extracts from contemporary literature ; J. E. HARTING's *The Ornithology of Shakespeare,* 1871 ; ROBERT PATTERSON's *Letters on the Natural History of the Insects mentioned in Shakspeare's Plays,* 1838 ; EMMA PHIPSON's *The Animal-Lore of Shakspeare's Time,* 1883. A scientific and comprehensive account is contained in A. E. SHIPLEY's article, ' Zoology in the Time of Shakespeare ', in *The Edinburgh Review,* July, 1912.

II. PLANTS

BY

Sir William T. Thiselton-Dyer

The study of plants has grown out of the necessities of life. The most primitive peoples learn by experience to use and distinguish the plants which may serve for food, for the various arts, or as remedies for disease. As far as the Greeks and Romans were concerned, their knowledge was summed up in the writings of Dioscorides and of the elder Pliny. And when the revival of learning took place in Europe, a vast and comparatively sterile literature was devoted to commentaries on Dioscorides and Pliny and to the attempt, only moderately successful, to identify in other countries the plants of Eastern and Southern Europe which they had described.

England alone possessed from the earliest times ' a wide knowledge of native plants and garden herbs, which was an original achievement ' and independent of tradition. The Anglo-Saxon stock, when rooted in English soil, burst out into literary accomplishment, to which that from which it sprang could produce nothing comparable. Its botany was confined, it is true, to ' herbal medicine '. But it was of purely native manufacture ; it was copious, and, unlike the custom on the Continent, for centuries the books in which it was described were written in the native tongue and were not intended merely for the learned, but for popular use. The principal surviving documents have been collected by Cockayne in his *Saxon Leechdoms*. He includes under the title *Herbarium* the eleventh-century Anglo-Saxon translation of the *De virtutibus herbarum* of Apuleius Barbarus, a late writer of obscure origin. According to Payne, ' the therapeutical part belongs to the lowest period of Roman medicine. But it was translated into Anglo-Saxon as the best work available in Europe on natural history in relation to medicine.' The fact that the Latin names were, when possible, replaced by English showed that, as far as botany was concerned, it added little to existing knowledge. Perhaps its chief interest is that it introduced to English readers the mythical properties of mandragora.

That the actual knowledge of plants at the time was copious is evident. Making all possible deductions from Cockayne's figures, Payne finds that Anglo-Saxon botany had 'about 500 English names of plants in use'. Apuleius has 185, and the earliest German Herbal, the *Herbarius* (1485), enumerates only 150. 'There must have been', says Payne, 'a popular and widespread love of flowers—a national characteristic which may still be recognized in the cottage gardens of the South of England.' All this was unintelligible to the Norman invaders, whose slender equipment in science only found a scanty expression in Latin and was merely literary. The Anglo-Saxons had accumulated a large body of fact and observation. The generalizations which would have followed were summarily quenched, and we may agree with Professor Earle that 'there was a great decadence in botanical knowledge in England between the eleventh and sixteenth centuries'. The development of what might have been an indigenous and independent school of botany was thus completely frustrated. Our later knowledge, as will be shown, was imported from the Continent. Many of the old English names became obsolete. Thus the herb they called 'bishopswort' was identified with the *vettonica* of Pliny and became 'betony'.

The Anglo-Saxon use of herbs for therapeutical purposes was purely empirical. It was superseded by a materia medica of an entirely different origin, which still persists. 'Even in our day', to quote Payne again, 'there exists a popular herbal medicine, strongly combined with the use of charms and magical ceremonies of very ancient origin, which still holds its place in popular belief. In this corrupt and undignified form we may still trace some features of the old Anglo-Saxon medicine.' In Gloucestershire, where this chapter was written, the writer met with a man collecting betony as he might have done a thousand years ago.

Gervinus has said that 'in Shakespeare's time nature had not yet become extinct'. But it was in process of becoming so, and Ellacombe says justly that Shakespeare is 'curiously distinct from all his contemporaries' in the use he makes of the popular botany, which was not literary but traditional. It is obvious that Spenser's language is purely

conventional and that he often did not know the plants
he names.   But Shakespeare was country-bred, and the
atmosphere of his plays is reminiscent of ' the hedgerows
and woods of Warwickshire '.   If Shakespeare introduces
a plant, he does it with faultless inspiration born of observation which no art can supply.   No other Elizabethan could
have written

> . . . whose perfect white
> Show'd like an April daisy on the grass.   (*Lucr.* 394–5)

He must have been familiar with the blooming of the wild
daffodil in the west which fills the country with a sort of
moonlight haze :

> . . . daffodils,
> That come before the swallow dares, and take
> The winds of March with beauty.
> > (*Wint. Tale* iv. iii. 118–20)

Shakespeare, when he is drawing on his country knowledge,
uses the native English nomenclature as in Dock, Daisy,
Elder, Harebell, Hemlock, with occasionally the Old French
—which in many names ousted the native tongue—as
in Burnet, Camomile, Eglantine, Fleur-de-Luce, Rue.
Shakespeare appeals to popular or, at any rate, general
knowledge; Spenser to one that is at least scholarly and
constantly reminiscent of the Roman poets.   Spenser's
' sayling Pine ' (*Faerie Queene*, I. i. 8) simply translates
Virgil's ' nautica pinus '.   ' Alcides' speckled poplar tree' (*An
Elegie*, 13) recalls Ovid's ' Herculeae populus alba comae ',
and ' as roses did with lillies interlace ' (*Faerie Queene*,
v. iii. 23), Virgil's ' mixta rubent ubi lilia multa Alba rosa '.
But if Shakespeare's botany is popular, it could appeal
to a quick intelligence on the part of his audience.   There
could not have been in the Elizabethan Age the sharp
division which now exists between urban and rural life, or
else his frequent references to things familiar in the country
would have been unintelligible.   ' Nature study', now
a plant of artificial cultivation, had a natural and sturdy
growth.

Not that Shakespeare is entirely lacking in echoes of
the Roman classics.   Such as there are, however,[1] are not
like Spenser's, the result of scholarly choice, but belong to

---

[1] No illustration is necessary here of the almost universal symbolism of
such plants as the laurel, the emblem of victory, and the olive, the token
of peace.

the literary atmosphere of a time when most educated
people could write and even, like the Queen, speak Latin.
Doubtless he would get many from Golding's translation of
Ovid (1567). Thus,

A purple flower sprung up, chequer'd with white
(*Ven. & Ad.* 1168)

recalls Ovid's 'flos e sanguine concolor ortus', Ben Jonson's
'Adonis flower'.

Nothing teems
But hateful docks, rough thistles, kecksies, burs,
Losing both beauty and utility (*Hen. V*, v. ii. 51–3)

suggests Virgil's

Segnisque horreret in arvis
Carduus : intereunt segetes, subit aspera silva,
Lappaeque tribulique,

where *lappae* are burdocks.

Darnel, and all the idle weeds that grow
In our sustaining corn (*Lear* IV. iv. 5–6)

is not unlike Virgil's

Grandia saepe quibus mandavimus hordea sulcis,
Infelix lolium et steriles nascuntur avenae,
(Virgil, *Ecl.* v. 36, 37)

where *lolium* is usually identified with darnel. The marriage
of the vine and elm is a purely Roman suggestion :

Thou art an elm, my husband, I a vine
Whose weakness, married to thy stronger state,
Makes me with thy strength to communicate.
(*Com. of E.* II. ii. 178–80)

Compare Ovid's 'amictae vitibus ulmi'.
It was an old jest that garlic hindered osculation :

Mopsa must be your mistress : marry, garlic,
To mend her kissing with. (*Wint. Tale* IV. iii. 162–3)

Martial said of leeks, equally obnoxious, 'edisti quoties,
oscula clausa dato.'
Describing by comparisons the hardness of Shylock's
heart, Antonio says :

You may as well forbid the mountain pines
To wag their high tops . . . (*Merch. of V.* IV. i. 75–6)

Shakespeare almost certainly never saw them, but an echo
of Virgil's 'abies in montibus altis' may have reached him.
To some these suggestions will seem far-fetched. Taken
as a whole, they show the way in which classical literature

dominated the language of the Elizabethan Age and the constant appeal that was made to it.

Of biblical plant-references there are very few, if any, that are beyond dispute.

> Sow'd cockle reap'd no corn　　(*Love's L. L.* iv. iii. 383)

may be reminiscent of the parable of the sower (Matt. xiii), where in the Rheims translation ' cockle ' renders ' zizania ' (tares).

> The food that to him now is as luscious as locusts
> > (*Oth.* i. iii. 354-5)

is obscure. It is probably a reference to the food of the Baptist (Matt. iii. 4), which was actually locusts, but was in later times believed to be the fruit of the carob, the ' husks ' of the Prodigal Son, which are certainly not luscious, though perhaps they came to be thought so from their association with ' wild honey' in the Bible.

Shakespeare names or alludes to more than 180 plants. The uses to which he puts his trees and flowers show nearly always delicate observation or something more than a passing interest. In one place it is an epithet, as in

> Usurping ivy, brier, or idle moss ;　　(*Com. of E.* ii. ii. 182)

in another it is the note of the careful observer, as in

> . . . cinque-spotted, like the crimson drops
> I' the bottom of a cowslip ;　　(*Cymb.* ii. ii. 38-9)

in another it is some traditional belief briefly summed, as in

> though the camomile, the more it is trodden on the faster it grows, yet youth, the more it is wasted the sooner it wears.
> > (*1 Hen. IV*, ii. iv. 446-8)

Again, we have unmistakably a few local touches. Such is the use of ' palm-tree ' (*A. Y. L.* iii. ii. 187) for willow, and the mention of the bilberry (*M. Wives* v. v. 51), the common name in the midland counties for the whortleberry, *Vaccinium Myrtillus*, familiar to those who know the hills of the district. Another is ' honey-stalks ' for the stalks of clover :

> With words more sweet, and yet more dangerous,
> Than baits to fish, or honey-stalks to sheep.
> > (*Tit. Andr.* iv. iv. 89-90)

The original application of ' honeysuckle ' was to the red clover, and it survives in Warwickshire and other parts of the Midlands.

Some of Shakespeare's scenes and songs are full of the colour and fragrance of herbs and flowers :

> When daisies pied and violets blue
> And lady-smocks all silver-white
> And cuckoo-buds of yellow hue
> Do paint the meadows with delight.
>
> *(Love's L. L.* **v. ii.** 902–5)

> I know a bank whereon the wild thyme blows,
> Where oxlips and the nodding violet grows
> Quite over-canopied with luscious woodbine,
> With sweet musk-roses, and with eglantine :
> There sleeps Titania some time of the night,
> Lull'd in these flowers with dances and delight.
>
> *(Mid. N. D.* **ii. i.** 249–54)

The advent of Polixenes and Camillo to the sheep-shearing in *The Winter's Tale* is the occasion of a lovely profusion of garden herbs and plants of the woods and meadows, disposed according to the seasons :

> *Perdita.* Give me those flowers there, Dorcas. Reverend sirs,
> For you there 's rosemary and rue ; these keep
> Seeming and savour all the winter long :
> Grace and remembrance be to you both,
> And welcome to our shearing ! . . .
> . . . Sir, the year growing ancient,
> Not yet on summer's death, nor on the birth
> Of trembling winter, the fairest flowers o' the season
> Are our carnations, and streak'd gillyvors,
> . . . Here 's flowers for you ;
> Hot lavender, mints, savory, marjoram ;
> The marigold, that goes to bed wi' the sun,
> And with him rises weeping : these are flowers
> Of middle summer, and I think they are given
> To men of middle age. You're very welcome.
> *Camillo.* I should leave grazing, were I of your flock,
> And only live by gazing.
> *Perdita.*   Out, alas !
> You'd be so lean, that blasts of January
> Would blow you through and through. Now, my fair'st friend,
> I would I had some flowers o' the spring that might
> Become your time of day. . . . O Proserpina !
> For the flowers now that frighted thou let'st fall
> From Dis's waggon ! daffodils,
> That come before the swallow dares, and take
> The winds of March with beauty ; violets dim,
> But sweeter than the lids of Juno's eyes
> Or Cytherea's breath ; pale primroses,

That die unmarried, ere they can behold
Bright Phoebus in his strength ; . . . bold oxlips and
The crown imperial ; lilies of all kinds,
The flower-de-luce being one.   (IV. iii. 73–127)

And in tragedy too the handful of herbs or the bundle
of weeds is made to play its part. So Ophelia in her last
mad moments upon the stage distributes her symbolic
bouquet :

There's rosemary, that's for remembrance; pray, love, remember:
and there is pansies, that's for thoughts. . . . There's fennel for you,
and columbines ; there's rue for you ; and here's some for me ;
we may call it herb of grace o' Sundays. O! you must wear your rue
with a difference. There's a daisy; I would give you some violets,
but they withered all when my father died (*Haml.* IV. vi. 174–84).

And in the midst of flowers she goes to her end :

There is a willow grows aslant a brook,
That shows his hoar leaves in the glassy stream ;
There with fantastic garlands did she come,
Of crow-flowers, nettles, daisies, and long purples,
That liberal shepherds give a grosser name,
But our cold maids do dead men's fingers call them :
There, on the pendent boughs her coronet weeds
Clambering to hang, an envious sliver broke,
When down her weedy trophies and herself
Fell in the weeping brook.   (IV. vii. 167–76)

Cordelia describes her raving father decked with a mad
medley of weeds :

Crown'd with rank fumiter and furrow weeds,
With hardocks, hemlock, nettles, cuckoo-flowers,
Darnel, and all the idle weeds that grow
In our sustaining corn.   (*Lear* IV. iv. 3-6)

The Elizabethan Age was pregnant with many things.
Amongst them was the rise of scientific botany, but
Shakespeare in no wise concerned himself with it.
In the contemplation of life in its largest aspects he
could disregard what was unessential for his purpose. He
was English to the core and could run the risk of even
seeming parochial. But the purpose of this chapter is to
describe the age as well as the man's position in relation
to its subject. Some account of the origin of modern
botany, which was contemporaneous with both, is therefore
necessary.

Modern botany found its starting-point in the general
revival of learning. But being at first purely literary its

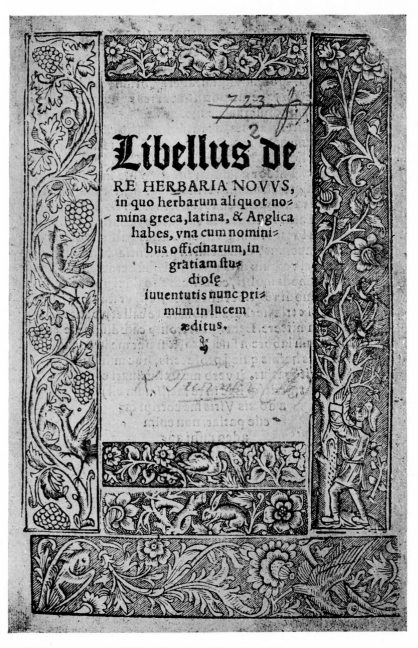

Libellus de
RE HERBARIA NOVVS,
in quo herbarum aliquot no-
mina greca, latina, & Anglica
habes, vna cum nomini-
bus officinarum, in
gratiam ſtu-
dioſę
iuuentutis nunc pri-
mum in lucem
æditus.

Title-page of WILLIAM TURNER'S *LIBELLUS* 1538

method was unscientific. It was subservient to medicine and, as Pulteney remarks, 'no drug used in medicine was esteemed true, unless found in Dioscorides'. The process by which botany gradually emerged in England into something more rational may be traced in his admirable pages, and it is one of the glories of the Elizabethan Age to have seen its foundations securely laid. The men who did the work were notable in many ways. The first and most remarkable of them was perhaps William Turner, who has been called 'the Father of English Botany'. He became a Fellow of Pembroke College, Cambridge, and while at the University bitterly denounced the neglect of botany:

Being yet a student of Pembroke Hall, whereas I could learn never one Greke, neither Latin nor English name, even amongst the physicians of any herbs or tre: such was the ignorance at that time.

He attached himself to Latimer, was imprisoned, and went abroad till the death of Henry VIII. He travelled about, making the acquaintance of many Continental botanists, finally finding his way to Ferrara, where he took the degree of Doctor of Physic. On his return he became physician to the Duke of Somerset, and was loaded with ecclesiastical preferment, ending with the Deanery of Wells. In 1548 he published *The Names of Herbes*, the historical importance of which consists in the fact that it tried to bring the native popular nomenclature into line with that which was current amongst scientific botanists abroad. During the reign of Mary he was in exile again. With Elizabeth, who had made his acquaintance at Sion, he had always been in high favour, and she promptly on her accession restored him to his preferments. He dedicated to her the complete edition of his *New Herball*, published at Cologne in 1568, and took occasion in the preface to compliment the Queen on her fluency in speaking Latin.

Turner's herbal was the first attempt in this country to define accurately familiar native and cultivated plants and to fix their nomenclature. Beyond this it had no scientific aim. But it bridges the gap between the old and the new botany. The names are given in alphabetical order, and the plants are illustrated with woodcuts mostly borrowed from Fuchsius. It is an odd coincidence that Turner had a garden at Kew. But it had no relation to the later one. To him belongs the merit of having intro-

duced lucerne into England. Turner's herbal was superseded by the *Niewe Herball* of Henry Lyte, ' of an ancient
family of Lytes-Cary in Somersetshire.' It was published
by Gerald Dewes in 1578, but was printed at Antwerp.
Unlike Turner's it was not original, but a translation from
the French version by Clusius of the Dutch herbal of
Dodoens or Dodonaeus,[1] printed in 1554. Lyte dedicated
his work to Queen Elizabeth. There were also complimentary epigrams by W. B., who was probably William
Bullein,[2] an ardent horticulturist who died in 1576, by
Thomas Newton, and W. Clowes. Lyte's herbal describes
1,050 plants, four-fifths of which are illustrated with foreign
blocks. It is a better arranged and more attractive book
than Turner's, but is still in method frankly herbalistic.
He explains in his preface that his purpose was

that even the meanest of my Countriemen (whose skill is not so
profounde that they can fetche this knowledge out of strange
tongues, nor their habilitie so wealthy, as to entertaine a learned
Phisition) may yet in time of their necessitie, have some helpes in
their owne, or their neighbours fieldes and gardens at home.

The book must have been popular and served its purpose
well ; in various forms it held its own for more than a
century. If Shakespeare looked into any botanical book
at all it was probably Lyte's book. But whether directly
or not, he certainly shows knowledge of its contents. When
he says :

> And shrieks like mandrakes torn out of the earth,
> That living mortals, hearing them, run mad,
>
> (*Rom. & Jul.* IV. iii. 48–9)

he recalls the old myth which the Anglo-Saxons learnt
from Apuleius ; and Payne is no doubt right in suggesting
that Falstaff's description of Justice Shallow,

for all the world like a forked radish, with a head fantastically
carved upon it with a knife (*2 Hen. IV*, III. ii. 337–9),

---

[1] Dodoens was physician for some time to the Emperor Maximilian and
his son.

[2] Bullein for a short time held Church preferment, but subsequently practised as a physician. He was personally acquainted with all the Elizabethan
botanists from Turner to Gerarde. Though he wrote a *Booke of Simples* in his
Bulwarke of Defence (1562), his own knowledge of botany appears to have
been slender. His chief merit consists in the efforts he made to improve the
cultivation of the land. He complained, as many do to this day, that ' Kitchen-
garden wares were imported from Holland, and fruits from France ', which
might equally well have been grown at home.

was reminiscent of some figure in a herbal, for he adds that they 'called him mandrake' (ibid. 342)[1]. Lyte simply touches on this, but his account is strictly scientific. It was an anodyne, and he revives from Dioscorides its use as an anaesthetic (apparently the earliest), that patients undergoing an operation 'shall feele no payne'. This would easily suggest Cleopatra's

> Give me to drink mandragora . . .
> That I might sleep out this great gap of time.
> *(Ant. & Cleop.* I. v. 4-5)

The influence of Lyte may account for the mention of 'hebona' or 'hebenon', which has been taken for the yew, but which the writer believes to be henbane:

> thy uncle stole
> With juice of cursed hebona in a vial,
> And in the porches of mine ears did pour
> The leperous distilment. *(Haml.* I. v. 61-4)

As a fact, it has been observed in a fatal case to produce 'a general congestion of dark-coloured liquid blood in the venous system '.[2] This would explain:

> whose effect
> Holds such an enmity with blood of man. (ibid. 64-5)

The pouring into the ears is in Pliny *(Nat. Hist.* xxv. 4. 17): 'oleum fit ex semine [hyoscyami], quod ipsum auribus infusum temptat mentem.' The external symptoms of general corruption seem like a poetical version transferred to leprosy of Lyte's description of the effects of henbane, which itself seems to have no basis in fact.

The . . . juyce . . . layde to any member or part of the bodie . . . doth mortifie and cause the sayde member to looke blacke, and at last doth putrifie and rot the same, and cause it to fall away.

Although the *Oxford Dictionary* fails to trace any other use of the name, there can be hardly any doubt that the 'insane root' is identical with henbane:

> have we eaten on the insane root
> That takes the reason prisoner? *(Macb.* I. iii. 84-5)

The name is reminiscent of the *Emmanes* of Apuleius, with its Latin synonym *Insana* (which Gerarde also gives). A case

---

[1] Bacon mentions 'Mandrakes; whereof Witches and Impostors make an ugly Image, giving it the form of a Face on the top of the Root'. (See p. 524 and plate.) The writer has been consulted about the authenticity of similar objects for the late Sultan of Turkey. [2] Taylor, *Poisons*, 2nd ed., 1859, 759.

is cited where monks who had eaten the roots for supper by mistake 'were seized in the night with the most extraordinary hallucinations, so that the place became like a lunatic asylum'.[1] Shakespeare might take 'as bitter as colo-quintida' (*Oth.* I. iii. 355–6) from Lyte, who has : 'The fruit . . . in taste very bitter,' and he might well get from him such knowledge of southern vegetation as would amplify what he took from Ovid. 'The soft myrtle' (*Meas. for M.* II. ii. 117) is not a very apt description of the somewhat harsh foliage ; but Lyte explains how 'certaine Her-boristes . . . with greate heede and diligence . . . preserve it from the colde of winter : for it cannot endure the colde of the Countrie'. Most of what Shakespeare has so superbly amplified about the cedar is to be found in Lyte :

The great Cedar waxeth very stowte and tall. . . . His limmes and branches be long and stretched out into length and breadth. . . . The great Cedar groweth . . . uppon the high mountaynes and places that be colde and moist, which are commonly covered with snow.

One passage will suffice for comparison :

He shall flourish,
And, like a mountain cedar, reach his branches
To all the plains about him.   (*Hen. VIII*, v. v. 53–5)

'Long heath' (for which 'ling, heath' is an unnecessary emendation of Hanmer's) makes another point of contact with Lyte, who gives two species, long heath and small heath, the first of which bears its flowers along the stems. Gonzalo on the sinking ship exclaims :

Now would I give a thousand furlongs of sea for an acre of barren ground ; long heath, brown furze, any thing (*Temp.* I. i. 70–2).

It is not necessary to go beyond Lyte for such equip-ment as Shakespeare needed for any reference to exotic plants. He would find there, for example, all that he needed about the date palm or the pomegranate. He was content with the common and available knowledge of his own day and did not trouble about curious or recondite allusions. There is scarcely a trace of any use of the later botanical literature of his time. A brief account of this is therefore all that is necessary.

From a scientific point of view, the greatest luminary in the botanical world of the time was Matthias Lobel, a countryman of Dodoens, who was born at Lille in 1538

---

[1] Taylor, loc. cit. 759.

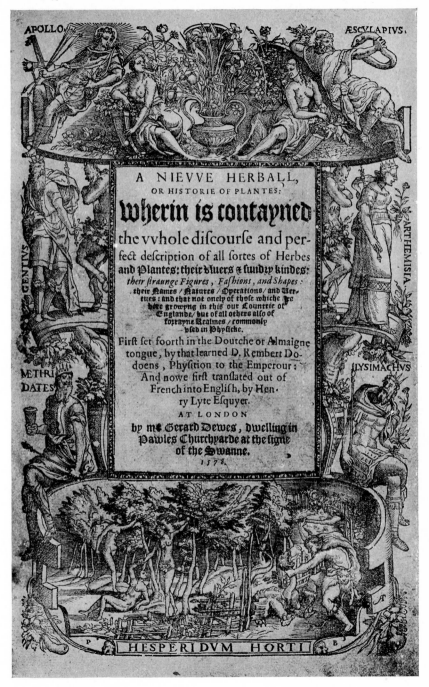

APOLLO.

ÆSCVLAPIVS.

ARTHEMISIA

GENTIVS

METHRI
DATES

LYSIMACHVS

A NIEVVE HERBALL,
OR HISTORIE OF PLANTES:

wherin is contayned

the vvhole difcourfe and perfect defcription of all fortes of Herbes
and Plantes: their diuers & fundry kindes:
their ftraunge Figures, Faſhions, and Shapes:
their Names, Natures, Operations, and Vertues: and that not onely of thofe whiche are
here growyng in this our Countrie of
Englande, but of all others alfo of
forrayne Realmes, commonly
vfed in Phyfike.

Firft fet foorth in the Doutche or Almaigne
tongue, by that learned D. Rembert Dodoens, Phyſition to the Emperour:
And nowe firft tranſlated out of
French into Englifh, by Henry Lyte Efquyer.

AT LONDON

by me Gerard Dewes, dwelling in
Pawles Churchyarde at the figne
of the Swanne.

1578.

HESPERIDVM HORTI

and died, it is said, in London, in 1616, the same year as
Shakespeare. He was physician to William, Prince of
Orange. Little is known of his history or why or when
he came to England. The study of botany still had its
headquarters on the Continent, yet Lobel printed and
published his *Adversaria* in London in 1571. It is in Latin
and was dedicated to the Queen. It preceded Lyte's
Herball, but is on an entirely different plane from works
intended for merely popular consumption. It was intended
for serious students, and one may wonder where they were
to be found. But the scientific history of the Elizabethan
Age still needs probing. Perhaps Turner left a school of
which little other trace survives. Lobel's work is at any
rate a landmark in the history of botany, for it contains
the first attempt at a classification of plants on the basis
of natural affinity. He appears to have been attached to
the mission to Denmark in 1598 conducted by Lord Zouche,
who was the patron of Ben Jonson, and he was superin-
tendent of a physic-garden, as it was called, maintained by
Lord Zouche at Hackney. In the second edition of the *Adversaria* (1605) Lobel calls himself botanist to King James.

It is evident from the life of Lord Herbert of Cherbury
that the new herbalistic art, which was of foreign origin
and quite independent of the older but still persistent
vulgar sort, was popular amongst the Elizabethan gentry.
He not merely thinks that 'it will become a gentleman
to have some knowledge in medicine', but would have
him 'know how to make . . . medicine himself, and afterwards prepare them with his own hands'. He does not
approve of 'chemic medicines', but thinks they are 'much
more happily and safely performed by vegetables'. In
a passage too long to quote in full, he says : 'I conceive
it is a fine study, and worthy a gentleman to be a good
botanic, that so he may know the nature of all herbs and
plants, being our fellow-creatures and made for the use of
man.' For the purpose he recommends to 'cull out of
some good herbal all the icones together'. By taking these
into the fields, 'one may presently find out every herb he
meets withal.' Lobel had in fact anticipated this by publishing in 1581, in a portable form, which became very
popular, the illustrations from his work with indexes of names
in seven languages.

In 1577 John Frampton, a merchant who had long resided at Seville and also translated Marco Polo, published a translation of the *Historia Medicinal* of Nicolas Monardes under the title of *Joyfull Newes out of the Newe founde Worlde*, which gives a good account of all its most valuable vegetable productions. This must have been a notable revelation, but Shakespeare wholly ignores it. Even to tobacco he makes no allusion.[1] The Potato may seem an exception. But in Shakespeare the potato of ' his fat rump and potato finger' (*Troilus* v. ii. 53–4), and ' Let the sky rain potatoes ' (*M. Wives* v. v. 20–1) was what is now called the Sweet Potato, which was found by the Spaniards in the West Indies as early as 1500. Gerarde called it the Common Potato, and that now familiar, the Virginia Potato. This epithet was erroneous, as the plant was neither native to Virginia nor cultivated there at the time. It was apparently brought by the Spaniards to Europe from Quito about 1580, and gradually found its way north-wards. Gerarde had it in cultivation in 1596, but it was doubtless still a rarity.

Whatever may have been the condition of the political atmosphere, the domestic life of England breathes the air of secure and ordered prosperity. To quote W. B. :

Elizabetha potens cuius moderamine solo,
Pax iucunda Anglis, atque arbor pacis oliva
Sic viget, ut passim per apricum incedere possit
Gens Britonum, tuto fragrantes carpere flores.

Such conditions would favour gardening, and this was the date of its systematic beginning, and it is coincident with the time at which botany ceased to be merely subservient to medicine. Plants were cultivated for their own sake and not as mere materia medica.

Lord Burghley had a fine collection of plants of which Gerarde had the superintendence, and he had also a large physic garden of his own at Holborn, which Pulteney thinks ' was probably the first of the kind in England, for the number and variety of its productions '. A passion for

---

[1] This is the more remarkable as Bacon (*History of Life and Death*, 305) says : ' Tobacco in our age is immediately grown into use.' Elsewhere (*Sylva Sylvarum*, 184) he describes the cultivation as extremely profitable, but notices that ' English Tobacco hath small credit, as being too dull and earthy '. This shows a cultivated taste. He discusses the remedy and comes very near the truth in finding it in heat.

collecting had grown up, and new plants were eagerly sought in every direction. Lord Zouche brought plants and seeds from Constantinople. Gerarde mentions Nicholas Lete, a London merchant, as ' greatly in love with rare and faire flowers, for which he doth carefully send into Syria, having a servant there at Aleppo, and in many other countries ; for which myself and the whole land are much bound unto him '. He speaks also of Lord Hunsdon, the Queen's first cousin, as ' worthy of triple honour for his care in getting, as also for his curious keeping, such rare and strange things from the farthest parts of the world '. England, as it has often done, repaid its debt to foreign learning, and the Continental botanists began to visit it for the sake of studying the new acquisitions.[1]

It is not surprising that they needed an illustrator ; Lyte's *Herball* had become wholly inadequate. As in our own day, a speculative bookseller saw his chance. He engaged Dr. Priest to make a translation of the latest work of Dodoens. Priest died and Gerarde was then employed. He appears to have had neither the scholarship nor the necessary botanical knowledge. He had, however, the assistance of Lobel, and using Dodoens as a foundation, he produced a book (1597) which was more comprehensive than anything existing. It was also the most copiously illustrated. Norton procured some 2,000 German blocks from Frankfort, and Gerarde had some others cut in this country. Gerarde died in 1612, and in 1633 Norton brought out a new edition, in which Gerarde's shortcomings were amended by Thomas Johnson, a thoroughly competent botanist. In its later form the book maintained a not undeserved reputation for at least a century.

So far botany had been occupied with the collection and nomenclature of plants and with some attempt at their classification. The plant itself as a living organism now began to be studied. The first attempt, by Cesalpino in his *De Plantis* (1583), was, as usual, built on the foundations

---

[1] Only two novelties in the later herbals are recognized by Shakespeare. One is the Crown Imperial (*Wint. Tale* IV. iii. 126) ; it was first described from Belgian gardens by Lobel in 1576, and is said to have been obtained from Constantinople. It soon found its way to England and became a popular plant. The other is the Sweet Potato, also described by Lobel, with ' Potades ' as the English name. Shakespeare may have learnt something about both from Gerarde.

laid by classical writers. Its influence did not reach England till the next century. But it would not be difficult to show, even from Shakespeare himself, that the eager curiosity of the Elizabethan Age was alive to the problem It is the subject of much elaborate, if unsystematic, speculation[1] by Lord Bacon in his *Sylva Sylvarum*, a book which, perhaps on account of its unsystematic character, has been completely ignored by botanists. Bacon peeled off effect from cause till he reached a core of general principle, and he hoped by combining such principles to arrive at a complete theory of the order of nature. But, though he must have the credit of first using experiment, his method was sterile since he rejected hypothesis. William Rawley, Bacon's chaplain, who published the book in 1627, quotes ' an usuall Speech of his Lordship; That this Worke of his Naturall History, is the World as God made it, and not as Men have made it; For that it hath nothing of Imagination'. The book, though now forgotten, must have had a wide popularity, for it reached the tenth edition. It contains much shrewd observation, but its chief value is the evidence that it affords of the trend of scientific speculation at the time at which it was written.

Shakespeare and Bacon were both attracted by a horticultural problem which doubtless was a subject of much interest at the time. Bacon tells us :

Take Gilliflowers seed, . . . and sow it, and there will come up Gilliflowers, some of one colour, and some of another, casually as the seed meeteth with nourishment in the Earth ; so that the Gardiners find that they have two or three Roots amongst an hundred that are rare and of great price, as Purple Carnations of several stripes.

He recommends that the ' experiment ' should be tried on other plants. Here Bacon was on the track of variation, the great discovery which had to wait for Darwin. But his explanation was futile, and he split on the same rock as Herbert Spencer in finding it in the environment.

Shakespeare makes Perdita and Polixenes discuss the question in *The Winter's Tale* (IV. iii. 81–97), and lifts it at once to a higher plane.

---

[1] ' He that looketh attentively into them, shall finde that they have a secret Order ' (*Sylva Sylvarum*, To the Reader).

Of Potatoes of Virginia. Chap.335.

Battata Virginiana siue Virginianorum, & Pappus.
Potatoes of Virginia.

with a light shew of yellownes, as though purple and yellow were mixed t
of the flower thrusteth foorth a thicke fat pointell, yellow as golde, with
pricke or point in the middest thereof. The fruite succeedeth the flowers,
bignes of a little bullesse or wilde Plum, greene at the first, and blacke whe

Perdita. The fairest flowers o' the season
Are our carnations, and streak'd gillyvors,
Which some call nature's bastards . . .
I have heard it said
There is an art which in their piedness shares
With great creating nature.
Polixenes. Say there be ;
Yet nature is made better by no mean
But nature makes that mean : so, over that art,
Which you say adds to nature, is an art
That nature makes . . .
this is an art
Which does mend nature, change it rather, but
The art itself is nature.

This is the insight of consummate genius. We are no longer left side-tracked in the environment, but face to face with the truth that nature contains the secret of its own evolution.

BIBLIOGRAPHY.—The works on plants by English authors bearing upon our period are : WILLIAM TURNER's *Libellus de re herbaria novus,* 1538 (title-page reproduced here), reprinted in facsimile by B. D. Jackson, 1877 ; *The names of herbes in Greke, Latin, Englishe Duche and Frenche wyth the commune names that Herbaries and Apotecaries use,* 1548, reprinted (ed. J. Britten) by the English Dialect Society, 1881, and the same author's *A new Herball,* 1551, the second part, 1562, and both with the third part, 1568 ; *A Niewe Herball, or Historie of Plantes. . . . First set foorth in the Doutche or Almaigne tongue,* by *that learned D. Rembert Dodoens : And nowe first translated out of French into English,* by HENRY LYTE, 1578 ; JOHN GERARDE's *The Herball or Generall Historie of Plantes,* 1597, which was enlarged by Thomas Johnson, 1633. A list of the plants cultivated by Gerarde himself appeared as *Catalogus arborum . . . in horto Joh. Gerardi* in 1596. THOMAS NEWTON's *An Herbal for the Bible,* 1587, contains descriptions of the forms and properties of biblical plants ; it is translated from the Latin of Levinus Lemnius. Important contemporary foreign sources and treatises are LEONHARD FUCHS' *De historia stirpium,* 1542 ; REMBERT DODOENS' *Cruydeboeck,* 1554 (which was also turned into French by Carolus Clusius, 1557); MATTHIAS LOBEL's *Stirpium adversaria nova,* 1570, 1576, &c.; *Plantarum seu stirpium icones,* 1581; ANDREA CESALPINO's *De plantis libri xvi,* 1583 ; PIERANDREA MATHIOLI's *Kreuterbuch,* 1590. On the history and progress of botanical science, should be consulted RICHARD PULTENEY's *Historical and biographical sketches of the progress of Botany in England, from its origin to the introduction of the Linnean system,* 2 vols., 1790 ; the introduction to JOHN EARLE's *English Plant Names,* 1880 ; SACHS' *History of Botany,* 1890; and J. R. GREEN's *History of Botany,* 1907. J. F. PAYNE treats the Anglo-Saxon treatises and figures and names of herbs in *English Medicine in the Anglo-Saxon Times,* 1904. The history of herbals is the subject of MRS. E. A. NEWELL ARBER's *Herbals, their origin and evolution, a chapter in the history of botany 1470–1670,* 1912 ; the relation of English to foreign herbals is traced by J. F. PAYNE in Trans. Bibliograph. Soc., ' read ' Feb. 17, 1908. The botany of Shakespeare is copiously treated in CANON ELLACOMBE's *Plant-Lore and Garden-craft of Shakespeare,* 2nd ed., 1884.

XVI

FOLKLORE AND SUPERSTITIONS : GHOSTS AND FAIRIES : WITCHCRAFT AND DEVILS

BY

H. LITTLEDALE

FOLKLORE

FOLKLORE, so far as it actually lives on among the folk, is orally transmitted from the old to the young, along the generations. It is only incidentally recorded in books, and there often in very imperfect forms. The folklore which Shakespeare embodies in his poetry is partly what he learned as a child at his mother's knee, or as a schoolboy beside the banks of Avon, and partly what in later years he derived from reading and observation.

Generally speaking, we may say that, in Shakespeare's folklore, the warp is indigenous, the woof is literary ; while in that of his more bookish fellow writers, the opposite is the rule. In other words, his work is more natural, theirs is more scholastic. Lyly, for instance, if

> Talking of Stones, Stars, Plants, of Fishes, Flies,
> Playing with words and idle Similies,

transfers whole pages from Pliny ; whereas Shakespeare more often goes directly to the countryside and the life of nature for his similitudes and his other illustrations from natural history. He frequently compresses the pith of a fable into a sentence. Thus in *Measure for Measure* (V. i. 294–5) the good Duke exclaims,

> But, O, poor souls !
> Come you to seek the lamb here of the fox ?

So, too, Richard II denounces the

> Snakes, in my heart-blood warm'd, that sting my heart !
> (*Rich. II*, III. ii. 131)

and Julia describes her own situation by reference to the parable :

> Alas, poor Proteus ! thou hast entertain'd
> A fox to be the shepherd of thy lambs ;
>
> *(Two Gent.* IV. iv. 98–9)

just as Suffolk says to Queen Margaret :

> were't not madness, then,
> To make the fox surveyor of the fold ?
>
> (*2 Hen. VI*, III. i. 252–3)

The poet in this manner constantly employs comparisons with animals, birds, and other creatures.

Some of these popular superstitions respecting animals are worth enumerating, and here in alphabetical sequence a few are given, which Shakespeare and his contemporaries accepted without demur.

First, of the Ape. To the mediaeval mind, every woman's destiny was marriage. She could become the bride of man or the bride of God ; and if she wilfully rejected both these alternatives, she was warned that after death her lot would be to lead apes in (or into) hell. (Cf. *Much Ado* II. i. 43–4).

The nocturnal Bat, from its ambiguity of structure, having wings like a bird and teeth like a mouse, was associated with works of darkness and things out of nature's course. The sprite Ariel flies on a bat's back, but fairies ' war with rere-mice [i. e. bats] for their leathern wings' (*Mid. N. D.* II. ii. 4).

The Cat was regarded as a familiar companion of witches. The belief that it was endowed with nine lives (*Rom. & Jul.* III. i. 83) might well be encouraged by its wonderful vitality, when hung up in a leathern bottle and shot at with crossbows, or worried by sportsmen like Bottom, who could play ' a part to tear a cat in, to make all split ' (*Mid. N. D.* I. ii. 32–3). Hogarth's ' First Stage of Cruelty' illustrates very forcibly these popular recreations of the good old times.

The Hare shared the cat's uncanny reputation. Camden, in the interesting account of Irish superstitions at the end of his *Britannia,* says that if the Irish find a hare amongst their herds of cattle on May-day, they kill her, ' for they suppose shee is some old trot, that would filch away their butter.' So Ben Jonson says that

> A witch is a kind of hare. . . .
> And marks the weather
> As the hare does.   (*Sad Shepherd* II. viii)

Hares were supposed to change their sex annually. The hare as a type of melancholy is coupled with an old lion, a gib cat, and a lugged bear ; they are all as gloomy as a lover's lute, the drone of a Lincolnshire bagpipe, or the swampy neighbourhood of Moorditch (*1 Hen. IV*, I. ii. 80–9).

The Hedgehog too was of evil name. Heywood (*Hierarchie*, 1635, p. 263) makes her an emblem of the Devil. The Latin name, *ericius*, through the Old French *iriçon*, gave us *urchin*, which meant both a hedgehog and a fiend with prickly skin. ' Urchin-shows ' (*Temp.* II. ii. 5)—apparitions of urchins—affright Caliban. Witches were thought to draw omens from the whining of the hedgepig (*Macb.* IV. i. 2).

The madcap Robin Goodfellow, or Puck, in likeness of a filly foal, beguiles the ' fat and bean-fed horse ' (*Mid. N. D.* II. i. 45). The horse which Dr. Faustus sold to the horse-courser (or dealer), when ridden into water, ' vanished away ', and the rider found himself sitting on ' a bottle of hay ', and was never so near drowning in his life. The Irish, according to Camden, believe that ' if they never give fire out of the house unto their neighbours ', their horses will live longer and thrive better. He adds that horses' lives are endangered by their owners eating an odd number of eggs.[1]

Concerning the Lion, Shakespeare gives us two items of popular lore :

> 'Tis
> The royal disposition of that beast
> To prey on nothing that doth seem as dead :
>   (*A. Y. L.* IV. iii. 118–20)

> The lion will not touch the true prince.
>   (*1 Hen. IV*, II. iv. 303–4)

Rats ' instinctively ' quit a doomed ship. In Ireland, as Rosalind could have learned from Colin Clout, they are ' rhymed to death ' (cf. *A. Y. L.* III. ii. 187–9) ; in ' drumming tunes ', Ben Jonson adds. The rat without a tail, in *Macbeth* (I. iii. 9), if not an early allusion to the guinea-

---

[1] Holland's translation, 1610, vol. ii, p. 146.

pig, must refer to the idea that witches could not complete their transformation into animal shapes.

In *The Winter's Tale*, Wolves and Bears are quoted as doing ' offices of pity ' (II. iii. 188) to babes exposed to perish ; an idea curiously widespread, from Cape Finisterre to Cape Comorin. Were-wolves or witch-wolves were, as Bishop Hall[1] states in his *Epistles*, ' witches that have put on the shape of those cruell beasts '.

We saw a boy there, whose halfe-face was devoured by one of them neere the village [in Ardenna] ; yet so as the eare was rather cut than bitten off. Not many dayes before our comming at Limburgh was executed one of those miscreants, who confessed on the wheele to have devoured two and forty children in that forme (1620, p. 270).

Drayton, describing a feast of shepherds to Pan, celebrated with ' Bonefires ', says that

> by night, with a devout intent,
> About the field religiously they went,
> With hollowing Charmes the Warwolfe thence to fray,
> That them and theirs awayted to betray. (*Poems*, 1619, p. 476)

In the margin Drayton explains ' warwolfe ' as ' men by sorcerie turning themselves into wolves '. The ' howling of Irish wolves against the moon ' (*A. Y. L.* v. ii. 120–1) may allude to the notion, recorded by Spenser, that the Irish ' were once every year turned into wolves, . . . and yet some of the Irish doe use to make the wolf their gossopp ' : an instance of totemistic survival.

The habits and movements of Birds have at all times provided matter for speculation and have been associated with omens, good or bad.

Cocks all the world over were considered the enemies of ghosts. The disappearance of ghosts before daybreak, and their absence at Christmastide, are due to the crowing of the cock. Ben Jonson wrote in his notes to *The Masque of Queenes* that

witches all confess that nothing is so cross, or baleful to their purposes, as that the cock should crow before they are done.

The names Basilisk and Cockatrice (although the former originally denoted a serpent supposed to be hatched out of a cock's egg) are used interchangeably by Shakespeare for a very deadly creature, that killed the beholder by

---

[1] ' Witch-wolves ' is Hall's equivalent for *loupsgarous* or λυκανθρώποι.

looking at him (*Wint. Tale* I. ii. 388; *Rom. & Jul.* III. ii. 27).
They played an important part in moral metaphor. Bishop
Hall tells us that

Crosses, after the manner of the cockatrice, die if they be foreseene.

In *The Phoenix and Turtle* (17–19) the lines :

> And thou treble-dated crow
> That thy sable gender mak'st
> With the breath thou giv'st and tak'st,

embody the curious beliefs that

> Ter tres aetates humanas garrula vincit
> Cornix,

and that the crow can change its sex at will.

That the Eagle kindled ' her undazzled eyes at the full
midday beam ', and that she tried the nature of her ' birds '
by making them gaze upon the sun, and cast them forth
from her eyrie if they blinked, were commonplaces in the
birdlore of the time. Richard Duke of York thus challenges
the Prince of Wales in *The Third Part of Henry VI* :

> Nay, if thou be that princely eagle's bird,
> Show thy descent by gazing 'gainst the sun. (II. i. 91–2)

Another wonder was the generation of the Barnacle
Goose. Bianca, in *The Malcontent* (III. i.), says that the man
who flatters greatness will grow great himself: ' like your
Scotch barnacle, now a block, instantly a worm, and presently
a great goose.' Max Müller traces the origin of this widely
diffused notion to the Irish bishops, who justified eating the
bird in Lent because it was really a transformed barnacle or
shell-fish; these *Hiberniculae* became *Bernicles*, and so *Barnacles*. Probably Caliban, when he fears that they will all be
turned into ' barnacles ', refers to this metamorphosis.

In some parts of England the country-people still hang
the stuffed skin of a Kingfisher by a cord out of doors,
to serve as a weathercock. Kent alludes to this custom in
his denunciation of roguish servants, who

> Renege, affirm, and turn their halcyon beaks
> With every gale and vary of their masters.
>
> (*Lear* II. ii. 83–4)

Juliet tells us that

> Some say the lark and loathed toad change eyes,
>
> (*Rom. & Jul.* III. v. 31)

but learned research has had to content itself hitherto
with the supposition that country-people consider the eye
of the toad more beautiful than that of the lark.

The Owl is Duncan's ' fatal bellman ' (*Macb.* II. ii. 4),
because it was the old custom for the bellman to visit
condemned persons the night before their execution and
bid them ' Good night '. Ophelia's ' They say the owl was
a baker's daughter' (*Haml.* IV. v. 42–3) is explained by
a Gloucestershire legend, of the transformation of a girl
who, through niggardliness, cut a large portion off some
dough that her mother was about to bake into bread for
Christ. Similar legends are told of the green woodpecker,
the lapwing, and the cuckoo.

The allegories of mediaeval preachers helped to popularize
certain notions of Oriental origin, such as those about the
Pelican, type of Christ, shedding its blood to feed its young :
the ' kind, life-rendering pelican ' (*Haml.* IV. v. 145) of
Laertes. On the other hand, Lear's ' pelican daughters '
(*Lear* III. iv. 74) would destroy him by bleeding him to death.

The notion that the Robin Redbreast and the Wren—two
' fire-bringing ' birds—

> with leaves and flowers do cover
> The friendless bodies of unburied men
> > (Webster, *The White Devil*, v. iv)

is no less beautifully alluded to in *Cymbeline* (IV. ii. 224–9),
where the ' ruddock ' in its charity would bring flowers, and
' furr'd moss', to the dead Fidele.

The song of the dying Swan is a belief as old as Plato,
and is recalled by Emilia's words in *Othello* (v. ii. 245–6),
as also by Portia's

> a swan-like end,
> Fading in music.　　　　　(*Merch of V*. III. ii. 44-5)

In the *Duchess of Malfi* (IV. ii),

> The screech-owl and the whistler shrill
> Call upon our dame aloud,

where Webster, as usual, copies Spenser's reference to

> The Whistler shrill, that who so heares, doth dy.
> > (*Faerie Queene* II. xii. 36)

Yarrell says that ' whimbrels are often spoken of, in the
south, as " the seven whistlers ", the rippling whistle being
repeated seven times ' ; but Mr. Swainson identifies the
whistler with the golden plover.

Fish-lore connects with bird-lore through the barnacle
goose and the osprey. Another general belief, not yet
by any means out of remembrance, was that if horses'

hairs fell into a stream they were turned into eels. As
Mark Antony says :

> Much is breeding,
> Which, like the courser's hair, hath yet but life,
> And not a serpent's poison.   (*Ant. & Cleop.* I. ii. 205–7)

Popular beliefs about bodily sensations were, as they
still are, numerous. Thus Desdemona asks whether itching
of the eyes ' bode weeping ' (*Oth.* IV. iii. 60), and Beatrice,
after overhearing talk about herself, exclaims : ' What
fire is in my ears ? ' (*Much Ado* III. i. 107). Ajax's ' fingers
itch ' (*Troilus* II. i. 27) to smite Thersites, and witches
take special note of such tinglings :

> By the pricking of my thumbs,
> Something wicked this way comes.   (*Macb.* IV. i. 44–5)

Children's games embody much antique tradition, for
children are the most conservative of mortals : to them
' the breach of custom is the breach of all ' (*Cymb.* IV. ii.
10–11). Quaint notions about diseases and popular remedies are also very enduring things. Fireside stories helped
to pass the long winter nights, and Richard II touches
their character when he bids his queen

> In winter's tedious nights sit by the fire
> With good old folks, and let them tell thee tales
> Of woeful ages, long ago betid ; . . .
> And send the hearers weeping to their beds.
>   (*Rich. II*, v. i. 40–5)

These old unhappy far-off things are the peculiar property
of folk-tale, which, in Sidney's words, ' holdeth children from
play, and old men from the chimney corner '.

Giants figured in many a place-name and many a legend.
Shakespeare alludes by name to Samson and Goliath
(*1 Hen. VI*, I. ii. 33), and his Warwickshire Sir Guy, and
Colbrand, whom Guy slew. In *Cymbeline* his mentioning their
' impious turbans ' (III. iii. 6) seems to indicate that he inclined
to class them with ' black pagans, Turks, and Saracens '
(*Rich. II*, IV. i. 95). Local traditions about giants are very
numerous and of great interest. Daniel finely characterizes
one such legend—that Stonehenge was brought from Africa
to Ireland by giants in a single night—as an example of

> ignorance, with fabulous discourse,
> Robbing fair art and cunning of their right.

Those celebrities of the nursery, Jack and Jill, in Sweden take the place of that Man-in-the-Moon, with his lanthorn and bush of thorn, once so ably presented before Theseus and Hippolyta at Athens. ' The Moon ' is the answer to Goodman Dull's riddle : ' What was a month old at Cain's birth, that is not five weeks old as yet ? ' (*Love's L. L.*, IV. ii. 36). There is a capital story from Vives, told in Sandys's *Ovid* (1632, p. 255), of an ass drinking up the moon. Just as the animal stooped to the water, a dark cloud passed across the moon's face, and the terrified rustics, seeing no reflection, at once cut open the luckless ass, to recover the missing luminary. The men of Wiltshire are still called moon-rakers, because of an alleged similar feat with a hay-rake. Possibly when Rosaline replies to the disguised King Ferdinand, that he is only asking for ' moonshine in the water ' (*Love's L. L.* v. ii. 209), Shakespeare may have had stories of this kind in his thoughts.

Like old wives' tales, nurses' talk is prolific of folklore. ' Good Mother,' says Littlewit in *Bartholomew Fair* (III. ii), ' how shall we find a pig, if we do not look about for 't ? will it run off o' the spit, into our mouths, think you, as in Lubberland, and cry wee, wee ? ' Lubberland is goblin-land— the land of the lubber fiends. Shakespeare, too, uses the formula of the old tale : ' It is not so, nor it was not so, but indeed, God forbid it should be so.' (*Much Ado* I. i. 226–8) [1]

Plant-lore is a vast subject. We need hardly linger over such popular usages as presentations of flowers at feasts, or strewings on graves, except to note that much attention was formerly paid to the emblematic significance of flowers. The attribute of causing love for the first person seen on awaking, given to the juice of Love-in-Idleness by Oberon (*Mid. N. D.* II. i. 168, 176–82), is taken from a well-known type of divination or of magic charm. The name of the plant or extract is not usually revealed, but Shakespeare was thinking less of the properties than of the name of his magic flower. Another juice, of a very different operation, is that of ' cursed hebenon ' (*Haml.* I. v. 62), probably the deadly yew-tree.[2] The ' dismal yew '

[1] See Halliwell's *Popular Tales*, p. 47, for this story.
[2] But see pp. 441, 509 *supra*.

(*Tit. Andr.* II. iii. 107) was planted in churchyards, perhaps in imitation of ancient heathen rites, or perhaps 'as an emblem of Resurrection, from its perpetual verdure' (*Hydriotaphia*, 4) ; or sometimes, perhaps, because the wood was good for bows, and cattle could not get at the poisonous leaves so easily there. The 'shroud of white, stuck all with yew' (*Tw. N.* II. iv. 55), of Feste's song seems, however, to denote a despairing death—yew-boughs instead of flowers being the hapless lover's 'strewments' (*Haml.* v. i. 255).

Learned opinion has varied as to the character of the elder-tree, and Shakespeare has nothing to say in favour of 'stinking elder' (*Cymb.* IV. ii. 59), unless he deemed it a merit that traditionally it formed the gallows of Judas Iscariot (see *Love's Labour's Lost*, v. ii. 607). It is associated with crime, as in *Titus Andronicus*, where the murderers' reward is fitly hidden for them 'among the nettles at the elder-tree' (II. iii. 272). The Mandrake (a popular etymologizing of Mandragora) played an important part in gruesome superstition, and Gerarde the herbalist tells us that this plant's natural habitat is under a gallows ; that it shrieked when plucked up ; and that as its shriek was fatal to the hearer, a dog was tied to the plant when a specimen was required. By his efforts to get free he pulled it out of the ground and instantly became a martyr to science. Shallow at Clement's Inn was

for all the world like a forked radish, with a head fantastically carved upon it with a knife (*2 Hen. IV*, III. ii. 337–9),

and so we catch in part the significance of his nickname, Mandrake. Some good plants thrive best in bad company.

> The strawberry grows underneath the nettle,
> And wholesome berries thrive and ripen best
> Neighbour'd by fruit of baser quality.
> *(Hen. V*, I. i. 60–2)

A part of Shakespeare's plant-lore is of classical origin, but his wonderful skill in touching with life his 'small Latin and less Greek' borrowings is shown in lines like these :

> Merciful heaven !
> Thou rather with thy sharp and sulphurous bolt
> Split'st the unwedgeable and gnarled oak
> Than the soft myrtle.   *(Meas. for M.* II. ii. 114–17)

Or these, of the Elysian beds of asphodel, when he makes
Troilus exclaim :

> give me swift transportation to those fields
> Where I may wallow in the lily-beds
> Propos'd for the deserver !   (*Troilus* III. ii. 11–13)

We need not linger over the receipt of fern-seed, by which
Gadshill walks invisible (*1 Hen. IV*, II. i. 96, 98–9) ; nor
over rue, sour herb-of-grace (*Haml.* IV. v. 181), symbol
of repentance ; nor rosemary, symbol of remembrance
(ibid. 174) ; nor the willow, worn by forlorn paramours, and
sung by the death-doomed Desdemona (*Oth.* IV. iii. 28).

Only one more plant can here be cited in connexion
with plant-lore : one that in Norse legend is wrought
beneath the waves by Marmendill, and that in classical
myth undergoes

> a sea-change into something rich and strange.

Shakespeare in his reference to coral made out of a drowned
man's bones (*Temp.* I. ii. 395–9) deviates from the Ovidian
notion, that coral is a sea-shrub which changes into stone
when taken out of the water. George Sandys in his *Travels*
(ed. 1621, p. 235) tells us that

it is a soft shrub, greene when under the water, and bearing a white
berry ;

> Hardnesse assuming from toucht aire alone,
> Vnder the sea a twig, above a stone.

And changeth into red.

Sandys in his *Ovid* (1632, p. 168) notes further that ' corall
sympathizes with the wearer, and waxeth pale with his
sicknesse '.

Popular comparisons embody much curious folklore,
mingled with direct humorous observation. For instance, in

> O ! he 's as tedious
> As a tired horse, a railing wife ;
> Worse than a smoky house (*1 Hen. IV*, III. i. 158–60)

we have a variant of a saying that Chaucer cites in his
Meliboeus, and that we find in the mediaeval rhyme :

> Fumus et mulier et stillicidia
> Expellunt hominem a domo propria.

Another example is

> As true as steel, as plantage to the moon,
> As sun to day, as turtle to her mate,
> As iron to adamant, as earth to the centre,
>   (*Troilus* III. ii. 184–6)

where we have the popular belief indicated that 'plantage'
(i. e. herbage), thrives best during the time of the moon's
waxing, and specially when at the full. Hundreds of
shorter comparisons and popular sayings occur. This,
for instance, is not from Sam Weller, but from Mabbe's
Celestina :

Everyone as he likes, as the goodman said when he kissed his cow.

Untamed shrews threaten to 'comb your noddle with a
three-legg'd stool' (*Tam. Sh.* I. i. 64). The speeches of
the aged have a character of their own : 'You and I are
past our dancing days' (*Rom. & Jul.* I. v. 35) ; 'We
have seen better days' (*A. Y. L.* II. vii. 120, *Timon*
IV. ii. 27) ; 'Well, we were born to die' (*Rom. & Jul.*
III. iv. 4). Many of these sayings, as in the old Proverbs of
Hendyng, and earlier even (like the 'ofost betost' of *Beowulf*),
are assonant, alliterative, or rhyming commonplaces. The
following are all Shakespearian : 'Things won are done'
(*Troilus* I. ii. 311), 'time must friend or end' (ibid. I. ii. 82),
'a little pot and soon hot' (*Tam. Sh.* IV. i. 6), 'hob nob'
(*Tw. N.* III. iv. 265), 'barnes are blessings' (*All's W.*
I. iii. 28), 'a young man married is a man that's marr'd'
(ibid. II. iii. 315). Phoebe's 'omittance is no quittance'
(*A. Y. L.* III. v. 133) is some noverint's version of a legal
maxim ; 'neither rhyme nor reason' (*Com. of E.* II. ii. 49)
is also a literary example.

John Lyly must have known an old wife of the
Mrs. Poyser type ; 'it will be a forward cocke that croweth
in the shell,' she may have said to him when a boy. He
varies the 'tedious prattling' of his *Euphues* and his
plays with many lively sayings of the proverbial sort.
Proverbs throw much light on the life of the folk. Thus
they prove (if it needs proof) that the goose was more in
evidence as part of the domestic environment anciently
than it is nowadays. 'It is a blind goose that knoweth
not a fox from a fernbush', and 'a blind goose that
cometh to the fox's sermon', are examples from *Euphues*.
So, 'three women and a goose make a market' explains
Costard's 'And he [the goose] ended the market' (*Love's
L. L.* III. i. 116). In *A C. Mery Tales* the 'olde proverbe'
is cited, that 'it is as great pyte to see a woman wepe as
a goose to go barefote'.

In Shakespeare's early plays especially, euphuistic use

them to the fhape of men & women; which falfifying practife hath confirmed the
the fimple and vnlearned people, who haue taken them vpon their report to
drakes.

The female Mandrake is like vnto the male, fauing that the leaues heereof be
or darke greene colour; and the fruite is long like a peare, and the other is rounde l

Mandragoras mas & fœmina.
The male and female Mandrake.

* *The place.*

Mandrake groweth in hot reg
and mountaines, as in mount (
lia, and fuch like places; we haue
ted in gardens, and are not elfev
in England.

* *The time.*
They fpring vp with their leat
flower in the ende of Aprill: th
Auguft.   * *The names.*

Mandrake is called of the Gr
of diuers ιυργαζι: and *Circæa* of (
who by Art could procure loue
thought that the roote heereof
loue: of fome αντίμμλον, *Anth*
Morion: fome of the Latines h
ræ malum, and *Terreftre malum*
lus: fhoppes and other nation
the Greeke name. *Diofcoride*
male is called of diuers ωλεωι: ar
another Mandrake by the name
is generally holden to be *Solanu*
fome *Circea lutetiana*, but not pr
we call it Mandrake, Mandrage.

* *The temperature*
Mandrake hath a predomina
as *Galen* faith, that is to faie c
degree: but the roote is colde
gree.

FOEMINÆ   MARIS

* *The vertues.*
Diofcorides doth particularly fet downe many faculties heereof, of which notw
be one proper vnto it, fauing thofe that depende vpon the drowfie and fleepin

THE   MANDRAKE

is made of proverbs in the snip-snap of witty repartee. Shakespeare also pleasantly represents the distortion of proverbial light in the darksome glass of an ignorant mind; and in *Coriolanus* he makes Marcellus note how the common people, when voicing their grievances, habitually use proverbial ' shreds ' (I. i. 214).

Reptiles, insects, and other crawling things are oftentimes referred to by Shakespeare, and we may suppose that allusions to

> Adders, spiders, toads,
> Or any creeping venom'd thing that lives
> > (*Rich. III*, I. ii. 19–20)

were meant to cause a sense of horror in the minds of the audience at the theatre.

Hence Richard is a ' pois'nous bunch-back'd toad ' (*Rich. III*, I. iii. 246), a 'bottled spider' (ibid. 242) ; and Edmund, in *King Lear*, is ' a most toad-spotted traitor ' (v. iii. 140). Poor Imogen, we are told, ' was as a scorpion ' in her stepmother's sight (*Cymb.* v. v. 45) ; and young Arthur is ' a very serpent' in John's way (*John* III. iii. 61).

Vindictive witches (like Middleton's Hecate) send snakes to suck the cows dry :

> The dew-skirted dairy wenches
> Shall stroke dry dugs for this.

Toads ' live upon the vapour of a dungeon ' (*Oth.* III. iii. 271), and ' infect fair founts with venom mud ' (*Lucr.* 850) ; just as spiders suck their poison up from the earth (*Rich. II*, III. ii. 14).

But there are occasionally compensations :

> The toad, ugly and venomous,
> Wears yet a precious jewel [the toadstone] in his head:
> > (*A. Y. L.* II. i. 13–14)

The spider is an exemplary weaver, and, moreover, may be drunk with impunity if one is not aware of its presence in the beverage : it is only when the ' abhorr'd ingredient' is seen, that 'violent hefts' ensue (*Wint. Tale* II. i. 38–44).

Women were a stock subject of popular satire ; wives' tongues and tempers and other strong points naturally formed a large part of everyday experience. More interesting, however, would be a collection of women's sayings about women. Rosalind's disguise enables her to make very free with her tongue on this subject ; and her descriptions of women are even better than Beatrice's, although Beatrice's have a peculiarly feminine 'tang' about them. Again, the wicked stepmother is one of the most important characters in folk-tale, and Shakespeare alludes to the common 'slander of most stepmothers' (*Cymb.* I. i. 71), without refuting it.   Jeremy Taylor [1] neatly illustrates the popular sentiment when he tells how

he that threw a stone at a dog, and hit his cruel stepmother, said, that although he intended it otherwise, yet the stone was not quite lost.

SUPERSTITIONS

'In our childhood,' wrote Reginald Scot,

our mothers maides have so terrified us with an oughlie divell having hornes on his head, fier in his mouth, and a taile in his breech, eies like a bason, fanges like a dog, clawes like a beare, a skin like a Niger, and a voice roaring like a lion, whereby we start and are afraid when we heare one cry Bough : and they have so fraied us with bull beggers, spirits, witches, urchens, elves, hags, fairies, satyrs, pans, faunes, sylens, kit with the cansticke, tritons, centaurs, dwarfes, giants, imps, calcars, conjurors, nymphes, changlings, Incubus, Robin goodfellowe, the spoorne, the mare, the man in the oke, the hellwaine, the fierdrake, the puckle, Tom thombe, hob gobblin, Tom tumbler, boneles, and such other bugs, that we are afraid of our own shadowes : in so much as some never feare the divell, but in a dark night ; and then a polled sheepe is a perillous beast, and manie times is taken for our fathers soule, speciallie in a churchyard, where a right hardie man heretofore scant durst passe by night, but his haire would stand upright.

Bishop Hall in his *Characters* has likewise given us an admirable picture of the kind of man that such childish teachings will produce. 'Superstition,' he says,

is godlesse religion, devout impietie.   The superstitious is fond in observation, servile in feare. . . . This man dares not stirre forth till his breast be crossed, and his face sprinkled : if but an hare crosse him the way, he returnes ; or if his journey began unawares on the dismall [2] day ; or if he stumble at the threshold.   If he see a snake unkilled, he feares a mischiefe ; if the salt fall towards him, he lookes pale and red, and is not quiet till one of the waiters have powred wine on his lappe ; and when he neezeth, thinks them not his

---

[1] *Holy Living*, p. 96.

[2] The dismal days, *dies mali*, or evil days, were the unlucky days of the Calendar.

friends that uncover not. In the morning he listens whether the
Crow crieth even or odd, and by that token pressages of the weather.
If he heare but a Raven croke from the next roofe, he makes his
will, or if a Bittour flie over his head by night : but if his troubled
fancie shall second his thoughts with the dreame of a fairie garden,
or greene rushes, or the salutation of a dead friend, he takes leave
of the world, and sayes he cannot live. He will never set to sea
but on a Sunday ; neither ever goes without an Erra Pater [almanac
with lucky days, &c., marked] in his pocket. Saint Paul's day and
Saint Swithune's with the Twelve, are his Oracles ; which he dares
believe against the Almanacke. . . . Old wives and starres are his
counsellors ; his night-spell is his guard, and charmes his Physicians.
He weares Paracelsian Characters for the toothach, and a little
hallowed waxe is his Antidote for all evils. . . . Some wayes he will
not goe, and some he dares not ; either there are bugges, or he
faineth them ; every lantern is a ghost, and every noise is of chaines.
He knowes not why, but his custome is to goe a little about, and to
leave the Crosse still on the right hand.

In Tudor times, superstition permeated man's life ; and
very limited success attended the efforts of the reformers
of religion to repress superstitious customs.

Shakespeare and his contemporaries bountifully illustrate
the superstitious credulity which guided their contemporaries' conduct, moulded many of their social customs, and
governed their habitual interpretation of natural phenomena. Superstition which crystallized into folklore absorbed
much that passed for scientific observation even among
the educated.

Around Birth and Marriage and Death and Burial, stars
rained influences, and omens hung, according to the teaching
of astrology. Fairies hovered about the cradle and sagacious
gossips shook their heads over portents, while they knapped
ginger and circulated the gossips' bowl.[1] Among the superstitious, belief in the efficacy of charms is always strong.
Sometimes charms were superstitious, ' some tricks, some
quillets, how to cheat the devil,' (*Love's L. L.* iv. iii. 288),
such as leechdoms and spells against evil influences and
prevalent epidemics ; or they were amulets—Joan of
Arc's ' periapts ' (*1 Hen. VI*, v. iii. 2)—and words of might,
to secure the welfare of the wearer or utterer ; or they were,
as in *Cymbeline*, dirges for the repose of the dead. The
Church had her conjurations and exorcisms, like Aaron's rod

[1] See *Merch. of V.* iii. i. 9–10 ; *Com. of E.* v. i. 406–8 ; *Mid. N. D.* ii. i. 47;
Rom. & Jul. iii. v. 174–5.

more potent than all others. This is exemplified in *Love's Labour's Lost*:

Write, ' Lord have mercy on us ' on those three ; . . . They have the plague (v. ii. 420–2).

Any infatuation was ascribed to charms. Thus, Mistress Quickly tells Sir John :

I never knew a woman so dote upon a man : surely, I think you have charms (*M. Wives* II. ii. 107–8).

Old Brabantio in sterner terms makes the same charge against Othello (*Oth.* I. ii. 73). Antony twice calls Cleopatra his ' charm ' (*Ant. & Cleop.* IV. x. 29, 38), in other words, his witch. Villains especially resorted to satanic spells. Thus Edmund, in *King Lear* (II. i. 41–2), says that Edgar stood

> Mumbling of wicked charms, conjuring the moon
> To stand auspicious mistress.

Even in the most trivial acts of life, charms were resorted to for good luck : Sir Politique Would-bee in *Volpone* (IV. i), having burst his spur-leathers,

' put on new, and did go forth ; but first' he ' threw three beans over the threshold '.

The change in men's ways of thinking is illustrated by the change in meaning that words like charm, crossing, shrewd, cursed, and many others were undergoing or had undergone. The Church, besides dispensing her blessings, set the example of solemn cursings, with bell, book, and candle ; and the stage was not slow to utilize this department of rhetoric. Many characters in Shakespeare declaim long imprecations. Queen Margaret offends in this manner in *Richard III* (I. iii. 216–33) ; and so does Suffolk in *2 Henry VI*, where poison, gall, cypress-trees, basilisks, lizard's stings, serpent's hiss, and boding screech-owls swell the note of execration (III. ii. 321–8). The queen, herself not unused to the practice, says, ' these dread curses ' recoil upon the curser (ibid. 330–2) ; just as Buckingham says that ' curses never pass The lips of those that breathe them in the air' (*Rich. III*, I. iii. 285–6), and harm no one but the speaker. Caliban's cursings—for he ' needs must curse' (*Temp.* II. ii. 4), like the savage that he is—are inherited from his mother's usage, or derived from her malignant witchery.

Deformity was regarded as a divine judgement. Queen

Margaret emphasizes the point to Richard, neither like his
sire nor dam,

> But like a foul misshapen stigmatic. (*3 Hen. VI*, II. ii. 136)

Elsewhere she says that he is ' elvish-mark'd ' (*Rich. III*,
I. iii. 228)—foul-featured like a changeling. In *Hamlet*,
Shakespeare ascribes such defects to ' nature's livery, or
fortune's star ' (I. iv. 32), and earlier, in *Lucrece*, he wrote
that

> Marks descried in men's nativity
> Are nature's faults, not their own infamy.   (ll. 538–9)

Divination, by many forms of inference, was widely
practised. The Bible was opened—*Stoicheiomanteia* this
was learnedly called—after the manner of the Sortes Vir-
gilianae, and the Talmudic Bath Col. Many domestic
superstitions, especially in the matter of future husbands,
had to do with divination, and the village crone, who
snatched a fearful joy from the awe that she inspired, on
such occasions often rendered her aid. Even the gallant
Touchstone, for Jane Smile's sake, seems to have resorted
to the practice known as peascod wooing, in which the
wooer plucked a pod from the pea-vine, crushed it, and
presented it to the lady, when the good omen depended on
none of the peas falling out of the husk (*A. Y. L.* II. iv. 50–3).

Divination and forebodings work together, for ' Fear doth
teach ' Venus's heart ' divination ' (*Ven. & Ad.* 670), and
such divination is often merely from the aspect of a bearer
of news. It was very unlucky, and even dangerous, to be
the bringer of bad news.

Shakespeare makes frequent use of dreams and their
interpretations. Morning dreams are true, says Jonson in
Love Restored. Dreams go by contraries, Lucullus finds, in
Timon (III. i. 6–7, 17). But every one did not believe
in dreams. ' You laugh ', says Cleopatra to Dolabella,

> You laugh when boys or women tell their dreams ;
> Is 't not your trick ?   (*Ant. & Cleop.* v. ii. 74–5)

Man is but an ass if he go about to expound Bottom's
dream (*Mid. N. D.* IV. i. 213–4).

Belief in the Evil Eye is shown chiefly by the terms
' overlooked ' and ' overseen '. Pistol, as a fairy, tells the
' vile worm ', Falstaff, that he was ' o'er-look'd ' even
from his birth (*M. Wives* v. v. 89) ; Lucrece actually plays
on the word :

> Thou, Collatine, shalt oversee this will ;
> How was I overseen that thou shalt see it !
>
> *(Lucr.* 1205–6)

Notions about Fate are also too widespread still to need exposition ; and Fortune is too false a huswife, too fickle, too harsh, sometimes too merry, sometimes too crooked, —all these epithets are Shakespeare's [1]—for us to have dealings with her. And yet Falstaff trusted the jade :

This is the third time ; I hope good luck lies in odd numbers. Away ! go. They say there is divinity in odd numbers, either in nativity, chance or death *(M. Wives* v. i. 2–5).

Cleopatra is variously called a witch, a spell, a charm, a gipsy ; and ' this great fairy ', this ' enchanting queen ', lets ' witchcraft join with beauty ' *(Ant. & Cleop.* IV. viii. 12 ; I. ii. 137 ; II. i. 22) ;—thus does Shakespeare indicate the closeness of association between Egyptians, gipsies, and magic arts.

Lyly has Gyptes, an Egyptian soothsayer, in *Endimion.* Desdemona's handkerchief

> Did an Egyptian to my mother give ;
> She was a charmer, and could almost read
> The thoughts of people. *(Oth.* III. iv. 57–9)

Similarly, Maudlin the witch, in *The Sad Shepherd* (II. iii), has an enchanted girdle, ' a browder'd belt with characters ',

> A Gypsan lady, and a right beldame
> Wrought it by moonshine for me and starlight.

Jonson's *Gipsies Metamorphosed* is a mine of gipsy-lore. One art that the Captain Gipsy there practises—palmistry for fortune-telling—is less ponderously expounded by that ' merry devil ', Launcelot Gobbo :

Well, if any man in Italy have a fairer table. . . . Go to ; . . . here 's a small trifle of wives : alas ! fifteen wives is nothing *(Merch. of V.* II. ii. 172–7).

Miracles, says Lafeu, are past ; and

we have our philosophical persons, to make modern and familiar, things supernatural and causeless *(All's W.* II. iii. 1–3).

In *Pericles,* an antique play, ' a fire from heaven came and shrivell'd up ' men's bodies (II. iv. 9) ; but such use of the miraculous is not common on the stage. Indeed, Shakespeare describes a fraudulent miracle—Blind Simpcox's

---

[1] See *Hen. V,* v. i. 85 ; *Rom. & Jul.* III. v. 60–2 ; *Ant. & Cleop.* IV. vi. 54 ; *Jul. Caes.* III. ii. 271 ; *Two Gent.* IV. i. 22.

restoration of sight at St. Alban's shrine—in *The Second Part of Henry VI* (ii. i. 59 ff.), just as Bishop Hall ridicules Lipsius's Two Ladies, Bluntstone's Boy, Garnet's Straw, and St. Wilfred's Needle, among the supposed miracles of his own time.

Certain natural phenomena were popularly regarded as presages of political trouble, and dramatic use was often made of omens, portents, and prophecies. Among omens, a man's stumbling was noted as very unlucky. Gloucester says :

> For many men that stumble at the threshold
> Are well foretold that danger lurks within.
> (*3 Hen. VI*, iv. vii. 11–12)

In *Love's Labour's Lost* we seem to get a survival of a propitiatory address to an unlucky object: ' Good night, my good owl ' (iv. i. 143). Delio, in *The Duchess of Malfi*, (ii. ii), sums this up when he says :

> How superstitiously we mind our evils :
> The throwing down of salt, or crossing of a hare,
> Bleeding at nose, the stumbling of a horse,
> Or singing of a cricket, are of power
> To daunt whole man in us.

Popular prognostications of some impending disaster to the State might be largely exemplified from Elizabethan literature, and prophecies seem to have had weight not only with the common people but even among the educated classes. Richard of Gloucester sends such ' inductions dangerous ' abroad, and employs supposed wizards to disseminate these ' drunken prophecies ', the better to set his brother Clarence and the King ' in deadly hate ' (*Rich. III*, i. i. 32–5). Joan of Arc has ' the spirit of deep prophecy ' (*1 Hen. VI*, i. ii. 55). ' Henry the Fifth did sometime prophesy ' (ibid. v. i. 31), as did the royal Saint, Henry the Sixth. Dying men utter prophecies, as old Gaunt does (*Rich. II*, ii. i. 31 ff.), and as Hotspur would do,

> But that the earthy and cold hand of death
> Lies on my tongue.   (*1 Hen. IV*, v. iv. 84–5)

Thus a few Elizabethan notions connected with superstition have been gathered ; but only a mere handful out of the heap. We have but ' run to the end of the rainbow to find a bag of gold, as they persuade children ' (Butler, *Characters*, p. 238).

GHOSTS

'A sad tale', says young Mamillius, 'is best for winter.
I have one of sprites and goblins . . . There was a man . . .
Dwelt by a churchyard' (*Wint. Tale* II. i. 24–9)—and so,
no doubt, many a creepy winter's tale was begun, in the
gloom of a flickering fire, while the rafters groaned and the
blasts howled above the wide old chimneys. Popular ideas
about spirits were very definite. One has only to glance
at the woodcuts in such old books as *The Kalendayr of the
Shyppars* (1503) to realize the kind of figures that the
imagination conjured up. The Church inculcated belief in
the good genius or guardian angel, told off to watch over
every human soul, and also in the hosts of evil spirits who
strove without ceasing to thwart the good angel's gracious
ministrations. In *Faustus* these opposing powers exhort
Faustus alternately, the one bidding him repent and be
saved, the other urging him to despair of salvation. So in
Shakespeare's *Sonnet* cxliv the poet has two loves, of comfort and despair, which 'like two spirits' do 'suggest' him
still—prompt him continually to good or evil thoughts ;
and the idea recurs elsewhere in many forms.

Students of occult lore, with wizards, witches, and the
like, were said to have entered into soul-destroying compacts
with these evil beings, who became their 'familiars', and
rendered them 'metaphysical aid' for a brief span of life.
Besides these spirits, celestial or infernal, the ghosts of the
dead also 'walked' on earth, and might show themselves
to men. There were family ghosts, like the classical Alastores
and the Irish Banshees, apparently genii, or goddesses of
the 'white lady' (Bertha) type, but sometimes actually
the perturbed spirits of departed human relatives. Thus
in *The Duchess of Malfi* (**v.** ii) the Cardinal says : ' None of
our family dies but there is seen the shape of an old woman,
which is given by tradition to have been murdered by her
nephews for her riches.' From *Hamlet* we can gather
many of the current notions regarding these ghostly
visitants. Coming after midnight, they must depart ere
cockcrow, or a fearful summons will hurry them away.
Scholars, able to speak Latin, and acquainted with the
formulae of exorcism, can conjure them ; but it is a perilous
thing to cross—confront and question—ghosts. They

THE ANGELL

Thom: Hammon Armig: Rich: Gethinge M. of ỷ pen.

'walk' usually because of some reparation to be made, or foul play to be disclosed, or to warn those dear to them of peril, private or public ; or to watch over hidden treasure. Their shapes are without substance, and weapons cannot harm them. They are recognizable figures, in well-remembered attire, wearing either shadowy armour, or in their habit as they lived; or they may appear in 'cerements' (*Haml.* I. iv. 48), the familiar 'winding sheet' of many an eerie tale. Ghosts can move swiftly, not merely through air, but through the earth, walls, doors, and the like solid obstacles. They will not speak unless they are questioned, and then only to those for whom they have a message. Until this is delivered they repeat their visits, if necessary appearing to others besides the person whom they specially seek. Their voices squeak and gibber ; but on the stage their airy tongues are distinct, and they move with warlike stalk. Ghosts are sometimes demons that lure men to death ; they assume a horrible form, and unsettle reason when their victim is on the verge of unseen destruction. The scholarly Hamlet knows this, but fearlessly follows whither the ghost leads, and hears from him, not the soul-freezing secrets of death's prison-house, which he durst not reveal, but the dreadful family history of incest and fratricide. We are told further that some ghosts fast by day in purgatorial fires, and during night, for certain hours, are at liberty to return to their earthly haunts. The ghost of Julius Caesar, like that of old Hamlet and that of Banquo, revisits earth and ' walks ' until he is avenged and can have rest. When Caesar's ghost appears, Brutus notices ' How ill this taper burns' (*Jul. Caes.* IV. iii. 274). In *Richard III*, when the ghosts of the king's victims have vanished, he exclaims,

> The light burns blue. It is now dead midnight.
> (v. iii. 274)

Ghosts sometimes appear in dreams, and the shadows of a dream may become visible hallucinations when one is awake. Brutus thus inclines to regard Caesar's spectre :

> Art thou any thing ?
> Art thou some god, some angel, or some devil,
> That mak'st my blood cold and my hair to stare ?
> Speak to me what thou art.
> *Ghost.* Thy evil spirit, Brutus.
> (*Jul. Caes.* IV. iii. 277-81)

In *Macbeth* there is an atmosphere of hallucination. Banquo—so soon to become a ghost himself—is at first in doubt of the reality of the weird sisters :

> Are ye fantastical, or that indeed
> Which outwardly ye show ?   (I. iii. 53–4)

Macbeth's vision of the dagger is pure hallucination of the over-wrought mind and eye. After the crime he is more prone to these attacks.

> Methought I heard a voice cry 'Sleep no more ! '
> (II. ii. 36)

This, like the air-drawn dagger, as his wife says, is the very ' painting ' (III. iv. 61) of his fear.

The popular ghost, like the stage ghost, was supposed to be an actual apparition from the grave. And yet there was some scepticism. Even in the old jest-book, *A C. Mery Tales*, out of which Beatrice had her 'good wit', we read that men feare many times more than they nede, which hath caused men to believe that sperytes and deuyls have ben sene in dyuers places, when it hath ben nothynge so.

Such shadows, as Shakespeare says, are 'the weak brain's forgeries' (*Lucr.* 460).

FAIRIES

Fairies are essentially the little people. With their whims and caprices and tempers, they are shadows of humanity in miniature, and act as tiny but potent guardians, blessing the homes, rewarding the minor virtues, and punishing the minor trespasses of ' human mortals ' (*Mid. N. D.* II. i. 101). Shakespeare's fays are not soul-endangering spiritual powers ; there is ever something childlike and irresponsible in their winsome ways. They are only with us during a few hours of the night, for ' fairy time ' (ibid. v. i. 373) begins after midnight, and closes at the rising of the morning star. Then the fairies follow night's shadow round the earth. When Puck tells Oberon that Aurora's harbinger is visible, and that wandering ghosts

> Troop home to churchyards : damned spirits all,
> That in cross-ways and floods have burial,
> Already to their wormy beds are gone,
> (ibid. III. ii. 382–4)

Oberon replies that the fairies 'are spirits of another sort', and adds the boast that in the shades of the forest he has often lingered until the sun has actually risen ! It is the child's pride at *staying up* beyond its usual bedtime. Yet though the fairies eat and drink and sleep, they are immortals themselves, and furthermore can confer conditional immortality on the human children who live with them, by dipping them in a 'virtuous well' (Fletcher, *Faithful Shepherdess*).

The changing seasons affect them. 'The summer still doth tend upon' Titania's state (*Mid. N. D.* III. i. 162), just as Ariel—who, as Pope saw, is not a fairy, but a sylph— flies after summer merrily (*Temp.* v. i. 92). In winter they pass to summer climes, where Indian votaresses watch the swelling sails by the margent of moonlit seas (*Mid. N. D.* II. i. 123–9).

Like children, Oberon's fays are naturally gladsome, tripping and skipping and dancing their fairy rings 'whereof the ewe not bites' (*Temp.* v. i. 37–8) ; but they are timorous too, and hide themselves when alarmed. Like children again, they are inclined to play mischievous tricks. Their knowledge has its limitations : Oberon does not know what form Titania will first behold on her awaking under the spell ; he is in doubt too whether Puck has merely mistaken his victims or has wilfully committed his knaveries. Puck, in fact, has made a blunder, but having done so, he rejoices over the 'jangling' caused by it (*Mid. N. D.* III. ii. 353). Yet with this mirthful weakness, Puck also has command over the powers of nature. He can cover the starry welkin with a fog, and can overcast the night (ibid. 355–7). This influence over nature is sympathetic. When the fairies are unhappy, nature is out of square, and man suffers ; for storms, fogs, floods, cold seasons, and murrain make their appearance. Even children have to share the general trouble : their playgrounds are full of mud !

> And this same progeny of evil comes
> From our debate, from our dissension :
> We are their parents and original.
>
> (*Mid. N. D.* II. i. 115–17)

Childlike themselves, they love children, and even steal them from their cradles, leaving foul misshapen changelings in their stead.[1] The little Indian boy, about whom Oberon and Titania quarrel, is not strictly a changeling in this sense, but an adoptive child, whose dead mother has been a ' votaress ' of Titania's ' order ' (ibid. II. i. 123). Thus Shakespeare connects Titania directly with Diana, and the votaresses of Diana's order are elsewhere mentioned by him (*Pericles* IV, Gower 4). He could not call his Fairy Queen Cynthia, for the name was appropriated to Elizabeth. Instead, he chose from Ovid (*Metam.* iii. 173) another of the moon's names, Titania, and made her love the ass-headed Bottom. Titania's love for a mortal, though due to a spell, is in keeping with the best traditions of fairy-lore. Sir Thopas fell in love-longing for a fairy queen, and fairies have loved men or women, as men or women have had fairy lovers, in many a well-known tale.

Just as in mediaeval romance there are many fairy queens, so Shakespeare has two : Titania, the sheeny fay of the moonlit woodland ; and Mab, the tricksy mischief-maker of the country homesteads. But Mab's portrait is drawn by no old gossip to the listening villagery : the lordly fancy of Mercutio, while preserving some of her homelier features, transports her to a more courtly sphere. Yet Mab, not Titania (not even our Tita) is Oberon's queen in Drayton's *Nymphidia* ; and in Jonson's *The Satyr*, ' there came tripping upon the lawn a bevy of fairies attending on Mab, their queen, who, falling into an artificial ring, began to dance a round.' The Satyr says :

> This is Mab the midnight fairy
> That doth nightly rob the dairy,
> And can help or hurt the churning,
> As she please, without discerning . . .
> She that pinches country wenches . . .
> This is she that empties cradles,
> Takes out children, puts in ladles. . . .

Let us add to this some part of Mercutio's description of her : she plaits horses' manes by night; she tangles hair in elf-locks ; she is the hag, or nightmare, and brings dreams to men (*Rom. & Jul.* I. iv. 89–95) : ' in elder times the mare that hight,' as Drayton says.

The name of Oberon Shakespeare took from the romance

---

[1] See the comic scene of Mak and the stolen sheep in the cradle, in the Townley Play. Compare *Wint. Tale* III. iii. 112 ; IV. iv. 677; *1 Hen. IV*, I. i. 86 ; Webster, *Devil's Law Case*, IV. ii. ; Jonson, *Sad Shep.* II. ii.

of *Huon of Bordeaux,* and its derivation through French
forms goes back to the Teutonic Alberich, the Elf King.
Puck too, or Robin Goodfellow, has nearly as many aliases
as he has transformations. The midsummer fairies do not
class Puck as one of themselves : he is bigger than they
are, and there is more of the Brownie or Leprechaun in
him. Puck, 'which most men call Hobgoblin' (*Nymphidia*),
is the Celtic Phooka, sometimes Robin Goodfellow, or Lob,
Lob-lie-by-the-fire ; the Lubber Fiend ; the ' lob of
spirits ', whose pranks are described in *A Midsummer
Night's Dream* (II. i. 34–41). In Shakespeare, Puck is
Oberon's court jester, the Sir Dagonet of Fairyland. Ben
Jonson, who does not disdain to mingle Shakespearian
fairy-lore with his classical borrowings, in his unfinished
Sad Shepherd introduces Puck-hairy; and in *The Devil is
an Ass* has a Pug with some of our Puck's attributes, but
otherwise with nothing Puck-like about him.

It is a hard matter to define the functions of certain
classes of elves and fairies, for they are as tangled as
elf-locks ; and in this respect they are on a par with much
other lore about ' the broken gods of creeds outworn '.
Shakespeare certainly did not trouble to keep the diverse
elements of his fairy-lore apart. Thus the spirits of *The
Tempest,* whom Shakespeare (taking the word ' elves '
from Golding's Ovid) makes Prospero address as

Ye elves of hills, brooks, standing lakes, and groves, (v. i. 33)

are more obviously descended from the classical nymphs
and fairies, and may be related also to the cabalists'
spirits of the elements. These spirits appear by day ;
the true fairies are nocturnal, and rank lower in the hier-
archy of the supernatural. Prospero's spirits belong
mainly to occult science ; Oberon's fairies are a part of
folklore.

Classical demonology and myth contaminated fairy-lore.
Dian and her nymphs modified the Celtic and Teutonic
notions about wild huntresses, while their spectral hounds,
' bred out of the Spartan kind ' (*Mid. N. D.* IV. i. 125),
yelled with the Gabriel hounds and the Celtic Cwn Annwn.
The Greek shepherd who beheld a nymph became a
nympholept ; Actaeon fared even worse ; and the fat
Actaeon of Herne's Oak, when the Windsor fairies drew
nigh, groaned in terror :

They are fairies ; he that speaks to them shall die.

(M. Wives v. v. 53)

In Chaucer's time the fairies had left England : the
' lymitour ' had banished them ; in Corbet's time, fairies
were things of the past :

> Farewell, rewards and fairies,
> Good housewives now may say,
> For now foul sluts in dairies
> Do fare as well as they.

In Hood's time, the Midsummer Fairies bade one more
long farewell ; and in our own time, only one remains :
' the oldest old thing in England,' Mr. Kipling's Puck.

WITCHCRAFT AND DEVILS

We have not here to investigate the ' noble and laud-
able' magic (in the Baconian sense) of the Elizabethan
men of science, but the ' impious and damnable ' magic,
the wizardry and witchcraft, that King James and his
witchfinders so indefatigably sought out and so pitilessly
punished. Shakespeare, although he makes Joan of Arc
a witch, probably believed little in witchcraft ; but the
King's interest in demonology sent all the court poets to
their occult studies, and the outcome is seen in many
Jacobean plays and poems and treatises that supply us
with illustrations of the black art. Sir John Harington
thus describes in 1604 his first interview with James :

His Majesty did much press for my opinion touching the power
of Satane in matter of witchcraft ; and askede me, with much
gravitie, if I did trulie understande why the Devil did worke more
with ancient women than others ? . . . His Highness told me [the
Queene his mother's death] was visible in Scotlande before it did
really happen, being, as he said, spoken of in secrete by those
whose power of sight presentede to them a bloodie head dancing
in the aire. He then did remarke muche on this gifte, and saide
he had soughte out of certaine bookes a sure waie to attaine knowledge of future chances.[1]

This letter gives us a very clear impression of James's
interest in psychic phenomena, and suggests further the
possibility of Shakespeare's having known of this strange
case of second sight when he contrived his apparition of
the ' armed head ' in *Macbeth* (st. dir., IV. i. 69).

[1] *Nugae Antiq.*, ed. 1779, vol. ii, p. 116.

To a scholar of imagination, the temptation of the fruit on the various forbidden branches of the tree of mediaeval science must have been almost irresistible. There was divination by water, by air, by fire, by smoke, by the crowing of cocks, by consulting the souls of the dead, by inspecting flour, by fish, by incense, by the hands, by the dead, by ventriloquism—and each of these branches had its exponents.[1] Many ecclesiastics and physicians, from Dunstan and Michael Scot and Roger Bacon to Cornelius Agrippa and Paracelsus, were reputed to have had dealings with the evil one:

> Lines, circles, scenes, letters and characters;
> Ay, these are those that Faustus most desires;

and the object of such studies was the attainment of power by intellectual means; for, as Faustus says,

> A sound magician is a mighty God.

References to common jugglers are of course frequent in the plays: they were mere fire-spitting mountebanks and conjurors, with their ' Hocos Pocos paucos palabros ' (Cf. *Tam. Sh.* ind. i. 5). Conjurors on the other hand were either exorcists or magicians. The exorcist (like good Dr. Pinch in *The Comedy of Errors*) might have to invoke the divine authority either over persons possessed by a devil (iv. iv. 56–9), or over persons obsessed, besieged, or assailed from without by wicked spirits.

The magician, on the contrary, summoned demons to render him service, and in repayment yielded them the reversion of his soul. Such magicians figure, though not prominently, in Shakespeare's earlier plays: Glendower's ' skimble-skamble stuff ' (*1 Hen. IV*, iii. i. 153) is not impressive. Prospero is a magician of a different cast. He is not the allegorical fiend in human shape, like Spenser's Archimago; nor is he outside ' the roll of common men ' (ibid. iii. i. 43), like the stagey Glendower; and still less is he the paltry juggler with mysteries, like Peele's Sacrapant. He may be compared rather with Faustus, if only for the sake of contrasting the two types of magician, the good and the bad. Faustus and Prospero both have the Renaissance love of learning, but Faustus studies magic because it is forbidden knowledge, Prospero because

---

[1] See *A Complete Christian Dictionary*, by Thomas Wilson, enlarged by A. Simson, 7th ed., 1661, art. ' Witchcraft '.

it is philosophical research. Faustus sells his soul to gratify his senses; Prospero's magic is 'not damnable', and he only uses it to work his deliverance from evil men. The magic that Faustus studies is the black art, diabolic and execrable; Prospero's 'art' is not malignant, not even 'mischievously good', like that of 'white witches'; it is simply the acquisition of extraordinary powers, by means of astronomy and of cabalistic studies. It is an art external to himself, depending on calculations and spells, and on magic paraphernalia, book, wand, and mantle; without these he is powerless. His soul is clear of all dealings with the evil one. Faustus has a magic wand too, and a girdle that confers invisibility, but his familiar is Mephistophilis; Prospero's is Ariel. In fact Prospero is more of the Hermetic philosopher than the regular magician; when he breaks his wand and buries his book, he is merely the learned prince.

Fuller, in his *Holy and Profane State*, lays down and proves at length certain propositions concerning witches.

(1) Formerly there were witches. (2) There are witches for the present, though these night birds fly not so frequently in flocks, since the light of the Gospel. (3) It is very hard to prove a witch. (4) Many are unjustly accused for witches. (5) Witches are commonly of the feminine sex. (6) They are commonly distinguished into white and black witches. The former heal those that are hurt, and help them to lost goods; the latter hurt and do mischief. Other writers speak of white, black, and grey: these last did good or evil as it chanced. Witches had power to transport human beings through the air, riding on a staff or on a 'coultree'. They could render themselves insensible to pain on the rack by using certain devilish unguents, 'or by swallowing a King of the Bees, who is prince ruler of the Hive'. Thus the village wise women—like old Mother Prat, or Gillian of Brentford—ran the risk of having worse powers imputed to them than they actually claimed, and the legal records of the 'witch-mania' are red with the blood of hundreds of these deluded creatures.

These 'beldam trots' were usually lame and palsied beings, withered and wild in attire, with beards, and skinny fingers. They dealt largely in fortune-telling and love-charms, and were suspected if a child fell sick or

S. MICHAEL ARCHANGEL

Vincit qui patitur

Ex Sumptib Harbottel Grimstone Armig: Iadrocsheut sculpt

From T HEYWOOD'S HIERARCHIE 1635

cattle did not thrive well. They generally had a black cat that shared their ill-repute. Witches higher in the profession dealt in crime. They fashioned images of wax, pricked them with needles, and buried them in dung-hills. The 'leperous distilment' in *Hamlet* (I. v. 64) is 'with Hecate's ban thrice blasted' (III. ii. 273); and Hecate, in Middleton's *Witch*, asks:

> Is the heart of wax
> Stuck full of magic needles? . . . .
> And is the farmer's picture and his wife's
> Laid down to the fire yet?

This Hecate (here become a mere witch) declines upon a lower range of feelings when she bewitches pigs, duck-lings, goslings, sheep, and milch kine, to revenge churlish refusals of flour, barm, milk, goose-grease, and tar. Medea's invocation of Hecate in Ovid (*Metam.* vii) was probably the channel by which her traditional mistress-ship of witches was preserved.

Harrison notes that the witches of the Isle of Man 'oftentimes sell winds to the Mariners, inclosed under certaine knots of thred', as the Lapland witches were said to do; and in *Macbeth* two of the witches offer winds to aid their sister's vengeance (I. iii. 11–13). Tempest and wreck and ruin are incidental effects of potent spells in operation. Witches hover through the murky air, and sail across perilous seas in sieves (*Macb.* I. iii. 8), cockles (*Pericles* IV. iv. 2), and eggshells (Jonson's *Sad Shepherd*). The habit of breaking empty eggshells to keep the fairies or witches from using them as boats is still inculcated in many nur-series—the schools of superstition. Such shipping is neces-sary, because water is a hindrance to demon journeys, although the Prince of Morocco says that 'the watery kingdom . . . is no bar to stop the foreign spirits' (*Merch. of V.* II. vii. 44–6). Joan of Arc knows that witches are wont to feed spirits with their blood, and she offers to 'lop a member off', in earnest of further benefits, if they will but help her once more (*1 Hen. VI*, v. iii. 15).

It is needless to recapitulate the particulars of witches that we meet in *Macbeth*. Shakespeare's 'weird women' (III. i. 2) are not mere exponents of erudite ritual of incanta-tion, deriving from Ovid and Bodinus, or from Lavaterus and Scot and Harsnet, although his scenic material and formal accessories, like much of his devil-lore, may be traced to such authorities. If his fatal sisters on one side follow the tradition from the Canidias and the Hecates, on another they take shape from his own imagination, and have intuitive affinities with the prince of the powers of the air, and the Parcae of Greek religion, and the death-decreeing sibyls of the North. There is little of this fatal prepotency in Middleton's witches; there is less in Jonson's; these writers aim at exciting our abhorrence; but Macbeth's juggling women-fiends are beings that rise above the grotesque to the terrible, and move us less to horror than to awe. Heywood (*Hierarchie*, p. 508), following Boece, says that Mackbeth and Banco-Stuart met 'white Nymphs' in a dark grove,

> Three virgins wondrous faire,
> As well in habit as in feature rare.

Shakespeare has created his 'freckled whelp, hag-born' (*Temp.* I. ii. 283), the man-monster, Caliban, part human toad, part changeling mooncalf, as a sort of link between the 'unfather'd heirs and loathly births' (*2 Hen. IV*, IV. iv. 122) of popular superstition, and the no less abhorred Brazilian cannibals, 'the savages and men of Ind' (*Temp.* II. ii. 61–2), of seafaring legend. We have no direct information, it is true, regarding Caliban's paternity, but the following account shows that there were 'sources' of information for Shakespeare which are perhaps lost to us.

In Brasilia, a barbarous woman by accompanying with one of these Daemons, brought forth a monster, which in a few hours grew to be sixteen handfuls high, whose back was covered with the skin of a Lisard, with big and swolne breasts; his hands like the pawes of a Lyon, with eyes staring, and seeming to sparkle fire; all his other members being deformed, and horrible to behold (*Hierarchie*, p. 541).

That Shakespeare was thinking of such a Brazilian demon is rendered more probable by the fact that he took the name Setebos—a Patagonian god—from the accounts of the Brazilian voyagers.[1] The belief that Devils took human brides is of great antiquity, a belief which is hinted at in:

> Or else the devil will make a grandsire of you. (*Oth.* I. i. 91)

Merlin and Robert the Devil were so fathered and mothered;

---

[1] See pp. 176, 182, and 186 *supra*.

and the common expression, the Devil's Dam, may mean either his *Dame* or wife, as in the story of Belphegor, or his *Dam* or mother, as in narratives of such mythic beings as Holda, or Grendel's mother, or the Vala.

In *The Historye of the Damnable Life and Deserved Death of Doctor John Faustus* we are told that

Lucifer himselfe sate in manner of a man all hairy, but of browne colour, like a Squirrell curled, and his taile turning upward on his backe as the Squirrels use.

In *King Lear* we are told that

The prince of darkness is a gentleman ; (III. iv. 147)

and in *The Virgin Martir* (III. iii), Harpax, an evil spirit, says that the Devil is

no such horrid creature, cloven-footed,
Black, saucer-eyed, his nostrils breathing fire.

Men's views of the embodied powers of evil varied in accordance with their form of creed and their grade of culture, and differed as widely as Old Iniquity, the roaring devil of the moral play, differs from Satan, the ruined archangel of the great Puritan epic.

BIBLIOGRAPHY.—Illustrative material may be found throughout the literature of the period and in modern commentaries thereon. The publications of various learned societies furnish evidence in the different departments of the subject, e. g. the Percy, Camden, Parker, Shakespeare, New Shakspere, Early English Text, and Folklore Societies. *The Gentleman's Magazine* and *Notes and Queries* contain rich stores of elucidatory matter.

On general folklore the following books are important : G. W. Cox's *An Introduction to the Science of Comparative Mythology and Folklore*, 1881 ; T. F. T. DYER's *English Folk-Lore*, 1878, and *Folk Lore of Shakespeare*, 1883 ; A. S. PALMER's *Dictionary of Folk Etymology*, 1882 ; G. L. GOMME's *English Traditional Folklore, Superstitions, Proverbs*, 3 vols., 1884, and *Folklore as an Historical Science*, 1908 ; LADY GOMME's *The Traditional Games of England, Scotland, and Ireland*, 2 vols., 1894, 1898.

For popular beliefs and superstitions may be consulted : J. AUBREY's *Miscellanies*, 1696, repr. 1890 ; J. BRAND's *Observations on Popular Antiquities*, 1777, ed. W. C. Hazlitt, 3 vols., 1870 ; [C. MACKAY's] *Memoirs of Extraordinary Popular Delusions*, 3 vols., 1841 ; W. H. D. ADAMS's *Curiosities of Superstition*, 1882. Popular rhymes and legends are collected or commented upon in J. O. HALLIWELL's *The Nursery Rhymes of England*, 1842, and *Popular Rhymes and Nursery Tales*, 1849 ; P. B. GREEN's *A History of Nursery Rhymes*, 1899 ; L. ECKENSTEIN's *Comparative Studies in Nursery Rhymes*, 1906. See also *Rustic Speech and Folk-Lore*, by Elizabeth Mary Wright, 1913.

The folklore relating to animals, plants, and the weather is treated in H. FRIEND's *Flowers and Flower Lore*, 2 vols., 1884 ; E. GOLDSMID's *Un-natural History, or Myths of Ancient Science*, 4 vols., 1886 ; C. SWAINSON's *The Folk Lore and Provincial Names of British Birds*, 1886, and *A Handbook of Weather Folk Lore*, 1873 ; F. E. HULME's *Natural History, Lore and Legend*, 1895 ; E. O'DONNELL's *Werwolves*, 1912 ; see also the bibliographies of Chapter XV, § 3.

For witchcraft, magic, and demonology the following are the chief authorities : R. Scot's *The Discoverie of Witchcraft*, 1584, ed. B. Nicholson, 1886 ; James I's *Dæmonologie, in Forme of a Dialogue*, 1597, 1603 ; S. Harsnet's *A Declaration of Egregious Popish Impostures*, 1603 (see *Notes and Queries*, ser. ii, vol. vii, pp. 144–5), from which Shakespeare took the names of the fiends Flibbertigibbet, Obidicut, &c., in *King Lear* ; F. Hutchinson's *An Historical Essay concerning Witchcraft*, 1718 ; [D. Defoe's] *A System of Magick*, 1727 ; Sir W. Scott's *Letters on Demonology and Witchcraft*, 1830 ; C. K. Sharpe's *A Historical Account of the Belief in Witchcraft in Scotland*, 1884 ; C. F. Smith's *John Dee (1527–1608)*, 1909 ; St. J. D. Seymour's *Irish Witchcraft and Demonology*, 1913 ; for angelology, T. Heywood's *The Hierarchie of the Blessed Angells*, 1635.

An extensive literature exists on the subject of fairies ; the following books deserve special mention : J. Ritson's *Fairy Tales, Legends and Romances, illustrating Shakespeare and other early English Writers*, 1831, ed. W. C. Hazlitt, 1875 ; J. O. Halliwell's *Illustrations of the Fairy Mythology of 'A Midsummer Night's Dream '*, 1845 ; Jabez Allies's *On the Ignis Fatuus, or Will-o'-the-Wisp, and the Fairies*, 1846 ; T. Keightley's *The Fairy Mythology*, 1828, &c. ; W. Bell's *Shakespeare's Puck and his Folkslore*, 3 vols., 1852–64 ; W. Sikes's *British Goblins*, 1880 ; E. S. Hartland's *The Science of Fairy Tales*, 1891 ; A. Nutt's *The Fairy Mythology of Shakespeare*, 1900 ; F. Sidgwick's *The Sources and Analogues of 'A Midsummer Night's Dream '*, 1908 ; F. Delattre's *English Fairy Poetry*, 1912.

PRINTED IN GREAT BRITAIN
AT THE UNIVERSITY PRESS, OXFORD
BY VIVIAN RIDLER
PRINTER TO THE UNIVERSITY